Text Organizational Web

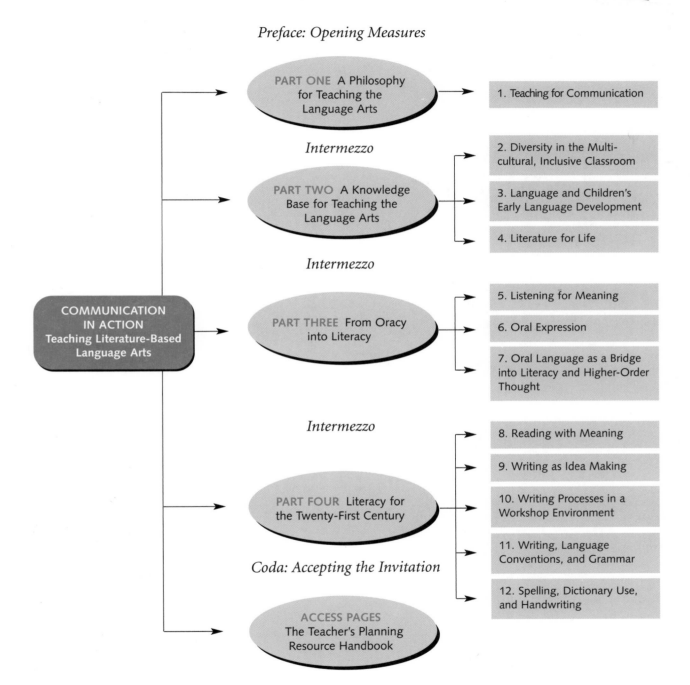

Preface: Opening Measures

PART ONE A Philosophy for Teaching the Language Arts

1. Teaching for Communication

Intermezzo

PART TWO A Knowledge Base for Teaching the Language Arts

2. Diversity in the Multi-cultural, Inclusive Classroom

3. Language and Children's Early Language Development

4. Literature for Life

Intermezzo

PART THREE From Oracy into Literacy

5. Listening for Meaning

6. Oral Expression

7. Oral Language as a Bridge into Literacy and Higher-Order Thought

Intermezzo

PART FOUR Literacy for the Twenty-First Century

8. Reading with Meaning

9. Writing as Idea Making

10. Writing Processes in a Workshop Environment

11. Writing, Language Conventions, and Grammar

12. Spelling, Dictionary Use, and Handwriting

Coda: Accepting the Invitation

ACCESS PAGES The Teacher's Planning Resource Handbook

COMMUNICATION IN ACTION Teaching Literature-Based Language Arts

COMMUNICATION IN ACTION

EIGHTH EDITION

COMMUNICATION IN ACTION

Teaching Literature-Based Language Arts

DOROTHY GRANT HENNINGS

Kean University

Houghton Mifflin Company   Boston   New York

To George, who continues to encourage, help, and care

EDITOR IN CHIEF: Patricia A. Coryell
SENIOR SPONSORING EDITOR: Sue Pulvermacher-Alt
SENIOR DEVELOPMENT EDITOR: Lisa A. Mafrici
EDITORIAL ASSISTANT: Sara Hauschildt
SENIOR PROJECT EDITOR: Kathryn Dinovo
SENIOR MANUFACTURING COORDINATOR: Priscilla J. Bailey
MARKETING MANAGER: Nicola Poser

COVER IMAGE: © Farida Zaman/The Stock Illustration Source
Part Opener Art:
Preface (Stonehenge, England): © Paul Almasy/CORBIS
Part One (Parthenon, Greece): © 2001 Index Stock Photography
Part Two (Carcassonne, France): © Roger Ressmeyer/CORBIS
Part Three (Great Wall of China): © 2001 Index Stock Photography
Part Four (Niagara Falls, New York): © Henryk Kaiser/Index Stock

Acknowledgment is made to the following authors and publishers for permission to reprint selections from copyrighted material:

"A Goblin" by Rose Fyleman from *Picture Rhymes from Foreign Lands* by Rose Fyleman. Copyright © 1935. Reprinted by permission of Basil Blackwell Publisher.

Alphabet and number guide from *D'Nealian® Handwriting* by Donald Neal Thurber. Copyright © 1987 by Scott, Foresman and Company. Reprinted by permission.

Flip charts © 1981 by Zaner-Bloser, Inc. Paper position graphics from *Creative Growth in Handwriting*. Copyright © 1975, 1978 by Zaner-Bloser, Columbus, OH. Reproduced by permission of the publisher.

Definition of *canopy* from *Webster's II Riverside Beginning Dictionary*. Copyright © 1984 by the Riverside Publishing Company. Reprinted by permission of the publisher.

Figure from "Sara's Story" by Anne Dyson in *Language Arts*, Vol. 58, No. 7. October 1981. Reprinted by permission of NCTE and the author.

Figures from Roger A. McCaid in *Perspectives on Writing in Grades 1–8*, Shirley Haley-James, ed. Reprinted by permission of NCTE.

Handwriting position charts from *Palmer Method, Cursive Writing, Grade 6*, teacher's edition, © 1976. Reprinted with the permission of the publisher.

"Helping" from *Where the Sidewalk Ends* by Shel Silverstein. Copyright © 1974 by Evil Eye Music Inc. Reprinted by permission of HarperCollins Publishers.

"How to Make a Hardcover Book" and "The Bridge They Said Couldn't Be Built" from *In Concert* by the Riverside Publishing Company. Copyright © 1989. Reprinted by permission of the publisher.

Emily Dickinson, "Moon" (first stanza only) from *The Complete Poems of Emily Dickinson*, © 1924. Reprinted by permission of the publishers and the Trustees of Amherst College from *The Poems of Emily Dickinson*, Thomas H. Johnson, ed., Cambridge, Mass.: The Belknap Press of Harvard University Press. Copyright © 1951, 1955, 1979 by the President and Fellows of Harvard College.

Excerpt from Nicholas Karolides, "Theory and Practice: An Interview with Louise M. Rosenblatt," as appeared in *Language Arts*, 77 (November 1999), pp. 158–170. Copyright © 1999 by the National Council of Teachers of English. Reprinted with permission.

Library of Congress Control Number: 2001093616

ISBN: 0-618-16601-7

3456789-DOC-05 04 03

Brief Contents

Contents

PART TWO

A Knowledge Base for Teaching the Language Arts   49

The Teacher's Planning Resource Handbook 487

American English is an amalgam with words derived or borrowed from many languages of the world. To understand and appreciate American English is to understand and appreciate the diversity that is America—a varied land of diverse peoples, cultures, and beliefs. Use the words here to clarify the early origins, especially basic Anglo-Saxon roots of American English and contributions from the Celts, the Viking raiders, and the Norman invaders after 1066.

Contributions from Old English (Anglo-Saxon)				Contributions from Celtic	Contributions from Old Norse (Viking/Icelandic)		Contributions from Old Norman French	
akin	pig	bead	whistle	cradle	sky	knot	parliament	catch
wife	thank	daughter	gut	crag	leg	outlaw	bailiff	beef
bride	hinge	buttock	mother	bald	berserk	husband	romance	pork
cow	stool	kith	daisy	breeches	bulk	Thursday	cream	toast
this	son	thumb	pit	bulge	knife	egg	cousin	
pail	berry	blood	whisper	bard	law		pocket	
ordeal	kiss	father			ugly		govern- ment	
man	the	bread			Wednesday		majesty	
girdle	gnaw	knit			bee			

Preface

Opening Measures

Audience and Purpose

I have written *Communication in Action: Teaching Literature-Based Language Arts,* Eighth Edition, to provide teachers and prospective teachers in language arts or combined language arts and reading courses with the knowledge base and practical ideas they need to plan and implement a literature-based language arts program in which children are actively involved in thinking and communicating. Linguists explain that the purpose of human language is thought and communication: People use language to construct and share meaning. Because language, communication, and thought are inextricably bound, I believe that language arts programs must heighten children's ability to use and interpret language, and children must be fully involved in thinking, speaking, listening, viewing, writing, and reading. I believe, too, that it is through meaningful interaction with others and with written text that young students refine their ability to use language to communicate, build their vocabulary, learn to formulate ideas, and develop understanding of the power and limitations of language.

My intent in *Communication in Action* is to describe an approach that integrates the language arts—speaking, listening, viewing, reading, and writing—into the total curriculum and in which literature is central. In this integrated, literature-based approach, children talk and write about a myriad of thoughts read and heard. They read stories, poems, and expository pieces, including newspapers and magazines. They listen to and/or view live performances, television productions, films, audio- and videotapes, recordings of music, and pictures, including great works of art. They use computers. They share their findings by dramatizing, telling, and showing. They contemplate and talk before writing. They collaborate as they compose, revise, and edit. They write and rewrite independently and celebrate by sharing what they have written.

As they read, write, and communicate orally with one another in a variety of authentic contexts, children develop strategies and skills when they need them to make and express meanings. In this respect, *Communication in Action* presents a creative, balanced approach in which children are actively engaged in real reading, real writing, real talking, and real listening. Simultaneously and as a part of those engagements, children are involved in contextually relevant lessons through which they develop and refine their reading and communication skills.

In short, *Communication in Action* presents a balanced design for the language arts that is based on my belief in the

- Integration of thinking, listening, speaking, viewing, writing, and reading into communication-centered experiences through which children learn to think and communicate naturally.
- Organization of language activities around the finest of literature across the curriculum. Within this framework, there must be sufficient attention to the development of basic strategies and skills.
- Development of the classroom as a community of learners who interact in large groups, teacher-guided instructional groups, and collaborative teams and who grow in literacy through personalized reading and writing.
- Organization of learning activities into ongoing literature-based and cross-curricular units of instruction that enable young learners to think critically and creatively.

These beliefs of mine arise out of formal research and investigations by teacher-researchers who are actively involved in language experiences with children.

Revisions in the Eighth Edition

Literature as Central

Among language arts educators today, there is continued interest in literature as the core element within the language arts. In *Communication in Action: Teaching Literature-Based Language Arts,* I have always emphasized the literature base of the language arts. Starting with the first edition published in 1978, I structured Chapter 4, "Literature in the Language Arts," as one of the foundation chapters of the book. As I stated in the preface to the 1978 edition, "Literature occupies a primary place in a dynamic language arts. . . . The best of story, poem, and nonfiction should fill the classroom so that children can read for the sheer pleasure of it and so that books can become stepping stones into further curricular experiences."

In developing the eighth edition, I maintain the emphasis of prior editions on an integrated language arts in which literature is central. In line with this continuing emphasis, I have honed Chapter 4 to clarify the elements of fine literature. I did this because I believe that unless teachers understand what makes a story "fine" and appreciate the way authors weave story strands together, they will have trouble engaging young readers in meaningful story responses. In addition, I have included thoughts on nonfiction, added material on linguistic responses, included new ideas relative to dramatic responses to story, and provided a new schematic for visualizing stories.

Word Study and Vocabulary Growth

Today there is also renewed interest among language arts educators in word study that leads to vocabulary growth and to appreciation of the way words in the English language are built, have come into being, and have evolved. For this reason, in the eighth edition I give greater attention to word elements and word origins than in prior editions. Those who have been friends of *Communication in Action: Teaching Literature-Based Language Arts* over the years will see this heightened attention at once as they note the new word-centered part openers, the entirely new section of Chapter 7 on word study and Word Walls, and the new short segments on morphemic relationships in Chapters 3, 8, and 12. Although a primary goal of language arts courses is for teachers to learn to love literature, a secondary goal is that teachers come to appreciate the wonder of words. I hope that these additions achieve this end.

The Teacher's Message Board: Instructional Strategies

Over the years, one of the distinguishing characteristics of *Communication in Action: Teaching Literature-Based Language Arts* has been its stress on providing elementary and early childhood teachers with a clear understanding of how to create interactive, balanced lesson sequences based on current theory and research. To continue this emphasis in the eighth edition, I have refined and expanded the sections of the prior edition in which I offer specific suggestions for functional, contextually relevant skills instruction. The outcome is a newly designed feature called **The Teacher's Message Board** where you will find posted a range of ideas relative to the teaching of skills in meaningful ways. You can use these ideas to plan mini-lessons, extended lessons, and independent workshop activities with and for children.

Issue Sites and the "Distinguished Series"

In the eighth edition of *Communication in Action: Teaching Literature-Based Language Arts,* two new features take the place of The Forums found in prior editions. The first new feature is called an **Issue Site.** In these features, I briefly introduce issues that educators are currently debating such as the merits of balanced instruction in the language arts or the literary merits of the Harry Potter books. Rather than setting forth a definitive point of view on the issue in an Issue Site, I quote an authority or two and offer discussion prompts so that readers come to their own conclusions relative to an issue. This, I hope, will foster critical thinking and prepare teachers to make reflective decisions about their teaching.

The second feature is what in my mind I call the **"Distinguished Series"**—specifically Distinguished Educators, Distinguished Children's Writers, and

Distinguished Poets. The idea for this came from a reviewer who said that she used the old Forums to introduce prospective and current teachers to the leaders in the language arts field. Based on her suggestion, I have constructed short, featured segments in which I introduce well-known educators and children's writers, offer a quotation from their writings, and provide a discussion prompt relative to the quotation. My hope here is that leaders in language arts become real people to classroom teachers, not simply names to be remembered.

Technology Notes

Another development in the past few years is the use of technology for information searches and person-to-person communication. Students and teachers are relying on computers to surf the Internet for additional information and to send email to one another. To highlight these applications, I have added a feature called **Technology Notes** to a number of chapters. There you will find Web addresses important to language arts instruction and ideas for using technology to facilitate learning and teaching, especially in the areas of speaking and writing.

A User-Friendly, Response-Eliciting Text

In revising *Communication in Action: Teaching Literature-Based Language Arts,* I have also given particular attention to making it as user-friendly and response-eliciting as possible. To make it a teachable text, I have:

- Placed technical terms in the margins to help pre- and in-service teachers learn the words educators use to talk about language arts instruction in a professional way;
- Labeled the different types of margin notes to cue readers as to the kind of information to be found there;
- Highlighted assessment guides with a special tab;
- Provided discussion and activity prompts relative to the vignettes and figures for use in university and college language arts classes;
- Added new subheadings to clarify main ideas;
- Reviewed the entire text to ensure its readability.

Other New Directions

In addition, the eighth edition of *Communication in Action: Teaching Literature-Based Language Arts* reflects changes that will affect the language arts well into the twenty-first century. In the new edition, I provide revised or added material on ways to organize the language arts classroom for instruction (Chapter 1); on children with ADHD, on LEP students, and on high-stakes testing (Chapter 2); on morphemic units and etymological investigations (Chapter 3); on aesthetic listening (Chapter 5); on choral speaking and speech giving (Chapter 6); on interactive writing (Chapter 7); on phonemic awareness, functional phonics, fluent oral reading, and decoding skills in upper-elementary grades (Chapter 8); on journals and on poetry (Chapter

9); on editing for language conventions (Chapter 10); on mini-lessons and sentence combining (Chapter 11); and on proofreading (Chapter 12). In Chapter 8, you will find a new lesson plan model related to teaching comprehension and oral reading fluency in upper grades. In Chapter 11, you will find a plan for a conventions-centered mini-lesson.

Organization

The overall organization of the eighth edition of *Communication in Action: Teaching Literature-Based Language Arts* follows the design of the seventh edition. The text has four parts, or movements. Part One develops a philosophy of teaching the language arts. It describes a literature-based language arts program in which reading and writing develop through meaningful interaction and includes a unit plan. The first movement sets forth what—based on current theory and research—I believe is important in helping children become well-spoken, literate human beings.

Part Two builds a knowledge base for language arts instruction. Chapter 2—the first in the movement—describes the characteristics of elementary school children and explains how to meet the needs of children who vary in behavior, language background, cultural background, ability, sensory perceptions, and speech. Chapter 3 presents basic concepts about the nature of language and language learning. Chapter 4 surveys children's literature, explaining the elements of fine literature and offering ideas for involving children in stories. It is positioned within Part Two rather than near the reading-emphasis chapter because in a literature-based language arts, literature is not only a base for reading but for listening, talking, and writing; literature is important across the curriculum.

The next eight chapters form Parts Three and Four—"From Oracy into Literacy" and "Literacy for the Twenty-First Century." Filled with detailed anecdotal descriptions of teaching and sketches of activities and lessons, each chapter emphasizes an area within the language arts: listening and viewing; oral expression; literacy and higher-order thinking; reading; idea making and writing; writing in a workshop environment; writing, language conventions, and grammar; the tools of writing—spelling, handwriting, and dictionary use. In each chapter, the title indicates only the focal point; all the language arts are integrated into each chapter and especially into each chapter vignette.

Between Parts One and Two, between Parts Two and Three, and between Parts Three and Four of the text are **Intermezzos** that offer the reader opportunity to move from theory into practice—to visualize a classroom where a teacher is actively experimenting with the ideas developed in the preceding part.

After the first chapter, which establishes the philosophical framework for the book, the chapters of *Communication in Action* can be read in an order that meets the course needs of instructors and their students. For example, instructors of language arts courses in which students take several additional reading courses may decide to treat Chapter 8—the reading-emphasis chapter—rather briefly, perhaps at the end of the course. In contrast, instructors of combined language arts/reading courses may have students read Chapter 8 in conjunction with Chapters 4 and 7 at the beginning of the course. This is possible because technical terms are redefined from chapter to chapter.

Features

Communication in Action has pedagogical features designed to make the material as accessible and relevant as possible:

Reflecting-Before-Reading Question/Schematic

Because I believe that readers should activate what they know before reading, each chapter opens with a question upon which readers reflect before beginning the chapter. The question is set in a schematic that also sets out key chapter headings and terms. Around an anticipatory web in their learning logs, readers can respond by jotting ideas that come to mind as they think about the Reflecting-Before-Reading Question and as they preview the chapter.

Teaching in Action Vignettes

As in all editions starting in 1978, each chapter begins with a sketch of a teaching episode. These sketches provide a view of what dynamic language arts teaching is like—from the teacher's vantage point. The vignettes model how successful teachers organize lessons and units so that students grow in ability to think and communicate. They demonstrate the diversity in background, ability, and interests that characterizes elementary children. In this edition, discussion prompts offer probes that encourage readers to respond critically and creatively to the vignettes.

Intermezzos

Between the major parts of the text, classroom teachers speak directly to the reader about action research they are conducting with their students. They explain how they are trying new practices and what they are learning from their classroom research. The purpose of the three Intermezzos and the description of teaching incorporated in the Coda is to give readers an idea of what they can do to make their own discoveries about teaching.

The Teacher's Message Board

As mentioned earlier, you will find Teacher's Message Boards throughout the book. They are set off from the running text and suggest activities and materials through which skills can be taught contextually as part of meaningful classroom activity, rather than through drill sequences and workbook pages. You will find Message Boards in almost every chapter of Parts Three and Four.

Issue Sites and the Distinguished Series

As mentioned earlier, Issue Sites and the Distinguished Series take the place of The Forums in prior editions. Issue Sites set forth current concerns about language arts instruction, provide statements by authorities in the field relative to the issue, and offer questions that readers can talk or write about in response. The Distinguished Series introduces leaders in language arts education and in children's literature to pre- and in-service teachers. Again there are discussion prompts to facilitate readers' response.

Technology Notes

Most chapters contain Technology Notes boxes that provide Web sites and ideas that relate to the use of technology in elementary classrooms. Readers should be encouraged to add their own favorite sites to those provided.

Margin Notes

To guide your reading and your teaching, you will find five kinds of margin notes:

- **Goal** notes next to the anecdotal descriptions of teaching. Goal notes state the objective being sought at the point in the teaching episode.
- **Word bank. . .** notes that list key vocabulary.
- **Go to. . .** notes that supply cross-references to other places in the book that deal with the same topic.
- **Read. . .** notes that offer titles of related articles or books on the topic being discussed.
- **Consider. . .** notes that provide related ideas and teaching suggestions.

Recurring References to Specific Children's Books

Several children's books are mentioned on more than one occasion or in considerable depth in *Communication in Action*, Eighth Edition. These books include *Sarah, Plain and Tall, Stone Fox, Maniac Magee, Hatchet, Thanksgiving Treasure,* and *A Taste of Blackberries.* This is done to encourage readers of *Communication in Action* to become readers of children's literature. Readers may wish to read one or more of these chapter books as they read *Communication in Action;* instructors using the text for a course may decide to ask their students to read one or more of these chapter books during the course and talk about the chosen chapter books as part of class conversations. Reading these children's books simultaneously with the reading of the text extends beginning and experienced teachers' understanding of the text itself.

Your Language Arts Portfolio

At the end of each chapter of *Communication in Action* are ideas for activities that readers might wish to pursue in response to the text and to include in their language arts portfolio. A language arts teaching portfolio is a compilation of materials through which a teacher can showcase him or herself as a knowledgeable practitioner. Today, some principals and superintendents are reacting positively to a job applicant who comes to an interview with a portfolio of materials that provides evidence that the applicant has control over fundamental teaching strategies and has a well-conceived philosophy of instruction. The activities listed at the ends of the chapters can be developed and organized as a portfolio as readers respond to the text.

Access Pages for Planning and Teaching

At the back of *Communication in Action* is a color-tabbed planning resource handbook called Access Pages. In these pages, you will find

- A list of Caldecott and Newbery Award–winning books;
- A list of books that children enjoy that make wonderful starting points for literature-based units;
- Unit plans that model ways of integrating language arts and literature into and across the curriculum;
- Examples of lesson plans, especially literature-based plans;
- Examples of mini-lesson plans, especially plans for teaching aspects of written language during writing workshops;
- Guides for evaluating computer software.

Beginning teachers and experienced teachers who are making the transition from basal-bound to literature-based instruction will find the Access Pages helpful as they start to plan lessons and units in which literature is central and as they organize mini-lessons based on children's demonstrated needs.

Instructor's Resource Guide with Test Items and Teaching Masters

Accompanying the text is a comprehensive, updated instructor's resource guide that provides

- Suggestions for teaching college courses in language arts and reading methodology, including questions to use in analyzing and talking about the Teaching-in-Action Vignettes and the other features;
- Additional reading lists;

- Course syllabuses including two syllabuses showing a non-chapter-by-chapter approach;
- Chapter, midterm, and final examinations including both multiple-choice and discussion-type questions;
- Ideas for portfolio compilation in language arts methods courses, including a checklist of teaching behaviors through which students can assess their development as teachers of the language arts;
- More than ninety teaching masters that can be made into transparencies for projection or can be duplicated for distribution.

Instructors who have not received a copy of the guide can request one from the publisher.

An Invitation to the Dance

Readers familiar with the previous editions of *Communication in Action* will recognize the continuing influence of Lewis Carroll on this edition. Although *Alice's Adventures in Wonderland* is a children's classic, Carroll has much to say to the adult, especially the adult involved in language arts instruction. Alice reminds the teacher of the importance of wonderland for children, the importance of

> Dreaming as the days go by,
> Dreaming as the summers die:
>
> Ever drifting down the stream—
> Lingering in the golden gleam. . . .

Alice reminds the teacher also of the wonderland of words that surrounds children, a wonderland where Alice can innocently ask, "Why did you call him Tortoise if he wasn't one?" and the Mock Turtle can emphatically reply, "We called him Tortoise because he taught us." The sounds and meanings of words dance through *Alice's Adventures in Wonderland*. Lewis Carroll knew all about word magic. He played with onomatopoeia, portmanteaus, the structure of language, puns, and word sounds, making the adult reader smile at the marvelously creative vehicle that language is. It is through active participation in that language and in the communication process that children grow in ability to speak, write, listen, read, and think about all manner of ideas. Welcome to that wonderland. Welcome to the dance.

Acknowledgments

I wish to express my appreciation to the colleagues and reviewers who helped me conceptualize my ideas as the manuscript evolved. First, I say "Thank you" to my friends at Kean University who continue to support *Communication in Action*. I also thank the four educators who reviewed the seventh edition and provided suggestions for the eighth:

Nancy L. Gibney	University of Detroit, Mercy
Lonnie R. McDonald	Henderson State University
Marlene J. Braunius	Florida Atlantic University
Anita S. Baker	Baylor University

This edition would have been far different if these reviewers had not approached their task with the thoughtful thoroughness that they did.

I am also indebted to the many exceptional teachers who shared ideas with me and tried activities in their classrooms. Chris Kazal, Micki Benjamin, Deejay Schwartz, and Lorraine Wilkening are real teachers who allowed me to see them in action and to use the ideas they are developing in their classrooms as teacher-researchers. Others like Jennifer Chou are composites of real teachers. For example, Ms. Chou is really Bernice Chin—an exceptional teacher—with a little bit of another teacher added to her. Others such as Aimee Williams, Louise Patterson, Sandy Mack, and Jennifer Krumm shared stories and art produced by their students.

Special thanks go to Margaret Kieltyka, Maureen Stawasz, Reginal Cantave, and Deejay Schwartz for their contributions to the Intermezzos and the Coda.

I wish to express my appreciation to the fine team from Houghton Mifflin Company who guided *Communication in Action,* Eighth Edition, from conception, through manuscript, and into final book form. I particularly thank Lisa Mafrici and Sara Hauschildt, my development editors at Houghton Mifflin, both of whom provided endless encouragement. I have worked with Lisa through many editions of *Communication in Action* and have found her to be a thoughtful, creative editor and simply a wonderful person. During the development of the eighth edition, I came quickly to appreciate the thoroughness to detail that characterizes Sara's work with manuscripts. I also thank Nancy Benjamin, who skillfully guided the production of the book; Theresa Flaherty, who served as project assistant; and Kathryn Dinovo, Senior Project Editor at Houghton Mifflin. I send my special thanks to Sue Pulvermacher-Alt, Senior Sponsoring Editor, who joined Houghton Mifflin just as the new edition got underway and added her support and enthusiasm for the project. This was a group of professionals with whom it was a delight to work.

As always, I send loving thanks to my husband, George, who commented on successive drafts, edited copy, checked galleys, located references, and offered both encouragement and constructive criticism. How fortunate I am to have his caring support.

Dorothy Grant Hennings
Warren, New Jersey

COMMUNICATION IN ACTION

Greek and Latin, the classical languages, are the source of many English words. To the Anglo-Saxon language, the early Romans contributed many basic words, especially ones with religious overtones. During and after the Renaissance, English helped itself to hundreds of word elements from both Greek and Latin.

Contributions from Old Latin	Contributions from Renaissance Latin			Contributions from Greek		
angel	benefit	pedestrian	anatomy	cosmos	chaos	poem
martyr	paragraph	bonus	candidate	titanic	barbaric	epoch
cap	congregate	capture	consecrate	acme	antithesis	theory
candle	egocentric	decade	migrate	dogma	enigma	stoic
priest	conducive	verbatim	hiatus	catastrophe	phobia	hubris
oyster	malignant	mortal	moral	basilica	stigma	stratagem
school	podium	circus	alumnus	charisma	pharmacy	hemorrhage
paper	pessimism	optimism	extrovert	hierarchy	hieroglyphic	heterogeneous

PART One

A Philosophy for Teaching the Language Arts

Where do we want to go through the language arts? What do we hope children will learn? In answering these questions, we discover the answer to Alice's question—Which way ought we to go from here?—a question that gets at our fundamental beliefs about teaching language arts. Part One develops four basic beliefs about language arts—beliefs in

- A balanced, integrated language arts,
- A literature-based language arts,
- The classroom as a social community of learners, and
- The development of ongoing literature-based units in which children listen, speak, read, and write.

CHAPTER 1

Teaching for Communication

An Integrated, Literature-Based Approach to the Language Arts

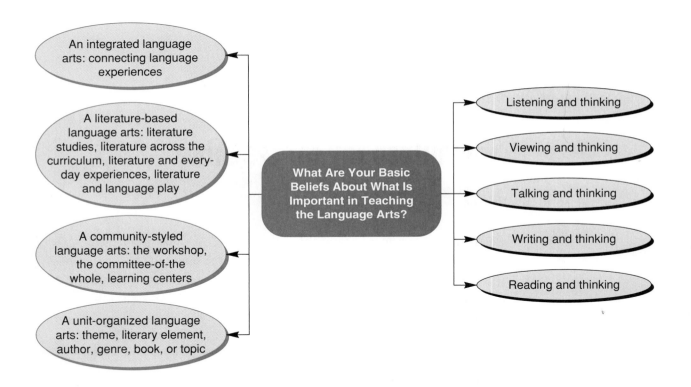

An integrated language arts: connecting language experiences

A literature-based language arts: literature studies, literature across the curriculum, literature and every-day experiences, literature and language play

A community-styled language arts: the workshop, the committee-of-the whole, learning centers

A unit-organized language arts: theme, literary element, author, genre, book, or topic

What Are Your Basic Beliefs About What Is Important in Teaching the Language Arts?

Listening and thinking

Viewing and thinking

Talking and thinking

Writing and thinking

Reading and thinking

Literature in Action *Walking with Rosie*

Students in Karin Topping's first grade clustered on the big blue rug in the communication center of the classroom. "Boys and girls," Ms. Topping began, "today I am going to share a picture storybook. However, as I read, I am not going to show you the pictures as I usually do. Instead, picture in your mind, step by step, what is happening. The story is *Rosie's Walk*. It is by Pat Hutchins."

Listen for sequence

Following her introduction, Karin Topping read the simple lines of *Rosie's Walk*. When finished, she asked the first-graders to retell the story in sequence. The children found this difficult. They recalled that Rosie had gone for a walk and had returned home for supper, but they were uncertain about whether she had traveled over, around, or by the haystack and whether she had done this before or after walking past the mill.

Reacting to the children's uncertainty, Ms. Topping asked them to take out their literature response journals. "Let's see if we can keep track of the action by making a picture of each event in order. Listen as I reread the story."

Visually represent story happenings

Karin Topping reread the first line of the story: "Rosie the hen went for a walk." Stopping there, she asked, "What picture can we draw in our response journals to show what these story words tell us and who the main character is?" One artistically talented child suggested that they draw a hen; the other children agreed.

Ms. Topping pressed on, "What can we do to make our picture show that Rosie was walking?" Another child volunteered that they could draw two pictures of Rosie and connect them with a dotted line with an arrow at the end. The other students liked this idea. To help them with their drawing, Ms. Topping suggested that they place their first picture of Rosie on the left side of a page in their journals and the second one a bit to the right and slightly above the first. She modeled this by drawing two hens on chart paper posted on an easel and connecting the hens with a dotted line.

When the children had drawn their two pictures, Ms. Topping returned to the book and read the next line, which tells where Rosie went first. Then she asked, "What can we draw to show this and help us remember the story action?" The first-graders decided to draw a yard with Rosie walking *across* it. Ms. Topping drew a yard and wrote the word *across* on her chart paper. Then she suggested that the students print that word in their journals next to their pictures of a yard.

Comprehend the meaning of relational words

After the children had drawn a picture to go with the first action of the story, Ms. Topping reread each line of the story, pausing after each reading to give them time to draw a sketch. She also asked the first-graders to choose what story words they might add to clarify the relationships described in the story. The children suggested the words *over*, *through*, and *past*. Ms. Topping added these words to her drawing as a model for those children who had trouble paying attention or who had difficulty understanding because their first language was not English. When they reached the end of the story, and Rosie returned home in time for supper, the children and Ms. Topping drew a line back to the beginning to show this last action. (See Figure 1.1.)

Having completed their rough sketches, the first-graders independently refined and colored what Ms. Topping had begun to call their *storymaps*. As they polished their work, Ms. Topping circulated, stopping to ask individual children—who had diverse abilities and backgrounds—to tell her what was happening at different points in the story.

Thinking Critically and Creatively

Recall story parts

The next day, the children shared their drawings. Using their storymaps as guides, or notes, they took turns recounting story actions. When they had retold the tale, Ms.

Figure 1.1
A Circular Storymap for *Rosie's Walk* by Pat Hutchins

Topping asked, "Did you like that story?" Without hesitating, the class answered with a unanimous yes.

Comprehend the need for conflict in a fully developed story; think critically; view

To encourage the children to think more critically, Ms. Topping replied, "You know, class, I did not really like the story as I shared it with you. There was something missing—something that good stories generally have. Think! Was anything missing?" No one answered, so Ms. Topping told the youngsters to look closely as she displayed the pictures from a big-book version. On the very first page, the children saw the fox hidden under the chicken coop, and they laughed as they saw the problems the fox got into as it tried to catch Rosie. They agreed that the story was better with the fox in it. The fox added a problem and suspense—elements that good stories have.

Then Ms. Topping guided the youngsters in creative, spontaneous role-playing. "I wonder what the fox was saying to himself as he looked out from under the coop at Rosie," she said.

Extend a story creatively

The first-graders talked out as though they were the fox. "I want that chicken for supper," "She looks nice and tender," "I am really hungry," were some of their ideas.

"I wonder what Rosie was saying to herself," Ms. Topping continued.

"This is a nice day for a walk," "The sun is shining," "It isn't raining," were ideas offered for Rosie.

Comprehend point of view

The children role-played each page of the story, talking out and making "mind talk" for each character. In so doing, they were reflecting the different points of view of each character in the story as well as using language creatively. When they finished, the first-graders decided to add drawings of the fox to their storymaps; the fox added suspense to the story.

Creating Stories Orally

Visualize a circular story

The next day, when Ms. Topping's first-graders gathered on the communication rug, they talked about the actions in *Rosie's Walk*. They analyzed the story and discovered that it ended where it began—at home—after the main character had had a series of adventures in the big world away from home. Ms. Topping explained that stories with this pattern are like circles. She drew a circle on the board, asked students to draw one in their literature response journals, and encouraged them to make large circles in the air with their hands to demonstrate how this story developed.

At that point, Ms. Topping introduced a puppet of Egor the horse. She told them they were going to make up a story like *Rosie's Walk*, using Egor as the main character. To begin, she asked the children to decide whether Egor was sad or happy. They unanimously decided that Egor was sad; they could tell by the expression in his eyes.

Then she thought aloud: I wonder where Egor lived. I wonder why he was sad. If Egor were to go for a walk as Rosie did, where could he travel that would make him happy? As the children made suggestions (zoo, circus, Disney World, beach), Ms. Topping printed them on the board. Of all the suggestions, most of the children liked the idea of a story about Egor's going to a circus; there were lots of things to do there to make you happy.

Create story sentences as part of a shared writing experience

Now Ms. Topping reminded the children of the first words in *Rosie's Walk* and asked them to think of a sentence about Egor to use in starting a similar circular-trip story about him. When one youngster proffered a sentence, she recorded it on large chart paper and asked for follow-up sentences to tell what Egor did at the circus and what happened at the end. She recorded the follow-up sentences in paragraph form on the chart paper, asking some students to insert the periods at the ends of the sentences and to inscribe Egor's name. The result was something like this:

Put in punctuation to represent sentence ends

> Egor the horse went to the circus. Egor saw clowns at the circus. Egor saw elephants. Egor saw lions. He bought a balloon. Egor came home and felt better.

Next, Ms. Topping asked the children to read the story as she moved her hand from left to right under the words. Then the children took turns reading and rereading the sentences.

Understand story structure; visualize story relationships

At this point, Ms. Topping noticed that some of the less mature first-graders were getting restless; the class had been talking for more than twenty minutes. She therefore asked the children to draw a map in their response journals to show the sequence of events in their Egor story and to connect the story events with a line to show that it—like *Rosie's Walk*—was a circular story that ended where it began.

Revising and Editing Together

The next day, Ms. Topping drew the children's attention to the shared story of Egor that they had written the day before. She had them read it aloud together, encouraging them to read in phrases and with rhythm.

That done, she asked the children to revise and edit their story. She did this by wondering aloud:

- How did Egor feel at the beginning? (sad) Where can we add *sad* to our story? (before *horse*)
- Look at the sentences *Egor saw elephants* and *Egor saw lions.* How can we make one sentence from these two? (*Egor saw elephants and lions.*)
- What do you think Egor saw the clowns doing at the circus? (doing tricks) How can we add this idea to our second sentence? (*Egor saw some clowns doing tricks at the circus.*)
- From whom did Egor buy a balloon? (balloon man) What color balloon was it? (blue) How can we add these ideas to the sentence? (*Egor bought a blue balloon from the balloon man.*)
- What would be a good title for our story? Let's think of many possible ones. (*Egor, Egor the Horse, Egor's Walk, Egor Goes to the Circus*) Which title do we like best of all? (*Egor Goes to the Circus*)

Expand and combine sentences; summarize through titling

As the children responded, Ms. Topping changed the big chart so that they could see their revisions and read their combined and expanded sentences. Again she had the youngsters read the sentences aloud together, stressing the natural melody of the lines. Their revised story went like this:

Interpret melody of sentence patterns

Egor Goes to the Circus

Egor the (sad) horse went to the circus. ~~Egor~~ He

saw clowns (doing tricks) at the circus. Egor saw elephants (and)

~~Egor saw~~ lions. He bought a (blue) balloon (from the balloon man.) Egor

came home and felt better.

Later that day, Ms. Topping keyed *Egor Goes to the Circus* into the classroom computer. She left the story on the monitor. The children could go to it in pairs, with each child reading the story with his or her reading buddy. Since the computers in this school were networked, children in other classrooms could read it as well.

Read and reread to build sight vocabulary

Listening, Visualizing, Role-Playing, Writing, and Reading

On successive days during communication time, Ms. Topping shared other stories with a circular pattern: *Three Ducks Went Wandering, Where the Wild Things Are, The*

Interpret story structure

During writing workshop, students can collaborate to help each other with stories they are drafting. (© *Jonathan A. Meyers*)

GO TO

Chapter 9, pages 324–332, for a discussion of emergent writing.

Grey Lady and the Strawberry Snatcher, and *The Camel Who Took a Walk.* In each case, the youngsters role-played the thoughts in the minds of major characters, drew storymaps in their response journals to depict main events, and compared the story to *Rosie's Walk.*

In a follow-up reading/writing workshop, students wrote their own stories of leaving home to explore the world out there. The first-graders did the best they could with spelling and went back to add interesting details as they had done in writing together. Later, some read their original stories to a reading mate; others shared them during a class communication time; still others placed their stories in the reading corner for classmates to read.

While the first-graders wrote their stories, Ms. Topping conferred one-on-one with four students. In conference, Ms. Topping listened as the youngsters told her about the stories they were drafting, helped with recording problems, and had students read aloud favorite parts from books they were reading independently and from personal journal entries they had made that morning. At times, she also spoke quietly with the children about behavior problems that had occurred earlier in the day and about personal concerns. Ms. Topping scheduled these conferences because in her multicultural classroom, the students had diverse language and social needs: Some were gifted learners already reading and writing with ease, others were slower and needed more support, and still others were learning English as a second language.

Similarly, in follow-up small-group sessions that Ms. Topping organized to meet special language-learning needs, students read more stories with a circular pattern. Again the youngsters drew storymaps depicting key actions. They drew lines to show the direction of story development. Finally, they made a critical decision: Of all the stories they had enjoyed in this literature-based unit, which was their favorite? The children unhesitatingly agreed that the best story was *Egor Goes to the Circus*!

Developing Language Facility Across the Curriculum

Even as Karin Topping was helping her first-graders to understand the structure of circular stories, the children were investigating melting and freezing as part of a science unit. Therefore, another afternoon found the class busily observing an ice cube balanced on a fork. This session began in the same way as the one with *Rosie's Walk*. The children described the ice cube—its shape, feel, and temperature. They talked about what it was doing—melting—and added the words *melt, melts, melted*, and *melting* to the word charts posted on the classroom walls. They drew pictures to show the ice cube melting. Then they held another cube in the sunshine to see whether it melted faster than one not placed in the warmth. They referred to pictures and captions in their science book to clarify their understanding. Later they filled some trays with water and put them in the freezer of the school refrigerator. They talked about what would happen to the water in the freezer. They compared putting the water in the cold freezer to putting the ice in the hot sunshine. With their teacher's guidance, the children drew diagrams that showed the cycle of water turning to ice and ice melting back to water. They drew lines to connect the parts of the cycle as they had done in mapping a circular story.

Writing After Talking

Because Karin Topping wanted her first-graders to learn how to write informational paragraphs as well as stories, she followed up with teacher-guided group, or shared, writing. First, she asked the children to tell what they had done to the ice cube and what had happened to it. Then she asked them to reflect on why this had happened. As the children responded, Ms. Topping wrote the sentences on the chalkboard. When the students had dictated six sentences, they went back to change words and expand ideas. The final publication draft is shown here:

Ice and Water

We put an ice cube in the sun. It began to drip. Then there was no ice cube. It melted. It became water. The ice cube melted because it got hot.

Judge stories critically

Build conceptual understanding and vocabulary

Perceive relationships

Write and edit expository prose

DISCUSSION PROMPT

■ What does Ms. Topping believe is important in teaching language arts?

■ What strategies does she use that are in keeping with her beliefs?

Ms. Topping keyed the composition into the classroom computer and had the computer print publication copies for the youngsters. As soon as they received their copies, the children read them and put them into their science learning logs—notebooks they kept for recording during unit study in science. As an extra project, some youngsters illustrated their reports and displayed them on the science bulletin board. The next day, in the same interactive manner, the youngsters cooperatively composed a report on freezing.

Planning for and Teaching the Language Arts: Developing a Philosophy of Instruction

WORD BANK

Integrated language arts

Balance in the language arts

Whole language

Unit study

Why did Karin Topping organize her unit as she did? What beliefs about language learning guided her approach? Following are four assumptions that are part of Karin Topping's philosophy of language arts instruction. These ideas determine in large measure how this teacher functions in planning for and teaching the language arts. Think about these beliefs as you develop your own philosophy of language arts instruction.

Belief 1: A Balanced, Integrated Language Arts   Children become more effective users of spoken, written, and visual language through social interaction in which they construct and communicate meanings and use language naturally in all its forms. Children learn through direct involvement in spoken language—the thread that should run through classroom activity from the earliest grades onward. Students need to talk prior to, during, and after viewing, listening, reading, writing, and respresenting ideas visually. Through talk, children link what they already know with what they are learning. They connect what they are seeing and reading with what they are writing. The language arts flow together as children use language to predict, raise and answer questions, think critically, and put new ideas together. The language arts—speaking and listening, reading and writing, viewing and visually representing—blend as children enjoy endless opportunities to communicate.

In a balanced, integrated approach, the language arts are in action across the curriculum. Children communicate as they explore the social studies and natural sciences and as they play with words and mathematical concepts. Teachers use the language arts as methods of teaching the content areas; children learn content through speaking and listening, reading and writing, viewing and visualizing. Children depend on spoken, written, and visual language as they learn through technology and make technology work for them. In a balanced, integrated approach, music and art flow meaningfully into the language arts.

In a balanced, integrated approach, children acquire literacy skills and understanding naturally through immersion in a language-rich environment. In addition, reacting to children's differing developmental needs, the teacher gives meaning-focused attention to skills where appropriate. Even as children are listening to and reading real books and reflecting and writing in response, the teacher draws on his or her understanding of individual differences to organize classroom experiences so that youngsters become more effective and efficient written language users—so that students

- Become more aware of the individual sounds of their language and develop the ability to associate the sounds of language with the written symbols through which we represent those sounds on paper.
- Become more able to make higher-order meanings as they read and listen and as they respond through writing and visualizing.
- Develop their functional vocabulary.
- Develop the ability to handle the conventional forms and patterns of spoken and written language.
- Become better spellers and more able scribes.

Where children demonstrate need for even more attention to particular skills, the teacher plans studies related to authentic reading and writing. In a balanced, integrated approach, skills are not taught in isolation, divorced from actual use, but as children need them to communicate. These ideas about skills instruction are derived in part from *whole-language* theory, a philosophy that stresses the importance of making meaning in reading and writing and involving children early on in making meaning with print. In part, too, these beliefs arise out of conversations educators are currently having about the importance of meaning-focused skills taught in a balanced way across the curriculum.

Belief 2: A Literature-Based Language Arts   Children become more effective language users by listening to, reading, and responding to great literature. At the same time, children learn to love books, stories, and poems and become readers-by-choice; they know books can supply them with understandings about the way the world works and the way language functions. For this reason, literature is central across the elementary school curriculum.

In a literature-based language arts, children become literate through meaningful encounters with real books, stories, poems, and articles rather than by completing discrete skill-building, workbook exercises or by reading only textbooks. Children build vocabulary through word studies rooted in the literature they are reading. They learn to make meaning with language as they read picture storybooks and novels as part of the reading program and as they read biographies and pieces of historical fiction in social sciences. They read informational books and articles from encyclopedias and off the Internet as they make natural science investigations. They learn about language by critically analyzing the way real authors use words to communicate meanings.

Belief 3: A Community-Based Language Arts   Children become more effective language users when they function in classroom communities in which they interact and collaborate with one another as well as work independently. Interaction in classrooms takes place as children function in pairs, small groups, and large groups. It occurs as children function in teacher-guided and child-guided groups. It occurs, too, as children pursue personalized reading and writing during workshop-type periods.

Accordingly, classrooms should be arenas for social interaction and collaboration in all its forms, and teachers should foster personalized, independent activity in which children use their growing language facility to read, write, and think. A community-styled language arts is vital in today's *multicultural, inclusive classrooms,* where children of diverse cultural backgrounds, children with emotional, physical, visual, hearing, and speech impairments, and talented and at-risk readers are learning together.

Belief 4: A Unit-Planned Language Arts   Children become more effective language users when their teachers plan ongoing, cohesive blocks of instruction—literature-based units—that enable them to function at their own level and pace, develop skills in functional contexts, and think critically and creatively. To this end, teachers must be dynamic in their planning, organizing a variety of language arts and content-based units in which literature is a major component and lessons and mini-lessons flow into one another to meet the special needs of children with differing abilities, personalities, learning styles, attention spans, and behavior patterns. To this end, too, teachers must hold themselves accountable for children's progress in meeting and exceeding basic standards in the language arts.

Distinguished Educator

Meet Regie Routman

Regie Routman is a language arts specialist in an Ohio school district who believes in meaning-focused approaches to literacy instruction. In her well-respected book *Invitations: Changing as Teachers and Learners K–12,* Routman writes, "Integration, or integrated language arts, is an approach to learning and a way of thinking that respects the interrelationship of the language processes—reading, writing, speaking, and listening—as integral to meaningful teaching in any area. Integration refers to integration of the language arts as well as integration of the language arts across the curriculum. . . . Integration also means that major concepts and larger understandings are being developed in social contexts and that related activities are in harmony with and important to the major concepts . . . that topics of study should be based on the 'big understandings' you are trying to get across from your curriculum. . . . The 'big understandings,' or major concepts to be developed, then become the root of unit planning" ("Integration," *Invitations: Changing as Teachers and Learners K–12* [Portsmouth, N.H.: Heinemann, 1994], 276).

DISCUSSION PROMPT

What is meant by integrated language arts?

How does Karin Topping, in the opening vignette, show that she believes in integrated language arts? In a literature-based approach? In teaching skills and strategies through authentic literacy events? In establishing her classroom as a community of learners? In unit teaching? Can you see yourself functioning as Ms. Topping does?

The remainder of this chapter elaborates on these beliefs:

1. A belief in a balanced, integrated approach in which spoken, written, and visual activities flow together, the language arts are part of the whole curriculum, and skills are taught functionally as children need them to communicate.
2. A belief in the centrality of literature in the language arts and across the curriculum.
3. A belief in organizing the classroom as a language-learning community with a blend of collaborative and personalized activities.
4. A belief that teachers should plan ongoing units of instruction that facilitate critical and creative thinking, skill development, and vocabulary growth.

Taken as a whole, the next four sections present a philosophy of language arts instruction that places communication and literature at the center of classroom activity. In reflecting on the ideas presented, ask yourself, "What do I believe is important in teaching the language arts?"

A Balanced, Integrated Language Arts

Teachers who believe in a balanced, integrated language arts organize their classrooms so that spoken language is the unifying thread across the curriculum. They blend the spoken, written, and visual language arts, and they teach skills in meaning-focused contexts when children need them.

The Spoken Language Base

WORD BANK

Integrated language arts

Reading/writing connection

Contextually relevant skill development

Functionally relevant skill development

Speaking and listening are channels through which children first encounter verbal and visual language. Through social interaction, young children acquire the meanings that members of their language community assign to word symbols and visual respresentations, and they learn to use and interpret written language.

In school, spoken language involvement continues to be important as children develop heightened facility with written and visual language and use language to learn. Through talk, children learn to think with words; through talk, they connect what they view and read with what they write. Figure 1.2 depicts the fundamental connection among the spoken, written, and visual language arts.

Spoken Language and Reading   Researchers have investigated the relationships between oral language facility and reading. In a classic study tracing the language development of 338 kindergartners over a number of years, Walter Loban (1963, 1976) found a positive correlation among speaking, listening, reading, and writing abilities. Youngsters with low oral ability tended to have little ability to read and write. As Terry Piper (1998) explains, "Children's reading and writing are, in a very real sense, extensions of their oral language. [Children] bring their life experiences, shaped

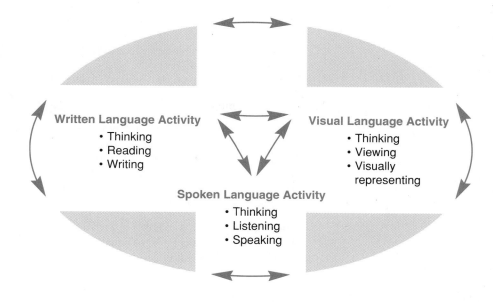

Figure 1.2
The Integrated Language Arts

first by oral language, to the task of learning to read and write." Initially their ability to handle the written language is dependent on knowledge of oral language. Only later, as children develop as written language users, does their ability to use written language become less dependent on oral language facility (Flood and Lapp, 1987).

The connection between children's ability to handle oral and written language can be appreciated by considering aspects common to listening and reading. As Robert Shafer (1974) clarifies, the task of the reader is similar to that of the listener: Both must go beneath the surface of a message to interpret underlying sentence structure and assign meaning. Further, both the listener and the reader must assign meaning to words. In their early years, children's understanding of words—their vocabulary—is acquired through listening and speaking. The more varied experiences children have with spoken words, the more meaning they bring to words as they read and write. In the words of David Pearson and Linda Fielding (1982), "Language in all its facets is an integrated phenomenon. Effects in one of its subsystems will show up in other subsystems. There appears to be a language comprehension system, of which reading and listening are but complementary facets."

One of these subsystems is the sound of language (Schreiber, 1980). Listeners use features of oral language—pitch, pauses, and tone—to help them understand what a speaker is saying. Schreiber proposes that in interpreting a written text, good readers add the "rhythms and melodies" of speech that are not fully communicated on paper, although punctuation marks supply some limited clues. Schreiber further proposes that one way to help children become better readers is to have them follow a written text as a teacher reads it orally. Involved in a shared reading of this kind, children use their stronger listening skills to comprehend; "listening along," they learn that the rhythms of speech are part of reading.

Spoken Language and Writing According to Christopher Thaiss (1990), research on written composition is beginning to give "overwhelming evidence of the importance of talk in the development of writing ability." When upper-grade students have the opportunity to participate in many forms of oral discourse, their writing shows greater fluency and awareness of audience. Their compositions are also livelier and more coherent.

Russell Stauffer and John Pikulski (1974, 1979) found the same to be true at the primary level. These researchers instituted a writing program based on the language experience approach in which first-graders had almost unlimited opportunity to hear stories, dictate stories and poems as their teacher recorded them on chart paper, see words from their original stories posted in the classroom, and reread stories they had created together. Later Stauffer and Pikulski analyzed the children's stories and found significant improvement in all dimensions of oral language evaluated—number of words to a sentence, number of sentences, number of different words, and number of different pronouns.

Spoken Language and Thinking Thought and oral language are similarly linked. According to Vygotsky (1962), thought and speech initially have different roots. Up to a certain point in a child's development, thought and speech follow different lines and are essentially independent. But at a certain moment at about age two, the lines of development converge. The child "makes the greatest discovery of his life"—that "each thing has its name." As Vygotsky explains, "This crucial instant, when speech begins to serve intellect and thoughts begin to be spoken, is indicated by two unmistakable objective symptoms: (1) the child's sudden, active curiosity about words, his question about every new thing, 'What is this?'; and (2) the resulting rapid, saccadic increases in his vocabulary." From this point, "thought becomes verbal and speech rational."

David Olson (1983) clarifies the relationship between thought and language: "Thought is simply speech which has linguistic form but isn't said. In other words, a thought is an utterance which remains unspoken. That's how thought is controlled. You engage in a dialogue with imaginary others or with yourself. The structure of words and expressions gives thought an orderly appearance."

Because oral language facility is a factor in children's ability to read, write, and think, conversation should occupy a significant portion of a child's school day. By stressing oral language, elementary teachers build a foundation for other curricular experiences—for word power, reading, writing, spelling, and study of grammar and usage patterns, as well as for study of the content areas.

The Reading/Writing Connection

To say that conversation should occupy a significant portion of the school day is not to downplay the importance of written language engagements from children's first moments in school. Most educators believe that children should not wait to read or write until they have strong control over oral language. They propose that children not wait to write until they know all their letters or have learned to read. From their earliest years, children should be involved in reading and writing because they want to know and communicate.

In the past, some educators viewed reading and writing as opposite and distinctive processes. They defined reading as a receptive language art and writing as an expressive language art. Today educators view reading and writing as overlapping processes suggesting that readers draw on their prior knowledge to construct meaning just as writers do (Squire, 1983; Kucer and Rhodes, 1986; Flood and Lapp, 1986; Musthafa, 1994; Moore, 1995). Just as with writing, reading is "meaning making" (Wells, 1986); it is active thinking that involves predicting, sorting, relating, questioning, creating, and critically evaluating.

Then too, as Bill Harp (1987) explains, "The act of composing reinforces concepts important to reading comprehension." Similarly, research tells us that the act of reading leads to heightened skill in writing: Avid readers tend to be good writers. Concepts central to reading, such as "word, sentence, topic sentence, main idea, supporting details, sequence, and plot," are central to writing as well. These are the kinds of reading/writing connections we need to reinforce within our language arts programs.

But although reading and writing are overlapping processes, they are still separate acts and offer "separate perspectives." As Timothy Shanahan (1997) tells us, "Reading a text and writing about it can provide alternative perspectives that deepen one's understanding of the text." As an example of the instructional significance of the alternative perspectives offered by reading and writing, Shanahan discusses a reader's awareness of the author as a choice-maker in a text and of the way an author's choices drive a piece of writing. Shanahan's research indicates that children become aware of the author "behind a text" later in their development as readers. However, writing "because it affords one an insider's view of this aspect of text, provides a powerful way of thinking about reading that would not be available if reading and writing were identical." By processing information through both reading and writing, people increase their chances of making meaning with text.

The Functional Teaching of Skills

As Beverly Bruneau (1997) explains, "Teaching appropriate skills and strategies is an important component of literacy instruction. . . . Children need experiences that help them figure out how to decode print, develop strategies for independent word recognition, and understand how our language works." Most educators concur, emphasizing that it is not a matter of whether teachers teach skills but how and when. Bruneau compares skills to dietary fat: "Too much of either one can be deadly," she writes. "Likewise, skills should not be 'consumed' alone. We usually don't eat butter or margarine right from the tub. We connect it to something substantial such as a bagel. Skills need to be connected to a real reading event. In this way they make sense."

In a balanced language arts, we teach skills when they are functionally and contextually relevant. *Functionally* means that instruction occurs when children demonstrate a need for a particular skill. *Contextually* means that instruction occurs as part of meaning-focused language experiences at the "point of use" (Price, 1998), not removed from real reading or writing. For a moment, think about how you were taught usage, punctuation, and other aspects of mechanics and sentence structure. Did you analyze sentences and complete exercises in a grammar book? Most probably. However, such instruction "is considerably more effective" in the context of writing. "Students revise their sentences and edit their writing more effectively when sentence revision and editing skills have been taught in the context of their own writing" (Weaver, 1996).

How are skills best taught?

Katherine Au describes her philosophy of skills instruction in the following way: "I now believe that instruction should begin with interest, with activities that students can find personally meaningful. Examples of such activities are reading and discussing a thought-provoking novel, such as *The Giver* by Lois Lowry (1993), or writing about events important in one's life. . . . *Once students are engaged in meaningful literacy activities, they have reasons to learn the skills and strategies they need to complete the activities successfully. . . . Students have the best opportunity to gain experience with the application and orchestration of skills and strategies when they engage in the full processes of reading and writing.* That is why authentic literacy activities—reading and writing that are meaningful—are central to a successful classroom literary program— especially for students of diverse backgrounds" ("Literacy for All Students: Ten Steps Toward Making a Difference," *The Reading Teacher,* 51 [November 1997], 187–188; italics added).

On the other hand, some teachers believe that children best learn to use their language by working systematically through sequences of language activities one after the other, generally out of the context of authentic reading and writing. These teachers ask children to complete discrete exercises that focus directly on the individual skills to be mastered. They reinforce the skills through drills and require that students master certain skills before moving on to higher-level ones.

Today, educators such as Dorothy Strickland (1994/1995), Jill Fitzgerald (1999), and a host of others are talking about *a balanced approach to literacy development* rather than a single best way. In a balanced approach, students develop skills and strategies such as "how to use phonics, how to use context in conjunction with phonics to guess at words" (Fitzgerald, 1999). They learn word meanings, basic spelling patterns, strategies for interpreting and responding to what they read, and strategies for writing their thoughts on paper. But as Fitzgerald explains, teachers who hold a balanced view value multiple ways of learning and arrange their literacy program "to incorporate diverse instructional techniques and settings." These teachers perceive themselves as specialists who can draw on their knowledge of what individual children need to know and develop varied instructional strategies to meet children's differing needs. ("What Is This Thing Called Balance?" *The Reading Teacher,* 53 [October 1999], 100–107).

DISCUSSION PROMPT

What advantages do you see in the position that Au espouses? What disadvantages do you see? What problems do you see in a more highly structured, systematic approach to skills development? What is your reaction to a balanced approach?

Literature-Based Language Arts

Diane Lapp and her colleagues remind us that "literature . . . is rich with opportunities for personal interactions and provides readers with an important way to learn about their world and themselves. Literature both educates and entertains; it stretches the imagination, allowing readers the opportunity to see their world and other worlds in many different ways" (Lapp et al., 1997). For these reasons, teachers who believe in literature-based language arts see literature as central in teaching and learning. These teachers use literature in a variety of ways:

- As the core of the language arts program.
- As an important resource within the content areas—social studies, science, health.
- As content to help children understand what is happening in their own lives and in the world around them.
- As material to extend children's experiences with language, their appreciation of the way the language works, and their ability to handle written and visual language.

In this section, we take a look at each of these contexts for language learning so that you get a general idea of what is involved in a literature-based approach. As you read, picture in your mind what is going on in these classrooms.

Literature Core Studies

Micki Benjamin is a third-grade teacher who has made literature the core of her language arts program for many years. Typically, Ms. Benjamin starts the school year by "doing" a series of advanced picture storybooks as read-alouds/talk-abouts/write-abouts. Her goals for children's beginning-of-the-school-year literary engagements are to broaden students' understanding of the elements of fine literature, help the third-graders respond to literature in a variety of ways, and provide them with tools to use as they interact with ideas through conversation and writing. And so, for several weeks, the third-graders "dance to the tune of stories"—listening to, conversing, and writing about short stories in their literature response journals during reading/writing workshops.

Dancing to the Tune of More Complex Stories   Having set the stage for the children's dancing to the tune of longer stories, Ms. Benjamin introduces her third-graders to Beverly Cleary's *Ramona Quimby, Age 8*. After an anticipatory conversation in which the children tell how they feel about coming to a new school building for the first time—which they have just done and which Ramona does in the story—the students study the cover and contemplate the title, predicting what this book is going to be about. Having listened to Ms. Benjamin read the first chapter aloud, they talk about it, deciding the kind of girl Ramona is and predicting whether they will like her. As they talk, they revisit the text, reading aloud lines that support the points they have been making, in the same way they had been doing with shorter picture storybooks earlier in September. After talking out their initial reactions to Ramona, students respond in their journals.

With that as the opening celebration to *Ramona Quimby, Age 8,* the third-graders read the book chapter by chapter to themselves. Usually, after they read a chapter on their own or to a buddy, the students respond in writing. During writing-response time, Ms. Benjamin's students can choose from a number of options that they explored during their initial study of picture storybooks: They can visually chart story happenings and in the process think out the roles of character and setting in the story, the way actions and reactions build up, or the function of conflict in the story. They can state opinions of characters or deeds. They can predict where the story is going. They can write as if they are a character and state their feelings from that point of view. Later, the third-graders gather for a Community Share in which some students start the conversation by reading their journal entries.

Students may also work with a reading buddy to select a couple of "power words"—words whose meanings they are not sure of but that they can figure out from the way the words are used in the sentence. Thinking together, workshop buddies propose a definition based on context clues and record it in the back of their journals to share with classmates. Students mount their power words on the classroom Word Wall, organizing them as a group with other words with which they share a meaning or spelling relationship.

Sometimes students turn to choral reading of lines, role-playing, dramatizing, pantomiming, or retelling after they have read a chapter. These are fun times in Ms. Benjamin's third grade, especially when the dramatizations are impromptu. Sometimes, too, Ms. Benjamin and her third-graders do a shared writing: The students orally craft thoughts that their teacher records on a chart, and they revise and edit together. This happens when students want to predict or sum up.

By November, Ms. Benjamin and her third-graders reach the final chapter of *Ramona Quimby, Age 8.* At that point, they have a grand celebration in which students share final drafts of selected literature journal entries that they have revised for this special share-fest. At that point, too, they have a class conversation in which students give their final opinions about the book.

Leaping Together into Other Books   With this, the time has come to leave Ramona and start another book. Because it is November, Ms. Benjamin introduces the class to *Thanksgiving Treasure* by Gail Rock. This book raises questions of right versus wrong at a level appropriate for third-graders; as a result, it is great for triggering the give-and-take of discussion.

In late November or early December, the class begins its third major chapter book; in most years, Ms. Benjamin selects John Gardiner's *Stone Fox,* a powerful story for children in the third and fourth grades. Reading it and writing in response, children compare and contrast characters and consider the motivation of characters. Ms. Benjamin also introduces the idea of multiple themes in a story.

In January, after the holiday break, Ms. Benjamin does a series of book talks. She tells a bit about several chapter books, displaying the covers and handing copies around so that children can do a "quick pick" the way they do when they go to the library to find a book to read. Based on this preview, the children vote on what book to read next as a class. Often their choice is Roald Dahl's *James and the Giant Peach;* the cover art intrigues children of this age.

A literature-study curriculum:

Class study of
picture storybooks
↓
Class study of
teacher-selected
chapter books
↓
Class study of
student-selected
chapter books
↓ ↓ ↓
Literature study
in literature circles
⋀ ⋀ ⋀
Buddy study of
self-selected books

Reading in Literature Circles and with Buddies After their class reading of *James and the Giant Peach,* the children begin to read and respond to books in literature circles, or teams, again making their choices based on a preview that their teacher presents. They respond by writing entries in their literature journals; they meet periodically with their literature circle and with Ms. Benjamin to talk out their reactions. From time to time, too, the teams gather as a class to participate in a brief languaging-together time, during which Ms. Benjamin gives them a literary clue to consider while they are reading their books—for example, the way the author uses similes or metaphors or the way the author builds the tension in the book.

Toward the end of the year, each student reads a book that only one other child in the class is reading at the same time—his or her book buddy. Book buddies generally read and respond on their own, although at times they may read orally in tandem with one another, collaborate on a written or visual response, or prepare a minidrama of a segment for class sharing. They talk together about "their book" during assigned chat times, confer periodically with their teacher, and from time to time report on their readings to the entire class.

When students in Ms. Benjamin's class arrive at the end of the school year in June, they do so without ever having filled in a workbook page or a book-related ditto and without ever having read an excerpted or doctored piece of literature. Instead they have spent much time conversing about stories and creating literature journals filled with personalized entries on stories they have read during the year; their journals provide evidence of how the students have grown as readers and as writers.

Literature Across the Curriculum

Literature can play an equally important role in content-area studies, with an outcome being that children not only learn content but also become skilled readers, writers, speakers, listeners, and viewers. Stop by for a time in Chris Kasal's fourth-grade social studies class to see how she used literature during a unit on Appalachia.

Beginning with Literature Ms. Kasal began a unit on Appalachia by having her students listen to Aaron Copland's *Appalachian Spring,* locate Appalachia on a classroom map, and brainstorm what they already knew about this region of the country. But quickly they turned to literature. Ms. Kasal orally shared Cynthia Rylant's *When I Was Young in the Mountains,* which has a repeating line—the title words. Children responded by talking about what life must have been like for Rylant as she grew up in Appalachia and about how her life differed from theirs. As they conversed, they webbed points in their learning logs.

Writing followed the read-aloud and the talking-together time, as it often did during this social studies unit. To the accompaniment of Copland's *Appalachian Spring,* some children created poems of their own in the listlike style of Rylant; others wrote paragraphs summarizing the points they had discussed; still others wrote paragraphs giving their reaction to *When I Was Young in the Mountains.* Having made first drafts, students gathered for a share-time to read their pieces and get input from their classmates before preparing final drafts.

Viewing, Listening to, and Reading a Variety of Genre On another occasion, having viewed photographs from *My Appalachia: A Reminiscence by Rebecca Caudill,*

GO TO

Chapter 9, pages 344–350, for samples of children's poems.

students responded by brainstorming ideas about that region of North America as a student scribe recorded the points on a big-idea chart. On still another occasion, the fourth-graders read articles about Appalachia from *National Geographic*, talked about the photographs, and collaboratively wrote descriptive paragraphs in response.

On yet another occasion, they listened to Judith Hendershot's *In Coal Country* and participated in a shared writing. As a class they summed up the main points of this book and crafted them in sentence form as Ms. Kasal recorded the points on chart paper. Then, working collaboratively in groups, they revised and edited the class summary. Later they regrouped as a class to share their final drafts, which they entered into the classroom computer so that other students on the school's computer network could read what they had written.

While these fourth-graders were reading and writing as a class, they were reading and writing on their own and in literature circles. Early in the unit, their teacher had given a brief book talk on a number of stories and novels set in Appalachia: Gail Haley's *Jack and the Bean Tree*, Lois Lowry's *Rabble Starkey*, Phyllis Naylor's *Shiloh*, Cynthia Rylant's *Missing May*, Katherine Paterson's *Come Sing, Jimmy Jo*, and Robert Burch's *Ida Early Comes Over the Mountain*. Based on the preview, students selected a book to read at home and in free moments in class. Students who had chosen the same book formed a literature circle, met periodically to talk about their book, and dramatically shared a little of their book during class share-times. Many students ended up reading more than one book during the unit, their interest having been piqued by what their classmates had presented.

As these students' activities indicate, children can be and should be going beyond their content-area textbooks as they investigate topics in the natural and social sciences. Children can be and should be looking at, listening to, and reading fine literature as they get involved with big ideas arising out of the subject disciplines. Children can be and should be drawing, writing, and speaking in response.

Clearly, no arbitrary separation exists between the language arts and the content areas. Children refine their communication and reading skills as they use them to learn across the curriculum. In the same way, there is no arbitrary separation of time blocks for reading, listening, speaking, writing, or thinking. One language activity flows into another in the classroom as in real life. Figure 1.3 depicts this flow.

Literature and Everyday Experiences

Although literature is central in the language arts, there are times when teachers may begin by tapping into other important resources and use literature to extend the experience. One of those resources is children's everyday experiences with people and things around them.

Elementary children want to talk about things that are happening to them and about things that are going on in the world around them. Research by Donald Graves (1983) and Lucy Calkins (1986) indicates that children enjoy writing personal narratives—stories arising out of their lives. If given personal journals, children willingly write on a daily basis. Functioning as authors, children like to share what they have written and get feedback from their audience to improve their writing.

In such contexts, literature facilitates conversation and writing; it helps children to see the meaning of events in their own lives. One sixth-grade teacher, for exam-

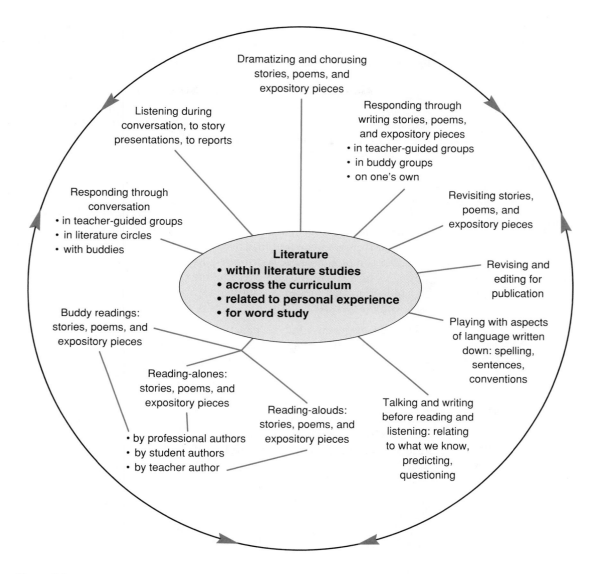

Figure 1.3
Language Arts Activities Within a Literature-Based Curriculum

ple, used literature for this purpose as students were talking about their television-viewing habits and preferences. She shared Chris Van Allsburg's *The Wretched Stone* and asked the youngsters to consider the meaning of the stone that glows in the dark and seduces the seamen into mindlessness. Much talk resulted. Students responded to the literature and the talk by writing in their literature journals. A second-grade teacher used a storybook in a similar way. When children in the class were experiencing friendship problems and were talking about why they should stick up for their friends, he shared Patricia McKissack's *Mirandy and Brother Wind*. Students responded with talk that went beyond platitudes and then with writing in which they described similar happenings in their lives. The flow of classroom events in Figure 1.3 relates also to this kind of personal experiencing.

Literature and Word Study

In Karin Topping's first grade, children build language facility as they react in oral and written form to people and ideas in literature. At times, however, this master teacher also engages children in active play with the language of writing and literature. Our complex language system presents endless avenues for creative word study through which students gain understanding of how their language works and learn to handle standard spoken and written forms. "Languaging together," children can play with the way we

- Represent speech sounds on paper.
- Build words from roots, affixes, and other words.
- Put words together in sentences and expand and transform sentences.
- Use punctuation marks, pauses, tone, and pitch of voice to communicate meaning.

Word Study in the Lower Grades   These types of word studies fit neatly into literature-based activities. For example, after children in one kindergarten class had listened to and chorused the old favorite "Polly Put the Kettle On," they highlighted with yellow marker the letter *p* in the charted copy in their class. Their teacher told them, "Boys and girls, I'm going to let you in on a great writing-down secret. When you are writing down your ideas and you hear the sound as at the beginning of *Polly* and *put,* you can use the letter *p* to put the word on paper." The teacher printed the words *Polly* and *put* on a section of the class Word Wall that she labeled *Pp.* She then listed other words starting with the same sound that students offered: *pen, pencil,* and *pet.*

Later in the afternoon, as part of a social studies read-aloud, these students listened while their teacher orally shared Peter Spier's *People.* As the students read the title several times together before listening to and looking at this book that celebrates diversity, they found the letter *p* at the beginning of *people* and *Peter* and added those words to their Word Wall. After the read-aloud, the teacher introduced the kindergartners to a Mexican puppet named Pedro. As the children manipulated Pedro's strings, they pretended they were he, spoke for him about why they should respect one another, and predicted the letter they would use to write his name on paper if they later decided to write a story about him.

On another afternoon, as part of the same social studies unit, the teacher shared Leo Lionni's *Pezzetino,* a book that celebrates the uniqueness of things. Students found the letter *p* at the beginning of Pezzetino's name and listened as they read his name for the sound to make when they saw the letter *p.* This time the children played with the letter *p* by making it in big strokes in the air and in big strokes on the chalkboard. Children could also respond to the oral language play by writing about Pezzetino if they chose. In so doing, they had opportunity to use the *p* to represent Pezzetino's name.

Word Study in the Upper Grades   The same kind of play with language has a place in upper grades (Invernizzi et al., 1997). For example, as part of their encounters with *Stone Fox* by John Gardiner—somewhere toward the end when students have taken ownership over the book—Ms. Benjamin's class plays with the sounds and spellings of *stone* and *fox:* They

- Brainstorm words that rhyme with *stone* and group them by spelling patterns.
- Brainstorm words that rhyme with *fox,* group them by spelling patterns, and consider the way words ending with *ox* form the plural.
- Check a dictionary to see how it indicates the vowel sounds.
- Organize their own word finds on the Word Wall, as shown in Figure 1.4.

The students also play with the sentence patterns of the story: They chorus story sentences, using their voices to signal the periods, exclamation marks, and question marks the author has provided to "show us how to read sentences." They orally compose similarly structured sentences, transforming them in creative ways as they think about why Gardiner crafted his sentences as he did. Research suggests that such oral play with sentences affects children's ability to write grammatical sentences (Martin in Porter, 1972).

Through language play—particularly literature-based word study—children can refine their ability to use language effectively and their understanding of how their language works. As part of literature-based language engagements, children can expand and tighten sentences, play orally with word order, and disassemble lengthy sentences. They can fatten and reduce words by adding and removing affixes. Almost every aspect of language is open to this kind of contextually relevant word study.

■ ● ● ●

READ

Marcia Invernizzi, Mary Abouzeid, and Janet Bloodgood, "Integrated Word Study: Spelling, Grammar, and Meaning in the Language Arts Classroom," *Language Arts,* 74 (March 1997), 185–192, which provides numerous examples of this kind of word study.

ōn			ŏx		
stone	moan	own	fox (foxes)	socks	Bach's
lone	bemoan	blown	box (boxes)	locks	
phone	roan	flown	lox (lox)	flocks	
shone	loan	shown	ox (oxen)	blocks	
clone				clocks	
tone				rocks	
drone					
prone					
bone					

Figure 1.4
A Literature-Based Word Wall Posting

The Organization of a Language-Learning Community

WORD BANK
Workshop
Mini-lesson
Collaborative group activity
Committee-of-the-whole
Learning stations and centers

Language arts educators, who believe that the classroom should function as communities of learners, organize activities so that children have diverse opportunities to think, write, and read on their own and to interact and collaborate. To these ends, an elementary teacher at times sets up his or her classroom as a workshop in which children pursue reading, writing, and discussion tasks. As youngsters work independently during workshop, the teacher is busy conferring with an individual child or with several children who have a problem in common. During workshop, the teacher also brings students together for short periods of instruction—for what today we call *mini-lessons*—and provides the children with the opportunity to collaborate in teams.

At other times, the teacher organizes his or her class as a committee-of-the-whole for purposes of instruction, discussion, and sharing. Additionally, he or she sets up classroom spaces, or learning centers, where youngsters can pursue interesting tasks in a relaxed setting. In this section, we focus on these organizational tools: the workshop with accompanying conferences, mini-lessons, and collaborative group activity; the committee-of-the-whole; and learning centers. You will want to consider these management tools as you organize student activity in your classroom.

The Integrated Language Arts Workshop

Today, many teachers organize classroom language activities as workshops in which children "go to it." Simply put, during workshop the students read, write, and discuss on their own. For example, one student may enjoy a book chosen for pleasure reading or read an Internet posting to find information to use in an investigation in progress. A second may revisit a story heard during a prior read-aloud, whereas a third may read a chapter from a book her group is studying. A fourth child may draft ideas that have been running through his head, and a fifth may revise something she had written the day before. At the same time, other students may be making a publication copy or doing follow-ups based on a recent lesson. During workshop, children also talk informally with one another about what they are reading and writing.

For purposes of accountability, some teachers require students to keep a record of how they spend their workshop time. Some require students at the beginning of a week to set goals they hope to accomplish and propose some "I-Must-Do" activities. Some set for each child a few "demand" tasks—tasks the child must complete by a certain date. Figure 1.5 provides an example of a student statement of goals. Other teachers take the "status of the class" at the beginning of workshop; they call each child by name and record his or her plans for workshop that day (Atwell, 1998). They do the same at the end of workshop, asking each child to account for how he or she used the time.

Teacher/Student Conferences   What is the teacher doing as children "go to it"? Workshop is a time for the teacher to help students with their individual problems. During workshop, the teacher confers one-on-one with students about early drafts of their writing, clarifies writing topics on which students may write in the future,

A PERSONALIZED WORKSHOP GUIDE

Name: _____ Week of: _____

	Date Started	Date Completed

Independent Reading:
Finish reading your book-of-choice: _____
    Write a response.
    Sketch or diagram a response.
    Select a part from this book for conferencing with the teacher. Pages selected: _____
    Get ready to talk about those pages.
    Reread with a partner: _____

Independent Writing:
    Select at least one piece from your writing folder for revision, editing, and publishing. Piece chosen: _____

    Confer with your editing mate at least twice about the piece.

    Begin to think about a new story to write. Get some first thoughts on paper. Possible writing topic: _____

I-MUST-DO Activity: _____

_____

Demand Activity: _____

_____

_____

_____

Figure 1.5
Personalized Workshop Guide

talks about personalized reading that students are enjoying, and asks students to read aloud sections from books they are reading to check on their oral reading fluency. As part of workshop, the teacher may bring together a few students who have demonstrated a similar reading or writing problem. In a shared conference, the teacher works with one student writer helping him or her to edit a piece of writing. Other

GO TO
Chapter 10 for more on mini-lessons and teacher conferences.

participants in the conference interject suggestions, too, and contribute examples from their papers that exhibit a similar construction problem.

Mini-Lessons   A second pivotal component of workshop is the mini-lesson. In a mini-lesson, the teacher provides direct instruction or a quick hint that has an immediate application as students get on with their work. The teacher decides on the substance of a mini-lesson by assessing students' needs, or he or she may interject a brief instructional sequence in response to a student query. For example, if upper-grade children are having trouble editing the punctuation of their complex sentences, their teacher may select that demonstrated problem as the topic for a mini-lesson. Or if children are having trouble getting started in responding to a piece of literature they are reading, a teacher may introduce an interesting, rather different form for expression, such as a list poem or a found poem.

A mini-lesson can last anywhere from a minute or two (in cases where the teacher

Children collaborate as they read together during a reading workshop.
(© Susie Fitzhugh)

offers a hint about language use or about how to complete a required task) to about fifteen minutes (in cases where the teacher provides some direct, explicit instruction with a bit of practice included). The teacher can address the mini-lesson to the entire class when almost everyone seems to need the instruction or to a small group when only a few students have demonstrated the need. A mini-lesson can occur at any time during workshop: (1) at the start, in which case it serves as an introduction to the workshop period, (2) at the end, in which case it serves as a summarizing activity, (3) at any point in the ongoing activity, especially when the teacher perceives a problem in the making.

Collaborative Group Activity   Another important component of workshop is small-group collaboration. During workshop, interacting in two- or three-person teams, youngsters can be involved in oral, written, and visual composing. Or during workshop, children can pair off to read to each other or prepare a mini-dramatization in response to a story they have been reading. Functioning in talk teams, children can discuss a literary selection, develop an outline of big ideas, and prepare themselves to share their newly found understandings with the class. In collaborating, a pair or a group of youngsters draws on one another's strengths (Berghoff and Egawa, 1991), gains a sense of belonging, and develops the esprit de corps that is common within sports teams and builds self-esteem (Glasser, 1986).

Some teachers rely on innovative organizational schemes to motivate children's collaborative group activity. For example, Mark Dressman (1999) described how one teacher—"Miss Wilson"—had her students cluster their desks into "colleges" in the "university that she and the students had decided to open. . . . Each college had its own bulletin board space on a nearby wall that announced its specialization as the College of Science, the College of Math. . . . The colleges' specialties were assigned by the students, each of whom enrolled in whichever one most interested them. . . . The norm [during university sessions] was for students to work together in small groups on topics of their own choosing. . . . The University was modified as new opportunities arose and new activities were suggested." When students gathered as Miss Wilson's University, their activities were "undeniably generative" and "intellectually engaging." As Dressman explained, ironically this was in distinct contrast to other classroom times when activity was highly skill driven and focused on helping children do well on state achievement tests.

Small-group collaboration can be student or teacher guided. At times, as was true at Miss Wilson's University, students are in charge of their collaborative group activity, with various youngsters taking turns assuming the roles of chairperson, recorder, and reporter. Sometimes the teacher may want to be a part of small-group activity; he or she functions as group leader, raising questions for student participants to consider and generally helping the group to maintain its focus on key considerations. Or he or she may simply listen in, contributing ideas just as any other member may do. As the teacher guides or listens in to one group of students during workshop, other students work on their own.

A major advantage of teacher- and student-guided group activity is that there is a social component—a component lacking when children work continuously on individualized activity. In some classrooms, children work hours completing dittos; with the advent of computers, they may spend many hours entering answers. In these classrooms, children may spend only a half-hour or so functioning as part of a teacher-guided reading group; however, because much of this time is occupied in

GO TO

The teaching-in-action vignette that opens Chapter 2 for an extended example of collaborative activity in an inclusive classroom.

READ

Mona Matthews and John Kesner, "The Silencing of Sammy: One Struggling Reader Learning with His Peers," *The Reading Teacher*, 53 (February 2000), 382–390, for a caution about collaborative studies.

silent reading, students have little opportunity for conversation. Peer-group collaboration is one way to avoid a neglect of oral communication.

Whole-Class Instruction, Guided Discussions, and Share Times: The Class as a Committee-of-the-Whole

Whole-class, teacher-guided activity—in which almost all students participate and the teacher offers instructional support—has a significant place and role in elementary classrooms. Whole-class activity serves a unifying function and develops the multicultural classroom as a community of learners (Berghoff and Egawa, 1991). It provides time for children to listen for informational content and to stories; develop ideas met through listening and reading; brainstorm, compose, and improvise as a class; dramatize and chorus together; refine basic understandings about literature and language; and hone needed skills. In 1985, the Commission on Reading of the National Institute of Education suggested a need for more direct, whole-class instruction, especially as children build reading facility.

For example, Ms. Topping—whom we saw in the action vignette that opened this chapter—shared *Rosie's Walk* with her entire class; the class responded to the story and together created a similarly structured tale about Egor the horse. As a class, too, the students listened to other stories with a similar design and later took part in a class lesson on melting and freezing. Through Ms. Topping's well-planned series of guided lessons, students developed an understanding of circular stories and acquired such "storymaking and writing-down skills" as assigning an emotion to a main character, combining and expanding on sentences, deleting words to avoid redundancy, and titling a story. In addition, through Ms. Topping's guided instructional sequence, they learned subject content and refined their ability to use the words *melt, melted,* and *melting* in talking and writing.

Students also can come together as a committee-of-the-whole to discuss ideas, share findings, and share pieces of writing that they have been drafting and revising during workshop. Teachers must know what they hope to achieve during a committee-of-the-whole session and have a clear idea of the sequence of activities they plan to use. Perhaps the most important factor in determining the effectiveness of whole-class discussion is the teacher's ability to raise questions and encourage broad participation. Does the teacher raise questions that primarily ask students to regurgitate facts? Or gently nudge youngsters to infer, compare, evaluate critically, decide, and generalize? Does the teacher respond to children's remarks by negatively evaluating and criticizing? Or respond by celebrating children's contributions and asking them to expand on what they have said? Does he or she encourage children to raise questions?

Learning Stations and Language Centers

A *learning station* is a way to personalize language learning. It is a classroom site where children work by themselves or in small groups to complete an activity outlined there. At the station are materials for completing the task and, in some instances, a self-assessment guide so that children who have finished the task can identify areas requiring further attention.

■—● ● ●

CONSIDER

Preplanning is essential if whole-class discussion and sharing are to succeed. The next section of this chapter explores strategies for planning units and lessons.

■—● ● ●

READ

Diane Lapp, James Flood, and Kelly Gross, "Desks Don't Move—Students Do: In Effective Classroom Environments," *The Reading Teacher,* 54 (September 2000), 31–33, for ideas for establishing writing, resource, listening, conference, computer, viewing, and teacher centers.

A teacher can set up learning stations in classroom corners, in alcoves created by placing bookshelves perpendicular to the wall, or along walls so that children face a bulletin board or chalkboard. At a station, he or she can organize tasks that require use of computers, videocassettes and players, audiotapes and recorders, flat pictures, realia, scissors, paste, and books. In some instances, several activities can be set in an alcove or on one bulletin board, in which case we call that classroom area a *learning center*. Learning centers that play special roles in language development include the following:

- An Interest Reading Nook, where there are books to read for pleasure and for information and a comfortable chair or two.
- An Interest Talk Corner, where two or three youngsters can discuss points from class lessons or share pressing concerns.
- A Language Production Center, where children write and illustrate. Here youngsters collaborate on writing and illustrating a literary magazine, parents' newsletter, or picture storybook using the production facilities available at the center, such as a laminating machine and a desktop, computer-based publishing setup.
- A Computer Communication Center, where children post and receive e-mail messages from one another, communicate electronically with students in other classrooms, and surf the Internet for information on topics they are writing about.

The Teacher's Message Board

Posted here are six organizing cores for literature-based units. Within literature units students build understanding of literature, hone their language skills, and develop vocabulary.

DISCUSSION PROMPT

- What are the advantages to students and teachers of developing children's literary engagements as ongoing units?
- Can you see yourself organizing such units?

- *Themes* such as these: people often must struggle to survive in the natural world; cooperation among peoples is necessary in a world filled with diversity
- *Literary Elements* such as characterization, verbal style, symbolism, story design and structure, tension and its sources, pictorial style
- *Authors* such as Arnold Lobel, Langston Hughes, Judith Viorst, Eloise Greenfield, Mirra Ginsburg, Chris Van Allsburg, Peter Sis, Jon Scieszka, Patricia MacLachlan, Patricia McKissack
- *Genres* such as tall tales, myths, fables, biography, autobiography, fairy tales
- *Chapter books* such as *Hatchet, Number the Stars, Stone Fox, Journey to Jo'Burg, Tales of a Fourth Grade Nothing, Journey to America, How to Eat a Worm*
- *Topics* such as the Westward Movement, Nature's Habitats, China in the Twentieth Century, the American Revolution, Discrimination in America—Yesterday and Today, Overcoming Fears, Survival in Nature

Language center experiences generally are outgrowths of small-group and whole-class activity. Through group or class interaction, children learn what they will be doing at a center and how to manipulate the hardware—the viewers, projectors, computers, printers, and scanners—necessary for successful completion of their tasks.

Creative Planning for Communication in Action

● ● ●

READ

Keith Barton and Lynne Smith, "Themes or Motifs? Aiming for Coherence Through Interdisciplinary Outlines," *The Reading Teacher,* 54 (September 2000), 54–63. These authors warn of the shortcomings of some topical units.

Creative planning is at the heart of effective teaching. To realize their long-term language goals, many teachers plan ongoing, cohesive blocks of instruction in which one lesson flows into another. They develop *integrated units* in which students respond to a series of related stories, poems, chapters, or expository selections and tap into related areas such as art, music, science, social studies, and technology. A well-organized unit lends continuity to children's language activity and provides a framework for daily lesson planning. See The Teacher's Message Board on page 31 for cores around which you can plan unit activity.

Each kind of core has a part to play in the curriculum; however, the topical unit has the potential to be superficial if teachers develop language experiences around such topics as chocolate, dragons, or monsters—shallow topics far too common in early childhood programs. As Timothy Shanahan (1995) rightly cautions, "Probably the worst mistake [that a teacher can make is to] develop units around topics rather than themes. . . . A topic is just a subject. . . . A theme, on the other hand, states a point of view or perspective." Topics that can lead to in-depth learning are grounded in the subject disciplines as are those posted on The Teacher's Message Board on page 31. Starting with these kinds of topics and reading both fiction and nonfiction, learners can develop significant generalizations about the social and natural worlds.

We turn next to a discussion of how to plan literature units and the lessons that comprise them. For an example of an integrated unit that starts with an organizing idea from science and in which children collaborate as they read and write, see the vignette that opens Chapter 2.

Designing Units

The first step in planning literature units is to identify the *objectives,* or learnings, being sought. Curriculum specialists recommend that teachers think in terms of specific behaviors students will acquire or refine. Examples of objectives, stated in terms of something students are able to do by the end of a unit, are, "Students will be able to write a critical response to a story that includes at least two supporting points"; "Students will be able to compose a series of paragraphs that describe the characters in a story." An example of an objective that involves a refinement of an existing skill is, "Students will be better able to use the illustrations on the cover of a book to predict key story elements."

The second step has two parts:

- Identifying the core literature and the themes that serve as the foci of the unit.
- Deciding how students interface with the literature.

In some schools, individual teachers are free to decide what literature children will read. In most cases, however, the school curriculum lists books for each grade level or provides options from which teachers—with input from their students—choose. At this stage in the development of a unit organized around a chapter book, teachers themselves must think deeply about the meanings of the main book to be read, because the ultimate truths of a story provide the unifying themes of the unit.

At this stage, as part of their planning, teachers decide how they intend to handle each chapter or piece of literature—as a read-aloud, a read-along, a read-alone, or a read-with-a-buddy. "Reading aloud" means that a teacher orally shares passages with the class. "Reading along" means that a teacher shares as students follow in their books. "Reading alone" means that students read silently to themselves after a discussion that establishes purposes for reading. "Reading-with-a-buddy" means that students pair off to take turns reading to each other—what some teachers call *share-pairing*. At this point, teachers consider the activities they plan to use with each chapter of the core book, or the *focal dimension* of the unit, and identify related literature that they plan to share with the class or that all students will read (*the integrative dimension*) or that they will make available in their classrooms for individualized reading (the *independent dimension*).

The third step in planning a literature unit is to determine how to celebrate the beginning of a class's journey into a book and its arrival at the end. Experienced language arts teachers build anticipation days before students embark on a book journey. They display book clues in the room—objects that relate to the book and maps that show the story location. They share a poem or story that strikes at the theme, and they involve students in related artistic, musical, physical, or conversational activity. For example, one fifth-grade teacher celebrated *Number the Stars* with a trip to a planetarium, a discussion of what a star means, and a reading of the psalm from which Lois Lowry derived the title of her book. A sixth-grade teacher celebrated the beginning of Avi's *Nothing But the Truth* with a singing of the U.S. national anthem and a discussion of how truth can be distorted.

Similarly, experienced language arts teachers heighten children's feelings about a book through a culminating celebration of literature. For example, one second-grade teacher culminated her students' journey into *Nate the Great* with a treasure hunt and a pancake feast—accompanied, of course, by talking and writing. In a fifth-grade classroom, the final celebration of *Shiloh* was the dramatization of story scenes and a debate of justice in the story and in real life. See Figure 1.6 for more ideas.

Another step in planning a unit is to decide on the listening, speaking, reading, writing, science, social studies, art, music, and physical activities that will be part of it and the topics of related mini-lessons through which students will develop vocabulary, specific language skills, and literary understandings. Obviously, the objectives determine in great measure the things the teacher and the students do with the

READ

Natalie Babbitt's "Protecting Children's Literature," *The Horn Book,* 66 (November/December 1990), 696–703, for a caution about making a good story "bear too much weight" by taking it apart to examine it critically. As Babbitt warns, "Fiction is a fragile medium."

A Thematic Unit Overcoming Fear

THE WEB

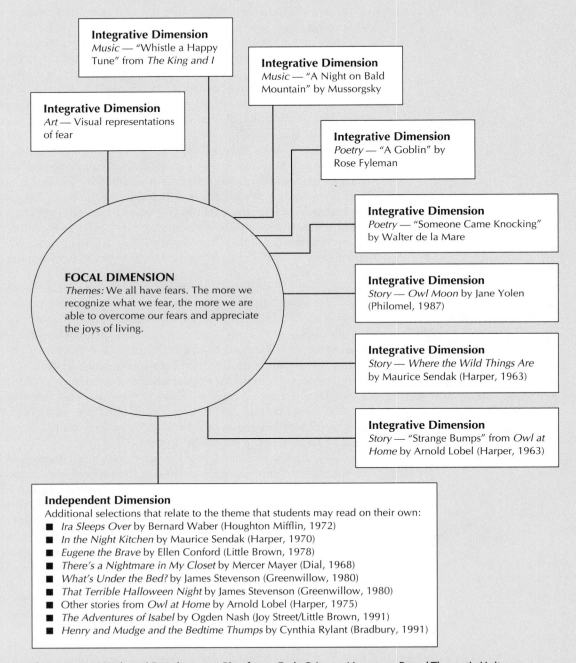

Integrative Dimension
Music — "Whistle a Happy Tune" from *The King and I*

Integrative Dimension
Music — "A Night on Bald Mountain" by Mussorgsky

Integrative Dimension
Art — Visual representations of fear

Integrative Dimension
Poetry — "A Goblin" by Rose Fyleman

Integrative Dimension
Poetry — "Someone Came Knocking" by Walter de la Mare

FOCAL DIMENSION
Themes: We all have fears. The more we recognize what we fear, the more we are able to overcome our fears and appreciate the joys of living.

Integrative Dimension
Story — *Owl Moon* by Jane Yolen (Philomel, 1987)

Integrative Dimension
Story — *Where the Wild Things Are* by Maurice Sendak (Harper, 1963)

Integrative Dimension
Story — "Strange Bumps" from *Owl at Home* by Arnold Lobel (Harper, 1963)

Independent Dimension
Additional selections that relate to the theme that students may read on their own:
- *Ira Sleeps Over* by Bernard Waber (Houghton Mifflin, 1972)
- *In the Night Kitchen* by Maurice Sendak (Harper, 1970)
- *Eugene the Brave* by Ellen Conford (Little Brown, 1978)
- *There's a Nightmare in My Closet* by Mercer Mayer (Dial, 1968)
- *What's Under the Bed?* by James Stevenson (Greenwillow, 1980)
- *That Terrible Halloween Night* by James Stevenson (Greenwillow, 1980)
- Other stories from *Owl at Home* by Arnold Lobel (Harper, 1975)
- *The Adventures of Isabel* by Ogden Nash (Joy Street/Little Brown, 1991)
- *Henry and Mudge and the Bedtime Thumps* by Cynthia Rylant (Bradbury, 1991)

Figure 1.6   A Web and Development Plan for an Early-Primary Literature-Based Thematic Unit

THE DEVELOPMENT PLAN

OBJECTIVES: Through interaction with literature and one another, children will be able to:
• Identify and overcome their fears, particularly of the dark and of the night • Predict what a story or poem is about based on title, cover, and other clues • Orally join in the chorusing of a poem and the reading of a story • Bring their feelings to bear on the interpretation of a poem or story • Express their feelings during talk time and in writing • Use context clues to predict the meaning of unfamiliar words, especially homographs such as *bump* • Perceive similarities and differences within several pieces of writing • Collaborate in the writing of a group poem or story using basic sentence-ending punctuation.

LEARNING SEQUENCE:

Opening Celebration: Sing "Whistle a Happy Tune" from *The King and I;* share times when we have been afraid; brainstorm things that scare us; make a finger painting.

"A Goblin" by Rose Fyleman: Predict what the poem is about based on the title and first line; listen for what the author feels; discuss our fears; read along while listening; chorus the poem together; dramatize scary things; draw a picture of the feelings expressed in the poem; write collaborative poems about our own fears; as a class, write poems with short lines in the style of Fyleman; write about times we were afraid; participate in a mini-lesson on use of sentence-ending punctuation as it relates to meaning.

"Someone Came Knocking" by Walter de la Mare: Predict what the poem is about based on the title; listen for what the author feels; draw a picture that depicts the feelings in the poem; hypothesize who came knocking; talk about when we have felt the same way; talk about when we are afraid; talk about why we are afraid; write about our fears; chorus the poem on several occasions; chorus "A Goblin"; decide how this poem is similar to "A Goblin" and how it is different.

"Strange Bumps" from *Owl at Home* by Arnold Lobel (Harper, 1975): Predict what the story is about based on the pictures; listen for how the main character feels; read along while listening; talk about why the character feels that way; tell when we have felt the same way; think about the multiple meanings of the word *bump;* dramatize the story; write about what makes us afraid; decide how this story is similar to "A Goblin" and "Someone Came Knocking" and how it is different.

***Owl Moon* by Jane Yolen (Philomel, 1987):** Predict what the story is about based on the title and cover; listen for how the main character feels; talk about why she is not afraid; talk about similar times when pleasure took the place of fear; use context to figure out word meanings; reread the story to a partner; dramatize the story; write about times when we were unafraid; decide how this story is similar to "Strange Bumps" and how it is different.

***Where the Wild Things Are* by Maurice Sendak (Harper, 1963):** Predict what the story is about based on the title and cover; listen for how the main character feels at the beginning of the story, in the middle, and at the end; decide how these feelings are similar to or different from those of the character in *Owl Moon;* talk about when we feel afraid, when we feel brave; write about our fears and our pleasures, using either poetry or story format; share our writings; dramatize our writings. Listen to *A Night on Bald Mountain.* Use our bodies to express meaning through extemporaneous movement.

Climactic Celebration: Sing "Whistle a Happy Tune." Share times when we have been brave. Tell stories we have read on our own. Share stories and poems we have written in this literature unit.

ONGOING ASSESSMENT: These activities will be a continuing aspect of the unit:
• Informal observations of children's reactions as they listen to poems and stories, their contributions to discussions held before and after they listen to a poem or story, and their contributions to choral speaking, singing, and dramatic activities • Analysis of students' written responses that they have revised, edited, published, and showcased in their portfolios • Checklists based on stated objectives and completed after individual conferences with students (e.g., in conference, ask students to predict based on the title and cover of an unfamiliar book; ask them to read along as you reread "A Goblin" and then have them tell about their feelings and about what the poem means to them) • Anecdotal records that describe student behavior.

literature they read or hear. Less obvious is the fact that students contribute to the planning. For example, as children read poems, novels, short stories, and expository pieces, they brainstorm writing options—things they would enjoy writing about in response to the literature. They also contribute by locating related stories and poems to read and identifying unfamiliar or interesting words to highlight on the Word Wall.

Still another important aspect of unit planning is deciding on how to evaluate students' progress toward the stated objectives. Today emphasis is on informal means of assessment: observation of student behaviors, anecdotal records, checklists, portfolios. Emphasis is also on children as participants in the assessment process. You will read more about these approaches later in this book.

GO TO
Access Pages 500–510 for unit examples.

Adapting a Basal Unit

In some school districts, teachers are required to organize children's reading/writing activities around a basal series containing selections grouped as units. When this is the case, teachers still function as the primary planners; they organize children's language experiences by drawing creatively and discriminately on the ideas and selections in the series.

Teachers adapting a basal unit may begin a unit by having students read the original, full-length, paperback version of a novel rather than the excerpted version in the series, using that novel as the focal dimension of the unit. Or teachers may begin with a series of poems or a novel of their own choosing that connects to the theme of a unit in the reading series. In working creatively with a mandated basal series in these ways, teachers do not have children read all the selections in the basal; rather, they select those that meet the needs and interests of the children in the class and add others that relate. They skip selections, suggesting skipped pieces as independent reading options, and they decide on the order in which they will use the pieces in the text. Creative teachers who view basals as anthologies sometimes skip entire units in the basal as they build alternate units with their students. Likewise, creative teachers omit activities suggested in the accompanying manuals and workbooks and involve students instead in ongoing writing, independent reading, and oral language activity.

Designing Lessons and Mini-Lessons Within Unit Frameworks

Just as teachers build units by identifying their objectives, the literary content, and the activities used to realize their objectives, so do teachers plan the extended lessons and mini-lessons within an ongoing unit by considering the learnings they hope to achieve, the activities they will use, and the materials needed.

What are the attributes of an extended lesson? Madeline Hunter (1982) proposes that the opening is especially important in that it sets the focus and motivates students; she calls that opening an *anticipatory set.* Hunter states that the teacher "should take advantage of the beginning of the class time to create an anticipatory set in students which will take their minds off other things and focus their attention. . . . An anticipatory set also can hook into students' past knowledge and trigger memory or some practice which will facilitate today's learning." The latter is especially true of the anticipatory set of a lesson that is part of an ongoing unit; the anticipatory set

---

A Lesson Plan Format

Context
Objective(s)
Sequence of activities
   Anticipatory set
   Instruction and
      modeling
   Closing set and
      independent
      applications
Materials
Related lessons
Evaluation

helps students recall and review the previous lesson in the unit and make the connection with what is to come. With mini-lessons, the anticipatory set is brief, often no more than a statement that gives the reason for the activity.

Students' responses to the anticipatory set may provide diagnostic information about the knowledge and skills students already possess. Obviously, any lesson that begins with the teacher telling students to turn to a particular page in their text, read it, and write an answer to the question at the end of the page fails to establish a motivating anticipatory set. Students become motivated by viewing and talking about pictures and maps related to the topic, chorusing a short poem, or webbing prior knowledge.

The main segment of a lesson includes *instruction* and *modeling* of processes that students will later have to perform on their own. Instruction can include the oral sharing of a story, poem, or informational selection; a discussion of key ideas; or the viewing of a video, filmstrip, or visuals from the World Wide Web. Modeling, in this context, means talking or doing together to demonstrate to students how to proceed as they study and learn. For example, students and teacher cooperatively create a poem following a pattern students may use later for independent writing. Or the teacher shares a paragraph similar to those children will later read, indicating aloud the thoughts that come to his or her mind while making meaning with the paragraph. Or in a mini-lesson during writing workshop, the teacher quickly models how to form a web of ideas as a way to get ready to write.

According to Mark Aulls (1986), a primary benefit of verbal modeling is that it makes otherwise "covert processes observable to the student." Aulls writes, "You cannot get some students to internalize a process by simply telling or even explaining what the steps are. . . . Verbal modeling provides the opportunity to show how to do something." As part of the instructional and modeling phase of a lesson, the teacher should check students' understanding. In checking for understanding, the teacher can ask students to respond with a nonverbal signal (e.g., holding up a question mark card if a sentence being displayed is a question), respond with choral responses, answer individually, or write a brief response.

Toward the end of the lesson, the teacher must pull the threads of it together and seek closure. During the *closing set,* students identify main ideas, summarize what they have learned, and generalize. If they have drawn or written, they share what they have composed. For mini-lessons closure is done quickly, with a student or two explaining applications to their own writing or reading.

Qualities of Successful Lessons

Lessons in the language arts are varied; no one lesson design works in all situations. Nevertheless, we can generalize about successful lessons:

- Successful lessons are based on meaningful content. This content is derived from literature, the subject areas, everyday experiences, or the nature of language itself.
- Lessons have an oral component, such as brainstorming, discussion, or dramatization. Students and teacher are verbally involved in communicating together.
- Reading and writing parallel the oral experiences. Students who are talking about or acting out ideas are often eager to write down their cooperative productions, write independently, and read more on the topic.

GO TO

Access Pages 512–522 for examples of this kind of lesson.

GO TO

Access Pages 512–524 for a series of lesson and mini-lesson plans.

- Children share what they have learned and produced. Oral sharing flows naturally from individual and group writing.
- One lesson or mini-lesson interrelates with others in a unit or is contained within a larger context such as a workshop. Small-group interaction flows out of periods of whole-class oral involvement; personalized study is based on small-group and whole-class work.

Rarely in teaching can lesson plans be implemented exactly. Children contribute suggestions. Unscheduled events or behavior problems interrupt plans. Activities that appear ideal in preplanning misfire. Modifications are to be expected given the variables functioning in elementary classrooms. Realizing this, one experienced teacher, Anita Baker, always has a backup plan ready. If her Plan A misfires, she shifts to her Plan B.

Trade Books, Textbooks, and Other Materials

Books are central in language arts. Clearly, a wide variety of books must be housed in dynamic classrooms—books galore to tease the senses, tantalize the imagination, and provide information; books that teachers read aloud to children; books that children read because they want to.

Many classrooms house a variety of graded textbooks as well. How are teachers to use these? The temptation is to open the language arts book and begin there. Some inexperienced teachers do just that. They introduce a lesson with, "Everyone turn to page 8. Keith, read the opening paragraph. Good. Pam, take the next. Are there any questions?" When none appears, such teachers continue, "Okay, complete the ten sentences beneath the two paragraphs." Used this way, the language arts text is a dead-end road resulting in minimal language use and no active involvement.

Language arts texts should play a reinforcing role. First, they can be used to back up understandings gleaned from oral encounters. For example, youngsters who together have played with a component of language go to the text to read about concepts with which they have already been orally involved. Second, language arts texts can provide word and sentence materials. If children are making sentence strips to cut into subject and predicate parts, expand into longer sentences, reorder, or transform into related patterns, the book gives examples. Third, some newer series offer poems and stories that children can prepare for choral speaking and individual oral interpretation. Some provide maps showing the origins of English, language trees, and selections from Old, Middle, and Modern English. These materials serve as content for class discussion. Finally, language text series provide a framework for instruction—a kind of scope and sequence guide. Even experienced teachers find texts beneficial as references, for they tell what skills and topics are important for children at a certain level and provide ideas that can be adapted.

Teachers will want to draw on other print materials: teacher-made classroom labels in early childhood classrooms, charts, word cards, samples of environmental print that serve diverse purposes, bulletin boards with a verbal component, magazines, newspapers. They will also want to tap into videos and filmstrips, particularly those relevant to content-area study. Videos provide background information and visual renditions of novels, which can be viewed after students have read a book and are ready to make comparisons. Audiotapes can similarly provide content for discussions and composition, especially recordings of interviews with children's authors. Today videocassette recorders (VCRs) allow teachers to store documentary and news programs for later retrieval. Camcorders enable students and teachers to produce videos of their own.

Computers and the Information Superhighway

Today microcomputers are being used for a variety of purposes within the language arts. One is the delivery of instruction. Commercially produced, computer-assisted instructional software packages (CAI) are available to teach vocabulary, content, and skills. Some of these programs are simulations that require the user to make decisions based on information supplied. Some are games with an educational intent. Others are drills—nothing more than workbook pages on a screen.

A second purpose of microcomputers is the management of instruction. Programs are available that allow the teacher to monitor student progress, compute grades, and keep numeric and anecdotal records. Given the nature of some computer-managed instructional (CMI) packages, the user must beware of the pitfall: overreliance on quantifiable data. Although the language arts teacher must maintain records, record keeping is not the goal of instruction; it should not be the tail that wags the dog.

A third purpose is presentation of literature. Today entire books are available on CD-ROM disks. Some CD-ROMs offer reference works. For example, *Microsoft Bookshelf* contains versions of *The American Heritage Dictionary, Roget's Thesaurus, The Columbia Dictionary of Quotations, The Concise Columbia Encyclopedia, Hammond Intermediate World Atlas, The People's Chronology, The World Almanac,* and *The Book of Facts.* This kind of computer material lends itself to use in literature-based units. Students can search *The Columbia Dictionary of Quotations* to find quotations that relate to topics and themes; they can use the atlas to locate places named in stories and articles they read; and they can use the encyclopedia, almanac, and fact book to track down related information. The thesaurus and dictionary are useful as children write in response to literature. *Microsoft Bookshelf* and other

Technology Notes

Some basic Web sites for language arts teachers are as follows:

www.ascd.org   Association for Supervision and Curriculum Development.

www.ash.udel.edu   Alphabet Superhighway Project.

www.ncte.org   National Council of Teachers of English.

www.pdkintl.org   Phi Delta Kappa professional organization.

www.readingonline.org   International Reading Association's on-line journal (*Reading Online*).

www.reading.org   International Reading Association.

GO TO

Access Pages 525–526 for an evaluative guide.

READ

Mark and Cindy Grabe's *Learning with Internet Tools: A Primer* (Boston: Houghton Mifflin, 1998), which spotlights the meaningful use of the Internet.

similar pieces of software are updated frequently, so if you order one, specify the latest version.

CD-ROMS today also offer versions of books, stories, and poems—especially versions of the classics. Available are computer-based versions of everything from fairy tales to works by authors from Shakespeare to Dickens to Dr. Seuss. Unfortunately some of what is being offered is of poor quality or may be abridged. As a result, when ordering books on CD-ROM, teachers must evaluate whether the computer-based version maintains the integrity of the original work and provides a truly literary experience.

Another purpose is word processing and desktop publishing. With the addition of a word processing program and a printer, a microcomputer functions as a typewriter with built-in editing capabilities. Used as a word processor, the computer is a powerful tool in teaching writing and reading and in the development of vocabulary. As we saw in Karin Topping's classroom, when children interactively create compositions together, the teacher or a student can type the texts directly into the computer; the children can immediately read on the monitor what they have written and shortly have a paper copy. In the same way, young people can use microcomputers for individual writing. As part of a literature-based unit, students can use desktop publishing programs to generate flyers, brochures, literary magazines, and books. They can add photographs to their publications, taken with digital cameras and fed into computers where the full-color images can be edited before being printed. Many educators believe that word processing and desktop publishing are among the most creative educational applications of the microcomputer for language arts programs. Using such systems, the student is a producer of ideas, not just a responder to a set of directions. In short, he or she becomes an active communicator—a meaning maker.

Still another purpose is communication and data retrieval via the information superhighway. When several computers are networked, one student or teacher can send a message to other students or teachers at other computers in the room or the school building. Similarly, if schools have the necessary software and a modem to make the connection, students and teachers can use their computers to send and receive e-mail to and from students and teachers in other buildings. In the same way, they can download information from the World Wide Web (WWW) and can join computer-based chat groups to "talk" on the net about common concerns. Schools are only now beginning to tap the potential of this exciting technology.

A Summary Thought or Two

Teaching for Communication

Chapter 1 sets forth a philosophy, or point of view, about teaching language arts. The chapter proposes that children become more effective language users by

- Interacting naturally as they create and actively communicate meanings within classrooms where listening and speaking, reading and writing, viewing and visualizing flow together and skills are taught functionally and contextually.
- Reading and responding to literature across the curriculum.

- Functioning in classroom communities in which they interact with one another and study independently in ways that meet their own needs.
- Functioning in classrooms where teachers plan ongoing literature-based units that involve children in all of the language arts: listening, speaking, reading, and writing.

If teachers begin in these ways, a blending of the traditional language arts results. Listening and reading, the processes through which people build an ever increasing repertoire of language meanings and garner input from others, have pivotal places in a language arts program. Speaking and writing, the processes through which people draw on their repertoire of meanings to transmit messages to others, flow parallel to listening and reading. At the same time, youngsters are actively involved in thinking critically about ideas they receive and produce. The result is integrated, literature-based language experiences in which reading, listening, speaking, writing, viewing, visualizing, and thinking are part of a larger whole: Communication in Action.

Your Language Arts Portfolio

Explanation

Today some principals and superintendents look favorably on applicants who come to a teaching interview with a portfolio that provides evidence of the teaching-related activities in which they have been involved. Because of this, you may wish to develop a teaching portfolio based on your language arts experiences. In preparing items for your portfolio, use a computer with word processing and drawing programs. This shows that you can use these pieces of software (and also gives your portfolio a neat, professional appearance). Here are items to include, based on Chapter 1 of *Communication in Action*:

- Read at least one article about literature-based instruction from each of these journals: *Language Arts, The Reading Teacher, The New Advocate*. Write a brief summary of the main ideas of each article. Note two classroom applications.
- Write a two-page paper in which you clarify your beliefs about teaching the language arts. Use the ideas in this chapter as a base for developing your philosophy.
- Subscribe to *School Talk* from the National Council of Teachers of English, Elementary Section. Read and make marginal notes on each issue. Compile the issues as a teaching resource.

Related Readings

Au, Kathryn, Jacquelin Carroll, and **Judith Scheu.** *Balanced Literacy Instruction: A Teacher's Resource Book.* Norwood, Mass.: Christopher-Gordon, 1997.

Carr, Janine. *A Child Went Forth: Reflective Teaching with Young Readers and Writers.* Westport, Conn.: Heinemann, 1999.

Five, Cora, and **Marie Dionisio.** "Teaching Reading and Writing: Organizing for Sensible Skills Instruction." *School Talk,* 4 (October 1998).

Hoffman, James. "The De-democratization of Schools and Literacy in America." *The Reading Teacher,* 53 (May 2000), 616–623.

Lindfors, Judith, and Jane Townsend, eds. *Teaching Language Arts: Learning Through Dialogue*. Urbana, Ill.: National Council of Teachers of English, 1999.

McIntyre, Ellen, and Michael Pressley, eds. *Balanced Instruction: Strategies and Skills in Whole Language*. Norwood, Mass.: Christopher-Gordon, 1996.

Raphael, Taffy, and Kathryn Au. *Literature-Based Instruction: Reshaping the Curriculum*. Norwood, Mass.: Christopher-Gordon, 1998.

Raphael, Taffy, and Elfrieda Hiebert. *Creating an Integrated Approach to Literacy Instruction*. Fort Worth: Harcourt Brace, 1996.

Routman, Regie. *Invitations: Changing as Teachers and Learners K–12*. Rev. ed. Portsmouth, N.H.: Heinemann, 1994.

Routman, Regie. *Conversations: Strategies for Teaching, Learning, and Evaluating*. Westport, Conn.: Heinemann, 1999.

Short, Kathy. *Literature as a Way of Knowing*. York, Me.: Stenhouse, 1997.

Sorenson, Marilou, and Barbara Lehman. *Teaching with Children's Books: Paths to Literature-Based Instruction*. Urbana, Ill.: National Council of Teachers of English, 1995.

Standards for the English Language Arts. Newark, Del.: International Reading Association and Urbana, Ill.: National Council of Teachers of English, 1996.

Tchudi, Susan, and Stephen Tchudi. *The English Language Handbook: Classroom Strategies for Teachers*. Westport, Conn.: Heinemann, 1999.

Wilde, Sandra, ed. *Making a Difference: Selected Writings of Dorothy Watson*. Portsmouth, N.H.: Heinemann, 1996.

A childish story take,
　　And, with a gentle hand,
Lay it where Childhood's
　　dreams are twined
In Memory's mystic band.

—Lewis Carroll, *Alice's
Adventures in Wonderland*

The Integrated Workshop in a Standards-Oriented Setting

Margaret Kieltyka is a fifth-grade teacher in an urban community in a state in which the state board of education recently issued standards for language arts literacy and competencies in five interrelated areas:

1. *Speaking*—All students will speak for a variety of real purposes and audiences in a variety of contexts.
2. *Listening*—All students will listen actively in a variety of situations in order to receive, interpret, evaluate, and respond to information obtained from a variety of sources.
3. *Composing*—All students will compose texts that are diverse in content and form for different audiences and for real and varied purposes.
4. *Reading*—All students will read, listen to, view, and respond to a diversity of materials and texts with comprehension and critical analysis.
5. *Viewing*—All students will view, understand, and use nontextual visual information and representations for critical comparison, analysis, and evaluation.

The standards document outlines specific competencies in these areas but explains that the competencies are not "discrete skills or content" to be attacked one by one; rather the language arts are interdependent processes that more often than not merge in an "integrated act of learning and knowing." The document insists that when engaging students in integrated literacy acts, teachers are *not* to develop lessons in step-wise fashion in order to achieve each objective outlined under each literacy area.

Last year, Maggie Kieltyka's principal asked for volunteers who would organize their classes as workshops and experiment with using chapter books rather than basal readers and language arts textbooks to help students build the mandated language competencies in the integrated manner set forth in the standards document. At that time Maggie wrote in her action-research report, "I had a class of 25 children whose scores on the Metropolitan Standardized Reading Test ranged from the fifteenth to the ninety-eighth percentile. I was eager to find out whether the workshop would be effective within a class with such variability, so I volunteered."

Since this was the first time she had structured her language arts program around a major piece of literature, Maggie picked the core book herself. She decided to use *The Cricket in Times Square* by George Selden as the focal dimension of an integrated

READ

Pat Meehan's "Beyond a Chocolate Crunch Bar: A Teacher Examines Her Philosophy of Teaching Reading," *The Reading Teacher,* 51 (December 1997/ January 1998), 314–324, for another teacher's description of how she developed a "new view" of teaching and experimented with that view in her classroom.

unit because the Selden novel is set in an urban area; she thought her fifth-graders would be able to relate and respond to it. Listen to what Maggie wrote about what happened as she and her students explored the story together.

Getting Started

"My students and I began *The Cricket in Times Square* with a lengthy discussion about New York City. This discussion arose out of our conversation about the title of the book and the illustration on the cover. We had analyzed both of these as a basis for predicting before reading.

"During our first talk time, the children expressed negative views of New York City. They made such comments as 'It's got rats and cockroaches.' 'There are a lot of murders there.' 'It's the city that never sleeps.' 'There's a lot of pollution there.' Because of the students' negative comments, I felt the need to elaborate on some of the theatrical, musical, and artistic opportunities that New York City has to offer. Together we viewed black and white photographs of some of the well-known sites in the city. Then following our conversation but before beginning the novel, we ventured some guesses, or predictions, in our literature response journals as to what the city was like in 1960 when Selden wrote his novel.

"Prior to beginning the novel, my class also enjoyed Paul Fleischman's poem, 'House Cricket.' Organized as two large groups, we chorused this poem for 'two voices.' Children loved making the 'crick-et-et-et' sounds, and I have to say that our class rendering was something to hear!

"With our ideas and predictions in mind and our cricket sounds echoing in our ears, we began the novel. I read Chapter 1 aloud to the class. As I read, children jotted down characteristics of Mario, a young boy we met in the story. Having heard the first chapter, we talked about Mario—what kind of person he was, whether we would want to meet him face to face. Then working collaboratively in literature circles, children created an attribute web about Mario."

On the Way

"Children read the next three chapters to themselves, reading independently during reading/writing workshop. After the reading of each chapter, we gathered to discuss the story. Students were invited to come to the book talk with one or two questions about the story. During our first group meeting, I described the kinds of critical thinking questions that they might bring to the talk time and distinguished such questions from simple fact-asking questions. I explained that I would like the class to lead the discussion as much as possible, that I would try not to ask too many of the questions. To my surprise, the book talk went more smoothly than I had anticipated. While the class did not function on its own, it did not rely 100 percent on my direction. Interestingly, children who did not normally participate in class discussions chimed in with stimulating questions and different points of view.

"After having read each chapter, students also responded to some aspect of it by writing in their literature response journals. I encouraged children to write about experiences of their own that related to what they were reading in *The Cricket in Times Square*. At times I suggested a writing prompt or two to get children started in their composing. One writing prompt was to compose a poem for two voices in the manner of Fleischman's 'House Cricket.' Another was to compose a list poem about a cricket or any other insect (Fagin, 1991). In suggesting these prompts, I organized a brief mini-lesson in which I modeled a way of brainstorming words and developing a repetitive phrase to use in creating ideas for poetry making. Children could experiment with these writing forms on their own or in coauthoring teams. As their writing developed and children chose some pieces for revision and editing, I invited them to share their entries. I knew that this writing was a success as children waved their hands wildly for a chance to share their poems.

"During the time when we were reading our novel, we observed some live crickets. Working collaboratively in pairs, my fifth-graders jotted down observational notes. Each member of a work pair shared a piece of note paper but independently jotted points on one end of the paper; then they compared notes and in the central part of their joint paper, or what we called a graffiti board (Short, 1995), jotted some key points that both felt were most significant. Work pairs made more notes as they observed their cricket after they fed bits of apple to it.

"Once each work pair had recorded a composite list of observations and behaviors, they collaborated in writing a paragraph. Grasping a teachable moment, I modeled a strategy for designing a logically organized paragraph: Start with a topic sentence that states your main point, or idea about the cricket; follow with supporting details. This experience turned out to be a fun viewing/writing time because some children in my class had only heard crickets; they had never had the opportunity to view one firsthand.

"From time to time, as we went on to complete *The Cricket in Times Square*, students would read a chapter together functioning as a pair share during workshop; students would read a chapter sitting next to one another, stop periodically to talk, and take turns reading 'great' parts to one another. At times, too, we would play chorally with other poems that related in some way to 'our' novel. For example, we played with Judith Viorst's 'My Cat' as we met Harry the Cat, another character in *The Cricket in Times Square*. We talked about character traits, contrasted Harry with Viorst's cat, and wrote poems in the style of Viorst. At the same time, as independent reading, some students enjoyed other books by Selden that are about the characters from *The Cricket in Times Square*: *Tucker's Countryside*, *Harry Cat's Pet Puppy*, and *Chester Cricket's Pigeon Ride*.

"From time to time, too, we would locate words that were new to us, use the context in which we found them to speculate on their meaning, check the dictionary if necessary to verify our hypothesized meaning, and then add the new words to a vocabulary chart we developed together. One day, our word study revolved around the word *cricket*. Students in groups brainstormed words like *cricket* that have two syllables and end in *et*. They identified such nouns as *picket, pocket, locket, rocket,* and *ticket* as well as *croquet, buffet, bouquet, ballet,* and *fillet.* Together we sorted the nouns into two categories: words in which the final *et* is pronounced with a short *i* and a *t;* words in which the final *et* is pronounced with a long *a* and the *t* is silent. We kept searching for more words to add to these categories, made two banners on which we displayed our words, and hypothesized about reasons for the different ways we handle the pronunciation in English. As you can see, this provided us with a functional context in which to talk about word derivations and to check the dictionary for clues as to the origins of words."

Looking Back

"In this manner, we read, talked, wrote, listened, and viewed our way through the Selden book. One day, I asked my students if they were enjoying *The Cricket in Times Square.* Words of approval rang through my classroom. Some students mentioned that they liked reading the novel and being able to talk about it in a group; they said they felt more mature. Some said it was just plain different and they liked it. Others mentioned that they enjoyed writing with a partner; they were never stuck for ideas because they could talk about the topic and get into it.

"I too enjoyed the experience. I deal with students who vary greatly in their ability to use language to communicate. Guiding the language development of such a diverse group is a challenge. Using the novel in a workshop environment, however, seems to offer me the opportunity to be a true teacher—one who teaches everyone every day (Roller, 1996).

"I also know that I was building the language arts literacy competencies set forth in the state curriculum standards. Obviously, I was working on the general competencies: My students were speaking, listening, and composing for a variety of real purposes, in a variety of forms, and at their varying ability levels; they were reading and viewing with comprehension; they were thinking critically.

"My fifth-graders were also building the specific competencies outlined in the state standards. For example, they were developing 'listening strategies, such as asking relevant questions, taking notes, and making predictions, to understand what is heard.' They were contributing 'to class and small group discussions' and participating 'in collaborative speaking activities, such as . . . reciting of poems.' They were using 'a variety of strategies and activities, such as brainstorming, listing, discussion . . . , note taking, and journal writing, for finding and developing ideas about which to write.' They were using 'prior knowledge to extend reading ability and comprehension and to link aspects of the text with experiences and people in their lives.' They were learning to 'take notes on observations' and 'report that information through speaking and writing.'

"I have taken the words within the single quotation marks in the last paragraph from the literacy standards of my state to show that we do not have to resort to the old drill approach of teaching skills devoid of any meaningful context to meet standards. We do not have to devise discrete lessons to address specific competencies.

DISCUSSION PROMPT

- What kinds of activities were part of Ms. K's reading/writing workshop?
- What was this teacher trying to achieve through those activities?
- In what creative ways could she have assessed her students' growth as language users?

Instead we must teach reading and writing strategies as part of ongoing units of instruction that will meet the diverse needs of children in classrooms like mine. We must provide varied opportunities for children to engage actively in reading real texts, talking about those texts, and responding critically and creatively to them through writing. This is the challenge I discovered as I experimented for the first time with a reading/writing workshop."

America is a land of immigrants who brought their home languages and cultures with them to their new land. Early immigrants were mostly Europeans who brought words from the Romance and the Germanic languages of Europe. Some of these words became part of English.

Contributions from French	Contributions from Spanish	Contributions from Italian	Contributions from German	Contributions from Dutch
bureau	rodeo	umbrella	frankfurter	cookie
cliché	canyon	alto	seminar	skate
bizarre	patio	spaghetti	blitz	cruise
butte	poncho	cupola	stein	cole slaw
parachute	buckaroo	pantaloon	hamburger	waffle
buffet	bonanza	sonnet	kindergarten	sleigh
bisque	alfalfa	staccato	pretzel	boss
denim	ranch	minestrone	pumpernickel	sauerkraut
rotisserie	coyote	parakeet	stollen	noodle

PART **Two**

A Knowledge Base for Teaching the Language Arts

What does it take to provide children with the best of educations—with extras? To answer this question, we must investigate the knowledge base that supports our instruction. Part Two focuses on the three-pronged knowledge base that undergirds language arts instruction: knowledge about

- The emotional, linguistic, cultural, perceptual, and expressive characteristics of the children whom we teach.
- The way children learn to use language to communicate and think and the way they learn to handle the components of their language.
- Fine literature and ways to engage children in it.

CHAPTER

Diversity in the Multicultural, Inclusive Classroom

Meeting the Social and Language Needs of All Children

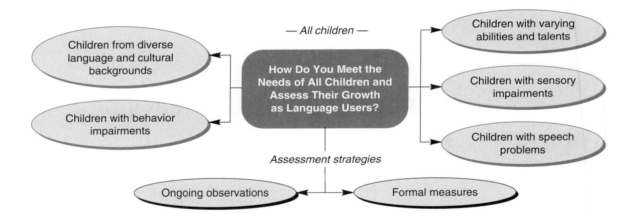

— All children —

| Children from diverse language and cultural backgrounds |
| Children with behavior impairments |

How Do You Meet the Needs of All Children and Assess Their Growth as Language Users?

| Children with varying abilities and talents |
| Children with sensory impairments |
| Children with speech problems |

Assessment strategies

| Ongoing observations | Formal measures |

A Learning Community in Action

Preserving Habitats: A Thematic Unit

As part of a literature-based, interdisciplinary unit, Beth Venezia and her third-graders were visiting the Fanwood Nature Center. The class had planned the trip based on the suggestion of two class investigative teams that were focusing their study on plants and animals in the environment. Earlier these students had written a letter to the center to set a time for a visit and had made a follow-up telephone call. In preparation, the teams had shown the class a map of the nature center and explained what they would see there. The teams had obtained their information from an explanatory brochure from the center.

Now, as the third-graders walked along, the members of the Plants-in-Our-Environment Investigative Team stopped by each labeled tree to record its name in their learning logs. Chandra checked unfamiliar trees in the pocket-size Golden

Learn to take notes based on direct experiences

Nature Guide *Trees: A Guide to Familiar American Trees*, which she had borrowed from the library. Walking and talking, the students described what they were seeing, reflecting aloud on relationships among the living things and identifying familiar plants like maples and ferns. Along on the trip was Lina Moreira, a signer, and two parent volunteers. Ms. Moreira translated what was being said into sign language for RuthAnne, a child with limited hearing, and translated the child's signs into speech. Each parent walked along with a hyperactive child who might have wandered if not watched closely.

Build vocabulary through direct experience

Shortly, the class came to a thicket, where the youngsters sat down to watch for birds. When the children sighted an unfamiliar bird, Janice and José, members of the Animals-in-Our-Environment Team, looked it up in Peterson's *Field Guide to the Birds* by comparing key features with illustrations in the guide. Reading the entry to herself, Janice summarized the information for the class. Ms. Venezia mentioned that several birds were nesting in the thicket. Mark, the word keeper for the week, recorded *thicket* in his learning log as the class talked about why the word was a good one for what they saw. Later he would add *thicket* to the power word section of the class Word Wall.

Learning in Collaborative Teams

Learn to cooperate with others in a workshop environment

Back in the classroom, the third-graders talked briefly as a committee-of-the-whole, reflecting on what they had seen at the center. Then they disbanded to work collaboratively in their investigative teams. On this afternoon, the Plants-in-Our-Environment and the Animals-in-Our-Environment teams merged to write a summary of their visit. The merged teams included Chandra from the Plants Team and Janice from the Animals Team, both of whom were gifted readers. Referring to their learning logs, team members talked about the trees they had noted—sassafras, sweet gum, tulip—checking the tree guide and trade books they had previously taken from the library for more information. As they proposed sentences, Lamal, who was a young computer hacker, entered them in the classroom computer.

After the six children from the two teams had drafted a paragraph, they checked punctuation, juxtaposed sentences to achieve a more logical order, and decided on a title. At that point, Ms. Venezia conferred with them, asking questions to guide their revisions and reminding them to run the computer spelling checker before Lamal printed a final publication copy to share with the class the next day.

Work on individual needs

Having prepared their next day's presentation, the six students turned to other cooperative or individual activities. Lamal printed publication copies on the computer and then went on-line to get some information for his report on reptiles; he entered the information he found into a computer database. José, who was talented in art and was learning English as a second language, worked with Janice, a linguistically talented child, on their bird book. José drew labeled sketches of birds based on illustrations in the Peterson guide, while Janice read in the guide for information to describe the birds. Later, chorusing together, they read a poem from Paul Fleischman's *I Am Phoenix*, which they were preparing to share with classmates. Alone at a table, Chandra wrote vigorously; she had completed her research on trees and was well into a revised draft of her report. When she had reached her saturation point and no longer felt like writing, she took out the book she had chosen for pleasure reading and settled back to enjoy. Frank was writing too, but slowly, a first draft on flowering plants, which he would later edit with Chandra, his writing buddy.

And then there was Bruce—a member of the Plants Team. Bruce walked about the classroom, shoved his desk around, and started to bother Chandra. At that point Ms. Venezia came over to him. She reviewed the rules of behavior the class had agreed on, emphasizing that in this class students did not disturb others. Then she reviewed with him the tasks that were his contribution to the unit, gave him samples of leaves, needles, and cones that the nature center had provided, and looked over his shoulder as he began to make sketches of them to illustrate the encyclopedia of plants he was writing. Later in the week, Ms. Venezia conferred with Bruce's grandmother, his primary caregiver. She suggested that the grandmother talk with Bruce each day about his accomplishments and read aloud with him each evening.

While the two teams were viewing, reading, writing, and sketching, the other students pursued individual or collaborative tasks. Behind the bookcase, in the viewing center, the members of the team investigating forest habitats were looking at a videotape on rain forests. The members of the team working on the seashore and oceans were in the library, where the librarian was helping them locate information for their booklike report on water pollution. The members of the Desert Habitat Team were taking turns reading aloud to one another from a book on desert cacti. The members of the team investigating rivers, brooks, and ponds were discussing the organization of the book they were cooperatively writing, with each third-grader (especially Stuart, who generally wanted things done his way) insisting that his or her chapter be the first in the book. When Stuart stood up and shouted out that his chapter had to go first, Ms. Venezia went to the team, told Stuart to sit down, and helped the students use reason to resolve the problem: "What topic logically belongs first?" she asked.

Managing Diversity in the Inclusive Classroom

While the students worked in teams and on their own, Ms. Venezia used her time to troubleshoot. She visited with individual students and groups that had problems in learning, socializing, or behaving. She kept alert to what the teams were doing and moved quickly to solve problems before they developed into unmanageable situations.

In addition, Ms. Venezia conferred more formally with students who had special needs and with the investigative teams. That afternoon she conferred with José and Erica, who were learning English as a second language. In conference, she had them orally generate sentences modeled after sentences she proposed with words from the outing (e.g., "I saw a maple tree"; "I saw a cardinal in the maple tree"). To clarify meanings, she displayed pictures of trees and samples of objects as she and the students generated sentences. She also reminded the students that they could run the English sentence-making program in the computer.

Ms. Venezia then conferred with the Desert Habitat Team. She helped them organize a web of ideas based on the material they were reading aloud. During the group conference, Ms. Venezia accepted variant language patterns; children who spoke a variant form of English (e.g., Black English) used their own dialect to express ideas. On the other hand, Ms. Venezia did not accept a four-letter word used by one youngster. She stopped, made eye contact with the child, and explained in no uncertain terms that this language was inappropriate in classroom discussion.

DISCUSSION PROMPT

■ Ms. Venezia believes in the team model of instruction to meet the varied needs of her students. What advantages do you see? Disadvantages?

Language Arts for All Children

The range of abilities and disabilities, interests and disinterests, previous experiences, and language backgrounds in most elementary classrooms is generally as broad as or broader than that in Ms. Venezia's third grade. This is especially so since the advent of the Individuals with Disabilities Education Act (IDEA), or Public Law 101–476, the major federal legislation mandating inclusive education. The law directs that "to the maximum extent appropriate, students with disabilities should be educated with students who do not have a disability, and that special classes, separate schools, or other removal . . . from the regular education environment occurs only when the nature or severity of the disability is such that education in regular classes with the use of supplementary aids and services cannot be achieved satisfactorily." Under P.L. 101–476, each state must establish procedures and standards for local school districts to follow to be in compliance.

Generally, state procedures and standards mandate that pupils with educational disabilities be placed in appropriate programs in the "least restrictive environment." This provision means that children with significant emotional, auditory, visual, speech, or physical disabilities are mainstreamed into regular classrooms, making these classrooms home to a diverse group of learners.

The range of differences within a classroom is further broadened by the presence of youngsters from diverse cultures whose first language may not be English and of others who speak variant forms, or dialects, of English. Learning side by side as well are youngsters who have severe learning problems, others who are talented in some way, and still others who are attention deficit, hyperactive, or simply turned off to learning.

How does a busy teacher meet the needs of thirty or more children in an inclusive elementary classroom? In this chapter, we examine possible answers to this tough question, keeping in mind what we observed in Ms. Venezia's third grade:

- The importance of providing a language-rich environment.
- The value of collaborative activities in enabling learners to read and write at their own levels and contribute based on their strengths.
- The value of ongoing literature-based units across the curriculum.
- The importance of maintaining a positive attitude toward all children and a close relationship with the home.
- The need for the teacher to cooperate with specialists—guidance counselors, psychologists, and school nurses.

Because space limitations prevent thorough coverage here, readers are urged to investigate topics in greater detail by studying texts on behavior impairments, multiculturalism, English as a second language, dialects, reading disabilities, and children with exceptionalities.

READ

Stephen Kucer's "Engagement, Conflict, and Avoidance in a Whole Language Classroom," *Language Arts,* 75 (February 1998), 90–96. Kucer uses a case-study approach to argue for a "fuller acceptance" of the individuality of the learner.

Children with Behavior Impairments

When Rolf's first-grade teacher, Maureen, talks about young Rolf, she begins, "He can be a charmer!" Then Maureen pauses and continues, "In the classroom, however, he wants 100% of my attention and the attention of his classmates. He can't keep quiet or sit to do his work. He's always on the move and fooling around. He can be violent too. Once in the boys' room and without provocation, Rolf slammed a trash can into another youngster. When I sent him to the office, the secretaries gave him their undivided attention and plied him with candy. He was charming to them, winning them over with his ready smile. The secretaries as well as the principal can't understand the challenge this boy can be. Rolf is a challenge because of his ADHD [attention deficit hyperactivity disorder], but what makes maintaining a positive classroom environment so difficult is the fact that I have two other youngsters who find it difficult to pay attention or sit for any length of time."

In today's elementary schools we find numbers of children like Rolf who suffer from a variety of emotional and social disorders. Some youngsters are hyperaggressive; they hit, push, swear, and want their own way. Some are hyperactive just as Rolf is; they cannot sit still, constantly get out of line, and fiddle around. Some have an attention deficit disorder (ADD) and pay attention for only short periods. Others are withdrawn and make few contacts with others. And still others are completely turned off to school, for whatever reason, or are bored with school and just act up.

Because behavior disorders are so diverse, it is hard to generalize about ways to handle them. Yet teachers must deal with youngsters who have behavior impairments if the classroom is to function as a community in which all children can learn happily together. In this section, we discuss two approaches to working with students with behavior impairments that relate directly to language arts instruction: the team model and literature-based unit learning. Then we consider guidelines for organizing classroom activity to minimize disruptive behavior.

The Team Model of Instruction

WORD BANK

Learning-team model versus an assignment model

In *Control Theory in the Classroom* (1986), William Glasser explains the importance of children's need for power in learning to read and write. By *power* Glasser means believing in oneself. Successful achievement, attention, and applause satisfy this need.

Glasser theorizes that the need for power affects children's learning to read and write. In their heads, people store pictures of activities that satisfy their needs. Initially, youngsters enter school with a positive picture of learning; they perceive reading and writing as exciting. But because of the way reading and writing happen in some classrooms, they fail. Failing, they "take the picture of reading [and writing] as a need-satisfying activity out of their heads." In its place they put a picture of themselves as nonreaders/nonwriters and as disrupters whose misbehavior entertains others. As a result, some practice what Adella Youtz (1996) calls "chronic oppositional behavior," saying no to whatever the teacher suggests.

How should teachers function so that students develop positive pictures of reading and writing and of themselves as learners? Glasser counsels patience in teaching young children to read and write. He suggests providing them with much opportunity to experience, make, view, listen, and speak. He advises that teachers read aloud to children, encourage them to join in the telling of stories, talk about literature with them, and expand vocabulary naturally through oral interaction. Teachers should stress ideas rather than letter-perfect renditions as young children begin to read and emphasize ideas over correct spelling as they begin to write. Teachers should keep the fun in early learning.

To some extent, the same is true in upper grades. Some upper-grade teachers rely on individual assignments rather than on activities that require interaction and cooperation: They assign students to read selections and write answers to follow-up questions without preliminary discussion; they assign homework and allocate blocks of class time to going over it. Glasser contends that this *assignment model of instruction* reinforces some students' view of themselves as nonreaders/nonwriters.

In place of an assignment model, Glasser proposes a *learning-team model*. Rather than reading and writing by themselves, behavior-impaired upper-graders may be

Collaborating to complete a science experiment as part of a cross-curricular unit, students gain a sense of accomplishment and build a positive self-concept.
(© *Joel Gordon*)

Children with Behavior Impairments ■ 55

better off reading and writing in teams. According to Glasser, "We are all social animals; we need the support and interest of others" to make reading and writing interesting. Collaborating on a learning team to complete a project, older students gain a sense of belonging, which builds a perception of self-worth. "Belonging provides the initial motivation for students to work, and as they achieve academic success, students who have not worked previously begin to sense that knowledge is power and then want to work harder." The better students fulfill their needs for power and friendship by helping those who are weaker (as Janice helped José in the opening vignette). The weaker students fulfill their needs by contributing to a successful group endeavor; working alone, they rarely experience success. Students begin to rely on themselves rather than totally on their teacher to guide their learning (Glasser, 1986).

Literature-Based Unit Learning

GO TO

Pages 32–36 for a fuller discussion of literature-based unit learning.

Marilyn D'Alessandro (1990) taught severely emotionally handicapped eight- and nine-year-olds in a multiethnic, special education setting in Brooklyn, New York. Some of her students were neurologically impaired, some came from chaotic homes, and some were foster children who had lived in many different homes. For this reason, she established an atmosphere that was "calm, regular, and above all, fair," with some rules that were nonnegotiable and applied equally to everyone.

While teaching these children, D'Alessandro found that when she changed from a basal-bound to a literature-based reading program, students' interest level went up and their attention and behavior improved. Students in her program read aloud in teacher-guided groups and discussed novels that appealed to them: *Charlotte's Web*, *Tales of a Fourth Grade Nothing*, the *Polk Street School* series, and *Journey to Jo'Burg*—an excellent cross section of books to include in the fourth-grade curriculum. They participated in numerous activities based on what they were reading, such as viewing videos, making visual representations, cooking, and visiting the zoo. D'Alessandro discovered that through this approach, the children "learned to control their emotions so that they did not interfere with comprehension while reading." Children whose normal behavior included shifting, pushing their desks, screaming, and fighting would "sit at a round [reading] table, crowded between other children, without panicking" and listen to a story that became an "avenue of escape" from their own problems. Most important, students came to view themselves as readers. They chose to read, were proud of their ability, and asked their other teachers to read with them in the same way.

Like Marilyn D'Alessandro, many regular classroom teachers are building their language arts programs around literature-based units. They also are building literature-based units into content-area studies, as we saw earlier in Ms. Venezia's inclusive classroom. Elementary teachers are moving in these directions because the explorations that are part of these units provide opportunities for individualizing instruction and encouraging children who have different learning preferences, or *modalities*. Some students pick up ideas more completely when they receive them auditorily. In contrast, some students prefer the visual mode; they are at their best when they receive input through their eyes and express it visually. For other stu-

READ

Rita Colasent and Penny Griffith, "Autism and Literacy: Looking into the Classroom with Rabbit Stories," *The Reading Teacher*, 51 (February 1998), 414–420, for a study that indicates that students with autism may "benefit from oral reading or story time, as do regular education students."

dents, touch is especially important in their thinking and learning. Still others are kinesthetic learners and thinkers; motion and action are significant factors in the way they interface with ideas.

Howard Gardner (1993, 1995) has developed a theory of multiple intelligences that is useful in considering the varied talents children bring to their learning. Gardner proposes that people have different kinds of intelligences that are rather distinctive; this does not mean, however, that if a person is strong in one area of functioning, he or she is weak in others. And of course, intelligences are not static; over time all people change in how they approach learning, one another, and the world at large. The value of Gardner's work is to make teachers aware of the diversity of learning styles to be expected in inclusive classrooms and of the need to organize children's activity in integrated units so all children have opportunities to experience success. See Figure 2.1 for a pinwheel that clarifies the multiple intelligences found in regular elementary classrooms.

Guidelines for Minimizing Disruptive Behavior

In every classroom—even under the guidance of experienced teachers who recognize the diversity within their classes—misbehavior occurs. Here are some general guidelines related to language arts instruction that help to minimize disruptive behavior:

- Establish guidelines for acceptable participation early on. (For example, we do not talk while someone else "has the floor"; we wait our turn; we do not "pump our hand" to get the teacher's attention.)
- Involve students in the formulation of classroom communication "rules." (For example, teacher and students cooperatively develop behavior contracts, which participants sign.)
- Establish procedures for classroom operation. (For example, at the sound of the drum, all must attend to the teacher; students place completed papers in the "in" basket; they do not sharpen pencils during class conversations, only during workshop.)
- Make sure that students know the tasks they are to do at times when the teacher is conferring with an individual or a small group. Make sure materials are availabel for completion of independent tasks. (For example, students work from chalkboard or duplicated lists of required and recommended tasks.)
- Be aware of children's special needs before problems arise, and plan activity based on a clear understanding of students' attention span. (For example, check for signs of restlessness and inattention during discussions and, when noted, switch tasks or means of instruction.)
- Maintain eye contact during discussions, move about the classroom, and bring as many students into a discussion as possible.
- Never use language activity or the withdrawal of it as punishment. (For example, do not assign compositions on why students should pay attention. *Written communication should never be punishment.*)

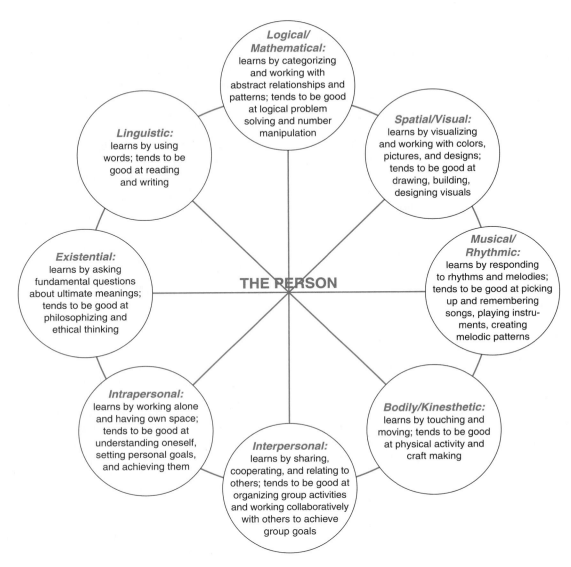

Figure 2.1
Gardner's Multiple Intelligences

Children with Diverse Language and Cultural Backgrounds

READ

"Children's Books: Perspectives,"
The Reading Teacher, 50
(December 1996/January 1997),
340–341, for children's books that
treat cultural diversity and
multiple perspectives.

GO TO

Access Pages 494–497, for a
bibliography of multicultural
books useful in developing a
curriculum.

In many of today's elementary classrooms we find students whose first language is Spanish, Portuguese, Vietnamese, Chinese, Arabic, or any of the world's other languages. These children learn with native English speakers for some or all of their school day and may be instructed by monolingual teachers. These children bring not only their diverse language backgrounds but their diverse cultures into the classroom.

Collaborative team activity and literature-based units—the two approaches discussed in the previous section—are as helpful in involving bilingual children in language learning as they are in engaging children with behavior impairments (Lim and Watson, 1993; Ernst and Richard, 1994/1995). Anna Compeau—a fourth-grade teacher in a school where many students are learning English as a second language and where class size averages around thirty-four—has found this to be true. One of the units she develops early in the school year focuses on the immigrant experience—the children's own experiences as immigrants and the immigrant experience in literature. The theme of the unit is that we all have our unique backgrounds, but we have common values too. In the unit, she shares *Watch the Stars Come Out, How Many Days to America: A Thanksgiving Story, Molly's Pilgrim,* and *Grandfather's Journey* in read-along fashion. As she reads a story aloud for a second time, students join in to read aloud with her in chorus, following her model as to pronunciation and rhythm. In response to the literature, students talk about and compare their own experiences to story happenings, role-play favorite parts of the stories, and collaborate to create pyramids to show key elements of the stories. They interview someone in their home or community who is an immigrant, collaborate in making visuals to clarify the sequence of the stories, use their visuals to retell stories to buddies, and create huge vocabulary charts that they post and use in writing.

Technology Notes

Check these Web sites for information about second language learning and diversity:

http://www.cal.org   The National Center for Research on Cultural Diversity and Second Language, a nonprofit group of scholars based in Washington, D.C., is a general source for materials on diversity and SLL.

http://www.handsonenglish.com/   This print journal helps teachers of English as a Second Language to develop games, projects, and lesson plans.

http://www.multilingualbooks.com/   *Multilingual Books* is an on-line catalogue that is a good source for videos, tapes, courses, and software.

http://www.tesol.com/   This is the site of the English Zone, which features a search facility, chat room, message boards, and learning materials.

Should limited English proficient (LEP) learners be provided with content-area instruction in their native language or is immersion in English the better way to go?

Annette Lopez (2000) explains that "bilingual education provides instruction in two languages, English and the native language of the learner, with some attention given to the learner's native culture and heritage." She further explains that some bilingual programs provide content-area instruction in the first language until students have a firm control of academic language, whereas other programs are early exit; students make a "quick transition to English literacy once they have acquired basic reading skills" in their native language. This is in contrast to immersion programs in which instruction is almost totally in English from the start "with some clarifications in the learner's home language" to ease the transition into English (2000).

Currently, the question of which is the more effective approach is being argued in the public press. (See "Bilingual Education Lives On," *The New York Times,* March 2, 2001, p. A23, by Ron Unz, who is leading campaigns to dismantle bilingual education in California and Arizona.) Some states continue to mandate programs that provide content-area instruction in the student's first language for many years, based on the notion that children should continue to get instruction in their native language so that they truly become bilingual—proficient in two languages. Other states now mandate the immersion approach, based on the assumption that children must learn English early and well to become fully functioning members of American society.

DISCUSSION PROMPT

What advantages do you see in providing content-area instruction in the native language as students develop their ability to handle academic English? What advantages do you see in an immersion approach? Why do you think that some states are turning away from bilingual education and to immersion programs?

Ms. Compeau also provides direct instruction to help her children learn English and encourages children who come from a variety of countries to share their culture with the class. In this section, we focus on the multifaceted role of the teacher in teaching English as a second language and developing the classroom as a multicultural community.

English as a Second Language (ESL)

Describing how he felt when he was younger and was a limited English proficient (LEP) learner, Marin, a student in Anna Compeau's class, wrote, "When I was little I only knew how to talk Spanish. I was born in the United States but no one in my family talked English. When I went to pre-K I did not know how to talk English. I met a friend and I talked to him. The teacher would tell me to talk in English. I did not understand what she said, so I asked my friend and he would tell me. Little by little I learned English. When I graduated I knew how to talk English."

Language arts teachers play four major roles in helping children like Marin develop English-language proficiency. First, teachers must accept the child's first language as an acceptable medium of communication and must not insist that a child with limited English proficiency speak only English. To help a child understand what is going on, teachers can pair a student with a child who has greater proficiency in English but also speaks the child's first language. When no other children are in the class who share the same home language as the LEP child, teachers should ask for bilingual volunteers from the community to visit the classroom for an hour or so during the week and to serve as translators. Bilingual volunteers can also make basic vocabulary charts with side-by-side entries for words in English and in the first language of LEP students in the class. Posted on the Word Wall, the multilanguage charts provide a ready referent for LEP students and give them a sense that their home language is part of their classroom environment. The charts also provide a reference for English-speaking elementary-grade students who are learning a second language as part of what today is called the "world language curriculum."

Second, teachers serve as speech models. Often those who are becoming *bilingual*—who are learning English even as they maintain proficiency in their native language—converse at home and in their community in their native language. As a result, their inability to communicate in English isolates them from neighborhood English-speaking children. Their major contact with English is at school, and their beginning attempts at English mimic the pronunciation, intonation patterns, and sentence patterns heard at school. The need for teachers who speak English well cannot be overemphasized.

Third, teachers must be aware that the child's native language differs from English not only in vocabulary but in the speech sounds that make up words, basic sentence patterns, intonation patterns, and even nonverbal behaviors. For example, Spanish speakers who have already learned their alphabet pronounce the vowels as /ah/, /ey/, /ee/, /o/, /oo/, not as /a/, /e/, /i/, /o/, /u/; thus, they have difficulty distinguishing among words such as *cut, cat,* and *cot*. There are structural differences, too. The descriptive adjective usually follows the noun in Spanish. Other basic structural differences include no *s* for the third-person singular verb; no use of the auxiliaries *do, does, did,* and *will;* substitution of the verb *to be* for the verb *to have;* and a different way of indicating questions and exclamations occurs in the two languages; so does the use of direct quotations.

Once aware of such differences, teachers can design oral sequences that focus on them. Much of this work occurs in small groups as a teacher gathers ESL learners together and provides practice with basic sentence and sound patterns. During sessions, conversations grow out of firsthand contact with objects and pictures, role playing serves as a context for using language, and pantomime takes the place of verbal language when communication breaks down. Sometimes visuals can help, as when one teacher, Judith Craig, used a time line to orient a young man from Thailand to English verb tenses—a concept difficult for him to understand because tense is not a part of verb functioning in the Thai language.

READ

Susan Watts-Taffe and Diane Truscott, "Using What We Know About Language and Literacy Development for ESL Students in the Mainstream Classroom," *Language Arts,* 77 (January 2000), 258–264. Watts-Taffe and Truscott explain that "social language skills develop more rapidly than academic language skills" and that "it takes an average of five to seven years for students to become proficient in academic language use."

GO TO

Pages 403–410 for specific strategies.

Specific strategies for building language facility that are described in Chapter 11 are especially helpful when applied orally:

1. *Expansions:* adding words at key spots in a sentence.
2. *Transformations:* transforming kernel sentences into questions, exclamations, and negative sentences.
3. *Sentence building:* creating sentences from subject and predicate parts.
4. *Sentence combining:* building one sentence from two short sentences.

Choral interpretation of sentences using typical English rhythm patterns, discussed in Chapters 3 and 6, is also helpful.

A fourth role is to communicate sincere appreciation for the culture of speakers of other languages. The goal of instruction is not only the acquisition of a second language but also the ability to function within both the American and the native cultures. To help all students achieve multicultural understanding, the teacher can allot time for sharing ideas about the customs that are part of the life of different peoples. Holidays celebrated by children who come from other parts of the world can be observed in classrooms, just as Halloween and Thanksgiving are celebrated

Distinguished Educator

Meet Gloria Ladson-Billings

Gloria Ladson-Billings is Professor of Curriculum and Instruction at the University of Wisconsin in Madison. She was a major contributor to the *Dictionary of Multicultural Education* and is known for her work on culturally relevant pedagogy. From a conversation with Gloria Ladson-Billings come these thoughts: "The major thing that I think people who are going to teach kids, any kids—not just kids different from themselves, but particularly if they're teaching kids who are different from themselves culturally, racially, ethnically, linguistically—is to understand that they, themselves, are cultural beings. . . . One of the major things I think is important for teachers to be successful, is not to decide, 'Oh, I've gotta go out and study these fifteen cultures.' Human beings group themselves in infinite varieties. You will never learn all the cultures there are to learn. But if you learn your own, it's one of the things that I think will help you understand that culture functions in particular ways. And so, while you may not know all the subtleties and nuances of culture, you can recognize its operation" ("A Conversation with Gloria Ladson-Billings" by Arlette Willis and Karla Lewis, *Language Arts*, 75 [January 1998], 63).

DISCUSSION PROMPT

Do you agree with Ladson-Billings that teachers must see themselves as cultural beings? What do you know about yourself as a "cultural being"? How does who you are affect your functioning in an inclusive, multicultural classroom?

there. Appreciating diversity, the teacher can encourage native English speakers to learn words introduced by Spanish, Vietnamese, or German speakers. In this way, native English speakers begin to appreciate diverse languages and cultures, and newcomers feel that the language and culture they bring are of value.

Language Arts for Migrant Children

■—● ● ●

READ

Catherine Whittaker, "'Voices from the Fields': Including Farm Workers in the Curriculum," *The Reading Teacher,* 50 (March 1997), 482–489, for a bibliography of books about migrant workers.

The United States and Canada have a relatively large population of seasonal migrants—workers employed in agriculture who follow jobs from place to place. Although not all migrant workers are bilingual and bicultural, many of those in the Southwest speak English as a second language. In the classroom, migrant children pose an additional challenge because they stay only a short time in school; most "attend at least two different schools each year, and some as many as six different schools in a year" (Whittaker, 1997).

In most programs geared to meet the needs of the migratory population, teachers must emphasize the development of a healthy self-concept. Children who move have less opportunity to develop close friends. Because they are often poor, speak a different native language, and have different cultural backgrounds, they may be the target of other children's taunts. However, these children have strengths. They may be more knowledgeable about geographical differences, having traveled more widely; they may be capable painters, vocalists, storytellers. Teachers must help these children display their talents, for success is necessary in the development of a positive self-concept. Teachers must also help children interact naturally with classmates, placing them in collaborative groups where they can learn, contribute, and feel good about themselves.

In the same way, teachers must emphasize target-language development for those whose native language is not English. They should supply extensive firsthand experience as a base for oral interaction and design lessons that involve considerable oral work to develop a functional speaking/listening English vocabulary. Shared writing is an important tool for making the transition between oral and written language. Students can dictate charts in both their native and target languages, going on to read what they have composed. In addition, teachers should share stories from the children's own cultures, using them as a base for informal conversations.

Finally, teachers and schools must assume responsibility for children's health problems, assuming that if children are poorly fed or in ill health, they will be less likely to acquire language facility. Many districts employ a home-school liaison to keep communication lines open and refer needy families to agencies supplying food, clothing, and advice. Educational service centers in Texas and other states provide consultants and workshops to assist teachers in meeting the special language needs of migratory children.

Children Who Speak Variant Forms of English

Most languages comprise a number of variant forms, or *dialects,* that differ in vocabulary, syntactic structure, and/or pronunciation. This diversity is to be expected, because language is always changing, and words and expressions mean different things to different peoples.

Linguists remind us that no dialect is inherently superior, none deficient. Variations of languages are different because they have changed in response to the needs of the people using them. In discussing dialects, the words *correct* and *incorrect* are inappropriate. The appropriate question is whether the dialect communicates clearly within the social community where it is functional. Linguists also point out that dialects are "well-ordered, highly structured, highly developed language systems" with extensive vocabularies and consistent rules for sentence making (Baratz, 1969).

Feelings about the desirability of certain forms, however, do exist. "I be goin'" communicates clearly, but the usage strikes a negative chord in the business world and hence inside the classroom. The same is true of such expressions as "I ain't got none" and "I done it." This negativism poses problems for youngsters coming to school speaking variants of English that rely on these expressions. The children who rely on these forms tend to test lower on standardized tests of verbal facility than their classmates who speak standard English, or what Marie Louise Gomez (in Willis and Lewis, 1998) calls "American edited English." This is to be expected since children's ability is being measured in a dialect other than their own. Unfortunately, however, because some of the structures of children's native dialect differ from American edited English, those children are at risk of falling behind in school.

Educational Approaches to the Dialectally Different

How to approach the education of children who speak dialects other than American edited English is a question of continuing concern. Logically, three approaches exist: to replace, to keep, and to add.

To Replace   The replace approach attempts to substitute American edited English for the nonstandard. As they speak, children are "corrected" to bring their speech in line with the standard. The problems with this approach are numerous. Children who are made to believe there is something wrong with their speech may stop speaking in school, which is counterproductive. Then, too, language is a social phenomenon; in requiring a complete dialect change, schools are striking at the core of a culture. For these reasons, most language arts educators reject the approach.

To Keep   The keep approach takes an opposite tack, maintaining that every dialect has equal communication potential, and children should not be forced to speak or write a dialect other than the one acquired within their social group or region. The dialect children bring to school should be accepted fully and should be the medium of instruction, say advocates of the keep approach.

READ

Kris Gutierrez, Patricia Baquedano-Lopez, and Myrna Turner, "Putting Language Back into Language Arts: When the Radical Middle Meets the Third Space," *Language Arts,* 74 (September 1997), 368–378, for interesting ideas about reaching across cultures.

The keep approach also has its problems. First, few books have been written with the sentence patterns and vocabulary of nonstandard dialects. Speakers who wish to read must be able to interpret the syntax and vocabulary of American edited English. Second, because nonstandard dialects are not used in many business situations, nonstandard speakers are less likely to find high-paying managerial and professional employment.

To Add   The add approach is a middle-of-the-road position. As Gloria Ladson-Billings explains this stance, teachers do not spend time trying to rid children of their vernacular forms. They respect the dialect that children bring to school and encourage them to communicate in their native dialect. However, because not introducing American edited English to children who speak other dialects can hinder economic advancement and would be unfair, teachers help youngsters learn English as a second dialect by contrasting vernacular forms with standard English forms. As Ladson-Billings further explains, teachers help youngsters understand where their native dialect is appropriate and how it translates; they say to children, "Well, this is how you translate that into standard form" (Ladson-Billings in Willis and Lewis, 1998).

As with the other stances, the add approach, has some problems. Even as children are learning to read, they must learn to handle the standard dialect in its oral form—something not required of children who grow up speaking American edited English. Despite this weakness, the bidialectal position is the most responsible approach: It accepts the economic realities of life in America today and respects children's native dialects as significant components of their culture. To teach standard English as a second dialect, elementary teachers can rely on the same strategies highlighted in the section of this chapter on ESL: lots of oral activity in which children build, transform, expand, combine, and orally interpret standard English sentence patterns; many opportunities to participate in shared writing and oral reading of the experience charts; and collaborative and unit learning.

Children Who Bring a Learning Disadvantage or Disorder

READ

Laura Robb, "A Cause for Celebration: Reading and Writing for At-Risk Students," *The New Advocate,* 6 (Winter 1993), 25–40. The article describes Robb's literature-based activities with at-risk seventh- and eighth-graders.

Another group that is the concern of the elementary school teacher consists of children whose academic achievement is below their peers'. Some children are at risk because of low IQs. Studies indicate that about 20 percent of the population have IQs between 70 and 90, that these youngsters usually learn in regular classrooms for most of the school day, but that "schooling is a strong force in forming and maintaining IQ" (Stephen Ceci in Wickelegren, 1999). Other children are at risk because they lack motivation or interest in school activities or have had limited experiences with language and books before coming to school. In a sense, these children bring with them a *learning disadvantage.*

Other students are at risk because they have, in the words of the Education for All

Handicapped Children Act of 1975, a disorder "in one or more of the basic psychological processes involved in understanding or in using language, spoken or written, which disorder may manifest itself in imperfect ability to listen, think, speak, read, write, spell, or to do mathematical calculations."

Children Who Bring a Learning Disadvantage

READ

Cathy Roller, *Variability Not Disability* (Newark, Del.: International Reading Association 1996), for an excellent description of a workshop approach to the broad variability in learning ability found in inclusive classrooms.

How does the teacher work with children who struggle with a learning disadvantage? Katherine Maria (1989) proposes that the teacher focus on what children know rather than on what they do not know. She recommends having children brainstorm before reading to activate their prior knowledge, focusing children's attention before reading on the concepts central in a selection, and using a variety of before-reading strategies.

Along similar lines, Michael Ford and Marilyn Ohlhausen (1988) suggest that the teacher

- Organize real, meaningful learning through the use of thematic units.
- Emphasize activities that capitalize on children's oral language skills.
- Implement whole-class activities (such as personalized reading and journal writing) that have built-in individualization.
- Use open-ended projects (such as the publication of a team booklet or class newspaper, or the production of a drama).
- Plan writing activities that allow individual students to respond at their own levels yet provide structure for writing.
- Use group incentives and internal competition (such as award of a bronze medal for 800 minutes of independent reading—a goal within the reach of most readers—a silver medal for 900 minutes, and a gold medal for 1,000 minutes) to motivate children to read.
- Implement a cross-grade sharing arrangement with a group of younger students in which slower upper-grade children read easy stories to a younger, receptive audience.

Also important are computers with voice output that level the playing field for youngsters who do not see themselves as readers.

In some schools today, resource room teachers (or Chapter 1 teachers) still give special instruction to children who are below grade level in reading and writing. These teachers handle a limited number of children at any one time and work in resource rooms equipped with materials to help children with learning problems. Often the classroom teacher must tell the resource room teacher what to emphasize with a child and provide ideas as to the instruction required. The classroom teacher called upon to set up an individualized learning plan for the child with reading and writing problems must remember that giving drill exercises to a child who does not like to read will probably make that child dislike reading even more. Instead, the classroom teacher must encourage the resource room teacher to engage children creatively in story listening, discussion, and group writing and to use interesting content from science, history, and geography.

Children Who Bring a Learning Disorder

According to an article in *Science* (Roush, 1995), there are more than 2.3 million schoolchildren now diagnosed with learning disorders. Findings, which are still controversial, "pin the blame on biology and suggest the problem could be even more widespread." Researchers suggest that as many as 20 percent of the nation's schoolchildren may have some form of learning disability.

One kind of disorder is dyslexia. According to Jack Westman (in Putnam, 1996), "The word *dyslexia* refers to difficulty in recognizing, articulating, comprehending, writing and spelling written words. As a neurological term, dyslexia calls attention to variations in the brain rather than deficiencies in instruction that underlie difficulties in reading and writing." Some children with dyslexia cannot visually track words with their eyes and may lose their place as they read. These children gain by following a line with a finger or a card. Some dyslexic children have difficulty recognizing words visually even though they can copy words accurately; for such children, letter-by-letter analysis is the only productive way of getting any meaning from print. Other children, with an auditory-linguistic dyslexia, cannot comprehend the meaning of words and may have trouble coming up with a word as they need it to speak. They also have trouble coming up with ideas in writing. For them, Westman recommends a whole-word method of teaching. Still other dyslexic children exhibit motor difficulties in writing and spelling, with the outcome being illegible handwriting and errors in spelling.

Given the variety of problems subsumed under the umbrella term of *dyslexia*, the teacher who is uncertain how to help a child with a severe reading or writing problem should consult a learning disability specialist, if there is one in the school district, for it is important to distinguish between problems caused by poor motivation or language background and those caused by a neurological dysfunction. It is important also to remember that people with dyslexia can be talented in other areas of performance; examples in point are Thomas Alva Edison, Woodrow Wilson, and William James.

CONSIDER

E. Paulesu et al. "propose that dyslexic brains are not able to mould connections between the sight, sound, and meaning of a word as efficiently as other brains" (*Science*, 292 [May 18, 2001], 1301.)

Academically Talented Children

In most elementary schools, at-risk and academically talented learners learn together in the same classroom. Lewis Terman (Terman and Merrill, 1960), the pioneer of intelligence testing, identifies three categories of academic giftedness: the high average (IQs ranging from 110 to 120), the superior (IQs between 120 and 140), and the very superior (IQs between 140 and 170). Children in these categories generally exhibit rapid language development, since most IQ tests are verbally based.

Yale psychologist Robert Sternberg (1984) questions heavy reliance on IQ tests in determining children's potential for learning. He notes that high IQ neither ensures intelligent performance in real-life situations nor correlates positively with success in

READ

Howard Gardner's work on multiple intelligences provides a comprehensive view of diverse learning styles. Check Figure 2.1 of *Communication in Action*. Read also Kevin Kelly and Sidney Moon, "Personal and Social Talents," *Phi Delta Kappan*, 79 (June 1998), 743–746, for a discussion of the importance of personal and social talents in achieving success.

life. In Sternberg's words, "intelligent performance in the real world centers on the ability to capitalize on one's strengths and to compensate for one's weaknesses and on the ability to modify the environment so that it will better fit one's adaptive skills." Sternberg also questions whether timed tests are true indicators of intelligence and proposes that such tests fail to identify the potential of children who have grown up in environments characterized by some type of deprivation. Clearly, too, giftedness can be expressed in diverse ways. Children can have musical, artistic, technical, personal, and/or social talents (Kelly and Moon, 1998).

Characteristics of Academically Talented Children

To identify youngsters with exceptional mental abilities, teachers should ask these questions:

- How rapidly does this child learn? How clearly does he or she perceive relationships?
- How probing are the child's questions? How curious is he or she?
- How extensive is the child's oral vocabulary?
- How easily does the child pick up and retain information?
- How divergent are the child's answers? How creative and novel are his or her approaches to problems?
- What level of questions does the child answer? Does the child respond well mainly at the factual level, or is he or she able to hypothesize, predict, and generalize?

A factor that confuses some teachers trying to identify academically gifted children is that this category includes youngsters who are disabled in speech, hearing, vision, or social adjustment. A noteworthy example is Helen Keller, who was both deaf and blind. A gifted child can be shy, restless, and inattentive; he or she can be a stutterer or exhibit articulation problems. Particular care must be taken in working with children who speak a different native language or dialect. Although these youngsters may do poorly on traditional tests, some obviously have the sharpness of mind that characterizes academic giftedness.

Programs for Academically Talented Children

READ

Joseph Renzulli, "A Rising Tide Lifts All Ships: Developing the Gifts and Talents of All Students," *Phi Delta Kappan*, 80 (October 1998), 104–111.

Academically gifted children tend to be rapid language learners. They read at an early age and may enter school as self-taught readers and writers. They have vocabularies that astound the average adult and perform higher-level cognitive tasks with ease. As a result, they require little drill with the basics, for they grasp ideas quickly. Instead of drilling, the teacher must open doors that encourage youngsters to discover, reflect, and think critically. The teacher should

- Provide an array of books that fascinate students who are already intrigued by words (the *Guinness Book of World Records,* an atlas, a world almanac, encyclopedias, a giant dictionary, field guides, an adult thesaurus).
- Schedule trips to the library to select books that stimulate curiosity and satisfy children's hunger to learn.

Personalized reading is a means through which academically talented learners can expand their knowledge and interests beyond the regular curriculum.

(© Jean-Claude Lejeune)

- Encourage surfing of the Internet for information.
- Schedule small-group discussions that treat subjects in greater depth than is possible in an inclusive class.
- Ask questions that lead readers to interpret, apply, analyze, synthesize, and evaluate.
- Encourage children to interrelate aspects of a particular experience and go beyond repetitive tasks to solve related problems.
- Suggest sophisticated assignments such as interviewing; researching; making tapes, videos, or slides; creating language games; and compiling a computer database.
- Encourage leadership by asking youngsters to lead a discussion, explain, or help others.
- Encourage children to participate in special events such as young authors' conferences and science fairs.

READ

Tom Rogers, "Fellow Nerds: Let's Celebrate Nerdiness!" *Newsweek* (December 11, 2000), 14, for a discussion of social problems that "book-smart" students face.

For language-talented children, writing must be wedded to reading as students develop the ability to handle diverse literary forms and styles. Writing original versions modeled after published story structures and styles, writing and sending letters to magazine and newspaper editors, writing critical reviews of stories, writing abbreviated encyclopedias, almanacs, atlases after researching a topic are all writing activities that flow naturally out of reading that language-gifted children can pursue independently or in teams.

As with dialectally different children, teacher attitude is important. James Gallagher (1975) reports that research studies "present us with a portrait of hostile feelings of teachers toward the gifted student." He suggests that these feelings are a reaction to the threat talented youngsters pose to teachers. A description of one academically gifted youngster's manner of interacting with adults hints at how a youngster may unknowingly intimidate a teacher (Hildreth, 1966):

> One day a visitor strolled over to the shelf of new books in a school library, picked out a book, and leafed through it. An alert ten-year-old stepped right up. "Here's a better book on horses than that one," he commented. "It has beautiful pictures." He exclaimed over details in the book, then picked out several others rapidly. "My favorite picture—lions in the jungle," and he sketched the story rapidly. The visitor turned the page, commenting on the next picture, "Leopards, no, wildcats." "Oh, no," said the boy, "those are cheetahs." "Have you read all these books?" inquired the visitor, indicating a row of 200 or 300 volumes. "Well, not quite all of them [modestly], but I know what most of them are about."

Children with Sensory Impairments

In the past, children with severe sensory impairments spent most of their school years in special classrooms instructed by teachers trained in educating students with disabilities. Today, as a result of Public Law 94-142 and aided by special educators, the regular elementary teacher must deal with youngsters who have hearing and vision impairments.

Children with Hearing Impairments

READ

■ Elizabeth Fielding, "Dealing with Auditory Processing Problems in the Classroom," *Reading Today,* 10 (June/July 1993), 28.

■ Nadeen Ruiz, "A Young Deaf Child Learns to Write," *The Reading Teacher,* 49 (November 1995), 206–217.

Although deaf children are generally not placed in regular classrooms, children whose hearing is impaired to an extent that interferes with normal language learning may spend some or all of their day in an elementary class. The teacher has a twofold responsibility to these youngsters: to identify those who have an impairment and to aid them in language development despite their disability.

Behaviors that are clues to some loss of hearing include speaking in a very loud voice, repeating answers already given, an inability to distinguish certain language sounds and make those sounds clearly, and playing a tape recorder at a high volume. Children who may have an impairment should be referred to the school health services for diagnostic testing.

Authorities advocate the use of specific procedures when working with hearing-impaired children in regular classrooms:

■ Seating children where they can see the teacher's lip movements; not standing before a strong light source that may prevent children from observing moving lips; forming children's chairs into circles during talk times; and refraining from talking while a child's back is turned.
■ Talking clearly and naturally in full sentences and writing important directions on the board.
■ Suggesting that children move around the room to be where they can hear best.
■ Encouraging children to participate in oral interaction.
■ Providing a computer that substitutes a blinking menu bar for the audible, attention-getting beep; encouraging students to communicate via e-mail or join a computer chatroom.

In terms of literacy development, children with hearing impairments may lag behind their hearing peers. Some have trouble acquiring basic decoding and comprehension skills. This difficulty arises from a combination of perceptual, communication, experiential, and instructional deficits (Wilson and Hyde, 1997). For example, phonics, which relies on perception of differences in sounds, may be physically impossible for some, requiring greater reliance on contextual clues, sight words, and structural analysis. Tactile, kinesthetic, and visual techniques for learning to spell gain in significance over approaches that stress sound-symbol relationships. For some children, speaking is a parallel problem; distortions of speech sounds occur because youngsters cannot hear the sounds.

Technology Notes

Check these Web sites for material on disabilities:

http://members.tripod.com/Caroline_Bowen/phonol-and-artic.htm
Bowen's article addresses speech disorders.

http://www.cchs.usyd.edu.au/csd/clinic/dyspraxia2.htm This article relates speech disorders to reading.

http://www2.edc.org This is the site of the National Center to Improve Practices in Special Education through Technology, Media, and Materials.

http://www.closingthegap.com This Web site provides information on assistive technology products that help students who have a disability to use technology, especially for writing.

In most, if not all, cases, children with a hearing impairment who are integrated into regular classes have some hearing, which can be amplified with hearing aids and used to facilitate interpretation and production of speech. Individualization is necessary, with the child being guided through an instructional sequence beginning with recognition of gross sounds and leading to the ability to discriminate speech sounds that look alike when formed on the lips. To assist children in producing difficult speech sounds, many schools make available a speech therapist, who can also help the teacher by providing suggestions, materials, and information on how to adjust the program.

Children with Visual Impairments

Like a hearing impairment, a loss of visual acuity can affect a child's ability to interpret and produce language. Often the elementary school teacher first recognizes a possible impairment by observing that a child bends the head down to the desk or holds a book up near the eyes when reading, squints at the board, covers one eye, blinks excessively, or thrusts the body forward to see. A youngster may say that he or she cannot see board writing or complain of blurriness while reading. A teacher should refer a child who exhibits a combination of these symptoms to the child's caregiver and to the school health service for eye examination.

Children with some vision loss, especially a loss that cannot be corrected with glasses, can be helped by

- Placement near the board.
- Instruction in small groups, clustered around an easel where words are written clearly in large print.
- Use of a reader-buddy, who reads directions printed on the board.
- Use of paper on which the lines have been darkened; use of darkened handwriting models; use of raised-letter models.
- Use of hearing, feeling, and touching rather than low-intensity pictures as a stimulus for speaking and writing.
- Preparation of special materials such as tests in large print; dictation of test questions.

- Provision of large-print versions of written materials and of computer technology that allows print magnification on the computer screen.
- Provision of chart paper on which to write down individual stories in large print.
- Provision of computers with voice or braille input, voice output, and an Internet connection. This enables children who have a severe visual impairment to access libraries worldwide and research ideas independently.

Children with Speech Problems

There are four major kinds of speech problems: articulation disorders, stuttering, phonation problems, and delayed or limited speech development. In most school systems, a speech therapist has direct responsibility for helping children with speech problems. The teacher's responsibility lies in identifying youngsters with impairments and providing a relaxed environment that encourages children to speak.

Speech Problems

Articulation disorders are the most frequent speech problems in children. Some youngsters substitute one sound for another, as in using the /w/ for the /r/ to produce *wed wose;* or the /t/ for the /k/ to produce a *tite* rather than a *kite;* or the /d/ for the /t/ or /th/ to produce *drain* for *train* and *dat* for *that.* Some youngsters omit sounds, especially those they find too difficult to produce or those they do not hear. Final-consonant sounds are commonly omitted, and a few youngsters produce no final-consonant sounds. A third form of articulation disorder is distortion. The /s/ is commonly distorted, accompanied by extraneous hissing or whistling.

Stuttering is another kind of speech disorder that in its most severe state is accompanied by exaggerated physical behavior—gasping for air, contortions of the face, blinking of the eyes, tensing of the body. Many children between three and five years of age typically repeat speech sounds, and adults often repeat in speaking. This is normal speaking behavior. Somehow, from normal speaking behavior severe stuttering develops with the physical manifestations associated with what specialists call *secondary stuttering.* Although it is not clear how secondary stuttering develops, it is considered a learned behavior. Attempts to avoid stuttering may to some extent be responsible for the accompanying physical behaviors.

Phonation disorders include problems related to intensity, pitch, quality, and rhythm of the voice. The husky, the monotone, the shrill, the nasal, and the too-soft voice are all phonation problems. Some are organic, resulting from a faulty mouth, nose, or vocal fold structure. Some are learned through associations with parents who speak similarly. Some may relate to psychological functioning.

A few children in early primary grades exhibit almost no speech at all. By twelve months, they do not speak the two or three words typical of most young children; by twenty-four months, they do not put together very simple sentences. Children generally are considered to have delayed speech development if they fall about twelve months behind these norms. Delayed development can result from overall mental retardation, hearing impairment, lack of speech stimulation, and emotional shock.

Teaching Children with Speech Problems

Remediating a severe speech disorder requires specialized training that most elementary teachers lack. For this reason, the need for highly qualified speech therapists cannot be overstressed. In school districts with insufficient personnel, teachers should work to see that the staff is expanded so that every speech-impaired child has access to specialized attention.

The classroom teacher can provide more generalized attention, especially in the lower grades. The teacher can involve children continually with the sounds of language. Informal conversations between teacher and students help youngsters see how pleasant speaking can be. Listening to stories and poems, chorusing and singing songs and rhymes, and playing games that require differentiation among sounds heighten children's sensitivity to language sounds. Greater sensitivity can be built through language activities that focus on particular speech sounds. Youngsters who have an articulation problem can practice producing different sounds as part of a teacher-guided play with sounds. The child works on a particular sound or problem, with the teacher *not* correcting or pointing out speech errors during general oral conversation activities. Constant correction makes speaking unpleasant and can worsen the problem.

Some attempt can be made to remediate phonation problems during oral interpretation of selections. Working within a group, children can vary pitch and loudness and experiment with different ways to project the voice. Choral speaking is an excellent way to develop vocal control as children interpret lines of poetry and prose, varying pitch, loudness, and tone to communicate meanings.

Stuttering is a more difficult problem. Teachers of young children must realize that repeating sounds is typical behavior at this stage. Labeling a child a stutterer and drawing this "condition" to parents' attention can be counterproductive. Kindergarten teachers in particular should help parents to accept the normal repetitions of youthful speech and encourage the child to talk.

The major contribution a teacher can make to an older child who has acquired the physical characteristics associated with secondary stuttering is to be patient, give the youngster time to contribute, and encourage other children to be patient and considerate. Teachers may be prone to urge children to speak more quickly or slowly, to stop and start over, to take a deep breath. Instructions such as these aggravate the situation, however, and may cause a young person with secondary stuttering characteristics to stop contributing. They also may result in aggravated physical mannerisms.

CONSIDER

Other productive activities include creative dramatics, puppet plays, role playing, reading along while listening, and audiotaping.

Continuous Assessment of Children as Language Users

READ

Robert Tierney, "Literacy Assessment Reform: Shifting Beliefs, Principles, Possibilities, and Emerging Practices," *The Reading Teacher,* 51 (February 1998), 374–390. Tierney suggests twelve principles to think about.

To provide children with experiences in line with their individual needs, teachers must assess children's strengths and weaknesses on a continuing basis. This applies to all children—those who have a disability, those who are "average," and those who excel. In this section, we turn our attention briefly to assessing children's growth as language users. Specific strategies are found in later chapters.

Assessment Through Ongoing Observation

Peter Winograd and his colleagues (1991) propose that viable assessment techniques are those that help students gain ownership of their learning. Students keep track of which books they find easy to read and which they enjoy most. They decide what writing they will edit and how they will edit it. They identify their own reading and writing goals. To this end, Winograd concludes that "teachers' informal observations and intuitions about children's needs are far more useful than are scores from formal tests; and that especially useful are observations of students' behaviors and responses while engaged in meaningful reading and writing tasks." Informal observation, or "kidwatching," provides data for making instructional decisions and helping parents understand their children's progress. To systematize their observations, teachers record segments of behavior on checklists and study work samples created over time. They schedule conferences or interviews in which they encourage students to assess their own progress (Parker et al., 1995).

Parents (or other caregivers) must be involved in literacy assessment. Caregivers "provide the multicultural link to the classroom both in terms of social and emotional support and in terms of providing teachers with important factual information about language and culture" and about their children (Quintero and Huerta-Macias, 1990).

Observations and Checklists   As teachers increasingly recognize assessment as an ongoing activity on which they base curriculum decisions, checklists are becoming more popular. An observational checklist itemizes literacy traits to be rated with some type of scale. The child

1. Chooses reading (or writing) as a free-time activity.
2. Revises and edits after writing a first draft that he or she has chosen for publication.
3. Uses guide words systematically to locate dictionary entries during editing.
4. Contributes relevant ideas to literature study group discussions.

Rating scales include such evaluative terms as *always, generally, never, poorly, adequately,* and *exceptionally.*

Some teachers develop a comprehensive checklist of traits, use the list to assess each child's growth several times a year, and share the checklist with parents. Other

GO TO

Pages 393–395 for a special kind of checklist—a rubric.

teachers develop a master list of traits related to a specific skill area, such as language facility in small-group discussions. Each child's name appears on the checklist, and the classroom teacher observes each child during group discussions over a period of several weeks and assesses his or her progress relative to the traits.

Sometimes home caregivers are asked to evaluate their children's attitude toward reading and writing and their children's reading/writing behaviors via a checklist. Anthony Fredericks and Timothy Rasinski (1990) propose an attitudinal scale for parents to complete periodically with the following items. The child

- Understands more of what he or she reads.
- Enjoys being read to by family members.
- Finds time for quiet reading at home.
- Sometimes guesses at words, but the guesses usually make sense.
- Can provide a summary of stories read.
- Has a good attitude about reading.
- Enjoys reading to family members.
- Would like to get more books.
- Chooses to write about stories read.
- Is able to complete homework assignments.

Caregivers respond by indicating whether they strongly agree, agree, disagree, or strongly disagree with the proposition. They also report what strengths they see, areas that need improvement, and concerns they have. In responding, caregivers get ideas for activities they can pursue with their children.

Observations and Anecdotal Records   Another aid to ongoing assessment is the anecdotal record, based on observations of student behavior. For example, during show-and-tell, Mattie brings in rocks she has collected and tells about each specimen, including the scientific name. During storytelling, Keith—who generally is unenthusiastic about most things—skillfully tells the story of Paul Bunyan. During collaborative study, Maria fools around. These tidbits are the stuff of anecdotal records. At the end of the school day, the teacher jots a few points in the folders of one or two children, making sure to record incidents that suggest strengths as well as weaknesses.

Some teachers like to make observations early in the year to establish a baseline against which to assess children's future growth. For example, first-grade teacher Karen West consciously chooses to observe her students during the first three weeks of the school year and makes notes on each child's responses in several settings such as during read-alouds, choral reading and shared reading, model writing, journal writing, independent or buddy-reading, listening and reading along with a story on tape, free choice, computer activity, and signing-in at the start of each school day. West "works to 'see' each child in several different settings" and starts a sheet of observational notes about each child's level and kind of performance. In this way, she begins a "descriptive story" of children's learning, which she continues to build throughout the school year (1998).

Portfolios of Children's Work   Especially in the area of written expression, work samples supply evidence of progress. Some teachers encourage each child to keep an active working portfolio, or folder, as well as a showcase portfolio of specially chosen

GO TO

Pages 390–393 for more on portfolios.

pieces to share with parents (described in more detail in Chapter 10). These teachers compare a child's pieces for signs of progress and areas in which instruction is needed. Some teachers involve children in the analysis of the dated pieces in their portfolios, encouraging them to identify their strengths and weaknesses. Teacher and child use a checklist of specific traits to compare dated items completed over several months and compiled in the portfolio (Farr and Tone, 1998).

Individual Conferences   The personalized conference is the ideal setting for assessing pupil progress. Listening to a child read in a one-to-one conference, listening to the child talk about a composition, or going through a portfolio with a child, a teacher can observe a variety of language behaviors. Observations can be recorded as anecdotal records and on checklists. Youngsters can participate by suggesting areas where they have made the greatest progress and areas that require attention.

Strengths and weaknesses noted in a conference determine both the kinds of group and individual tasks to be undertaken and the content of those tasks. A teacher can also note problems to refer to learning specialists—the psychologist, reading specialist, and speech therapist. These specialists—the instructional team—can help the teacher design lessons to meet unique needs and can contact parents, educating them on how best to help their children at home.

READ

■ Lucy Calkins et al., *A Teacher's Guide to Standardized Reading Tests: Knowledge Is Power* (Westport, Conn.: Heinemann, 1998). The authors provide an overview of tests and guidelines for interpreting test results.

■ James Hoffman et al., "High-stakes Testing in Reading," *The Reading Teacher*, 54 (February 2001), 482–492.

Formal Measures, Including High-Stakes Testing

Some understanding of children's growth in language skills can come from the standardized tests administered in most school districts. The typical battery of achievement tests, such as the Iowa Tests of Basic Skills and the Metropolitan Achievement Tests, contains subtests that measure vocabulary, reading comprehension and speed, understanding of the mechanics of writing, spelling, and so forth. However, these tests measure skills out of context; children who can handle spelling on tests or tell how the language is used do not necessarily apply these tools in writing. But used in conjunction with ongoing assessment of literacy, the tests supply specific diagnostic information (Cooter, 1989). As the IRA/NCTE Joint Task Force on Assessment reminds, the basis for use of such standardized measures is "teachers' knowledge about learning and literacy. The more teachers know about literacy development in general and . . . about the literacy development of individual students, the more they will be able to make sense of what students do and the better equipped they will be to provide appropriate instruction" (1994).

Another kind of formal measure is high-stakes testing—standardized testing mandated by states and other agencies outside school districts. High-stakes testing programs are used in some cases to determine whether school districts meet standards and to make comparisons among school districts. The National Council of Teachers of English has resolved "to support and mobilize growing opposition and resistance to high-stakes testing conducted by private testing agencies, states, and other agencies" (Bianchini, 2000; see also Harman, 2000). Given that schools are accountable to the people whom they serve, readers may want to debate the appropriateness of high-stakes testing programs and develop statements of their own regarding them.

A Summary Thought or Two

Diversity in the Multicultural, Inclusive Classroom

Who are the children who are learning in today's elementary schools and whose needs the teacher must meet? Today's elementary students are youngsters with diverse emotional, linguistic, cultural, academic, perceptual, and expressive characteristics that affect their language learning. This chapter has described these children and has detailed ways teachers can involve them in language and learning.

Two ideas evolved as chapter themes. First, the teacher's role is to employ strategies that engage children actively and naturally in language and literature: collaborative team learning and literature-based and content-area–based units that provide opportunities for talking together, reading aloud, oral composition, dictation to the teacher, use of concrete materials, and oral play with language. These strategies allow students to work at their own level within a multicultural, inclusive classroom.

Second, the teacher has a role in early identification of language-learning problems. For this purpose, the teacher relies on such ongoing assessment tools as checklists, anecdotal records, portfolios, and individual conferences, as well as more objective, standardized measures. The teacher uses information gleaned through informal and formal assessments as a basis for planning personalized and group instruction, requesting assistance from learning specialists, and soliciting assistance from the home.

Your Language Arts Portfolio

■ Observe in a classroom or resource room where a child with an impairment is learning. Make organized notes on his or her learning behavior. Write a paragraph describing a successful instructional strategy that the teacher is using and explain why this strategy seems effective.

Related Readings

Allen, Janet, and **Kyle Gonzalez.** *There's Room for Me Here: Literacy Workshop in the Middle School.* York, Me.: Stenhouse, 1998.

Barkley, Russell. *ADHD and the Nature of Self-Control.* New York: Guilford Press, 1997.

Barrera, Roslinda, Verlinda Thompson, and **Mark Dressman,** eds. *Kaleidoscope: A Multicultural Booklist for Grades K–8.* 2nd ed. Urbana, Ill.: National Council of Teachers of English, 1997.

Calkins, Lucy, et al. *A Teacher's Guide to Standardized Reading Tests: Knowledge Is Power.* Westport, Conn.: Heinemann, 1998.

Carreiro, Paul. *Tales of Thinking: Multiple Intelligences in the Classroom.* York, Me.: Stenhouse, 1998.

Farr, Roger, and **Bruce Tone.** *Portfolio Assessment: Helping Students Evaluate Their Progress as Readers and Writers.* 2nd ed. Fort Worth: Harcourt Brace, 1998.

Ford, Donna. *Reversing Underachievement Among Gifted Black Students.* New York: Teachers College Press, 1996.

Freiberg, Karen, ed. *Educating Exceptional Children: Annual Editions, 01/02.* Guilford, Conn.: McGraw-Hill/Dushkin, 2001.

Glazer, Susan. *Assessment Is Instruction: Reading, Writing, Spelling, and Phonics for ALL Learners.* Norwood, Mass.: Christopher-Gordon, 1998.

Henkin, Roxanne. *Who's Invited to Teach for Equity and Social Justice?* Westport, Conn.: Heinemann, 1998.

Keefe, Charlotte. *Label-Free Learning: Supporting Learners with Disabilities.* York, Me.: Stenhouse Publishers, 1996.

Martinez-Roldán, Carmen, and Julia López-Robertson. "Initiating Literature Circles in a First-Grade Bilingual Classroom." *The Reading Teacher,* 53 (December 1999/January 2000), 270–281.

Oyer, Herbert, Barbara Hall, and William Haas. *Speech, Language, and Hearing Disorders: A Guide for the Teacher.* 2nd ed. Boston: Allyn and Bacon, 1994.

Phi Delta Kappan, 79 (June 1998). The issue focuses on talent development.

Putnam, Lillian, ed. *How to Become a Better Reading Teacher: Strategies for Assessment and Intervention.* Upper Saddle River, N.J.: Merrill/Prentice, 1996.

Roller, Cathy. *Variability Not Disability.* Newark, Del.: International Reading Association, 1996.

Shannon, Patrick. *Reading Poverty.* Westport, Conn.: Heinemann, 1998.

Short, Ruth, Mary Kane, and Tammy Peeling. "Retooling the Reading Lesson: Matching the Right Tools to the Job." *The Reading Teacher,* 54 (November 2000), 284–295.

Sidelnick, Mark, and Marti Svoboda. "The Bridge Between Drawing and Writing Hannah's Story." *The Reading Teacher,* 54 (October 2000), 174–184.

Spear-Swerling, Louise, and Robert J. Sternberg. "Curing Our 'Epidemic' of Learning Disabilities." *Phi Delta Kappan,* 79 (January 1998), 397–401.

Willis, Arlette, and Karla Lewis. "A Conversation with Gloria Ladson-Billings." *Language Arts,* 75 (January 1998), 61–70.

Wood, Karen, and Bob Algozzini, eds. *Teaching Reading to High-Risk Learners.* Boston: Allyn and Bacon, 1994.

CHAPTER 3

Language and Children's Early Language Development

Social Interaction—The Key

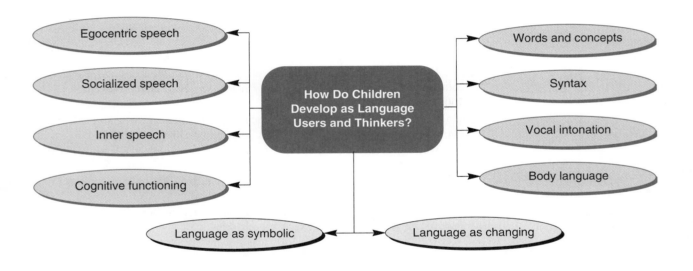

Language Learning in Action

Mushrooms Now

Three-and-a-half-year-old Eric approached his Aunt Dorothy to read him a story. Eric had been to his aunt's house before, and he knew that there were lots of great storybooks there, for she was a teacher. Together they rummaged through a stack of books to find one to read. Eric discarded this one and that one until he came to *Mushroom in the Rain*. He said, "This one. I want this one now!" When Eric's aunt asked why, Eric said, "I want the animals. I want them now."

Just a few months earlier, when Eric and his aunt had read together, Eric did not have the patience to look at the book's cover; he truly wanted the story *now!* But this time—a bit older—he willingly joined into a conversation about the animals on the cover. He pointed to and named each one and identified the colorful objects he saw on the cover as mushrooms. He listened and watched while Aunt Dorothy read the title and ran her hand under the title words. He even helped to reread the title with a lilting expression when his aunt told him that today he was going to read the story with her.

Aunt Dorothy was about to open the book when Eric spied the fox on the back cover. "The fox. Mushrooms. In the rain," he said.

"Yes," expanded his aunt, "the fox is under the mushrooms, and it is raining." With that, the two settled down in the green plush recliner to enjoy the story.

And Eric did enjoy it. He joined in to say, "Move over," as more animals crowded under the mushroom. Toward the end of the story, Eric's sister, Chelsea, climbed into the chair with Eric and Aunt Dorothy. "It's getting crowded here with Chelsea," Eric said.

"Yes," replied his aunt. "We must move over so that she can fit in this chair too. It is getting crowded, just like under the mushroom."

When the story was over, Eric grabbed the book. "Again. Again. Read again." And so they read again, starting with the title, with Eric reading along and running his hand under the title words with his aunt. This time Chelsea, who was in first grade, read the first page. And this time, as Aunt Dorothy read the move-over lines of the story, Eric, without prompting, read too. When they finished, Eric said, "The mushroom grew big."

"Mushrooms grow when it rains," agreed his aunt.

Later that afternoon, after Eric had had a grand—and active—time eating and talking, swimming and talking, playing and talking (Eric loves to talk!), he cornered his uncle. "I want *Mushroom in the Rain*. I can read that book." And so he settled down to join in the reading of his now favorite book with his uncle, who added animal noises to the story, which Eric began to add as well.

Still later, Eric approached his aunt with the same request, "*Mushroom in the Rain*, now." She suggested that instead they play the mushroom game. "Let's chant some words from the story and march to the sounds we make: 'Mushroom, mushroom; move over, move over; make room, make room; march, march, march.'" Eric agreed. In a rhythmic pattern, Eric and his aunt chanted and marched together. As they did this, Aunt Dorothy invited, "Listen, Eric, to the sounds at the beginning of the words we are saying. *Mushroom, move, make,* and *march* all start with the same sound." And so they chanted, marched, and listened again. Aunt Dorothy explained, "These are all 'mushroom words.' They have the same sound as we start to say them. Let's chant and march some more." They chanted, marched, and added other 'mushroom words' to their chant—*Mother, Michael* (a cousin's name), and *mouse* (from the story).

A couple of weeks later, Eric said to Grandma Ruth—as they were talking and enjoying another story together—"*Mrs. Mooley* is a mushroom word." Then Eric (who has a 10 percent hearing loss as a result of continued ear infections) said to Grandma Ruth, "I can read now. I read *Mushroom in the Rain*." He was still thinking and talking about this story that he had enjoyed so much. The reading of *Mushroom in the Rain* had been a significant literacy event for him.

Use language naturally to communicate meanings

Hear the sounds of language: become phonemically aware

DISCUSSION PROMPT

■ How can teachers use similar literature-based classroom events to involve children in the meanings and sounds of language? Why is it important to do this?

How Young Children Learn to Communicate and Think

By using language to express ideas important to them, children like Eric refine their ability to use language to communicate and think and grow in general cognitive facility. In this section, we consider these two aspects of language development—aspects especially important in the years before children enter school and the early years they spend with us in classrooms.

Development of Communication and Thinking Power

Jean Piaget (1965) supplies teachers with an interesting framework for studying children's growth as language users. According to his theory, toddlers go through two developmental stages in their progress toward a mature use of language to communicate and think: the *egocentric* and the *socialized* (see Figure 3.1). Young children's speech is egocentric in that they talk aloud without reference to an audience. Piaget describes three kinds of egocentric speech:

- *Repetition:* Toddlers repeat sounds for the sheer pleasure of hearing them. These sounds may be words, but little meaning exists in the repetitive stream.
- *Monologue:* Youngsters talk aloud to themselves without addressing a listener. Listen to a child before he or she falls off to sleep. Often there is a steady stream of words—crib talk.
- *Dual or collective monologue:* Youngsters talk aloud in the presence of another person, who may not be attending and does not respond.

Piaget explains that youngsters' early speech is mainly egocentric. As late as ages six and seven, some form of egocentric speech exists; kindergartners, for example, talk in monologue as they work independently or in a dual monologue as they work next to someone else.

With maturity comes socialized speech—talking with and to another person. Michael Halliday (1975, 1977) has studied the way children develop socialized speech and the functions for which they use it. He explains that it is through interaction with others that young children learn to use language for a variety of purposes and to communicate a variety of meanings. Youngsters learn early to communicate that they want something. This is what Halliday calls the "I want," or the *instrumental*, function of language. Children also learn to use language to mean "do as I tell you." By using language in this way, children control the behavior of others in their environment; this is the second, or *regulatory*, function of language. Third, children learn to use language to mean "me and you"—an *interactional* function through which youngsters greet and name specific people and manage the social environment.

A fourth function of language, according to Halliday, is the *personal;* at times children use language to express their awareness of self and to express feelings. This is the "here I come" function. The fifth function of language is to mean "tell me why"; expecting answers, children begin to use language to ask all manner of ques-

WORD BANK

Egocentric speech
Socialized speech
Inner speech or mind talk

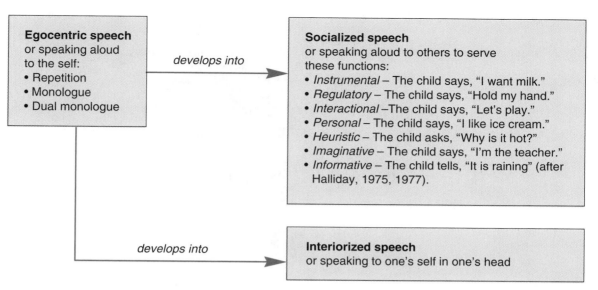

Figure 3.1
Forms of Speech and the
Functions of Language

tions about the world around them—the *heuristic* function. Then there is the *imaginative* function, or what Halliday calls the "let's pretend" function. Using this, children create a universe of their own—a universe that at first is just sound plays but ultimately develops into the make-believe of story and poem.

By eighteen months, Halliday notes, toddlers have learned to use language to express these six kinds of meanings. Only somewhat later do youngsters begin to use language to mean, "I've got something to tell you." Halliday writes that "the idea that language can be used as a means of communicating information to someone who does not already possess that information is a very sophisticated one which depends on the internalization of a whole set of linguistic concepts that the young child does not possess." Although it emerges later than the other functions, the *informative* function is the dominant one in the adult's use of language.

Even as children are developing the ability to use language to carry on these communication functions, they are developing the ability to use language to think. The talking aloud to the self that youngsters do is key to the development of thinking ability. Lev Vygotsky (1962, 1986) believes that in older children, thought is related to *inner* (or *interiorized*) *speech*—talking to oneself in one's mind. As children mature, egocentric speech diminishes and becomes interiorized. Inner speech—mind talk— is a mechanism on which the adult relies when thinking through a difficult problem. It is the basis of complex thought and is especially important in listening, reading, and writing.

GO TO

Chapter 10 for a discussion of the role of inner speech in writing and Chapter 8 for a discussion of inner speech and reading.

Early literacy events, as when a parent reads to a child, are important in the child's language development. (*© Elizabeth Crews*)

As the title of his book *Thought and Language* suggests, Vygotsky emphasizes the relationships between thought and verbal language. In teaching language, we are essentially teaching thought. Vygotsky writes:

> Thought and language, which reflect reality in a way different from that of perception, are the key to the nature of human consciousness. Words play a central part not only in the development of thought but in the historical growth of consciousness as a whole. A word is a microcosm of human consciousness.

As children develop the ability to use words to think and to communicate, conversation with adults is essential. Adults supply "the ready-made meaning of a word, around which the child forms" an idea cluster. Adults do not pass on to the learner their modes of thinking; rather, according to Vygotsky, they pass on words and word patterns that already have common meaning within the human community.

How School Programs Contribute to Communication Power

If we base school language programs on the ideas of Piaget and Vygotsky, conversation becomes the bridge to continued cognitive and language growth. Clearly, children must have opportunities to use inner and socialized speech, and teachers must model out loud how they talk to themselves in their minds as they read, write, and listen. Although little research evidence exists that suggests how to assist children, we can hypothesize some strategies.

Facilitating Inner Speech   To encourage growth in productive mind talk, teachers can do the following:

- Supply "let's pretend" telephones and microphones in preschool, kindergarten, and first grade. Children go to the Talking-to-the-Self Center to explain something into a telephone or microphone.
- Establish an Explaining-Aloud Center in second and third grades. Children go there to explain something studied—a process, idea, topic—into a tape recorder or to another student.
- When children do tasks composed of a series of steps, suggest that they tell themselves how to perform each step as they do it.
- Encourage talking to the self "whisper style" when a job gets tough. When youngsters find a job hard to do, suggest that they speak to themselves. Children can do this as they cut, paste, draw, read, and write.
- Do group talking out loud as part of reading, writing, and problem solving. Ask children to say what they are thinking during these activities.
- Encourage children to tell themselves stories read or heard. Have them create stories of their own first by talking out loud to themselves, then by talking to themselves in their heads.
- Divide children into talking-out-idea pairs. Children tell their buddies a story they have invented before writing it down.

Facilitating Socialized Speech   It almost goes without saying that children in classrooms should be involved orally in using language to achieve the full range of language functions and in using language to reflect on all kinds of experiences, both direct and vicarious. Unfortunately, however, research indicates that relatively little time is allocated in many classrooms to the natural give-and-take of conversational discussions. A study by Joanna DeStephano, Harold Pepinsky, and Tobie Sanders (1982) indicates that much classroom interaction requires only one-word answers by children, that teachers do most of the explaining and talking, and that little actual dialoguing occurs, especially during group instruction in reading. David Dillon and Dennis Searle (1981) find a similar pattern in their study of oral interaction in a first grade. They note that the functions for which children use language in the classroom are restricted and in no way reflect the diverse functions for which children use language in the home environment.

CONSIDER

Use *Iktomi and the Boulder* by Paul Goble (New York: Orchard, 1988) to introduce children to the idea of mind talk. In Goble's book, smaller print is used to give the thoughts in Iktomi's mind.

Distinguished Educator

Meet Brian Cambourne

Brian Cambourne is head of the Centre for Studies in Literacy at Wollongong University in Australia. In an article in *The Reading Teacher,* Cambourne describes an experiment by Ruth Weir in which Weir studied the presleep monologues of very young children and suggested that "learner-talkers need time away from others to practice and employ (perhaps reflect upon) what they've been learning." Cambourne further explains, "Just as the presleep monologues that Weir noticed seemed to be a necessary component of language learning, so 'monologue with oneself' (which is a form of reflection) seems to enhance" our transformation of the meanings and/or skills that someone else has demonstrated to us into a set of meanings and/or skills that are uniquely our own ("Toward an Educationally Relevant Theory of Literacy Learning: Twenty Years of Inquiry," *The Reading Teacher,* 49 [November 1995], 186, 188).

DISCUSSION PROMPT

How do you use inner speech before sleep? During conversation? During reading? During writing? In what other situations do you use inner speech? How much do you use it? For what purposes? Is your mind ever blank? If so, when? How can a teacher help children use inner speech more effectively, especially during reading and writing?

To assist young children as they refine their ability to use language for a variety of social functions (i.e., interactional, heuristic, informative), some teachers use a Communication, or Magic, Circle. Upon entering the classroom, children gather in the circle, clustering on a central rug to converse. Examples of Communication Circle activities include the following:

- Sharing completed work, such as compositions and drawings, with listeners saying what they liked.
- Sharing objects from home on a topic being studied. For example, when studying community helpers, children bring in magazine pictures or objects they associate with a particular helper. They explain what they have brought in, and listeners comment on things shared.
- Repeating stories. Children take turns telling parts of a story they know. Each child tells a bit. Another child takes up the story where the previous one stopped. Here children function as "socialized listeners" to continue the story.

These activities require the socialized, or two-way, speech that characterizes mature adult interaction. They are essential at all levels, especially in the early grades.

Cognitive Development: Concrete to Abstract

To use language to make these kinds of meanings with an increasing degree of sophistication, a person must be able to compare, categorize, generalize, and think critically. Piaget (1965) provides teachers with a framework for understanding the way children at different age levels are likely to think about objects and events. Piaget hypothesizes four stages in children's cognitive development:

Concrete

Abstract

Stage 1: Sensorimotor (birth to age 2)	A period of visual and manipulative exploration of the physical environment
Stage 2: Preoperational (age 2 to age 7)	A period of rapid language development when the child begins to think with words, imitates adult behavior, and judges objects in concrete terms
Stage 3: Concrete operations (age 7 to age 11/12)	A period when, through manipulation of objects, the child mentally transforms concrete data into generalizations about reality and concepts based on similarities and differences
Stage 4: Formal operations (ages 11/12 and older)	A period when the child goes beyond the concrete to use language in an abstract way

In sum, as children mature, they learn to think in more abstract terms and become less dependent on firsthand experience as a basis for thought.

Today theorists prefer a less rigid interpretation of children's cognitive development. Nonetheless, if applied flexibly, Piaget's framework is a useful tool for looking at overall patterns in child development. Knowledge of the stages is important as the teacher asks students to think about, talk about, and visually represent all kinds of ideas. For example, researchers have studied how children think about and respond to stories. In extended studies, Alan Purves (1975) has found that the way children respond varies with age, as suggested by Piaget's stages. Third-graders think literally, making such comments as, "It's about a rock" and "He got a whole bunch of cats." Their evaluative statements express their feelings about a story and omit reasons for their judgments. They make comments such as, "It sounds good" and "It's funny."

According to Purves, fourth-graders make similar responses except that the older children comment more about personal relations and attempt comparisons between story characters and themselves. Thinking more critically, they may cite reasons: "The reason I liked that was because I like curious people" and "I like it because it sounds true." In contrast, fifth-graders begin to comment on literary aspects: "Because it rhymes and I like the words," "the feeling of the words," "the way he said it."

Research demonstrates similar results when children are asked to think critically about story acts. As Myra Weiger (1976) has found, second-graders judge story as well as real acts in terms of clear-cut categories of right and wrong set down by adults. Justice is administered by authority figures, as shown in such comments as, "My mother don't like us to tell lies. She'd keep us in the house"; "That's what my father does to me"; "I don't like fighting 'cause I know it makes God mad." Weiger explains that many fourth-graders still judge by referring to adult authority. Some, however, function at higher levels, as shown in this comment: "They kept bothering her and she couldn't take it no more so she just moved away and they learned a lesson."

By sixth grade, many students respond in terms of a concept of equity. A typical sixth-grader's response to Pinocchio is: "Since he was just a puppet, he wouldn't know better." This response considers extenuating circumstances. Based on her findings, Weiger proposes that children need more opportunity to react to moral dilemmas so that they develop a mature sense of justice. She concludes that "children's literature provides an effective method of developing moral judgment in children because it deals with moral experience at every age." In language arts, children should have numerous opportunities to think critically and talk about a variety of topics. In this way, they develop their ability to operate intellectually on ideas they receive and to communicate their own ideas to others.

CONSIDER

A fine book for a values discussion is Phyllis Reynolds Naylor, *Shiloh* (New York: Atheneum, 1991). Ask upper-graders to judge the rightness of Marty's actions. Use Naylor's Newbery acceptance speech (*The Horn Book*, 68, July/August 1992, 404–411) in conjunction with the novel.

How Children Develop Language Facility

The word *communicate* comes from the Latin *communicare*, which means "make common or make known"; *communicare* derives from *communis*, which means "common." This suggests that communication is a social process whose ultimate purpose is a common understanding—a unity within the social group. Through social interaction in a variety of situations, children acquire language facility. They learn to use the (1) words and sounds, (2) syntax, or sentence structure, (3) intonation patterns, and (4) nonverbal language and social conventions that are inherent aspects of their language. We now look at these four aspects of language that children acquire as they develop as language users.

Words and Sounds

Language—the arbitrary sound symbol system humankind has devised to represent things, events, and ideas in the world around them—is the bedrock of communication. The words of language are the repositories of humankind's collective and individual experience. Through words, humans think with a degree of clarity and precision superior to that of organisms lacking verbal speech. The ability to use words to speak thoughts has enabled *Homo sapiens* to escape the present. John McCrone (1991) explains,

> Mammals, like dogs and apes, live only in the present. Chimps may often look as if they are thinking even when simply sitting in the shade of a tree, yet they are still being driven by the changing world around them rather than responding to chains of internal thoughts. . . . Their wordless minds can react only to

the events that surround them at a particular moment. Human minds, however, have broken free. We can think about the past, make plans for the future, and fantasize about imaginary events. . . . Language is the key.

W. N. and L. A. Kellogg's (1933) classic study of the child and infant chimpanzee reared in the same home for a year attests to the primacy of verbal language in human thought. The Kelloggs found that the chimp kept up with the child in its intellectual development until the child began to talk. After that the chimp dropped behind, limited by its inability to use spoken words.

At ten to thirteen months, children utter their first word—a naming word such as *mama* or *dada,* which they apply to any person who supplies food, a smile, or a change of diaper. In a few months' time, many children control about ten words, which are likely to include nouns like *ball* and *doggy,* specific names like *Mommy,* and action words like *give* and *bye-bye.* By twenty-four months children's vocabulary averages 150 words, and by three to four years about 1,000 words. Words acquired early tend to be nouns and verbs, with a very few prepositions used to show relationships. Of course, these parameters are general. Philip Dale (1976) cautions, "Age is not a good indicator of language development. Children vary greatly in their rates of development."

WORD BANK
Concept
Assimilation
Accommodation
Schema

Concept Formation and Word Power   Children gain control over words by gradually attaching symbolic labels to things they encounter in their world. These are the same labels they hear members of their family use in interaction with them and others in their immediate environment. The wagonlike vehicle in the family garage is called *car;* so are those shorter and lower models seen on the highway. As youngsters attach the label *car* to numerous models that differ in many respects but share a number of characteristics, they build a concept of *car.* They have developed a construct in their heads that allows them "to place stimuli in or out of the category" (Howard, 1987). That mental construct is a *concept.*

Concepts differ in their level of abstraction. *Car* represents a concrete concept, for a person can point to this sample and to that one. In contrast, concepts such as *honesty, pleasure,* and *thoughtfulness* are more abstract. They represent traits to which one cannot point directly.

According to Hilda Taba et al. (1964), concept formation begins with recognizing the essential qualities of things and differentiating the qualities of one thing from the qualities of another. A simple example will clarify this process of differentiation, which is at the heart of conceptualizing. Looking at a cat and hearing an adult apply the label *cat* to it, young Jemel may repeat in telegraphic form the sentence the adult has spoken. If Mommy has said, "Look at the cat there in the tree," the boy may reduce and repeat, "Cat there." Later, seeing another animal with four legs that is meowing and has a coat of fur, Jemel may point and say, "Cat," meaning "There is the cat." Still later, spotting another four-legged, furry animal (holding an acorn in its paws), the child repeats and says, "Cat come," meaning "I want the cat to come here."

At this point, in conversational style the adult may say, "That's a squirrel." At still another point, as parent and child look at pictures in a storybook and interact verbally, Jemel may apply the word *cat* to lions and tigers.

Piaget (1964) uses the terms *assimilation* and *accommodation* to describe the processes through which children "fatten up" their concepts. He explains that as youngsters experience new situations, they assimilate, or integrate, new data into their conceptual understanding. At the same time, they must change—or accommodate—the concepts they build as they meet new data that do not fit their existing conceptual schemes; they reconstruct their existing concepts in light of their new experiences (Barnes, 1993). In this way, youngsters fine-tune their use of the word labels they apply to phenomena in the world around them. Viewed from this perspective, concept formation is an active, fluid process of exploration and discovery; it requires numerous encounters and interactions that allow youngsters to assimilate more details and refine their growing understanding.

Individual concepts do not function in isolation; rather, they are related to other concepts in a hierarchical framework that theorists term *schema* (plural *schemata*). A person's concept of "cat," for example, is part of a more comprehensive concept, "pet," which in turn is part of a larger concept, "animal." The network of these interrelated concepts—a schema—is stored in the brain in such a way that it can be modified as children encounter new but related examples. From this perspective, what children already "know" (or what schemata children already possess) determines to a great extent what they learn in new situations. From this perspective, too, what teachers do before children listen, read, and experience is extremely important. Teachers should organize lessons so that children can relate their past experiences to what they are about to hear or read. In this way, children's learning in the new situation is heightened.

Word Building Blocks: Phonemes, Rimes, and Graphemes   The words of a language are made up of speech sounds, or *phonemes*. Roger Brown (1958) defines a *phoneme* as "the smallest unit of speech that makes a difference to a listener or a speaker." Take, for example, the words *bat, hat, fat, sat.* The change of the consonant sound at the beginning of each word (in the *onset* position) makes a difference in the meaning sent to a listener. Each word starts with a different phoneme. Now substitute a different vowel sound in each word: *bit, hit, fit, sit.* An English speaker hears a difference in the middle sound of a pair like *bat* and *bit.* Again the speaker is dealing with two different phonemes: the short *a* and short *i* sounds. Linguists have identified about forty phonemes that make up the English sound system.

Now repeat aloud the words *bat, hat, fat, sat,* focusing on the final sounds. How are the final sounds of each word similar? Obviously, these words rhyme: All end with the same two phonemes—the /a/ and /t/. Today linguists call such combinations of phonemes found at the ends of several or more words *rimes* or *phonograms.* Researcher Edward Fry (1998a, 1998b) has identified 38 rimes from which more than 650 one-syllable English words are built. Here, moving across the rows, are these rimes (or word families) in the order of their frequency, or number of uses in one-syllable words:

-ay	-ill	-ip	-at	-am	-ag
-ack	-ank	-ick	-ell	-ot	-ing
-ap	-unk	-ail	-ain	-eed	-y
-out	-ug	-op	-in	-an	-est
-ink	-ow	-ew	-ore	-ed	-ab
-ob	-ock	-ake	-ine	-ight	-im
-uck	-um				

WORD BANK
Phoneme
Onset
Rime
Phonogram
Alphabetic system
Grapheme

GO TO
Page 444 for a discussion of onsets and rimes in spelling.

■ ● ● ●

CONSIDER

The onset of a word is the consonant or consonant blend before the first vowel sound, for example, the /m/ at the beginning of *mine* and the /tr/ at the beginning of *trunk*. The remainder of each word—the *-ine* and the *-unk*—are rimes.

■ ● ● ●

READ

■ Hallie Yopp, "Developing Phonemic Awareness in Young Children," *The Reading Teacher*, 45 (May 1992), 696–703, and "A Test for Assessing Phonemic Awareness," *The Reading Teacher*, 49 (September 1995), 20–29, for ways to increase and assess children's phonemic awareness.

■ Hallie Yopp, "Supporting Phonemic Awareness Development in the Classroom," *The Reading Teacher*, 54 (October 2000), 130–143.

English writing is an *alphabetic system* in which the printed form attempts to represent the sounds of the language. The written language provides one or more graphic symbols, or *graphemes,* for each of the sounds that comprise words. Although there is no one-to-one correspondence between speech sounds (phonemes) and their graphic symbols (graphemes), there is a strong correspondence in the English language.

How do children learn to communicate with the phonemes, rimes, and graphemes of their language? According to Patricia Kuhl and her associates (1992), babies show a similar pattern of phonetic perception regardless of where they are born: "They discern differences between the phonetic units of many different languages, including languages they have never heard, indicating that the perception of human speech is strongly influenced by innate factors." Early experiences within a particular language community, however, reduce infants' ability to perceive differences among speech sounds that do not make a difference in their native language. As Kuhl explains, "Adults exhibit a pattern of phonetic perception that is specific to their native language, whereas infants initially demonstrate a pattern of phonetic perception that is universal." Her research suggests that infants' phonetic perception is altered very early by their exposure to the particular language in which they are reared. Working with American and Swedish babies, Kuhl and her colleagues discovered that as early as six months of age, an infant's ability to discern phonemes begins to be limited to those sounds that make a difference in his or her native language. This is much earlier than the age at which infants acquire word meanings.

Although children discern phonemes at an early age, they do not learn language by segmenting words into phonemes or generating meaning in reference to discrete phonemes. Research suggests that children cannot separate words into phonemic segments with any degree of accuracy until the end of first grade. After analyzing many studies in this area, Maryanne Wolf and David Dickinson (1985) report that separation of words into phonemic segments is "virtually impossible" until the end of first grade, when 70 percent of children can segment. However, these researchers posit a "strong relationship between early segmentation skills and later reading and spelling: *the more aware the child is of the sound system, the easier it is to learn to read.*"

Children learn to speak their language by interacting with people and gradually building and refining their conceptual understanding and the related word symbols. The same is true in reading. David Olson (1983) reminds us that as children learn to read, larger units of meaning are more significant than discrete phonemes. In generating meaning in reading, children should use the "context of larger structures first," focusing on story, conversation, and sentence meanings before words and on words before phonemes and graphemes. The strong correspondence between the English speech sounds and their graphic symbols assists students as they learn to read and write, but only as an aid to meaning-based clues. This is the theory behind a balanced philosophy of skills instruction.

The paragraph you have just read, however, does not mean that children's ability to hear the phonemes and combinations of phonemes of their language, especially the onsets and rimes, is unimportant. Just the opposite is true: Young children who are highly aware of sounds of their language—who are what we call *phonemically aware*—generally develop more rapidly as readers and writers than youngsters

Children begin to develop as language users as they interact naturally with family and friends. (© *Zefa Visual Media–Germany/Index Stock*)

who do not understand that words are made up of individual speech sounds. This is probably true because in English, a substantial, consistent correspondence exists between the speech sounds and the graphemes used to represent them. To make use of that correspondence in decoding and encoding, students must be able to hear the individual language sounds (the phonemes) and groupings of word-ending sounds (the rimes). For this reason, it is imperative that teachers draw young children's attention to the sounds within words during literature-based literacy events in ways that are playful and that do not detract from the joy of reading. You saw this happening in the opening vignette as Eric and his aunt played with /m/, where this sound was found at the onset of words in a story Eric was enjoying.

Word Building Blocks: Morphemes   A *morpheme* is the smallest meaning-bearing unit of language, a meaningful sequence of phonemes that cannot be subdivided without destroying the meaning of the unit. Consider the word *boys*. Its meaning can be analyzed: *boy* means "young man" and cannot be subdivided without losing that meaning; *-s*, in this instance, means "more than one." *Boy* and *-s* are morphemes—true building blocks—for words are constructed systematically with them. Some morphemes stand alone as words; *boy, cat, sing, two, five, of* are free

WORD BANK
Morpheme
Prefix
Suffix

morphemes. On the other hand, bound morphemes cannot function alone. English prefixes and suffixes like *-ness, -y, dis-, pre-,* and *mini-* are bound morphemes, as are inflectional endings like *-ed, -ing, -s,* and *-er.*

Children learn early how to handle the word-building characteristics of English. Jean Berko (1958) studied the word-building skills of four- to seven-year-olds to determine whether young children could generate the plural and possessive forms of nouns; the present tense, third-person singular and past tense forms of verbs; and the comparative and superlative forms of adjectives. Berko found that children of that age were beginning to function according to the systematic word-building rules of English. They had acquired this ability to use the basic word-building forms of English in a natural way by listening and talking to members of their speech community.

On the other hand, upper-elementary-grade students can benefit from some attention to the more sophisticated Graeco-Latin (G-L) word-building elements of English. This is especially true for children who grow up in homes where multisyllabic words based on Greek and Latin prefixes, suffixes, and roots are not commonly used. According to David Corson (1985), most of the specialist vocabulary of English is Graeco-Latin in origin and is generally used in talking about the social and natural sciences. People, especially of working-class backgrounds, tend not to use specialist vocabulary in everyday speech. As a result, students who have had little out-of-school contact with G-L–based words must jump what Corson calls "the lexical bar" when they study advanced social studies and the sciences starting in the third and fourth grades. These students meet numbers of unfamiliar words in their social studies and science textbooks.

To help students jump the lexical bar, a teacher can draw students' attention to such morphemic units as prefixes, suffixes, and roots as they grapple with big ideas across the curriculum. Consider, for example, the element *ced-* or *cess-,* meaning "to go or to yield." Here are just a few words derived from that Latin root; see how the word tower in which they are organized highlights the morphemic relationships:

se	CEDE		
se	CES	sion	
se	CES	sion	ist
re	CEDE		
re	CES	sive	
re	CES	sion	
re	CES	sion	al
con	CEDE		
con	CES	sion	
ex	CEED		
ex	CESS	ive	

When upper graders encounter the words *secede* and *secession* as they read about the American Civil War, they can organize a *ced-* word tower and can include other related words in it (for example, *succeed, success, succession, successive, successor, proceed, procedure, precede, precedent*). By constructing word towers organized around

How should the teacher approach word studies with children?

Terry Piper talks of the naturalness of language: "It would appear that acquiring language—oral and written—is part of children's nature. The stories of Helen Keller and of a girl named Genie who managed to acquire her first language at the age of 13.5 after nearly 12 years spent in isolation, speak to the intensity of the human drive to acquire language. Language is so very much a part of human nature that the most interesting thing about language acquisition may be the failure to acquire it. . . . The naturalness of language should not be read as an invitation to ignore language in the school curriculum. Rather, it should be read as a challenge to design language programs in school that build upon children's real experience of learning and using language and to integrate oral and written language across all subjects of the curriculum" (*Language and Learning: The Home and School Years,* 2nd ed. [Upper Saddle River, N.J.: Merrill/ Prentice-Hall, 1998]).

David Corson points to the fact that specialized English contains numbers of words that "begin with prefixes such as 'circum-,' 'contra-,' 'homo-,' 'mono-,' 'ultra-,' 'semi-,' 'sub-,' 'retro' "; multisyllabic words based on such prefixes and Greek and Latin roots are "alien" to many young learners. These children find "this lexis a strange one when it is first encountered in *school* or in a *book* or in a *newspaper,* and may reject all three in consequence to some extent." Words based on G-L elements such as prefixes, suffixes, and roots are not at all a "natural" part of some children's functional vocabulary; these words are more liable to be a "rarity" (*The Lexical Bar* [Oxford: Pergamon Press, 1985]).

DISCUSSION PROMPT

Piper suggests that language learning is natural. Do you agree? Disagree? Do students learn specialized language naturally? What does all of this imply about children's experiences with language in elementary school? Is there a place for direct attention to elements of the English language, especially those elements derived from the Greek and Latin languages? When and where might this kind of instruction be most effective?

commonly found roots (e.g., *port-, scrib-, vert-, rupt-, stru-, tract-, spect-,* and *spir-*), students make explicit their knowlege of such prefixes as *con-, re-, se-, pre-, pro-, ex-,* and begin to visualize a multisyllabic word not as a string of separate letters but as a series of meaningful elements. Word study of this kind can have a positive effect on both vocabulary development and spelling.

Syntax, or Sentence Structure

WORD BANK

Syntax

Transformational-generative grammarians

To learn a language is not only to acquire meaning-filled word symbols; it is also to acquire the syntax of that language. *Syntax* refers to the arrangement of words into meaningful and grammatical sentences. Just as people use words to send messages, so do they use word order to communicate thought. There is a world of difference, achieved by a shift in word order, in the messages sent by these two sentences:

> *As dusk fell, John saw the tiger.*
> *As dusk fell, the tiger saw John.*

Theories Regarding Acquisition of Syntax Today educators look to *transformational-generative grammarians* to explain the way language works. Transformational-generative grammarians describe the way language users build (generate) sentences and change (transform) them. These linguists postulate that there is a significant difference between the surface features of a language and its deep structure. This becomes clear by thinking about two sentences that on quick examination appear similar:

> *John is easy to please.*
> *John is eager to please.*

Noam Chomsky (1968) points out that these sentences differ in both their meaning and underlying structure. In the first, someone else is pleasing John; in the second, John is the pleaser. Furthermore, a different underlying structure is suggested by the fact that the first sentence can be changed, or transformed, into a completely sensible sentence: "It is easy to please John." The same transformation performed on the second sentence results in, "It is eager to please John," which does not make sense.

The ability to use and interpret the deep structure of their language is what children develop as they acquire language facility. They learn to speak in the noun phrase/verb phrase pattern that typifies language; they learn to handle question making, command making, negation, and modification by trying out these patterns. In so doing, they produce original utterances that adhere to the recurring patterns of their language. By the time children enter school, they generally can manipulate their language in all of these ways. In this respect, although youngsters coming to school do not know the terminology used to describe their language—do not know how to label and talk about nouns, verbs, and so forth—they have a relatively good command of its grammar.

Chomsky explains children's ability to generate original sentences by suggesting that what children are doing is grasping the underlying "rules" governing sentence production. Children do not consciously think out, verbalize, and apply these linguistic rules but gradually develop an intuitive sense of how to put words together in meaningful units. This generative theory of language development explains a speaker's capacity to create sentences he or she has never heard or read. The speaker functions in terms of the rules for sentence building that he or she has internalized through hearing spoken sentences. Such functioning is possible because of the human being's innate predisposition for language (Chomsky in Putnam, 1994).

David Rumelhart and James McClelland (1987) question the theory that children learn language by intuitively learning "rules." Based on their work with computer models, they propose that children learn language by learning analogies, by reasoning that "this word sounds like that word," by making associations. To support their view, Rumelhart and McClelland cite the reasoning of a five-year-old boy. Asked what grade comes before the seventh grade, the boy replied, "Sixth." Asked what grade comes before the sixth grade, he replied, "Fifth." Before fifth, the boy answered, "Fourth." Before fourth, the boy said, "Thirdth," before third, "Secondth," and before second, "Firsth." Interestingly, when Rumelhart asked the five-year-old the grades starting with kindergarten, the boy stated all the words correctly. Rumelhart and McClelland propose that the boy was reasoning by analogy rather than functioning on a "rule" that he had internalized.

Pinker and Prince (1987) debate the meaning of Rumelhart and McClelland's work: They agree with Chomsky that children internalize language-making rules when they learn language. Kolata (1987) sums up the current, split views of language acquisition: "There is still no consensus on how children learn" to put words together to form sentences. Are they working with internalized "rules" or reasoning by analogy? Educators are still debating that question.

Research on Syntax Acquisition   Researchers have studied how young children gradually learn to form grammatically correct sentences. Roger Brown and Ursula Bellugi (1966) report that imitation of parental statements plays a part; a very young child may repeat a sentence produced by a parent, in the process reducing it to the essential elements while retaining the original word order, or syntax. Where the parent says, "The dog was barking," the child reduces the sentence to a two-word utterance: "Dog barking." At other times, the child produces original utterances that are reductions of typical English sentences. A parent conversing with a young child, according to Brown and Bellugi, tends to repeat and expand the child's utterances, adding auxiliaries, determiners, and prepositions to the basic words. For example, when the child says, "Mommy glasses," the parent expands to, "Yes, Mommy has her glasses" (see Figure 3.2).

Glenda Bissex (1981), whose book *GNYS AT WRK* (1980) describes the literacy development of her young son Paul, summarizes a fascinating point about children's early speech. Children do not start speaking in single words or sounds but in meaningful one- and then two-word sentences. In a child-parent conversation, "Car" may really mean, "I hear a car"; "Sweater chair" may really mean, "My sweater is on that chair." Within the context of the social interaction between parent and child, the telegraphic sentence of the child takes on extended meaning—a meaning that the parent expands in responding.

Bissex writes, "Children learn to talk by interacting with an environment that provides rich information about language: they learn by speaking, being spoken to, asking questions, and listening to speech. From models of older speakers they learn the values and functions of speech; they receive feedback, support, and encouragement. . . . Children learn to talk by talking in an environment that is full of talk." In that environment, the parent functions as a conversation coach. According to Gordon Wells (1979), a relationship exists between the extent to which parents support and expand their children's contributions to a conversation and the youngsters' lin-

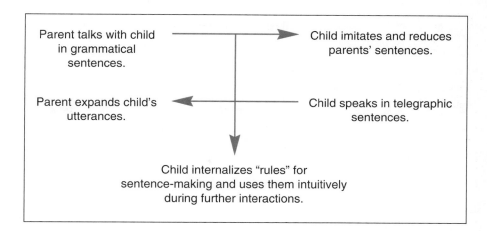

Figure 3.2
A Social, Interactive Model of Early Language Development

guistic level when they enter school. Parental support and expansion of children's conversations also have a positive effect on children's later reading achievement.

Social Interaction and Literacy   Social interaction is key in children's literacy development. In the words of William Teale (1982), "Natural literacy development hinges upon the experience the child has in reading or writing activities which are mediated by literate adults, older siblings, or events in the child's everyday life." Teale contends that interactive literacy events are essential in children's development of reading and writing ability. To learn to read and write, youngsters must participate fully in story reading or writing, conversing actively as part of their encounter with print.

This suggests why reading and talking about stories with children matters so much, both at home and at school, and why school programs that require much filling in the blanks are unproductive. Solitary fill-in-the-blanks activity fails to provide the social interaction between child and adult so important in continued language development—an interaction that does occur during a shared literary experience of which natural conversation is a part. The same is true of language programs that put greater stress on individual letters and sounds than on meaningful sentence and story units.

It also suggests why writing must occur within a social context and mean more to young children than an exercise in letter formation. According to R. Kay Moss and John Stansell (1983), young children generally do home writing because they like it; its language reflects more completely children's full range of language resources. In contrast, early school writing tends to be less creative, reflecting children's belief that this writing is done not to communicate or to enjoy but to practice letter forms, spelling, and page arrangement. Then, too, school writing generally is done without social interaction. Children must be quiet. Yet, as Anne Dyson (1981) points out, "Talk is an integral part of beginning to write"; it provides both meaning and the systematic means for getting that meaning down on paper. Writing, as well as reading, is an interactive process.

WORD BANK

Stress

Pitch

Pause

Intonation Patterns

Even as some linguists provide ideas on how people generate meaningful sentences, others—the *structural linguists*—describe the structures through which speakers communicate meaning. One element of communication that structural linguists have been investigating is intonation. Intonation is an integral and distinctive part of a language system. It is the rhythmic pattern, the melody of speech; it plays a significant role in the overall sound of English and other languages as they are spoken and read orally or ultimately written down and read silently. The features of intonation are

- *Stress:* the emphasis, or accent, given to syllables, words, or phrases.
- *Pitch:* the highness/lowness level, or frequency level, of the voice.
- *Pause:* the juncture that separates units of speech.

Carl Lefevre (1973) sees wide applications of understandings about stress, pitch, and pause to language arts instructions—applications ranging from basic rhythms in primary grades to acting, artistic interpretations of poetry, and punctuation in upper grades.

Stress   Through changes in stress (or accent), speakers can alter the way words function in sentences. On what syllable do you put the stress in the word *present* in each of the three sentences given here? How is the difference in stress reflected in the way *present* functions in the sentence?

> I received a valuable *present.*
> I will *present* the award to the recipient?
> I will write in the *present* tense.

Accented on the first syllable, *present* functions as a noun or adjective; accented on the second syllable, *present* functions as a verb. Speakers whose first language is English have little difficulty handling this distinction, but for those learning English as a second language, the distinction is one that teachers may have to highlight. However, play with similar pairs of homographs can be interesting for all children Youngsters can search for examples and post them on the classroom Word Wall in sentences that relate sound and function. Marcia Invernizzi et al. (1997) provide these samples:

Stress in First Syllable	Stress in Second Syllable
subject (noun, adjective)	subject (verb)
conduct (noun, adjective)	conduct (verb)
rebel (noun, adjective)	rebel (verb)
console (noun, adjective)	console (verb)

Pitch   Pitch refers to the highness or lowness of the voice, or its rise and fall—not in loudness but in frequency. Men's voices tend to be lower in pitch than women's.

Changes in pitch can convert utterances from declarative into interrogative and exclamatory sentences, for there is a relationship between the vocal fall or rise at the end of an utterance and a speaker's intent to state, question, or exclaim. Try this sentence: "The water is boiling." By shifting the pitch pattern, you can convert the statement into a question or an exclamation.

The ability to perceive pitch patterns in speech helps writers punctuate sentences they are drafting. Writers who perceive the drop-stop of the voice at the end of a sentence can use that sound signal as a clue for inserting a period; those who perceive the rise-stop of the voice at the end of a sentence can use it as a question-marking clue. Similarly, writers can use the sound of an exclamation to punctuate exclamatory sentences. During editing conferences as children polish their writing for publication, teachers need to draw children's attention to this fundamental relationship between sound and sentence-ending punctuation and encourage them to read their drafts aloud, listening for the sentence-ending sounds.

Pause   Pause, or juncture, refers to the ways speakers terminate their speech flow. At times speakers make quick breaks in their speech to distinguish between expressions like *a name* and *an aim*, *I scream* and *ice cream*, *illegal* and *ill eagle* (Lefevre, 1973). Speakers pause slightly longer at the comma stops in *Margaret, my friend, is at home*. When pausing at the comma stops in this sentence or ones containing parenthetical expressions or series constructions, the voice does not go up or down but stays level. We use a similar pause at the comma stop in the sentence *Our grass needs cutting, but our mower is broken* and at the semicolon break in *The star performer arrived; then the program began*.

Longer stops occur at the ends of sentences and generally are accompanied by downward drops or upward rises of the voice. Speakers typically end declarative statements with a fade-drop; the flow of their speech fades and drops before they begin another utterance. They end some questions with a fade-rise. Without conscious thought, speakers rely on fade-drops and fade-rise stops to divide speech into oral sentence units and in so doing, clarify what they mean. The fade-drop stop at a sentence end signals "I'm stating." The fade-rise stop at a sentence end signals "I'm asking"; only in sentences that begin with question-signaling words like *how, when,* and *why,* is the rise of the voice at the end of an utterance unnecessary.

Clearly, these rises, drops, and pauses in speech bear a direct relationship to punctuation in writing. Teachers must help students to listen for these sentence sounds and to include commas, periods, question marks, and exclamation marks to signal them on paper. For example, Nancie Atwell (1998) teaches her uppergraders to listen for sentence spots where their voices "drop and stop" as they edit their writing. This proves a useful tool for students who are struggling with comma splices (sentences that they incorrectly separate with a comma rather than with a period or semicolon) and with run-on sentences (sentences that they fail to separate at all).

Interpretive Intonation   Most people are aware that the way they speak communicates how they feel—fearful, bored, excited. Linguists distinguish among these emotional aspects of vocal expressiveness and grammatical aspects such as pitch, stress, and pause, which are dictated by the structure of the language system. Emotions expressed vocally are an "over story," placed on top of the sentence structure of the utterance. In no way, however, does this fact downgrade the significance of tone of voice.

CONSIDER

Robert Frost wrote, "A sentence is a sound in itself on which other sounds called words may be strung. You may string words together without a sentence-sound to string them on, just as you may tie clothes together by the sleeves and stretch them without a clothes line between two trees, but—it is bad for the clothes."

Nonverbal Language and Social Conventions

To communicate, one must be able to use and interpret the very pronounced gestures and more subtle posturings and eye movements that accompany speech. Albert Scheflen (1972) notes the purposes nonverbal language serves as an adjunct to verbal language. Some moves that speakers make frame and punctuate verbal interaction. A nonverbal expression may say, "I am finishing my statement" or "I am beginning a different idea." Some body movements instruct, suggesting "Sit there," or "I am in charge." Others warn of consequences: "That's wrong," "Don't do that," "Be careful!" In such instances, body language is regulatory and may be used purposefully for social control. Still other body movements communicate bits of information: "Yes," "No," "Maybe." Some movements, such as shaking hands, taking someone's arm in walking, or opening a door, are part of the rituals society uses to maintain the social order and make that order agreeable. Other movements communicate feelings: fear, pleasure, excitement, anger. According to Stephen Norwicki and Marshall Duke (1992), in face-to-face interaction only 7 percent of emotional meanings are sent through words; 55 percent are sent through facial expressions and 38 percent through tone of voice, posture, and gestures.

● ● ●

READ

Roger Arles, *You Are the Message: Secrets of Master Communicators* (New York: Dow Jones–Irwin, 1988), for more on nonverbal communication. See also Norwicki and Duke (1992). These authors have found that 10 percent of children have one or more problems in sending or receiving nonverbal signals—a condition they term *dyssemia*.

Listeners use body language to communicate without speech. They sometimes regulate who is next to speak by turning and focusing attention on the person chosen. Listeners indicate their lack of understanding or disagreement by frowning, their agreement by nodding, their interest by leaning forward. They indicate desire to speak verbally by a variety of gestures. Such cues make verbal pronouncements of who is to speak next unnecessary; they also tell a speaker how clearly he or she is getting the message across, whether the person is talking too quickly, or perhaps whether he or she is boring a listener.

Like verbal behavior, nonverbal behavior is learned through social interaction. For example, children learn turn taking in conversation at an early age through interaction with their parents (Snow, 1977). Also like verbal behavior, nonverbal behavior does not have a single universal meaning. To English speakers a smile generally is a sign of joy, excitement, friendship; but at times English speakers smile not because they are happy but because smiling is expected of them. Moreover, people from diverse cultural backgrounds do not draw on an identical nonverbal vocabulary. Persons from some cultures use touch more than do persons from others; they may stand more closely in communicating and use more gestures. In this respect, "silent languages" are as numerous as the languages differentiated by the linguists.

Instructional Implications

In this section, we have considered what is important in early language acquisition. From the ideas presented, three generalizations about language instruction emerge:

- Social interaction—communication—should be central in language arts programs and across the curriculum, because through interaction, children learn to use spoken, nonverbal, and written language.
- In a language program, students should be actively involved with words, sentence and intonation patterns, and the nonverbal behaviors and social conven-

tions of their language. This involvement occurs in social situations and is a necessary part of reading and writing, as well as of oral activity.

■ Because language is speech and writing is the representation of speech sounds, students should have some opportunity to play with the relationships between speech sounds and graphic symbols and between intonation patterns, meaning, word function, and punctuation signals.

How Children Learn About Language

To know a language is to know how to use that language—its words, syntax, intonational patterns, and nonverbal signals. Accordingly, to teach language arts is first to develop children's ability to communicate. This is the thesis of Chapter 3. But there is another way to know a language: to know *about* it.

The Symbolic Nature of Language

The human mind has devised arbitrary systems as vehicles for communication and for thinking. Words are actually symbols without meaning in and of themselves. Over the years, people have attached meanings to the combinations of articulated sounds that comprise words and to the arrangement of these words in phrases and sentences; they have attached meanings to the intonations of voice and the nonverbal behaviors that are part of language. Over time these words, patterns, and behaviors have changed and grown into languages. Some knowledge about language is essential as a background for communicating with others, especially in a pluralistic society.

Take, for example, the fact that language is an arbitrary system. The linguist Robert Hall (1960) explains that there is no inherent relationship between an object and the word symbol created to represent it. The meaning of the symbol is derived from the situations with respect to which it is used. The words *dog, chien, Hund,* and *sobaka* all refer to the familiar canine friend, depending, of course, on where the speaker lives. No one of these words is inherently better than any other. This is an important understanding to acquire, for one should not view another person as superior or inferior because of the particular language or dialect he or she speaks.

Activities that further children's appreciation of the symbolic nature of language can be fascinating. Here are a few ways to involve children with this fundamental characteristic of language:

■ *Symbols around us.* Children make a collection of the visual symbols that surround them—symbols such as those for peace, danger, and good luck; the signs used to represent professional groups; the logos adopted by industries to represent their products. They analyze the symbols to see whether a relationship exists between the symbol and the meaning attached to it. Young people who have

CONSIDER

Use Vladimir Vagin and Frank Asch, *Here Comes the Cat!* (New York: Scholastic, 1989) to help children appreciate language diversity. Use Ann and Paul Rand, *Sparkle and Spin: A Book about Words,* reissued ed. (Abrams, 1991), for a playful look at language.

studied the visual symbols of their culture enjoy creating symbols for a product they invent, a family crest, a school logo, or a class symbol.

- *Pictographs.* Ancient peoples wrote down thoughts in picture form; they might have drawn a horse, for instance, to represent that animal. Students use a modification of picture writing by creating rebus stories in which they use pictures to represent words.
- *Hieroglyphics.* Upper-graders can study samples of highly stylized pictures recorded by the ancient Egyptians. For example, was the stylized picture, or *hieroglyph,* that represented water. In the case of a hieroglyph, it is relatively difficult to determine from the picture what is being represented; thus, the picture is called an *ideograph* rather than a *pictograph.*
- *Chinese characters.* Some Chinese characters are compound ideographs—a combination of stylized pictures that, taken as a whole, communicate the desired meaning. For example, ▢ represents the sun, while ——— represents horizon. The symbol for dawn combines the two signs ▢ , while three suns represent the idea of clear or crystal. Moon is represented ▢ , while bright is communicated through the symbol ▢▢ . Can you figure out why?

Technology Notes

Check these Web sites for material about words:

http://ablemedia.com/ctcweb/showcase/roots.html   See "Roots of English: An Etymological Dictionary," a Windows software program that emphasizes etymologies from Latin and Greek and can be downloaded.

http://www.m-w.com/cgi-bin/mwwod.pl   The site provides a word of the day with the definition, an example, a sample sentence, information about the word, and related words.

http://www.m-w.com/lighter/flap/flaphome.htm   This is a source on American youth slang.

http://www.onelook.com   Go to this general dictionary clearinghouse site for a variety of more specific dictionary sites: dictionaries of technology words, science words, sports words, and so forth.

http://www.randomhouse.com/jesse   See Jesse's Word of the Day.

http://www.wordorigins.org/thelist.htm   The site gives explanations of how words and popular expressions came into the English language. See Wilton's Etymology Page.

http://www.wordorigins.org/source.htm   At this site is an annotated list of etymological sources with links.

Language Origins and Change

Another kind of knowledge about the English language centers on its origins and evolution. During the late nineteenth century, *historical linguists* began to study the development of the English language. They identified English as belonging to the Indo-European language family and recognized it as a Germanic language more akin to Dutch, German, Icelandic, Norwegian, Danish, and Swedish than to Latin and the Romance languages (see Figure 3.3). The historical linguists developed generalizations about English language origins and evolution based on a comparative study of the vocabulary, syntax, sounds, and spellings of the various languages. Today, generalizations commonly encountered in language arts programs include the following:

Language is constantly changing.
Supporting Ideas:

1. New words are constantly being added to a language to meet the demands of a changing lifestyle and environment (e.g., *sport utility vehicle, minivan, modem, Internet*).
2. Word-making mechanisms include compounding, development of words that are analogies of existing words, incorporation of slang expressions, and merger of parts of other words.

CONSIDER

Robert MacNeil writes, "The consensus among most scholars is that linguistic change is neither positive nor negative, rather that language ebbs and flows like the tides" ("Language, Reading, and Pleasure," *The Reading Teacher*, 49 [September 1995], 8–14).

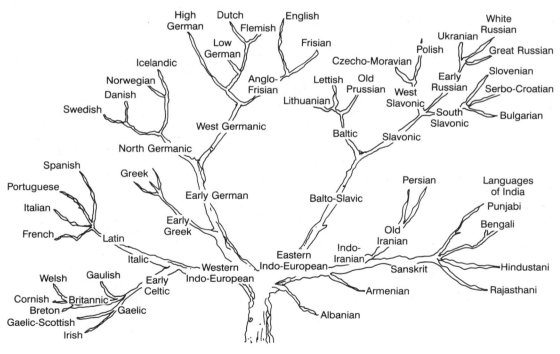

Figure 3.3
The Family of Indo-European Languages

3. New words enter a language through borrowing from other languages; this occurs when language groups interact. Scientific words may result through conscious construction of words based on Latin or Greek roots and affixes.
4. Some words drop from common usage as the need for them lessens.
5. Existing words may acquire new meanings, pronunciations, and spellings.
6. What is considered acceptable usage may become unacceptable, and vice versa.
7. As dialectal groups interact, language cross-fertilization occurs.
8. Dictionaries are records of word spellings, meanings, and pronunciations; dictionaries change to reflect changes in the language.

Forces exist to stabilize language.
Supporting Ideas:

1. Books about language, such as dictionaries, style manuals, and grammars, have a stabilizing effect on language, holding back changes in written expression that appear in everyday oral expression.
2. Rapid means of transportation and communication—e-mail, telephone, television, radio—unify language.

Some languages are related through common ancestry.
Supporting Ideas:

1. Similarities among languages related through common ancestry are generally greater than among those not so related.
2. Major language groups are called *families;* families trace their origins to a common ancestor.
3. English belongs to the *Indo-European language family*, which can be traced back thousands of years to a location in eastern Europe. The closest language relatives to English are the Germanic languages, including Dutch and German.
4. American English is most similar to other dialects of English, such as British English; however, major differences in vocabulary, syntax, and pronunciation exist among dialects.
5. Word changes can be traced back thousands of years so that one can find out when and how most words entered the language.

Ways to Handle Historical Relationships

■■■ ● ● ●
READ
Robert McCrum, William Cran, and Robert MacNeil, *The Story of English* (New York: Viking, 1986), and *Word Mysteries and Histories* (Boston: Houghton Mifflin, 1986).

References such as *The Story of English* by Robert McCrum, William Cran, and Robert MacNeil and *Word Mysteries and Histories* offer background on language origins and change. Having read about the way language has developed, a teacher may be tempted to share the material by telling and explaining; the material *is* fascinating and storylike. But children can discover some of the relationships for themselves. By studying samples of different languages, youngsters gain appreciation not only of language as a changing medium of communication but of the way linguists operate.

One form that historical investigation can take is the comparison study. Youngsters use English–foreign language dictionaries to discover equivalent words in other languages for common English words. Later, they analyze their word discoveries to see whether they can generalize about the languages that are most closely related. Similarly, students can systematically track word origins and hazard an educated guess as to when and how a particular word came into English. (See Figure 3.4 for a time line charting linguistic events in the history of English.) One way to begin is to consider idioms, where figurative meaning differs from literal. Children can think

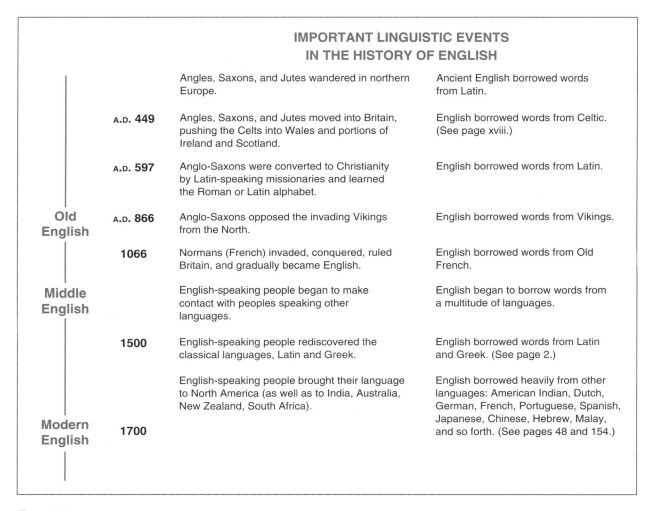

IMPORTANT LINGUISTIC EVENTS IN THE HISTORY OF ENGLISH

		Angles, Saxons, and Jutes wandered in northern Europe.	Ancient English borrowed words from Latin.
	A.D. 449	Angles, Saxons, and Jutes moved into Britain, pushing the Celts into Wales and portions of Ireland and Scotland.	English borrowed words from Celtic. (See page xviii.)
	A.D. 597	Anglo-Saxons were converted to Christianity by Latin-speaking missionaries and learned the Roman or Latin alphabet.	English borrowed words from Latin.
Old English	A.D. 866	Anglo-Saxons opposed the invading Vikings from the North.	English borrowed words from Vikings.
	1066	Normans (French) invaded, conquered, ruled Britain, and gradually became English.	English borrowed words from Old French.
Middle English		English-speaking people began to make contact with peoples speaking other languages.	English began to borrow words from a multitude of languages.
	1500	English-speaking people rediscovered the classical languages, Latin and Greek.	English borrowed words from Latin and Greek. (See page 2.)
Modern English	1700	English-speaking people brought their language to North America (as well as to India, Australia, New Zealand, South Africa).	English borrowed heavily from other languages: American Indian, Dutch, German, French, Portuguese, Spanish, Japanese, Chinese, Hebrew, Malay, and so forth. (See pages 48 and 154.)

Figure 3.4
Time Line Showing the Development of English

DISCUSSION PROMPT

■ At what point could you make this kind of material part of your language arts program?

CONSIDER

An interesting reference is Isaac Asimov, *Words on the Map* (Boston: Houghton Mifflin, 1962). Invite older students to browse through Asimov's *Words of Science* (Boston: Houghton Mifflin, 1962). His *Words from History* (Boston: Houghton Mifflin, 1968) is equally inviting.

about how expressions such as *a bee in his bonnet, flipped his lid,* and *walking on thin ice* came into being.

Students enjoy tracing the origins of words to discover the manner and time of their introduction into English. Since English has borrowed words from all the languages of the world, the investigation takes on multicultural, geographical overtones as students search dictionaries to find words with Chinese, Arabic, Russian, Hebrew, and other origins. Some interesting words to investigate are *coffee, sauna, tea, banana, koala bear, babushka, succotash, apostrophe,* and *batik.* Other interesting words are *hamburger, turkey, danish,* and *frankfurter*—words that quite literally come off the globe.

Language Investigations and the Social Studies

Word study fits easily into social science units, for the development of language parallels the development of people. Language change reflects migration, conquest, and trade patterns. Similarly, language tells much about the social relationships and values of people past and present. It reports scientific, technological, and industrial progress as well as geographic and economic factors overcome in an attempt to build and maintain a way of life. In this respect, the surfacing of new words in a language and the falling into disuse of others serve as a barometer on which investigators can read changes in human activity.

CONSIDER

A search of one state map—Idaho—produced these names: Moscow, Salmon Creek, Sun Valley, Lewiston, Silver City, Twin Falls, Butte, Bonner's Ferry, Yellow Pine, and Coeur d'Alene.

In terms of classroom study, as students trace the development of their country, they consider not only how their nation changed but how their language changed in response. One way to correlate language and social study is through map investigations. In thinking about the early settling of New England, children search maps for town, city, and state names that reflect the origins, values, and way of life of the colonists, as well as the geography of the new land. Looking at the settlement of the middle colonies, children compare the names they find on maps of New Jersey and New York with place names in England, Holland, and Germany. As they trace the westward movement, they search maps for names that indicate who the pioneers were, what their interests and religions were, what perils they encountered, and even what the first industrial, agricultural, or mining ventures were.

Etymological investigations, in which young people discover the origins and historical development of words based on their component elements, also fit neatly into content-area studies. Suppose readers encounter the word *aqueduct* as in this sentence: "The Romans constructed an aqueduct in Nîmes, France, sometime during the first century A.D." Readers run a dictionary check to determine the meaning of *aqueduct* and discover the etymology of it: *aque* from the Latin *aqua* meaning water, and *ductus,* from the Latin verb *ductere* meaning to lead. In the same section of the dictionary, students find other words derived from the Latin *aqua: aqua, aquamarine, aquanaut, aquarium, aqueous, aquifer.* They list those on a section of their Word Wall that they label "Etymological Relationships." (Do not hesitate to use powerful terms like *etymological.*) Similarly, they can brainstorm other words built from the Latin root *ductus (conduct, conductor, induct, induction, reduce, reduction, deduce, deduction,* and so forth) and create webs with the root at the center and the words built from it radiating outward. Using a colored marker, upper-graders can highlight the element the words have in common and hypothesize their meanings based on the meaning of the root. See Figure 3.5 for an example of an etymological word web.

Tracing the etymology of words in contextually relevant word studies, upper-graders come to appreciate the diverse origins of their language. They also use their knowledge of word elements to increase their vocabulary and begin to see component elements as meaningful units of words. To help you lead this kind of etymological investigation, you may want to keep such books as Bob and Maxine Moore's *NTC's Dictionary of Latin and Greek Origins* (1997) or Donald Ayers's *English Words from Latin and Greek Elements* (1997) available on your bookshelf.

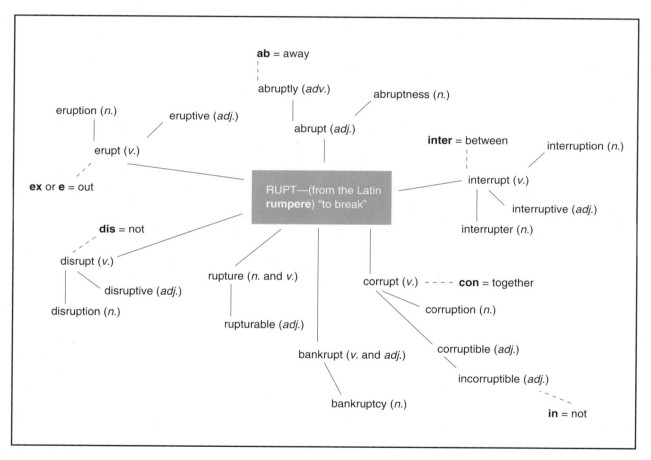

Figure 3.5   An Etymotogical Word Web

ACTIVITY PROMPT

Create a word web based on the Latin *gratus,* which means "beloved, pleasing, dear." Prefixes used in conjunction with *gratus* include *con-, un-, dis-,* and *in-.*

A Summary Thought or Two

Language and Children's Early Language Development

Children develop language facility through social interaction. As young children meet and use language in a variety of social situations, they grow in their ability to handle the ideas for which words are symbols. Talking to themselves and to others, they also grow in their ability to think abstractly and use the words, sentence structures, intonation patterns, nonverbal behaviors, and social conventions that characterize their language. As Cambourne (1995) writes, "Transformation is the process that enables learners to 'own' or be responsible for their learning. . . . My classroom data show that the process of transformation is enormously enhanced through discussion with others. . . . *Just as toddlers can learn to control the oral language of the culture into which they're born only by socially interacting with others, older learners also need a myriad of opportunities to interact with others.*"

Because conversation is key in children's developing as oral language users and ultimately as literate human beings, talk must be the integrating thread across the elementary curriculum. This is a major conclusion of Chapter 3. A second is that conversation with children in the family setting is extremely important as they develop language facility. As this chapter suggests, the kinds and extent of children's early conversations within the home determine the ease with which youngsters use language to communicate and think when they get to school. Within the family, some children—like young Eric who opens Chapter 3—have been active participants in oral language–based literacy events; they have been talking (and talking about literature) since they were very young. Others only rarely have sat down with an uncle, granny, father, or mother to talk and to read (Purcell-Gates et al., 1995).

To encourage family conversation and reading, schools must establish family conversation/literacy programs and establish early contacts with those who care for toddlers. Schools must schedule workshops for new parents and send home brochures that teach parents the importance of conversation and also of reading aloud to children. Where there is no district-wide family conversation/literacy program in place, the kindergarten teacher must take the initiative in communicating with the home, encouraging family talk and reading. Language learning does not begin within schools; it begins within the family.

Your Language Arts Portfolio

- Using the main headings of Chapter 3, create a data chart in which you delineate terms, definitions, and main ideas of the chapter. If you can do this, you will be better able to guide children in making data charts for recording during reading.

Related Readings

Barinaga, Marcia. "Priming the Brain's Language Pump." *Science,* January 31, 1992, 535.

Begley, Sharon, et al. "Mapping the Brain." *Newsweek,* April 20, 1992, 66–70.

Berko-Gleason, Jean. *The Development of Language.* Columbus, Ohio: Merrill, 1985.

Cambourne, Brian. "Toward an Educationally Relevant Theory of Literacy Learning." *The Reading Teacher,* 49 (November 1995), 182–190.

Corson, David. *The Lexical Bar.* Oxford, England: Pergamon Press, 1985.

Fox, Sharon. "Research Update: Oral Language Development, Past Studies and Current Directions." *Language Arts,* 60 (February 1983), 234–243.

Harste, Jerome, Virginia Woodward, and Carolyn Burke. *Language Stories and Literacy Lessons.* Portsmouth, N.H.: Heinemann, 1984.

Hennings, Dorothy G. "Contextually Relevant Word Study." *Journal of Adolescent and Adult Literacy,* 44 (November 2000), 268–279.

Lindfors, Judith. *Children's Language and Learning.* 2nd ed. Englewood Cliffs, N.J.: Prentice-Hall, 1987.

MacNeil, Robert. "Language, Reading, and Pleasure." *The Reading Teacher,* 49 (September 1995), 8–14.

Newman, Susan, Billie Casperelli, and Cara Kee. "Literacy Learning, A Family Matter." *The Reading Teacher,* 52 (November 1998), 244–252.

Piper, Terry. *Language and Learning: The Home and School Years.* 2nd ed. Upper Saddle River, N.J.: Prentice-Hall, 1998.

Putnam, Lillian. "An Interview with Noam Chomsky." *The Reading Teacher,* 48 (December 1994), 328–333.

Reading Teacher, 49 (April 1995). This is a themed issue on family literacy. It includes an article on teachers' choices in classroom assessment.

Voss, Margaret. *Hidden Literacies: Children Learning at Home and at School.* Portsmouth, N.H.: Heinemann, 1996.

Vygotsky, Lev. *Mind in Society: The Development of Higher Psychological Processes.* Cambridge, Mass.: Harvard University Press, 1978.

Wells, Gordon. *The Meaning Makers: Children Learning Language and Using Language to Learn.* Portsmouth, N.H.: Heinemann, 1986.

Wood, David. *How Children Think and Learn.* Oxford, England: Basil Blackwell, 1988.

Related Readings About the Nature and History of Words

Ayers, Donald M. *English Words from Latin and Greek Elements.* 2nd ed. as revised by Thomas Worthen. Tucson, Ariz.: University of Arizona Press, 1986.

Hennings, Dorothy G. *Vocabulary Growth: Strategies for College Word Study.* Upper Saddle River, N.J.: Prentice-Hall, 2001. See the etymological segments at chapter beginnings and endings.

Kennedy, John. *Word Stems: A Dictionary.* New York: Soho Press, 1996.

Merriam-Webster New Book of Word Histories. Springfield, Mass.: Merriam-Webster, 1991.

Moore, Bob and Maxine Moore. *NTC's Dictionary of Latin and Greek Origins: A Comprehensive Guide to the Classical Origins of English Words.* Chicago: NTC Publishing Group, 1997.

Pei, Mario. *The Story of Language.* Rev. ed. New York: Signet Classics, 1966.

Robinson, Andrew. *The Story of Writing.* New York: Thames and Hudson, 1995.

Literature for Life

Journeying into and with Books

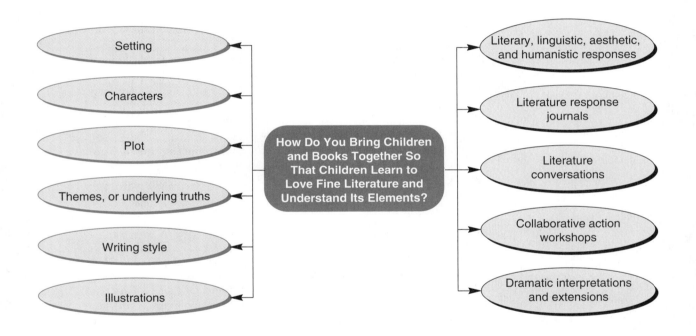

Setting

Characters

Plot

Themes, or underlying truths

Writing style

Illustrations

How Do You Bring Children and Books Together So That Children Learn to Love Fine Literature and Understand Its Elements?

Literary, linguistic, aesthetic, and humanistic responses

Literature response journals

Literature conversations

Collaborative action workshops

Dramatic interpretations and extensions

A Literature Conversation in Action

Racing Life with Willy

The students had been reading John Gardiner's *Stone Fox* for about two weeks. Today, they were gathered in their literature conversation circles to talk about Chapter 7, "The Meeting." The instructor gave just a few prompts to start the students on their way: She suggested, "You may want to start your conversation by talking about what happens here and how it affects you, how you feel toward Willy and Stone Fox, how perhaps the two are similar. . . . Don't write anything down. Just talk."

Exploratory Conversations

The conversation in one group began like this:

Maria: Little Willy went into the barn.

Dawn: It was just like him to do that . . . to go into a dark barn.

Donna: Yes, it was like him. He isn't afraid.

Denise: He is curious . . . just like when he asked Dr. Smith all those questions in Chapter 1. Grandfather brought him up that way.

Maria: How old is he?

Denise: Ten.

Dawn: Yah, and he doesn't cry when he gets hit.

Maria: Like here, it says that it was night when he had to go out for Grandfather's medicine. He wasn't afraid to go out in the night.

Dawn: North Road must've been pretty deserted, dark and all.

Maria: A scary place . . .

Donna: He isn't scared, though.

Talk toward understanding—aesthetic responding

Maria: It was a different time and place, though. There probably weren't so many things to be afraid of.

Denise: I guess he put his fear away. He had to, for Grandfather. Just like he was doing the race for Grandfather.

Maria: He is still polite, even after Stone Fox hits him. He says, "Mr. Stone Fox." It's interesting that the dogs don't jump all over him.

Denise: That's right. The dogs didn't even bark. They knew he was okay.

Donna: Stone Fox is that way, too. He is an animal person. That's how they are the same. They both have a way with animals.

Denise: They were both doing the race for someone else. . . .

After the students had talked in their circles, they gathered for a class Community Share. What they did was continue the discussions started in their conversation circles, talking about the kind of people little Willy and Stone Fox were. Students explored what Stone Fox was thinking as he stood unmoving and silent. They recalled why he was silent—because he did not like white people, for they had taken the Indians' land—and they hypothesized why he had struck little Willy. One student mentioned the relationship between the characters' names and their personalities. Was this intentional? The instructor interjected the idea that behind each character is an author and sometimes we have to think why an author like Gardiner is crafting his story in the way he is. The instructor asked a question to bring closure to the class discussion: "If you had one hundred dollars and you were a betting person, on whom would you place your money?" Most of the students bet on Stone Fox. As Heidi said, "There's no way little Willy can win." Others agreed: "He doesn't have a chance—no way." But JoAnne proposed, "Stone Fox is going to give his winnings to little Willy. He sees himself in Willy. And books like this have to have happy endings. Gardiner is going to make it come out."

Think from the point of view of the author

Over the next week, the students read Chapters 8 and 9. They came together after reading the chapters to explore ideas in their literature conversation circles and to talk briefly in a follow-up Community Share with the instructor. And then it was time to read the final chapter—"The Finish Line." The instructor read the chapter aloud, as students followed in their books or just listened if they preferred. Students gasped when the instructor read the line, "Her heart burst. She died instantly." The instructor paused for a moment before continuing the reading—and her voice cracked as she read to the dramatic close.

Reflective Writing

Reading the last words, the instructor sat back in her chair. She said nothing. Then, when moments had passed, she said, "I have trouble talking right now. Let's write our feelings. That's what I want to do—in my literature response journal. You try that too." Here is what some of the students wrote:

> I am in shock! It is so sad for Willy. He didn't have anyone to begin with but his Grandfather. But he always had Searchlight. Now she's gone. (Lisa)

> I have to admit that after I had read the first few chapters, I went home and had to finish the book. When I got to the end, I cried. Even now, I got all choked up and I couldn't have spoken if I'd wanted to. There is a dignity to the last chapter . . . to Stone Fox. (B.J.)

> I feel sad for Willy because his dog died. However, I am happy for him because he won the race. I have to wonder though why Stone Fox let Willy win. It does not make sense to me that he would hit him in one chapter, and let him win in another. . . . But Stone Fox may have seen a little of himself in Willy . . . trying to achieve the unachievable. (Sean)

> I am absolutely shocked. I did not believe that Searchlight would die. I misunderstood Stone Fox. My feelings for him turned right around. (Janice C.)

> Willy now has the money for Grandfather and the land, but he has lost his best friend. The final picture is so sad. Powerful. (Laurie C.)

> My grandmother passed away last Monday. She was my best friend and she is all I can think about. Searchlight was Willy's best friend. Each loved the other more than anyone in the world. To lose someone that close is devastating, especially since Searchlight died to save little Willy and Grandfather and the farm. I was surprised at the end. I really thought that Stone Fox was going to win the race and give the money to little Willy. (JoAnne S.)

When the students had written, they came together as a community to share their entries. Shortly, entry sharing spontaneously gave way to a "grand conversation." Several students remarked that they had cried at the end, but Dawn said she didn't feel that way at all. Denise commented that she could never figure out how people could get so upset when their dogs died, that it was only when she got a dog herself that she understood. She asked Dawn whether she was a "dog person"; Dawn answered that she was not. The instructor interjected that she had cried and yet she was not a "dog person" in the least. Maria explained, "You were not crying for Searchlight, then. You were crying for little Willy and maybe even for Stone Fox."

Most of the students agreed that they had not anticipated the ending. Denise, however, disagreed. She said that she had seen it coming. "Look," she said, "on page sixty-three where Grandfather tells Willy, 'There are some things in this world worth dying for.'"

Maria added, "Maybe this is saying that we must sacrifice to achieve the really important things in life. You have to give up something to get something."

Recognize instances of foreshadowing

At this point, the instructor grasped the "teachable moment" to interject, "The line that Denise read is an example of what literary critics call *foreshadowing*. Authors at times gently hint at what is to come; they foreshadow future events, to prepare us for them. You have to read with care to pick up a point like this one that Denise has given us. Look for evidence of foreshadowing in the novels you are reading on your own."

The students went on to bring up other points. The hometown crowd was rooting for little Willy not from prejudice against Stone Fox but because little Willy was the hometown boy, just as today the locals root for the local team. Stone Fox was an outsider, always on the move from race to race and not really getting close to anyone. Stone Fox saw himself in little Willy and was able to get beyond his hatreds (but one student believed that Stone Fox didn't do it for Willy but for Searchlight—that Stone Fox was an "animal person"). The writing is terse; those short sentences, especially at the most dramatic points, are very powerful. Searchlight represents what we must give up to accomplish our dreams. When a student made the last point, the instructor introduced the term *symbol:* What the student was saying was that Searchlight may be perceived as a symbol. She may stand for something—an idea, a truth—that is bigger than she is. Another teachable moment!

Make symbolic meanings

DISCUSSION PROMPT

■ What is the teacher's role during literature-based conversations? What did this teacher do to increase students' understanding and love of literature?

The Teacher and Literary Engagement

You have just visited not an elementary classroom but a college seminar in which future teachers were reading a children's chapter book, talking about it in literature conversation circles and Community Shares, and writing in response in their literature response journals. Today, many educators believe that elementary teachers must participate in literary conversations and write in response to stories they are reading, just as the students in this vignette are doing (Cardarelli, 1992; Hennings, 1995).

In this chapter, you will read about the elements of fine stories and about instructional strategies for developing literary engagements that help children become aware of these elements. In reaction to the chapter, form a literature conversation group with other teachers (or future teachers) to explore stories and poems through talking together. Also keep a literature response journal in which you reflect on and express the feelings you have as you read. To be a successful teacher of literature, you must be a lover of literature; you must enjoy exploring your responses to literature by talking and writing.

Ways to Analyze Children's Stories—Qualities That Trigger Responses

Fine literature is the red blood of a language arts program. It carries the content—the oxygen, so to speak—for language experiences. But more important, literature sustains life by transfusing it with rhyme and reason, escape and enchantment, joy and sorrow. Consequently, selecting books with literary qualities that evoke a deep response is crucial in language arts teaching. Teachers face an abundance of stories from which to choose, selections so varied that understanding what makes a book fine is essential for making wise choices.

Charlotte Huck (1993) defines literature as "the imaginative shaping of life and thought into the forms and structures of language" and defines the subject of literature as "the human condition; life with all its feelings, thoughts, and insights." The reader responds to this aesthetic ordering of life's experiences in great stories and is transported beyond immediate perceptions to feel deeply—to care, to want, to cry, to laugh, to love, to hate, and perhaps to understand for the first time. Some writers can weave so complete a spell with words that the story becomes reality and for a moment the real world ceases to exist.

A reader's response arises out of his or her prior experiences with life, literature, and language; yet the author's skill in telling a story is an equally significant determinant of the reader's response. To catch a reader in the web of a story, an author must establish a setting in which the characters can function with integrity, create believable characters, interweave elements of plot, develop themes that pull story threads together, and make words sing in the mind. In books for the younger reader, the illustrator must contribute pictures that tell the story as forcefully as the words and stimulate equally strong responses. *Setting, character, plot, themes, style,* and *illustrations:* These are the major elements of a story.

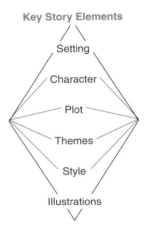

Key Story Elements

Setting

Character

Plot

Themes

Style

Illustrations

■ ● ● ●
CONSIDER

A good book for clarifying the relationship between setting and plot is Jerry Spinelli, *Maniac Magee* (Boston: Little, Brown, 1990). See Figure 4.1 for a setting map a fifth-grader made based on his reading of the book.

Setting

Rebecca Lukens (1995) identifies two kinds of story settings: a *backdrop setting* that has little influence on a story and an *integral* setting that has considerable influence on the characters, plot, theme, and mood. Some authors develop settings that tap into the reader's senses of smell, taste, hearing, sight, and touch. They use setting to "reveal traits and changes in the characters," move the plot forward, and heighten feelings (J. Watson, 1991). When setting is integral, it can "drive" the story, controlling characters and plot.

In an interview with Cyndi Giorgis and Nancy Johnson (1999–2000), Louis Sachar talks about the setting he created in his Newbery Award–winning *Holes.* He relates, "To me the story was always about the place, more than the characters. Normally when I start a book, I start with characters, and it all comes out of them. In this case, I started with the place, and everything grew out of that." Sachar set *Holes* at

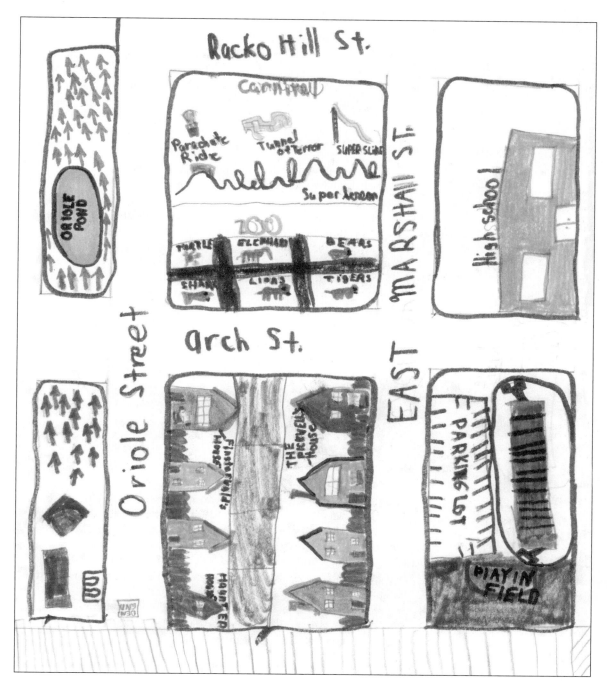

Figure 4.1
A Map Based on *Maniac Magee* by a Fifth-Grader Who Read the Book During a Class Novel Unit. See Figure 4.2 for another visual that came out of the same unit.
Source: Courtesy of Derek Jamiolkowski and Dena Underwood.

Camp Green Lake in the scorching heat of a Texas summer. Camp Green Lake was not your typical fun-filled pleasure spot; rather it was a camp for delinquent boys run by the merciless Warden. There was no lake, and nothing at all was green. Clearly, that setting is an integral aspect of the story—a story that Sachar considers far "grander . . . than any of the others" he had written before.

Author Katherine Paterson is equally aware of the important role setting plays in story. While writing *Jacob Have I Loved,* she investigated island life off the Maryland shore, and her descriptions of her Rass Island setting are as clear and sharp as a documentary video. Visualize this scene in your mind's eye:

> The ferry will be almost there before I can see Rass, lying low as a terrapin back on the faded olive water of the Chesapeake. Suddenly, though, the steeple of the Methodist Church will leap from the Bay, dragging up a cluster of white board houses. And then, almost at once, we will be in the harbor, tying up beside Captain Billy's unpainted two-story ferry house, which leans wearily against a long, low shed used for the captain's crab shipping business. Next door, but standing primly aloof in a coat of fierce green paint, is Kellam's General Store with the post office inside, and behind them, on a narrow spine of fast land, the houses and white picket fences of the village. There are only a few spindly trees. It is the excess of snowball bushes that lends a semblance of green to every yard. (Katherine Paterson, *Jacob Have I Loved* [New York: Crowell, 1980], 1–2).

According to Paterson, the patterns of life on this remote island dominated by marshes, a church steeple, ferries, crabbing, and watermen determine what the characters are and what they do. The place—the Chesapeake—melds character and plot.

So does time. Paterson sets *Jacob Have I Loved* in the early 1940s, which saw the trauma of Pearl harbor. As they read, readers know that the remoteness of Rass Island cannot protect its inhabitants from the events of the times. Time, as well as place, affects story.

Character

Central in story are the characters who inhabit the setting the author has crafted. Some characters remain in the mind for many days. Readers remember Maniac Magee because that special young man becomes real to them. Maniac is a full-blown character. Even in their first meeting, readers see Maniac Magee as "one part fact, two parts legend, and three parts snowball." They see him as a persistent kid who keeps at Amanda until she loans him a book. They see him as a fleet runner and an "ace" punter who snatches a football right out of the hands of James "Hands" Down. They see him as a brave rescuer of the weak who saves Arnold Jones from the torments of older boys and from a case of the "finsterwallies." Throughout, readers know that Maniac really cares about people.

The Multidimensionality of Characters   According to Donald Graves (1991), almost without exception professional writers "cite the preeminence of character over plot; that is, events occur because of the nature of the characters involved." The power of *Maniac Magee* lies in its central character. Maniac has qualities that all of us possess, for who has not longed for a place where he or she belongs? But Maniac goes

READ

Jerry Spinelli, *Wringer* (New York: HarperCollins, 1998) and E. B. White, *Charlotte's Web* (New York: Harper & Row, 1952) for superb examples of characterization.

GO TO

Figure 4.2 for a character web that highlights the multi-dimensionality of Maniac Magee. Use it as a model for webs that connect descriptive inferences to character actions.

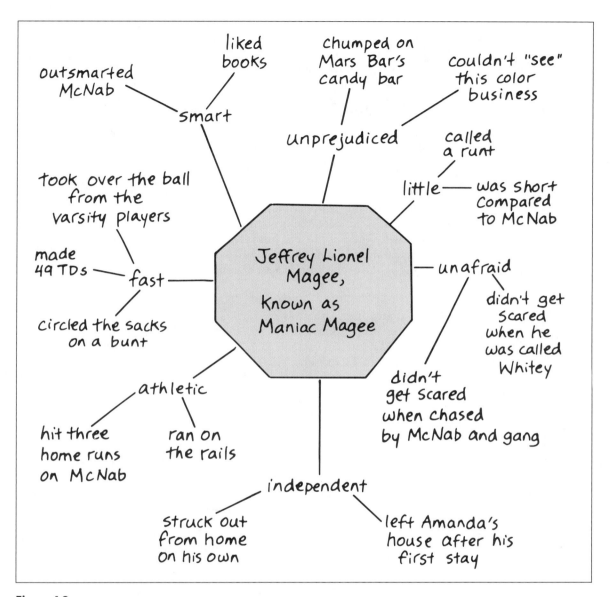

Figure 4.2
Character Web Based on the First Sixteen Chapters of *Maniac Magee*

ACTIVITY PROMPT

Web a character in a book you are reading.

beyond the ordinary. Spinelli paints Maniac larger than life so that the reader cannot help but turn the page to find out what this modern-day tall-tale hero will do next. Yet in some ways readers already know, for Maniac performs with a certain consistency. He rarely steps out of character to become other than his independent, tough, fearless, racially open, and essentially caring self. Because Maniac is multidimensional, human but larger than life, consistent in his actions, and has an underlying caring streak, *Maniac Magee* becomes a friend readers remember.

Strong characterization is essential in books for intermediate graders. Gilly, for example, is *the* story in Katherine Paterson's *The Great Gilly Hopkins*. Eleven-year-old Gilly knows that she is nobody's real kid. Brilliant but bratty, she moves from foster home to foster home with her feelings masked behind her barracuda smile. It is Gilly who has learned not to care because of the hurts the world has heaped on her. It is Gilly who finds a place of her own in the most unlikely place of all—with ungainly, illiterate Maime Trotter and "retarded" William Ernest, who love her for herself. And it is hurting, human Gilly Hopkins, with all the growing-up feelings of rejection and loneliness, who makes the reader read on. Most good books for maturing young people have at least one strong character like Gilly.

GO TO

Access Pages 494–497 for a list of children's books that have a multicultural thrust as do Maniac's, Gilly's, and Jennifer's stories.

How Character Is Developed   Through their *descriptions* of emotional and physical attributes—the way characters feel, look, and dress—authors begin to turn "story people" into real people. In *Jennifer, Hecate, Macbeth, William McKinley,* and *Me, Elizabeth,* for example, E. L. Konigsburg introduces Jennifer through the eyes of Elizabeth, the narrator, who sees Jennifer feet first. Elizabeth thinks, "They were just about the boniest feet I had ever seen. Swinging right in front of my eyes as if I were sitting in the first row at Cinerama."

But description takes the reader only to Jennifer's surface. Her *words*—to herself and to others—and her *actions* take the reader inside to see her whole self. Jennifer says things like

> Witches convince, they never argue. But I'll tell you this much. Real witches are Pilgrims, and just because I don't have on a silly black costume and carry a silly broom and wear a silly black hat, doesn't mean that I'm not a witch. I'm a witch all the time and not just on Halloween.

CONSIDER

Ways to Know a Character

Jennifer does original things, too, like writing notes in a strange script and operating masterfully on trick-or-treat night. Through the descriptions, dialogue, and deeds, the reader perceives Jennifer as a "really sharp cookie."

Characters are less fully developed in books for early-primary-grade youngsters. Still, in picture storybooks the reader generally finds a group of characters or one character who is the focus. Take as an example Marjorie Sharmat's *Frizzy the Fearful,* in which the reader meets Frizzy Tiger. Frizzy, the reader quickly learns, is afraid of everything, which is something no self-respecting tiger should ever be. He tries to hide his cowardice from his friends because he is especially scared that they will discover he is a "fraidy cat." But they do! Despite his embarrassment at being found out, Frizzy cannot overcome his fears until the day he musters all his courage to rescue Nova Cat, who is stuck up a tree—only six inches up! Although communicating a fundamental message about overcoming one's weaknesses little by little, the story is short, and nearly all a reader knows about Frizzy is his fearfulness. This is the single dimension of personality that the reader sees; yet it is enough for the young child, who still can identify with the tiger.

Identifying with the Character   Stories that enthrall readers are those in which they can almost completely identify with a character. What readers bring to a story determines to a great extent whether such identification occurs. This suggests that not all good books are good for all readers. With the young child, it matters not whether the main character is male or female; the young child is able to identify with Frizzy Tiger because feelings of fear and embarrassment are part of childhood. With older children this is not so true, for the problems of growing up male and growing up female differ. As a result, boys can identify more easily with some characters, girls with others.

Despite these differences, some characters attract a wide readership. Usually these characters do things that children wish they could do or feel emotions that lie at the heart of growing up. Astrid Lindgren's *Pippi Longstocking* continues to appeal because every youngster has imagined how it would be to do exactly as she or he wants. What youngster has not dreamed of being the hero of the moment? Likewise, even though Mildred Taylor's *Roll of Thunder, Hear My Cry; Let the Circle Be Unbroken;* and *The Friendship* tell what it is like to grow up black in a place where being black means being poor and harassed, they have almost universal appeal because of the intense emotions they engender. The reader feels with Cassie and her brothers and in the process is changed even as the characters are changed by the unfolding events.

Plot

Huck (1993) discusses the importance of plot in fiction: "Children ask . . . , 'Does the book tell a good story?' The plot is the plan of action; it tells what the characters do and what happens to them." But a plot is more than a sequence of events. To be effective, it must have tension-building conflict. Something must be at stake; some difficulty must be overcome. It is to see the resolution of the conflict that most readers continue to read until the end of the story.

Plot Structures in Picturebooks   In most picturebooks, the plot is relatively simple. There is one main sequence of events, with few or no subplots to deflect attention from the main character, and one central problem, or conflict, to be resolved. Generally, each action flows from earlier ones; as a result, the reader can anticipate what will occur and what the final outcome will be. Take, for example, Paul Goble's *The Girl Who Loved Wild Horses.* The story is simple. The Native American girl has a deep understanding of horses and enjoys special moments with them. Then one day a squall drives the horses and the girl into a far-off valley, where she meets a magnificent wild stallion. She lives there with the wild horses until her human family finds her. Home again, but discontent, she explains, "I love to run with the wild horses. They are my relatives. If you let me go back to them, I shall be happy for evermore." The reader knows then that the girl who loves wild horses will someday run free among the Horse People. In this as in many picture storybooks, the action rises step by step, coming to a simple yet satisfying end that the reader can anticipate.

Often that end is the place where the action began, which gives the story a circular structure (see as in Figure 4.3). An example is Chris Van Allsburg's *The Garden of*

Figure 4.3
A Second-Grader's Pie Chart of *Farewell to Shady Glade* by Bill Peet. The story has a modified circular design in that the animals end up not back in Shady Glade, but in a place like it. *Courtesy of Sandy Mack and Courtney Breese.*

GO TO

Access Page 516 for a lesson plan that includes this book.

Abdul Gasazi. The tale begins with Alan and Miss Hester's dog, Fritz, standing on the porch watching Miss Hester leave for a visit with her cousin. After an active morning, Alan and Fritz nap on the couch and then go for a walk that brings them to the garden of Abdul Gasazi. Alan loses Fritz in the garden, only to have the mysterious Gasazi say that he has turned Fritz into a duck, for he hates little dogs. Heartbroken, Alan heads home with Fritz the duck under his arm, but the duck flies off with Alan's hat and Alan returns to Miss Hester dogless and duckless. There he finds Miss Hester and Fritz; Alan feels silly for believing that Abdul Gasazi could turn the dog into a duck. But after Alan leaves, Miss Hester finds Fritz on the porch with Alan's hat in his mouth, leaving readers to figure out what really happened. Stories such as this are "turn-about" tales, because though the action rises step by step, the ending takes an unexpected twist.

In some stories, especially folktales that have been retold over the ages, plot develops through repetition of the action. An example is the classic tale of the father and son who leave their village in the Nigerian bush country to seek wisdom in the world beyond. When they start out, the man and the boy ride the family camel, but meeting criticism, the man has his son climb down and walk. Meeting criticism as they continue, they change places: The boy rides; the father walks. Once more they are criticized, and they decide that both will walk. This, of course, brings more criticism. What does the man decide to do? What has he learned about the wisdom of the world? The reader knows before the third repetition. This is a "just imagine story" because the reader can just imagine what is to happen before it comes to pass. Figure 4.4 summarizes plot patterns commonly found in children's stories.

Structure in Chapter Books   Plot in books for middle-graders is more complex, with one or more subplots that underlie the main action and often carry the theme of the story. Despite this complexity, however, a central question binds the story together—a question that emerges early on in the tale that must be answered in some way by the story's end (Zindel, 1992).

For example, think for a moment about Gary Paulsen's powerful survival story, *Hatchet. Hatchet* has a finely crafted structure: It is essentially a story-within-a-story with an underlying symbolic metaphor that ties the two parts together. The first story is of Brian's struggle to survive in the Canadian wilderness. Alone in the wilds of Canada, Brian undergoes multiple trials, or tests, starting when he realizes that he must land the small plane in which he is riding and climaxing when he goes back into the submerged plane to retrieve the survival kit. This last test is what has been called the "pit experience." Brian passes each test aided by his hatchet; with his passing of the pit experience, Brian emerges as a new person, one who has learned to control his environment. In the story, the hatchet is a significant "player." Without the hatchet, Brian would probably not have survived. In the context of the story, therefore, the hatchet takes on added significance: The hatchet can be seen as a symbolic metaphor of people's need for something to support them in their fight for survival.

The second story is about Brian's inner struggle to accept his mother, knowing "The Secret"—her secret—as he does. Boarding the plane, he rejects his mother, turning away from her; but it is she who gives him the hatchet that saves his life. In the wilderness his thoughts return again and again to "The Secret." At the end as Brian returns home to his mother, he has learned to live with "The Secret" just as he has learned to survive in the wilderness.

Figure 4.5 depicts the story-within-a-story structure of *Hachet*. It shows the outer and inner stories, the cross-over between the two, Brian's growth as a result of his experiences (the ending is higher than the start), and the significance of the hatchet in the story. Visualizing a story's structure schematically helps the reader to see the author's hands at work, weaving the strands of the story together. For readers who are visually oriented learners, conceiving of a story in this way extends the pleasure of the reading experience (H. Gardner, 1993, 1995).

Tension   The author's effectiveness in weaving plot can be judged not only by the structure he or she crafts to tell the tale but also by the tension, or emotional pull, that he or she generates. Tension in a story is a direct outgrowth of conflict; it rises and falls in longer stories and chapter books, reaching a climax at some point and then generally tapering off as the author ties up the loose ends.

Finely crafted stories draw the reader into the plot by building tension from the very beginning. Paul Zindel calls the author's initial tension-builder the "catalytic grabber." Read Lois Lowry's grabber on the second page of *Number the Stars* when Annemarie, the protagonist, hears the soldier's "Halte" directed at her and her

PROGRESSIVE PLOT PATTERN	DESCRIPTION	GRAPHIC TO CLARIFY THE DESIGN
Linear	Events follow one another in a simple progression with little rise in the emotion level. Example: Peter Sis, *Starry Messenger* (San Diego: Harcourt Brace, 1995).	beginning ⟶ end
Step-by-step: rising action/falling action	Events flow logically as the action/emotion level peaks and then falls off to a satisfying ending that can almost be anticipated. Examples: Patricia MacLachlan, *Sarah, Plain and Tall* (New York: Harper Row, 1985); Lois Lowry, *Number the Stars* (Boston: Houghton Mifflin, 1989); Wilson Rawls, *Where the Red Fern Grows: The Story of Two Dogs and a Boy.* (Garden City, NY: Doubleday, 1961).	climax / beginning / end
Step-by-step: rising action	Events flow logically one into the next as the action/emotion level rises to a stunning climax at the very end. Ending can almost be anticipated. Example: James and Christopher Collier, *My Brother Sam Is Dead* (New York: Four Winds Press, 1974).	end / beginning
Turn-about	Events flow logically one into the next with the action/emotion level rising, but the ending takes an unexpected twist that readers may not fully anticipate. Examples: Chris Van Allsburg, *The Garden of Abdul Gasazi* (Boston: Houghton Mifflin, 1979), John Gardiner, *Stone Fox* (New York: Crowell, 1980).	end / beginning
Circular or modified circular	Events flow logically one into the next with tension building, but the final action carries the main character back to where he or she began. Example: Maurice Sendak, *Where the Wild Things Are* (New York: Harper & Row, 1963, 1988).	end / beginning
Repetitive	Events repeat; each repetition varies slightly, but the repetitive action can generally be anticipated. Example: Janet Stevens, *Tops and Bottoms* (San Diego: Harcourt Brace, 1995).	beginning / repetition / end

Figure 4.4
Progressive Plot Patterns in Narratives

DISCUSSION PROMPT

■ Patterns are general designs, with variations possible. Stories can fit into more than one category. For example, repetitive stories sometimes are circular. How can your understanding of patterns support instruction as you bring children and books together?

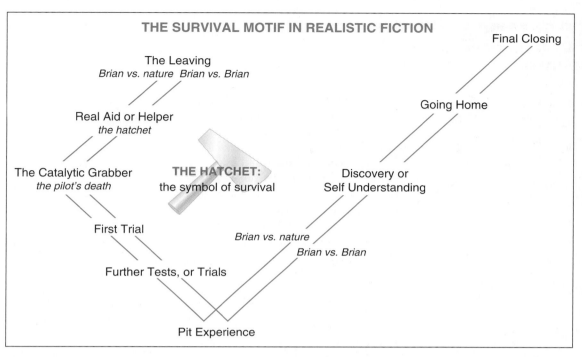

Figure 4.5 A Web of Story Elements and Relationships in *Hatchet*

laughter stops. Read the first two pages of Sonia Levitin's *Journey to America,* see the two uniformed men who patrol in front of the house, hear Mother's warning to never mind if the doorbell rings for everything will be all right, and learn that Father must go away. In the first chapter of Hans Richter's *Friedrich,* check the description of Germany in the 1920s when "hardship and unemployment were on the rise." Each of these beginnings establishes a feeling of unease and a sense that *everything will not be all right!* These kinds of tension-building starts grab readers emotionally and keep them reading.

Once the master storymaker has grabbed up readers emotionally, he or she continues to build the tension. Lukens (1995) identifies four sources of conflict out of which tension develops. One kind of tension pits the person against nature. The driving question of the story becomes, Will the person literally be able to survive? This struggle for survival against nature creates the surging tensions of *Hatchet,* as we have just seen. A second kind of tension pits the person against the self. A main character struggles with an inner problem or internal weakness with the driving question of the story being, Will the person gain control over him or herself? Again we have seen this kind of tension at work in *Hatchet:* Brian has to grow beyond "The Secret" that has immobilized his being if he is to tap into his inner resources and survive.

A third kind of conflict pits person against person. There is some of this in John Gardiner's *Stone Fox.* Little Willy, the protagonist, must fight for his grandfather, his home, and the way of life he loves. Ultimately, he must face Stone Fox, the Native American antagonist, who is fighting for his land and his people. What will happen

Distinguished Author

Meet Paul Zindel

Speaking at the 37th Annual Convention of the International Reading Association (May 7, 1992, Orlando, Florida), Paul Zindel, author of the young-adult novels *The Pigman* and *My Darling, My Hamburger,* identified six elements in a successful novel that are also part of a reader's life:

- The theme—the meaning the author is trying to convey (according to Zindel, "theme is most important in story").
- The catalytic grabber—the way the author gets the action going (see pages 121–123).
- The need—the purpose for which the main character strives (in Zindel's words, "the need drives the characters").
- The central question—the question in a reader's mind that must be answered by story's end.

- The turning point(s)—one or two events that turn the story in a new direction.
- The subplot—the plot underlying the main action that often carries the theme.

DISCUSSION PROMPT

You can ask questions about a novel based on these elements: How does the theme relate to your life? How and why does the catalyst affect you? How does the need apply to you? What is the theme of your life at this stage? What catalysts exist in your life? What needs drive you? Read a young-adult novel and use Zindel's elements to analyze it. Respond by writing in your literature response journal where you keep notes about books you are reading.

on the day of the race when the two competitors face off? The author gives us a glimpse when the two main characters meet the night before the race and Stone Fox strikes out physically at Willy. This raises the tension level of the story, a level that climaxes on the day of the race.

Stone Fox also provides an example of a fourth kind of conflict: the person against society. Little Willy is being squeezed by society, for he must pay the taxes that have accrued over the years. If he cannot pay, he loses his farm and his grandfather. When the bank turns him down for a loan, Willy must solve the tax problem on his own. In solving that problem with Willy, the author raises the tension to an almost unbearable level.

At times an author seems deliberately to provide relief from the escalating tension. For example, that delightfully laughter-filled episode in Patricia MacLaughlan's *Sarah, Plain and Tall* where Sarah and the children slide down their hay dune offers relief by pushing from the foreground into the background (momentarily at least) the question that drives the novelette: Will Sarah stay? In reading a story, it is fun to note "hot spots," see the hand of the author controlling the tension level, and talk about the function of comic relief in plays and stories. By doing this, we are reading like a writer. At the same time, we are growing in our knowledge of "how literature works" (Brock and Gavelek, in Raphael and Au, 1998).

And then, of course, there are the endings of a story to consider. First, endings must be believable, consistent with everything the reader knows so far about the characters and plot. Second, endings must be emotionally satisfying, regardless of whether they are shockers or gentle closings. An ending that is a shocker is Collier and Collier's dramatic close to *My Brother Sam Is Dead*. Here the reader knows what is coming because this coauthoring pair has warned us in the title, but nonetheless, the ending is dynamite, so powerful it leaves the reader gasping in horror. In contrast is the ending to *Sarah, Plain and Tall*, a gentle, aesthetic closing down of the story that is touching in the extreme. Both are emotion-filled endings—final grabbers that leave readers to contemplate the meaning of this thing we call life and leave them with the question as they close the book, What is *it* all about?

Themes, or Underlying Truths

What is *it* all about? That question brings us to a consideration of themes in fiction. As Lukens (1995) points out, themes are the underlying truths about life: the big ideas that unify a story. Generally, the successful author communicates the themes through events and characters rather than through an overt statement, as in a fable. Byrd Baylor never directly tells readers of *Hawk, I'm Your Brother* that enslaving another being is wrong, but that truth is there. The Indian boy frees his beloved hawk, who reaches its glory soaring above the Santos Mountains.

The Russian critic Mikhail Bakhtin (in Paul, 2000) has categorized stories as either dialogic or monologic. Dialogic texts allow for multiple interpretations; bringing their unique backgrounds into their interaction with a story, different readers make different meanings with it—make highly personalized themes with the "stuff" that the author has given them. In contrast, according to Bakhtin, "a monologic text allows for only one meaning," much in the way that propaganda is slanted to encourage a particular interpretation.

This is not to suggest that an author does not have underlying truths about the world in mind as he or she begins to develop a story. Just the opposite is true, as Christopher Collier, the historian behind the book *My Brother Sam Is Dead,* attested in a speech he gave at the University of Connecticut in 1998. In his presentation, Collier explained that he starts any historical novel with a theme—a big idea that will hold his story together. As an example, Collier told how he started to research *My Brother Sam Is Dead* during the Vietnam War era. Through his book, Collier, a pacifist, said that he wanted to show the horror of war; the horror and his revulsion toward it became the twine through which he bound his story together.

Because authors do have thoughts in mind that they layer into their stories, Louise Rosenblatt believes that readers can legitimately talk about an "author's probable intention"—"probable" because readers "can never enter into the author's mind." Readers can "look for clues that may reflect the intention that guided the actual writing process" and may "look for external 'background' information that will suggest or confirm the internal." Rosenblatt, however, warns that readers cannot argue, "That's what the author says is the intention, so that's what the text 'says.'"

Rather, "readers may find various possible interpretations different from the author's and different from each other" (in Karolides, 1999).

What do these ideas suggest to the teacher of literature? First, teachers must be wary of texts that clearly preach a particular point of view and do not allow for multiple interpretations. Instead, they must encourage the reading of dialogic stories into which young readers can read their own life stories. Second, teachers must be open to multiple interpretations of stories; they must keep wondering, "What other truths are layered into this story?" Third, teachers can help students to consider an author's "probable" intent. Together teachers and students can wonder, "What ideas did this author have in mind that guided his or her writing of the story?"

Writing Style

According to William Anderson and Patrick Groff (1972), "The foremost determinant of literary effectiveness is language. Only through language can literature communicate; whether written or spoken, the essence of literature is always verbal."

Word Sounds   Word sounds play a major part in books for younger children. Theodore Geisel, better known as Dr. Seuss, was a true "sound smith." Dr. Seuss wrote with a rhythm so natural that an oral reader feels the words must always have belonged in that order. He played with alliteration and rhyme to achieve spectacular effects; it is Horton who hatches the egg and lazy Mazy who claims it in the end in *Horton Hatches the Egg.* Humor comes, too, through repetition, simple at times, as in, "My goodness! My gracious! My word!" and more involved at other times, as in the recurring line, "An elephant's faithful one hundred percent!" Dr. Seuss also played with onomatopoeic words like *whizz, thumping, bumping,* and *squeak.* Many of the same effects splashed in large scale by Dr. Seuss are found in other stories children enjoy, albeit painted with a more muted stroke.

Word Pictures   Through an artful choice of words, an author can craft pictures more vivid than some photographers can take. Picture this snapshot of Little Ann, Billy's beloved coon hound in Rawls's *Where the Red Fern Grows:* "As graceful as any queen with her head high in the air, and her long red tail arched in a perfect rainbow, my little dog walked down the table. With her warm gray eyes staring straight at me, on she came. Walking up to me, she laid her head on my shoulder" (p. 155). A simple metaphor—the dog's colorful tail is called a rainbow; common words—mostly one syllable; yet that metaphor and those words draw readers into the picture to be there with Billy and Little Ann.

Look also at this verbal snapshot from the same book, told (as is the entire book) from Billy's first-person point of view: "Raising the ax high over my head, I brought it down with all the strength in my body. My aim was true. Behind the shoulders, in the muscular back, the heavy blade sank with a sickening sound. The keen edge cleaved through the tough skin. It seemed to hiss as it sliced its way through bone and gristle" (p. 194). As you can see here, sharpness of detail is a central element of Rawls's style, but so is a choice of words that relates to the mood. Rawls's words at this point are filled with harsh sounds that communicate the harshness of the moment.

Look at a final snapshot that Rawls provides in *Where the Red Fern Grows—*a

■━ ● ● ●
READ
Barry Lane, *After the End: Teaching and Learning Creative Revision* (Portsmouth, N.H.: Heinemann, 1993), about how an author creates verbal snapshots.

Issue Site

Are books such as those in the Goosebumps and the Harry Potter series really literature?

In a recent PBS interview on the *NewsHour,* Harold Bloom criticized the highly popular Harry Potter books by J. K. Rowling as lacking in "literariness." Bloom, a renowned literary critic and author of more than twenty books, noted that the Harry Potter books are heavy with clichés and that the characters lack depth. Other critics have condemned the books because of their focus on wizardry and magic. Such criticism has landed the Potter books on the most frequently banned or challenged book list, according to the American Library Association's Office for Intellectual Freedom.

On the other hand, many young readers are adamant supporters of Harry. For example, one young fan—Julia—discovered a commentary on the Internet called "Harry Potter Takes Drugs," written by Family Friendly Libraries. The commentary suggested that the books' witchcraft fantasies were not appropriate for taxpayer-funded schools and libraries. Julia responded with an e-mail in which she wrote, "If they followed the logic they used against Harry Potter, they could have banned Buddhism." Julia's e-mail came to the attention of the American Library Association, which awarded her a $100 savings bond for her protests against censorship.

In an article in *Language Arts,* Leslie Perry and Rebecca Butler analyzed the negative criticism that has also been heaped on books in the Goosebumps series, especially the supposed scariness of the stories and lack of "literariness." Perry and Butler concluded that R. L. Stine, the author of the books, "should be applauded for almost single-handedly making reading *COOL.*" They ended their article with two questions and a three-word answer: "So, are Goosebumps books real literature? Who cares?! *Reading is reading!* ("Are Goosebumps Books Real Literature?" *Language Arts,* 74 [October 1997], 454–456).

DISCUSSION PROMPT

What is your take on scariness, witchcraft, and magic in books for children? Should children be "allowed" to select their own books for independent school reading even when children's selections are books such as in the Potter and Goosebumps series? Why? Why not?

Sample books in each of these series. Develop your own conclusion: Are they real literature?

---

closeup of the graves of Little Ann and Old Dan, viewed through Billy's eyes: "When I walked up close enough to see what it was, I sucked in a mouthful of air and stopped. I couldn't believe what I was seeing. There between the graves, a beautiful red fern had sprung up from the rich mountain soil. It was fully two feet tall and its long red leaves had reached out and in rainbow arches curved over the graves of my dogs" (p. 209). How powerful this image is—a gem so sharp, focused, and ultimately moving; yet this is more than an emotion-packed picture. Yes, with Billy, readers see the rainbow arches of the red fern curved over the graves, but they also see the rainbow arch of Little Ann's long red tail in their memory. Here Rawls has crafted a striking metaphor that carries a rainbow message of hope and love and brilliant color that lasts long after readers have read the final lines.

Rawls is a master of the written snapshot that zooms in to magnify significant detail. So are other fine authors who are part of children's literary heritage. Listen to the pictures of Maine that Robert McCloskey paints beautifully with words in *Time of Wonder* and *One Morning in Maine.* See winter through Berta and Elmer Hader's verbal snapshots in *The Big Snow.* Search for an owl with Jane Yolen during the time of the *Owl Moon,* feel the cold, and listen to the quiet of night. This is what "literariness" is all about.

Pictorial Style

GO TO

Access Pages 488–490 for a list of recent Caldecott and Newbery winners.

Readers of *Time of Wonder, The Big Snow,* and *Owl Moon* find their experience with literature heightened by the illustrations. Books for the younger child tend to be picture stories in which meaning is communicated through words and pictures, and pictures at times dominate. The importance of pictures in these books is indicated by the fact that each has been recognized for artistic excellence by being awarded the Caldecott Medal, presented yearly by the American Library Association to the artist of the most distinguished American picturebook for children. In contrast is the Newbery Medal, awarded each year to the author who has made the most distinguished contribution to American literature for children.

Harmonizing Words and Pictures Through Color   Successful storybooks are illustrated with pictures that harmonize with the words. Illustrators achieve this harmony in a number of ways. One is to use color, or the absence of it, to enhance story meanings. For example, in the Caldecott winner *The Funny Little Woman* by Arlene Mosel, Blair Lent's illustrations washed in soft greens, yellows, and browns show where the action is occurring. When the funny little woman is tucked cozily in her little house, it is filled with color; but when she falls down the hole after her dumpling, the underworld blooms with color and the little house appears as a black-and-white sketch, probably as it remained in the woman's memory while she lived in the realm of the oni. Later, when the woman escapes to the upper world, the lower one fades into black and white while color lights up the little house.

Harmonizing Words and Pictures Through Size   In Dr. Seuss's *And to Think That I Saw It on Mulberry Street,* the pictures get larger and larger as Marco's imagination takes over and return to normal size only when Marco tells his father what he actually saw on Mulberry Street. Similarly, in Maurice Sendak's *Where the Wild Things Are,* the pictures occupy more and more of the page as Max travels farther and farther from his very own room into the land of the wild things. Changes in picture size can be an effective way to communicate meaning.

Harmonizing Words and Pictures Through Detail   When Max becomes king of the wild things, Sendak shows him wearing a crown. When Peter in *The Snowy Day* walks with his feet pointing out like "this" and pointing in like "that," Ezra Jack Keats shows tracks in the snow doing just "this" and "that." And when Squire Lovel of Trove in *Duffy and the Devil* loses all the clothes that his wife has contracted

NARRATIVE GENRES	CHARACTERISTICS	TITLES FOR READING ALOUD AND ALONE
Account	A retelling of events that actually happened	*Susanna of the Alamo: A True Story* by John Jakes (1986); *Two Lands, One Heart: An American Boy's Journey to His Mother's Vietnam* by Jeremy Schmidt and Ted Wood (1995)
Biography	True account of a person's life written by another person (Note: When children write biographies, suggest that they use the first person. This adds freshness.)	*Amos Fortune, Free Man* by Elizabeth Yates (1950); books by Jean Fritz; *Lincoln: A Photobiography* by Russell Freedman (1987); *Anthony Burns: The Defeat and Triumph of a Fugitive Slave* by Virginia Hamilton (1987)
Autobiography	True account of a person's life written by the person	*Little by Little: A Writer's Education* by Jean Little (1988); *Starting from Home: A Writer's Beginnings* by Milton Meltzer (1988); *A Girl from Yamhill: A Memoir* by Beverly Cleary (1988); *Eastern Sun, Winter Moon: An Autobiographical Odyssey* by Gary Paulsen (1993)
Historical fiction	A story based on events that actually took place	*Sarah, Plain and Tall* by Patricia MacLachlan (1985); *Night John* by Gary Paulsen (1994)
Realistic fiction	A story in which a character solves a problem in a realistic way	*Tales of a Fourth Grade Nothing* by Judy Blume (1972); *Shiloh* by Phyllis Naylor (1991)
Mystery	A story in which a character unravels a series of clues to solve a mystery; filled with suspense and action	Encyclopedia Brown stories by Donald Sobol; *From the Mixed-up Files of Mrs. Basil E. Frankweiler* by E. L. Konigsburg (1967); *The Westing Game* by Ellen Raskin (1978)
Fantasy	A story in which magical things happen and in which there are magical beings such as wizards and dragons	*The Wizard of Oz; Alice in Wonderland;* Arthur Yorinks' *Hey, Al* (1968); J. K. Rowling's Harry Potter books
Talking-beast tale	A fantasy in which animals are personified; they talk and act as people do	*Charlotte's Web* by E. B. White (1952); old tales such as *The Little Red Hen* and *The Three Little Pigs*
Fable	A tale told with an acknowledged moral	Old fables by Aesop and La Fontaine; modern fables by Arnold Lobel, *Fables* (1980)
Pourquoi tale	A story that creatively explains a custom, a natural phenomenon, or an animal characteristic	*Why Mosquitoes Buzz in People's Ears* retold by Verna Aardema (1975); the *Just So Stories* by Rudyard Kipling
Tall tale	A story in which a main character can do impossible deeds; a tale filled with superlatives	Old stories about Pecos Bill, John Henry, Paul Bunyan; McBroom tales by Sid Fleischman

Figure 4.6 Kinds of Narrative Genres

Use Mitsumasa Anno et al., *All in a Day* (New York: Philomel, 1986), to help children understand differences in art styles. The book, which touches on the theme of cultural diversity, has art by nine distinguished illustrators.

READ

■ "Using Nonfiction Literature," *School Talk*, 5 (January 2000), for ideas for using nonfiction in the classroom, especially in social studies.

■ Donald Graves, *Investigating Nonfiction* (Portsmouth, N.H.: Heinemann, 1989).

with the devil to make for him, Margot Zemach shows a squire clothed only in shoes, clutching his hat in front of him. In each case, words and pictures are in harmony.

At times, too, illustrations supply additional detail. In Ann Grifalconi's *The Village of Round and Square Houses,* the softly muted drawings provide a picture of life as it is lived in the village of Tos. In the same way, the muted drawings in Judith Hendershot's *In Coal Country* provide the details of setting for that story.

In books for upper-graders, pictures play a lesser but still significant role. In most cases, the pictures are pen-and-ink sketches scattered sparingly through the book. The effect, however, can be powerful, as in Paula Fox's *The Slave Dancer;* here Eros Keith's illustrations are stark, communicating a sense of overwhelming horror.

Nonfiction in the Curriculum

Children should be introduced to a variety of story forms: picturebooks, traditional tales, modern fantasy, contemporary realism, and historical fiction. See Figure 4.6 for examples. As Carl Smith (1991) explains, "Each type of literature presented to a young reader serves two functions: to develop a schema for that literary genre and to encourage the application of thinking skills in a variety of literary engagements. . . . Reading a variety of literary genres has a related positive effect on writing."

Children should also be introduced to a variety of nonfictional forms. Foremost in selecting informational literature are accuracy and authenticity. Nonfiction authors must research their subjects so that their facts are correct and interesting details are plentiful enough to make the text come alive. Second is structure. Authors must organize their ideas so that the reader can anticipate where the text is going. To do this, authors must craft tight paragraphs that focus on important ideas. They must develop their ideas in a sequence that is clear and at the same time creative. And they must use relation-indicating words *(first, next, after that, finally; for example; however, but; in contrast, on the other hand; if-then; because)* to make smooth transitions between ideas and clarify connections among them.

Style is a third factor in the success of nonfiction writing. As Stephanie Harvey explains (in "Using Nonfiction," 2000), reading nonfiction gives youngsters opportunities to explore their "passionate curiosity" about their world. To respond to children's questions about the world, however, authors must craft their texts artfully: They must use choice words, paint vivid pictures in their readers' minds, and set up creative comparisons that stretch the imagination.

The National Council of Teachers of English has established the Orbis Pictus Award for Outstanding Nonfiction for Children to honor authors who have written informational books that are accurate, clearly organized, and stylistically fine. See the list posted on the Teacher's Message Board on pages 131–132 for authors and books that have been honored since 1990. On the list thrice is Russell Freedman, in 1997 for *The Life and Death of Crazy Horse,* in 1995 for *Kids at Work: Lewis Hine and the Crusade Against Child Labor,* and in 1991 for *Franklin Delano Roosevelt.* Freedman is also a winner of the Newbery Award—one of the few nonfiction writers so recognized—for his *Lincoln: A Photobiography* (1987). Listen to one paragraph from Freedman's wonderful winning book. Visualize in your mind the picture Freedman is painting of young Lincoln. Watch for how he crafts his paragraph simply to focus

The Teacher's Message Board

Posted here are the winning and honor books for the Orbis Pictus Award since 1990. They are wonderful books for children to read; through them, readers can discover what makes for great nonfiction writing. Reading these books, too, young people can pick up clues for use in their own informational writing. You can use them as content for read-alouds in which you demonstrate key features of the genre.

■ *2000* The Winning Book: *Through My Eyes* by **Ruby Bridges** (Scholastic)
Honor Books: *At Her Majesty's Request: An African Princess in Victorian England* by **Walter Dean Myers** (Scholastic); *Clara Schumann: Piano Virtuosa* by **Suzanna Reich** (Clarion Books); *Mapping the World* by **Sylvia A. Johnson** (Atheneum); *The Snake Scientist* by **Sy Montgomery,** illustrated by Nic Bishop (Houghton Mifflin); *The Top of the World: Climbing Mount Everest* by **Steve Jenkins** (Houghton Mifflin)

■ *1999* The Winning Book: *Shipwreck at the Bottom of the World: The Extraordinary True Story of Shackleton and the* Endurance by **Jennifer Armstrong** (Crown)
Honor Books: *Black Whiteness: Admiral Byrd Alone in the Antarctic* by **Robert Burleigh**, illustrated by Walter Lyon Krudop (Atheneum); *Fossil Feud: The Rivalry of the First American Dinosaur Hunters* by **Thom Holmes** (Messner); *Hottest, Coldest, Highest, Deepest* by **Steve Jenkins** (Houghton Mifflin); *No Pretty Pictures: A Child of War* by **Anita Lobel** (Greenwillow)

■ *1998* The Winning Book: *An Extraordinary Life: The Story of a Monarch Butterfly* by **Laurence Pringle,** paintings by Bob Marstall (Orchard Books)
Honor Books: *A Drop of Water: A Book of Science and Wonder* by **Walter Wick** (Scholastic); *A Tree Is Growing* by **Arthur Dorros,** illustrated by S. D. Schindler (Scholastic); *Charles A. Lindbergh: A Human Hero* by **James Cross Giblin** (Clarion); *A Reporter's Story* by **Wilborn Hampton** (Candlewick); and *Digger: The Tragic Fate of the California Indians from the Missions to the Gold Rush* by **Jerry Stanley** (Crown)

■ *1997* The Winning Book: *Leonardo da Vinci* by **Diane Stanley** (Morrow Junior Books)
Honor Books: *Full Steam Ahead: The Race to Build a Transcontinental Railroad* by **Rhoda Blumbert** (National Geographic Society); *The Life and Death of Crazy Horse* by **Russell Freedman** (Holiday House); and *One World, Many Religions: The Ways We Worship* by **Mary Pope Osborne** (Alfred A. Knopf)

■ *1996* The Winning Book: *The Great Fire* by **Jim Murphy** (Scholastic)
Honor Books: *Dolphin Man: Exploring the World of Dolphins* by **Laurence Pringle,** photographs by Randall Wells (Atheneum); and *Rosie the Riveter: Women Working on the Home Front in World War II* by **Penny Colman** (Crown)

■ *1995* The Winning Book: *Safari Beneath the Sea: The Wonder World of the North Pacific Coast* by **Diane Swanson** (Sierra Club)
Honor Books: *Wildlife Rescue: The Work of Dr. Kathleen Ramsay* by **Jennifer Dewey** (Boyds Mills Press); *Kids at Work: Lewis Hine and the Crusade Against Child Labor* by **Russell Freedman** (Clarion Books); and *Christmas in the Big House, Christmas in the Quarters* by **Patricia C. McKissack** and **Fredrick L. McKissack** (Scholastic)

Message Board, cont.

■ *1994* The Winning Book: *Across America on an Emigrant Train* by **Jim Murphy** (Clarion Books)
Honor Books: *To the Top of the World: Adventures with Arctic Wolves* by **Jim Brandenburg** (Walker); and *Making Sense: Animal Perception and Communication* by **Bruce Brooks** (Farrar, Straus & Giroux)

■ *1993* The Winning Book: *Children of the Dust Bowl: The True Story of the School at Weedpatch Camp* by **Jerry Stanley** (Crown)
Honor Books: *Talking with Artists* by **Pat Cummings** (Bradbury Press); and *Come Back Salmon* by **Molly Cone** (Sierra Club Books)

■ *1992* The Winning Book: *Flight: The Journey of Charles Lindbergh* by **Robert Burleigh** and **Mike Wimmer** (Philomel Books)
Honor Books: *Now Is Your Time! The African American Struggle for Freedom* by **Walter Dean Myers** (HarperCollins); and *Prairie Vision: The Life and Times of Solomon Butcher* by **Pam Conrad** (HarperCollins)

■ *1991* The Winning Book: *Franklin Delano Roosevelt* by **Russell Freedman** (Clarion Books)
Honor Books: *Arctic Memories* by **Normee Ekoomiak** (Henry Holt); and *Seeing Earth from Outer Space* by **Patricia Lauber** (Bradbury)

■ *1990* The Winning Book: *The Great Little Madison* by **Jean Fritz** (Putnam)
Honor Books: *The Great American Gold Rush* by **Rhoda Blumberg** (Bradbury); and *The News About Dinosaurs* by **Patricia Lauber** (Bradbury)

on one main idea, includes interesting anecdotal detail that relates to his main point, uses direct quotation to add interest, and provides a mind-stretching simile:

> By the time he was sixteen, Abraham was six feet tall—"the gangliest awkward feller . . . he appeared all joints," said a neighbor. He may have looked awkward, but hard physical labor had given him a tough, lean body with muscular arms like steel cables. He could grab a woodsman's ax by the handle and hold it straight out at arm's length. And he was one of the best wrestlers and runners around. (p. 14)

Read Freedman's paragraph aloud to yourself to see how smoothly the words flow together, how nicely they sound. Freedman, although a writer of nonfiction, is a wordsmith as are others such as Jim Murphy, Jean Fritz, Laurence Pringle, and David Macaulay who work this genre.

Bringing Children and Books Together

Today educators are turning to fine literature and using it as the core material of the language arts and across the curriculum; they are organizing a variety of unit experiences in which stories, poems, and nonfiction are central. As early as 1992, Lea McGee noted, "The move toward literature-based instruction around the United States might fairly be characterized as a revolution." In the last ten years, there has been much attention to reader response—the transaction of a reader with a text. In this section, we consider aspects of reader response and identify ways to heighten children's response to fiction and nonfiction. Finally, we look at some issues that teachers should consider as they move into literature-based language arts.

The Nature of Reader Response: Literary, Aesthetic, Humanistic

According to Louise Rosenblatt (1978), a person carries on a "dynamic, personal, and unique activity" as he or she interacts with and responds to a text. One kind of reader response is what Rosenblatt terms *efferent*. Efferent meaning-making requires readers to disengage "attention as much as possible from the personal and qualitative" aspects of a piece and focus on "information, concepts, and guides to action." Important in efferent reading response is what remains *after* the reading—the understanding acquired, the inferences made, the conclusions developed, the opinions generated.

Especially as they read expository content, efferent readers may have to focus on getting the facts straight and understanding an author's big ideas. But, efferent readers may also want to look with an analytic eye and consider the way an author crafted a story. For example, making-meaning with fiction, readers may consider how the author ensnared readers' emotions early on, foreshadowed coming events, built up and relieved tension, and relied on progressively more complex metaphors to create supporting themes. Similarly, efferent readers may compare the way one author crafted his or her text with the way another author did it. Responding in these ways, readers are looking at text from a *literary* perspective, "reading like a writer," crawling into the writer's mind and under his or her skin to perceive how that author is plying the writer's craft.

An interesting way to view text from a literary perspective is to look at the words a writer chose to tell his or her story. In most instances, the specific words a writer used was a matter of choice, not chance, and considering that choice helps the reader perceive the author behind the text. For example, readers of Bernard Waber's *You Look Ridiculous, Said the Rhinoceros to the Hippopotamus* can consider why Waber chose the word *ridiculous* for his title rather than the synonym *silly,* which means almost the same thing. Was this a purposeful use of alliteration? Did Waber have in mind the comparably long length of the words *Ridiculous, Rhinoceros,* and *Hippopotamus* when he opted for *ridiculous*? Working from a literary perspective that in this case has *linguistic* overtones, students are taking an efferent—an analytical—stance.

WORD BANK

Efferent

Literary

Linguistic

Aesthetic

Humanistic

Distinguished Educator

DISCUSSION PROMPT

Rethink your own responses as you have read stories, poems, and articles. When has your transaction with text been primarily public and efferent, with emphasis on "take-away" knowledge? When has your transaction with text been more private and aesthetic, with emphasis on feelings and emotions? Describe specific transactions you have had that fall into each category and others that fall "nearer the middle" of the continuum.

Meet Louise M. Rosenblatt

Louise M. Rosenblatt is known for her two major books—*Literature as Exploration* (1938; 2nd ed., 1970; 3rd ed., 1976; 4th ed., 1983; 5th ed., 1995) and *The Reader, the Text, and the Poem* (1978), in which she set forth her oft-quoted theory of literary transaction. Rosenblatt graduated from Barnard College in 1925 and received a doctorate in 1931 in comparative literature from the Sorbonne in Paris, having written her dissertation in French. She then taught in liberal arts departments at Barnard and at Brooklyn College; in the Schools of Education at New York University, Rutgers University, Michigan State University, and other prestigious institutions. In the year 2000, if you had paid a visit to the University of Coral Gables, you could have seen her teaching there. Dr. Rosenblatt was honored by the National Council of Teachers of English as the 1999 Outstanding Educator in the English Language Arts.

In a 1999 interview with Nicholas Karolides, Rosenblatt talked about her theory of literary transaction: "What readers make of their interplay with a text depends on what they bring to it, in linguistic and life experiences, in assumptions about the world, and in personal preoccupations. . . . Meaning 'happens' during the interplay between the text and the reader."

In the interview, Rosenblatt clarified the distinctions between efferent and aesthetic readings of a text: "In efferent reading . . . from the Latin *efferre*, to carry away . . . a greater proportion of attention is centered on the public, generally shared meanings, and less on the privately felt aspects. This is the kind of meaning the scientist aspires to—impersonal, repeatable, verifiable."

Continuing, Rosenblatt explained what she meant by an aesthetic (in contrast to an efferent) stance in reading: "Instead of attention mainly to facts and ideas abstracted for use afterwards, the reader of, say, a lyric by Keats would focus on what was lived through during the reading, on the ideas as they are embodied in the images, the sensations, the feelings, the changing moods. Attention would be given to the public, referential aspect, but mainly to the aura of feelings and attitudes surrounding it. I called this *aesthetic* reading."

But Rosenblatt reminded educators that today she was "emphasizing the range of possible stances between the efferent and the aesthetic poles. Between the two poles, there is a sequence of possible proportions of attention to public and private aspects of sense. I have been citing reading events whose selective attention clearly placed them at one or the other end of the continuum. But there are many, perhaps most, reading events with the proportion falling nearer the middle. Thinking of different reading transactions as places on a continuum solves the problem most theorists have about such texts as Emerson's essays, or *The Book of Isaiah*, or Lincoln's Gettysburg Address" (Nicholas Karolides, "Theory and Practice: An Interview with Louise M. Rosenblatt," *Language Arts*, 77 [November 1999], 158–170).

In contrast, *aesthetic* meaning-making is subjective and personal. Responding to a story or poem, aesthetic readers crystallize "from the stuff of memory, thought, and feeling a new experience. . . . This becomes part of the ongoing stream of our life experiences to be reflected on from any angle important to us as human beings" (Rosenblatt, 1978). What readers are "living through" —what they see, hear, and feel—as they interact with text is important. Rosenblatt calls this process of selecting ideas, sensations, feelings, and images and making something unique and personal with them "the literary evocation." Readers who assume an aesthetic stance connect emotionally with a story or poem they are reading to become as one with it. They are, in the words of Judith Langer (1995), envisioning "text worlds in the mind."

Another perspective—that perhaps is a melding of efferent and aesthetic—is what can be termed the *humanistic.* In responding humanistically, readers reach far beyond the words of a text to "read the world" within it (Freire and Macedo, 1987). "Reading the world" means that readers focus on life lessons—what the text means in terms of the human experience—past, present, and future. Whereas responding to text from a literary perspective suggests reading like a writer and responding from an aesthetic perspective suggests reading from the heart, responding from a humanistic perspective implies reading like a philosopher: Readers scaffold off the themes the writer embeds in the text to create their own lessons relative to the meaning of life and living, the nature of right and wrong, and the nature of human interaction in a diverse world. Readers take away from the text re-viewed ideas about the self, the self in relation to others within the social milieu, the self in relation to societal institutions, and the self in relation to the environment.

Not only can reader response be considered in terms of literary, linguistic, aesthetic, and humanistic stances, but it can also be considered in terms of the modality of the response. Children can respond to literature visually by sketching or representing schematically; verbally by writing; orally by dialoguing, dramatizing, and chorusing; kinesthetically by moving and acting out. By building opportunities for varied responses into the curriculum, teachers give children with different learning preferences an opportunity to work from their talents. In the sections to follow, you will consider ways of organizing children's varied experiences with literature to facilitate multifaceted responses.

Literature Response Journals (LRJs)

One means of encouraging students to reflect on what they read is the *literature response journal.* Students record in their LRJs as they get ready to read, while they are reading, and after they read stories, poems, and expository pieces. They use whatever form of expression they choose—story, poem, or exposition; description, explanation, or free association; words, pictures, or graphic organizers.

Some teachers give students a prompt or two to think and write about, during and after reading. For example, as her third-graders read a chapter of *Thanksgiving Treasure* by Gail Rock, Ms. Benjamin asked readers to consider whether it was ever right to lie or to do something underhanded, as the story character did in the chapter read. Children responded to the prompt by writing in their literature response journals. Later they enthusiastically shared their entries and talked about them. Good prompts for triggering active responses while reading are ones such as Ms. Benjamin's that ask for inferential, critical, or creative thinking—not just fact calling.

Patricia Kelly (1990) suggests three prompts for triggering a written response to literature: (1) *Literary:* What did you notice in the story? (2) *Aesthetic:* How did the story make you feel? (3) *Aesthetic:* What does this story remind you of in your own life? In using these prompts with third-graders, the teacher provides a five-minute writing time and an opportunity for students to share their responses with the class. Kelly finds that one-line entries dominate initial attempts, but as students become familiar with responding to literature in this way, their responses become more detailed and go beyond literal retelling. Students progressively are more able to put their feelings into words and actually display fewer errors in sentence structure.

Another approach is the generic response guide, as in Figure 4.7. This kind of guide does not focus on any one story and can be used in a variety of contexts. Teachers can encourage children to keep a copy of the suggested response options, which tend toward the aesthetic, on the inside cover of their literature response journals.

Some teachers, like Marjorie Hancock (1992), do not provide any prompts as they ask children to respond in their journals. These teachers encourage students to record "the thoughts going on in their heads." They stress "honesty and trust" in writing responses, downplay correct spelling and mechanics, and reply to students' entries by making encouraging, nonevaluative comments. As an example of this kind of freewheeling, aesthetic written response, Hancock provides these entries by a sixth-grader:

> Reaching out, don't you understand it's just trying to grab a hold and not let go, search until you find your answer. I know you can understand, Dicey. Just try, you can. I know *you. I* know you can. (a response while reading Cynthia Voigt's *Dicey's Song*)

> Was there really a face in the window? Was someone watching you Ned? What if dad was watching you or mom or Mrs. S. Are you in trouble could you have shot an animal? Listen to your conscience. (a response while reading Paula Fox's *One-Eyed Cat*)

Carole Cox and Joyce Many (1992) provide an example of eleven-year-old Winke's response to E. L. Konigsburg's *A Proud Taste for Scarlet and Miniver.* Winke's first responses were simply retellings of the book. Then she made a connection with another book and began a story of her own based on it. Finally, she came "face to face with her own beliefs as a result of reading":

> I wonder about life. That lots of people change, even when they are older. Which disagrees with a thought I had—it was harder to change when you are older. Maybe you couldn't change at all. This book makes me disagree with that.

Cox and Many suggest that as Winke wrote, she began to construct her own reality. Her response became aesthetic and centered on her own images, feelings, mood, and ideas. She began to picture the story in her mind, to extend the story by hypothesizing how it could be different, and to relate associations to her own life. For this kind of aesthetic response to happen, Cox and Many propose that students must be

AN AESTHETIC-RESPONSE GUIDE
Try one of these ways for taking off with a story you have read. Express your feelings and thoughts in your journal. You may use any medium you wish: a story, a description, an explanation, a poem, a picture, a visual of any kind. Remember you won't have to share your most personal feelings during conversation time. Mark your private entries. • How does this make me feel? What is my mood as I read? Why do I feel this way? • When in my life have I felt the same way? Why did I feel that way? • When has a similar thing happened to me? How did I feel then? Why did I feel that way? • What connections do I make between what is happening in the story and my own life? • What questions do I ask as I read? Why do I raise these questions? • What questions do I answer as I read? What are my answers to the questions? • What do I want to say to a character as I read? • What more do I think a character wants to say to me beyond what is in the story? • What do I wonder as I read? • When have I acted in the same way as a story character? Why did I act that way? • Of what does this remind me: a book, a film, a story, a piece of music, a piece of art? • What touched me the most in this story or poem? Why was I so affected?

Figure 4.7
An Aesthetic Response Guide (After Hennings, 1995)

granted the freedom to make choices about how they will "organize their evocation of a text"—as a poem, a vignette, or whatever else. The open-ended prompt these authors suggest is simply, "Write anything you want about the story you just read." These authors also stress the importance of providing time for children to respond, opportunity for responding over time, and opportunities for students to talk to themselves, to each other, and to the teacher.

Free verse works especially well as a trigger for aesthetic expression. Poetry liberates children from the idea that they must retell, summarize, or even criticize and allows them to pour out their feelings. An easy introduction to responding through poetry is the modified found poem. Children simply "find" a phrase or two in a story they are reading, set them down in the line-style of poetry, and adapt and expand on the original words to express their own feelings (Weiger, 1971; Hennings, 1997–1998). Here is an example based on phrases from *Sarah, Plain and Tall:*

You must have a garden;
we must have a garden;
I must have a garden—
Zinnias and marigolds and wild feverfew,
dahlias and columbine and nasturtiums—
You must have a garden;
we must have a garden;
I must have a garden wherever I am.

growl

grin

Of course, creative storymaking is always a response option. Children can respond in their journals by creating new stories that incorporate elements of stories heard or read. Students can write about the further adventures of a character, perhaps using the first person to speak in the voice of a story character. They can write a story that expands on the theme of one read or emphasizes the same emotions. They can write in the style of an author read or use a similar pattern of development. For example, responders may rely on the running-out-of-breath sentences that are part of Judith Viorst's distinctive style or model their stories after the *growl/grin* pattern of a story they have just finished—a story that starts with a problem and finishes with the resolution of it.

Literature Conversations

Children not only write in response to literature; they talk. Talking about ideas helps readers to explore relationships and expand their thinking. Children who have listened to or read a poem, story, or some nonfiction can gather immediately as a class to share journal entries and expand orally upon them. To further the class conversation, teachers can invite children to go beyond factual retelling to

- *Infer and predict*: What kind of person was little Willy? Why do you think Stone Fox hit little Willy?
- *Express opinions*: Was it right for the townsfolk to leave little Willy on his own to solve his problems?
- *Express feelings*: How do you feel about Stone Fox when he hits little Willy? Why do you feel like that?
- *Relate happenings to their own lives*: When have you felt the same as little Willy? When has something similar happened to you?

Literature Circles A teacher-guided, team approach to conversation about literature is the Literature Circle (Peterson, 1987; D. Watson, 1988; Short et al., 1999), in which four or five children choose the same book to read and explore together. They read that book independently and respond to it by writing in their literature journals. When children gather in their Literature Circle for discussion with their teacher, their purpose is to reflect and exchange ideas in a dialogue. As Dorothy Watson explains, teachers begin the dialogue by asking children to read from their journals or by asking a question that is "an invitation to dialogue":

What do you think? How are you different now from when you started this book? What do you know or think about now that you didn't know or think about before you started this book? Would you like to share something with us? What would you like to ask the author, or someone in the group, about the book? Does this book remind you of any other literature you know? How did the author get you to think? How did the author get you to feel happy, scared, sad? Do you see any patterns in the pictures or in the story?

Notice that none of Watson's "invitations to dialogue" ask for facts; rather, they are personal-reaction probes. After students have reflected together on a selection, the teacher can review with members of the Literature Circle the kinds of questions

READ

Carmen Martinez-Roldan and Julia Lopez-Robertson, "Initiating Literature Circles in a First-Grade Bilingual Classroom," *The Reading Teacher,* 53 (December/January 2000), 270–281, which concludes that "young bilingual children, no matter their linguistic background, are able to have rich discussions if they have regular opportunities to engage with books from a transactional perspective."

that facilitated their dialogue. Children can ask themselves these kinds of questions when writing in their response journals as and after they read a selection.

Maryann Eeds and Deborah Wells (1989) caution a teacher, who is conversing with a group of children, about the overuse of questions as invitations to dialogue and turning real discussions into "gentle inquisitions" in which questions have one correct answer—the one in the teacher's head. They contend that in a true classroom dialogue, the teacher functions simply as a comember of the group, not as the authority on the meaning of the text. In this context, literary conversations become "grand" conversations with ideas flowing naturally just as ideas flow back and forth across the table at a dinner party.

Key Literary Elements   How does a teacher prepare for grand conversations? Before meeting with a Literature Circle, a teacher reads the story the children are exploring, once to live through it (as Rosenblatt would say) and again to read like a writer, noting ways in which the author is developing the text. In doing this, the teacher considers the story in terms of key literary elements (after Eeds and Peterson, 1991):

■ *Time and place:* How does the author communicate a sense of time and place? How does the author use setting to further the story?
■ *Point of view:* From whose point of view is the story told? How does the author develop the story to make me one with the character who is telling the tale?
■ *Character:* Why do I (why do I not) believe in certain characters? How do the characters grow as people through the story events?
■ *Tension:* How does the author grab me and my emotions at the start? How does the author continue to build the tension? When and how does he or she relieve it? How does the author ultimately resolve the tension-generating conflict? Am I satisfied with the ending? Why or why not?
■ *Structure:* What pattern(s) do I see in the development of the story?
■ *Snapshots:* What pictures does the author craft that transport me into the story and give me a sense of "I am there?"
■ *Mood:* What mood does the author create? How does he or she make me feel? How does he or she bring me to this state of feeling?
■ *Themes:* What meanings do I develop as a result of this story? Are there any big truths about life and living that I see revealed?
■ *Symbol and extended metaphors:* What symbols does the author weave into the story? What extended metaphors do I perceive?

GO TO

Pages 110–113 to see this in action.

In preparing for literature conversations, the teacher does not think through each and every question he or she will use to heighten children's awareness of these elements of story. Rather, the teacher delves into a book first to make his or her own meanings with it and then to see how the author works behind the scenes plying the writer's craft. As children talk together about a story, the teacher senses a "teachable moment"—a natural opportunity to clarify something about the nature of storying. For example, a teacher may pick up on a student's comment that a particular story character seems to be changing and interject that this is often the case in finely crafted stories. Characters grow through experiencing events; it is something to

■ ● ● ●

READ

- T. Raphael and E. Hiebert, *Creating an Integrated Approach to Literacy Instruction* (New York: Harcourt Brace College Publishers, 1996).

- S. McMahon and T. Raphael, eds., *The Book Club Connections: Literacy Learning and Classroom Talk* (New York: Teachers College Press, 1997).

- T. Raphael et al., *Book Club: A Literature-Based Curriculum* (Littleton, Mass.: Small Planet Communications, 1997).

- T. Bond, "Giving Them Free Rein: Connections in Student-Led Book Groups," *The Reading Teacher,* 54 (March 2001), 574–607.

watch for as we talk and reread. Or a teacher may pick up on the students' disagreeing as to the meaning of a story or poem and interject that stories and poems can have multiple themes, or meanings, adding that really good stories have layers of meaning that make it possible for a reader to respond in more than one way (Eeds and Wells, 1989). To do this, of course, teachers must be "into" stories—they must have some understanding of what makes a story finely crafted.

Book Clubs   In some cases, especially after having had prior opportunities to dialogue with their teacher, children can meet on their own in groups to talk about a book they are reading. A group of three to six students, who have chosen to read a particular book, meet as a Book Club (Raphael, 1992). Students in a Book Club read the selection on their own, keeping literature response journals. Periodically they meet with other members of their club to participate in Book Club discussions. In contrast to Literature Circle discussions, Book Club discussions are student led; such roles as facilitator emerge as the group functions as a unit. In their club meetings, students generally begin by sharing their LRJ entries and then go on to react to them. Also, periodically, students get together with their classmates and their teacher in Community Shares. During Community Shares, they have the opportunity to talk about ideas that they are exploring in their groups and learn about literary elements to consider in their Book Club discussions—characters, mood, symbols, and so forth.

Collaborative Literature Action Workshops

Working collaboratively in small groups (perhaps in their Book Club groups), children can also "do thinking things" with literature. One form that response can take, a form with both a written and a visual/pictorial dimension, is charting (Roser and Hoffmann, 1992). "Physically a Language Chart is constructed from a large piece of butcher paper ruled into a matrix." On one axis children plot titles (and authors/illustrators) of the books or chapters of a book being read as a unit; on the second axis, they plot response elements—efferent, aesthetic, and humanistic—which they choose cooperatively as they talk about what they have read.

For example, Nancy Roser and James Hoffmann describe one group of young children who read a series of books centering on the theme "Being Different Is Being Special." In the first column of their reaction chart, they collaboratively recorded titles and authors; in the second column, they named the person who was different. In the next two columns they told how the character was different and what made the character special. To add an element of the aesthetic to these basically efferent reactions, students could record their own feelings about the character in a fifth column, or tell how the story related to their lives.

Similarly, as students respond to books by one author as part of an author-focus unit, they might record book titles in the first column, special elements of each book in the second, common and unique elements in the third and fourth, and their feelings about each book in the last. Clarifying relationships in a chapter book, students might note key events of each chapter in the first column, characters' feelings in response to the events in the second column, and their own feelings in the third. Clarifying character relationships and roles, students name the characters in a first column, list the role of each character within the community in the second, and hypothesize the role of each within the structure of the story in the third (protagonist, or hero; antagonist, or villain; supporting actor; extra).

An advantage of the response chart is that its production requires visualizing as well as using words for labels. Other kinds of collaborative literature action projects (CLAPs) have a visual dimension too:

- Geographical mapping, as students translate verbal descriptions of story places into an actual map that shows geographical relationships replete with a north/ south direction compass, title, key, and scale indicator (revisit Figure 4.1).
- Webbing story relationships, such as character and idea webbing (Bromley, 1996; revisit Figure 4.2).
- Flowcharting story events to show cause-and-effect relationships or predict (see Figure 10.4).
- Graphing the rise and fall of story action and emotion (see Figures 5.5 and 4.8).
- Construction of a time line to show time relationships (see Figure 10.3).
- Creation of a schematic of some kind that clarifies story themes and/or symbols (see Figure 4.9).

Figure 4.8
A Group's Feeling Graph Based on Their Reading of *Bridge to Terabithia.*
Courtesy of teachers Aimee Williams and group members Casey O'Mara, Zack Mish, Casey M. Herrlich, and Kevin Britton.

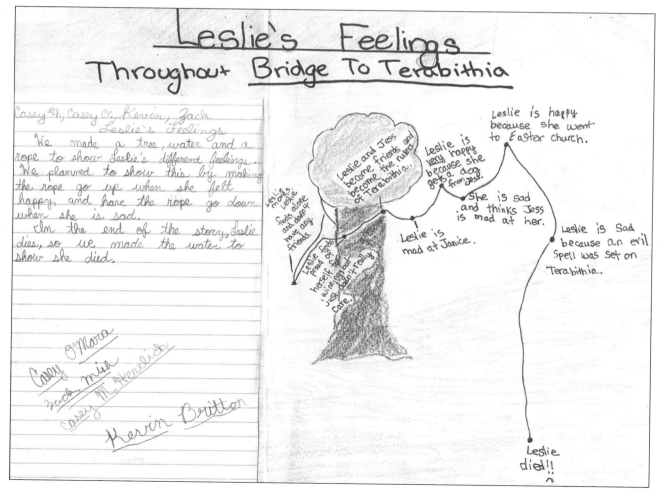

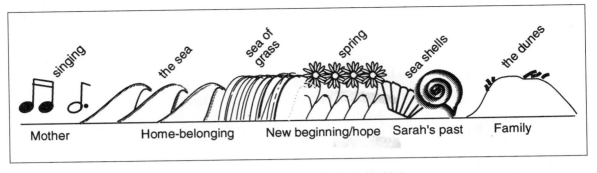

Figure 4.9
Symbols in *Sarah, Plain and Tall. Courtesy of Karen Anolick, Patricia Weber, and Denise Antonazzi*

These activities, some of which are applicable to both fiction and nonfiction, require children to analyze and infer—to see into the writer's craft. Students do not simply retell nor do they spend lots of time building, cutting out, or coloring and painting—which can take time away from reading and reflecting about reading without any valuable learning outcome (Zarillo, 1989; Reed, 1997–1998).

Another activity that works well in a collaborative workshop and requires and calls for analytical and creative thinking is titling, or "finding names that 'mean'" (Hennings and McCreesh, 1994). Students can analyze chapter titles in a novel to see "if there is a pattern, logic, or purpose to them." They can develop similar patterns as they provide titles for untitled chapters in books they are reading. In doing this, students are playing with main ideas, key emotions, and important characters. They may be playing also with parts of speech if they create titles that are in the noun-verb pattern ("Sarah Came"), are in the adjective-noun pattern ("The Violent Wind"), or end with a particular suffix ("Realization," "Indecision," "Creation")—strategies that students can observe in the titles of books they are reading.

Dramatic Interpretations and Extensions—Spontaneous and Prepared

GO TO
Pages 193–194, 197–199 for more on this.

After reading a story, children can use drama to respond collectively, collaboratively, or individually. With little preparation as in the manner of comedians who extemporize on television or with a bit of preplanning of what they will say or do, children can play out scenes they have read, using nonverbal activity and making up dialogue to fill in the blanks of a story. Or a student can "become" a character in a story and speak for him or her, recounting what happened and how he or she felt about it. He or she can become the author of the tale, explaining the thoughts he or she had in mind in writing it and the elements of his or her background that may have fed into the story. Or two or three students can become characters in comparable stories and talk together from the point of view of the characters; in other words, a Cinderella can compare notes with Snow White, with one young person talking as Cinderella and the other as Snow White. These kinds of mini-dramatizations are really interpretations and extensions of a story; young dramatists go beyond the tale the author has presented to develop in heightened fashion the events, the characters, and the feelings.

Spontaneous and preplanned dramatic responses to stories require risk taking, and because of that, students may feel uneasy at the start. To help students begin to enjoy dramatic interpretations and extensions of stories, the teacher should schedule spontaneous, total class activities. For example, responding to Pat Hutchins's *Rosie's Walk,* some kindergarteners can become hens, others foxes, and still others yards, lakes, windmills, and beehives. With everyone having a verbal and physical role in the mini-drama, students move about the room, interpreting their character or object. Hens strut about, repetitively cackling a line such as, "What a fine day for a walk. Too bad nothing exciting is happening." Foxes slink about and say something like, "I'm going to get that hen! Nothing is going to stop me." Lakes ripple; yards sway; windmills rotate their blades. And everyone has fun.

Other simple stories with limited dialogue work equally well with beginning dramatizers. Maurice Sendak's *Where the Wild Things Are,* Mirra Ginsburg's *Mushroom in the Rain,* Eric Carle's *The Rooster Who Set Out to See the World,* and Leo Lionni's *Swimmy* are examples that are useful at the kindergarten and first-grade levels.

Similarly, second- and third-graders can become the characters in Jane Yolen's *Owl Moon,* which has only limited dialogue as conceived by the author. Numbers of youngsters become the daughter who goes out owling with her father, the father who hoots owl-like as the two plod through the quiet of the winter night, and the owl that finally swoops down. With the light of an overhead projector glowing like the owl moon, all the students become players: daughters, fathers, or owls. They walk and search; they hoot; they stop—their body motions communicating the feelings and the mood of Yolen's story. In this case, most of the story can be performed nonverbally, with only occasional hoots and the final line, "Let's go home," disturbing the quiet of the wintery night.

With more complex stories, a student or teacher narrator can retell the story orally as dramatizers tell it through body motion. A story such as Tomie De Paola's *Strega Nona* works well within this kind of framework. Several dramatizers become the pasta pot, others the pasta, others the townspeople, while one child plays big Anthony and another Strega Nona. Working from this type of dramatization, individual students can spontaneously begin to make up and contribute lines; they speak as the pot, the pasta, the townspeople, Anthony, or Strega Nona would. Stories that are a bit humorous—for example, Janet Stevens's *Tops and Bottoms*—are particularly good for collective dramatic rendering. Only after young people have had several opportunities to interpret and extend a story through a collectively rendered dramatization should the teacher encourage collaborative group renderings and eventually individual ones.

An Instructional Concern: Significant Topics and Controversy

Sibling relationships, divorce, aging, death, sex, terrorism, female and male roles, discrimination, and drugs are just a few of the significant topics popular with authors writing for young people. A case in point is Katherine Paterson's Newbery Medal–winning *Bridge to Terabithia.* In it, death breaks up a close friendship

Who has the right to write the stories of a particular culture?

Writing in *The Reading Teacher* (May 2000), Howard Miller discussed the criticism that Judi Moreillon met in response to her children's book *Sing Down the Rain* (1997). Because Moreillon is a white woman, some people questioned her right to write about the Tohono O'odham culture—despite Moreillon's careful scholarship in researching the rainmaking ceremony that she wrote about in the book to ensure that *Sing Down the Rain* met tough standards of authenticity and accuracy.

Miller raised some sensitive questions as he considered the situation: "Should the inability to truly live another's life be the determining factor in deciding whether an 'outsider' has the right to relate the stories of another culture? Can Gary Paulsen legitimately write about slave life in *Nightjohn* (1993, Laurel Leaf)? Was it acceptable for Steven Spielberg to make the movie *Amistad* (1998, DreamWorks), depicting inhumane treatment of captured Africans during the Middle Passage? Both of these are white men, after all, with no personal knowledge of slavery."

DISCUSSION PROMPT

Should the ethnicity or race of a writer influence a reader's judgment of a piece of writing by that author? Can someone of a particular racial or ethnic background write effectively about characters who are far different from himself or herself? Should a teacher share with students pieces such as *Nightjohn* and *Sing Down the Rain*—pieces written by a person of a different background than the major characters in the stories? Give reasons to support your position on the issue.

between a young boy and girl. How overwhelming death is comes across clearly to the reader as Paterson writes: "*God—dead—you—Leslie—dead—you*. He ran until he was stumbling but he kept on, afraid to stop. Knowing somehow that running was the only thing that could keep Leslie from being dead." This book engenders controversy. It is on some banned-book lists for its treatment of death, religion, and boy/girl relationships.

Some parents object to books that treat sex and drugs in explicit terms. Cases in point are Beatrice Spark's *Go Ask Alice*, the diary of a fifteen-year-old who turns to drugs and sex and finally dies from overdosing, and Norma Klein's *Mom, the Wolf Man, and Me*, the story of a youngster who lives in a nontraditional family arrangement with her never-married mother and her mother's significant other. The same is true of Judy Blume's *Forever*, which is sexually explicit. Whereas Blume's *Blubber* is widely acclaimed for its clear, honest, and humorous treatment of the problems of growing up, *Forever* is controversial. Books like it belong in libraries for young people to select, read, and judge critically. It is difficult, however, to make this explicit fiction an integral part of the elementary school language arts curriculum.

GO TO

Access Pages 494–497 for an annotated bibliography.

A number of books vividly describe the treatment of minorities. *Behind Barbed Wire* by Daniel Davis tells in a forthright manner the story of the internment of Japanese Americans during World War II. Milton Meltzer's *Never to Forget: The Jews of the Holocaust* focuses on the Jewish experience during that war. Russell Freedman's *Indian Chiefs* depicts the problems Native Americans faced as they were pushed from their land. Gary Paulsen's *Nightjohn* forcefully tells about the horrors of slavery in America. These books as well as ones dealing with special-needs children have a role in elementary classrooms, especially as part of literature-based social studies units. Portions can be read aloud. Students can respond by talking and writing in their journals. In so doing, students may begin to comprehend the extent of the crimes humans have committed against one another and become more compassionate, humane beings.

An Instructional Concern: Stereotyping

Some books, especially ones written numbers of years ago, are flawed: They present a stereotypical view of people and the roles people play in society. One form that stereotyping can take is sexual. Women are depicted engaged primarily in passive pursuits, following—never leading—their male counterparts. Their concern is primarily with clothes, their appearance, and finding Prince Charming. In contrast, men are depicted in more active pursuits—participating in sports, working, solving problems.

In recent years, some progress has been made. Today most books portray women in more active and varied roles, and girls as well as boys are clever, capable, and athletic. Today, too, men in stories are portrayed as having tender feelings and crying when overcome with those feelings; men also are shown assuming homemaking tasks and opting for careers in the nurturing professions—nursing and preschool teaching. However, since children continue to read the older stories, they still come in contact with the old stereotypes.

A second form of stereotyping is ethnic. Until recently, few storybooks featured main characters who were members of racial or religious minorities or showed adult members of minority groups operating within the full range of available occupations. Few books celebrated the cultural diversity that is part of the American experience.

Things are changing. One of the first books to treat African Americans in a natural way was Lorraine and Jerold Beim's *Two Is a Team*. A picture storybook of the 1940s, it describes a friendship between two boys, Ted and Paul, one of whom is black and the other white. Other landmarks were Ezra Jack Keats's *The Snowy Day*, which tells of the delight of Peter, an African American boy, as he plays in the snow, and E. L. Konigburg's *Jennifer, Hecate, Macbeth, William McKinley, and Me, Elizabeth*, another story of an interracial friendship. More recently we have seen Vera Williams's *A Chair for My Mother* and Faith Ringgold's *Tar Beach* named as Caldecott Honor Books, the first in 1983, the second in 1992. Both feature main characters who are from minority groups in the United States. The winner of the Ezra Jack Keats Award in 1995 was Cari Best's *Taxi, Taxi*, a story featuring a Latina child. In 2000, Christopher Paul Curtis's *Bud, Not Buddy* won both the Newbery Medal and the Coretta Scott King award. *Bud, Not Buddy* is the story of an African-American boy's search for his father, a legendary jazz band leader. But these books have only scratched the surface. If children are to acquire a meaningful view of life within a

CONSIDER

The Ezra Jack Keats Award is given periodically to an outstanding first book by an author, especially a first book that relates to life of a minority group.

pluralistic society, they need many more books that depict diverse ethnic groups interacting in a variety of situations

Obviously, teachers must be aware of the stereotypical images books covertly and overtly send to readers. They must keep alert for instances in which one group of individuals is treated differently or in a discriminatory manner. Once teachers are alert to this problem, they will find many instances, since most of the folktales and fairy tales of the past present stereotyped images. Should schools discard these pieces of literature in favor of more relevant stories? Should they rewrite the stories of the past? Huck (1987) takes a middle-of-the-road position on these questions, especially as they relate to sexual stereotypes:

> There is no point in denouncing fairy tales for their sexist portrayal of beautiful young girls waiting for the arrival of their princes, for evil stepmothers or nagging wives. Such stories reflected the longings and beliefs of a society long past. To change the folktales would be to destroy our traditional heritage. . . . But today's books must reflect a liberated point of view.

Teachers must help children to see folk literature as a reflection of a different time and place. They can ask children to consider how a particular tale might be different if it had been written today. At the same time, teachers must bring children together with stories that introduce them to a variety of diverse cultures and help them appreciate that diversity.

A Summary Thought or Two

Literature for Life

The underlying theme of this chapter is that fine literature is an essential component of elementary school programs and that children should be encouraged to read a variety of good books. The fundamental goal of continuing contact with literature is that children learn to love books and to respond from literary, linguistic, aesthetic, and humanistic perspectives. To achieve this goal, teachers must bring to literature study a joy in life: an interest in little things like mushrooms, measuring worms, and minnows that occupy such an important place in children's stories; a delight in the sounds of language; an intense desire to find out; a commitment to understand people and living; and ultimately a love of books and an understanding of what makes literature fine. Without a love of books, teachers find it hard to instill such a love in children and to encourage a full response.

A second theme of the chapter is that through contacts with fine books, children can acquire a host of other learnings. Specifically, they can learn to

CONSIDER

Teachers can use these behaviors as items on an assessment checklist.

- Appreciate excellence in the writing and illustrations they find in books.
- Select books that meet their particular needs and interests.
- Interpret and evaluate stories, poems, and selections of nonfiction.
- Write in many different forms (picture, picture story, fable, realistic story, and so forth).
- View the world and living from an expanded horizon stripped of traditional stereotypes.

Such learnings are possible if teachers introduce children to books in which character, plot, setting, themes, words, and illustrations are skillfully interwoven and build literature-based units with children that tap the word, sentence, story, picture, and content power of books.

Your Language Arts Portfolio

- Participate in a "grand" conversation with your peers in which you talk about a children's chapter book in the manner described in Chapter 4. Then write a brief summary of the conversation and include what you learned about literature as a result of the discussion.
- Keep a literature response journal in which you respond aesthetically to stories and poems. Also keep in your journal an annotated bibliography of children's books and poems as you read them.
- Read several chapter books for children in grades 3–8. Select one and write an analysis of it in terms of the characteristics of fine literature explained in Chapter 4.
- Write a lesson plan based on one chapter of a children's novel. Include the elements of a lesson plan, as in the model plans provided in the Access Pages (see pages 512–522).

Related Readings

Bamford, Rosemary, and Janice Kristo, eds. *Making Facts Come Alive: Choosing Quality Nonfiction Literature, K–8.* Norwood, Mass.: Christopher-Gordon, 1998.

Bromley, Karen. *Webbing with Literature: Creating Story Maps with Children's Books.* 2nd ed. Boston: Allyn and Bacon, 1996.

Evans, Karen. *Literature Discussion Groups in the Intermediate Grades: Dilemmas and Possibilities.* Newark, Del.: International Reading Association, 2001.

Frank, Carolyn, Carol Dixon, and Lois Brandts. "Bears, Trolls, and Pagemasters: Learning About Learners in Book Clubs." *The Reading Teacher,* 54 (February 2001), 448–462.

Galda, Lee, Shane Rayburn, and Lisa Stanzi. *Looking Through the Faraway End: Creating a Literature-Based Reading Curriculum with Second Graders.* Newark, Del.: International Reading Association, 2000.

Harris, Violet. *Using Multiethnic Literature in the K–8 Classroom.* Norwood, Mass.: Christopher-Gordon, 1997.

Hill, Bonnie, Nancy Johnson, and Catherine Noe, eds. *Literature Circles and Response.* Norwood, Mass.: Christopher-Gordon, 1995.

Hillman, Judith. *Discovering Children's Literature.* Upper Saddle River, N.J.: Merrill/Prentice-Hall, 1995.

Jacobs, James, and Michael Tunnell. *Children's Literature, Briefly.* Upper Saddle River, N.J.: Merrill/Prentice-Hall, 1996.

Langer, Judith. *Envisioning Literature: Literary Understanding and Literature Instruction.* New York: Teachers College Press, 1995.

Language Arts, 69 (November 1992). The focus of this issue is literature-based language arts programs.

Lehr, Susan, and Deborah Thompson. "The Dynamic Nature of Response." *The Reading Teacher,* 53 (March 2000), 480–493.

Technology Notes

Check these Web sites for material on children's literature:

www.ala.org/booklist/best.html   ALA BEST LISTS

www.Amazon.com   Amazon Electronic Bookstore

www.crocker.com/rebotis/   Carol Hurst's Children's Literature Site

www.ucalgary.ca/dkbrown/index.html   Children's Literature Web Guide

www.users.interport.net/fairrosa   Fairrosa Cyber Library of Children's Literature

www.scils.rutgers.edu/special/kay   Vandergrift's Children's Literature Page

Individual authors also have home pages such as this one posted by Avi: **www.avi-writer.com.**

Lukens, Rebecca. *A Critical Handbook of Children's Literature.* 5th ed. New York: HarperCollins, 1995.

Lukens, Rebecca, and Ruth Cline. *A Critical Handbook of Literature for Young Adults.* New York: HarperCollins, 1995.

Moss, Joy. *Using Literature in the Middle Grades: A Thematic Approach.* Norwood, Mass.: Christopher-Gordon, 1995.

Norton, Donna. *Through the Eyes of a Child: An Introduction to Children's Literature.* 5th ed. Upper Saddle River, N.J.: Merrill/Prentice, 1999.

Pavelka, Patricia. *Making the Connection: Learning Skills Through Literature.* York, Me.: Stenhouse Publishers, 1998.

Reed, Elaine Wrisley. "Projects and Activities: A Means, Not an End." *American Educator,* 21 (Winter 1997–1998): 26–27, 48.

Roser, Nancy, and Miriam Martinez, eds. *Book Talk and Beyond: Children and Teachers Respond to Literature.* Newark, Del.: International Reading Association, 1995.

Russell, David. *Literature for Children: A Short Introduction.* New York: Longman, 1994.

Sorensen, Marilou, and Barbara Lehman, eds. *Teaching with Children's Books: Paths to Literature-Based Instruction.* Urbana, Ill.: National Council of Teachers of English, 1995.

Sutherland, Zena. *Children and Books.* 9th ed. New York: HarperCollins, 1997.

Tomlinson, Carl, and Carol Lynch-Brown. *Essentials of Children's Literature.* 2nd ed. Boston: Allyn and Bacon, 1996.

Journals That Relate to Children's Literature

Bulletin for the Center for Children's Literature
The Horn Book
The New Advocate
Tall

Intermezzo

There was a book lying near Alice on the table, and while she sat watching the White King . . . she turned over the leaves to find some part she could read, "—for it's all in some language I don't know," she said to herself.

—Lewis Carroll, *Through the Looking Glass*

CONSIDER

Ms. Stawasz suggests developing the integrative dimension of the unit by orally sharing "Secret Talk," a poem by Eve Merriam; "Poem" and "Youth" by Langston Hughes; and Carol Carrick's story *The Accident*. Weave in a musical thread—Rimsky-Korsakov's "The Flight of the Bumblebee" and Debussy's "Nuage" (Cloud). Ask students to look through a book of art masterpieces for a painting that creates the same mood as *A Taste of Blackberries*.

A Literary Journey

Dorothy Strickland reflects on the changing character of the educational researcher. Whereas in the past Strickland went into classrooms to do research, today she collaborates "on research teams where classroom teachers are involved in every aspect of the investigations. Indeed, it is frequently the teachers themselves who initiate much of the research." These teachers "are encouraged by a need to construct their own knowledge about things that are important to them" ("The Teacher as Researcher: Toward the Extended Professional," *Language Arts,* 65 [December 1988], 754–764).

Maureen Stawasz is such a teacher-researcher. Having taught reading with a basal text to students grouped by ability, Ms. Stawasz decided to experiment with a class reading of a chapter book by taking her sixteen sixth-graders on a journey into Doris Buchanan Smith's *A Taste of Blackberries*. She explained, "Through my unit, I hoped that the students—my travelers—would share the lives of the characters and the painful, yet healing, plot of the story. I hoped that my travelers would freely express themselves both in discussion and writing, relating their personal experiences and feelings to the story events. Students' written responses throughout the unit would comprise a literary magazine, a memento of their journey with *A Taste of Blackberries*." Here is Maureen Stawasz's description of that literary journey.

The Travelers

"My sixteen travelers were sixth-graders with varying levels of reading skills and interest. Most read on or above grade level. One youngster had received Resource Room services for reading until this year. Another child had arrived from Poland four months before and had just started to pick up English. Two or three others were passive readers; they would read, but they usually needed considerable motivation. All the students responded well to teacher read-alouds.

"Most of the students in the class had experienced death in some form—the death of a grandparent, a parent, a friend, a pet. This was important background, for *A Taste of Blackberries* is based on the sudden, incomprehensible death of a young boy and the feelings experienced by a friend left behind."

The Journey

"An aura of suspense surrounded the start of *A Taste of Blackberries*. It took us two days before we were prepared with the necessary 'supplies' for the trip. To start, I publicized the trip: 'Wednesday is the day we start our book, *A Taste of Blackberries*!

Get ready for Wednesday!' This aroused curiosity; students knew that this was going to be something different from their weekly skip through the basal stories.

"It was important for the children to become familiar with our 'destination.' What do blackberries taste like? Each child received two blackberries because black-berries were out of season and very costly. Since each had only two berries, they could not gobble them up. Instead, they savored each berry. Together, we inhaled the sweet smell. We placed a single berry on our tongues to feel the softness and the bubbly sacs of juice. Slowly we pressed the berry to the roofs of our mouth to let the juice inside run over our taste buds and slip down our throats. We let our teeth take over to finish off the berry. On charts in our response journals, as well as on a master chalkboard chart, we described the LOOK, FEEL, TASTE, and SMELL of our berry.

"In a section of our response journals, we wrote the title and author of the book. Then we looked at the cover. It shows two boys picking blackberries on the outskirts of a small town. On the cover is the quote, 'We planned to have fun all summer. . . .' We talked about the title, predicting the setting, the characters, the traits of the characters, and the kind of fun two boys could have in the summer.

"The next day, I read aloud the first chapter. Students listened to identify the characters and their traits. Having listened, students worked in pairs to make a character web for each of the main characters introduced in the chapter. We came back together to share our webs and talk about Jamie and the narrator. Our journey had begun.

"With the exception of the last chapter, students read the following chapters—one a day—to themselves. Generally we used the pictures in a chapter to get ready so that the weaker readers were able to handle the text on their own. We made responses in our journals and shared our thoughts after reading. The children initi-ated these discussions; they were eager to ask questions about things they didn't understand and to tell about similar experiences that had happened to them and how they had felt. We identified power words in a chapter and used the context to figure out meanings. We suggested a chapter title since chapters are untitled in the novel. We proposed writing options that we could try during writing workshop.

"It was slow going at first. The children were getting used to the characters and the buildup of the plot. More advanced readers were quick—too quick—with their responses during follow-up discussions; more reluctant readers sat further down in their seats, happy to let the others take over.

"The 'travelers' were hooked after Chapter Three when tragedy strikes Jamie, a major character. Everyone was eager to read Chapter Four, only to have their worst fears confirmed; the character they were getting to know was dead. Their question was, 'What will happen next?' The sixth-graders predicted events to come.

"The travelers journeyed on; this trail of death was familiar. Could we use our own experiences with death to get us through this unexpected turn? This we did; we shared our experiences, our confusion, and hurt with honest openness. We began to compile our deeper understandings in our class literary magazine, dedicating it to loved ones we had lost.

"At the suggestion of a student who at the start was content to let the others do the talking, we read the last chapter aloud. It seemed as though the travelers, who

CONSIDER

Maureen recommends independent reading during the unit, suggesting books that get at the meaning of friendship: Betsy Byars's *The Cybil War,* Jean Little's *Look Through My Window,* and Zilpha Snyder's *The Egypt Game.*

were responding emotionally at this point, wanted to come together and celebrate the final leg of the journey. Every traveler applauded spontaneously as I read the last word. We had become a community that had shared the specialness of the book, our thoughts, and our writings. We had created the literary magazine, *Tasting Blackberries,* as a showcase portfolio of our experiences with the book. In groups, we had researched, formulated ideas, composed, edited. At the end of the unit, each one of us had a copy of our class magazine."

The Destination: Assessing Where We Had Been

"Assessment of a literary journey of this type must be in terms of individual reading attitudes as well as skills. I gave no worksheets, I distributed no vocabulary lists, I gave no tests, and I did not ask children to write answers to comprehension questions at the end of each chapter. How could I determine language growth?

"Obviously, I had to use informal assessment through observation and work products. For example, as we read, the children debated who the two characters on the cover were. We knew one was Jamie, the boy who died, and the other was the narrator. We studied the traits of each character and debated as to which character was which on the cover. Kristy, one of my sink-in-the-chair readers, made a clever discovery that excited us all. In Chapter Five, Smith mentions that the narrator needed help parting his hair. Kristy pointed out that only one of the characters on the cover had a part in his hair; he must be the narrator. I was elated for Kristy and noted in my anecdotal records for the day that Kristy was able to read for details, make connections, and draw conclusions.

"Dana took awhile to come around. She generally didn't participate unless asked directly. But she was the one who announced she didn't want to wait another day to find out how the story would end, and 'Couldn't we *please* read this last chapter out loud together today?'

"Jarrett, a tough little guy, cried softly to himself in class. Was he identifying with the characters and plot? Of course. Monique wrote me a letter saying she tried to open up but it was hard because she almost started to cry. Michelle, Diana, and Jackie had great ideas for sequels and asked if they could have more time to write their ideas down. Everyone wanted to know other books by Doris Buchanan Smith, so one day we headed to the library to check the card catalog.

"Through their journals and the magazine, the children were involved in different writing forms. They wrote personal narratives, messages from the point of view of one of the characters, letters of sympathy to the deceased boy's mother, and poetry. One writing option at the end of Chapter Seven was to write a eulogy for Jamie. Only one child attempted it initially. When Monique shared her eulogy with the class, five others decided to write eulogies for the literary magazine. Others edited paragraphs they had written in their journals and wanted to include in the magazine. They rewrote them so they would sound exactly as they wanted them. Were they writing to a specific audience? Were they claiming the writing as their own? Were they revising to communicate their ideas? Most certainly.

■━ ● ● ●

CONSIDER

Writing options the children tried: People Who Are Gone But Not Forgotten; A Character Speaks; Poetry for Jamie; A Eulogy for Jamie; A Letter to Jamie's Mom; Stages of "Good Grief"; Blackberry Recipes; An Interview with a Character; What to Do When Stung by a Bee; A Report on Bees; A Report on Allergies; A Biography of D. B. Smith.

"The sixth-graders were very positive about both the reading and the writing. They volunteered to take on extra assignments to add to the magazine. They referred to the story at times other than when they were reading *A Taste of Blackberries* or writing in response. For example, the word *environment* came up in science discussion one afternoon. 'Yeah, you know,' said Jackie, 'Like Mrs. Mullins's garden had a peaceful environment. That's why the kid went in there after Jamie died.'"

Reflecting Back

"When I was a high school freshman, I had an English teacher named Miss Rice. As a child, I had devoured any books I could get my hands on. That is why my mother and I could not understand how it was that I could never pass one of Miss Rice's book reports. I could tell everything that happened in the book, but I could not satisfy Miss Rice. I realize now that my teacher wanted me to respond to the meaning of the book. I read the book *A Separate Peace* three times before my oral book report conference with Miss Rice. Before the conference I said to her, 'The only thing I don't understand is what was the separate peace?'

'That, Maureen, is the whole question of the book,' she answered.

"Through my experiences reading *A Taste of Blackberries* with my sixth-graders, I am convinced that children need more quality experiences getting at the underlying meanings of a book—at the personal meanings a book has for them. I am not referring to decoding skills. I am not referring to retelling skills. I am referring to helping children to relate to the characters, feel with them, and develop even as the characters are developing. I am referring to involving children in an aesthetic experience that is so intense that students want to continue reading and cry and clap in response. Students need to grasp the pleasure of a book. They need to explore beyond the words and relate the plot to their own lives.

"Reading *A Taste of Blackberries* with my students has convinced me that teachers must demonstrate the pleasure and the emotional pull of reading. This cannot be done through lectures, worksheets, and assigned book reports. The way to make children want to read is to travel with them through a few books, creatively expanding their literary journey through writing whenever possible. In time students will get hooked; they will select reading as a way to fill their time and writing as a way of responding.

"My experiment with *A Taste of Blackberries* has also convinced me that reading chapter books is particularly effective with slower readers. When chapter books are read over a period of days, these readers have time to get to know the characters and are grabbed up by the dynamics of the plot. They begin to look forward to reading. They anticipate what will happen next to the characters. I can honestly say that reading a chapter book made a difference for my slower readers.

"My sixth-graders now 'own' *A Taste of Blackberries*. They own it because it became a part of them and they became a part of it. It's a good feeling 'owning' a book.

GO TO

Page 135 for a definition of *aesthetic* as used in this context.

DISCUSSION PROMPT

■ In what ways did Maureen Stawasz change the way she approached reading and literature with her sixth-graders? How did she change the way she assessed their learning?

"I teach at the elementary school in the same town where I went to high school. In about three years, many of my students will be sitting in Miss Rice's English class. I have faith that their book conferences with Miss Rice will be better than mine."

As Americans traveled to the Near East and Far East and as immigrants from these areas of the world arrived in the United States, American English and the American culture were enriched.

Contributions from Arabic	Contributions from Persian		Contributions from Hindi (an Indian language)	Contributions from Japanese	Contributions from Chinese
sofa	taffeta	veranda	bandanna	kimono	shantung
almanac	orange	lilac	chintz	soy	sampan
mohair	caravan		cummerbund	tsunami	pekinese
algebra	awning		gunny (as in gunny sack)	hibachi	tea
zenith	shawl			ginko	kowtow
apricot	scarlet		shampoo	bonsai	chow
nadir	lemon			tempura	china
sherbet	turban			jujitsu	shanghai

"The time has come," the Walrus said,
"To talk of many things:
Of shoes—and ships—and sealing wax—
Of cabbages and kings—"
—Lewis Carroll, "The Walrus and the Carpenter"

PART Three

From Oracy into Literacy

How do we encourage children to talk of many things—significant things such as shoes (industry), ships (commerce), and sealing wax (human communication); everyday things such as cabbages; and things that are at the heart of stories, such as kings and faraway places? In answering this question, we must consider how to involve children in listening, speaking, and critical thinking. Part Three focuses on oral communication within a literature-based language arts program:

■ Listening for meaning—learning to listen and listening to learn.
■ Expressing through speaking—the classroom as a talking place.
■ Talking, reading, and writing together—from experiencing to critical thinking.

CHAPTER 5

Listening for Meaning

Learning to Listen and Listening to Learn

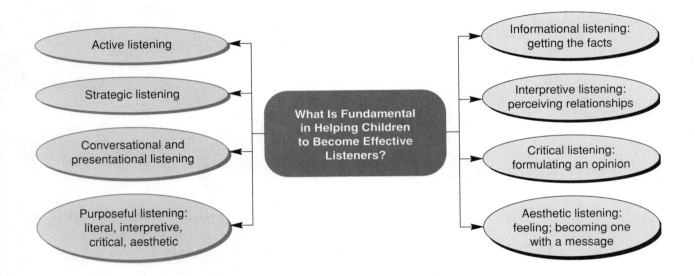

Active listening		Informational listening: getting the facts
Strategic listening		Interpretive listening: perceiving relationships
Conversational and presentational listening	**What Is Fundamental in Helping Children to Become Effective Listeners?**	Critical listening: formulating an opinion
Purposeful listening: literal, interpretive, critical, aesthetic		Aesthetic listening: feeling; becoming one with a message

Listening in Action *Getting at the Root of Conflict*

It was read-aloud time in Ann Arnold's sixth-grade social studies class. Youngsters sat with learning logs open as Ms. Arnold displayed a page of an expository selection that she was going to read to them as part of their unit on medieval times. To start, she pointed to and read aloud the title of the selection: "How People Resolve Conflict." She told the class that when she reads a heading in an informational book or when she listens to an informational video or a report, she thinks for a moment about what the title brings to mind and predicts what it is about. Based on the title, the sixth-graders did the same, brainstorming aloud. A student scribe recorded points on the chalkboard in a weblike arrangement to show connections (see the upper half of Figure 5.1).

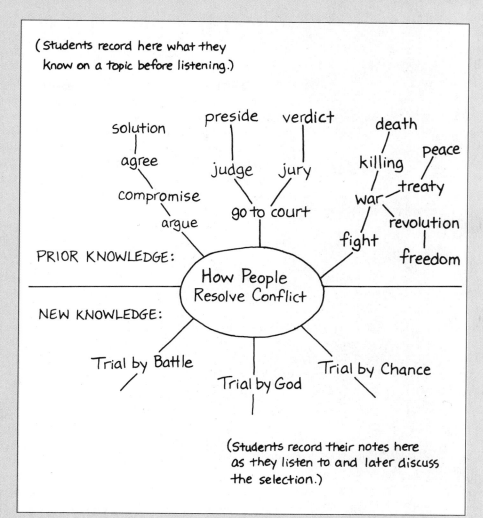

Figure 5.1
A Web for Recording Before and During Listening

DISCUSSION PROMPT

■ What is the structure of this visual?

Modeling Listening Strategies

Having activated students' prior knowledge (the anticipatory-set phase of her lesson), Ms. Arnold read aloud the introductory section, modeling as she went along the thoughts that came to her mind as she read. Then she held up the book she was sharing to show the first subheading: "Trial by Battle." She explained, "I always look at all the subheadings before reading to get an overview. I use them to predict what the subsections are about and propose questions to ask myself while reading. When I listen, I do the same thing. I ask myself questions and listen for answers. This helps me keep my mind from wandering. Let's do that now together. What is this section about? What questions will you keep in mind as you listen?"

Next Ms. Arnold pointed to the other subheadings in the selection ("Trial by God" and "Trial by Chance"), and the children predicted what those subsections were about and proposed questions to keep in mind while listening to them. The teacher reminded them that when they viewed a video or listened to a report or a lecture, they could not look ahead at subheadings; rather, they had to listen for signal words to predict what a speaker would say next.

At that point, Ms. Arnold divided her class into three listening teams with specific tasks to perform while she shared the selection. Students in Team One were to listen and take notes on the content of the first part of the selection, "Trial by Battle," using their proposed questions as a listening guide and writing their notes on the lower half of the conflict web (see Figure 5.1). She explained that taking notes based on questions proposed before listening is an efficient strategy for handling ideas presented during a lecture. Students on the other two listening teams were to write down at least two questions to ask the note takers.

Listen to follow directions; listen to take notes

In the same way, Team Two students were to become note takers as the teacher shared the second part, "Trial by God," and Team Three students were to function as note takers as she shared the last segment, "Trial by Chance." In each case the others were to think of questions to ask the note takers. Good listeners always raise questions in their minds while listening.

Listening to Learn

When the directions were clear, Ms. Arnold read each section aloud, modeling fluent reading. From time to time, she would stop in midsentence to tell the class a thought that occurred to her. She would add, "Did that thought go through your mind, too, as you listened?"

Discussion followed, with the students who had written questions based on what they had heard directing their questions to the note takers. The students tended to ask factual questions like, "What is a duel?" To encourage interpretive and critical thinking and to model question raising while listening, the teacher thought aloud: "Do you believe that few people really were killed? Why? What were the advantages of this way of settling conflict? Disadvantages?" As the sixth-graders talked about the second and third sections of the selection, they began to ask these higher-order questions of their peers, and a general discussion evolved in which students considered examples of when these ways of settling conflict were used in their country. They talked of the duel between Burr and Hamilton (which they had studied in fifth grade) and of the way trial by the will of God was applied during the Salem witch trials (examples not in the text). They recalled Frank Stockton's short story "The Lady or the Tiger?" which they had read earlier, and categorized it as trial by chance.

Listen to participate in a discussion

Finally, Ms. Arnold asked, "If you were living then and you had to settle a conflict, which of these ways would you prefer? You must pick one." Students thought, picked, and shared their choices and reasons.

Listen critically to formulate an opinion

Again a discussion—at times rather intense—ensued. Students began to say, "None of these is right," and the teacher suggested that they think of an alternative. The students suggested trial by jury based on the evidence in a case. The teacher asked the students to write a paragraph in their learning logs convincing someone why trial by jury would or would not be a fairer way to settle conflict. She told them that they would start their next discussion by sharing their persuasive paragraphs while others listened to think critically about this question, "What is the fairest way to resolve conflict?"

Seeking Closure

As the discussion ended, Ms. Arnold sought closure. She asked students to review the steps they had taken in preparing to listen and in actually listening. Students described the way they had predicted the topic and thought about it before listening, raised questions before and while listening, taken notes based on their questions, and used their notes to guide their thinking during the follow-up discussion.

Ms. Arnold explained to the class that the strategies they had just used were the same ones they could use when they listened and read on their own. In listening and reading, they should identify the topic and think about what they already know about it before beginning. In listening and reading, they should talk to themselves in their heads, watch for major changes in subtopics, raise and answer questions in their minds, review what they have heard or read, and jot down main ideas for later reference. The last is particularly important in listening, since one cannot go back to the text to check out misconceptions. Ms. Arnold also explained that when the students went to junior high school, their teachers would expect them to be able to take notes on class presentations and discussions. That is why they would be practicing their note-taking strategy as they listened to informational content during the next few days.

CONSIDER

People's understanding of how they learn and know is called *metacognition*. The final section of this Listening in Action vignette is geared to develop metacognitive understanding. Go to Chapter 8 for a discussion of metacognition.

DISCUSSION PROMPT

- What does Ms. Arnold believe is important in teaching content-area studies? What instructional techniques does she use based on her beliefs?

Listening and Learning

If you had chatted with Ann Arnold while her sixth-graders were writing busily and asked her to state the language arts objectives that were incorporated into her social studies lesson, she would probably have said something like this: The children will be better able to

- Bring their prior knowledge to bear on what they are hearing by predicting what is to come.
- Follow a presenter's or conversationalist's train of thought, using the speaker's signal words to predict what he or she will say next.
- Take notes while listening, using questions to guide their note taking and to keep their attention focused on the main ideas.
- Access their notes as an information source during follow-up discussion.

To achieve these objectives, Ms. Arnold had used her own behavior as a model of what to do in listening and had involved her students actively; they had webbed, talked, written, and shared. For each objective as well, Ms. Arnold had helped the sixth-graders to develop a strategy that they could apply knowingly in the future. During the lesson, too, students had had opportunity to listen both conversationally and presentationally. Additionally, Ms. Arnold encouraged her students to set a purpose for listening—a purpose that was essentially efferent. In this section, we will consider these aspects of listening instruction: making listening *active, strategic, both conversational and presentational,* and *purposeful.*

Active Listening

In classrooms, listening should be an active process, with students reacting rather than passively receiving. Active listening goes beyond reception or even retention of ideas. It requires listeners to generate and express thoughts both verbally and nonverbally through bodily movements and changes. In Elizabeth McPike's words, "Effective listening is . . . perhaps the hardest, *most active* work any learner is called upon to do" (in Armstrong, 1997–1998).

Outward signs of active listening are (1) physical or vocal expressions of feeling, (2) cooperation with others in a group, (3) expressions of acceptance toward others in a group, and (4) expressions of desire to keep an open mind (Faix, 1975). Other signs are asking relevant questions and making pertinent comments (Brent and Anderson, 1993). In classrooms, listening responses can be overt. Children may respond physically by choosing, manipulating, or organizing materials; by purposefully using their bodies to respond; or by moving spontaneously. They may respond by telling, writing, dramatizing, visually representing, and/or reading.

Franklin Ernst (1968) indicates that listeners' responses are almost continuous if listeners are attending fully. He explains: "Listening is an activity evidenced by movement on the part of the not-now-talking person. It is manifested in the behavior by the physical, visible motion of the listener's body. . . . To listen is to move, to be in motion for the words of the talker." Motions include changes in position, movement of muscles in rhythm with a speaker's sentences, and changes in facial expressions. The truly involved listener is mentally active, with activity reflected physically.

Working for active response is essential if schools are to overcome the passivity to oral communication that teachers have observed. A 1992 study by the National Assessment of Educational Progress (NAEP) reports that 62 percent of fourth-graders, 64 percent of eighth-graders, and 40 percent of twelfth-graders say they watch at least three hours of television daily (Stout, 1992). This diet of televiewing has turned some children into couch potatoes, for televiewing can be a simple receptive act. Teachers must help children become more critical listeners as well as more actively involved ones.

Strategic Listening

Listeners function most efficiently if they have strategies that they apply systematically and of which they are aware. For example, one general strategy relates to prediction: Effective listeners predict before listening, basing their predictions on the topical and structural signals a speaker sends early on; they continue to listen to test their predic-

Literature-based read-alouds encourage active listening and make the reading connection. *(© Elizabeth Crews)*

tions and summarize by talking to themselves in their minds while and after listening. This strategy is the Directed Listening-Thinking Activity, or DL-TA (Stauffer, 1980). Another general strategy relates to the main ideas of a presentation. Some effective listeners apply a main-idea-making strategy as they listen; they keep asking themselves the question: "What big idea is this person trying to tell me?" Once they grasp the main idea, they ask the backup question, "What details is this person giving me in support of the idea?" Related strategies are talking to oneself in the mind and note taking based on signal words a speaker uses. All of these strategies help listeners to block out distractions, focus on the ideas, and keep the mind from wandering. They are strategies that teachers can and should model for students.

In the remaining sections of this chapter, you will find descriptions of more specific ways to help children become strategic listeners. Let us at this point, therefore, consider some general ideas concerning this approach. First, listening strategies are best acquired across the curriculum. Children listen to learn as part of mapping activities, graphing and measuring activities, and natural science investigations; they do so as part of their experiences with music, art, and literature. To complete a map, graph, or investigation, youngsters must listen for detail, sequences of steps to follow, and key words. If teachers model these aspects of listening in meaning-focused contexts, students are more likely to develop the requisite strategies. During music-related experiences, youngsters must listen to lyrics, looking for words that paint a

Meet William Armstrong

William Armstrong, the author of the 1970 Newbery Award–winning book, *Sounder,* contends that listening is made more difficult by the fact that the listener has to coordinate his or her "mental powers with an outside force—the person or thing to which the listener is listening. This demands the discipline of subjecting the mind of the listener to that of the speaker. . . . When you begin to train yourself to be a good listener, you are faced with a difficulty not unlike that of trying to drive a car without brakes. You can think four times as fast as the average speaker can speak. . . . Only by demanding of yourself the most unswerving concentration and discipline can you hold your mind on the track of the speaker. This can be accomplished if the listener uses the free time to think around the topic—'lis-tening between the lines.'" In a classroom situation, according to Armstrong, this means "anticipating the teacher's next point, summarizing what has been said, questioning in silence the accuracy of what is being taught, putting the teacher's thoughts into one's own words . . ." ("Learning to Listen," *American Educator,* 21 [Winter 1997–1998], 24–25, 47).

DISCUSSION PROMPT

Armstrong is an author. Why do you think he is concerned about listening? What strategies do you use to help you listen to learn? How did you learn to anticipate, summarize, and question? How can the teacher help young listeners acquire oral processing strategies?

clear picture. During art-related experiences, they must listen as the teacher describes how to hold a brush and mix paints. And during story time, they must listen for words that send a happy message or a sad one.

Second, strategic listening blends naturally with the other language arts. As you saw in the opening vignette, writing can be a way of responding to and summarizing ideas just heard. In the same way, listening and reading go together. Many of the strategies useful in listening are equally as important during reading.

Conversational and Presentational Listening

Listening takes place in conversational and presentational settings. In conversational listening, there is an immediate give-and-take that results in a cross flow of ideas. Face-to-face discussions, for example, are conversational, with one person and then another assuming the talking role and others taking the listening role; conversationalists switch roles frequently as they exchange ideas. Elements important in conversational listening are making eye contact with the speaking person, indicating with the body that one wants to speak, not interrupting when a speaker is in the middle of saying something, not hogging the speaking role, and when it is time to speak making one's remarks connect with what has gone before. These are human-relational components of listening and are dependent on what Francine Falk-Ross (1997) calls metacommunicative awareness—explicit knowledge of the implicit routines that characterize and facilitate conversations. According to Falk-Ross, some students with language difficulties have real trouble handling these "implicit rules of conversation"; they require a language program focusing on "strategies for participating in classroom discourse" that make them aware of what is important in conversational listening.

In presentational listening, one person, a group of people, or a medium of some kind maintains the primary speaking role. Elements important in presentational settings include making eye contact when the speaker looks in the listener's direction, indicating interest and understanding by body stance (such as leaning forward in the seat) and by changes in facial expressions, using an acceptable behavior (such as raising one's hand) to ask a question. Again these are human-relations elements of which some students are not fully aware; their lack of metacommunicative awareness can present problems in classrooms where they must function at times as presentational listeners.

Organizing for Conversational Listening   Andrew Wilkinson (1970) advocates more classroom time spent in conversation and discussion circles "in which two or three or half-a-dozen are sitting around and ideas get discussed and pushed around." Today some educators call such discussions *grand conversations* and suggest that students have grand conversations especially as they get involved with the great ideas in books they are reading.

Another social situation for building human-relations skills relative to listening is a more informal chat group. After a school holiday, assembly, or individualized reading time, youngsters meet in chat groups or with chat buddies to talk about things done, enjoyed, or read. Sometimes the topics for chat groups or buddies are wide open; children decide what they will talk about. Such conversations pay added dividends. Through conversation "we build communities in our classrooms" (Dickinson, 1993).

The tasks that several youngsters complete together are also functional contexts for developing human-relations skills relative to listening. Working cooperatively, children must listen closely to make a verbal response that maintains a logical conversational flow and ultimately gets the job done. Here are some tasks that lead to growth in conversational listening skills: creating visual representations in response to a story, poem, or piece of nonfiction; coauthoring or coediting poems, stories, letters, and reports; deciding how to organize a group report; preparing for dramatizations; planning parties and trips; investigating a science problem in teams.

Before students begin a discussion, buddy conversation, or group task, the teacher offers reminders in the form of a brief mini-lesson geared to increasing *metacommunicative awareness*—children's explicit awareness of the "rules" of discourse. He or she may remind, "Remember to be respectful of others' ideas by listening closely and not interrupting. Give your buddy a fair share of the speaking time; don't be a time-hog. Try to respond in terms of what your buddy has been saying." After children have worked and talked together, they can evaluate themselves on how they performed in relation to these reminders. On future occasions, students themselves

GO TO

Page 214 for more on conversations that build a sense of community.

Listening skills can develop as students work together on a purposeful task, such as the editing of one child's writing. *(© Susie Fitzhugh)*

express the reminders before discussions begin. In addition, children who have severe problems adhering to the general routines of classroom discourse may need language support from a specialist who helps them with their response by "guiding their language participation within and on the periphery of the classroom" (Falk-Ross, 1997).

Organizing for Presentational Listening   A wonderful presentational-listening setting is the read-aloud. During a read-aloud, the teacher orally shares a segment of text, as in the opening vignette. Jim Trelease, the recognized leader of the read-aloud movement, explains that "listening comprehension comes before reading comprehension, and it's usually two or three years ahead. A child reading on a fourth-grade level may be able to listen to books written on a sixth-grade level. It is the child's listening vocabulary that feeds his reading vocabulary" (Trelease in Schwartz, 1995).

As you saw in the opening vignette, read-alouds are especially useful in the content areas for helping children to function as listeners within presentational settings. For example, before sharing a book on rivers with second-graders, the teacher may suggest that one group of children listen to find out where and how rivers start, a sec-

Issue Site

Is reading aloud to children a valid use of instructional time, especially in middle grades?

Jim Trelease advocates reading aloud to students. He proposes that reading aloud exposes "the student listener to a positive reading role model; new information, the pleasures of reading, rich vocabulary, good sentence and story grammar; a book he or she might not otherwise be exposed to; fully textured lives outside the student's own experience; and the English language spoken in a manner distinctly different from that in a television show. Simultaneously the student listener's imagination is being stimulated, attention span stretched, listening comprehension improved, emotional development nurtured, the reading-writing connection established, and, where they exist, negative reading attitudes reshaped to positive. Is there a textbook or workbook that will accomplish all that in a 15 minute period or even an hour?" ("Jim Trelease Speaks on Reading Aloud to Children," *The Reading Teacher*, 43 [December 1989], 200–206). Find and read this reference as well as Trelease's popular *The New Read-Aloud Handbook*.

DISCUSSION PROMPT

Some educators who believe in skill-based programs question whether limited instructional time can be used in more productive ways. They ask, "Shouldn't students be using scarce time to read to themselves, to discuss, or even to do skill-building exercises? Isn't there an age when we should stop our reading aloud to young people?" What do you think?

ond group listen to find out how rivers get bigger, and a third group listen to find out where the rain comes from. Groups share their findings in follow-up discussions and then together go on to hypothesize why rivers are important. In much the same way, the teacher can handle informational films and videos as well as magazine and newspaper articles he or she is sharing during current events.

Similarly, oral reporting can be organized to facilitate the development of presentational listening skills. Teach students to begin their presentations by announcing and displaying on a chart the main topic and the subtopics about which they will speak. Suggest that listeners divide into the same number of teams as there are subtopics; each team assumes responsibility for getting the facts, raising questions relative to its subtopic, and orally summing up the main ideas after the presentation. Before reporters begin and to help develop metacommunicative awareness, ask children to review the behaviors expected of them as respectful listeners: Keep your eyes on the speaker; don't interrupt to ask questions until the agreed-upon time; then raise your hand politely to ask your questions; make your face show that you are paying attention.

Purposeful Listening

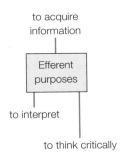

Listeners are generally most successful when they listen with a purpose in mind. Their purpose helps listeners concentrate on the message, keeping their thoughts from wandering off into unrelated areas. Some listening purposes are efferent in that emphasis is on picking up facts and ideas to take away: Listeners listen (1) to get information, (2) to interpret the information they are receiving, and/or (3) to think critically about that information—its content, its form, and even its sender. Such purposes are particularly appropriate as people listen to expository selections being offered in read-alouds and as they listen to lectures and subject-centered reports. In these instances, listeners are primarily concerned with making sense of the facts and ideas of a message. They try to be objective as they look at details, make connections among them, and weigh evidence. This was what you saw when you looked in on Ann Arnold's lesson.

Of course, at other times, Ms. Arnold helps children to set purposes for listening that are aesthetic. An aesthetic stance is especially appropriate as children listen to stories, poems, historical novels, and even biographies. Here, youngsters are less concerned with taking away facts and ideas and more concerned with their own feelings and emotions, of becoming one with what they are hearing.

As Funk and Funk (1989) remind, classroom listening should be purpose filled. In the following sections, you will have an opportunity to read about the kinds of purposes that children can set for their listening as they learn across the curriculum: efferent purposes (literal/informational, interpretive, critical) and aesthetic purposes. Figure 5.2 enumerates specific listening objectives relative to each of these purposes. You can use it as a checklist to assess children's development as effective listeners.

Informational, or Literal, Listening

W O R D   B A N K

Sequence-signaling words

Topics

Main ideas

Supporting details

While they listen, people at times function as literal thinkers; they concentrate on getting the facts straight. In informational listening, their purpose may be to

- Use key sequence-signaling words to follow the steps in a set of directions.
- Make sense of and visualize story and expository sequences in a presentation, being especially alert for sequence-signaling words.
- Identify topics and subtopics, main ideas, and supporting details of an oral presentation.
- Take useful notes by relying on signals a speaker sends to help them perceive the organization of the presentation and the relative importance of the ideas.
- Summarize the key ideas and terms of a discussion or presentation.

This section of *Communication in Action* clarifies ways to help children develop cognitive strategies that they can apply knowingly to carry out these information-gathering purposes, especially as they make forays into the content disciplines and listen to learn.

STUDENT ASSESSMENT: A LISTENING CHECKLIST

	I am able to	Always	Most of the time	Some-times	Never
HUMAN-RELATIONS ASPECTS	1. Perform politely in conversational settings, making eye contact with the speaker, indicating with my body that I want to speak, not interrupting when a speaker is in the middle of saying something, and making my remarks relate to what has gone before.				
	2. Perform politely in presentational settings, making eye contact when the speaker looks in my direction, indicating interest and understanding by body stance (such as leaning forward in my seat) and by my facial expressions, using an acceptable behavior (such as raising my hand) to ask a question.				
INFORMATIONAL ASPECTS	3. Follow the sequence of steps in directions given to me.				
	4. Make sense of and visualize story and expository sequences in a presentation or video, being especially alert for sequence-signaling words.				
	5. Identify topics and subtopics, main ideas, and supporting details of a presentation or video.				
	6. Take useful notes (including a summary of main ideas and important terms) by relying on signals that help me perceive the organization of a presentation or video and the relative importance of the ideas.				
	7. Summarize the key ideas and terms of a discussion, presentation, or video.				
INTERPRETIVE ASPECTS	8. Infer relationships among ideas by contrasting and comparing, categorizing, proposing reasons and causes, making predictions, generalizing, citing related examples, and hypothesizing effects.				
	9. Infer a speaker's feelings and point of view based on the verbal components of the message—the kinds of words chosen to communicate it.				
	10. Infer a speaker's feelings and point of view based on visual and vocal cues—the speaker's gestures, facial expressions, large body motions, and intonation patterns.				

Figure 5.2
A Checklist for Assessing Listening Behaviors. Using this checklist, teachers can assess children's growth as listeners. Children can use the same checklist to self-assess.

Informational, or Literal, Listening ■ 167

CRITICAL ASPECTS	11. Begin to recognize the difference between fact and opinion, categorize a statement as opinion rather than fact, and decide whether a stated judgment is valid.				
	12. Formulate opinons, preferences, and judgments of my own and develop a proof in support.				
	13. Evaluate stories heard by assessing characters, plot, and style.				
	14. Weigh the quality of a TV show, movie, video, or sound filmstrip I have viewed.				
	15. Identify some messages as "propaganda" and evaluate them as harmless or harmful.				
AESTHETIC ASPECTS	16. Take genuine delight and pleasure in what I am hearing.				
	17. Feel deeply in response to what I am hearing.				
	18. Create relationships that are new and personal.				

Name of student _____   Date _____

Figure 5.2 (cont.)

DISCUSSION PROMPT

■ How do these listening behaviors relate to behaviors important in reading? How can the teacher make the listening/reading connection?

Following Directions

The normal activities of a classroom provide opportunities for children to develop workable strategies for making sense out of a set of directions. Each day, teachers tell children how to complete specific learning tasks. In giving directions, teachers should try to use clear transitional, or sequence-signaling, words (*first, next, then, when, finally*) and model how to use these words to keep track of what to do. Even young children should be asked to repeat segments of a set of directions, ticking off the steps on their fingers as they recap: *first . . . , second . . . , next . . . , then. . . .* In the process, they practice a strategy that efficient listeners use when faced with a set of directions: repeating in abbreviated form, step by step. When directions are more complicated, teachers can encourage students to draw a series of pictures or a schematic to clarify what to do step by step; again this is a strategy efficient listeners rely on.

Making Sense of Story and Video Sequences

The ability to follow directions relates in certain basic respects to the ability to follow sequences of events in stories and informational content. Both abilities require the listener to pick up on such sequence-signaling words as *first, second, then, next, after that, finally.*

● ■ ● ● ●

CONSIDER

Children's magazines are a fine source of stories and articles to read to middle-graders. Check *Boys' Life, Cobblestones, Cricket,* and *Monkeyshines.*

Story Sequences   At times as children listen to a story, the teacher can suggest, "Let's listen to see what happens step by step." After listening, young children can volunteer to retell portions of the story "step by step"; as they retell, they draw pictures of story events on a time line in the order in which those events occurred in the story, as in Figure 5.3. The result is children's first set of functional listening notes: points put down on paper to use in reviewing what listeners have heard.

On a second listening, children focus on the language clues, or signal words, in the story that tell them what is happening and when. A particularly good story for sequence listening is Judith Viorst's *Alexander and the Terrible, Horrible, No Good, Very Bad Day* in which phrases that tell the time of day and verb tenses are clues to sequential development. Children can add these sequence-signaling words to their picture notes.

Middle-graders to whom the teacher reads a chapter of a novel on successive days can use time lining in a similar way. Each day, they revisit story events by posting them on a time line to show the step-by-step progression of the story and perhaps to clarify events that are not in chronological sequence as is the case with flashbacks. As they retell story events on paper in schematic fashion, the teacher encourages the use of the sequence-signaling words as an aid to tracking what happened and remembering the order of events.

Video Sequences   Listening to informational videos as part of content-area studies, students can do much the same thing. To help students build an idea-tracking strategy for listening, the teacher can introduce a social studies video with the suggestion, "Let's listen to the introduction to discover how many points the video is going to present and the order in which the video is going to cover them." Or, the teacher can suggest, "Listen closely for signal phrases such as *to begin with, the next point, in conclusion* that help us to keep track of where the video is going. I always pay close attention to phrases like these that guide me through the ideas." After upper-graders have watched the video, they go over the major points. Encouraging recall of the transitional words that let them in on what was happening in the video, the teacher can suggest, "What was the first point covered, the second point? Use the number words—enumerating words—as you recap the points." Students can add the enumeration-signaling phrases to the classroom Word Wall, and review the video to see whether they picked up on the signals being sent.

When a video in the social and natural sciences incorporates a series of events, students can listen for sequence, again paying close attention to pick up the words that are clues to the chronological or step-wise progression. The teacher begins, "Let's listen to find out the sequence in which the events took [or take] place. Keep

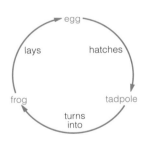

Figure 5.3
A Story Line of *A Bear Before Breakfast* by Eth Clifford

ACTIVITY PROMPT

A linear story like this one makes an easy beginning for picture-based note taking. Make a similar story line based on a story of your choosing.

alert for sequence-signaling words. I always look out for sequencing words when I listen because they keep me on track." After watching a video that describes natural science cycles—such as the egg-tadpole-frog-egg cycle, the egg-caterpillar-cocoon-moth-egg cycle, the water cycle, the rock cycle—students can visually represent the stages on a circular time line and explain the steps in the cycle by relying on the sequence-signaling words. This kind of activity is also appropriate with biographies and historical documentaries in which authors use clue phrases as well as verbs to indicate time changes and to which students can respond by visualizing chronological relationships on a time line.

Getting the Gist of a Message

Getting the gist of a message—grasping its main ideas—is at the heart of informational listening (and informational reading as well). How can teachers help children build a comprehensive strategy to accomplish this purpose?

Topic Finding   Most educators recommend that teachers help children identify the topic of a communication before considering main ideas (Aulls, 1986), for the gist is the main ideas being made *about the topic*. To grasp the main ideas, one must know the topic.

The title of a formal speech, a documentary video, or a report often provides a first clue to the general topic to be covered. Speakers often identify their general topic and some of their subtopics up front by saying something like this: "This afternoon I'm going to be talking about. . . . In presenting this topic, I'll be considering three areas: the first . . . the second . . . the third. . . ." A speaker may even emphasize the general topic in his or her opening statement by repeating the topic word; a lecturer may display his or her main subtopics on a chart or overhead transparency. For these reasons, listeners must learn to be especially alert during a speaker's (and their teacher's) introduction—to be ready "to go" from the very first words spoken.

To help students develop a strategy for using a speaker's first words as clues to the topic and perhaps subtopics *(First-Words Strategy)*, an upper-elementary teacher should begin a class discussion or a lesson by clearly stating the topic and indicating the two or three things students will be doing during the session. The teacher may clarify where the class is going by webbing the topic and subtopics on the chalkboard. In this functional context, the teacher can ask, "What signal about the organization of our lesson did I just send you? What did you think in response? Did anyone do anything in response?"

This is the time to introduce the importance of students' having their learning logs open, ready to go at the start of a lesson; working to get a clear conception of the topic; and noting down key points for future reference. This is a good opportunity to show students various ways to indicate the start of a new topic in their learning logs (by drawing a wavy line of separation, by printing the new main topic in big letters, and/or by highlighting the topic word with a colored marker or through underscoring). And this is the time to clarify a *Signal-Response Strategy* for making sense with a speaker's message—a listening strategy based on asking oneself two questions: "What *signal* is the speaker sending?" and "What do I—the listener—think and do in *response* to that signal?" In this instance, the signal the speaker is sending is what the topic will be; the students' response is to record and highlight that topic in their learning logs.

The teacher should model topic-finding in instances where a speaker does not send an explicit signal. The teacher may say, "When I listen and a speaker does not announce his or her topic or give me clear signals as to where he or she is going, I keep asking myself, 'What is this person talking about? What's his or her topic?' For example, suppose I hear this at the beginning of a report or a video.

> Rain, snow, wind, heat, and cold are all part of weather. Weather is the way the air is at a certain time. The weather may change from day to day or even from hour to hour. It might be sunny this morning and cloudy this afternoon. Or it might be dry today and wet tomorrow.

As I listen, I keep asking myself, 'What is this about?' I listen for any significant words that keep repeating. I do not wait until the end. I keep talking to myself in my head, trying to figure out the topic. In this case, the word *weather* keeps repeating. All the sentences relate to the weather, so I know weather is the topic. If I had not been ready to listen or not been concentrating at the beginning, I would have missed the topic. Knowing the topic guides me as I listen."

Main-Idea Making   Keeping the topic in mind, a listener identifies the main idea. Again the teacher should model a strategy—in this case, the *Main-Idea-Making Strategy.* He or she may say, "When I listen, I keep sifting through the points being made, and I keep asking myself, 'What point is the speaker making about the topic?' Again, I keep talking to myself in my head, gradually putting the main idea together. In this case, the main idea is that weather is the way the air is at a particular time— sunny, rainy, snowy. All the details relate to that point."

Having modeled the Main-Idea-Making Strategy, the teacher should encourage students to use it to learn. The teacher might read aloud a piece of nonfiction and ask children to identify the topic and the main idea, telling how they arrived at both. For example, a teacher might share this content during a weather unit:

> A useful tool that tells us something about the weather is called a thermometer. Thermometers are used to measure the temperature of the air. Another way of saying this is that a thermometer tells us how hot or cold the air is. If you had a thermometer hanging outside your window, you would be able to tell if it was cold enough to need a coat outdoors or if the weather was warm enough for you to wear shorts.

Then the teacher reviews the strategic question-answer sequence that he or she uses to identify the topic:

"What is the topic?"

"Thermometers."

"How do we know?"

"The word *thermometer* keeps repeating; the whole thing is about thermometers."

Here listeners are identifying the topic and telling the strategy they use to arrive at it.

In the same way, students propose that the main idea is that thermometers are used to measure the temperature of the air. The way they arrive at this conclusion is to keep asking themselves, "What's the big idea about thermometers that this passage is getting at?"

Children can practice their strategies for topic finding and main-idea making as they listen across the curriculum. While viewing a video, students ask themselves, "What's the topic? What is this video saying about the topic? How do I know?" They ask the same strategic questions as they listen to a panel discussion, an oral report by other students, or a radio news report. Through continued work in a variety of contexts, children refine their listening strategies. Reading comprehension also improves, since the strategies for finding topics and making main ideas in listening apply equally to reading.

Relating Main Ideas and Supporting Details   In content-area study, listening for main ideas flows naturally into working with significant details. For example, during unit study a teacher can read a passage aloud from a children's science book and stop at key points to encourage youngsters to talk about how they found the topic and made a main idea. The teacher can then reread the passage, asking them to give key details that support the main idea. The strategy students use in listening for detail is to ask themselves as they listen: "Does this detail help support the main idea or is the detail simply icing on the cake?"

Taking Notes That Include Main Ideas and Supporting Details

Most college students would agree that being able to take class notes in an organized fashion is a major determinant of how well they ultimately do. They would also agree that they had acquired their skills as note takers on their own by trial and error. How can elementary-grade teachers prepare students for the rigorous note taking that is so important for success in high school and college? The answer is teacher modeling of note-taking strategies with plenty of opportunity for students to experiment with the demonstrated strategies and develop a style of their own.

Modeling Ways to Respond to a Speaker's Signals   A great context for modeling the Signal-Response Listening Strategy is the viewing of informational videos because teachers can replay a video and have students focus on words and phrases that give particular guidance to a note taker. In that context and through a series of mini-lessons, teachers can demonstrate note-taking strategies by sharing the ideas that went through their own minds and the notes they took in response.

In a series of mini-lessons, a teacher can show how he or she

- Recorded the major subtopics early on as the video announcer enumerated the topics to be covered. Replaying the video, students can review the signal words that the announcer gave in the introduction that were hints as to what was to come—a statement of his or her purpose, the number of points to be covered, the order in which the points were to be covered—and see how the teacher responded by jotting down the subtopics.
- Picked up on the major transitional words that the announcer used to signal the start of the next subtopic, for example, "Now let us turn to the next area. . . . The next topic will be. . . ." Students replay these segments of the video and identify how their teacher indicated the change of subtopic in his or her notes in response.
- Listened for and responded to clues a speaker sent to indicate what points were very important and what points were really icing on the cake—how he or she wrote down in an abbreviated, quick form the points the speaker stressed.
- Listened for signal phrases that indicated the announcer was getting to the end and had begun the closing remarks: *In conclusion, Let me sum up,* or *Let me review my four points.* Again the teacher should replay the video, ask students to listen for the signal phrases, and identify how he or she responded to these signals.

Modeling Ways to Organize Notes   In other mini-lessons, the teacher can model various ways to organize notes: The teacher can show how he or she

- Sketched labeled drawings the speaker displayed and incorporated them into the written notes.
- Jotted down key terms with definitions and highlighted those terms to make them stand out.
- Left plenty of space between points written down and at the sides so that additional points could be inserted as the items came to mind.
- Placed a question mark in the sidebar where he or she had a question to ask when time permitted.

Modeling Possible Formats for Note Taking   At some point, the upper-grade teacher should model various note-taking formats. One traditional format is the outline, which is a strategy for highlighting relationships between main ideas and supporting details that may help some students to take a systematic set of notes. In this context a teacher reviews how to use a speaker's signal words to determine the

CONSIDER

A listening guide for an outline:
I. Main idea
   A. Supporting detail
   B. Supporting detail
   C. Supporting detail
II. Main idea
   A. Supporting detail
   B. Supporting detail

GO TO

Pages 308–312 for more on webs and charts for note taking.

main subtopics, how to record those as main headings within an outline (for example, *I*), and how to record subordinate points, or supporting details, beneath the subtopics (for example, *A, B, C*)—not word for word but in a shortened, quick form. And of course, the teacher shows how he or she often goes back to revise the developing outline. At some point, students apply the same techniques, share their notes, and consider fix-up, or revision, strategies they had to use. Experimenting with formal outlines, some students may decide that they function better using a simple listing technique without worrying about *A*s, *B*s, or *C*s. Some may develop a system of color coding and underscoring that better meets their needs for noting relationships and indicating higher-levels of importance.

Drawing a graphic that depicts relationships among ideas is a note-taking strategy that may be more useful than outlining to some students. The teacher can model how to use a graphic organizer to record main and subordinate ideas during listening by saying, "Sometimes it helps me to visualize the relationships between a main idea and the supporting details. I record the main idea in a box and hang the supporting details from that box. I use a similar strategy when I read. I write the main idea in a box. Then I turn my sheet and write down supporting details connected to the main idea." (See Figure 5.4.) After listening to a portion of an informational video or hearing a paragraph read aloud to them, students can cooperatively create similar graphic organizers that visually clarify relationships among ideas. In the same way, a teacher can model how to use webs and data charts for recording while listening.

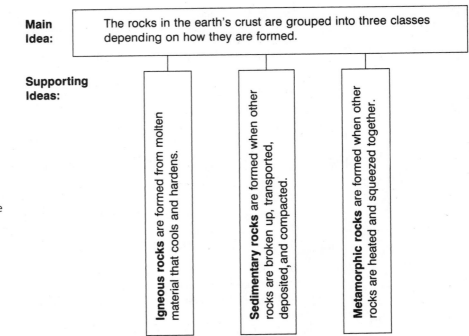

Figure 5.4
A Graphic Organizer for Relating Main and Subordinate Ideas

ACTIVITY PROMPT

Create a visual structured differently to show the information given in this "hanging visual."

The Teacher's Message Board

Note these functional contexts for developing informational listening skills.

- **Introduce Your Partner.** On the first day of school, pair off students. Student pairs chat, telling each other key facts about themselves. Youngsters introduce their buddies to the class. Encourage students to chat with classroom visitors to gather information to share when introducing the visitor to the class.

- **Take the Message Home.** At the end of the afternoon, encourage children to recap the things they learned during the day. Ask several listeners to repeat the points. Suggest that upon arrival home, they tell a caregiver what they did in school that day.

- **Story Notes.** Read a story to a group. Ask children to respond by drawing three visuals, the first telling what happened at the beginning , the second telling what happened in the middle, the third telling what happened at the end. Students use their story notes to retell the story to other students who were not in their listening group. Remind them to take care to use clear sequence-signaling words in their retellings.

- **Interview.** Encourage the collection of data through interviewing. Demonstrate how to organize a series of questions in preparation for an interview and for note taking during it. Good contexts for interviewing are biography writing, study of local history and leaders, and current events issues.

- **Mock Interviews.** A student can take the role of a person from the past whom he or she has researched. Other students prepare a question outline for interviewing the visitor who comes out of history and use the outline for listening and recording.

Summarizing a Message: The Recap Strategy

Another strategy for processing oral messages is to summarize important points. Following a class discussion, the teacher can model this strategy by saying, "We have been discussing the relationships between weather and climate. After I have been involved in a discussion, I often review in my mind the important points. Let's run through and list the most important ideas." As a way to seek closure to class discussions, on successive days, the teacher can ask children to sum up important points and note them on the chalkboard. On other occasions, he or she can ask students to recap by talking to themselves in their heads and then sharing their thoughts with others in small groups. The groups organize lists of key points covered in the discussion. Research indicates that summarizing after listening and reading is one of the best ways to learn new material.

In the upper-elementary grades, teachers from time to time should give a mini-lecture to help students take notes in their learning logs by applying the same strategies they have used in response to a video. This is a good context in which to teach summarizing. After students have made notes on the mini-lecture, a teacher might say, "Now, based on your notes and in a space at the end of them, write down three major ideas that recap what I have been saying. Then record two or three terms you think are important for you to remember. Write a clear definition of each. Having taken notes, I always use this Recap Strategy to help me review and remember the important points. Try it. You may like the strategy, too." Upper-graders share their recaps, decide whether they have missed something really important, and consider the advantages of the Recap Strategy.

Listening to Interpret

WORD BANK

Inferences
Connotations

Informational listening involves getting the facts straight. Interpretive listening, in contrast, occurs as people delve into the facts and go beyond to think about relationships—to make *inferences*. People listen to interpret when they

- Infer relationships among ideas by contrasting and comparing, categorizing, proposing reasons and causes, making predictions, generalizing, citing related examples, and hypothesizing effects.
- Infer a speaker's feelings and point of view based on the verbal components of a message, especially the *connotations* of the words chosen to communicate it.
- Infer a speaker's feelings and point of view based on visual and vocal cues—the speaker's gestures, facial expressions, large body motions, and intonation patterns.

As this list indicates, interpretive listening is an analytical process in which people get at implied meanings that are often not stated explicitly—that are not "right there." It relates to informational listening because inferring requires an information base if interpretations are to be valid.

Inferring Relationships Among Ideas

One way to make connections during listening and go beyond the facts that a speaker states explicitly is the "And So What . . . ?" Question-Raising Strategy. When listeners have summarized a message they have heard by listing several important main ideas, a teacher who is modeling the strategy queries, "And so what does this mean to us?" To help listeners make higher-level connections, the teacher can post a chart listing "And So What . . . ?" questions that listeners can ask themselves to go beyond explicitly stated ideas, as shown here:

- *Compare/contrast.* In what ways are these events, people, stories, characters the same? different? Are there happenings and people in our lives that are similar? different?
- *Categorize.* What label can we attach to this event or story that tells what kind it is? For example, was this a period of hardship or ease? Is this character the protagonist or antagonist?

- *Give reasons.* What reasons can we think of to explain what happened or why people acted as they did? For example, why did Stone Fox make the decision he did? Why did Benedict Arnold do what he did and become a traitor to the American cause?
- *Make predictions.* What will happen now? What evidence do we have to support our prediction?
- *Generalize.* What big conclusion can we draw about life or literature based on what we have heard?
- *Cite examples.* What other examples can we think of where our conclusion applies? Where and when has the same kind of thing happened?
- *Hypothesize.* What would happen if . . . ?

The teacher encourages students to ask these kinds of "And So What . . . ?" questions, propose answers, and add some of their answers to their learning-log notes. In this context, the teacher might suggest, "You can add a sentence to your notes that goes beyond the facts—that represents your own thinking. You might want to do that as a sidebar, recording your own ideas down the side of your learning-log notes in a space you leave for your extensions. That's what I do. Or you can make a visualization that represents relationships."

This is the time to demonstrate forms that visualizations can take. For example, students who ask, "How are Stone Fox and Little Willy alike?" can make U-charts: On one downward arm of a U, they record the unique attributes of Stone Fox; on the other downward arm, they record the unique attributes of Little Willy; and on the connecting arm, they record shared attributes. Elementary students find a U-chart visualization easier to manage than the overlapping circles of a Venn diagram, which is a common visual way to represent a comparative relationship. Similarly, students who ask predictive questions can create "if-then" charts: two boxes joined by an arrow. In the left-hand box, students write what they know—the current conditions; in the right-hand box, they indicate their predictions based on their knowledge. Encourage students to design original visualizations to represent other relationships.

Students should be urged to use the "And So What . . . ?" Question-Raising Strategy as they listen and read independently. The teacher models his or her use of the strategy by saying something like this: "I don't just take in the facts. I think about them to make them my own by asking, 'And So What . . . ?' When I take notes, I add my 'And So What . . . ?' ideas."

Inferring Point of View and Feelings

In *Language in Thought and Action,* S. I. Hayakawa (1964) distinguishes among the emotional meanings, or connotations, of words that determine a speaker's impact on listeners. He calls words like *louse* and *slob* "snarls," for they carry negative connotations, and more positive words like *sweetheart* and *home* "purrs." Nonverbal and vocal expressions similarly carry negative or positive messages. This means that as children listen, teachers must stress the way meanings are being expressed.

Comprehending Implied Meanings   Primary-graders can learn about the emotional wallop of words through a search for "happy" and "sad" words. To begin, children in two-person teams cut two large clown faces from light-colored construction

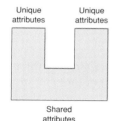

Unique attributes   Unique attributes

Shared attributes

A U-chart

■ ● ● ●

CONSIDER

Teach children a strategy for inferring point of view. Teach them to ask:"What do the kinds of words this speaker is using tell me about how he or she feels toward his or her subject?"

The Teacher's Message Board

Note these functional contexts for developing interpretive listening skills.

- **Are They the Same?** As children consider a community or national issue, share with them two articles, reports, editorials, or letters to the editor. Ask: Are both articles saying the same thing? If they differ, what is the difference? Use a U-chart to compare and contrast.

- **Snarls and Purrs.** Read related letters to the editor to students who are studying an issue. Ask children to identify the snarls and purrs.

- **Adjective Play.** As children learn about adjectives, ask them to make inferences about the characters in stories they hear by identifying adjectives that describe them. Children must give reasons for their choice of adjectives.

- **Story Variations.** Different versions of the familiar fairy tales exist. Read two or more versions of a tale such as Cinderella, and ask youngsters to listen for ways they vary. Again suggest U-charts for highlighting comparisons.

paper. One face is happy, the other sad. Instead of drawing the facial expressions with lines, however, children print "happy-meaning" words in the shape of eyes, mouth, hat, and so forth. In the same fashion, they draw the features of the sad clown with "sad-meaning" words.

Once children have identified words with happy and sad connotations, they listen for very pleasant, angry, ugly, bored, and/or excited words in stories. They pencil these on other faces and add words found in the dictionary and thesaurus that communicate a similar feeling.

Upper-graders can handle connotation in greater depth. They can identify purrs and snarls in videos, especially those on controversial issues. After viewing a video, students think about those narration words that sent a positive or negative message.

Inferring Feelings   While listening to poetry, elementary children can pinpoint the feelings the poet is conveying. Shel Silverstein's poems are great for oral sharing. Students laugh as they hear Silverstein's "Sick," "The Planet of Mars," and "Boa Constrictor" from *Where the Sidewalk Ends.* They smile at "Something Missing," "Messy Room," and "Here Comes" from *A Light in the Attic.* While listening to poems like these, youngsters visualize meanings and then sketch or paint the feeling communicated by the poet. Later, they convert their pictures into a word collage by adding key words from the poem.

During a story read-aloud, children can listen to infer the feelings of the characters. Teacher Barbara Woods has devised a simple listening guide to stimulate youngsters to analyze characters' feelings. Across the top of a duplicated sheet, she draws a row of smiling faces and across the bottom, a row of frowning faces. As children listen to stories, they decide which characters are generally happy and which are unhappy, and they write the names of the characters under the appropriate listening-

CONSIDER

Check your local video library for *Hailstones and Halibut Bones* and *Attic in the Wind* from Miller Brody (New York) in their video versions. Use them for listening for feelings.

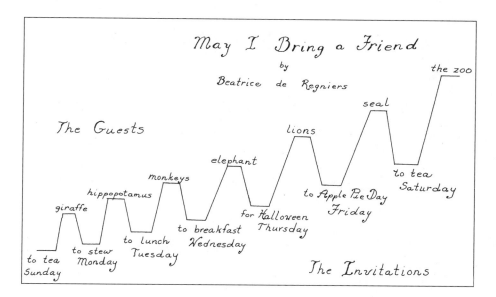

Figure 5.5
A Story Graph

guide faces. Since changes occur in a story and unhappy characters become happy, students may write the name of a character beneath both a happy and an unhappy face and draw an arrow from one to the other to show the direction of change.

In the same way, intermediate students can graph the emotional swings of a story. On the vertical axis of a graph, they plot words that describe emotional extremes, such as *very happy, very sad* or *high hope, despair*. On the horizontal axis, they plot *story beginning, story middle, story end*. Then, as they listen to a particular story, they construct a graph line starting on the far left at *story beginning*. The graph line flows up and down to reflect mood swings in the story.

Upper-graders can plot several graphs for one story or poem. Each graph is from the point of view of a different character or group of characters. For example, students can plot emotional highs and lows first for Mudville and then for the opposing team as they listen to *Casey at the Bat* (Thayer, 2000). Figure 5.5 is a sample graph based on the story *May I Bring a Friend?* by Beatrice Schenk de Regniers; it contains words suggesting story happenings.

Inferring from Nonverbal and Vocal Expressions

Words and sentences are vehicles through which people communicate orally. In addition, people use nonverbal and vocal expressions to get their feelings and ideas across. Often what Sara Lundsteen (1979) calls the "person-context" determines a listener's response. By *person-context*, Lundsteen means a speaker's facial expression, eye focus, gestures, stance, gross body motions, tone of voice, inflections of voice, pauses, loudness, and pitch, as well as changes in these characteristics.

Because nonverbal and vocal expressions can engender strong feelings in a listener and even cause him or her to tune out, a listener should know how a speaker is using those expressions and what effect they have on his or her reactions. This is

INTERPRETING IMPRESSION MANAGEMENT ON TELEVISION

1. How does the performer use gestures as part of the message?

2. How does the performer stand, sit, and position his or her head?

3. Does the performer use facial and eye expressions as part of his or her communication? If so, how?

4. How does the performer vary his or her tone of voice, pitch, and loudness of speech?

5. Evaluation: Is this performer using nonverbal and vocal means of communication effectively?

Figure 5.6
A Television Listening Guide

CONSIDER

Use picture viewing to introduce a storybook to be shared; ask listeners to study the cover picture and predict what might happen in the story.

especially true in situations where conversationalists purposefully manipulate their nonverbal and vocal expressions to achieve a desired effect.

Picture Viewing   Picture viewing offers an easy introduction to meanings sent nonverbally. Mrs. Jaye, a kindergarten teacher, snipped from magazines pictures showing people in different interactive situations. She mounted each picture on construction paper and drew comic strip balloons from each mouth. In a talk session, her children brainstormed what the people were thinking. They discussed: Do the people like one another? How do we know? How do the people feel? How do we know?

The children produced amazingly perceptive inferences. One picture showed a woman holding a potato masher. The children inferred that the woman was angry; the expression on her face and the way she held the masher told them that. The thoughts they gave her were: "My husband is not home yet, and this food will go bad. I'm mad."

Becoming Aware of Impression Management   In the upper grades, a more sophisticated study of impression management as employed on TV commercials and political telecasts is possible. Students in one sixth grade watched TV commercials and studied how performers manipulated vocal and nonverbal language. They used a TV listening guide as shown in Figure 5.6.

These sixth-graders had a great time with commercials in which business executives advertise their own products. Using the understandings they had built up in interpreting commercials, they went on to analyze videotaped speeches of politicians to see if they could detect instances of impression management. Later they analyzed messages sent by people they knew: parents, siblings, teachers. To this end, they constructed guides for recording aspects of body and vocal language. Through their study, these youngsters became more aware of the impact of vocal and nonverbal messages.

Listening Critically

WORD BANK

Fact versus opinion

O/P/O

Propaganda

GO TO

Page 298, for a discussion of critical reading.

Listening also involves judgment making, with listeners deciding about the rightness, goodness, or harmfulness of ideas and the manner in which those ideas are being presented. People engage in critical listening when they

- Begin to recognize the difference between fact and opinion, categorize a speaker's statement as opinion rather than fact, and decide whether a stated judgment is valid or has elements of bias.
- Formulate opinions, preferences, and judgments of their own and develop a proof in support.
- Evaluate stories heard by assessing characters, plot, and style.
- Weigh the quality of a TV show, movie, videotape recording, or sound filmstrip they have viewed.
- Identify some messages as "propaganda" and evaluate them as harmless or harmful.

Lundsteen (1979) contends that in the past, schools have failed to emphasize listening in which judgments are a part and that there is danger in this neglect. Today the mass media, particularly television, bombard young and old with ideas. Are people selective and critical in choosing programs? Do they question the ideas they hear? Do they support their opinions with evidence? Or are they nondiscriminating and gullible? Following are some ways to build judgmental listening into the curriculum so that youngsters become more discriminating viewers.

Recognizing Opinion

Listeners must be aware of the differences between factual and judgmental statements and be able to spot judgmental statements when they hear them. This is no easy task, and even upper-graders may require a mini-lesson or two to help them perceive the differences. To this end, the teacher can extract examples of both kinds of statements from a video the students have just viewed:

1. Oranges are grown in California and Florida. (*fact*)
   Orange juice tastes better than apple juice. (*opinion*)
2. The temperature reading at noon today was 26°C. (*fact*)
   The water is too cold for swimming. (*opinion*)

Based on the examples, students generalize about the nature of factual and judgmental statements: Opinions represent people's personal preferences or feelings. The truth or falsity of a factual statement can be proved by pointing to specific instances whereas opinions cannot be proved definitively. Different opinions can be stated on the same topic; people's opinions differ. Opinions contain elements of "should," "must," "best," "bad," "too much." Words and phrases such as these (as well as more explicit phrases such as "I believe . . ." and "My opinion is . . .") are clues that a statement is opinion, not fact.

Later as students listen and view independently, teachers can encourage them to ask, "Is this fact, or is it the speaker's opinion? If it is opinion, let's clarify the opinion by restating it in our own words." Having identified a particular statement or presentation as opinion, students can ask the next questions: What proof does the speaker provide in support of the opinion? Is the proof sufficient? Is the judgment biased because of the speaker's "reading the world" from a particular cultural perspective (Creighton, 1997)?

Formulating Opinions, Preferences, and Judgments

Children who have identified and critiqued the opinions of others must take the next step: express opinions of their own and support them with evidence, or a proof. This is especially true as children listen and respond to opinion-stating material in the content areas and in current events. In these contexts, the obvious next questions are: Given the opinion stated in the report, the video, the film, what do I think? What is my opinion? What proof can I assemble to support my opinion? Another sequence of questions that trigger judgmental thinking is: Given a choice among those possibilities, which would I choose? Why did I choose as I did?

With students I like to call this strategy O/P/O to clarify the sequence of questions that critical listeners ask themselves when working with opinions (Hennings, 2002). The first O stands for "opinion"; the listener must first ferret out the opinion of the speaker by focusing on clue words that signal an opinion-in-the-works. The P stands for "proof"; the listener must evaluate the proof that the speaker offers in support of his/her opinion and consider the biases of the speaker—where the speaker "is coming from." The last O stands for "opinion"; the listener formulates an opinion of his/her own, provides reasons to justify the position being taken, and considers his or her own biases. Here is where students must be urged to ask, "Why do I believe the way I do? What is there about me that has brought me to this opinion?" Students can design their own schematics for visualizing a speaker's opinion, his or her supporting proof, and their own opinions formulated in response, again with a supporting proof and an assessment of their own biases. (See Chapter 7, page 251, for an example of a visual for representing opinions and proof.)

Judging Story Characters and Actions

Critical thinking can be—and should be—a part of story listening. Children listen to comprehend what is happening and to make judgments about characters and actions. In this context, Barbara Woods's guide for analyzing happy and unhappy

Figure 5.7

A Character Study. Children write the name of a story character next to each line of faces. As they listen to the story, they draw features on the faces and adjectives below the faces to show changes in feelings.

Courtesy of Maxine Owens and Cindy Davis

characters described earlier can serve as a strategy for judging good and evil characters, particularly in fairy tales, where the line between the two is clearly drawn. The format of the guide remains the same: two rows of faces—one with pleasant expressions, the other with frowning faces. Youngsters who have listened to a story print the names of good characters under the pleasant faces and those of evil ones beneath the leering faces. For example, when judging characters in *Hansel and Gretel,* young children might list Hansel and Gretel on the top row and the witch and the stepmother on the bottom. Supporting their judgments with specifics, they print the deeds performed by the characters on the faces. See Figure 5.7 for a variation of this type of guide.

Upper-graders can progress to multifaceted judgments to make a second sheet for a story, this time considering whether characters are shrewd or gullible. Shrewd ones are labeled across the top and gullible ones across the bottom. By doing this, evaluators become aware that good characters sometimes are gullible while evil ones may be shrewd. Students in upper grades are able to identify other contrasting qualities, such as quick versus slow or wise versus foolish, and they can make similar judgments as they respond in their literature journals to stories they have read.

In the same way, older students can judge story actions rather than characters. They begin by sequentially recording story actions on a time line. Having plotted the major happenings, they decide which acts were morally right and which were morally wrong, and they indicate their judgments on the time line by circling items with different-colored markers. If a task team consists of several children and each child evaluates right and wrong independently, there will be differences of opinion—differences that stimulate discussion. Youngsters will be eager to justify their opinions, by giving reasons.

The Teacher's Message Board

Note these functional contexts for developing critical listening skills.

- ■ *What Do I Believe?* Students formulate opinions whenever they listen to editorials, presentations, videos, and so on. Remind them to ask, "What do I believe is good about this? Bad? What proof do I have? What are my personal and cultural biases?" Emphasize respect for judgments that are supported rationally.

- ■ *"The One" of the Year.* In almost any context, students can name "The One" of the Year—the event, the film, the person, the book that shines in some way. For "The One" so designated, students must give reasons and decide what biases of their own helped to determine their choice. Similarly students can develop "Best-Seller Lists"—lists of the "best" in a field.

- ■ *Rating on a Scale.* Encourage upper-graders to develop scales (or rubrics) for rating anything and everything: their own handwriting, characterization in books they read, actions of countries past and present, web sites. Encourage interesting terms for the rating categories: master, journey person, apprentice; two thumbs up, one thumb up, one thumb down, two thumbs down.

- ■ *Doublespeak.* Ask students to look for doublespeak and euphemistic language in telecasts and broadcasts. Examples of doublespeak are calling a shovel a "combat implacement evacuator" and calling slums "inner cities." The National Council of Teachers of English considers doublespeak dangerous, because language is distorted purposefully to hide important facts. A euphemism is a positive-sounding word substituted for a word that carries a negative connotation. Examples are calling a road a "parkway," a factory district an "industrial park," a lavatory a "powder room."

With youngsters who have had little experience with critical listening, first attempts should be group ones that model how to do it. For instance, before sharing a story in which an essentially good character does something wrong but for a good purpose, such as Patricia Coombs's *The Magic Pot*, the teacher draws a line on chart paper. As each event in the story occurs, a volunteer writes a summary phrase on the line. Then children and teacher go back to judge each act, circling good acts in red and wrong ones in blue and giving reasons to support their judgments. Older students can talk about extenuating circumstances.

Students who have joined in teacher-guided critical listening can form groups to plot other stories. First, they listen to a story as a class; afterward, they form three-person task teams. Each team summarizes story events, judges them, and develops a proof. Later, teams compare their evaluations and orally support them.

Judging a Performance

People pass judgment on things seen and heard. Leaving a movie, they say, "I liked that. It was good." Flipping from one TV program to another, they remark, "I can't stand any more of that!" People often judge quality informally and fail to consider what specifically they like or dislike. Is it the content, the delivery, or a combination of both?

Because young people spend so much time televiewing, they need to be able to assess the quality of performances to make wise use of their viewing time. One way to get children to look critically at TV programs is to have them name favorite programs, with names recorded on the board. As follow-up, they vote to determine their five favorite programs as a class—programs that deserve the rating "excellent." As part of the discussion that occurs, upper-graders should ask themselves: What qualities must a program possess to be judged excellent? In contrast, what qualities must a program possess to be judged average or poor? Later, youngsters form their own lists of excellent, good, and poor programs, indicating one reason for each program listed.

Identifying Propaganda

Commercials occupy a considerable amount of telecast time and may distort facts to create particular impressions. The result is what we call *propaganda.*

Commercials distort facts in a number of ways. One way is through use of glittering generalities—claims so general they could not possibly be true. A statement such as, "Product X outperformed the other leading competitor on absolutely every test," is an example of a glittering generality. A second form that distortion can take is the bandwagon effect: The advertisement claims that everyone is turning to the product, especially people "in the know." It plays on people's desire not to be different or left out. Commercials may also include personal endorsements or testimonials by celebrities—celebrities who may not even use the product and are being paid merely for the use of their names. A fourth sales strategy is to stack the deck, citing only the good points and omitting the weak ones. When this occurs, a commercial contains half-truths. Finally, advertisers attempt to associate their product with things that carry a positive connotation—for example, cigarette ads used to show smokers amid sparkling clear brooks, green grass, fresh air—the antithesis of the dirty air smokers create.

Upper-graders find it challenging to view, listen, and read for examples of these forms of propaganda. They may start with newspaper and magazine advertisements and analyze how facts have been distorted. Working from an outline such as the one in Figure 5.8, students categorize statements they have identified. Later they turn to TV commercials to identify other examples.

DEVICES FOR MANIPULATING FACTS IN ADVERTISING		
Purpose: To discover examples of fact manipulation in commercials and advertisements		
Task: View and listen to TV commercials and study magazine ads. Find statements that fit each of the categories.		
Type	**Definition**	**Examples**
1. Glittering generality	A statement so general that it could not possibly be true	
2. Bandwagon effect	A statement suggesting that everyone is turning to the product	
3. Testimonial	A statement by a celebrity or company representative attesting to the merits of the product	
4. Deck stacking	A statement giving only the good points and ignoring the obvious weak ones	
5. Positive association	An attempt to associate the product with pleasurable things	

Figure 5.8
A Guide for Categorizing Commercials and Advertisements

Listening Aesthetically

WORD BANK

Aesthetic stance

Feelings and emotions are key in aesthetic listening. People assume an *aesthetic stance* when they

■ Take genuine delight and pleasure in what they are hearing, whether that be a conversation, a story, a poem, a drama, or a piece of expository prose.

- Feel deeply in response to what they are hearing—so intensely that they take on the mood of the message, feel the feelings, and become one with the story, poem, or drama.
- Create relationships that are new and personal out of a story or poem by picturing story happenings, extending the story, and relating it to their own lives.

Sharing poems, stories, and plays in a dramatic manner is one of the best ways to encourage students to listen aesthetically. With poems and stories, it is not the information that listeners take away that is important, but what they are "living through," what they are "burning through"—the fact that they are perhaps being changed by the experience. Listening, they "pay attention to the associations, feelings, attitudes, and ideas" that the words of story or poem arouse within them. They listen to themselves, as Louise Rosenblatt (1978) tells us in her landmark book *The Reader, the Text, the Poem*. In short, listeners become "moment-to-moment" participants in the story or poem. Let us consider the aesthetic stance by thinking about some examples.

Taking Genuine Delight and Pleasure

Scenario: Teacher Anne Grant opened Leo Lionni's *The Biggest House in the World* and read the title on the first page. At the same time, she turned on a recording of "Serenade" from the wonderful ballet *Les Millions d'Arlequin* by Ricardo Drigo. As Ms. Grant dramatically read about the snail whose dissatisfaction with being so little caused him to grow bigger and bigger until he was too large to move to another cabbage, the music created a mood in harmony with the story. When the story action peaked, so did the music, and when the snail realized the folly of his dissatisfaction, the music lilted once more. Listening, Ms. Grant's young students were entranced by the story and music; their faces reflected their oneness with the little snail and their joy at the ultimate solution.

Scenario: A group of third-graders listened to their teacher recite Judith Viorst's poem "My Cat." Having heard the poem once, they rose to their feet, and following their teacher's lips, they chorused it together. They chorused "My Cat" again and again, trying to recite the long "running-out-of-breath sentence" in one "lung-full" and physically moving their bodies in harmony with the rhythm and feelings of the poem. Smiles spread across the classroom as the students began to "own" the poem—began to recite it from memory with confidence and delight. Smiles got bigger as the students listened to their teacher read aloud another delightful piece by Viorst, *Alexander and the Terrible, Horrible, No Good, Very Bad Day*. Here, when the teacher got to the repeating line based on the title as well as to the "kick line," "I think I'll move to Australia," the third-graders joyfully joined in. They were having a good time visiting with Judith Viorst and were loving everything about the story: the silly illustrations of Alexander with his great facial expressions, the things that happened to him in the story, and the sounds of the words. Having had terrible, no good days themselves—days when they wished they were anywhere but there—they felt with Alexander, but they also appreciated the humor in the situation.

Vivian Yenika-Agbaw describes a time when she responded to the beautifully crafted pictures of a story much as these third-graders responded to Viorst's story and poem. Hear her as she talks of her first encounter with *Christmas in the Big House, Christmas in the Quarters* by Patricia McKissack and Fredrick McKissack:

> Flipping through the pages of *Christmas in the Big House, Christmas in the Quarters,* I was enthralled by the beauty of the pictures that extended the story for me. The characters looked so familiar in their distinct outfits that reflected who they were on this historical plantation. Thompson, the illustrator, succeeds in capturing the fall foliage in an exquisite manner that is alluring, and communicates a feeling of tranquility and serenity. I grinned with satisfaction after going through all the pictures. I truly enjoyed the experience. (1997, p. 447)

In each of these contexts, to listen aesthetically is to laugh, to smile, to grin. It is to be enthralled, to respond with joy and appreciation, to join physically into a story or poem, to feel light, to feel bubbly, to appreciate. Listeners feel in these ways when the illustrations, events, words, and sounds of story or poem resonate for them.

How can elementary and middle school teachers help listeners feel the fun of literature? The answer is really simple: Make a read-aloud dramatic. Teachers need to use their voices expressively and move their bodies in harmony with the story. They must use their facial expressions as a storytelling vehicle. At the same time, they can embellish a story or poem with and for listeners by reading to music, asking students to join in on repeating lines, and encouraging children to use body motions as they chorus and rechorus poems together. They can ask students to listen for words or phrases they particularly like that tickle their funny bones or delight their senses. The result is what Yenika-Agbaw (1997) calls "pleasurable reading."

Feeling Deeply–Living Through

Listen, now, as Katie Wood (1994) describes the "living through" of a story that occurred as a group of teachers together reached the end of Cynthia Rylant's *Missing May:*

> For a few moments no one spoke, and what was held within that first response of silence was what had been pushing us to this place all week—a deep sense that we had been a part of something powerful, something somehow separate from the rest of the world. If anyone from the outside had walked into our room at that moment, they would not have understood the feeling they found there. Intruders would have known they were interrupting something more powerful than words.

Teachers can help children feel equally deeply in response to the tug of story. Young children can use the pictures of a story as they make aesthetic meanings. One first-grade teacher chose Paul Galdone's *The Horse, the Fox, and the Lion* to get her pupils to become one with the story. She began by focusing on the pictures, because an aesthetic response to literature "reaches further into the artistic world when we expand our transaction to include illustrations as well as text" (Madura, 1995). Having shared the story, the teacher asked, "How do the pictures make you feel? Show me with your faces. Show me with your bodies. Where in the story lines do you feel that sadness?" In response, the children put a sad look into their eyes and onto their faces and hung their heads down just as the horse was doing in the story. The students said that the line from the story—"The horse, feeling very sad, wandered away till he came to a forest where he might find shelter under the trees in bad weather"—made them feel unhappy along with the horse. "How bad," one child responded, "to have no place but under the trees to get out of the rain—no home to go home to."

Whereas the illustrations in a picture storybook help young listeners to become one with a story, older listeners who are hearing a chapter from a novel read aloud to them must see in their own minds what is happening in a story. Responding aesthetically, they "enter into the world of the characters and envision what it would be like to be the characters themselves" (Cox and Many, 1992). In so doing, listeners experience the pathos, or dramatic sadness, of a story.

To encourage students to assume an aesthetic stance, the teacher can invite listeners to pretend they are a character in a story they are hearing, to climb into his or her body, and to feel with that character. Feeling intensely, children and teacher may talk in their minds to a character, tense their muscles in anticipation, frown or grimace, and at times weep with a character. Who can listen to the dramatic final chapter of *Stone Fox* and not come away teary? Who can listen to the final chapter of *Sarah, Plain and Tall* and not plead, "Stay, Sarah! Please stay. We need you!"? Who can listen to the final chapters of *My Brother Sam Is Dead* and not clench his or her teeth? Each of these is not a response to the literature; it is a "living through" of the literature.

Creating Relationships That Are New and Personal

A third-grade girl listens to a reading of Allen Say's *Grandfather's Journey* and recalls tales her own grandfather told her about his feelings when he left his home in Russia and came to America. A fifth-grade boy listens to Katherine Paterson's *Bridge to Terabithia,* feels with Jess as he experiences the loss of his best friend, Leslie, and relates the death of Leslie to the death of his younger brother. Responding to the story, the boy tells how he felt when he lost his baby brother—his own disbelief, his own feelings of loneliness. Similarly, a sixth-grade girl listens to Betsy Byars's *The Summer of the Swans,* experiences Sara's terror as she searches for her brother who is mentally disabled, and thinks about her own sibling whom she sometimes loves and sometimes seems to hate.

Carole Cox and Joyce Many (1992) suggest that extending and relating are ways to assume an aesthetic stance when listening to or reading a literary work. By *extending,* Cox and Many mean that listeners go beyond the actual text to propose what would have been or could have been *if . . .* In making this kind of extension, listeners create stories of their own based on what they are feeling. By *relating,* Cox and Many mean that listeners think about their own "personal experiences that had generated similar emotions in the past."

Teachers can encourage extending and relating by wondering, "What if . . . ?", by asking, "When have you felt the same way?", and by recounting their own feelings in similar circumstances. This is the time to connect listening with writing. The teacher can suggest, "I'm too filled with feelings to talk right now. I want to climb into my own skin, feel, and write my feelings in my journal." It is the time also to connect listening with drama and have children play scenes from stories they are listening to and show how they and the story characters are feeling.

A final caveat before closing: Do not think that aesthetic listening occurs only in reference to fiction. Some pieces of nonfiction have the potential to elicit aesthetic responses. Peter Sis's *The Starry Messenger,* Jean Fritz's *Traitor: The Case of Benedict Arnold,* and Russell Freedman's *Lincoln: A Photobiography* are examples. Listeners can walk with Galileo in the pages of Sis's book and feel his agony as he was forced to recant his theories about the solar system. They can become Benedict Arnold in the pages of Fritz's biography and sense a bit of themselves in this one-time hero who was driven by his obsessions. They can live through the events of the American Civil War and feel the horror of battle as they listen to the lines of Freedman's biography and study the photographs. To help listeners go beyond efferent meanings and assume an aesthetic stance, the teacher prompts, "How does this make us feel deep inside?"

A Summary Thought or Two

Listening for Meaning

This chapter has set forth four basic principles relative to listening instruction (see Figure 5.9). First, listening in classrooms should be active. To this end, teachers must encourage students to generate ideas in relation to a message rather than simply sitting and passively receiving. Responses can be physical, oral, or written. Second, teachers must model specific strategies that students can use to become more effective listeners. In this respect, some classroom listening should be strategic. Third, teachers must recognize that all listening is not the same: Some is conversational,

Figure 5.9
Facets of Listening

ACTIVITY PROMPT
Make a visual clarifying literal listening.

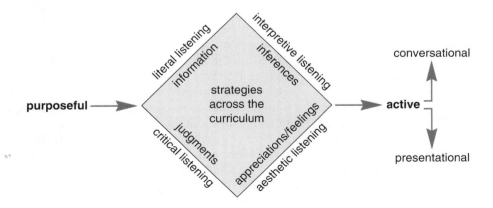

some presentational. As a result, teachers must organize classroom activity so that students take part in the give-and-take of conversation and respond to oral reports, read-alouds, films, and tapes. Fourth, people listen for a variety of purposes that language arts educators today characterize as efferent or aesthetic. Students should have the opportunity to listen in order (1) to identify main ideas and supporting details, (2) to make inferences, and (3) to judge—efferent listening purposes important in high school and college learning. At times, students should also be asked to assume an aesthetic stance in which their feelings and what they are living through are more significant than the information they take away. Although an aesthetic stance is especially appropriate as children listen to stories and poems, it is appropriate too as children respond to nonfiction.

Your Language Arts Portfolio

- Select one major segment of Chapter 5. Create a schematic that includes key points from the segment. If you can make an original schematic of a segment of text, you will be more able to guide children in making schematics based on their own reading and listening.
- Devise a lesson plan based on a children's story in which youngsters listen interpretively, critically, and aesthetically.

Related Readings

Armstrong, William. "Learning to Listen." *American Educator,* 21 (Winter 1997–1998), 24–25, 47.

Brent, Rebecca, and **Patricia Anderson.** "Developing Children's Classroom Listening Strategies." *The Reading Teacher,* 47 (October 1993), 122–126.

Choate, Joyce, and **Thomas Rakes.** "The Structured Listening Activity: A Model for Improving Listening Comprehension." *The Reading Teacher,* 41 (November 1988), 194–200.

Creighton, Donna. "Critical Literacy in the Elementary Classroom." *Language Arts,* 74 (October 1997), 438–445.

Falk-Ross, Francine. "Developing Metacommunicative Awareness in Children with Language Difficulties: Challenging the Typical Pull-out System." *Language Arts,* 74 (March 1997), 206–216.

Hennings, Dorothy Grant. *Beyond the Read-Aloud: Learning to Read by Listening to and Reflecting on Literature.* Bloomington, Ind.: Phi Delta Kappa, 1992.

Jalongo, Mary R. "Promoting Active Listening in the Classroom." *Childhood Education* (Fall 1995), 13–18.

Pearson, P. David, and **Linda Fielding.** "Research Update: Listening Comprehension." *Language Arts,* 59 (September 1982), 617–629.

Schwartz, David. "Ready, Set, Read—20 Minutes Each Day Is All You Need." *Smithsonian,* 25 (February 1995), 82–91.

Seitz, Ernest R. "Using Media Presentations to Teach Notetaking, Main Idea, and Summarization Skills." *Journal of Adolescent and Adult Literacy,* 40 (April 1997): 562–563.

Trelease, Jim. *The New Read-Aloud Handbook.* New York: Penguin, 1989.

———."Have You Read to Your Kids Today?" *Instructor,* 105 (May/June 1996), 56–60.

————. "Jim Trelease Speaks on Reading Aloud to Children." *The Reading Teacher,* 43 (December 1989), 200–207.

Winn, Deanna. "Develop Listening Skills as a Part of the Curriculum." *The Reading Teacher,* 42 (November 1988), 144–146.

Wood, Katie. "Hearing Voices, Tell Tales: Finding the Power of Reading Aloud." *Language Arts,* 71 (September 1994), 346–349.

Oral Expression

The Classroom as a "Talking-Place"

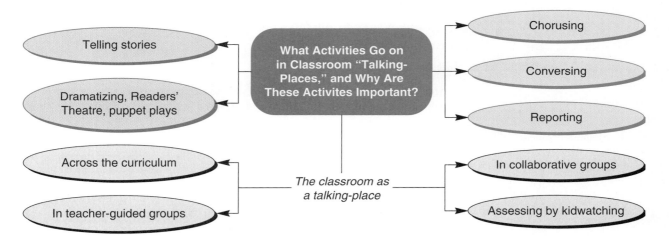

Telling stories

Dramatizing, Readers' Theatre, puppet plays

Across the curriculum

In teacher-guided groups

What Activities Go on in Classroom "Talking-Places," and Why Are These Activites Important?

The classroom as a talking-place

Chorusing

Conversing

Reporting

In collaborative groups

Assessing by kidwatching

A Talking-Place in Action — *Dramatizing "The Three Billy Goats Gruff"*

Everyone was ready. The flannelboard was propped on the easel of Karin Topping's first grade. The children's eyes were alert, watching as Ms. Topping began to tell "The Three Billy Goats Gruff."

Creative Storytelling and Conversation

"Trip, trap, trip, trap," the children echoed softly as the littlest billy goat Gruff went over the bridge. "Trip, trap, trip, trap," they chorused more loudly as the middle goat Gruff went over. "It is I, the middle billy goat Gruff, going over the bridge," they contributed, based on what had happened to the littlest goat. "Why don't you wait for my big brother Gruff," they suggested, again based on what had happened to the littlest goat. "Oh, no, you're not!" they roared for the troll, using their meanest voices. Because "The Three Billy Goats Gruff" is a repetitive tale, the children were able to predict what the characters would say; they could readily contribute repeated words

Respond to story patterns by predicting

even as their teacher demonstrated story action by placing and moving pieces on the flannelboard.

Having heard the story, the first-graders were eager to talk about it and "do" it again. This time some decided to become little Gruffs, some middle Gruffs, some big Gruffs, and others mean trolls. Now, as their teacher narrated the story, youngsters from the role-playing groups contributed the speaking words, improvising as they went along to add to what the characters said. Standing up, they used their bodies to express movements to go along with the "Trip, trap, trip, trap." They shook their heads and stomped their feet to simulate goat or troll actions—at times encouraged by their teacher, who asked, "What else do you think the goat said? How do you think the troll moved his eyes and face as he spoke? Tell me. Show me."

Express thoughts through voice and body

The result was conversation and an impromptu retelling of the story that bordered on creative drama. Later that day, with the music of Edvard Grieg's "March of the Trolls" playing softly in the background, the children made paper bag puppets to go along with "The Three Billy Goats Gruff." Some made trolls, some goats, depending on their personal preferences.

Creating a Drama Together

The next day, when the children gathered on the communication rug, they brought their troll and goat puppets with them and gathered in groups according to the characters they had chosen.

Create original story ideas through spontaneous drama

"Let's go on with our story, children," Ms. Topping proposed. "Goats, you are now in the field on the other side of the bridge. What are you doing? Feeling? Saying to one another?" The children responded in terms of the delicious grass they were eating and how glad they were to get rid of the mean troll.

"Stand up, trolls! Move like trolls!" directed the teacher. "Look, billy goats, here comes a band of other trolls. Why do you think they are coming? What can you say? What do you do? Trolls, what do you say? How do you move your bodies? Your face? Your eyes? Goats, how do you feel as the trolls get nearer?"

Guided by their teacher's organizing questions, the goats and the trolls spontaneously created and acted out a drama in which the trolls came after the goats and the goats outwitted the trolls, this time by hiding under the bridge.

That sequence played out, Ms. Topping asked, "But suppose you trolls were not bad ones after all. How could you have moved your bodies and faces to show this? What could you have said to the goats? What would you goats have said to the trolls?" The children responded by doing, speaking, and adding sounds like *clump, clump, clump* as they moved their puppet heads and took the parts of the characters represented by those puppets.

Role-Playing to Understand Content

The children in Ms. Topping's first grade had enjoyed dramatizing "The Three Billy Goats Gruff." They talked about what they had done and asked if they could play out a story again. So another afternoon found them in the Communication Center, listening to another picture book: *Ox-Cart Man* by Donald Hall.

Create original dialogue to go with a story

This time, the teacher began by reading the book and sharing the pictures. After an initial reading and discussion, the children went back to interpret the pictures, reading into each the thoughts and words of the man and the other people depicted.

They spoke out as though they were the characters in the story, different children contributing different lines, prompted by their teacher's probing questions: "How do you think the man felt as he said good-bye to his family? What did he say? What else? What did they answer? What expressions did he have on his face?"

Because *Ox-Cart Man* tells the story of the cycle of the seasons and the way one family in early nineteenth-century New England reacts to those changes, the drama the children produced was a serious one. In proposing what characters were thinking, saying, and doing, the children encountered a lot of content. They had to talk about the seasons and what each member of the family did; they had to consider the differences between life in early nineteenth-century America and life today.

The children most enjoyed dramatizing the part where the man sold the wool and the shawl, the candles and the shingles. They called out, like the man, "Come and buy. See what I've got." To do this, they selected objects from the classroom to hold up and "sell," describing their goods much more fully than in the story. The result was a marketplace of activity through which the children handled major social studies concepts—goods, trade, production—as they created orally and spontaneously together.

Ms. Topping's classroom is what Dorothy Watson (1993) calls "a talking-place." It is a place where children use talk to respond to stories and create dramas, express poems in choral fashion, converse about everything and anything, and present their ideas more formally during share-times. In this chapter, we consider these ways to make our classrooms become active talking-places.

DISCUSSION PROMPT

- Why is it important that classrooms become "talking-places"?

Storytelling and Dramatics: Let's Make a Story Together . . .

READ

- Olga Nelson, "Story Telling: Language Experience for Meaning Making," *The Reading Teacher,* 42 (February 1989), 386–390.
- R. Craig Roney, "Back to Basics with Storytelling," *The Reading Teacher,* 42 (March 1989), 520–523.
- Karen Gallas, "When the Children Take the Chair: A Study of Sharing Time in a Primary Classroom," *Language Arts,* 69 (March 1992), 172–182.

Elementary-school youngsters should have numerous opportunities to hear stories and poems and to react orally and creatively, as we saw happening in Ms. Topping's classroom. Ways to achieve this goal are through participatory story listening and storytelling, spontaneous drama, Readers' Theatre, pantomime, more formal drama-festival times, and choral speaking. Through these experiences, children learn to

- Put words together to express ideas in mind.
- Rely on their voices and bodies to highlight ideas.
- Use visuals to add clarity to a message.
- Express themselves orally with some degree of confidence and poise.
- Think creatively, extending a story to predict, imagine, and propose.

Participatory Storytelling

In *An Exchange of Gifts,* Marion Ralston (1993) suggests that the sharing of a story is like the giving of a gift. "It is a gift of preparation and imagination from the storyteller to the audience. It is also a gift of shared appreciation from the audience to the storyteller." "Storytelling creates for our listeners a sense of mystery, of wonder, of reverence for life" (Cooper and Collins, 1991). It is an integral part of teaching. Telling stories while they teach, teachers clarify and illustrate points and model storytelling strategies for children who themselves are becoming spinners of stories.

Participatory storytelling as part of story listening is a fine beginning for developing children's ability to express themselves orally. Stories have a straightforward sequence that provides a ready introduction to sequencing and pacing of ideas. They have an inherent appeal for children; youngsters love to hear stories and can easily develop interest in sharing similar tales. Also, stories for children are action filled. In telling them, youngsters must vary intonation, express meanings through face and body, use props where appropriate, and select the most expressive words.

Research shows that oral activity related to stories increases children's ability to use language effectively. In a study by Dorothy Strickland (1973), youngsters in an experimental group were exposed to a literature-based oral language program. They enjoyed a daily story, which was followed by a period of storytelling, puppetry, creative dramatics, role-playing, choral speaking, or discussion. Children in a control group listened to stories but did not participate in oral activities. Strickland found that both groups showed increases in language facility, but those involved in oral follow-ups made significantly greater gains.

A similar study by Maryellen Cosgrove (1987) also showed gains in reading as a result of story listening. In Cosgrove's study, fourth- and sixth-graders listened to stories three times a week for twelve weeks. The students evidenced significant improvement in reading attitudes, independent reading, and comprehension when compared to a control group that did not hear stories. Likewise, Patricia Kelly (1990) reported heightened student interest in literature when third-graders were involved in story listening, Readers' Theatre activities, role-playing, and choral speaking.

Researchers have been investigating the effect of having children retell stories after listening to or reading them (Morrow, 1985a and b, 1986; Gambrell, Pfeiffer, and Wilson, 1985; Gambrell, Koskinen, and Kapinus, 1985; Brown and Cambourne, 1989). Using retelling in classrooms, teacher-researchers share a story, model retelling of that story, provide opportunities for children to retell stories after hearing and reading them, and encourage children to create original stories. The research indicates that oral retelling significantly improves children's comprehension, their sense of story structure, and the language complexity of original stories they dictate (Morrow, 1986; Koskinen, Gambrell, Kapinus, and Heathington, 1988).

Oral sharing of stories belongs in the upper as well as primary grades. Jim Trelease (1989) describes one remedial sixth-grade class where the teacher, Mrs. Hallahan, simply read each day from the book *Where the Red Fern Grows*. Trelease explains:

> A hardened, street-wise, proud group (mostly boys), they were insulted when she began reading to them. "How come you're reading to us? You think we're babies or something?" they wanted to know. After explaining that she didn't think anything of the kind but only wanted to share a favorite story with them, she continued reading *Where the Red Fern Grows*. Each day she opened the class with the next portion of the story and each day she was greeted with groans. "Not again today! How come nobody else ever made us listen like this?"

READ

■ Denny Taylor and Dorothy Strickland, *Family Storybook Reading* (Portsmouth, N.H.: Heinemann, 1986), for a treatment of the importance of story listening in young children's language development.

■ W. Nikola-Lisa, "Read Aloud, Play a Lot," *The New Advocate*, 5 (Summer 1992), 199–213, for a discussion of language play and dramatic play as responses to literature.

But [Mrs. Hallahan] persevered, and after a few weeks (the book contained 212 pages), the tone of the class's morning remarks began to change. "You're going to read to us today, aren't you?" Or, "Don't forget the book, Mrs. Hallahan."

"I knew I had a winner," she confess[ed], "when on Friday, just when we were nearing the end of the book, one of the slowest boys in the class went home after school, got himself a library card, took out *Where the Red Fern Grows,* finished it himself, and came to school on Monday and told everyone how it ended."

In this case, story sharing by the teacher led naturally into storytelling by a student and could easily have developed into dramatic retelling.

Similarly, social commentator Richard Rodriguez (1981) explains how he was affected by a teacher's reading aloud to him as part of remedial instruction:

> Most of the time we took turns [reading]. I began with my elementary text. Sentences of astonishing simplicity seemed to me lifeless and drab. . . . Then the old nun would read from her favorite books, usually biographies of early American presidents. Playfully she ran through complex sentences, calling the words alive with her voice, making it seem that the author somehow was speaking directly to me. I smiled just to listen to her. I sat there and sensed for the first time some possibility of fellowship between a reader and a writer, a communication, never *intimate* like that I heard spoken words at home convey, but one nonetheless *personal.*

Creative oral story sharing, storytelling, and story retelling are not frills of the elementary language arts; they are integral components that lead to a heightened ability to use both oral and written language.

Spontaneous Drama

Informal classroom drama also has a major place in the oral language curriculum. The Joint Committee of the National Council of Teachers of English and the Children's Theatre Association (1983) explains, "Informal classroom drama is an activity in which students invent and enact dramatic situations for themselves, rather than for an outside audience. This activity, perhaps most widely known as creative drama, . . . is spontaneously generated by the participants who perform the dual tasks of composing and enacting their parts as the drama progresses. This form of unrehearsed drama is a process of guided discovery led by the teacher for the benefit of the participants."

An easy introduction is the repetitive story. To begin, children decide how key words should be spoken and take turns playing the lines over and over. For example, in dramatizing "The Little Red Hen," children decide how the hen must have gone about her tasks and how she would have spoken her important line, "Very well then, I will do it myself!" The teacher asks, "How do you think the hen worked when she planted the field? Reaped the wheat? Took it to the mill?" Youngsters answer by showing. They repeat the recurring hen line and the lines of the other animals, each time varying their voices to show differences in meaning. Then, guided by the teacher, they improvise the words and actions of the Little Red Hen when she is faced by three other animals who want to take her bread away.

GO TO

Pages 164 and 165 for more on read-alouds.

READ

Miriam Martinez, "Motivating Dramatic Story Reenactments," *The Reading Teacher,* 46 (May 1993), 682–688. Martinez describes "spontaneous, child-initiated, child-directed" dramatic activity in early primary classrooms.

Isn't drama a "frill" that takes away time from reading and writing?

Some teachers contend that they have no time for dramatic activities in their classrooms. They call drama a "frill" and say that time spent in dramatic activity cuts into the time available for reading and writing. From their perspective, there are just more important ways to use valuable instruction time.

Jennifer McMaster, a third-grade teacher in Fayetteville, New York, thinks this is very wrong. Ms. McMaster speaks of the value of drama in the language development of her children: "One of the important features of drama is the variety of communication experiences it offers to children. Drama is thinking out loud; it develops oral language skills as the child defines, articulates, expresses, and verbalizes thoughts in the context of improvised activities. By participating in drama activities, children develop listening skills. . . . Children experience the chance to improve their speaking skills as they take on different roles, selecting the language most appropriate to the situation. . . . Children engaged in dramatic play use literate language. This language use, which includes defining references to pronouns, clarifying ambiguous terms, choosing objects to symbolize other objects, and clearly introducing topics, will later transfer into their learning of written language" ("'Doing' Literature: Using Drama to Build Literacy," *The Reading Teacher*, 51 [April 1998], 574–584).

DISCUSSION PROMPT

Is drama a curricular "frill"? If not, what are the purposes of creative oral expression in the elementary language arts? What specific strategies did Karin Topping use to involve her students in dramatization during storytelling? What other strategies are available to you? What learnings might result?

READ

- Martha Combs and John Beach, "Stories and Storytelling: Personalizing the Social Studies," *The Reading Teacher*, 47 (March 1994), 464–471.

- Jenifer Schneider and Sylvia Jackson, "Process Drama: A Special Place for Writing," *The Reading Teacher*, 54 (September 2000), 38–51, for a description of ways to use drama in developing social studies understandings and writing ability.

Dorothy Heathcote (1983), noted for her work with creative drama, goes beyond stories to organize dramatic activity around historical periods and events. Heathcote describes how she uses drama to help older children get a sense of the events relative to General Wolfe's siege of Quebec. Children do not look at Wolfe from "over there" or "outside." They become Wolfe, who must decide what to do when faced with the imperative, "Give us your orders." Children must draw on their relevant knowledge about Wolfe, the military and political situation at Quebec, the weather, and the soldiers to make a response.

As Heathcote explains, now "there is a sudden pressure on the learners: 'These guys are expecting me to tell them what to do.'" Responding to this pressure, participants in a drama "unpack" previously held conclusions; they actively use information encountered and make new and different connections. Here the teacher's role is that of "journeymaker"—to take students on a "journey of learning." The teacher must press and ask if participants are to discover the meaning behind the material they are studying. Often it is the teacher who must pose the problem situation that begins the drama—the what-if question that gets participants thinking.

Readers' Theatre

■ □ ● ● ●

READ

■ Barbara Larkin, "Can We Act It Out?" *The Reading Teacher,* 54 (February 2001), 478–481, for a description of one first-grade teacher's experiences with Readers' Theatre.

Another exciting form that classroom drama can take is Readers' Theatre. Using Readers' Theatre, students read a story aloud, with different students reading the parts of various story characters and using variations in intonation, pitch, and reading rate to bring the story alive. Typically, one child reads each character's part. Linda Hoyt (1992) suggests variations on this format: Children read parts chorally or read in small groups. This lets every child participate, helps slower readers "experience reading at a rate that approximates oral speech," and "encourages repeated readings for fluency."

Children can dramatically read directly from a text, using the quotation marks to tell them when the narrator is speaking and when each character comes in. At times, children read dramatically from scripts on which individual roles have been specially marked. But as Hoyt believes, the most effective scripts for Readers' Theatre are those designed by students. Students can list the main characters and then choose portions of the story to read aloud dramatically. The teacher's role here is to prepare for dramatic oral reading by modeling for the students ways to use the voice to express thoughts, feelings, and mood.

Youngsters can translate nonfiction trade books into Readers' Theatre scripts as well. Books such as those in the *Magic School Bus* series and shorter informational picture books are particularly adaptable (Young and Vardell, 1993). Children can also adapt portions of longer trade books, such as *Lincoln* and *The Wright Brothers,* both by Russell Freedman.

Terrell Young and Sylvia Vardell suggest that students skim a potential book before scripting it, choosing a portion that is particularly interesting. Working from a reproduction of the chosen section, students delete lines that are less critical to the development of the ideas and decide how to render others so that they "weave into a coherent whole." Students volunteer to read parts, add a prologue to introduce the reading, and practice reading their lines (perhaps working in reading pairs). Young and Vardell propose that this is a more effective way of integrating nonfiction into the curriculum than the discredited round-robin reading of the past.

Pantomime

Pantomime is important in language programs. First, through pantomime children can loosen their inhibitions about expressing themselves nonverbally. Second, they gain control over their nonverbal expressions, which are as significant in face-to-face communication and in creative drama as they are in pantomime. Third, they begin to realize the importance of body language in communication and become aware of the nonverbal messages that others send.

Pantomime should start as a class activity, with all children interpreting an action or feeling. Children express more freely when everyone, including the teacher, is involved. A beginning for the very young is Let's Pretend play. Children pretend they are

- Rubber bands stretching or masses of clay being flattened.
- Balls rolling, bouncing, and hurtling through the air.
- Animals such as snakes, horses, kangaroos, sea gulls, tigers.
- Machines such as helicopters with propellers, windmills on a breezy day, jackhammers tearing up the street.
- Natural phenomena such as waves rolling shoreward, winds gusting, snowflakes floating earthward, clouds bouncing.

Kindergartners and preschoolers can interpret these actions to music. With desks pushed back, they stretch, roll, spin, and wiggle as the music inspires them.

Many types of stories lend themselves to pantomimed telling:

- *Nursery rhymes.* Several youngsters pantomime rhymes such as "Little Miss Muffet," "Little Jack Horner," and "Jack and Jill," as watchers try to guess the rhyme.
- *Fables.* Several children pantomime the actions of fables such as "The Wind and the Sun," "The Reed and the Oak," and "The Miller, the Boy, and the Donkey," while a narrator reads the fable.
- *Talking-beast tales.* Children pantomime the actions of tales such as "The Three Little Pigs" while a narrator reads. Then they pantomime the story, trying to tell it totally through actions.

Upper-graders who have seen comedians perform humorous pantomimes on TV can make up original skits to share wordlessly. Humor is achieved in pantomime through exaggeration, so children should select topics that can be exaggerated— catching a mosquito or scratching an itch when one's arms are full.

Drama Festivals and Formal Drama

CONSIDER

Teachers must guide children as they begin to function, circulating among collaborative teams, making suggestions, and helping children prepare by trying out words and gestures.

Children who have experienced participatory storytelling, spontaneous drama, and pantomime can go on to tell and dramatize stories, grouped in "little theater companies." At times, all the members of the class can contribute to a story festival that focuses on tales from a particular country, by one author, on one theme, or of one genre (myths, fables, tall tales). More often, only a few students contribute to a briefer sharing time. Those who wish to share sign up, indicating their story title, their medium (puppet, pictures, filmstrip), their name, and their little theatre company (see Figure 6.1).

To get things started, one teacher assembles a collection of books related to a unit in progress; these books form the independent dimension of the unit. In each book, she slips a card. Students who read a particular book sign its card. When several signatures appear, those students gather as a performing company to share the book with others.

Classic tales are particularly useful in this context. A classroom Dramaland Book Shelf should hold collections of Grimm, Andersen, Asbjornsen, and Moe; adaptations of French tales by Perrault; modern tales like E. B. White's *Charlotte's Web,* P. L. Travers's *Mary Poppins,* and Astrid Lindgren's *Pippi Longstocking;* collections of myths; storybooks that tell just one fable, such as Brian Wildsmith's version of

A Visit with Hans Christian Andersen
• The Life of Hans Christian Andersen: a presentation by the Andersen Reporters—Tom, Kev, Jake, and Marcia. • "The Steadfast Tin Soldier": a puppet show by the Danish Puppeteers—Melissa, Karen, Moose, Gil, Mary, and Bob. • "The Ugly Duckling": a dramatization by the Playing Five—Marti, Max, Janey, Jill, and Jason. • "The Little Mermaid": a shadow play by the Four Keys—Nate, Herb, Kathie, and Sallie. • "The Emperor's New Clothes": a filmstrip-telling by the Script Writers—Jennifer, Phyllis, Frank, and Joe. • Talking with Andersen: an interview with the Star Interviewers—Angela, José, and Marie—and with Hans Christian Andersen, played by Milt. • Some Andersen Riddles: all participants. Today's Announcer—Rose

Figure 6.1
Example of an Upper-Grade Drama Festival Program

READ

Jennifer Catney McMaster, "'Doing' Literature: Using Drama to Build Literacy Classrooms," *The Reading Teacher,* 51 (April 1998), 574–584, for a discussion of purposes of drama in classroom instruction.

LaFontaine's "The Rich Man and the Shoemaker"; and books that relate one old fairy tale, tall tale, or legend (Peltzman, 1994).

Children working cooperatively in little theatre companies need ways to avoid memorization of stories they tell and dramatize. They can experiment with these approaches:

- A narrator who reads long descriptive passages, simulating the wandering storyteller of yore.
- Cue cards held up and changed by a "stagehand."
- Notes written behind scenery objects.
- Scrolls containing the lines that players hold and unroll as the playlet progresses.
- Spontaneous adaptations of the lines; children know "about" what they are going to say but make up specific lines as they go along.

At times youngsters enjoy dramatizing original playlets. Students who have collaborated in the writing of a short play share it dramatically with the class. Acting out is followed by conversation in which listeners tell which actions or words in the story they liked. At other times individual youngsters who have written short stories convert them into playlets or pantomimes for group dramatizing.

During actual sharing sessions, informality is the key. Although the sharing may be dramatic, it is not a magnificent production with elaborate props and scenery, nor do children practice extensively or memorize lines. Rather, emphasis is on enjoying language and literature. The only audience is classmates and teacher; contributions are not graded, and children feel no pressure to produce perfect performances. Upper-graders generally add to the fun by hamming it up—a positive addition, for relaxed players enjoy performing.

Materials to Support Storytelling and Dramatics

Once a teacher has told a few stories, children assume the role of storyteller; they tell stories or parts of stories they have read or made up. In their storytelling, children use the same materials teachers use to extend story meanings: pictures, puppets, flannel pieces, and so forth. Let us next consider some of the techniques children can use as they share stories.

Using Pictures to Tell Stories   Flat pictures add impact to story sharing. Several children who have written or read a story can render key scenes in picture form. These can be hung sequentially on a story line as the children share their story with the class. Or, if only two or three children share a story, they can mount key story scenes they have reproduced on each of the six faces of a good-size box. As they share the story, they display appropriate pictures. Children who do not enjoy drawing can snip pictures from magazines to mount on their story boxes or on construction paper to hang on the story line during sharing.

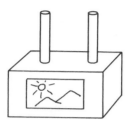

The story roll is a related device for sharing. Individually or in groups, children draw story scenes on a roll of paper. They attach the short ends of their completed story rolls to cardboard tubes, slip them into circles cut into a viewing box, and rotate them to pull the roll through the box so that the pictures are visible through a large rectangular cut in one side. Displaying their pictures sequentially, students relate the story happenings.

If facilities for making transparencies are available, children can use them for sharing stories. Each child in a listening group selects a picture from the storybook. With the aid of a thermofax machine, the teacher makes transparencies of the selected pictures; then each child adds color to his or her selection. Later, in story sequence, each child places the transparency on the "stage" of the overhead projector to tell about that part of the story.

Students can produce original, single transparencies based on an exciting incident in a book read. Projecting a transparency, a student tells about the incident in question, not revealing the outcome but relating the exciting buildup. This sharing format can turn into a book sale, with a speaker enticing listeners to read the whole story.

If a filmstrip of a story is available, that strip—without the audiotape that may accompany it—can serve as the medium for sharing by youngsters who have read the original book version. A small group follows up a reading or listening experience with a viewing of the silent strip. Then they use their memory of story events to devise their own version, which they share with others while showing the strip.

Using Puppets in Drama and Storytelling   Few youngsters or oldsters can resist the appeal of puppets. Students can make hand puppets from various materials:

- Paper bags to which features have been added with markers, crayons, construction paper, or yarn.
- Socks, stockings, or work gloves to which features have been added with buttons, yarn, or scraps of material.
- The hand by marking features directly on the fist or fingers.
- Styrofoam or Ping-Pong balls stuck on the fingers or on ice cream bar sticks, with glitter, buttons, and yarn forming the features.

Students can make head puppets that they hold directly over their faces from these kinds of materials:

- Paper plates, with features drawn with marker pen and eyes cut through the plates.
- Full-size paper bags in which eye, nose, and mouth openings have been cut.

They can make body puppets from a variety of things:

- Large cartons from which one side has been removed and through which a head hole has been cut in the opposite side; the cartons can be painted colorfully.
- People-shaped and -size cutouts. Youngsters stretch out on a piece of heavy-grade cardboard, and their classmates trace their body outline; the youngsters cut out the outline, color themselves in, and hold their puppets in front of them during drama time.

Most of these puppets require little time to assemble and little artistic talent to produce—and the results can be striking.

Some teachers who include puppet play among the options from which children can choose as they share stories keep a Stuff Sack in the classroom with ribbons, bows, twine, scraps of fabric, lengths of old yarn, paper bags, worn-out but clean socks and gloves, paper plates, buttons, and other odds and ends. Children contribute to the Stuff Sack and draw materials from it as they assemble puppets for story sharing. Sometimes children will be creative in the construction of their puppets, choosing materials not in the bag or using a design not attempted before.

Shadow puppets, which are part of the culture of Indonesia, can become a lively part of creative classroom dramatics as well. In Indonesia, puppets are made from hard leather in which tiny holes are punched to outline facial and body features. The puppets are held up behind a thin curtain, and a strong beam of light is shone from behind the puppets through the curtain. In a room that is otherwise darkened, the puppets appear as silhouettes that walk, lean over, and even raise their arms, since arms are attached to the body with clips and each arm is connected to a separate stick that is moved up and down to operate it. Upper-elementary pupils can construct a shadow puppet from heavy-grade cardboard, punch tiny light-passage holes in the manner of the traditional Indonesian puppet, and mount the puppet shape—which can be anything from a person to a tree or house—on a stick. For a stage, a good-sized piece of thin sheeting is suspended vertically. The light source is an overhead or slide projector.

Here are a few general suggestions for handling puppets:

- Don't involve too many puppets in a show; three or four are about all elementary students can manage.
- Help children in upper grades arrange cue cards to avoid memorizing lines. Suggest that they tape cue cards to the back edge of the table behind which puppeteers are performing or down the sides of a box or regular puppet stage. Remind students that notes on unattached pages will get disarranged during telling and cause confusion. Or designate a narrator who reads most of the lines; performers interject the words said by the puppets they are manipulating.

CONSIDER

The overhead projector can also be used to flash puppet shadows on a screen.

Informal dramatic performances should emphasize the pleasure of sharing stories and should involve children in a variety of creative storytelling strategies. *(© Jonathan A. Meyers)*

- Suggest that each child manipulate only one puppet so that he or she can effectively interpret the action through puppet motion. Talk about the messages sent through a nod and a shake of the head, the slump of the body, the tilt of the head, the way people walk. At some point, have all children take a puppet in hand to express feelings like tiredness, happiness, sadness, wide-awakeness, and anger.
- Help children play with their voices to express feelings vocally. Children can experiment with expressing fear, pleasure, fatigue, warmth, dislike. They can make their voices sound young or old, faraway or nearby, high or low pitched, loud or soft. They can produce story noises like growls, snarls, hoots, chuckles, groans. Sound is fundamental in puppet plays, so do some preparatory work in which students hold puppet heads they have made and experiment with different ways to vary voice pitch and loudness.

Choral Speaking: Let's Do a Poem Together . . .

The story-sharing and dramatic techniques just described can be adapted for sharing poems. Some stories are actually verses, especially picture storybooks such as those by Dr. Seuss. Dr. Seuss's *Green Eggs and Ham* and *The King's Stilts* are particularly suitable for class pantomime while a narrator reads the lines.

Choral speaking is another way to interpret poems. It is a group approach through which participants gain a feel for poetic sounds and relate oral interpretation techniques to the communication of meaning. Although most choral speaking is used with poetry, the techniques can be applied to prose selections.

Introducing Children to Choral Speaking

Speaking chorally, children, led by a conductor, recite the lines of a poem either together or in turn. In the lower grades, the piece is usually a short one that the teacher first recites to the class. Having heard the teacher recite it several times, the children join in. In the lower and middle grades, the piece may be printed as a chart: a Poetry Broadside. Still, the teacher must orally introduce the piece, perhaps pointing to the words while speaking. In the upper grades, the piece may be on a duplicated sheet or in a book that children have.

Choral-Speaking Roles   Because a class chorus resembles an orchestra, the role of conductor is pivotal. The conductor is responsible for establishing the rhythm, indicating when groups will contribute their parts, and keeping everyone together. For these reasons the teacher-conductor must speak clearly and lead the chorus with hand or arm. A drum helps maintain the beat; the conductor beats the drum with one hand and leads the chorus with the other.

After a time, a youngster assumes the role of Keeper of the Rhythm, striking the drum as the class choruses to the beat. Or the Keeper of the Rhythm converts a rhythm band stick into a baton and conducts with it. To choristers, a flick of the stick means "halt" and a point of the stick means "join in." After a time, some children will want to assume the role of Conductor of Chorus: The volunteer takes baton in hand to lead the class.

Another role that adds to the pleasure of choral speaking is Title Giver. Rather than having the entire class chorus the title and author of the piece, one chorister contributes it. Responding to a point of the stick, the Title Giver recites title and author. This is especially effective when the piece is by a class member; the young poet is reinforced by hearing not only the selection recited but his or her name as well.

Children as Orchestrators of Choral Speaking   Children should participate in the orchestration of choral-speaking selections. While working on a piece, students decide how they will chorus it—which lines to recite loudly or softly, smoothly or haltingly, with greater or lesser emphasis. By participating in these orchestrational decisions, children encounter fundamental elements of oral communication. They relate elements such as loudness/softness, short pause/long pause, high pitch/low pitch to meanings being communicated. They interpret punctuation vocally, pausing longer at a period stop than at a comma stop and longer at a semicolon stop than at a comma stop.

A popular piece for children to orchestrate together is Rose Fyleman's "Goblin," for its meaning is evident and the punctuation and italics are easy to translate vocally:

A Goblin

A goblin lives in our *house, in* our *house, in* our *house*
A goblin lives in our *house all the year round.*
He bumps
And he jumps
And he thumps
And he stumps.
He knocks
And he rocks
And he rattles at the locks.
A goblin lives in our *house, in* our *house, in* our *house.*
A goblin lives in our *house all the year round.*

One group decided to speak the beginning and ending sections in unison, stressing the word *our*. They decided too that it would be most effective if they spoke the first "all the year round" in a staccato whisper. They made the second reading of the refrain louder and louder to suggest that the goblin was getting closer and closer. This contrasted with the quiet of the last four words, "all the year round," which they again whispered.

The class decided that the short lines in the middle should be recited by individuals. The lines should be spoken quickly, with each child in the chain contributing promptly. To help the children do their parts, the conductor pointed from one to the next to keep the action going.

Different Ways to Chorus a Piece

As the previous example implies, it is possible to arrange a selection and choristers in a variety of ways. These are six formats for class chorusing.

Refrain In refrain choral speaking, the teacher reads or recites the main verse, and the children join in on the refrain. Poems with repetitive refrains lend themselves to this kind of choral speaking. A piece that works well is Robert Louis Stevenson's "The Wind" from *A Child's Garden of Verses*:

The Wind

I saw you toss the kites on high
And blow the birds about the sky;   } *lines spoken by*
And all around I heard you pass,   *a narrator*
Like ladies' skirts across the grass—
   O wind, a-blowing all day long,   } *lines recited by*
   O wind, that sings so loud a song!   *the choral group*

■ ● ● ●

CONSIDER

Rose Fyleman, *Picture Rhymes from Foreign Lands* (New York: J. B. Lippincott, 1935, 1963). Children can compose original versions by substituting sets of rhyming verbs—for example:

   He flips
   And he dips
   And he clips
   And he slips.
   He calls
   And he falls
   And he wanders in
   the halls.

> *O you that are so strong and cold,*
> *O blower, are you young or old?*
> *Are you a beast of field and tree,*
> *Or just a stronger child than me?*
>   *O wind, a-blowing all day long,*
>   *O wind, that sings so loud a song!*

} *lines spoken by*
a narrator

} *lines spoken by*
by the choral group

Children can also contribute the sound of the wind (*Swishhhhhhhh*) as the narrator reads the initial four lines of each stanza. Other poems that lend themselves nicely to refrain chorusing are David McCord's "Song of the Train," Laura Richards's "The Umbrella Brigade," Walter de la Mare's "Quack," Kate Greenaway's "Jump—Jump—Jump," and Margaret Wise Brown's "Little Black Bug."

Unison   A conductor can lead an entire class group in chorusing a piece. Especially with children in the lower primary grades, the selection initially should be short, probably no longer than the two to four lines of the refrains they have been contributing as part of refrain chorusing. Also, because children have trouble coordinating their voices, they should begin with a rhythmic poem such as this one:

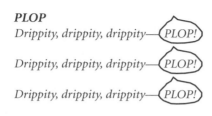

PLOP

Drippity, drippity, drippity— PLOP!

Drippity, drippity, drippity— PLOP!

Drippity, drippity, drippity— PLOP!

That's the song of a DROP.

Kindergarten and first-grade teachers recommend nursery rhymes such as "Pat-a-Cake" and "Pease Porridge Hot" for unison chorusing. Little rhymes such as Robert Louis Stevenson's "Rain" and "Time to Rise" also work well.

Older children can chorus more serious prose and poetry pieces in unison. For example, as part of a fifth- or sixth-grade social studies unit on the founding of their nation, students can chorus these lines from the Preamble to the Constitution:

> WE THE PEOPLE of the United States, in Order to form a more perfect Union, establish Justice, insure domestic Tranquility, provide for the common defense, promote the general Welfare, and secure the Blessings of Liberty to ourselves and our Posterity, do ordain and establish this Constitution for the United States. . . .

Within the same unit, upper-graders can chorus stanzas from Henry Wadsworth Longfellow's "Paul Revere's Ride" (which begins with the well-known lines: "Listen, my children, and you shall hear/Of the midnight ride of Paul Revere . . .") and Ralph Waldo Emerson's "Concord Hymn" (which contains the oft-quoted lines, "Here once the embattled farmers stood,/and fired the shot heard round the world.") Later, as upper-graders learn about more recent events in the history of their nation, they can chorus short segments from some of the powerful speeches and documents of the past: Abraham Lincoln's "Gettysburg Address," Martin Luther King's "I have a dream" speech, John F. Kennedy's inaugural address that contains the memorable

CONSIDER

For unison chorusing:
  Spring is showery,
    flowery, bowery;
  Summer is hoppy,
    croppy, poppy;
  Autumn is wheezy,
    sneezy, freezy;
  Winter is slippy,
    drippy, nippy.
  —Mother Goose

lines, "Ask not what your country can do for you. . . ," and the Preamble to the United Nations Charter. As students chorus such pieces, they begin to sense the beauty of language when it is handled with style.

Line-a-Child or Line-a-Group   A series of children or groups can, in turn, speak a line or two of poetry. Verse with short lines and distinct line endings lends itself to line-a-child chorusing in the lower grades.

For the older voice choir, more sophisticated pieces are appropriate. For example, junior and senior high school students often read "Cuccu Song" as part of their study of early English literature. Composed about 1250, the song goes like this:

Cuccu Song
Sumer is icumen in;
  Lhude sing cuccu!
Groweth sed, and bloweth med,
  And springeth the wude nu.
Sing Cuccu!

Cuccu, cuccu, well singest thu, cuccu:
  Ne Swike thu naver nu;
Sing cuccu, nu, sing cuccu,
  Sing cuccu, sing cuccu, nu!

Groups of choristers can recite lines that communicate meaning: "Sumer is icumen in," "Groweth sed, and bloweth med," "And springeth the wude nu." Another group recites lines that incorporate "Sing cuccu." As they chorus, upper-graders acquire a feel for the piece and an increased understanding of the meaning that the medieval poet was trying to communicate. At this stage too, students consider the punctuation and make their pause patterns reflect it.

Sound Groups   Dividing a class into students with high-pitched and low-pitched voices and having the contrasting groups speak different sections of a poem is a form of choral speaking sometimes termed *antiphonal*. For this, poems with segments that can be distinguished according to meaning and mood are appropriate.

One piece for two-voice interpretation is "If You Ever" (author unknown): One group choruses the lines that repeat "ever, ever, ever" and the other the lines that repeat "never, never, never."

If You Ever
If you ever ever ever ever ever } *first group*
  If you ever ever ever meet a whale
You must never never never never never } *second group*
  You must never never never touch its tail
For if you ever ever ever ever ever } *first group*
  If you ever ever ever touch its tail
You will never never never never never } *second group*
  You will never never meet another whale.

CONSIDER

For line-a-child chorusing, use John Ciardi, "The River Is a Piece of Sky"; Eve Merriam, "A Lazy Thought," "Mean Song," and "Conversation," in *There Is No Rhyme for Silver* (New York: Atheneum, 1962); Vachel Lindsay, "The Potatoes' Dance," *Collected Poems* (New York: Macmillan, 1925).

CONSIDER

For sound-group chorusing, use the following:
  Whisky, frisky,
  Hippity hop!
  Up he goes
  To the treetop!
  Whirly, twirly,
  round and round!
  Down he scampers
  To the ground.
  Furly, curly,
  What a tail!
  Tall as a feather,
  Broad as a sail!
  Where's his supper?
  In the shell,
  Snap, cracky,
  Out it fell.
    —Anonymous

Some of the poems of A. A. Milne can be chorused pleasurably in sound groups. "If I Were King" is good for two-sound interpretation, and "The Four Friends" works effectively with four sound groups, each group speaking the lines about one of the four friends. Both poems are in the classic *When We Were Very Young*.

Simultaneous Voices, or Rounds A variation on the group format is to have two groups speak different words at the same time. Paul Fleischman's *Joyful Noises: Poems for Two Voices* contains poems set up to be chorused in this way, as does his earlier *I Am Phoenix: Poems for Two Voices*. After chorusing Fleischman's poems about insects and birds, children can create and chorus poems for two, three, or even four voices.

Similarly, a main group can chorus the words of a poem while other groups simultaneously contribute repetitive chanting sounds. If each group joins the chorusing several seconds after the preceding group, the result is roundlike. To make rounds from poems, the teacher should select pieces with a steady rhythm, such as nursery rhymes. Starting with one like "Hey Diddle Diddle," teacher and students repeat it until all are familiar with the words and rhythm. They keep the beat through an even striking of a drum. Once children know the rhythm, one group repeats a simple but related chant such as "Moo, Moo. Moo, Moo." After the chanting group is in full swing, the rest speak the lines, maintaining the same beat as the chanters.

Body Chants and Finger Plays Children can add actions to their interpretations of many poems. Verses filled with action words are ideal for body chanting and chorusing. An old favorite is "Hickory, Dickory, Dock!":

Hickory, Dickory, Dock!
Hickory, dickory, dock!
The mouse ran up the clock.
The clock struck one.
The mouse ran down.
Hickory, dickory, dock!

As young children chorus the first two lines, they climb their hands upward in step-like increments. When chorusing the third line, they use their arms to strike one o'clock. On the last two lines, they make descending motions with their hands.

Not all students need contribute the same actions to a body chant. A class may identify several actions that fit the meaning and form into sections, with each section contributing a different action. For example, while interpreting "Hickory, Dickory, Dock," one section may decide to move heads left and right, a second to tick index fingers left and right, and a third to swing arms back and forth. Since members of each section must synchronize their motions, designate one member of each section as Concert Master. At a signal from the Conductor, the Concert Master of a section starts the motions; others in that section synchronize with the Concert Master.

Very young children in nursery school and kindergarten enjoy the action of finger plays. In finger plays, children speak or sing a short, rhymelike piece, simultaneously interpreting it with fingers and body. Through finger play, children come to enjoy the

CONSIDER

Hey diddle diddle!
The cat and the fiddle!
The cow jumped over the moon.
The little boy laughed to see such sport,
And the dish ran away with the spoon.

CONSIDER

Turn a simple verse like this into a poem for three voices by having one group repeat "tick tock" and another "tickety tock" as a third group choruses the rhyme.

CONSIDER

Sources of finger-play ideas are Sarah Hayes and Toni Goffe, *Clap Your Hands: Finger Rhymes* (New York: Lothrop, Lee & Shepard, 1988); Liz Cromwell and Dixie Hibner, *Finger Frolics* (Lavonia, Mich.: Partner Press, 1983); and Kay Cooper, *Too Many Rabbits and Other Fingerplays* (New York: Scholastic, 1995).

sounds and rhythms of poetry and increase their control over the fine muscles of their fingers. Also, some rhymes include number or directional concepts. As children interpret the numbers and directions with their fingers, they increase their understanding of number sequences, elementary addition and subtraction, and *left/right*, *up/down*, and *through/into*.

Traditional plays that you may recall from childhood are "Eensy-Weensy Spider," "I'm a Little Teapot," and "Where Is Thumbkin?" A teacher can also convert familiar poems into finger plays with the assistance of children. One young group created this play based on "It's Raining":

It's raining. It's pouring.	(Move hands up and down as fingers simulate rain.)
The old man's a-snoring.	(Make snoring noises.)
He went to bed	(Bend head to pretend sleep.)
And bumped his head	(Rub head.)
And couldn't get up in the morning.	(Bend head again to pretend sleep.)

Here are two newer pieces for finger and action play that reinforce understanding of number and spatial concepts (on successive repetitions of the first finger play, children substitute words like *rabbits*, *children*, *squirrels*, and so forth for *fingers*):

Climb and Hide

Fingers climb up ladders.	(Make fingers walk upward.)
They tumble down the slide.	(Make fingers slip downward.)
Fingers run quite quickly	(Run with the fingers.)
To find a place to hide.	(Put both hands behind back.)

Plop, Plop, Plop

One great, green frog sitting on a rock	(Stick the thumb of one hand through the fist of the other.)
Jumps into the water and makes a big plop.	(Dive the thumb off the hand that simulates the rock.)
Two great, green frogs sitting on a rock	(Stick two fingers of one hand through the fist of the other.)
Jump into the water and make a bigger plop.	(Dive the two fingers off the "rock" hand.)
Three great, green frogs sitting on a rock	(Stick three fingers through fist of the other.)
Jump into the water and make the biggest plop.	(Dive the three fingers off the hand that simulates the rock.)

Choral Speaking in the Language Arts Choral speaking fits into the overall language program in many ways. Children can chorus poems they have read and ones they have written, write pieces that pattern like the poems they have chorused, expand choral speaking into spontaneous dramatizations—and in the process make discoveries about writing style, punctuation, and sentence patterning. Not only can

READ

- Sonja Dunn, *Butterscotch Dreams* (Markham, Ontario: Pembroke, 1987).
- Joyce and Daniel McCauley, "Using Choral Speaking to Promote Language Learning for ESL Students," *The Reading Teacher*, 45 (March 1992), 526–533, for a discussion of choral speaking in English as a Second Language programs.

children interpret poetry through verse choirs, but they can also interpret prose selections. In the process, they begin to understand the repetitive patterns of prose.

Choral speaking also has a role in content-area study. As youngsters study different periods, places, and peoples, they can read and chorus related poetry. For example, Native American chants, songs of pioneers, railroaders, and canal builders, and laments for those lost in battle are appropriate for chorusing as part of the study of American history. Translations of Chinese nursery rhymes, African chants, and Old English verses are appropriate as part of the study of history and sociology. Through chorusing poetry, students get a better sense of the time, place, and people they are studying.

Should choral speaking be used for assembly programs and presentations? Many language authorities have suggested that to get children to speak a poem in perfect coordination is difficult and requires endless repetition, especially if children are to perform a lengthy piece in unison. Practicing the same selection over and over for a performance, however, causes children to lose interest. Although a short, simple choral-speaking selection may be included at times in an assembly program, chorusing has its value mainly as a learning, rather than performance, activity.

Conversations: Let's Talk Together About . . .

Dorothy Watson (1993) writes, "If the personalization of knowing and the socialization of learning are to become a way of life, it falls on teachers to create with their students a community in which meaning-making is their intention, and it can't be done without talk." As we learned in Chapter 3, children do little talking in some classrooms, which is a grave matter given that classroom talk serves so many vital purposes. In this section, we look at those purposes and then at some of the ways to organize our classrooms as talking-places.

The Purposes of Classroom Talk

READ

The December 1996 issue of *Language Arts;* its focus is oral language.

Purposes of classroom talk include the following:

- Advancing children's learning of the linguistic and social conventions of conversation.
- Advancing children's learning of content and ways of intellectually processing that content.
- Building the classroom into a community of learners.

Talking to Learn the Linguistic and Social Conventions of Conversation A primary purpose of classroom talk is to help children develop the language facility and interpersonal skills they must have to function effectively as conversationalists in the world at large—a basic goal of the language arts. More specifically, classroom talk can help children learn to select the appropriate words for communicating their ideas in social situations, to use sentence patterns in making their ideas easy to follow, and to shift from formal to informal language patterns depending on the situation. Classroom talk can provide children with opportunities to (1) follow the line of thought of previous speakers and comment in related terms, (2) put ideas together in a logical and clear way, (3) see the relationships between ideas being discussed and what they can contribute, (4) move a conversation forward by generalizing and summarizing, and (5) become aware of the needs of listeners and make "conversational repairs" when they know their listeners do not understand what they are saying (Piper, 1998). Furthermore, by talking together as they learn, children can acquire some of the social aspects of polite conversation: waiting their turn to comment and refraining from monopolizing a conversation, encouraging others to comment, courteously contributing with confidence and poise.

Talking to Learn and to Write: Content and Process   A second purpose of classroom talk relates to the learning of content and to the ability to think about content. Douglas Barnes (1993) explains that "learning is not a matter merely of adding new information" to what people already know. Rather, people modify, or reconstruct, what they know in light of "new experiences, new ideas, new ways of thinking and understanding" that they are encountering. This kind of reconstruction of knowledge is no simple task, especially when the new ideas to be accommodated are unfamiliar.

It is in this context that talk is essential to learning. Through talk, learners have opportunity to relate new ideas to their "existing expectations. And this takes time, for learning of any importance seldom happens in a moment." Learners must revisit material they are learning, "working upon understanding" and talking at it from a variety of vantage points, "each time reconstructing and extending some aspect of the topic." Barnes calls this kind of talk *exploratory.*

Distinguished Educator

Meet Dorothy J. Watson

Dorothy Watson is a professor at the University of Missouri-Columbia, where she teaches courses in reading. Watson is an advocate for whole language and is a believer in turning classrooms into "talking places." She explains that creating meaning is a "dynamic process of bringing forth personal knowing in a social place." In this context, productive classroom talk "encourages real questions, is informative and hesitant, is natural, and is a way of connecting ideas; it expands a learner's knowledge and allows each learner to emerge as a resource" ("Community Meaning: Personal Know-ing Within a Social Place," in *Cycles of Meaning,* ed. Kathryn Pierce and Carol Giles [Portsmouth, N.H.: Heinemann, 1993], 8–9).

DISCUSSION PROMPT

What purposes does talk serve in the elementary classroom, according to Watson? How do you react to a classroom in which children are talking vigorously to one another in small groups? To a classroom in which children are working silently on their own?

Working in groups or pairs, children refine their conversational skills as they build understanding of the content areas. (© *Elizabeth Crews*)

In classrooms, exploratory talk must be central. Barnes stresses that classrooms should be places where children talk about things that matter to them and to other children operating within the classroom community. For talk to be productive, that community must be supportive, and interaction must be based on the premise that what children already know is of value and worthy of expression. Only then will children become risk takers, try out ideas orally, and learn.

What Barnes calls "traditional forms of instruction, based primarily upon the teacher's presentation followed by question and answer and individual written tasks," will likely discourage students from making meaning through talk. Students wait for their teacher's questions and contribute only what they think he or she wants to hear. The talk that results is "unnatural," not at all like real conversation that takes place in social situations (Piper, 1998).

Talk is essential not only as an aid to children's growth in understanding of a topic, but also as a medium through which children develop thinking power. This is especially true as children pursue investigations in the content areas. Kathy Short and Junardi Armstrong (1993) have investigated the role of talk in classroom inquiry. They explain that it is through talk that children are introduced to ways of thinking about ideas "other than reciting facts and story details." As part of inquiry cycles, children use talk "to consider new perspectives, to build on the ideas of other

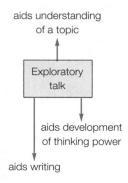

aids understanding
of a topic

Exploratory
talk

aids development
of thinking power

aids writing

students, to hypothesize and explore half-formed thoughts, to ask questions, to develop a focus." Through exploratory talk of this kind, children grow as thinkers.

Exploratory talk of the kind that Barnes, Short, and Armstrong describe is an aid to writing. Jean Dickinson, a fourth-grade teacher, tells about mornings in her classroom when children have come to school excited about something that has happened to them. She provides time for the children to share their "personal stories" with their classmates, who often show their appreciation through applause. Having orally shared, children come to appreciate their own stories and turn to writing to save them. As Dickinson (1993) summarizes, "Through talk, we support the writing of stories."

Stories children write, of course, go beyond the personal to encompass aspects of the curriculum. Students who have been talking exploratively about what life was like for early settlers on the American great plains, why a lighted candle goes out when a tumbler is placed on top of it, or how their bodies digest foods can write paragraphs of summary or explanation. Talk is a natural bridge into writing, especially when content to be written is a bit technical.

Talk That Builds the Classroom as a Community   A third purpose of talk in classrooms relates to the classroom community. As teacher Jean Dickinson (1993) reminds, "Through talk we build learning communities in our classrooms. . . . Talk is the means by which the students and I come to understand one another. It is through talk that we create a safe and secure learning environment conducive to risk taking." In Dickinson's classroom, read-alouds with multicultural picture books, chapter books, and poems and the talk used before and after contribute especially to a sense of community.

Judy Collier, a kindergarten teacher, uses classroom talk to support her young students as they work toward their learning goals. Talk provides encouragement—not the encouragement of indiscriminate praise but encouragement that focuses on students' efforts and on specific aspects of their endeavors. For example, Judy comments, "Mary and Layla, you two have been working on your book all morning! You have written a lot about the Stegosaurus. Will you read it to me when you're finished?"

Collier also uses talk as a means of conflict resolution in her classroom, an important factor in maintaining the kindergarten learning community. To this end, this teacher has two "Blue Chairs" that children occupy when they have an interpersonal problem to resolve. Sitting in those chairs and using guidelines their teacher has modeled, children talk out the conflict, thus ensuring the smooth running of the community (in Burke, 1993).

Ways to Bring Social and Curricular Conversations into Being

Conversations occur in a variety of places and contexts in classrooms. Some are conversations-in-passing, as when children and teacher chat in the playground and share their feelings about a game just played or when youngsters talk informally as they return from a class outing. Some spontaneous talk occurs in the classroom when the teacher discovers a child who is bubbling with excitement about something

WORD BANK

Exploratory talk

Grand conversations

Instructional conversations

Life-centered conversations

important to him or her. At times the teacher draws the child aside, and they chat together. At other times the teacher does what Dickinson does, gathering a group of youngsters so that the child can tell everyone. On still other occasions, when students have much to talk about, the teacher schedules a chat time so that friends can talk. Some teachers pair children for social conversations so that no one is left out; during conversation breaks, chatting pairs get together to talk. Other teachers identify a corner of the room as a conversation center, where two or three youngsters can meet for informal conversation.

Often conversation serves curricular purposes. This is true when children gather as a class or in small groups to explore ideas. Let us look next at these kinds of conversations.

GO TO
Pages 138-140 for a description of literary conversations.

Class Curricular Conversations Eeds and others (Eeds and Wells, 1989; Eeds and Peterson, 1991; Roller and Beed, 1994) use the term *grand conversations* to describe ongoing, story-based discussions in which teacher and students dialogue, with the teacher helping students to "extend and deepen their literary experience." When conversations become "grand," children direct their talk to what really matters to them in a story and how that has affected them. We considered this kind of conversation earlier, in Chapter 4. You may want to revisit that material.

Claude Goldenberg applies the term *instructional conversations* to comparable discussions that can occur as children learn across the curriculum (1992–1993; see also Barrentine, 1996). In Goldenberg's words, "Instructional conversations, or ICs, are discussion-based lessons geared toward creating richly textured opportunities for students' conceptual and linguistic development." ICs are instructional in that they promote learning, conversational in that they appear to be "natural and spontaneous"—free from the traditional teacher-asks-a-question, student-answers, teacher-accepts-or-rejects-answer pattern. More specific characteristics of this kind of freely flowing conversation are as follows:

Instructional Elements
1. A thematic focus—or big idea—threads through the conversation.
2. Children's existing knowledge is brought to bear as the theme unfolds.
3. Where necessary, the teacher teaches a skill or concept.
4. The teacher elicits extended contributions by inviting children to expand (e.g., "Tell me more about that"; "What do you mean by that?").
5. The teacher probes for supporting arguments or reasons.

Conversational Elements
1. Often discussion revolves around questions having no one correct answer.
2. The teacher (although having an initial game plan) is responsive to students' statements.
3. Utterances build one upon the other.
4. The teacher tries for a challenging but nonthreatening atmosphere.
5. The teacher encourages general participation and does not hold the "exclusive right" to determine who talks next (Goldenberg, 1992–1993).

CONSIDER
Other phrases encourage children to expand on their ideas: and so . . . , so what . . . , so then . . . , go on . . . , yes?

To facilitate instructional conversation, children circle their desks so that they make eye contact with one another, and they establish some simple guidelines for participation—unobtrusive ways that they can signal their desire to join in.

Kathy Short (1995) suggests a strategy to help children keep their attention focused during class conversations—the graffiti, or sounding, board. As they participate in a class conversation, two or three students share large pieces of chart paper on which they jot or sketch images or phrases that come to mind. When class discussion lags, sounding-board buddies meet briefly to explore the points they have scattered randomly on their sounding boards and web the points to highlight relationships. Talking buddy-to-buddy, students do some of these exploratory think-tasks: restating ideas to clarify them; summarizing points just made; devising questions to raise later; responding to questions previously raised; diagramming relationships in an original way; generalizing and concluding based on ideas presented so far; developing an opinion; or deciding on next steps.

An advantage of sounding-board buddies' meeting and talking briefly and periodically during instructional conversations is that when the class reconvenes, students can share the ideas they have explored with their buddies. "Quiet children, and especially quiet girls [who] often get overlooked," (Fredericksen, 2000) may now feel more confident and join in. Also, students in inclusive classrooms who have short attention spans get a change of pace. In instances where many children in the class suffer from restlessness and inability to attend for an extended period of time, teachers can swing back and forth between total class discussion and sounding-board buddy exchanges: Students discuss as a Committee-of-the-Whole for only five to ten minutes, then shift to converse on the same topic with a buddy or two for just a few minutes. This cycle repeats.

Small-Group Conversations About All Manner of Ideas   Instructional conversations as well as grand conversations occur not just as children talk in groups with the teacher serving as facilitator. These kinds of conversations—what I like to call *life-centered conversations*—occur also as children talk together in groups, on their own, about everyday matters and issues. D. Ray Reutzel and his colleagues describe conversations that occurred as part of one fifth grade's study of the Vietnam War. Having developed some knowledge of Vietnam through an introductory series of teacher-guided activities, the fifth-graders organized into groups of four or five. Together they read, explored through talk, taped their talk, responded to their taped talk, and crafted their talk as a "dialogical book" about Vietnam. The teacher circulated, assisting where necessary. As a result of their ongoing conversations, these fifth-graders came away with increased ability to interact orally to get a job done. They came away, too, with an in-depth understanding of the Vietnam War (Reutzel et al., 1995).

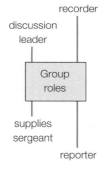

Conversations that result in this kind of learning do not just happen. Teachers must prepare students for small-group interaction. Mrs. Tyler, the teacher of the class that was studying the Vietnam War, prepared in several different ways. She showed her students how to use a researcher's notebook to gather information so that their conversations and writings would have substance. She had students role-play "being polite and taking turns in a conversation"—something that is vital if students are to work compatibly. She encouraged each group to elect a leader "who would facilitate the management concerns and conversations of the group." She made sure that during conversations, each participant had specific responsibility for some aspect of the topic.

Some teachers structure small-group activity in a more formal way, especially when students have had few prior experiences learning and talking together in groups. They provide questions to get children's small-group, life-centered discussions off the ground. Kathleen Berry (1985) did this as she involved upper-graders in a study of economic factors surrounding the early fur trade in Canada. She gave her students questions like those in Figure 6.2. Students used the questions as jumping-off points to explore definitional, historical, hypothetical, relational, and ethical aspects of the topic. Starting with the given questions, the students veered off into other areas that interested them.

Donna Alvermann (1991) recommends merging groups as a way to expand thinking during life-centered conversations. She suggests a think-pair-share format in which individuals think about what they want to say and then pair up to discuss their ideas with a partner. Partners then merge with another pair of students to explore their ideas further and work toward consensus. Finally, the two sets of partners decide on ideas to share during follow-up class discussion.

Reports: Let Me Tell You About . . .

Conversing is one dimension of speaking. A second dimension is reporting. Children need considerable support if they are to learn to present ideas in front of others in a clear, self-confident way, especially when those ideas are based on information reporters must gather systematically. In this section, we consider ways to help children develop oral presentational skills and ways to organize the class to facilitate reporting. Later, in Chapter 8, we look at study strategies (note taking and organizing) that are also important as students gather and prepare material for reporting.

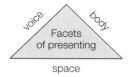

Tools for Reporting: The Voice, the Body, and Space

The voice plays a major role in holding listeners' attention. Good speakers change the speed of their voices, vary loudness, pitch their voices attractively, and avoid mannerisms that may affect listeners negatively.

Young people need to experiment with variations in speed, pitch, loudness, and tone. Probably the best way to experiment is to record an oral report on tape. This technique is especially good if the presentation is a team endeavor, for group members can listen to themselves in playback, assessing their vocal expression, the overall organization and clarity of their presentation, and their general knowledge of the topic.

Effective communication is as dependent on dynamic use of the body as it is on dynamic use of the voice. The use of visuals is one way to encourage appropriate gesturing and body movement in oral reporting. The student who uses a time line to show relationships will point to each entry on the line as he or she talks; the student who works from a map will point to locations on it; and the student who uses a picture he or she has painted will hold it up (see Figure 6.3). Pointing, moving toward, and holding up are all nonverbal communication devices necessary when using a visual. These gestures add action and force to a presentation.

If the school or community owns a camcorder, it can be used to videotape presentations for self-study. Each student views his or her contribution to a program and evaluates it in terms of such questions as, Did I make eye contact with my audience? Did I gesture automatically? Did I change my facial expressions as required? In viewing a videotape, young people often can spot their own problems and without prompting improve on them during future reporting sessions.

Definitional Questions

- What does *exploration* mean?
- What does *discovery* mean?

Hypothetical Questions Requiring Projections and Guesses

- Why was fur trading especially important in Canada?
- Do you think that fur trading would have been as important in the American Southwest as it was in Canada? Why? Why not?
- Why were furs important then?
- For what were they most likely used?
- Do you think furs were considered of more value then than they are today? Why? Why not?
- Why do you think people back then wore fur garments?
- Why do they wear them today?

Background Information Questions

- Who were the people important in the fur trade?
- What methods did the fur traders use to get furs?
- What means did they have to trade their furs?
- How was the fur trade organized?
- Where and when in Canada was fur trading important?

Questions to Encourage In-depth Curricular Discussions

Relational Questions

- What is the relationship between the price of furs and the cost of production?
- What is the relationship between the price of furs and people's desire for them?
- At what point would you say that prices are too high?
- What examples from your own life can you relate to the pricing of goods?

Ethical Questions

- Is it morally right to kill animals for their skins to use in making clothing? Why? Why not?
- Do you think that it was "more right" to do that back in early Canadian days than it is today?
- Do you think that it is "more right" to do it today? Why? Why not?

Figure 6.2
Kinds of Questions to Encourage Content-Area Conversations

DISCUSSION PROMPT

- How do these questions connect to what you know about Bloom's taxonomy?

Figure 6.3
Children's Art: A Means of Making a Report More Dramatic
Source: Courtesy of Ndungu Muthegu, age 11, Nairobi, Kenya

Arranging a classroom to facilitate communication invites forceful student presentations. This means that a presenter need not share by standing alone in front of the class; rather, he or she selects a comfortable position that fits the message. Perching on a high stool, sitting on a swivel chair, standing next to a projector are possible positions. Listeners may sit in groups or in a circle, on the floor or in chairs as the situation requires.

Settings for Reporting

Major formats for reporting include the small feedback group, the panel, and the individual report. By functioning in a variety of settings in a relaxed classroom environment, children anticipate sharing rather than fear it and gain poise in reporting to others.

The Small Feedback Group   Too often teachers think of oral reporting as a whole-class activity in which one or two youngsters speak to the class. This setting, however, may be the least productive. A much more productive setting is a small *feedback group* in which listeners can more easily ask questions.

One way to organize the class for reporting is the Idea Fair. Here one or two reporters share with a group of between four and ten students. In this organizational pattern, several reporters function simultaneously and must repeat their presentations as listening groups move through the Idea Fair. A variation of the Idea Fair is to have a team of reporters set up in a corner of the classroom. As two or three students complete an assignment, they visit the Idea Corner to listen to the team describe its findings. Eventually all students hear the presentation.

Three advantages accrue from this organizational pattern:

- Students must repeat their reports, and in so doing they refine their presentations.
- Listeners in small groups are more willing to render verbal feedback. Similarly, reporters are more at ease when presenting to smaller groups.
- Because each group may have heard a slightly different presentation, the whole-class discussion that follows revolving-group reports is more likely to serve a summarizing function.

Technology Notes

Check out these computer applications as they relate to children's oral reporting and storytelling:

- *Presentation Programs Such as PowerPoint.* Programs for preparing slides to display with a computer and a liquid crystal display projector during oral presentations result in professionally styled visuals to integrate into an oral (or written) report.
- *Clip Art Programs.* These programs provide a ready source of art to include in presentation or storytelling slides.
- *Camcorders and Digital Cameras.* Students who are studying their communities, social phenomena, land forms, and life forms can produce their own videos and photographs to share as they talk about important ideas. They can project videos and computer-edited movies as part of their oral presentations, especially presentations that relate to the social and natural sciences.
- *Scanners.* Students can transfer illustrations into a computer from various sources to use in storytelling and reporting.
- *LCD (Liquid Crystal Display) Projectors.* Students can display visuals during presentations using LCD Projectors in conjunction with an overhead projector.
- *"Smart" Classrooms.* Classrooms that are equipped with computers and display cameras make it convenient for students and teacher to project all kinds of visual and oral materials.

CONSIDER

The panel presentation format works especially well in content-area studies.

The Panel Presentation   During a *panel* presentation, each reporter presents information on one aspect of a larger topic. In some instances, after reporting, panelists discuss points developed during the reporting phase; listeners pose questions and offer opinions.

One advantage of the investigative-reporting-team approach is that young people must work together to select information and organize their reports. Cooperating, they acquire small-group interaction as well as search skills. A second advantage is that several students investigating a topic must subdivide it into smaller segments, so that each member can focus on one segment. In so doing, young people learn to identify manageable subdivisions. Third, students have an opportunity to try out on their classmates' ideas about content and ways of presenting that content visually. Others supply feedback, so that final presentations are forceful and interesting. Fourth, students presenting as part of a panel support one another; no one stands alone.

Younger students serving on a panel can share books they have read. A panelist simply retells an episode, and the audience contributes questions. Similarly, younger students can sit as a panel to share their impressions of a common experience—an exciting event witnessed, a TV program viewed, a trip taken together. At first, a teacher moderates panel presentations in primary classes so that children develop an understanding of the moderator's role in introducing the topic and the panelists, calling on questioners, and thanking panelists. Shortly, students assume the role of moderator, modeling their activity after the teacher's.

The Individual Report   As a format for sharing, the *individual report* has wide applicability at all grade levels. One form of reporting is the announcement, in which a child very briefly, and with little preparation, tells about a coming event. At the opposite end of the continuum is the investigative report, in which a student shares information acquired through considerable study. Show-and-tell is another form of individual reporting, as is the monologue, in which a youngster assumes the identity of a personality of the past, the present, or fiction and explains happenings from that person's point of view. Children doing monologues may don simple costumes to get a feel for the people whose identity they are assuming. For example, a pair of glasses pulled down on the nose can turn a reporter into a Benjamin Franklin who shares his thoughts on the Revolutionary War. An old oil lamp held in hand transforms another monologist into a Florence Nightingale who tells of the Crimean War. Similarly, a monologist may assume the identity of a favorite author. The monologist tells events in the author's life and ways those events influenced his or her writing.

Assessing Children's Growth as Oral Language Users

It is important to be able to share a story or poem expressively, converse naturally, and report clearly in this world of ours, for ultimately most social interaction is oral.

The person who has control over the various forms of oral expression has a "foot up" over those who are less sure of themselves. Elementary language arts must give young people this "foot up." To do this, teachers must truly become "kidwatchers," assessing children's development on a continuous basis.

Assessment Guidelines: Oral Expression

In assessing children's growth in oral communication, teachers should design programs with three major characteristics:

1. Children should be involved in the assessment. They should apply clearly stated criteria to the evaluation of their own activities and later discuss their self-assessments with the teacher who supplies feedback one-on-one and offers suggestions for improvement.
2. Fear of failure should be minimized. A teacher should put youngsters at ease by establishing an informal, nonevaluative atmosphere. External evaluation in front of the group should be avoided. Asking listeners to criticize a presentation strips the pleasure from reporting and introduces fear. Keeping a marking book open and writing down a grade at the close of a report adds uneasiness.
3. Assessment should be in terms of a number of behaviors. Teachers and students can identify specific learnings to be acquired and help children assess themselves with respect to those learnings. In this way, youngsters can identify strengths as well as weaknesses.

Using Performance Checklists to Assess Growth

Performance checklists are lists of basic learnings to be acquired. Because learnings are stated rather precisely as observable behaviors, they make self-analysis a relatively easy process. For example, a learning that might appear on a performance checklist of oral language skills is, "I comment in terms of what others have said."

In assessing their progress in reference to such a statement, students may use categories such as Very Often, Often, Sometimes, Never; or Very Easy Task for Me, Easy Task for Me, Hard Task for Me. For each learning, the self-evaluator checks the appropriate category. Or students may rank-order a number of learnings from one requiring the most improvement to one requiring the least. This forces youngsters who tend to evaluate themselves positively in all areas of their performance to identify areas that need work.

Figure 6.4 provides a checklist for upper-elementary students and summarizes the learnings in this chapter. Of course, a teacher must modify the list to meet the needs of his or her students and the curriculum. Students complete a series of checklists over time and keep them in their showcase portfolios along with other work products that indicate growth. Periodically the teacher also uses the checklist to assess children's oral expression. At the end of a marking period, teacher and student talk about the checklists and work products and set goals for the coming months.

A CHECKLIST FOR ORAL EXPRESSION			
Specific Learnings	**The Rating Scale**		
	Always	Some-times	Never
A. EXPRESSING STORIES AND POEMS			
1. I speak clearly when I share stories and poems.			
2. I use my voice, face, and body expressively in sharing.			
3. I use props naturally as part of storytelling.			
B. SPEAKING WITH OTHERS			
1. I speak clearly when I converse.			
2. I choose appropriate words to communicate my ideas.			
3. I make my comment relate to what others have said.			
4. I contribute ideas that interest others. I avoid boring others.			
5. I wait my turn and do not interrupt.			
6. I do not "hog" the discussion.			
7. I am confident when I contribute.			
8. I am courteous in speaking with others.			
C. SPEAKING IN FRONT OF OTHERS			
1. I speak clearly when I report.			
2. I make eye contact with my listeners.			
3. I gesture and move smoothly.			
4. I use visuals effectively.			

WHAT I CAN DO TO BECOME A BETTER SPEAKER:

Name of student _____ Date of self-evaluation _____

Date of teacher/student conference _____

Figure 6.4
A Self-Evaluation Checklist for Assessing Oral Expression

A Summary Thought or Two

Oral Expression

The major point of Chapter 6 is that classrooms should be talking-places in which children listen to and tell stories; participate in spontaneous dramas, Readers' Theatre, pantomimes, drama festivals, and puppet plays; and join in to chorus the best of poems and stories. In classroom talking-places, children converse for a variety of reasons and in the process heighten their ability to use language to communicate, to think, and to learn. Conversation helps to build the classroom as a community of learners in which youngsters function courteously with one another. In classroom talking-places, children at times present their ideas more formally. As they report, they learn to use their faces, their bodies, visuals, and space as part of their message; and they become more comfortable sharing their ideas in different ways—in small feedback groups, panel presentations, and individual reports.

All these talking-place activities occur across the curriculum. During literature-based units, children dramatize and tell stories, "do" poems together, converse, and report. They converse, dramatize, and report in relation to social studies and science, art and music, health and mathematics. They do these things as they read and as they write. Oral language activity is the integrating thread in elementary school learning—something we will think more about in the next chapter.

Your Language Arts Portfolio

- Prepage a minidrama for presentation to a group of your peers. Use a creative approach. Perhaps develop an original script. For example, become Pippi Longstocking replete with braids and freckles and talk about "yourself" and "your" adventures. Or working with a friend, you "become" a story character such as Bud, Not Buddy while your friend "becomes" Maniac Magee; "you" compare "your" lives. Write a brief summary of what you did and how you felt doing it.

- Develop a series of instructional questions based on a topic in the manner of the questions in Figure 6.2 on page 218. Be sure to develop questions that fall into these categories:

  1. Definitional questions.

  2. Background information questions.

  3. Hypothetical questions requiring projections and guesses.

  4. Relational questions.

  5. Ethical questions.

- Experiment with computer-based presentational software such as PowerPoint. Develop visuals using the software so you become efficient at producing computer materials.

Related Readings

Booth, David, and **Carol Thornley-Hall,** eds. *The Talk Curriculum.* Portsmouth, N.H.: Heinemann, 1992.

Combs, Martha, and **John Beach.** "Stories and Storytelling: Personalizing the Social Studies." *The Reading Teacher,* 47 (March 1994), 464–471.

Cooper, Pamela, and **Rives Collins.** *Look What Happened to Frog: Storytelling in Education.* Scottsdale, Ariz.: Gorsuch Scarisbrick, 1991.

Cottrell, June. *Creative Drama in the Classroom: Grades 1–3.* Lincolnwood, Ill.: National Textbook, 1987.

———. *Creative Drama in the Classroom: Grades 4–6.* Lincolnwood, Ill: National Textbook, 1987.

Dudley-Marling, Curtis, and **Dennis Searle.** *When Students Have Time to Talk: Creating Contexts for Learning Language.* Portsmouth, N.H.: Heinemann, 1991.

Dwyer, John. *A Sea of Talk.* Portsmouth, N.H.: Heinemann, 1991.

Flynn, Rosalind, and **Gail Carr.** "Exploring Classroom Literature Through Drama." *Language Arts,* 71 (January 1994), 38–43.

Fredericksen, Elaine. "Muted Colors: Gender and Classroom Silence." *Language Arts,* 77 (March 2000), 301–308.

Gambrell, Linda, and **Janice Almasi,** eds. *Lively Discussions! Creating Classroom Cultures that Foster Interpretation and Comprehension.* Newark, Del.: International Reading Association, 1996.

Gillard, Marni. *Storyteller, Storyteacher: Discovering the Power of Storytelling for Teaching and Living.* York, Me.: Stenhouse Publishers, 1995.

Heathcote, Dorothy. *Drama as Context.* Aberdeen: National Association for the Teaching of English, 1980.

———. "Drama as a Learning Medium." *Language Arts,* 65 (January 1988). This issue focuses on drama and learning.

Heinig, Ruth. *Improvisations with Favorite Tales: Integrating Drama into the Reading/Writing Classroom.* Portsmouth, N.H.: Heinemann, 1992.

Hill, Bonnie, Nancy Johnson, and **Catherine Noe.** *Literature Circles and Response.* Norwood, Mass.: Christopher-Gordon Publishers, 1995.

King, Nancy. *Storymaking and Drama.* Portsmouth, N.H.: Heinemann, 1993.

Martinez, Miriam. "Motivating Dramatic Story Reenactments." *The Reading Teacher,* 46 (May 1993), 682–688.

McCaslin, Nellie. *Creative Drama in the Classroom.* 5th ed. White Plains, N.Y.: Longman, 1990.

McMaster, Jennifer. "'Doing' Literature: Using Drama to Build Literacy Classrooms." *The Reading Teacher,* 51 (April 1998), 574–584.

Morado, Carolyn, Rosalie Koenig, and **Alice Wilson.** "Miniperformances, Many Stars! Playing with Stories." *The Reading Teacher,* 53 (October 1999), 116–123.

Paratore, Jeanne, and **Rachel McCormack,** eds. *Peer Talk in the Classroom: Learning from Research.* Newark, Del.: International Reading Association, 1997.

Pierce, Kathryn, and **Carol Giles,** eds. *Cycles of Meaning.* Portsmouth, N.H.: Heinemann, 1993.

Ralston, Marion. *An Exchange of Gifts: A Storyteller's Handbook.* Markham, Ontario: Pippin Publishing, 1993.

Roe, Betty, Suellen Alfred, and Sandy Smith. *Teaching Through Stories: Yours, Mine, and Theirs.* Norwood, Mass.: Christopher-Gordon, 1998.

Schneider, Jenifer, and Sylvia Jackson. "Process Drama: A Special Space and Place for Writing." *The Reading Teacher,* 54 (September 2000).

School Talk. (August 1995). The theme of the issue is "Key Principles in Language Learning: Talk, Text in Context, Role Playing, Collaboration, and Drama." *School Talk* is a publication of National Council of Teachers of English.

Smith, Patricia, ed. *Talking Classrooms: Shaping Children's Learning Through Oral Language Instruction.* Newark, Del.: International Reading Association, 2001.

Stewig, John, and Carol Buege. *Dramatizing Literature in Whole Language Classrooms.* 2nd ed. New York: Teachers College Press, 1994.

Wagner, Betty Jane. *Educational Drama and Language Arts: What Research Shows.* Westport, Conn.: Heinemann, 1998.

Wilhelm, Jeffrey, and Brian Edmiston. *Imagining to Learn: Inquiry, Ethics, and Integration Through Drama.* Westport, Conn.: Heinemann, 1998.

Young, Terrell, and Sylvia Vardell. "Weaving Readers' Theatre and Nonfiction into the Curriculum." *The Reading Teacher,* 46 (February 1993), 396–406.

CHAPTER 7

Oral Language as a Bridge into Literacy and Higher-Order Thought

The Integrated Language Arts

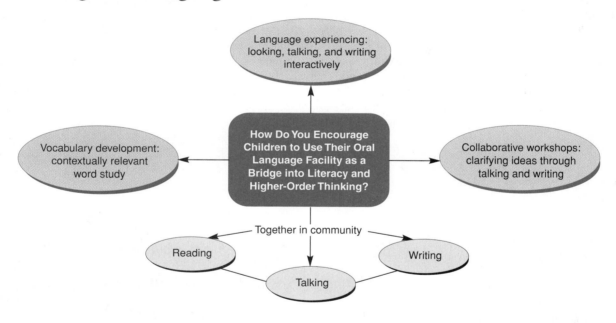

Language experiencing: looking, talking, and writing interactively

How Do You Encourage Children to Use Their Oral Language Facility as a Bridge into Literacy and Higher-Order Thinking?

Vocabulary development: contextually relevant word study

Collaborative workshops: clarifying ideas through talking and writing

Together in community

Reading

Talking

Writing

Language Experiencing in Action

Billy Goat

It was spring, and Karen Donovan's first-graders were learning about farms. They were listening to and reading lots of books about farms and talking about farm life. As part of their integrated language arts, science, and social studies unit, the class visited a farm. Spying cows, pigs, horses, chickens, and goats, the first-graders bubbled with joy. Jumping and pointing, the children exclaimed, "Look at the goat. It's on the roof of the house!" "Look at the chickens. They are fighting!"

Excitement ran high as the children returned to their city school. Without prompting, the first-graders talked about things they had seen, described animals they liked, and proffered their opinions. There was much joyful, spontaneous talk, starting with, "Did you see . . . ?" as the children asked others if they had noticed this or that.

Talking and Writing Together

Back in the classroom, Ms. Donovan clustered her first-graders around the recording easel, on which she had mounted a piece of chart paper. "Let's write about the animals we liked best. We'll start by listing the animals we like and the reasons we liked them."

As the youngsters excitedly called out animal names and offered reasons for their choices, the teacher recorded their ideas as a two-column table on the chart paper. Next, she asked Chen-li to select the animal he liked best. He chose "The Brown and Black Horse." Other children who also chose the horse raised their hands. The youngsters did this for each animal, in the process registering their preferences for the best-liked animal. The winner was Billy Goat. Most of the children had been fascinated by the way Billy sat on the roof of his house. Furthermore, this was the first time many of these urban youngsters had seen a goat.

Before composing, the children talked about the goat; most contributed an idea to the brief discussion. Then six children volunteered their reasons for choosing Billy. Each child dictated a sentence, as the teacher recorded it on the chart paper with children assisting at key points. Some helped by inscribing the word *He* at sentence beginnings; others added the sentence-ending periods.

> **Billy**
>
> The billy goat is cute. He has a long beard. His legs are long and skinny. He has a big belly. He looks funny sitting on the roof of his house. He might get hurt if the roof didn't have those bumps.

When Ms. Donovan had printed the experience-story chart, she read it aloud with the children and asked them for a title that would sum it up. They volunteered suggestions, which she listed; then they gave reasons to support the titles they liked best. After much reflection and discussion, the youngsters chose "Billy." One youngster came forward to inscribe the letters of Billy's name at the top as Ms. Donovan and the other students stretched out the sounds and helped by suggesting letters to represent these sounds.

[margin notes:]

Express an opinion supported with reasons—simple critical thinking; arrive at consensus through listening and voting

Summarize a judgment

Title a composition based on the main idea

The teacher encouraged the children to reread the story. Youngsters took turns coming to the easel to read aloud each sentence and pointed to the words as they read. Sensing a teachable moment, Ms. Donovan also wrote the contraction from the story—*didn't*—on the section of the classroom Word Wall titled "Word Connections." She asked, "What two words make up *didn't?*" One first-grader offered *did not*, which the teacher printed on the Word Wall next to the word *didn't*. She showed them how *didn't* was formed from *did not* by combining the two and using the apostrophe to take the place of the letter *o* in *not*. Under *didn't*, she recorded *isn't* and asked students to figure out the two words that *isn't* comes from. She recorded *is not* next to *isn't* on the Word Wall and began to use *contraction* in a natural way to talk about this kind of word. See Figure 7.1 for the Word Wall listing that resulted from this mini-lesson that Ms. Donovan interjected briefly into the ongoing language experience sequence.

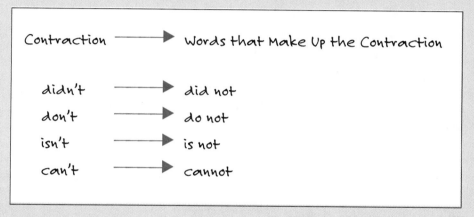

Figure 7.1
A Word Wall Listing: Contractions

Writing and Dictating Individually

The next day, as the children worked on a variety of personal writing activities, Ms. Donovan and an aide conferred with individual children, talking and writing about other animals they had seen. For example, Chen-li, a gifted child who was hesitant about writing down his ideas because his native language was not English, dictated lines about his favorite horse. The aide recorded them on lined paper pasted on one side of a large piece of construction paper, helping him when he ran into trouble finding the English word to express what he wanted to say and cluing him in to a point or two about how English sounds are represented on paper. Chen-li read his own words back to the aide, again finger-pointing the words. Later Chen-li drew the brown-and-black horse, added more ideas to the story, and read it to his classmates, who applauded his offering.

Meanwhile, on their own, other youngsters wrote about their favorite animals, giving reasons for their choices. In writing, these students used invented spelling—a combination of print, numbers, and pictures to get their ideas on paper. They had been told to use whatever symbols they knew to hold their thoughts on paper so that they could share the ideas later. The teacher also conferred with these youngsters, encouraging them to reflect more critically on why they liked the animals they had chosen to write about.

When each child had completed a page by dictating or writing and had orally shared his or her work, the teacher published the papers by posting them around the perimeter of a bulletin board captioned "Animals We Saw and Liked." In the center, she mounted the large story chart about Billy Goat, to which the children attached a blue ribbon.

What Was Happening: Instructional Strategies in Action

Had you gone along with Ms. Donovan and her first-graders on their trip and visited their classroom on their return, you would have seen children actively talking and writing together about things they had just experienced. You would have seen children using oral language as a bridge into and between writing and reading. You would have seen children developing vocabulary and language skills at a point when they needed them to speak and write.

To encourage her first-graders to become more aware of things around them, think and write in response, and grow simultaneously in language facility and understanding, this teacher was relying on time-proven instructional strategies. These strategies arise out of the language experience approach of the 1970s, whole language beliefs that surfaced more recently, and the word study movement of the 1990s and 2000s. Among the strategies, which are as valuable in the upper-elementary grades as they are at the primary level, are the following:

■ Full-class language experiences to which children respond by talking together and contributing to teacher-guided group writing.
■ Mini-lessons in which children focus on particular words as those words surface during talk time.
■ Collaborative workshops in which students think critically as they react to a shared experience and write interactively in response.

During full-class language experiences, mini-lessons, and collaborative workshops, students talk and write together, functioning as communities of learners and using oral language as a vehicle for reacting to their firsthand and literature-based experiences. As a result of this integrated approach to the language arts, children come away with an expanded vocabulary and greater control over both oral and written language. In Chapter 7 you will consider these three components of an integrated approach to the language arts—an approach in which oral language activity serves as a bridge into literacy and higher-order thought.

Language Experiencing: Looking, Talking, and Writing Interactively

■ ● ● ●

READ

- David Whitin and Phyllis Whitin, "Inquiry at the Window: The Year of the Birds," *Language Arts,* 73 (February 1996), 82–87.

- David Whitin and Phyllis Whitin, "Learning Is Born of Doubting: Cultivating a Skeptical Stance," *Language Arts,* 76 (November 1998), 123–129. The Whitins remind us that "inquiry begins with looking closely," and "learning is born of doubting."

■ ● ● ●

CONSIDER

Plato once wrote, "The mark of the true philosopher is the capacity for wonder."

n *The Art of Teaching Writing,* Lucy Calkins (1994) talks about the value of living with a sense of awareness, of "pausing to look" more deeply at things that many people simply overlook. She tells how grateful she is for special moments in her life—moments spent in mountain meadows full of wildflowers, on moonlit ski trails, and by cascading waterfalls. She tells how grateful she is for the laughter in her home, and the sense of adventure that fills it. These moments of awareness and the feeling she has about living are what make her the person and *the writer* she is.

Language arts educators must provide children with experiences that awaken them to the world around, observe with a "wondering eye," and feel deeply about things and events in their lives (Whitin and Whitin, 1996). Language arts teachers must do this if children are to read and write with the intensity of spirit that carries them beneath the surface of an experience to create personal meanings. That, after all, is the purpose of literacy instruction.

To accomplish this, teachers must tap into the excitement of childhood and encourage it, as Karen Donovan was doing with her first-graders during their farm visit. They must encourage students to talk about what they are experiencing and feeling. And ultimately, teachers must inscribe for and with children as they craft stories orally together, encouraging children to read over and over again what they have composed interactively. Let us look at ways to accomplish this.

Walkabouts, Community Adventures, and Projects That Elicit Talk

Walk with children outside. Look. Touch. Listen. Laugh together, as the city children in Ms. Donovan's class did on their visit to the farm. Then talk. Just a brief time spent outdoors can conjure up wondrous words and impressions.

For example, on a day when the first snow of the year covers the ground, youngsters can go outside to make footprints in the snow, shake snow from branches, and draw pictures in the snow with a twig. To build anticipation before children venture forth, a teacher may share Ezra Jack Keat's *The Snowy Day.* Returning to the warmth of their classroom, children are eager to talk. On other occasions, children can walk through woods or parks filled with crisp leaves, across dry desert sands, or by a brook that is home to water striders and mayfly larvae. Youngsters may pause to talk about whatever nature is offering that day—birds, a lizard, a turtle.

In urban areas, a walkabout offers different experiences that lead to heightened awareness. As sidewalk engineers, children can "direct" construction at a local building site, experiencing the thrill of watching a worker stride across a beam stretched over empty space. Will the worker stumble? Children hold their breath as they watch and let out their breath with relief as the worker reaches the other side. Or children

Firsthand experiences outside can invite children to "pause and look." Such moments can provide the content for thinking, talking, and writing together. *(© James Carroll)*

can pause and listen to the sounds of their city, covering their eyes to focus on the sounds around them.

Youngsters can venture farther to visit places of interest in their community—for example:

- Shops in the community, particularly a bakery, bank, pet shop, or barber shop.
- Buildings, such as the local courthouse, police station, firehouse, or library.
- Industrial parks and shopping complexes. On the school bus, youngsters drive through these areas, stopping from time to time to focus on particular sights and talk.

Community adventures such as these are as appropriate with middle-grade students as they are with younger ones, especially if those adventures are accompanied by the jotting down of impressions. Elementary students can keep Writing Notebooks, small idea books in which they note things they pause to look at on the way to school, in the playground, in their classroom, and on class adventures. These impressions are thoughts that Calkins (1994) says are too great to be forgotten. They are the "bits and pieces" of youngsters' lives, embryonic ideas that "may or may not emerge someday as major pieces of writing," but they do give young writers a start.

That start can also come from classroom experiences. In one kindergarten class, Fluffy, a well-loved guinea pig, is a popular resident. Each week, a kindergartner assumes responsibility for feeding and observing Fluffy. Each week, children gather to talk about Fluffy's reaction to food, her appearance, and her activity during the week. In another class, Yellow Back, a box turtle, roams freely and competes for space with two-legged residents. Groups of children take turns observing Yellow Back and recording notes in their Science Logs.

Beginning in second grade, cross-curricular observational and investigative projects can open children's eyes to the wonders of the world. Students can plant evergreen or palm seedlings, tend to them, make periodic observations, and record findings in their Science Logs. Similarly, they can make periodic weather observations, conduct discovery-type science investigations, and make sociological number counts (the number of students who use school facilities during different hours of the school day). These kinds of projects encourage children to stop, observe, and ultimately analyze. If children then talk about their observations and findings and read in related references, they are building a storehouse of ideas for writing.

Teacher-Guided Group Writing: Experience Stories, Shared Writing, and Interactive Writing

READ

Sylvia Ashton-Warner, *Teacher* (New York: Simon & Schuster, 1963), for a discussion of oral composition as a basis for reading and writing. It is an education classic.

Having observed and having talked about what they have seen and found, the students can compose an experience story as a class. In experience story writing, the children suggest ideas, which the teacher inscribes for them on chart paper. The students watch as the teacher records the letters and words of the sentences they are dictating. For example, on Friday in Fluffy's kindergarten, students gather on their big red rug to dictate their weekly report: "February 5: This week Fluffy did not move around much. She just sat in the corner. Fluffy was very tired." As their teacher records, one child volunteers to take the marker and make the letters in Fluffy's name, a name she has learned to spell because it has appeared in the weekly report on so many prior occasions. Another child volunteers to record the number 5. Having dictated their observational report, the children reread it in choral style; they follow along as their teacher points to the syllables and words with a Magic Reading Wand. They take turns leading the choral reading. Sometimes one child volunteers to read a sentence. Sometimes, too, the teacher takes advantage of the linguistic characteristics of the language experience chart to teach or reinforce an understanding about how words work on paper. You saw Ms. Donovan do this through her mini-lesson on contractions.

Language Experience Approach   Russell Stauffer (1979) is credited with conceptualizing what has been called the *language experience approach* (LEA) in which young children experience, talk, dictate related ideas, and then reread what they have composed together. Stauffer explained that by composing group language experience charts and then rereading their dictated stories several times, children would gradually and naturally come to recognize the letters of their language and would develop a sight vocabulary of words they could read. Stauffer also proposed that teachers take dictation from individual children; in rereading their personalized stories, children would find reading to be a meaningful and exciting endeavor.

In proposing the language experience approach, Stauffer was rebelling against the stifling use of workbook pages and uninteresting basal reader stories as the one way to introduce young children to reading. In 1973, Van Allen summarized the philosophy behind the approach in this way:

- What I can think about, I can talk about.
- What I can say, I can write—or someone can write for me.
- What I can write, I can read.
- I can read what I write, and what other people can write for me to read (in Burns, Roe, and Ross, 1999).

Shared and Interactive Writing   More recently, teacher-guided group writing has evolved into what today is popularly known as *shared writing*. In shared writing, just as in the language experience approach, students dictate sentences and their teacher records them; then children read and reread what they have crafted. We can note a few differences, however, between the earlier language experience approach and today's more focused shared writing activity.

One major difference is that advocates of shared writing more definitively emphasize the value of using teacher-guided group writing not only as a follow-up to direct experiences but also in the context of listening and story reading. These teachers may read a story to their children and follow the read-aloud with talk and shared writing. Writing together with their teacher, children may retell key events in sequence from the story, tell their favorite parts, or suggest an alternate ending. At other times, teachers may ask students to use the pictures to predict what will happen in a story, print the students' predictions on a chart, and then ask students to read to verify what they have predicted.

A second difference is that adherents of language experience often asked their young charges to copy the story charts as a way to teach sight words. You will still see

WORD BANK

The LEA Sequence:
Experience
Talk
Dictate
Reread

WORD BANK

Shared writing
Interactive writing

some teachers asking students to copy the stories they have written together, but most advocates of shared writing object strongly to copying activities. As follow-up, these teachers prefer that youngsters create related stories using whatever they already know about writing; these teachers encourage very young students to use a combination of pictures, symbols, and letters to "hold" their story ideas on paper.

Third, advocates of shared writing propose that teachers record children's dictated sentences in paragraph form, indenting the first word of the first sentence and using the words *sentence* and *paragraph* naturally in talking about what they are doing. In the past, many language arts textbooks depicted language experience stories with sentences recorded as lists, sometimes as numbered lists. This happened because LEA was conceived as more of a way to teach young children to read rather than an integrated oral language/writing/reading strategy. Today, advocates of shared writing realize the value of having teachers model the way print works and the way inscribers think when they are writing ideas down on paper. In this context, teachers' own spelling, knowledge of conventions of written language, and penmanship skills are important teaching tools. Teachers must model standard spellings, standard language conventions, and clear handwriting because what they record for their children becomes a demonstration of the correct way to do it.

Fourth, advocates of shared writing activity suggest that at times the teacher encourage students to "take control of the pen" and become active contributors to the recording of letters, words, and punctuation that they need to represent their stories on paper. When students contribute directly to their class stories by helping to write them down, shared writing becomes a more powerful instructional tool: *interactive writing* (Button et al., 1996). Writing a story interactively, children and teacher cooperate to "construct it letter by letter, word by word" (Pinnell and Fountas, 1998, pp. 183–194). As they do this, the teacher draws children's attention to strategic processes that young readers and writers must learn to handle, being "careful not to focus on too many details in any one" session. Because students gain more when they are active players in a lesson, interactive writing has become the major form of teacher-guided group writing advocated today by language arts specialists.

Fifth, advocates propose that interactive writing is important across the curriculum at every grade level, not just in early primary grades. For example, middle-graders can meet as a class after conducting a science-mathematics small-group investigation in which they have devised and performed an experiment to find out the characteristics of materials that sink when submerged in water and the characteristics of materials that float. They orally compose their findings, which students and teacher cooperatively inscribe on the board or on a large paper chart. Together, they talk about what they have found out, attempt to explain their findings, and add their conclusions to the chalkboard or the chart. One student may make a copy on the computer to print out so that all students can add it to their Science Logs.

Language Learning Outcomes of Interactive Writing

Interactive writing pays dividends related directly to the skills of reading and writing. We know that at all levels, children benefit from firsthand experiences and conversations about those experiences as they read and write. Without direct involvement, children may have few beginning points for writing and may approach reading of a

● ● ● ●

READ

Kathryn Button, Margaret Johnson, and Paige Furgerson, "Interactive Writing in a Primary Classroom," *The Reading Teacher*, 49 (March 1996), 446–454.

The Teacher's Message Board

Posted here are steps in the interactive writing procedure.

1. *Experience* something vicariously through story or poem or directly through firsthand involvement.

2. *Talk* about high points of the experience: What was the greatest part? What were our overall feelings?

3. *Construct sentences interactively.* Students take turns offering sentences; sometimes several students offer a sentence to use (especially for use as the introduction or conclusion), and the class decides which one or ones to use to express their main points.

4. *Write down sentences.* When teachers inscribe, they synchronize pronunciation of the words and syllables with their recording of them, stretch out words as they write them, and think aloud the spelling decisions they are making. When young students record, as a group they sound and think their way letter by letter, word by word through onsets and rimes. They make decisions together about paragraph indentations, capitalization, and end-of-sentence punctuation. Older students do most of the recording with students' talking out their decisions about how to inscribe multisyllabic words and about what kinds of punctuation to use.

5. *Reread.* During inscription, students read sentences that the scribe has just recorded. Afterward, students chorus together the sentences they have written interactively, using their voices to "read with meaning." Volunteers offer to reread particular sentences with expression.

6. *Revise and edit.* Students—especially upper-graders—go back to check that their story says what they want it to do and proofread for mechanical problems.

7. *Focus on skills.* Students participate in a mini-lesson based on a writing or reading problem that surfaced during the interactive writing. At the kindergarten and first-grade levels, mini-lessons generally focus on construction of a meaningful title, sentence reordering, sound/symbol relationships, end-of-sentence punctuation, and beginning capitalization. In the later years, mini-lessons deal with sentence combining, subject/verb agreement, verb tenses, punctuation, or whatever other mechanical skill students need.

Teacher Cautions

- Model excellence in manuscript or cursive writing.
- Model conventional use of written language. Write in paragraph form with conventional paragraph indentations. Spell in standard patterns.
- Title the composition after completing it. What is the main idea we are trying to get across? What choice words can we use to express that point?

selection with little prior knowledge. This is especially true for at-risk learners who have had limited experiences with the world and with books and few opportunities at home to use language to reflect on their experiences. It is equally true for children learning English as a second language.

In Early-Primary Grades   Shared and interactive writing help young children understand the way print works. In serving as the scribe and asking children's help in recording letters, words, and punctuation, teachers model basic principles of written language:

- Thoughts are made up of individual words.
- Words are made up of sounds.
- Sounds are recorded with letters.
- Words are written down from left to right and top to bottom.
- First letters of beginning words are written in uppercase letters.
- Periods end sentences.

To teach these aspects of written language, teachers must make transparent the thoughts that go through their minds as they record ideas on paper. They model those thought processes by stretching out "like rubber bands" the sounds of syllables and words as they record letters on paper, by spelling out words letter by letter and syllable by syllable in recording, and by saying such things as, "We are starting a new paragraph; let's indent." Or, "We are starting a new sentence. What kind of letter must we use?" Or, "What sound do we hear at the beginning of the word *baby*? What letter do we need to record the sound at the beginning of *baby*? Will someone enter it? What vowel sound do we hear next? Let's put the letter *a* down next. Let's stretch out the word *baby*. What sound do we hear after the long *a*? Beth, you add *b* because it's the letter that starts your name. We record the final *e* sound of words like *baby* with the letter *y*. I will add the *y* to *baby*. We sometimes pronounce the letter *y* with a long *e* sound when it comes at the ends of words."

In the Later Grades   At upper levels, students can learn even more complex things about inscribing ideas. For example, fourth-graders conducting a "Sink or Float? investigation" learn how to organize a science report under four headings: materials, procedures, findings, and conclusions. As they interactively compose their report on chalkboard, chart paper, or computer, the teacher records these definitive headings to indicate the subsections of the report, models how to enumerate procedures step by step, helps students to differentiate between findings and conclusions, and models how to write paragraphs that express conclusions succinctly. Similarly, third-graders who are creating a fairy tale together learn how to record dialogue: to start a new paragraph whenever someone different speaks, to put words spoken within quotation marks, and to put a comma after introductory clauses such as, "He said, . . ."

Teacher-guided forms of group writing are also important in teaching the tools of revision. You will read more about that application in Chapter 10.

Vocabulary Development Through Contextually Relevant Word Study

Firsthand experience accompanied by conversation and interactive writing pays another kind of dividend: the expansion of children's functional vocabularies and word knowledge. As children talk about events they have experienced and dictate their ideas, they begin to use words that other students and their teacher have been using. Additionally, during mini-lessons that the teacher offers at contextually relevant spots during class discussions, students zero in on a word they have begun to use orally and make connections between it and related words. In the process, children's vocabulary can grow exponentially. In this section, we consider a series of contextually relevant word study strategies that can help children expand their vocabularies in a natural and meaningful way as part of oral interaction. This expansion is vitally important because vocabulary is a significant determinant of reading and listening comprehension.

A Word Study Mini-Lesson: A Scenario

Consider the following scenario: A class of second-graders visits an airport as part of a social studies unit. On their visit, they stand in an observation lounge and talk about how the airplanes are taking off and landing on the runway. For youngsters who come from families where flying is an infrequent occurrence, *runway* may be an unfamiliar word that they learn to handle through on-the-spot group talk.

Returning to their classroom, students gather around a piece of chart paper for a contextually relevant mini-lesson. In the middle of the paper (as in Figure 7.2), the teacher prints the word *way* and asks the second-graders whether they can remember a word from their airport trip that ends with it. Students offer *runway;* a volunteer prints it at the end of a line extending outward from the central word *way.* To aid the recording, the teacher asks the class, "What two simple, little words do we hear in the word *runway?* How do we spell each of the simple words?"

The teacher continues, "Let's brainstorm as many other words as we can that end with the word *way.* We call longer words that are made up of short ones *compound words.*" As students provide such compound words as *highway, parkway,* and *driveway,* the teacher helps the second-graders record them in web style, encourages youngsters to give the meanings of the words as they add them to their *way* web, and helps them mount their *way* web on the Word Wall. He or she keeps using the phrase *compound word* to refer to words like *runway* that are made from two smaller ones; he or she keeps reminding the students to work from the meaning of the two little words in figuring out the meaning of a compound one.

Because word search-and-ask missions are an ever-present feature of their class activity, students know that they should be on the lookout for other *way* words to add to their *way* web. They can search for words in their reading and ask people at

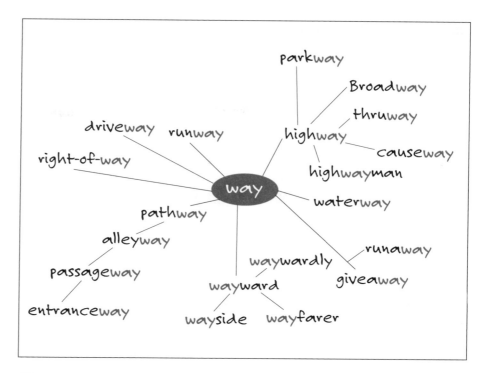

Figure 7.2
A Word Wall Web: Compound Words

home for *way* words that come to mind. On successive days, based on their ongoing search-and-ask mission, students expand their Word Wall web, adding familiar nouns such as *pathway* and *alleyway;* less familiar nouns such as *causeway, waterway,* and *passageway;* proper nouns such as *Broadway;* other kinds of words such as *away, giveaway, runaway,* and *right-of-way;* and eventually words that begin with *way,* such as *wayward* and *wayside.* As students offer words, they sort them into categories and organize the words in their *way* web to highlight commonalities and differences. They rely on a dictionary as a reference tool, checking on the meaning of a word that they may have found through search-and-ask but that is new to them.

A Second Scenario

In a similar way, upper elementary-grade students can brainstorm, search for words, and use visual means to clarify the interrelationships within and among words they encounter in content-area investigations. For example, when sixth-graders meet the word *astronomy* in a science video, they may hypothesize its meaning based on the context in which they have heard it. As follow-up, they can brainstorm, search for, and "phone a friend" for assistance in locating other words that contain the element *astro-*. As they uncover a host of related words, they make a word tower to which they add more *astro-* words: *astronaut, astronomer, astronomical, asteroid, asterisk, aster, astrodome* (which are easy to find because they are located in the same section of the dictionary). As they work with these words, they discover the meaning common to all *astro-* words: "star." They recheck the dictionary and make a further discovery: that *astro-* can be traced back through Latin to the Greek word *astron*, which also means "star" and that *-nomy* means "science of" and can be traced to the Greek word *nómos*, meaning "custom or law." (See Figure 7.3.) Through word study minilessons that help them to focus on elements within words and on elements common to a series of related words, students expand their vocabularies. Upper-graders also begin to recognize some of the Greek and Latin affixes and roots that are particularly important in the specialized vocabulary of the natural and social sciences.

Word Study Strategies: Brainstorming, Searching, and Discovering

As these two examples demonstrate, brainstorming is a useful strategy to encourage children to go beyond firsthand observation and perceive relationships among words. In group brainstorming, students contribute words and phrases on a topic about which they are talking and reading; the teacher posts the words on the wall so that students can readily access them as they need them to write. The advantages are obvious: The strategy is an oral one that helps youngsters tap into their speaking vocabulary as they begin to write. Similarly, students who have trouble getting started have a reservoir of words available as they get ready to write. These words

CONSIDER

Remember that brainstormed lists are not examples of interactive writing. Interactive writing is teacher-guided group writing that is recorded in sentence and paragraph form and models how print works.

Figure 7.3
Word Interrelationships: Etymology on the Word Wall

ACTIVITY PROMPT

Create a similar chart to show interrelationships and derivation of the word *president*. Include other words with *pre-* and *sid-* (*sed-*, *sess-*). Use a dictionary.

from Greek
<u>astron</u> meaning "star"

from Greek
<u>nómos</u> meaning "custom or law"

astro- = star

-nomy = science of or system of laws governing

astronomy

astronomical
astronomer
astronaut
aster
asterisk
asteroid

economical
economy   economist
taxonomy
agronomy
gastronomy
gastronomical

become the ideas—the "stuff," so to speak—of their writing. Then too, having the visual images of the words on constant display helps in spelling.

Search is a natural follow-up to brainstorming: To search is to keep alert for related words and ideas as one goes on to read, listen, and talk. Search also means asking. Students ask anyone and everyone for words to add to their Word Wall web or tower. Through an ongoing search-and-ask mission, students discover a variety of words that they sort into categories based on shared features; they add those words to their webs or towers in locations that highlight relationships within and between the words. Based on their word finds, students make discoveries about the meaning of word elements (prefixes, roots, and suffixes); they generalize about how words in their language work (Fresch and Wheaton, 1997). In this way, young people build their vocabularies and their knowledge of how words are structurally and etymologically interrelated in the English language. They begin to see that words are not simply made up of strings of letters; they have component parts—affixes and roots—that in and of themselves have meaning.

Kinds of Word Walls

Gay Su Pinnell and Irene Fountas (1998) describe interactive Word Walls as tools "to use, not simply to display." They propose that interactive Word Walls not only foster reading and writing and provide support for children during their reading and writing but also can be designed to "support the teaching of important general principles about words and how they work, . . . promote independence on the part of young students as they work with words in writing and reading, and provide a visual map to help children remember the connections between words and the characteristics that will help them form categories." For these reasons, Word Walls are dynamic teaching tools that can be used in a variety of ways.

Words We Are Using and Studying   Children can reserve a section of bulletin board space for "Words We Want to Use"—words that surface in talking and reading that are powerful ones to use in writing. For instance, students may choose to add *bulge* and *bulges* to their Power Words list after they listen to Leo Lionni's *The Biggest House in the World* in which Lionni writes that the little snail learned to make large, pointed bulges. Students who write in their literature journals in response to the story can refer to the Word Wall and choose *bulge* and *bulges* to describe the plight of the snail who wanted to be the biggest and the most beautiful one in the cabbage patch.

Similarly, the teacher and students can title a section of Word Wall "Words on a Topic We Are Studying." For example, having listened to Ferde Grofé's "Cloudburst" from the *Grand Canyon Suite,* listeners might brainstorm describing words and naming words to list on the Word Wall in a section of their topical board labeled "Storm Words":

Describing words: noisy, banging, crashing, breaking, striking, wet, spattering, dark, blowing, bending, tossing

Naming words: storm, cloudburst, thunder, bolt, streak, lightning, rain, wind, shower, flood, danger, disaster, warning, alarm, thunderheads, clouds

CONSIDER

Other fine selections include Grofé's *Mississippi Suite*, Rimsky-Korsakov's "Flight of the Bumblebee," Grieg's "March of the Dwarfs," Donaldson's *Once Upon a Time Suite,* and Saint-Saëns's "Danse Macabre."

Meet Janiel Wagstaff

Janiel Wagstaff is a classroom teacher who is continually searching for better ways to help her young charges develop an understanding of the way words work. She explains how she makes words a visual part of her primary-grade classroom: "In my years of teaching second grade, the Word Wall was an important classroom feature. . . . We built the Word Wall with key words containing chunks or rimes. These chunks, such as *ake* in *cake* and *art* in *dart*, help students read and write unknown words by analogy to words they already know rather than sounding out letter-by-letter or using phonetic rules." Wagstaff then became a kindergarten teacher. Describing her kindergarten teaching, she writes, "These students needed work in phonemic awareness and recognizing letters, letter names, and beginning consonant sounds. In second grade, we selected our Word Wall words from the context of humorous poetry. Since I had experienced great success with this method, I immersed my kindergartners in familiar rhymes, poems, and chants as a means of building a different type of Word Wall: an ABC Wall. . . . Our first familiar rhyme was 'Jack and Jill.' After reading, reciting, and dramatiz-

ing the nursery rhyme, we selected *Jack, water,* and *pail* as first key words for our ABC Wall. I emphasized the beginning sound of each word, helping students hear and say the sound and notice how they made the sound with their mouths and tongues. We then practiced writing the first letter in each word and evaluated other words for like beginnings. . . . We worked with the new letter-sound correspondences for one week through varied wordplay activities, then added them to the ABC Wall" ("Building Practical Knowledge of Letter-Sound Correspondence: A Beginner's Word Wall and Beyond," *The Reading Teacher,* 51 [December 1997/January 1998], 298–304).

DISCUSSION PROMPT

What specific objectives is this teacher seeking to achieve through her Word Wall? How did her objectives differ from second grade to kindergarten? How were they similar? What rationale can you suggest in support of what she is doing? What other instructional strategies can be used in conjunction with a Word Wall?

When students write creative stories in response to the listening/talk time, they can tap into their brainstormed word bank to trigger their own thinking.

In the same way, students can brainstorm topically related words for the Word Wall as part of content-area studies. During study of the water cycle, for example, third- or fourth-graders can develop topical listings of such related words as water cycle words (evaporation, condensation, clouds, and precipitation), forms of precipitation (shower, rain, snow, hail, sleet), and bodies of water (brook, stream, river, lake, pond, ocean). They use their words as they write summary paragraphs.

Related Words Another kind of Word Wall list highlights phonological, structural, etymological, or semantic relationships. In the lower grades, where phonological relationships are most significant as children learn to spell and read, children can listen for words that start with the same consonant sound (the *onset*) or belong to the same word family and end with the same sounds (the *rime*). For example, youngsters who have been dictating stories, as those in Karen Donovan's first grade were doing, can list on a section of the Word Wall labeled "Words That Start the Same" a word they have used in their interactive writing chart, such as the word *house*. They can reread the story and search for other words that start in the same way as *house: his, he, have, hurt*. They list those words beneath *house,* perhaps highlighting the letter *h* that we use to represent the beginning sound by inscribing it with a colored marker. As they go on to listen and read, they brainstorm and search for other words with the same onset; they also make a discovery about the way to record the sound they hear at the beginning of words like *hurt*. You will learn more about phonological applications of Word Walls in Chapter 8 as you read about the development of decoding skills.

In much the same way, third- and fourth-graders can play with words that share a structural relationship. For example, they list on the wall a word such as *unpleasant* that they have been using to talk about something that has happened in their classroom and about which they have written interactively. They brainstorm other words that start with the prefix *un-: unhappy, unfortunate, unclear,* and *unnecessary*. They search the dictionary for still others. Based on their word finds, students make a word discovery: The prefix *un-* usually means "not." Third- and fourth-graders can record their *un-* words on webs that they sketch on a section of the Word Wall labeled "Word Connections." To make a prefix web, they write the prefix in the center of the web with its meaning and words with that element on spokes extending outward from the center. Students can do the same with suffixes.

During content-area unit studies, upper-graders can make webs that highlight etymological relationships and add them to the Word Wall. Many English words are built from Greek and Latin roots. Encountering a word such as *nominate* in their social studies textbook, sixth-, seventh-, and eighth-graders can check its origins in a dictionary, discover that *nominate* can be traced back to the Latin word *nomen,* brainstorm and search for other words that have a similar etymology, and record all such words that they discover on a tower on the Word Wall. One advantage of a word tower is that the shared feature (in this case *nom-*) is listed in columnar, color-highlighted style to emphasize the kinship among the words (Hennings, 2000). Figure 7.4 is a Word Wall example that shows how focusing on one word element can lead to functional understanding of a host of related words.

nom- = name, from the Latin *nomen*

	nom	i	nate	
	nom	i	na	tion
	nom	i	na	tive
	nom	i	nee	
	nom	i	nal	
	nom	i	nal	ly
	nom	en	cla	ture
	noun			
re	nown			
de	nom	i	na	tion
de	nom	i	na	tor

Figure 7.4
A Word Tower That Highlights a Common Etymology

■ ● ● ●

CONSIDER

A word source: W. Cabell Greet, *In Other Words: A Beginning Thesaurus (K–2)* (Glenview, Ill.: Scott, Foresman, 1969), and *In Other Words: A Junior Thesaurus (3–6)* (Glenview, Ill.: Scott, Foresman, 1969).

At times, teachers reserve sections of the Word Wall to clarify semantic relationships among words:

■ Synonyms—words with almost the same meaning, such as *large/big*.
■ Antonyms—words with opposite meanings, such as *large/small*.
■ Homophones—words with the same sound but differing in spelling, origin, and meaning, such as *their/there/they're, pail/pale*.
■ Homographs—words with the same spelling but differing in origin, meaning, or sometimes pronunciation, such as *bar, go, run* with their multiple meanings.

As students come upon examples of these kinds of words during literature or content-area studies, the teacher can schedule mini-lessons in which everyone brainstorms and searches for examples. In the process, students make exciting discoveries about word meanings relative to origin, sound, and spelling.

Teachers do not keep all of these sections of the Word Wall up and running at any one time. The kinds of words on display are ones that are contextually relevant—that relate in some way to the ongoing activities across the curriculum. Words on the wall change as children turn their attention to other subjects. Recall the caveat that opened this part of this chapter: "Word Walls are tools to use, not simply to display."

A related caveat is one offered by Janet Allen (1999): Keep "literature at the heart of vocabulary instruction." Obviously, today's teachers avoid "deadly word lists" and do not require students to copy dictionary definitions, write sentences based on those definitions, and regurgitate definitions and sample sentences on tests. They know that vocabulary instruction works best when it is part of contextually relevant word studies in which students come upon a word, brainstorm and search for related ones, and make discoveries about how words work in the English language.

Collaborative Workshops: Clarifying Ideas Through Talking and Writing

Children must have ample opportunity to experience their world. As you have been learning in this chapter, children must experience both life firsthand and life as depicted in books. Experience alone, however, is not enough. Children must talk out their ideas in response to their varied experiences if they are to make sense out of them, and they must compose together in teacher-guided groups if they are to develop strong written-language skills. In addition, children must focus on some of the words they are using as they talk about their experiences if they are to develop the functional vocabularies they need to read with understanding and write with clarity. Oral language activity is the main bridge into literacy.

Oral language experiences are important not only at the primary-school level but also in the upper-elementary and middle grades as young people encounter "meaty" content. In the upper grades especially, children should be encouraged to think critically and deeply about what they are experiencing and reading. As Michelle Commeyras (1993) reminds us, "Students need to be critical thinkers in order to cope with the complexity of the age of information because as citizens and consumers they will be bombarded with conflicting information, some of which is misleading or erroneous." To help children develop the ability to think in depth requires lots of talking out of ideas! In this section, we will highlight the collaborative workshop as a context for involving children in higher-order thinking processes. In so doing, we will emphasize the second half of the thesis of the chapter: that oral language activity is the main bridge into higher-order thought.

Higher-Order Thinking: What Is It?

Educators often use the general term *critical thinking* in talking about higher-order thought processes. Robert Ennis (1987) defines critical thinking broadly as "a practical reflective activity that has reasonable belief or action as its goal. There are five key ideas here: *practical, reflective, reasonable, belief,* and *action.* They combine into the following working definition: *Critical thinking is reasonable reflective thinking that is focused on deciding what to believe or do.* Note that this definition does not exclude creative thinking. Formulating hypotheses, alternative ways of viewing a problem, questions, possible solutions, and plans for investigating something are creative acts that come under this definition." The National Council of Teachers of English Committee on Critical Thinking in the Language Arts (Bosma, 1987) agrees: "Critical thinking is a process which stresses an attitude of suspended judgment, incorporates logical inquiry and problem solving, and leads to an evaluative decision or action."

More recently, theorists have begun to focus on critical thinking as it occurs during the reading act; they use the phrase *critical literacy* to refer to the process of analyzing the words and illustrations of a text for the "author's point of view, intended audience, and elements of inclusion or bias" (Creighton, 1997). In this context, a critical reader/thinker asks: What assumptions about society, culture, and individual rights underlie the text? Are these assumptions valid or are they biased? If they are biased, in what ways? What is there about this author's background that makes him or her believe and write in the way he or she does? What is there about my own prior and present cultural and gender experiences that make me respond as I do? According to Donna Creighton, the critical reader/thinker must attempt to understand the relationships between power and marginalization of any group of people within society that are reflected in what he or she is reading and take steps to overcome them. From this point of view, critical thinking not only involves problem solving, decision making, and rendering judgments but also uncovering underlying biases within a text and taking action to remediate inequities.

How does the classroom teacher build critical-thinking behaviors, especially when critical thinking is conceived as encompassing not only evaluation but decision making, problem solving, and action? The answer lies in discussions about literature and life. Because thinking and "languaging" go hand and hand, children should have endless opportunities to make evaluative judgments as they study literature and the content areas. These opportunities should start orally, for oral language activity can model for students how to use language to think. Students should talk together about literature, especially literature that speaks to injustice, people's inhumanity to one another, and environmental issues. As Bigelow (1992) explains, "Instead of merely absorbing the authors' words, children can begin to argue with them. Significantly, to invite students to question the injustices embedded in text material is implicitly to question the injustices embedded in the society." In talking together about literature, children can also begin to recognize their own biases and gather alternative ideas (Lehman and Haynes, 1985; Smith, 1990).

This section describes a lesson sequence that occurred in one sixth grade. It provides a format for designing a similar sequence of higher-order thinking experiences and clarifies what an instructional conversation is all about.

■▶▶▶

GO TO

Chapter 3 for material on children's developing ability to make critical judgments, Chapter 5 for material on critical listening, Chapter 6 for questions that encourage in-depth thinking, and Chapter 8 for material on critical reading.

Collaborative Workshop in Action

The Lorax

It was after lunch. Returning to their classroom, Henry Dag's sixth-graders spied a marqueelike sign mounted on an easel at the doorway:

In 1984, Theodor Seuss Geisel received a special Pulitzer citation "for his contribution over nearly half a century to the education and enjoyment of America's children and their parents" (*The New York Times*, April 17, 1984).

> **The Think Tank**
> Those entering must be ready to think!
> Video Showing Today at 1:00 P.M.
> *The Lorax*
> by
> Dr. Seuss
> (pseudonym for Theodor Geisel)
> Discussion Today at 1:30 P.M.
> Reporting After 2:15 P.M.

A rotating spotlight flashed colors in sequence across the sign. The classroom was dark, ready for viewing the video.

With no preliminaries, the teacher flicked on the VCR, and the reds, yellows, blues, and greens of *The Lorax* danced across the screen. The students sat entranced watching the Onceler systematically destroy the land as the Lorax warned of impending disaster.

Clarifying Thinking Through Talk

At the story's end, Mr. Dag asked, "How many of you liked the Onceler in the film? Wave your hand if you do." No hands went up. "How many of you liked the Lorax? Wave your hand." There was a flurry of hands, and the teacher continued, "Let's talk about why we all disliked the Onceler. What are some of the specific things the Onceler did that we didn't like?"

At that, children began to contribute. One told of how the Onceler had dumped Gluppity-Glupp and Schloppity-Schlopp into the rivers, a second of how the Onceler had polluted the air with fumes, another of how the Onceler had cut down the Truffla Trees, and still another of how the Onceler had scarred the earth to construct roads. At one point, to jog students' memories, the teacher pantomimed an Onceler act: smoking a big cigar and shaking ashes onto the floor. He asked students if they could pantomime another act. One youngster portrayed nonverbally how the Onceler had peeled a banana and carelessly thrown the peel out the window. During this stage, a student served as scribe, recording examples.

"Did the Onceler do anything that was good?" queried Mr. Dag. Children pondered. Then one volunteered that the Onceler had supplied jobs, which meant better homes and food for the Onceler people. A second suggested that the Onceler had saved the last Truffla Tree seed so that Truffla Trees could grow again.

Next children pondered why the Onceler had done what he had and who the Onceler really was. Almost unanimously the sixth-graders decided that greed was the motive and that the Onceler was "big business."

"Do you think that the Onceler was really just that?" the teacher pressed. The scribe read an item from the list the class had previously developed: that the Onceler had cut down all the Truffla Trees. "Has anyone here caused a tree to be cut down unnecessarily—just *once?*" To jog ideas, the teacher rolled up a piece of paper and tossed it into the basket. At that, many hands went up as the children related times when they had thrown away paper items they could have reused. One youngster described something he had recently read about how used paper is changed back into pulp and converted into new paper products. Item by item the youngsters went through the list recorded by the scribe and described when they themselves had just once acted like the Onceler. Gradually, they began to perceive that *they were the Onceler* and that greed was too general a reason to explain acts like those in the video. They began to comprehend the importance of suspending judgment until they had considered the facts of a case.

Students focused now on the Lorax. "Why did everyone like the Lorax? What did the Lorax do that we liked? What biases do we hold that make us judge as we do?" The children supported their earlier vote by describing specific acts of the Lorax. "Whom did the Lorax stand for in real life?" The children decided that the Lorax represented everyone who speaks up even when others take an opposite stand.

Build background for higher-order thinking through viewing and listening

Identify specific examples to support an opinion

Go beyond stereotyped explanations

(Note: It is important to stress that the Onceler represents all of us—not big business—if we are to avoid an anti-industry bias.)

Perceive relationships

Contribute ideas to class discussion

A POLLUTION EVILS BOARD

The Litterbug ☐ ☐

A man is driving along an open stretch of a major interstate highway. He decides to have some candy; so he opens a package, pops a piece into his mouth, and tosses the wrapper out the window.

The Smokestack ☐ ☐

A large electrical generating plant produces power by burning a high-sulfur coal. It emits thick gases into the air.

The Hog ☐ ☐

A child asks for an extra big piece of dessert, but finds that he or she is too full to eat the whole thing, so leaves the rest to be thrown out.

The Dumper ☐ ☐

An oil tanker cleans its tanks by dumping what is left offshore. The oil washes ashore, gumming up miles of beach and marshland.

The Puffer ☐ ☐

The sign in the people-filled, unventilated room reads: "No Smoking." A woman lights a cigarette and smokes until the room is smoke-filled.

Figure 7.5
A Task Sheet for Rank-Ordering Opinions

ACTIVITY PROMPT
Make a similar task sheet for rank-ordering events, characters, people in the news.

Contribute ideas to consensus group; support an opinion with proof

Convincing Others

After the class had spent a good deal of time considering "what" and "why," Mr. Dag shifted gears. "So far," he announced, "we have been judging the rightness and wrongness of acts. As we have seen, some acts seem worse than others. Now we are going to rank acts in terms of which ones are worse than others. I have a sheet in which I have described acts very similar to the ones committed by the Onceler. Put a number 1 in the first box next to the name of the offender you consider to be the worst one, a number 2 next to the name of the offender you consider to be a little less bad, and so on down the line." The teacher distributed the task sheet in Figure 7.5, and the children individually rank-ordered the offenders.

When each student had completed a sheet, the teacher divided the class into five teams. The teams were to arrive at a compromise sheet that to some extent embodied the thinking of each member. Those whose opinion differed from others' with respect to the rank-ordering of items had to convince others on the team. In so doing, the children became actively involved in trying to change opinions so that the composite ranking would reflect reasons they believed were significant. Mr. Dag waited until the teams had compiled their composite rankings, which they recorded in the second box next to each name on the task sheet. At that point, the Team

DATA TABLE					
Team No.	The Litterbug	The Smokestack	The Hog	The Dumper	The Puffer
1	4	2	3	1	5
2	4	1	5	2	3
3	4	2	5	1	3
4	5	1	4	2	3
5	3	2	5	1	4

Figure 7.6
A Data Table for Recording Opinions

Secretary recorded the consensus on a chart the teacher had outlined on the chalk-board. The team findings are shown in Figure 7.6.

Together the class analyzed the results, considering how the team rankings, although different, were similar. They noted that all teams had ranked the Smoke-stack and the Dumper as very bad, and they gave reasons for those high rankings: the fact that the acts hurt more people and were committed by groups rather than by individuals. Teams ranking the Dumper higher than the Smokestack (and vice versa) gave reasons to support their rankings. In like manner, participants considered acts they had generally ranked as least offensive: littering and puffing. Again, they verbalized the criteria they had used to formulate their judgment.

Defend a position orally

Interactive Writing: Poetry

To wrap up the session, Mr. Dag turned to *The Lorax*. He opened to the page toward the end that shows a memorial-like pile of rocks bearing the imprint *UNLESS*. "What significance does the word *unless* have in the story?" he asked. Remembering the video, the children explained that unless everyone was more careful, the earth would be no more. The teacher wrote the main clause on the board and followed it with a series of *unlesses* in the following pattern:

The earth will be no more
    unless _____
    unless _____
    unless _____
    unless _____

Summarize key ideas through interactive writing

On the spot, the class composed a list poem consisting of a string of specific *unless* clauses:

The earth will be no more
    unless we protect the forest from being cut away,
    unless we stop the fouling of the air,

unless we halt the reckless dumping into our waterways,
unless we work together to save the land.

Their summary poem-making ended the Think Tank Session for the afternoon.

Reading and Composing Alone

The next afternoon, Mr. Dag's sixth-graders saw a sign that said "The Writing Box" spread across the doorway marquee, and they entered the Box to write allegories modeled after *The Lorax*. To introduce the form, the teacher asked the children to read a second allegory by Dr. Seuss, *The Butter Battle Book*. Then they talked about how the story communicated its message and compared it with *The Lorax*. They quickly perceived that in allegories, story characters stand for persons in real life and story acts stand for real-life acts. They saw that by using a representational technique, writers send a message to readers. Following talk-time, the children spent the afternoon composing allegories. Most worked in writing teams. At the suggestion of Mr. Dag, they signed their finished stories with pseudonymns, adding the word *pseudonym* to their Word Wall because it was one that had been new to them and that they had begun to use in reference to Dr. Seuss. In posting the word, they bracketed *pseudo-* and marked its meaning as "false." They bracketed *-nym* and marked its meaning as "name."

Clearly Mr. Dag's sixth-graders were going beyond the facts in the story to create extended meanings. To move children beyond what was "right there" in the story and to think more critically about it, Mr. Dag was using a series of interactive, oral-language-based strategies. We will look at those strategies next.

DISCUSSION PROMPT

- Mr. Dag believes in an integrated language arts. What evidence of his beliefs do you see in the way he teaches?

Reflecting on Meaningful Content

A first strategy that triggers higher-order thinking is to lay a foundation with meaningful content about which children want to talk. Substance or content is essential if instructional conversations in elementary classrooms are to touch on fundamental problems, issues, and ideas. How do children acquire the background necessary for higher-order thinking? The answer lies in oral language activity.

Thinking Aloud About Literature Ideas in books are the warp and woof of instructional conversations and eventually of writing. Talking together about ideas met in stories becomes oral pondering as youngsters identify key strands, note relationships among strands, weave them together into generalizations, and ultimately formulate opinions and judgments. Interactive writing becomes a means of recording ideas discussed and of summarizing and clarifying them.

In the episode just described, an allegorical video supplied the content for higher-order thought. Other kinds of stories provide content more suited to the cognitive abilities and interests of early-primary children. A teacher can share a short story or poem, which the children later ponder as a group. Very young children can ponder a feeling book like Judith Viorst's *I'll Fix Anthony*—the internal talking of a

READ

Claude Goldenberg, "Instructional Conversations: Promoting Comprehension Through Discussion," *The Reading Teacher*, 46 (December 1992/January 1993), 316–326.

GO TO

Chapter 3 for a discussion of developmental stages. Teachers must organize activities based on their understanding of children's cognitive development.

little brother as he tells himself what he will do "when he is six" to get back at his big brother. Children decide whether they like Anthony and whether they like the little brother. They identify mean acts and good acts. They think about why the little brother has mean thoughts. They describe times when they felt just like the little brother and said, "I'll fix _____." Children who are six go on to write their own repetitive lines patterned after Viorst's: "When I'm seven, _____ ."

Thinking Aloud About Content-Area Issues   Youngsters can also think out loud about issues related to social studies, science, and current events. For example, a teacher can share a news clipping that describes a controversial current event. Students listen, identify key points, and formulate opinions. Historical events can be treated in the same fashion. Studying events such as the "treason" of Benedict Arnold, the "civil disobedience" of the Boston Tea Party, and the duel between Aaron Burr and Alexander Hamilton, youngsters read several accounts of the events. They identify key factors and note discrepancies. They ponder reasons for actions, try to view an issue from all sides, and try to overcome their own biases. Ultimately, discussants formulate their own positions, take sides, and support their positions with reasons. The word *positions* in the preceding sentence is significant, for within discussion groups, all children need not arrive at the same opinion. The judging scale in Figure 7.7 is one way to help children visualize the weighing of evidence pro and con in arriving at a judgment.

Graphic information can also provide a context for thinking aloud. Several political cartoons about the same event, a series of graphs or maps, or data from experimental studies can be examined and discussed in teacher-guided or student-led groups. The possibilities are endless.

Going from the Simple to the Complex

A second strategy that triggers higher-order thinking is to lay the foundation for more complex thinking tasks by starting with lower-order ones. The teacher in *The*

WORD BANK
Strategies Leading to Higher-Order Thinking:
Reflecting on meaningful content
Going from simple to complex
Voting
Rank-ordering and defending
Writing and reading interactively

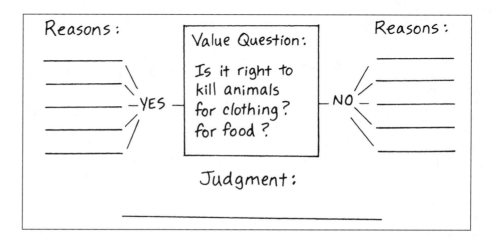

Figure 7.7
A Judging Scale for Critical Thinking
Source: After Alvermann, 1991.

Distinguished Educator

Lorax vignette did this when early on he asked students to name the acts committed by the Onceler. Specifying examples is a lower-order task. Higher-order tasks include

1. Describing things and events.
2. Grouping related items together.
3. Labeling groups or categories.
4. Formulating generalizations and inferences.
5. Identifying criteria for judging and developing judgments based on these criteria (Taba, 1964).

Hilda Taba's research (1967) indicates that if children are asked to perform a higher-order, more abstract thinking operation before identifying specific examples, they typically are not able to perform the higher-order task, and discussion founders. It indicates that to involve children in thinking about complex interrelationships, a teacher should generally move from less to more abstract, as Mr. Dag did in the preceding vignette. See The Teacher's Message Board (p. 253) for question sequences that lead to higher-order thinking as a critical response to literature.

The Teacher's Message Board

Posted here are questions to encourage deep thinking.

QUESTIONS THAT ENCOURAGE CHILDREN TO THINK DEEPLY ABOUT A BOOK OR STORY THEY HAVE READ

Background Questions

- Who are the characters? How does the story begin? How does it develop? How does it end? Why does the author end it this way? What is the story saying to you? What is its message?

Higher-Order Questions

- What part of the story do you like best/least? What makes you like/dislike it?
- What character do you like best/least? What did that character do/not do that makes you like/dislike him or her? Why does that act appeal/not appeal to you? When has anything similar happened to you?
- What picture do you like best/least? What is it about that picture that makes you like/not like it?
- What words appeal/do not appeal to you? Why do you like/dislike those words?
- Is the message or the story a valid one? Does it give a truthful picture of what happens in the real world? Why? Why not? What biases do you hold that influence your judgment?
- Are there stereotypes in the story? Give some examples. How do you react?

Summary-Evaluating Questions

- Would you like to read this story again? Why? Why not?
- Would you like to share this story with a friend? Why? Why not? What kind of person would like/dislike this story? Why?
- Is this a good story? What evidence do you have to support your judgment?

QUESTIONS THAT ENCOURAGE CHILDREN TO THINK DEEPLY ABOUT STORY AND EVERYDAY ACTS

Background Questions

- What did the character (person) do or say when . . . ?
  (Ask children to describe a particular act.)

Higher-Order Questions

- Was it right (fair, just, smart) for the character (person) to do that? Was it right for the character to say that? Why? Why not?
- What happened as a result? How did that act affect other people?
- What circumstances led him or her to do that?
- What was his or her reason for doing that? Was that reason a good one? What evidence do you have to support your judgment?
- What moral principles, or big ideas about right and wrong, are behind what you are saying?
- What would you have done if you had been the character? Why would you have done that? How would other people have judged your act? Why?

Taba's work verifies that guiding a discussion to involve children in higher-order thinking is not easy. When planning a discussion, teachers may want to think about some questions through which to guide youngsters in pondering diverse ramifications. Although in the actual discussion teachers will diverge from their plans, considering some possibilities in advance is helpful. In essence, teachers must have a discussion plan and, as they teach, apply that plan flexibly to involve children in productive thinking and talking.

Voting

A third strategy for involving children in higher-order thinking is voting. The teacher in *The Lorax* vignette opened the session with a simple vote; listeners indicated by waving their hands whether they liked or disliked a character. Sidney Simon et al. (1972) advocate judgmental voting, especially as an icebreaker. In voting, every participant is involved; no one sits back while others talk, since everyone reacts with a nonverbal signal: hand waving. Simon suggests five nonverbal signals students can make, although one can stick to simple hand waving if preferred:

- Thumbs up and waving if reactors are in high agreement.
- Thumbs up if reactors like or agree.
- Thumbs down if reactors dislike or disagree.
- Thumbs down and waving if reactors dislike or disagree violently.
- Arms crossed if reactors have no comment.

That the first response is nonverbal and in unison has advantages, according to Simon. A nonverbal response is easier to make than a verbal one. Reactors need not phrase a sentence; rather, they react almost spontaneously. For children fearful of participating orally, a unison response allows immediate participation as their responses blend into the group's. Also, the fact that children are contributing even though their contribution is part of a unison response accustoms them to joining in. The initial involvement breeds greater involvement as youngsters are caught up in an issue.

Rank-Ordering and Defending

A fourth instructional strategy that encourages children to think deeply is rank-ordering and then defending that ordering. In ranking, discussants choose among alternatives and explain the reasons for their choices. In so doing, they discover that issues are often more complex than is first apparent. The teacher in *The Lorax* vignette used this approach when he asked children to rank the five acts on the Evils Board. Students had to make choices, defend them to their team, develop a group consensus, and defend their consensus before the class.

The value of ranking and defending lies in the fact that students must go beyond the simple labels *good* and *bad* and judge the extent of good and evil. In doing this, youngsters function within a gray area in which there is no absolute right or wrong. Since not all children in a class rank a series of alternatives in the same way, the strategy elicits differences in opinion, and those differences are a key to involved discussions. Youngsters typically are eager to defend their team's reasoning, and discussion becomes fast and furious.

In the lesson with *The Lorax,* the teacher devised the alternatives that students ranked and organized as a task sheet. A teacher can vary the technique by delivering the options orally. With this variation, students will refine their listening skills. Using an oral approach in lower grades, a teacher may limit alternatives to three so that youngsters are able to recall significant details. Or the teacher can work with a writing team to compose alternatives related to a social science or current events topic being studied, a story read, or a film viewed. In that case, individuals from the writing team present the alternatives orally to the class for rank-ordering. Or if youngsters have pondered an Evils Board of the teacher's making, individually they can devise a follow-up sheet of related evils for rank ordering and discussion.

Writing and Reading Interactively

In teaching thinking, writing and reading are fundamental strategies, especially when used in concert. Writing is a way to make thoughts stand still so that they can be examined. It is a form of communication that forces one to handle relationships and organize ideas logically. At its highest level, reading requires the interpretation of meanings not explicitly stated in the text, the generation of comparisons and contrasts, the classification of ideas, and the formulation of generalizations and judgments. Research by Robert Tierney (1990) indicates that evaluative thinking and perspective shifting increase when reading and writing occur together. Both reading and writing foster critical thinking, but when used together, they pack a powerful punch.

As the previous literature-based vignette suggests, writing is a natural outgrowth of thinking aloud. To follow an instructional conversation with interactive writing is an effective way to focus on key points and model summary writing. At the same time, the teacher discovers whether students have control over the major points discussed and can distinguish the significant from the insignificant.

Specific interactive writing activities to use as follow-up to an instructional discussion are numerous, especially in science and social studies. For example, children who have discussed the meanings expressed in a graph can compose a one-paragraph summary. Those who have talked about a series of pictures can compose a paragraph or two explaining relationships. Others who have orally analyzed a series of maps can organize a paragraph that translates into verbal form the ideas shown visually. In this way, development of thinking and writing skills becomes an objective of content-area teaching. Writing and thinking skills are taught contextually as youngsters work with meaningful content.

Similarly, reading is a natural component of think-aloud sessions. Youngsters can read to find supporting facts and ideas, categorize facts and ideas, contrast one selection with another, generalize, and criticize.

The teacher is the key factor in determining whether reading leads to critical thinking prowess. The focus he or she gives to classroom reading determines what levels of

READ

- P. David Pearson and Dale Johnson, *Teaching Reading Comprehension* (New York: Holt, Rinehart and Winston, 1978), 157–164, for "text explicit," "text implicit," and "script implicit" reasoning in reading.
- Taffy Raphael, "Question-Answering Strategies for Children," *The Reading Teacher*, 36 (November 1982), 186–190, for the Question-Answer Relationship (QAR) strategy. Using QARs, children identify the three ways they find answers to questions. Answers to "Right There" questions are in the text; answers to "Think and Search" questions must be put together from ideas in the text; answers to "On My Own" questions are found within children's knowledge base.

thinking children pursue—whether they read only to get the facts explicitly stated, read for ideas implied in the text, and/or rely on their own background information and associations in their interpretation of the text. In the previous teaching-in-action vignette, Mr. Dag asked his sixth-graders to compare Dr. Seuss's *The Butter Battle Book* with *The Lorax,* a selection about which they now had considerable understanding. Thinking through similarities, the children discovered the characteristics of allegory, which they went on to use in their own writing, and also discovered fundamental meanings that they could apply to problems of everyday life. In the process, they were using language to reflect on experience, something Anne Dyson and Celia Genishi (1983) call the "essence of critical verbal thinking."

Planning for Higher-Order Thinking

Oral language involvement is essential in a language arts program that teaches higher-order thinking. By using oral language to reflect on their experiences, chil-

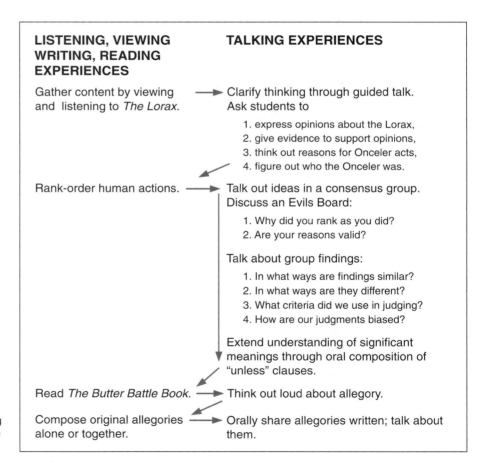

Figure 7.8
A Plan for Interactive Learning

DISCUSSION PROMPT

- How does this kind of planning lead to an integrated language arts?

dren can try out and refine thinking processes fundamental to reading and listening with comprehension, to writing and speaking with clarity, and to general problem solving. To this end, the teacher may want to plan sequences of oral language activity that help children bring their prior knowledge to bear on a particular situation at hand—a story to be interpreted, a project to be completed, a question to be resolved.

Figure 7.8 clarifies the general listening, talking, reading, and writing activities that Mr. Dag used in relation to *The Lorax*. It highlights the oral interactions children will experience. A teacher can design similar sequences based on hypothetical problems in social studies (You Are There at the Boston Tea Party—What Will You Do?), current issues (You See a Classmate Copying During a Test—What Do You Do?), a science demonstration (What Happens to Ice Held in Sunshine?). The purpose here is to get children thinking aloud so that they learn to use language to reflect on experiences—direct experiences in the real world and vicarious experiences from the world of books—and to use language to think critically.

A Summary Thought or Two

Oral Language Activity as a Bridge into Literacy and Higher-Order Thought

Children must have opportunities to look at and wonder about the world around them. They must talk with others to celebrate their experiences with the real world and the world of books; they must write interactively as they begin to acquire the ability to handle words on paper; and they must have opportunities to focus on words by brainstorming, searching for, and discovering connections. The classroom must be filled with the words that children are beginning to use as they talk and write together. Ultimately, too, children must have opportunities to think beyond the apparent and to become critical listeners and readers. As children experience, talk, write interactively, read what they have written, and focus on words, they use their oral language facility as a bridge into literacy and higher-order thinking. Viewed from this integrative perspective, Chapter 7 is a "bridge" chapter: It highlights the connections between oral and written language and between language and thought.

Your Language Arts Portfolio

- Go on a walkabout. Pause, look, and wonder at what you see. Make jottings in your Writing Notebook, which can be part of your portfolio.
- Assess yourself. Are you naturally curious about the world around you? Do you wonder why? Do you find joy in words? Write a paragraph in which you describe your interests and your "curiosities."
- Select and read a book for children. Create a series of questions that you could use to nudge children into literacy and higher-order thinking.
- Plan a lesson that includes discussion, interactive writing, and a vocabulary-development activity. Teach your lesson to a child or two. Assess your ability to lead a discussion, guide interactive writing, and develop a Word Wall for vocabulary building.

Related Readings

Allen, Janet. *Words, Words, Words: Teaching Vocabulary in Grades 4–12.* York, Me.: Stenhouse Publishers, 1999.

Baron, Joan, and Robert Sternberg, eds. *Teaching Thinking Skills: Theory and Practice.* New York: W. H. Freeman, 1987.

Beyer, Barry. *Practical Strategies for the Teaching of Thinking.* Boston: Allyn and Bacon, 1987.

Booth, David, and Carol Thomley-Hall, eds. *Classroom Talk: Speaking and Listening Activities from Classroom-based Teacher Research.* Portsmouth, N.H.: Heinemann, 1992.

Busching, Beverly, and Betty Slesinger. "Authentic Questions: What Do They Look Like? Where Do They Lead?" *Language Arts,* 72 (September 1995), 341–351.

Commeyras, Michelle. "Promoting Critical Thinking Through Dialogical-Thinking Reading Lessons." *The Reading Teacher,* 46 (March 1993), 486–493.

Dewey, John. *How We Think.* Special edition of the 1933 classic. Boston: Houghton Mifflin, 1998.

Fountas, Irene, and Gay Su Pinnell, eds. *Voices on Word Matters: Learning About Phonics and Spelling in the Literacy Classroom.* Westport, Conn.: Heinemann, 1999.

Gallagher, Pat, and Gloria Norton. *A Jumpstart to Literacy: Using Written Conversation to Help Developing Readers and Writers.* Westport, Conn.: Heinemann, 2000.

Ganske, Kathy. *Word Journeys: Assessment-Guided Phonics, Spelling, and Vocabulary Instruction.* New York: Guilford, 2000.

Griss, Susan. *Minds in Motion: A Kinesthetic Approach to Teaching Elementary Curriculum.* Westport, Conn.: Heinemann, 1998.

Hennings, Dorothy Grant. *Beyond the Read Aloud: Learning to Read Through Listening and Reflecting.* Bloomington, Ind.: Phi Delta Kappa, 1992.

Johnson, Dale D. *Vocabulary in the Elementary and Middle School.* Needham Heights, Mass.: Allyn and Bacon, 2001.

Klooster, David, et al., eds. *Ideas Without Boundaries: International Educational Reform Through Reading and Writing for Critical Thinking.* Newark, Del.: International Reading Association, 2000.

Makler, Andra, and Ruth Hubbard. *Teaching for Justice in the Social Studies Classroom: Millions of Intricate Moves.* Westport, Conn.: Heinemann, 2001.

Marzano, Robert. *Cultivating Thinking in English and Language Arts.* Urbana, Ill.: National Council of Teachers of English, 1991.

———. "Language, the Language Arts, and Thinking." In *Handbook of Research on Teaching the English Language Arts.* Ed. J. Flood et al. New York: Macmillan, 1991, 559–586.

McCarrier, Andrea, Gay Su Pinnell, and Irene Fountas. *Interactive Writing: How Language and Literacy Come Together, K–2.* Westport, Conn.: Heinemann, 1999.

Nielson, Allen. *Critical Thinking and Reading.* Urbana, Ill.: National Council of Teachers of English, 1989.

Olson, Carol. *Thinking Writing: Fostering Critical Thinking Through Writing.* New York: HarperCollins, 1992.

Pinnell, Gay Su, and Irene Fountas. *Word Matters: Teaching Phonics and Spelling in the Reading/Writing Classroom.* Westport, Conn.: Heinemann, 1998.

Ross, Elinor. *Pathways to Thinking: Strategies for Developing Independent Learners K–8.* Norwood, Mass.: Christopher-Gordon Publishers, 1998.

Short, Kathy, and Jerome Harste, with Carolyn Burke. *Creating Classrooms for Authors and Inquirers.* 2nd ed. Portsmouth, N.H.: Heinemann, 1995.

Smith, Patricia, ed. *Talking Classrooms: Shaping Children's Learning Through Oral Language Instruction.* Newark, Del.: International Reading Association, 2001.

Sternberg, Robert J. "Critical Thinking: Its Nature, Measurement and Improvement." In *Essays on the Intellect.* Ed. Frances Link. Washington, D.C.: Association for Supervision and Curriculum Development, 1985.

Whitin, David, and Phyllis Whitin. "Learning Is Born of Doubting: Cultivating a Skeptical Stance." *Language Arts,* 76 (November 1998), 123–129.

Wooten, Deborah. *Valued Voices: An Interdisciplinary Approach to Teaching and Learning.* Newark, Del.: International Reading Association, 2000.

Intermezzo

before going on

"What is a Caucus-race?"
said Alice; not that she
much wanted to know, but
the Dodo had paused as if
it thought that somebody
ought to speak. . . .

"Why," said the Dodo,
"the best way to explain it
is to do it."

—Lewis Carroll, *Alice's*
Adventures in Wonderland

■ ■ ● ● ●

READ

Jeffrey Glanz, *Action Research:*
An Educational Leader's Guide to
School Improvement. Norwood,
Mass.: Christopher-Gordon
Publishers, 1998, for information
on how to become an action
researcher.

CPR in the Classroom: An Oral Communication Unit

Reginal Cantave has been teaching sixth and seventh grades in an urban community for several years. As the years have gone by, he has become more and more concerned about the oral communication skills of his students, especially their lack of ability to listen with understanding. As Mr. Cantave explained, "Each morning in my school, the principal makes announcements over the public address system. On several occasions to test my hypothesis that my students were poor listeners, I asked them afterward to recall something said during morning announcements. The most popular response was, 'I don't know.'"

Mr. Cantave thought about why this was so and decided to investigate ways to improve his students' oral communication skills. In a paper describing his action research, he wrote, "The students I teach are from similar environments and I have found that those with poor listening skills are those whose environments are most similar of all. Almost all of them unfortunately have experienced prenatal drug exposure and have now what some would consider a nontraditional home life.

"For these reasons, I decided to experiment with a series of activities that focused on both listening and speaking and that required both conversational and presentational involvement. My general goal was to help my students to become more attuned to what people around them have to say. More specifically, I was concerned with teaching my students 'to wait attentively to perceive a signal and to heed it'— the definition of listening according to *Webster's College Dictionary*."

The Interactors

"The community where I teach is more than four square miles in area; there are close to 10,000 elementary and junior high school students. Nearly all these children see the same things around them every day: En route to and from school, they pass rundown buildings, littered lots that are their playgrounds, and crack vials and syringes. Most of them must walk through gang territories to go to the store for milk. Many do not live in two-parent homes; some do not live with either a mother or father but are cared for by a well-meaning aunt or grandmother who may not have the strength to impose the strong discipline that they sadly may lack. Each of these factors reinforced my desire to do something different in terms of language arts instruction, something that required greater attention and personal involvement on the part of my students.

"I decided to use one seventh-grade and one sixth-grade class as my experimental sample. Homebase 746 consisted of twenty-seven students. Five of the twenty-seven were repeating seventh grade and close to half could not comprehend or write at grade level; almost all had trouble paying attention and learning through listening. Homebase 646 had twenty-three students. None had been retained from the previous year; however, only five were working at grade level. The average reading comprehension score of these fifty students whom I met daily as their language arts teacher was actually at a third- or fourth-grade level. More than 90 percent of the school's population is (as I am) African American with most of the remainder being Spanish speakers; my classes reflected this diversity."

The Action

"Because the principal's announcements over the PA system are an integral part of the opening of school each morning, I began with them. My students and I talked about why the announcements were being made and what significance the announcements had for them—to remind them of things they had to do and to get them to places on time during the day. I explained that we would be listening in teams to the announcements for the next week. The job of each team was to listen to an announcement and be ready to retell it to the class. I demonstrated how I would point to a team as the principal began a new announcement to indicate which team was responsible for that particular announcement.

"We began this different, highly structured, team-based approach. After the announcements, each team came to the front and told the topic of an announcement and the main point of it. At first, as a team reported, I stood at the board and recorded the topic and a few points about it. Quickly, however, I assigned the recording job to a student from the team. Shortly thereafter, listeners had to record these points in their notebooks before we summarized them on the board together.

"Even as students were retelling and relistening to the announcements, I introduced two criteria for evaluating our progress as speakers and listeners: *presentation* and *respect*. As a class, we developed scoring rubrics for both. We used these categories under 'presentation': I could follow the speakers without any problem. I had some trouble following the speakers and the points. I didn't get it. We used these categories under 'respect': I paid great attention. I paid OK attention. I was out of it.

"Now I was ready to start my oral communication unit. I explained that since we had had some experiences with listening and speaking, we were going to do something more sophisticated that they would enjoy. We were going to give speeches, interview one another, and present commercials. On different days, I modeled each form: I gave a speech in which I played the role of a Student Council nominee seeking election since SC elections were in progress in the school. I had one of the security guards in the school join us in the classroom and I interviewed him. And I presented a commercial for a popular product.

"Students listened for what I was saying and for how I was saying it. They rated me on my presentation and themselves on respect toward the presenter using our scoring rubrics. I also introduced a third criterion—creativity—and we decided on a three-point scale for rating it. I now had my assessment instrument in place—an instrument that we began to call **CPR**—**C** standing for the creativity of a presentation, **P** for the clarity of the presentation, and **R** standing for the respect listeners showed their classmates during a presentation.

"After my sixth- and seventh-graders had talked about my presentations and their own attention during them, they were given time to work in pairs or teams to interview or to prepare and present a speech or commercial. Most of the activity of the pairs and teams was oral as students talked and listened to one another and practiced what they would present. When in the afternoons we gathered for our "Give It Your Best Show" times, students made their presentations and completed a brief questionnaire for each presentation they had viewed and heard. They had to rate the presentation on the **C** and **P** scales and themselves on the **R** scale on the questionnaire. Additionally, they had to indicate the one element they liked most, the one element they liked least, and one point they learned (my LLL scale). Each student had an opportunity to work on each form of communication—a speech, an interview, and a commercial."

The Outcome

"Most of my students presented well. Some presented very well, especially those who are creative and are natural actors. Many lost points during the first one or two presentations on the Respect scale, but improved during successive presentations. I saw some improvement from each student by the time he or she had made his or her third presentation. I also saw improvement in the collaborative team activity that preceded the presentations, with more time-on-task and less disruptive behavior.

"Most important, the students enjoyed the three-week unit. They seemed eager for the opportunity to work cooperatively together in pairs and teams rather than individually on text-based tasks. They also seemed eager to work at a task that required creativity. In each class, the students asked if they could do assignments like this 'again in the future' and if they could continue to work collaboratively on their assignments as they had been doing. Jarrod made my day when he commented, 'You've got it, Mr. C!'"

Reflections

"What did I learn from my experiment? One thing I learned was the power of collaborative activity. The students worked hard in their pairs and on their teams to get ready to present. Second, I learned the importance of my modeling as a basis for the development of a rating scale; students saw how I did it and saw themselves doing the same kinds of things. Third, I learned to organize my classroom to 'leave students wanting more.' When teachers find something of value that students enjoy, I think it's important that they let them go with it. Especially in schools where students have been turned off to learning, teachers must look for activities where children can succeed and find enjoyment. My students have not been successful as readers and writers; they can, however, perform orally when functioning in

DISCUSSION PROMPT

■ What assumptions about teaching and learning underlie the way Mr. Cantave functions as a teacher? What is this teacher's philosophy of language arts instruction?

a structured environment with clear criteria. In such an environment, they catch the spark.

"Sadly some of my coworkers do not see these as valuable parts of their instruction. They rely on worksheets and more worksheets to teach communication skills. I know this doesn't work—that what does work is starting orally with activities that students can enjoy and do well. Having succeeded orally—as my students did—maybe, just maybe, I can spark their interest in reading and writing."

African Americans and Native Americans contributed words from their first languages. At the same time, the act of living in America gave rise and continues to give rise to new words and different ways to use existing words. In the nineteenth and twentieth centuries, too, as people made discoveries, their names were attached to what they had discovered, and even more words became a part of the English-language mosaic.

American Contributions		Contributions from Various African Languages		Contributions from Native American Languages		Words Based on People's Names	
gerrymander	gobbledygook	jazz	banana	caucus	papaya (Carib)	sandwich	bloomer
boondoggle	blizzard	giraffe	goober	squash	manatee (Carib)	quisling	bowdlerize
jeep	chad	yam	zombie	woodchuck	buccaneer (Carib)	cardigan	quixotic
radar	sonar	gumbo	koodoo	caribou		burnsides	einsteinium
grouchy	tuxedo	buckra	kola, also cola	moccasin		poinsettia	
hayseed	pesky	tote		succotash		crapper	
		zebra		hickory		boycott	

PART Four

Literacy for the Twenty-First Century

How do we help children to become masters of words—especially written words?
How do we help children to make meaning with words as they read and to say what
they mean when they write? In answering these questions, we must delve into how
readers and writers function, think about how children develop as readers and writers, and consider the kinds of written communications that children read and write.
Part Four focuses on written communication within a literature-based language arts
program—literacy for the twenty-first century:

- Reading with meaning—involving children with authentic reading.
- Writing as idea making—engaging children in all forms of writing and reading
  (stories, poems, and nonfiction).
- Writing processes—encouraging children to function as authors.
- Language patterns, usage, and grammar—helping children to manage their
  language.
- Spelling, dictionary use, and handwriting—helping children to refine the tools of
  writing.

Reading with Meaning

Becoming Literate

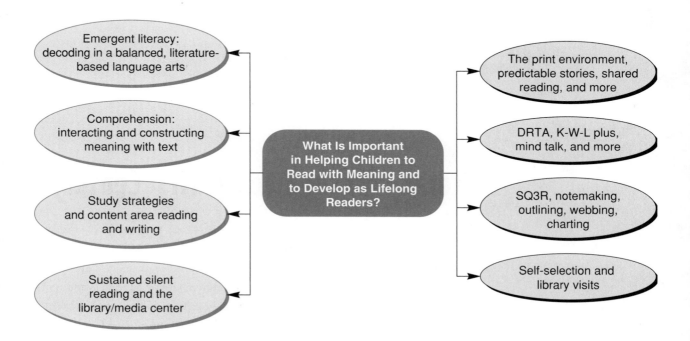

Emergent literacy: decoding in a balanced, literature-based language arts

Comprehension: interacting and constructing meaning with text

Study strategies and content area reading and writing

Sustained silent reading and the library/media center

What Is Important in Helping Children to Read with Meaning and to Develop as Lifelong Readers?

The print environment, predictable stories, shared reading, and more

DRTA, K-W-L plus, mind talk, and more

SQ3R, notemaking, outlining, webbing, charting

Self-selection and library visits

Reading/Writing in Action *From Communication Circle into Reading-Writing Workshop*

It was a crisp Monday morning. As was their daily custom, the sixteen kindergartners gathered along the perimeter of the bright red rug that set off the Communication Circle in their large classroom.

Attendance checking followed the flag salute and the introductory song. Pointing, the kindergartners counted heads around the circle. Reaching sixteen and knowing eighteen were in the class, they decided two were absent and identified missing class-mates. Then their teacher, Lorraine Wilkening, recorded the date in the corner of the chalkboard—a date the children read aloud with her. At that point, the teacher gestured toward a bulletin board chart that contained six words: *milk, paper, blinds, Fluffy, plants, chairs.* "Let's decide who will help with tasks this week," she suggested. Boys and girls volunteered to feed Fluffy, the class pet, to help water the plants, and so forth. Next to the appropriate word on the chart, Ms. Wilkening listed the names of two volunteers, and the entire class "read" back the completed chart so that all would remember their tasks.

Listening and Talking Together

Several books in hand, the teacher settled in a rocking chair at the front of the red rug. "Boys and girls," she announced, "during reading/writing workshop this morning, we are going to read a story about two animals, a hippopotamus and a rhinoceros. Let's look first in the encyclopedia to see what these animals are like." She opened a volume to display a picture of a hippopotamus. Prompted by a question or two, the children described the animal and pantomimed the way the hippo was wallowing in the mud. Then they examined a large picture of a rhinoceros, again describing it, especially the two horns on its nose. Encouraged by their teacher, they compared the rhino's nose with the hippo's. They talked about the rhino's horns and considered possible uses.

Then the teacher read the title and displayed the cover of the picture storybook *"You Look Ridiculous," Said the Rhinoceros to the Hippopotamus* by Bernard Waber. She asked the children to think about the meaning of *ridiculous* and to guess why the author had used that word rather than *silly.* She asked them to predict why the rhino might have said such a mean thing to the hippo. In response to the first question, the children proposed that the word *ridiculous* started the same way as *rhinoceros* and sounded better with it. Responding to the second question, the kindergartners suggested that maybe the rhino might think that the hippo looked ridiculous because it was all covered with mud or because it didn't have horns on its nose.

Ms. Wilkening now began the story. Each time before the hippo repeated the question, "Do I look ridiculous?" the teacher looked at the class, particularly at those children whose attention was wandering. Anticipating the story question, the students joined in the repetition. When the story ended, the teacher asked the class questions that highlighted story feelings and structure:

- Who is the main animal in the story? Who is the troublemaker?
- What did the rhino do to make trouble? Why did he do this?
- How did this make the hippo feel? Why did she feel this way? How did you feel at this point in the story? Why?
- What did she decide to do? Why? What would you have done? Why?
- Whom did she ask first for advice? What answer did she get?
- Whom did she ask next? Then next?
- How did she feel as she went from one animal to the next?
- How did she finally solve her problem?
- How did the hippo feel at the end? Why did she feel better? How did you feel? Why?
- Has anyone ever made you feel the way the rhino made the hippo feel? When? Is it right to say things like the rhino said?
- Did you like this story? What was good about it? Bad?

Recognize written words

Develop meaningful concepts before reading

Predict to develop a framework for reading

Build an understanding of story structure

As the children talked about the characters, sequence of events, and feeling changes in the story, they used the vocabulary of the story. Soon *ridiculous, rhinoceros, hippopotamus*—big words for kindergartners—were tripping off their tongues. Soon they were talking, too, about how wrong it is to tell anyone that he or she is ridiculous because he or she is different. Doing that makes the speaker ridiculous.

Going back through the story, Ms. Wilkening asked the children if they would like to draw pictures of the story animals and write about them with their invented spellings. Children volunteered to draw and write about the hippo, the rhino, the lion, the giraffe, the other animals in the story, and the hippo bedecked with the parts she wished she had. Ms. Wilkening told the youngsters they would use their drawings and writings to review the story action and feelings the next day.

Pantomiming Meanings

Because the children had been listening and interacting for more than fifteen minutes, and the class contained several attention-deficit children, Ms. Wilkening now scheduled a physically active animal time. The children stood up and, to a recording of Saint-Saëns's *Carnival of the Animals,* pantomimed the way the animals in the story moved. To prompt the activity, Ms. Wilkening had pasted photocopied story pictures on cardboard. As she held up the elephant, children became elephants; seeing the monkey, they moved like monkeys.

Listening for Language Sounds

This active time merged into a thinking and listening time. At the top of a strip of chart paper, the teacher wrote the word *ridiculous.* "Now," she announced, "we're going to think about words that begin with the same sound as *ridiculous.* Let's pull on our thinking caps." The children put their hands to their heads and pretended to pull on thinking caps. As they did so, under a lowercase *r* written on the chart, Ms. Wilkening recorded *rain* as she said it. The children repeated *rain* and *ridiculous* and contributed words with the same beginning sound: *red, rabbit, road,* and *right.* When they could not think of another word, the teacher presented a riddle: "I'm thinking of an animal, a little bigger than a mouse. It eats cheese." With this clue, the children produced *rat.* She encouraged, "Who in our class has a name that begins just as *rabbit* does?" With this, they produced *Ruth* and *Rod,* which she recorded under an uppercase *R.* She stapled the strip to a hanger, which she hung from a light fixture. At that point, Ms. Wilkening told the children that when she heard the sound like that at the beginning of *rat,* she used the letter *r* to write it down. This was a "secret" of writing that they might wish to use, too.

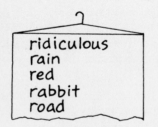

When they had produced a list of words, the children interactively composed a troublemaker story, with individual children contributing sentences with words from the brainstormed word chart. As children contributed sentences, Ms. Wilkening recorded them on chart paper. Whenever the teacher ended a sentence, one child added the period. Once the story was written, the children read it with their teacher, who moved her hand under the lines from left to right as they read. They read it several times, working on speaking the words in "chunks" of meaning. In so doing, they read the last line with so much feeling that Ms. Wilkening asked one child to substitute an exclamation mark for the period "to show how to read it." Then individual children came to the chart to read lines as the teacher's moving hand indicated clusters of words to read as units. Their story went like this:

> ## The Ridiculous Rat
>
> The rabbit saw a red rat. The rat was sitting by the road. The rabbit said to the red rat, "You look ridiculous. You are red and you look ridiculous."

Reading Writing

Discriminate visually among words; visual discrimination—the ability to distinguish one letter form from another—is important in early reading.

Quickly Ms. Wilkening took scissors and cut the story chart into punctuation marks and clusters of words read as units. She clipped the first sentence between *The rabbit saw* and *a red rat,* the second between *The rabbit was sitting* and *by the road.* Then she distributed the pieces. "Let's see if we can find story words that are the same as the ones on our chart list. Who has a piece that has *rat* on it?" Those holding a piece with *rat* came forward to hold their pieces next to that word on the list as others checked to see if the two words were visually the same.

Reconstruct story sentences

When they had discovered all possible matings, the children—with much teacher guidance—reconstructed the story from the cards. Ms. Wilkening called forward the two holding parts of the first sentence. The children decided which of the two parts went first and which second, laying the parts side by side on the rug and reading the sentence. Youngsters holding parts of successive sentences did the same until the story was together again. During the activity, Ms. Wilkening kept two children closely beside her; these two were youngsters whose attention had been wandering.

Listening for and Spelling More Sounds

Develop phonemic awareness; distinguish the sound represented by *r*, reinforcing what has been learned

At that point, the teacher distributed to each kindergartner a card inscribed with *r*. She announced, "Boys and girls, I'm going to call out words. Some will begin with the same sound as *rabbit, rat,* and *ridiculous;* some will not. When you hear a word that begins with the same sound, hold up your card. What letter is on the card?" The unison response was "*r*."

"Yes," continued the teacher, "the letter *r*. We use the letter *r* to write the sound we hear at the beginning of *rat* and *rabbit*. Point to another word on our chart that has the letter *r* at the onset." Children hopped up to point out words.

When all were back in their seats, Ms. Wilkening began a fast word call. Hearing words like *rabbit* and *rat,* the youngsters held up their *r* cards. Hearing words not beginning in the same way, they lowered their cards.

Developing Number Concepts

Develop meaningful concepts as a base for reading and thinking

A fast finger play came next, sequenced in especially for youngsters who had trouble attending and needed a lot of physical involvement: "There were ten little _____ in the great big bed, and the little one said, 'Roll over! Roll over!' They all rolled over and one fell out. There were nine and the little one said. . . ." On previous occasions children had done the play with kittens, lions, and bunnies. Now they did it with rabbits. The youngsters stood up, sang together, held up fingers to show the decreasing number of rabbits in the bed, and rolled their arms to show rabbit motion. "Did anyone hear any other words in the song," the teacher asked, "that begin with the same sound as *rabbit?*" The children knew the answer and called out *"Roll over"* in the same rhythm they had used in singing.

Emerging as Readers and Writers—The Workshop

The kindergartners and their teacher had been engrossed for almost thirty minutes—a long time, given the short attention spans of these young learners. Action had been fast, with numerous changes in activity to keep attention. Now Ms. Wilkening explained what the children would do when they went into the independent phase of reading/writing workshop. Some would go immediately to the writing center, where they would draw pictures of a rhino, a hippo, or another animal selected from the story *"You Look Ridiculous"* and write about the animal. Others would pair off with their reading buddies to take turns reading aloud to each other from books that the teacher had previously shared with the class and they had chosen to reread. Here reading meant telling the story based on the pictures, the words they could read, and their memory of the story. Still others would draw on the reverse sides of their *r* cards a picture of something beginning with the same sound as *rabbit* and *rat.* The cards would be shared during the languaging-together session on Tuesday morning, with other children guessing the objects and words represented.

At the same time, children met individually with Ms. Wilkening. Some met with her to dictate stories (as in Figure 8.1) or to read stories they had written on their own using invented spellings. For example, Jo dictated an original troublemaker story, reread the story to her teacher, illustrated it, and then read it to a group of working classmates.

Ruth, a language-talented kindergartner, read aloud to Ms. Wilkening from a storybook that she had been reading on her own and explained why she liked the story. After reading to Ms. Wilkening, Ruth shared the story with those at the writing table. In this setting, Ruth, Jo, and the others were emerging as readers and writers in ways that met their unique learning needs.

Seeing Sequence and Structure in Stories

Understand the structure and sequence of the story

Tuesday morning saw this class of young children gathered again in the Communication Circle. Completing the opening exercises and attendance taking, they began this time by sharing their animal drawings and writings and using them to retell the story of the hippopotamus and rhinoceros. As the children retold the story—at times referring back to the book "to get it right"—Ms. Wilkening had them glue their pictures to a large piece of brown paper stretched across the floor. The children glued

Figure 8.1
A Kindergartner's Original Troublemaker Story

A DICTATED STORY:
"The lion lives in a cage. He lived in a forest, but a man who worked for a zoo grabbed the lion and put him in a cage. The lion is sad. He would like to get out, but he can't."

DISCUSSION PROMPT

- What were Ms. Wilkening's objectives for this series of lessons?
- What strategies was she using to help her students grow into literacy? What are advantages and disadvantages of her approach?

their pictures in "story order," starting with the hippo in the mud, continuing with the rhino coming along, and including in sequence each animal the hippo met. The last picture they glued down was the hippo wallowing happily in the mud.

With that accomplished, Ms. Wilkening asked the children to decide when in the story the hippo was happy and when she was sad. As the children decided, volunteers hopped up and drew happy or sad faces above the glued-down animal pictures on the storymap they were developing together. They noticed that in this story the hippo started out happy and ended up happy as well. They starred the rhino as the troublemaker. Then they retold the story together, using their storymap as a guide.

Later during workshop, children wrote their own troublemaker stories with pictures that showed story action and with words spelled as children heard them. They had an opportunity to share their stories with Ms. Wilkening and another student in the kindergarten. They posted their stories in the corridor to be "read" and "reread" as children waited in line to go outside or to the auditorium.

Decoding/Encoding in a Balanced Literature-Based Language Arts

WORD BANK

Graphophonic cues

Phonemic awareness

Phonological awareness

Functional phonic ability

Semantic cues

Syntactic cues

Onset and rime

CONSIDER

Attention to ways speech sounds are represented on paper is what we mean by phonics. See *School Talk,* "Phonics Fuss: Facts, Fiction, Phonics, and Fun." National Council of Teachers of English, 1 (November 1995) for ideas by Regie Routman and Andrea Butler on how to teach phonics contextually.

Perhaps the most demanding teaching endeavor of all is the one Ms. Wilkening is performing: helping young children gain control over the sounds and the written symbols of language so that they can comprehend and enjoy reading and express themselves in writing. Ultimately, to read and write, children must be able to distinguish visually among the graphic symbols of language (for example, between the letters *d* and *b*) and recognize some words on sight and attach meaning to them—words that we say are part of their sight word vocabulary.

Also important in emergent reading and writing are other insights and abilities that make it possible for youngsters to respond to the *graphophonic* cues (symbol and sound-based clues) embedded in language:

- The insight that words are composed of units of sound (phonemes) smaller than the syllable and rhyming units of their language; the ability to hear and differentiate among the individual sounds that comprise a language—what today we call *phonemic awareness.* For example, a phonemically aware child is able to hear a difference between the beginning consonant sound of *bat* and the onset of *cat* and can offer other words that start with the same sounds, segment the word *bat* into its individual sounds (/b/, /a/, and /t/), and blend a string of isolated phonemes (/t/, /i/, and /p/) to form a recognizable word (*tip*).

- The insight that words are composed of combinations of sounds consisting of more than one phoneme: rimes, blended sounds, and syllables—what today we call *phonological awareness.* For example, a phonologically aware child is able to hear the rime at the ends of the words *cat* and *mat* and supply other words that end with the same rime (*pat, bat, fat*); hear the blended sound at the onset of *troll* and provide other words that start with the same blend (*trip, trap, trick*); and clap the syllable units in a word such as *window.*

- The ability to associate the speech sounds of language (the *phonemes*) with the letter or letters (the *graphemes*) through which we represent the speech sounds on paper—what we call *functional phonic ability.* For example, the child with functional phonic ability records the letter *b* when he or she is writing down the sound he or she hears at the onset of the words *boys, bake,* and *boat* and pronounces a /b/ sound when he or she reads a word that starts with the letter *b.*

Good readers interpret the graphophonic cues with little conscious thought, but research—especially the research on phonemic awareness—indicates that young children can profit from some attention to the sounds and symbols of language. This attention can be an integral and enjoyable part of actual reading and writing, when children need the phonemic awareness, phonological awareness, and phonic ability to make meaning with text. Children use the graphophonic cues in conjunction with meaning-based clues (*semantic cues*)—the overall context in which a word occurs. In relying on semantic cues, readers predict what word belongs in a particular slot in a sentence by deciding whether a word makes sense there.

Good readers also perceive the melody of sentence sounds and appreciate the relationships between melody, word order, and meaning. In the elementary grades, children gain appreciation of the cadence and sentence patterns of written words by hearing tuneful sentence sounds in stories read to them, rhythmically chorusing lines of stories together, and creating word magic as they interact to compose stories together. By playing orally with sentence sounds, children intuitively gain control over the word order and sentence patterns that characterize their language and use their knowledge of those patterns to figure out words as they read. When children use their intuitive knowledge of English word order and of sentence patterns to relate words in their spoken vocabularies to words on paper, they are said to be using *syntactic cues.*

How do teachers—especially teachers who believe that meaning is most significant in early literacy events—help children to develop their abilities to use these three cuing systems: graphophonic, semantic, and syntactic? In this section, we attempt an answer to this question that emphasizes the importance of teaching children decoding and encoding strategies through authentic, meaningful reading and writing rather than through the discrete skills sheets and workbook pages that have been the basis for much early skills instruction in decoding and encoding in the past.

A Print-Rich Environment: Written Language All Around

Preschool and kindergarten teachers who believe in an approach to early literacy in which decoding skills are taught in functional contexts design their classrooms as print-rich environments. Enter Ms. Wilkening's kindergarten and you see labels everywhere. You see children's desks labeled with their names, the door labeled *door,* and windows, chairs, and walls are labeled as well. You see number words hanging from the ceiling next to the numbers themselves and color words hanging next to colored balloons. As children and teacher talk together, they refer to the labels; children locate letters and labels that apply to what they are talking about. They help their teacher make labels to affix to other things in their room. In addition, students and teacher paper the walls of their classroom with words from stories they read together and words they simply like; the result is a Word Wall—a wall of words as we talked about in Chapter 7 (Wagstaff, 1997–1998).

Students also gather to construct and share ideas that their teacher and they record on big pieces of paper: a plan-ahead chart—a list of things children are looking forward to doing during the day; a summary chart—a sentence or two about an activity they have just completed; an idea chart—a list of grand ideas they have at some point in a class conversation. The resulting charts hang everywhere in this print-rich environment, to be read and reread from one day to the next.

In Ms. Wilkening's classroom, books are everywhere, too, for this teacher has set up an environment that invites participation (Holdaway, 1986). There are little books and big books. There are books of stories, books of poems, and books about the world of nature and the world of people. Some of the books are propped up, their colorful covers clearly visible; some are shelved in the reading center where children can browse; a

GO TO

Pages 231–237 for a comprehensive discussion of shared and interactive writing.

Is there a "best" method for teaching children to read?

In the past decade, in an attempt to raise educational standards, the legislatures in 26 states have introduced legislation "encouraging or requiring the direct, explicit, and systematic use of phonics and related word skills in beginning reading instruction. . . . Comparable commands for heavy skills teaching have appeared at the local level, as in the Los Angeles schools, where the superintendent ordered . . . that phonics lessons should 'stand alone as a teaching tool'" (Cole, 2000). States have also instituted statewide testing programs to see that children are learning what they are supposed to. The outcome has been that some teachers are focusing on narrow skills through decontextualized exercises that prepare students to pass the tests.

As Gerald Duffy and James Hoffman explain, "The rationale seems to be that teachers and teacher educators cannot be trusted to make good instructional decisions on their own, so we must find the 'perfect method' for teaching reading and force this 'silver bullet' on everyone." Duffy and Hoffman contend, however, that "the answer is not in the method; it is in the teacher. It has been repeatedly established that the best instruction results when combinations of methods are orchestrated by a teacher who decides what to do in light of children's needs. . . . Hence, reading instruction effectiveness lies not with a single program or method but, rather, with a teacher who thoughtfully and analytically integrates various programs, materials, and methods as the situation demands"—what today is termed a balanced approach ("In Pursuit of an Illusion: The Flawed Search for a Perfect Method," *The Reading Teacher,* 53 [September 1999], 10–16).

DISCUSSION PROMPT

Is there a best method for teaching reading? Should teachers be given the latitude to choose the methods and materials they will use to teach reading? Why or why not? Should legislatures make instructional decisions? Why or why not? What advantages and disadvantages do you see in putting teachers in the instructional decision-making seat? What advantages and disadvantages do you see in putting legislators in the decision-making seat?

few are open on the floor in corners, waiting for children to pick them up and read. Ms. Wilkening uses books creatively as she reads aloud to children and in the context of real reading simultaneously clues in the children to ways they can match the sounds of language with the symbols they are seeing in stories. In Ms. Wilkening's kindergarten, children are learning to read by reading, just as they are learning to write by writing.

Building Phonemic and Phonological Awareness Through Predictable Stories and Poems

READ

Phonemic Awareness and the Teaching of Reading: A Position Statement of the International Reading Association. Newark, Del.: IRA, 1998.

Ms. Wilkening shared the story *"You Look Ridiculous," Said the Rhinoceros to the Hippopotamus* as a read-aloud because it is great for joining in. Filled with repetition, the story allows children to use both semantic (meaning-based) and syntactic (sentence-structure, or word-order) cues to predict words and events. We call such pieces *predictable stories.*

Bill Martin (1974) describes the response of children who are listening to a selection containing repetitive lines that pattern "Brown bear, brown bear, what do you see?" In successive lines of the story, brown bear becomes red bird and then yellow duck. Hearing the lines, children readily pick up the sentence pattern; when their teacher reads the third repetition, "Yellow duck, yellow duck," without prompting, they join in on the repeating question, "What do you see?"

As Martin explains, children who do this "have figured out how the author put his story together and they are using this information to help them read pages not even read to them yet." They can anticipate actively because they have learned "how the text works." They are using semantic as well as sound-related cues to guide their listening.

Many traditional tales have predictable words and lines: "The Little Red Hen," "The Gingerbread Boy," "The Three Little Pigs." These stories prompt children to join in while listening as their teacher reads aloud; in the process they are learning how stories develop, or are structured.

Young children can do much the same with poems and at the same time develop an awareness of the onsets and rimes that comprise words. An *onset* "is the part of the syllable that comes before the vowel and is always a consonant or consonant blend"—for example the /p/ in *pig.* "The rime is the rest of the unit"—for example, the sound of the /i/ and the /g/ in *pig* (Routman and Butler, 1995). Children begin by listening to their teacher start a couplet:

To market, to market, to buy a fat pig,
Home again, home again, jiggety- . . .

READ

Phyllis Trachtenburg, "Using Children's Literature to Enhance Phonics Instruction," *The Reading Teacher,* 43 (May 1990), 648–654, for a bibliography of trade books that contain repeating phonic elements.

As their teacher pauses before adding the final word *jig,* the children use their growing sense of the sounds of language to join in on the rhyming last word. They do the same with a second couplet that the teacher recites, using their recognition of the repetitive pattern and their growing ability to distinguish sounds of onsets and rimes to predict the final word:

To market, to market, to buy a lamb chop,
Home again, home again, hippity, hop.

The children go on to create their own versions, using words that start with the same onset as a preceding word and that end with the same rime as the word at the end of a previous line:

To market, to market, to buy a red hat,
Home again, home again, clickity, clat.

Lots of fun-filled, traditional nursery rhymes and picturebooks are available that can help children focus on the individual sounds of their language: For example,

As children listen to their teacher share a big book, they can see the illustrations and follow the enlarged lines of print. (© *Frank Siteman/Stock Boston*)

both "One, Two, Buckle My Shoe" (a nursery rhyme) and Barbara Emberley's *Drummer Hoff* (a picturebook with illustrations by Ed Emberley) are excellent for encouraging choral participation and in the process heightening children's awareness of the individual sounds of their language.

Building Sight Word Vocabulary and Graphophonic Understanding Through Shared Book Experiences

An excellent context in which children can functionally develop their decoding/encoding skills is the *shared book experience*. In conducting a shared book experience, the teacher orally reads a story to children and the children follow along with the text. Helpful here are big books in which the text and illustrations have been

WORD BANK

Shared book experience
Contextually relevant word study
Matching
Masking
Sentence reconstruction

enlarged so that youngsters can listen and watch as the teacher reads the words and moves the Magic Reading Wand from top to bottom and left to right. There are many ways to use shared books to develop children's decoding abilities in a contextually relevant manner. Here are a few examples.

A Scenario: A Shared Book Experience Don Holdaway (1982) describes a group of young children who gathered to listen to a big book. The story was *The Teeny Tiny Woman*. When the teacher got to the repeating line, "Give me my bone!" the children spontaneously joined in, correctly decoding the words *me* and *my* based on syntactic and semantic cues. When the teacher drew students' attention to the graphophonic distinction between the two (and children's attention should be drawn to elements of print such as this), they had no trouble visually distinguishing the two words. Rather quickly they added those words to their sight vocabulary.

Teachers can take advantage of words children hear and see in big books to help them make connections between the sounds of language and the letters used to write down those sounds. For example, Ruth Kiel asked her kindergarteners who had heard *The Teeny Tiny Woman* to help her record *me* and *my* in the letter *m* section of their ABC Word Wall and to offer other words that began the same way. One bright child offered *macaroni*, which Mrs. Kiel listed under *me* and *my*. Other youngsters suggested *Mary* and *Mike*, the names of children in the class, which Mrs. Kiel listed under an uppercase *M*. The teacher at this point explained a basic phonics relationship simply by saying, "I'll give you a reading hint. Whenever you see the letter *m*, read it with the sound that you make when you start the words *me* and *my*. Whenever you want to write down a word that starts with the same sound as *me* and *my*, use the letter *m*." With that, Mrs. Kiel had the students stand up and draw little *m*'s and big *M*'s in the air with their fingers as they chorused, "Give me my bone!"

At noon, when the kindergartners were eating their lunch, Mrs. Kiel suggested that they look at their milk cartons. "What letter do we use to write down the sound that we hear at the beginning of the word *milk*?" she asked. Students found the word *milk* on the carton and recorded it on their ABC Word Wall with other *m* words. Later the same day during share-time when Rick was telling about his recent trip to Disney World, he mentioned seeing Mickey Mouse. Sensing an opportunity to reinforce a phonics understanding, the teacher asked the children to chorus the name *Mickey Mouse*. When they had done that, a student called out, "Those are *m* words, too, Mrs. Kiel," and Mrs. Kiel added Mickey Mouse to the *M* section of the ABC Wall. With that, another child interjected, "Put *monkey* up there. It's an *m* word." Later that afternoon as the children were getting ready to go home, Tim's mother dropped by the classroom. Again grasping a teachable moment, the teacher said, "Let's all say 'Hello' to Tim's mom." When the children chorused, "Hello, Tim's mom," the teacher called attention to the word *mom*: "What sound do you hear at the beginning of the word *mom*? What letter do we use to write down that sound? Let's add *mom* to our ABC Wall."

Basic Instructional Strategies Using a literature-based, balanced approach to phonics instruction, primary-grade teachers can introduce a host of graphophonic relationships in much the same way as Mrs. Kiel did. Such a lesson has these elements:

- Children listen and follow along as the teacher shares a story, poem, or song inscribed in large print. The teacher points to the words as he or she reads them.

READ

Donald Richgels et al., "Kindergartners Talk About Print: Phonemic Awareness in Meaningful Contexts," *The Reading Teacher*, 49 (May 1996), 632–642. Richgels suggests asking children, "What can you show us in the print?" before reading big books aloud. Children "show" letters, sounds, and words they recognize.

CONSIDER

On the Word Wall

me

my

macaroni

milk

mom

Mary

Mike

Mickey Mouse

- Children join in on the repeating lines.
- Children talk about the story, poem, or song—what they like about it and why.
- From the piece, the teacher extracts a couple of words that share a graphophonic feature and that children can recognize on sight. Children chorus those words and see if they can figure out the shared feature. The teacher clarifies the graphophonic relationship by verbalizing something about how the language works on paper.
- The teacher records words with the shared graphophonic feature in an appropriate section of the Word Wall, highlighting the shared letters, perhaps by inscribing them in a different color from other letters. Children volunteer related words then and later, whenever words surface during reading and talk times.

In developing phonics lessons based on a shared reading of a big book story or a poetry/song chart as Mrs. Kiel was doing, kindergarten and first-grade teachers generally start by highlighting the consonant sounds as those sounds occur in the onset position rather than by highlighting vowel sounds. Teachers tend to do this because consonant sounds are more consistent in pronunciation and spelling than are the vowels and because sounds in the onset position seem to be easiest for children to differentiate.

Once the children have some control over initial consonant sounds such as /b/, /t/, /g/, and /r/, teachers can do literature-based activities with what are called consonant blends—sounds such as those we hear at the beginnings of words such as *tree, grass, bridge, draw,* and *cry.* For example, having listened and followed along as their teacher read "The Three Billy Goats Gruff," first-graders can think of other words that start with the same blended sound as the word *troll.* They remember the tuneful repeating line from the story, "Who's that going trip, trap, trip, trap over my bridge?" and roar it together. In this story context, children readily proffer *trip* and *trap* as words that start with the same sound as *troll.* They eagerly roar out other words to add to their growing number of *troll* words listed on the Word Wall under the consonant blend *tr: trick, tree, tripped.* In this context, too, children can think of other words that start with the same blended sound as *Gruff* (*grass, green, greedy*) and the same blended sound as *bridge* (*bright, bring, brave*). Teachers can help students to generalize by saying, "Use the sound you make at the beginning of the word *troll* when you see the letters *tr* at the beginning of a word." As follow-up, children keep alert for "troll" words as they read other big books together.

Simultaneously, teachers can use rhyming stories, poems, and songs to help children gain control over common phonograms, or word families such as *-at, -an, -or, -op, -et,* and *-ight.* After they have listened to and chorused a poem such as "Plop" several times as on page 207, students read it together from an enlarged chart version. Having read it over and over following the teacher's Magic Reading Wand as it guides their eyes from word to word across and down the page, children listen and look for a word that has the same rime at the end as does the word *plop.* They find *drop* and brainstorm *hop, cop, pop,* and *top,* all of which they record in columnar and highlighted fashion on the Word Wall. There are about thirty-eight phonograms of this kind, as we have seen in Chapter 3. Teachers should keep alert for stories, poems, and songs that are natural contexts for highlighting the sound/symbol relationships associated with word families.

■ ● ● ●
CONSIDER
On the Word Wall
plop
drop
hop
cop
pop
top
mop

The Teacher's Message Board

Posted here are instructional techniques for teaching decoding and encoding in functional contexts.

READING/WRITING ACTIVITIES IN FUNCTIONAL CONTEXTS

DECODING/ENCODING STRATEGIES TO EMERGE

■ **Shared reading:** Children reread a big book or chart as the teacher or a student volunteer follows the lines of print from left to right using the Magic Reading Wand.

➤ Children learn to follow and create print going from top to bottom and from left to right.

■ **Reading aloud with joining in:** Children can listen to rhyming stories and poems and join in on the rhyming words. They listen to stories in which there are many words that start with the same beginning sounds of words (onsets) and join in on chorusing them.

➤ Children become more aware of the sounds of their language, especially the rimes and onsets.

■ **Sharing writing:** Children listen while the teacher records dictated sentences on an experience chart, says the words of the sentences syllable by syllable, and stretches out the sounds used to represent the letters; finding in a shared-writing (or language experience) chart words that start with the same consonant or blend, for example, the onset at the beginning of *nest*.

➤ Children begin to hear the phonemes and rimes of their language; discriminate orally among the sounds; realize that words are composed of smaller units of sound (phonemic awareness).

■ **Matching letters:** Children match a letter printed on a sticky note with that letter found in a big book or chart, especially as the first letter of a word; they match a sticky note that contains a common phonogram (such as *ig*) with that phonogram found in a big book or chart.

➤ Children begin to discriminate visually among letters of the alphabet and name the letters (visual discrimination and letter recognition).

■ **Matching sight words:** Children match a short word such as *the*, *I*, and *you* printed on a sticky note with that word in a big book or shared writing chart.

➤ Children recognize short words on sight.

■ **Masking:** Children propose what letter to use to write the first letter of a word that has been masked out on a chart or in a book, with a sticky note; they write that letter on a sticky note the way they would do when using one letter to place-hold in invented spelling.

➤ Children hear beginning word sounds (onsets) and can associate speech sounds (phonemes) with the symbols (graphemes) used to represent those sounds.

■ **Reconstruction:** Children reconstruct individual sentences from a language experience chart or big book (the teacher cuts a copy of each sentence in half in preparation for this activity); they reconstruct several sentences from a language experience chart in the order in which those sentences appear in the chart or big book.

➤ Children use context clues to make meaning, recognize words on sight, and follow the sequence of a story.

Even as teachers are focusing children's attention on onsets and rimes during shared reading, they should help students use their growing understanding to figure out unfamiliar words. After a shared reading, teachers can remind children of what they know about print and how they can use that knowledge to decode new words. "Remember," Mrs. Kiel reminds her kindergartners, "when you are reading a word and see -op at the end, say the same sounds that you hear at the ends of *plop* and *drop*." Similarly, Mrs. Kiel reminds her students at the conclusions of other mini-lessons that deal with different onsets and rimes to keep alert for letters at the beginning and end of words that they "know how to read." Eventually, as she begins to focus students' attention on phonograms, she reminds them to keep alert for "family members" they already know. She tells them, "With what you know about how words start and how they end, you can generally guess what an unknown word is by thinking about what the story is saying at that point." Mrs. Kiel reminds her students of this strategy for unlocking new words after most shared readings and mini-lessons. She also gives her kindergartners opportunity during some shared reading times to figure out new words using their strategy and their growing knowledge of onsets and rimes.

Matching, Masking, and Reconstructing Story Sentences   Don Holdaway has explained several shared-reading instructional techniques to help children relate language sounds with the symbols of written language. One technique is to use sticky notes to make letter and word slips to accompany the text of a big book. After a shared reading, children go back to *match* the slips with the letters and words of the text, sticking them where they belong. For example, after one shared reading, children may look for words that start with the onset *b* and match those words with a sticky note that has a *b* on it. Or youngsters may match a sticky note with a sight word such as *the, me,* or *I* on it to that word in the big book. A related technique is to *mask* a particular consonant where it appears at the beginning of a word (such as the /m/ in the activities as described above), ask students to guess the letter that is masked, and ask them to insert the letter necessary to represent the sound they hear at the beginning of the word. To mask, the teacher simply puts a sticky note over the letter where it appears in the big book story.

Teachers can also prepare a cut-up version of key sentences in the big book story by printing out those sentences on chart paper and cutting apart sentences into chunks of meaning. Using their growing understanding of graphophonic and semantic cues, readers *reconstruct* the sentences. They add periods between the sentence units.

In planning activities such as these through which children develop strategies for decoding text, teachers must remember that the main goal of shared reading is youngsters' enjoyment of books. In a balanced approach, word study activities generally come *after* oral experiences in which children listen to, chorus, and talk about stories and poems. Graphophonic activities are organized as mini-lessons in which the teacher provides examples of words that share a sound/symbol relationship, encourages students to think of related words, and briefly clues in the children to an element of text that will aid them when they read and write on their own. See the Teacher's Message Board on page 279 for a chart that clarifies these functional approaches to phonics instruction.

Word Study in the Upper Elementary Grades

At second grade and beyond, students focus in much the same way on the *morphemes,* or the meaningful word units of their language: prefixes, roots, and suffixes. For example, listening to and following along with a social studies text that uses the words *replace* and *remake,* third-graders can focus on them. They clap the two syllables, note how the words are the same, brainstorm other words that begin with the prefix *re-,* and list them on their Word Wall. Based on the way in which *replace* and *remake* are used in the text, they hypothesize the meaning of *re-* ("again") and apply that meaning to other words they have listed on the Word Wall. As students continue to read, they keep an eye open for other words that start with the prefix (and other words such as *read* that might at first appear to contain the prefix but do not). Commonly used prefixes that upper-elementary students should focus on at some point are posted on the Teacher's Message Board on page 282.

In the same way, students in upper elementary grades can begin to look more closely at word roots or bases. Linda Livolosi is a sixth-grade science teacher who has found that focusing children's attention on roots can lead to more rapid understanding of technical vocabulary as well as everyday words. Teaching about invertebrates, she has her science students clap the syllables in the word and list it on the Word Wall to highlight the four syllable units. Students recall the prefix *in-* means "not" and quickly propose that an invertebrate is "not a vertebrate." They check the dictionary for *vertebrate,* discover that a vertebrate is an animal that has a backbone or spinal column, and propose that an invertebrate must be an animal without a backbone. Probing more deeply, Ms. Livolosi's sixth-graders check the word *vertebra* in the dictionary and see that it comes from the Latin verb *vertere,* meaning "to turn." Ms. Livolosi reminds her students that they have encountered lots of other words that come from that same Latin verb. She suggests the word *reverse.* Students suggest some others, list them in columnar style on the Word Wall, and highlight the *vert-* root with a colored marker: *revert, reversal, divert, diverse, diversity, invert, version, introvert, extrovert.* Some of the more commonly found Latin and Greek roots are posted on the Teacher's Message Board on page 282.

Although many upper elementary school students are ready for the kind of meaning-focused word study in which Ms. Livolosi involves her sixth-graders, teachers are finding that numbers of youngsters in grades three and up have severe decoding disabilities. One teacher told me, "Many of my fourth-graders are reading at a low primary-grade level and still have trouble connecting the sounds of language with the graphemes through which we represent the sounds. They are almost illiterate. What do I do?"

Clearly, these upper-graders are still in need of oral language activities that can help them become more aware of the sounds of language and the letters we use to represent those sounds in writing. They need to

- Be involved orally with rhyming poetry, joining in on the final rimes.
- Focus on the beginning sounds of words and in their notebooks develop their own Word Banks of words that start with the same onsets.
- Make personalized alphabet books with pages that include lots of words that start with the same sounds.

The Teacher's Message Board

Posted here are word elements to discover as part of ongoing reading. Encourage readers to figure out meanings of prefixes and roots based on the way a word is used in a sentence they are reading. Encourage them to search for other words with an element.

Prefixes

Prefix	Meaning	Sample	Prefix	Meaning	Sample
ab-, a-, abs-	away, from	abduct	ad-	to	admit
anti-, anta-	against	antiwar	pro-	for	prowar
inter-,	between	interstate	intra-	within	intrastate
in-, im-, il-	not	impossible	non-	not	nonsense
un-	not	unhappy	contra-, counter-	against	contrary
re-	again	review	ex-, e-	out of	eject
pre-	before	preview	post-	after	postpone
sub-	under	submarine	super-	above	superior
circum-	around	circumvent	se-	apart	secede
trans-	across	transfer	con-, co-	together	cooperate

Roots or Bases

Root	Meaning	Sample	Root	Meaning	Sample
bene-	good	benefit	mal-	bad	malice
scrib-, script	to write	scribble	-graph	writing	phonograph
bio-	life	biology	geo-	earth	geology
prim-	first	primary	uni-	one	unite
bi-	two	bicycle	duo-	two	duet
tri-	three	triple	cent-	hundred	century
fact-	to make	manufacture	cred-	to believe	credit
ject-	to throw	eject	port-	carry	export
vert-	to turn	revert	duct-	to lead	conduct
-logy	study of	geology	ped-	foot	pedal

In short, these students need the same kinds of meaning-focused, oral language activities that we have just been talking about and that are posted on the Teacher's Message Board on page 279.

Additionally, teachers need to work with their upper elementary grade students to help them to build oral reading fluency. The strategies that upper elementary grade teachers use to help disfluent readers are the same strategies that primary-grade teachers have found useful: teacher modeling, choral and repeated readings, buddy and assisted reading, guided oral reading, and reading aloud to oneself as part of guided reading. In the next section, we will clarify these strategies.

Oral Reading Fluency

Most of us remember being in a class where we had to take a turn reading a paragraph of text aloud. Those of us who had problems reading aloud may remember hoping we

WORD BANK

Fluent oral reading

Choral and repeated readings

Share-pairs and assisted reading

Guided oral reading

Reading aloud to self

would get a part with easy words—words we could pronounce without stumbling. We may remember that we did not think much about what we were reading; instead we concentrated on getting the words right so that we would not look foolish.

Experienced teachers recognize the pitfalls in round-robin reading regardless of the level of schooling where a teacher may use it. They realize that in many cases, students who read aloud are simply saying words and that a student's being able to render a passage orally does not mean that he or she is comprehending it. They also realize that during round-robin reading, teachers in the past gave little attention to the skills important in a fluent oral rendering of a text. According to Meribethe Richards (2000, p. 535, based on Zutell and Rasinski, 1991, and on Dowhower, 1991), three skills underlie *fluent oral reading*:

- *Rate,* or the ability to pace an oral reading of a selection appropriately.
- *Smoothness,* or the ability to recognize words automatically and quickly.
- *Phrasing,* or the ability to read with expression and to express the rhythmic and melodic patterns of a passage.

There is some evidence that these skills are necessary if readers are to comprehend what they read and enjoy reading (Nathan and Stanovich, 1991; Rasinski, 2000). For readers to "interact meaningfully with a variety of texts, they must be competent in word recognition, read at a suitable rate, and understand how to project the natural intonation and phrasing of the spoken word upon the written word" (Richards, 2000). As Timothy Rasinski (2000) summarizes, "Excessively slow, disfluent reading is associated with poor comprehension."

Teacher Modeling Perhaps one of the best ways for a teacher to teach the skills associated with fluent oral reading is to read aloud to students, who follow the text in their books. The teacher reads expressively. He or she varies the rate of reading depending on the meanings and feelings he or she senses in the text, clusters words in meaningful phrases, varies pitch and loudness to heighten meaning, uses pause for effect, and interprets punctuation through vocal changes. Having shared a dramatic portion of text, the teacher draws students' attention to characteristics of his or her oral rendering by asking, "What did I do with my voice to draw you into the story? Where did I slow down? Where did I speed up? Where did I speak more loudly? Where did I speak more softly? Where did I pause? Where did I get excited? Why do you think that I did this?" (after Rasinski, 2000).

Choral and Repeated Readings Having modeled and encouraged students to think about the way he or she used vocal changes in reading a passage aloud to them, the teacher asks children to reread orally and together the portion of text they have just heard. The teacher urges, "Let's all try to read this aloud, using our voices to show the meanings and our feelings, just as you heard me do." Over the years, educators have recommended *choral reading* as a way to help children interpret the sounds and rhythms of poetry (Miccinati, 1985). Clearly, chorusing poems expressively as a class is an approach that helps children hear the melody of their language, but choral reading works equally well as a way to develop oral reading fluency as it relates to prose. Teacher and children chorus and rechorus a passage, experimenting with different ways of varying the voice to express underlying meanings. Once the class has performed a passage together several times, individual children can volunteer to perform a read-aloud of it.

By doing this, the teacher is tapping into the power of another strategy important in the development of oral reading fluency: *repeated readings.* With repeated readings, children gain control over the hard words; they begin to pronounce them smoothly and confidently. They also gain control over aspects of phrasing. They begin to cluster words into meaningful chunks and interpret the cues embedded in the punctuation marks. These skills practiced in the context of one passage carry over to other passages, which in turn increases fluency in both oral and silent reading. Repeated readings have also been shown to increase comprehension (Samuels, 1997).

Share-Pairs and Assisted Reading   During workshop periods, the teacher can divide listeners into *share-pairs* who take turns rereading to each other a story they have already heard or even a story they have read silently to themselves. Two buddies may curl up under a desk to reread a story, two others may find a quiet corner where they reread, while two others may take turns rereading a class big book mounted on an easel. At the same time, other buddies may reread to each other trade books they have chosen for independent reading. Because repeated readings have been shown to increase both reading fluency and comprehension, students should be encouraged to reread the same material on several occasions. Remember, too, that rereading, practiced orally, is as helpful at upper levels as it is in the primary grades; it is particularly useful when a teacher is working with children who have a reading disability or are learning English as a second language.

Another form that oral reading can take is *assisted reading,* in which two or more students together read aloud a passage that they have already read silently or that the teacher has read to them. Assisted, or paired, reading gives readers a sense of security and enables the better reader to assist the weaker one with hard words.

Guided Oral Reading   At times, teachers rely on *guided oral reading* as a follow-up to silent reading. For example, after fourth-graders have read a chapter of *Stone Fox* to themselves, the teacher says, "Let's find a part that shows little Willy's determination." Students revisit the text and a volunteer reads aloud words that Willy speaks that show he is determined; classmates follow the text in their books. Or the teacher says, "I felt scared with little Willy. Where in the chapter did you feel scared with him? Let's read the lines together and show our concern in our voices."

Here children are sharing lines that they have read silently and have chosen for a particular purpose. They have prepared the lines for oral reading by rereading them in their minds. Once volunteers have shared lines they have chosen, the entire group can chorus and rechorus them, working on a fluent and meaningful rendering.

Reading Aloud to Oneself as Part of Guided Reading   Guided reading is an approach to reading instruction that is based on the premise that children need some explicit skills instruction. The approach draws heavily on strategies developed as part of Reading Recovery, a program carefully structured to help young children catch up on skills that they need. Using guided reading, the teacher introduces a new book to children by "walking them through it." Children predict based on the cover and read the title and author's name; the teacher gives a brief overview of the story and may introduce some words or word patterns from the story. After that, all the children in

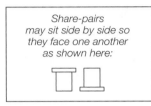

Share-pairs may sit side by side so they face one another as shown here:

GO TO

Chapter 6, page 199, for detail on Readers' Theatre, another strategy for developing fluency.

the group *read aloud to themselves.* As children read aloud, the teacher keeps alert for children who may be struggling with the text. The teacher may help students who seem to be having trouble with particular words, giving them a strategy for handling a part in the text that is posing a problem to them. At times, he or she may sit next to a student who is struggling and read chorally with that youngster.

After the first read-through, children reread, concentrating this time on oral reading fluency and comprehension. Choral reading and teacher modeling of selected sections can follow, as can a skill-building mini-lesson that the teacher feels is needed based on problems that he or she has picked up as the youngsters have read aloud to themselves. Lessons deal with onsets and rimes, interpretation of punctuation, chunking of works into meaningful phrases, changing tone and pitch of voice when a different character speaks—in short, with any element of oral reading that children need to succeed.

One-on-One Reading for Instruction and Diagnosis of Decoding Problems

With children who read on a sound-by-sound basis or generally have trouble decoding the sounds of their language, the teacher is wise to schedule time for individual oral reading. During a reading conference held while other youngsters are reading to themselves or to a classmate, the teacher may engage one child in assisted reading. The teacher may also take these steps:

1. Ask the child to read aloud a short passage at his or her instructional level and talk about what he or she has read.
2. Praise the child for doing something well, particularly with respect to *self-monitoring*—going back to self-correct a decoding *miscue,* or error.
3. Discuss one or two miscues the child did not self-correct.
4. Provide a fast mini-lesson relative to a specific miscue the child has shown. This last step can occur in a small group that the teacher has put together based on a common miscue problem.

Barbara Taylor and Linda Nosbush (1983), who have researched one-on-one oral reading of this kind, report that through its use, poorer readers begin to employ more self-correcting behaviors.

One-on-one reading provides a setting not only for instruction but for diagnosing a child's ability to decode, or crack the written code. In an individual conference, as the child reads aloud, the teacher interprets his or her pattern of decoding errors and determines to what extent the miscue disrupts meaning. *Miscue analysis* provides valuable clues to a reader's interaction with a text (Y. Goodman, 1997).

Summarizing ideas about miscue analysis, Burns, Roe, and Ross (1999) suggest five kinds of questions the teacher should consider in reference to a child's decoding errors:

1. Is the miscue a result of the reader's dialect? If a child says *foe* for *four,* she may simply be using a familiar pronunciation that does not affect meaning.
2. Does the miscue change the meaning? If a child says *dismal* for *dismiss,* the substitution makes no sense, showing that he is not using semantic cues in decoding at this point in the text.

READ

Yetta Goodman, "Reading Diagnosis: Qualitative Versus Quantitative," *The Reading Teacher,* 50 (April 1997), 534–538.

3. Does the reader self-correct? If a child says a word that does not make sense but self-corrects, he realizes that something isn't right, based on the semantic cues in the text.

4. Is the reader using syntactic cues? If a child says *run* for *chase* (and substitutes the same part of speech), she shows reliance on syntactic cues; but if a child says *beautiful* for *boy,* she is failing to use the underlying sentence structure to help in decoding the word.

5. Is the reader using graphic cues? A child who substitutes *house* for *horse, running* for *run,* and *dogs* for *dog* is not using all the graphic cues available.

By analyzing a child's miscues, the teacher gathers information on what cues—semantic, syntactic, and/or graphophonic—to emphasize with a particular reader.

Summary Thoughts on Decoding and Oral Reading Fluency

In this section of Chapter 8, you have been considering ways to help children handle print with ease and assurance. The emphasis has been on helping children to develop graphophonic strategies "within the context of meaningful reading and writing activities" so that they are able to apply "phonics concepts as they read and write" (Dahl and Scharer, 2000, p. 594). The emphasis has also been on helping students to perceive the structural elements that comprise words—the affixes and roots—and to develop as fluent readers within the context of authentic reading and writing activity.

As Regie Routman and Andrea Butler (1995) remind us, "Good teachers . . . never abandoned phonics. They always acknowledged that phonics had an important place in the reading and writing process without being an end in itself. We believe the issue has never been whether or not phonics should be taught, but when, how, how much, and why." Similarly, we can say that good teachers never abandoned study of word elements or oral reading engagements to develop fluency. Again, the question has not been whether but how.

In this section, you did not visit with teachers who were teaching decoding strategies by assigning worksheets in which children circled pictures of items whose names started with the same sound or letter or in which children circled the prefixes in a series of words. You did not look over the shoulders of children who spent most of their language arts time "sounding out" rather than reading. You did not see children reading in round-robin style. What you did see were teachers helping youngsters acquire sound-letter knowledge, word understanding, and fluency through authentic reading, writing, and oral language activities.

Elementary teachers have a vast repertoire of exciting, literature-based strategies and materials for getting children started down the road to literacy: big books, predictable stories, rhymes, choral reading, Word Walls, matching and masking, shared reading, shared writing, teacher modeling, assisted reading, rereadings, guided oral reading. To put it bluntly, teachers who rely on worksheets and workbooks to teach sound/symbol relationships and who allocate most of children's language arts time to the teaching of phonics are more likely to make children dislike reading rather than help them see the joyful endeavor that it truly is.

Comprehension: Interacting and Constructing Meaning with Text

Kurt selected a book. He had read other books by the same author, and the cover and title of this one struck his fancy. He read the jacket blurb and then flipped through, looking at the black-and-white line drawings and the chapter titles. The book appeared to be an adventure story—a chase—and he was in the mood for some exciting reading, so he decided to try it.

Sprawling on the floor, Kurt began to read. In the first chapter, he met Jake, the main character, and learned what Jake's problem was: His father had died, leaving Jake and his dog—Jim Ugly—alone. Reading between the lines, Kurt figured out that Jake must be about his age. He made a fast judgment, too: He decided that he was going to like this book because he could relate to Jake. Shortly, he was immersed in the story, so engrossed that he visualized himself participating in the action. Later, having read several chapters, Kurt heard his mother call and had to put down the book, but in doing so he took Jake with him. Now, in his imagination, he spun a tale of his own, of meeting Jake and the adventure the two would have together.

An Interactive-Constructive (I-C) Model of Comprehension

WORD BANK

Interactive-constructive model

Schemata

Metacognition

Good readers like Kurt interact with texts they are reading. They have personal expectations about what they will get from a selection, and they bring those expectations to bear as they read by predicting and testing their predictions. They actively create meaning by constructing, or generating, relationships between what is within the text and what they already know. This view of reading is called *interactive-constructive* (I-C). Proponents of an interactive-constructive model of comprehension believe that the meanings a reader makes depend on what both the reader and the author bring to the text, as shown in Figure 8.2. In contrast, a bottom-up, or text-driven view of comprehension sees meaning as residing in the text. The reader's job is to "get at" that meaning by working from the parts (sounds, letters, individual words) to the whole (the story meanings). An interactive model contrasts, too, with a top-down, or reader-based, view, which sees meaning residing entirely in the reader. According to top-down theory, what the reader makes of a text is what that text is all about (Miller, 1988).

World Knowledge and Comprehension   In constructing meaning, good readers draw on their prior knowledge of the subject—their "world knowledge." Readers have networks of prior understanding about a topic, what theorists call *schemata*. A schema is a set of expectations, or what George Miller (1988) calls "an abstract knowledge structure stored in long-term memory." In reading, readers modify and add to their existing schemata. From this perspective, the prior knowledge readers have about a subject has as much to do with their comprehension of a passage as the actual words written in it.

Researchers have investigated the effect of prior knowledge on comprehension. In

Figure 8.2
An Interactive-Constructive
Model of Comprehension

DISCUSSION PROMPT

■ An I-C model suggests that
each child's interaction with a
particular text differs and that
each child constructs meanings
that are uniquely his or her
own. Instruction based on an I-C
model includes considerable
individualization. How will your
understanding of I-C theory
affect your teaching?

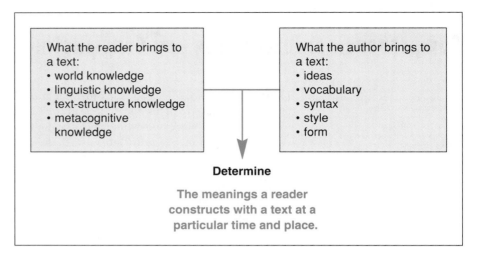

What the reader brings to
a text:
• world knowledge
• linguistic knowledge
• text-structure knowledge
• metacognitive
  knowledge

What the author brings to
a text:
• ideas
• vocabulary
• syntax
• style
• form

Determine

**The meanings a reader
constructs with a text at a
particular time and place.**

one study (Miller, 1988) sixth-graders were asked to read two passages—one about the game of horseshoes, which was familiar to them, and one about an unfamiliar game. The children's comprehension of the passage about the familiar game of horseshoes was greater than their comprehension of the passage about the unfamiliar game. As Miller explains, the children's existing "horseshoe schema" helped them to "organize and remember the information in the text about the game of horseshoes."

Some theorists (Hirsch, 1987; Ravitch and Finn, 1987) suggest that educators have not given enough attention to the development of children's world knowledge. They contend that young people lack the network of information necessary to read news magazines and newspapers with any degree of comprehension. For example, some high school seniors cannot identify the country on the southern border of the United States and cannot name the New England states. To help children comprehend, these theorists propose, the school must provide a curriculum that requires them to read significant content.

Linguistic Knowledge and Comprehension   As Figure 8.2 shows, in making meaning good readers also draw on their knowledge of how language works—their "linguistic knowledge." They apply their understanding of how written symbols are used to represent speech sounds, how punctuation marks are used to break messages into thought units, how sentences are structured (word order), and how ideas are linked into a cohesive message. Look, for example, at this paragraph:

> The monkey swung from tree to tree. When she found a ripe banana, she would
> stop and pick it, peel it, and eat it. Then she would continue her trip through
> the trees.

To understand this paragraph, readers obviously must be able to decode the words—relate the phonemes and syllables of English to the graphemes through which they are represented on paper. But equally important, readers must understand linguistic

Distinguished Educator

The National Council of Teachers of English and the International Reading Association are the premier organizations in the United States dedicated to the advancement of literacy. In the words of the *Standards for the English Language Arts,* developed by these organizations, "Before even beginning the first sentence of a text, knowledgeable readers know how to approach and frame a reading experience with a sense of purpose, need, and direction. Becoming a knowledgeable reader, however, takes time and many experiences with different kinds of texts. Young learners soon recognize that they must orchestrate several different kinds of information in text. Drawing upon their sense of phonological awareness (their conscious awareness that spoken words can be broken into separate sounds and/or sound units), their knowledge of word meanings and language structure, and their knowledge of the world, they develop strategies for making meaning from many experiences with a variety of texts. . . . One of the most important

functions of English language arts education is to help students learn to interpret texts—that is, to reflect on textual meaning from their own perspectives—and to evaluate texts—that is, to use critical thinking to identify particular text elements, such as logic, emotional appeal, and purpose. As students interpret and evaluate texts, they explore their own feelings, values, and responses to the ideas presented. Thus, they make their own responses to texts an integral part of their reading experience" (Newark, Del. and Urbana, Ill.: IRA and NCTE, 1996, pp. 31, 33).

DISCUSSION PROMPT

How can you help children become "meaning makers" as they read? How can you help them "orchestrate several different kinds of information in text"? What kinds of experiences with text should children have within the language arts curriculum, especially a curriculum based on an interactive-constructive view of comprehension?

relationships. They must link the pronoun *it* with its antecedent, *a ripe banana.* They must recognize the time relationships implied by *when* and *then.* They must link the *trip through the trees* in the last sentence to the monkey swinging from tree to tree in the first. Today reading specialists suggest that an important aspect of comprehension is being able to make the linkages suggested by linguistic clues such as these, which give coherence to a selection (Moe and Irwin, 1986).

Knowledge of Text Structure and Comprehension   The knowledge of text structure that readers bring to a selection affects comprehension as well. A story has a structure that includes setting and characters, problem, action and reaction sequences leading to a resolution of the problem, and a theme that binds the story together. In contrast, an informational passage develops logically, often starting with an introduction that sets forth the thesis, or main idea, and the points that are to come. Headings indicate major sections of the text, and a summary reviews main points. A poem may have a repeating pattern. Various genres work differently because authors construct them to serve different social purposes. Good readers use their knowledge of the genres to make choices as they construct what a particular text means.

Metacognitive Knowledge and Comprehension   A reader's metacognitive knowledge also determines the meanings that a reader makes with a text. *Metacognition* refers to people's awareness of how they learn, know, and read; it refers to their awareness of how they go about making meaning and how they monitor their own comprehension during reading. Good readers monitor their comprehension knowingly as they read. They raise and answer questions in their heads, they visualize, they predict, they correct their predictions as they go along, they summarize to themselves, and they reread to "fix up" when they know they do not understand. In short, good readers have reading know-how. They know how they approach reading, and they vary their strategies depending on their purpose and the material they are reading. According to Ann Brown et al. (1986), metacognitive control is highly important in reading success.

   In sum, readers bring knowledge and awareness to reading that affect their comprehension: world knowledge, linguistic knowledge, text-structure knowledge, and metacognitive knowledge. In the remainder of this section and in the next, we will think about ways to help children activate what they already know as they make meaning with text. We will begin by talking about before-reading activities that heighten comprehension, move to consider things good readers do while reading, and then consider after-reading strategies.

Before Reading: Building a Framework for Comprehending

WORD BANK
Directed Reading-Thinking
Activity (DR-TA)
K-W-L Plus
Word webbing

As we saw in the vignette that opens this chapter, Ms. Wilkening involved her kindergartners in a before-reading talk-time that prepared them to function as interactive-constructive readers. Displaying the encyclopedia pictures, Ms. Wilkening first sparked children's talk about the hippopotamus and how it wallows in the mud, using the word *wallows* in the before-reading talk-time and pantomiming the action. Next, Ms. Wilkening shared the encyclopedia pictures of the rhinoceros and got children talking about the rhino's horns—world knowledge important to comprehension in that the hippo's lack of horns is the problem that starts the story action. Then she involved them in a discussion of the meaning of *ridiculous*. These activities made it possible for children to predict reasons for the rhino's saying to the hippo, "You look ridiculous."

Predicting—The Directed Reading-Thinking Activity (DR-TA)   At some point, teachers need to do what Ms. Wilkening was doing—teaching children to predict what they think will happen in a selection they are going to read or what will happen next in the selection they are reading. Before reading an expository piece, readers must make a brief survey of the text in order to predict.

   According to Russell Stauffer, prediction gives readers a purpose and a framework for understanding what they read. Children read to test their predictions, or hypotheses. This strategy—predicting before reading a portion of text, reading to test predictions, and clarifying ideas through discussion after reading—is essentially the strategy of a *Directed Reading-Thinking Activity,* or *DR-TA* (Stauffer, 1980).

Predictive questions teachers can ask young readers before they read include these:

1. Read the title, study the cover, look at the pictures, and then predict: Who is this about? When did it happen? Where did it happen? What is going to happen?
2. Look at the way the words are put on the pages and the lines are organized. Predict: Is this a story? A poem? Is it about facts?
3. Set your purpose: What do you want to get out of this? Fun? Facts? Feelings?
4. Decide: How should you read this? Fast? Carefully?

Teachers can expand these questions as upper elementary readers read expository texts:

1. Read the title. Study the cover, pictures, charts, graphs, and tables. Predict: What is this going to be about? What do you already know about this topic? Do we need to get more information before we read?
2. Survey the text. Decide: How is the selection organized? Is there an introduction? A summary at the end? Some study questions? How are the headings and sub-headings laid out? What kinds of graphics are there?
3. Decide: How will you read this? Just skim for big ideas? Read fast? Read for details? Take notes?

These questions are the same ones youngsters themselves should raise as they prepare for independent reading. By asking these predictive questions during before-reading conversations and making readers aware of them, teachers are modeling a strategy students can use as they read and study on their own.

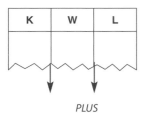

CONSIDER

| K | W | L |

PLUS

sort, categorize, organize, and/or web to highlight relationships

Activating Prior Knowledge—K-W-L Plus   Donna Ogle (1986) suggests a slightly different teaching model to help children to activate what they know prior to reading; Ogle calls her teaching model *K-W-L Plus.* The *K* in K-W-L Plus stands for "What I *Know,*" the *W* for "What I *Want* to Learn," the *L* for "What I *Learned,*" and the Plus for the categorizing and organizing of material learned. Before reading an informational piece, Ogle suggests that students survey it to get an overview of what it is about. Based on their before-reading survey, students talk about what they already know on that topic, recording in the first column of a three-column chart words, phrases, and sentences that come to mind. Students also set a purpose for their reading: They talk about what they hope to learn from reading the selection, and each youngster records his or her projections in the central column of his or her K-W-L Plus chart. Having read the selection, students add to the chart information they have found out, categorize the information they have listed, and create a graphic organizer to clarify relationships (Carr and Ogle, 1987; Shelley et al., 1997). Although K-W-L Plus is a general instructional model that teachers can use to organize classroom reading activities especially in relation to expository text, readers can use the strategy as they study material on their own. Students construct their own three-column charts on which they make notes before, during, and after reading.

Developing Vocabulary   Teachers can also prepare children for reading and help activate readers' prior knowledge by interjecting into the before-reading talk some of the vocabulary from a selection. Ms. Wilkening did this by using the words *rhinoceros, hippopotamus,* and *ridiculous* before reading and by having children recall that *ridiculous* means "silly." During the reading, she did it, too, by having the children chorus the repeating line, "Do you think I look ridiculous?" Research indicates that understanding of the vocabulary of a selection is a primary determinant of a reader's comprehension of the ideas developed in that selection.

Using the words of a selection during before-reading conversations is perhaps the most natural way to clarify pivotal vocabulary, but there are other ways, too, to activate what children already know and at the same time interject key words. One is brainstorming, followed by *word webbing.* Using this strategy, the teacher asks children to call out words, phrases, or ideas that come to mind when they think of the topic of a selection they are about to read. The teacher offers words as well—especially words that are key to understanding the main ideas of the selection. The teacher or a student records the brainstormed words on the board or a chart. Together, participants organize the words into a web or chart that highlights relationships.

WORD BANK

Mind talk

Thinking aloud

While Reading: Mind Talking

As was explained in Chapter 3, much of young children's speech is egocentric: Toddlers talk aloud to themselves. With maturity comes the ability to direct thoughts to others and the diminution of egocentric speech. Lev Vygotsky (1962) believes that as children mature, egocentric speech is internalized; instead of speaking aloud to themselves, children learn to talk to themselves in their heads. This is inner speech, or *mind talk,* which is directly related to thought in older children and adults.

Mind talk is what good readers do as they read. They respond continuously to what they read by talking to themselves in their heads (Davey, 1983). They respond by

- Forming pictures in their minds of what they are reading (*visualizing*).
- Linking what they are reading to what they already know.
- Predicting what is going to happen.
- Clarifying confusing points.
- Raising and answering questions about the text and its structure.
- Evaluating and criticizing what they are reading.
- Correcting errors in comprehension.

Thinking Aloud Beth Davey (1983) and James Baumann, Leah Jones, and Nancy Seifert-Kessell (1993) recommend that the teacher orally model the process of mind talking while reading. Here modeling means *thinking aloud:* reading aloud and describing the thoughts that come to mind before, during, and after reading a particular selection. Essentially, what the teacher does is show students how to talk to themselves as part of reading—how to respond by generating their own text and how to monitor their own comprehension. As Allan Collins, John Seely Brown, and Ann Holum (1991) explain, "One needs to deliberately bring the thinking to the surface, to make it visible."

How does a think-aloud sound in action? Here is an example with the teacher's think-aloud comments in italics and the text by the author in regular print:

CONSIDER

This selection is from Lee Sheridan, "The Bridge They Said Couldn't Be Built," in *In Concert* by Leo Fay et al. (Chicago: Riverside Publishing, 1989).

The Bridge They Said Couldn't Be Built

From the pictures I know this is about the Brooklyn Bridge, near New York City, about how the bridge was built. I wonder why they said it couldn't be built.

New York in the Winter of 1866–1867

The winter of 1866–1867 *That was just after the Civil War* was one of the worst ever recorded in the history of New York. Snow covered most of the area, and great blocks of ice clogged the East River between Manhattan and Brooklyn. *The East River must separate Manhattan and Brooklyn.* Often the Fulton Street ferryboat was unable to cross the East River. *That was because the ice blocked the river.* So people trying to get to work in Manhattan or return home to Brooklyn were jammed up at each river bank. *I guess the Brooklyn Bridge hadn't yet been built.* What's more, with no electricity and no telephones, there was no way of communicating across the river except by boat.

John A. Roebling

One person who didn't think a bridge was impossible was an engineer named John A. Roebling. Roebling was known throughout the world as the expert bridge builder of the day. *I guess he had made a lot of bridges.* Suspension bridges were his specialty. *The Golden Gate Bridge is a suspension bridge.* A suspension bridge is a bridge suspended by wire cables hung over towers and fastened on the land at both ends. *That's the definition of a suspension bridge—suspended by wire cables hung over towers and fastened on the land at both ends. I can picture that.*

Roebling had founded his own Wire Rope Company to manufacture the cables for suspension bridges. *He called it wire rope because he was making wire cables.* In 1866 he had just completed the longest suspension bridge ever built—a bridge in Cincinnati over the Ohio River. If anyone could build a suspension bridge over the East River—a length of half a mile—John A. Roebling was the one to do it. *The East River Bridge is half a mile long.*

Several years earlier, Roebling had submitted a plan for a suspension bridge connecting Manhattan and Brooklyn. No other kind of bridge could be built across an area as wide as the East River and also allow ships to pass underneath. *The East River must have been an important shipping route because of New York City.* Still, the officials of both New York and Brooklyn had doubts. They rejected Roebling's first plan as impossible. *It says first plan, so he must have kept trying.*

Farr (1987) suggests that children who have followed a text while listening to a teacher do a think-aloud identify the strategies the teacher used to think about the selection and record the strategies brainstorm-fashion on the chalkboard. They might identify the teacher's before-reading predicting based on the title and the pictures, reading to test predictions, visualizing, questioning and answering, relating content to facts already known, fixing up earlier interpretations, clarifying relationships in the text, inferring, and restating key information. Children pair off to practice mind talking while reading. Eventually they practice the strategies while reading to themselves.

Davey (1983) recommends using self-assessment checklists to monitor thinking-while-reading behaviors. An example is given in Figure 8.3. During follow-up discussion, youngsters describe the thoughts that went through their minds as they read.

SELF-ASSESSMENT CHECKLIST: MY THOUGHTS WHILE READING			
	Never	Some	A Lot
1. I made predictions.			
2. I made pictures in my mind.			
3. I asked myself questions and answered them.			
4. I thought about things I already knew.			
5. I corrected my predictions as I read.			
6. I explained things to myself in my head.			
7. I figured out word meanings from the context of the sentence and the structure of the words.			
8. I reread to fix up when I knew I did not understand.			

Figure 8.3
A Checklist of Thinking-While-Reading Behaviors

ACTIVITY PROMPT

Read a story. Then categorize your mind talk using this guide.

GO TO

Figure 8.3 and note 7.

Using Context and Word-Structure Clues   One kind of thought that goes through readers' minds relates to word meanings. Able readers do not know the meaning of every word they meet, but they do have a strategy for handling an unfamiliar one: the Skip-Over Strategy. They simply skip the unfamiliar word if they can get the overall sense of a sentence from the other words and if the purpose of their reading is enjoyment or general information, as would be the case in reading novels, newspapers, or magazines. This is in contrast to less able readers who, frustrated when they meet an unfamiliar word, come to a grinding halt and may give up on reading.

The reading of technical selections calls for a different set of strategies. When able readers are studying complicated texts and meet an unfamiliar technical term, they do pause to consider the meaning of the new word:

- *Strategy 1*. They look for *context clues* the author has built into the sentence: a synonym somewhere near the unfamiliar word; words or phrases of opposite meaning somewhere nearby; an explicit definition or explanation of the technical term.
- *Strategy 2*. At times, they find a clue to meaning within the word itself—a *word-structure clue* such as a prefix or root they know.
- *Strategy 3*. They talk to themselves in their minds, *restating* the meaning of the term and sometimes writing a definition in their learning logs.
- *Strategy 4*. When able readers cannot tell themselves the meaning of a technical term, they look it up in the *glossary* of the book or in a *dictionary*.
- *Strategy 5*. Then they try out the given definition in the context of the sentence they are wrestling with.

● ● ● ●

CONSIDER

Word-Cracking Strategies:
 Context analysis
 Word-structure analysis
 Restating
 If still in doubt
  Dictionary check
  Context application

Typically, though, able readers rely on context clues, checking a dictionary only when they cannot crack the meaning through analysis of sentence and word relationships.

Teachers should model for readers the way they use mind talk to figure out word meanings from context and word-structure clues. They must model the different approaches: getting the meaning from the overall sense of the sentence; focusing on synonym, antonym, and word-structure clues; pausing to restate definitions of technical terms encountered in study reading; deciding whether to check the glossary; applying the dictionary definition to the context. Teachers should be cautious about suggesting that students stop to look up each unfamiliar word; frequent halts destroy fluency, continuity of thought, and interest.

After Reading: Talking and Writing in Response to Stories

When children talk about a text that they are reading, teachers may invite youngsters to think about meanings they have been making in their minds. In responding aloud, children talk through their thoughts—something they do in their heads when they read independently. After the discussion, teachers can encourage students to identify the kinds of thinking they have been doing during the discussion. Teachers can explain that these are the same kinds of thoughts and feelings readers pursue as they respond on their own.

Literal Comprehension At times, readers *think literally:* They think in terms of the facts, sequences of events, main ideas and supporting details, causes and effects stated directly in a text. Readers tell themselves these aspects of the text, restating them in their minds and perhaps organizing them in an attempt to remember them. This way of responding to a text is, of course, efferent: Emphasis is on taking away information from a text (Rosenblatt, 1978). As Burns, Roe, and Ross (1996) explain, however, literal comprehension is fundamental; it requires a thorough understanding of word, sentence, and paragraph meanings and is necessary if readers are to make more complex meanings.

To trigger reconstructions of what children have been reading, a teacher may say, "Let's talk about what's going on here." Having read a story, children may tell who the characters are and some of the things that happen—this before going on to consider more complex relationships. Having read an informational piece, children may tell some of the main ideas and supporting details and organize them as a data chart, time line, or flow chart.

GO TO

Pages 170–172 for main-idea–making strategies.

Interpretive Comprehension At times, readers *interpret* information they have read: They read between the lines, generating information and ideas not directly stated. In doing this, readers make inferences. They may infer time relationships, such as the year, time of day, or season when a story takes place; geographical relationships; cause-and-effect relationships; the ages, feelings, family relationships of characters; and main ideas and generalizations if these points are not stated explicitly in the text.

Interpretive reading also involves ferreting out meanings communicated through idioms, literary allusions, and figures of speech. The author who writes of a person, "He had no heart," does not mean this literally but is relying on an idiom. The author who describes a man with a Midas touch is communicating something special, too—something meaningful only to the reader who recognizes the allusion to the

The Teacher's Message Board

Posted here is a lesson plan to teach comprehension, fluent reading, and paragraphing through authentic reading and writing. Try modeling your literature-based lesson plans after this plan by teacher JoAnn Peterson.

A Third-Grade Lesson on Chapter 1 of *The Courage of Sarah Noble*

Objectives:

The students will be able to show empathy for the characters, Sarah and John Noble, by putting themselves in the characters' shoes; make inferences about the characters based on their actions and words; make predictions about the story based on events in Chapter 1. They will be better able to read aloud in a fluent manner; they will be better able to construct logically developed paragraphs.

Anticipatory Set:

■ Introduce the book by showing the cover and asking students to brainstorm based on the cover and the word *courage.*

■ Guide a talk-about on the topic of courage with students giving examples from their lives. Teacher and students interactively will create and record in paragraph form a prereading chart that explains the meaning of courage.

■ Guide children to predict what the story is about based on the cover. Teacher and students interactively will create and record a second paragraph on their prereading chart that enumerates their predictions.

Guided Instruction and Modeling:

■ Set a purpose for listening to Chapter 1: Pretend you are Sarah. How do you feel about being in the wilderness? Why do you want Father to tell you about home? What kind of person are you, Sarah? What kind of person is Father?

■ Hang a shiny star from the ceiling. Ask students to get comfortable on the floor. Turn out most of the lights to simulate night. With flashlight in hand, read aloud the first chapter of the story to the students while emphasizing the animal sounds. Read with a variable voice tone to show the nervousness of Sarah and the calmness of Father. At the end of the chapter, pause a moment before turning on the lights to allow the students to reflect.

■ Ask students if they think that Sarah is courageous and tell why or why not. Distribute copies of the book to students and ask them to find lines to read aloud that support their inference that Sarah was courageous. Encourage fluent oral reading through choral reading and rereading of lines suggested.

■ Encourage talk about how students felt when they pretended to be Sarah, how they felt about being in the wilderness, and why Sarah kept asking Father to tell about home.

■ Ask students to take out their literature response journals (LRJs) and write in response: What kind of person is Sarah? Father? Follow with sharing and talking about entries. Based on what the children contribute, interactively create a character comparison chart on the chalkboard, recording together the characteristics that Sarah and Father share, and those that are unique to each character.

Sarah's Unique Characteristics

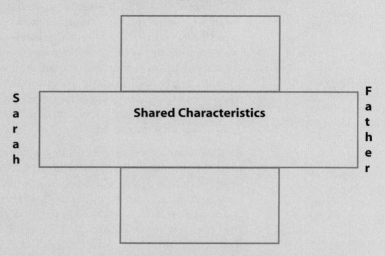

S
a
r
a
h

Shared Characteristics

F
a
t
h
e
r

Father's Unique Characteristics

Concluding Set:

■ Discuss: What does it take to be courageous? When do you think the story takes place? What do you predict will happen next?

Follow-up Activity:

■ Organize students into read-aloud pairs. One student in each pair is to be Father, the other Sarah. Have the students read aloud the dialogue between the two characters as given in Chapter 1. Before starting, model fluent oral reading that shows emotions and chorus some lines together.

■ Talk about the words *courage, cloak,* and *musket* as used in the story. Add them to the power section of the Word Wall.

Materials:
Multiple copies of *The Courage of Sarah Noble,* chart paper, marker, easel, flashlight, star, students' LRJs.

Assessment:
Teacher will assess students' ability to feel deeply with a story character, infer, and predict based on their contributions to the class discussion, their contributions to the interactive writing, and their entries in their LRJs. Teacher will assess children's development as paragraph writers based on their contributions to the interactive writing and their LRJ entries.

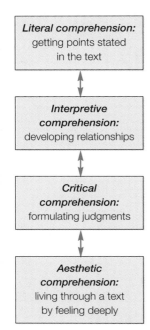

WORD BANK

Literal comprehension: getting points stated in the text

↕

Interpretive comprehension: developing relationships

↕

Critical comprehension: formulating judgments

↕

Aesthetic comprehension: living through a text by feeling deeply

king who wanted everything he touched to turn to gold. When Alfred, Lord Tennyson, wrote of "crossing the bar," he was referring metaphorically to death, not speaking literally of crossing a sand bar. Some of the most difficult interpretations readers must make relate to these kinds of references. Readers must bring to bear their previous experiences with language, literature, and life in constructing meanings.

Guiding literature discussions, teachers may need to nudge children beyond the reconstructions that reflect literal thinking to develop interrelationships. Teachers do this by wondering aloud: "I wonder why the author designed the story that way," or "I wonder why that character did that," or "I wonder if the character will win." Working with nonfiction, teachers also wonder: "I wonder how these two points are related," or "I wonder why this happens," or "I wonder what would happen if. . . ." And for both stories and expository text: "Wonder this way when you read on your own. That's what I try to do."

Critical Comprehension   To *think critically* requires making judgments. Readers judge the accuracy of facts, the validity of conclusions, the author's style and competence. They may decide whether they like the way the author began the piece, developed it, ended it, used examples to illustrate the main point, clarified difficult ideas, and used figurative language. They may decide whether an act of a character in a story was fair or unfair, dumb or smart. At its best, critical reading requires the reader to suspend judgment until all the evidence is in, give reasons for the judgment, and state the criteria used in making it.

Teachers can nudge children into critical thinking by raising the issues of goodness, fairness, rightness. Again, during literature discussions, teachers can use a variation of mind talk to model critical thinking in response to reading: "I wonder whether it is right . . ."; "At one point, I really didn't like that character . . ."; "I'm not really sure I like the way the author handled the end of the story because. . . ." And in follow-up, "Do you have a place where you wonder?" "Do you have something you don't like?"

Aesthetic Comprehension   In Chapters 4 and 5, we talked about Louise Rosenblatt's (1978) definitions of efferent and aesthetic stances. Recall that when readers function literally, interpretively, and critically, they generally assume an efferent stance. The ideas readers take away from the text are of primary importance. In *aesthetic reading,* on the other hand, the actual experience of "living through" a text is most important. Readers live through a text when they completely immerse themselves in it, become one with it, feel deeply with it.

Teachers need to draw attention to their response to stories as a way of modeling aesthetic meaning making. One teacher may say, "I was so scared here that my hands were shaking." Another may say, "I was crying inside when I read that. My voice broke when I read it to you." Still another may say at some point, "I hated Sarah for not telling the children she was staying. I felt that was mean." Some aesthetic responses, like this last one, overlap with the critical. That is to be expected, for although some responses are clearly efferent and others clearly aesthetic, some responses have shades of both. As with any distinction, the dividing line is not always clear-cut.

A Caution   One point before moving on: A problem often perceived in reading instruction is a predominance of teacher prompts and activities that require literal thinking. As mentioned in Chapter 4, some teachers carry on a "gentle inquisition" that passes for instruction: They ask questions that require students to find the answers in the text and then stand as authorities as to the correctness of youngsters' responses (Eeds and Wells, 1989). Teachers need to consider a different model of reading instruction and assessment. They should structure conversation times in which students and teacher dialogue together—yes, reconstructing parts of a story, but going on to wonder about relationships and meanings, critique the text, and talk about their feelings. At the same time, teachers "kidwatch"; they observe individual children's participation in the talking-together-about-literature times, later recording anecdotal comments on an assessment guide (see Figure 8.4).

TEACHER OBSERVATION AND ASSESSMENT GUIDE: THINKING ABOUT FICTION	
Student _____ Date _____ Book/Author _____	
Reading behaviors	**Comments**
1. Told the main events of the story (literal).	
2. Identified the big idea of the story (literal and/or interpretive).	
3. Used a graphic organizer to map story relationships (interpretive).	
4. Compared this story to other stories he or she had read (interpretive).	
5. Identified parts he or she liked or disliked and told why (critical).	
6. Told how he or she felt as a result of reading the story (aesthetic).	
7. Related the story to his or her personal experiences (aesthetic).	
8. Wrote and shared a story of his or her own based on a story read (aesthetic-creative).	

Figure 8.4
An Anecdotal Record Form for Observing and Assessing Reading Behaviors: Story Contexts

ASSESSMENT GUIDE

After Reading: Talking in Response to Expository Texts

Most of the examples in the previous segment relate to conversations that occur after children have read stories. You may have been asking yourself in your head (mind talking), "How do teachers organize after-reading discussions when those discussions evolve out of the reading of an expository text? How do teachers assess children's growth as efferent readers based on far-reaching discussions of factual content?"

The Guided Reading Procedure   Anthony Manzo (1975, 1985) suggests a structured approach to after-reading discussions that are based on expository texts, a Guided Reading Procedure (GRP) in which teachers prepare students for reading by first activating what they know about the content and then setting purposes for reading. Students read with this purpose in mind. Having read, they brainstorm the facts and ideas they remember as a scribe records these data—whether correct or incorrect—on the board. Children then reread to find data they forgot and to correct what they have recorded.

To help the children perceive relationships, the teacher encourages them to manipulate the data—grouping them to clarify relationships such as cause-effect and sequence. At times students group data into charts, grids, webs, or time lines. When students have experienced the Guided Reading Procedure on several occasions, the teacher verbally reviews the steps in the strategy, for students can use these same steps as a comprehension strategy when they read on their own.

Reciprocal Teaching   Annemarie Palincsar and Ann Brown (1985) recommend reciprocal teaching as a discussion strategy after students have read nonfiction. Teachers begin the after-reading discussion by formulating a question based on a paragraph, summarizing the material, and making a prediction or a clarification of any difficult parts. Having modeled how to take an efferent stance of this kind, the teacher asks readers to do the same with another paragraph. The approach is called *reciprocal* because teacher and students take turns being the teacher and asking the questions. Here the students are building a comprehension strategy and developing metacognitive awareness—awareness of how to raise and answer questions as they read. According to Palincsar and Brown (1986), "Reciprocal teaching has been effectively implemented in both small and large group settings, in a peer tutoring situation, in content area instruction, and most recently in listening comprehension instruction."

Assessment   Diagnosis of learning is an ongoing part of teacher-student dialogue of the kinds just described. Even as children contribute to a discussion, the teacher is observing and diagnosing their response behaviors. During any one discussion period, the teacher focuses on one or two students, using an anecdotal record form as in Figure 8.5. After the discussion, the teacher takes a moment alone to write brief comments about the student or students observed. Or the teacher can use such a

TEACHER OBSERVATION AND ASSESSMENT GUIDE: THINKING ABOUT NONFICTION

Student _____ Date _____

Book/Author _____

Reading behaviors	Comments
1. Identified the main topic of the selection (literal).	
2. Identified major ideas and supporting details (literal).	
3. Used new terminology in talking about the selection (interpretive).	
4. Proposed related examples (interpretive).	
5. Organized data graphically (interpretive).	
6. Drew pictures to highlight relationships (interpretive).	
7. Wrote a summary of major points (literal and interpretive).	
8. Told points with which he/she agreed/ disagreed and gave reasons (critical).	
9. Related ideas to his or her prior experiences (aesthetic).	

Figure 8.5
An Anecdotal Record Form for Observing and Assessing Reading Behaviors: Nonfictional Contexts

form after a teacher-student conference that focuses on a child's independent reading. The teacher initiates a one-on-one discussion based on the items on the form, noting afterward the student's response on the guide.

Writing in Response to Expository Text

Writing is a natural follow-up to the reading of expository text. As James Squire (1983) explains, "Composing is critical to thought processes because it is a process which actively engages the learner in constructing meaning, in developing ideas, in relating ideas, in expressing ideas. . . . To possess an idea that one is reading about requires competence in regenerating the idea, competence in learning how to write the ideas of another."

M. C. Wittrock's research on generative reading (1983) suggests that asking students to generate a summary sentence for paragraphs they read significantly increases their retention and comprehension of the text. Interestingly, students who also are given paragraph headings to use in their summary sentences double their retention and comprehension.

Some elementary-grade teachers ask their students to keep learning logs in which they write their responses to expository text. Responses to expository text are generally efferent in nature rather than aesthetic. Responding in their learning logs, students are intent on getting the ideas straight, summarizing points clearly, inferring, comparing, or judging. Responding aesthetically in their literature response journals, students are more in touch with their feelings and emotions.

The teacher's role here is many-faceted: to help children see purpose in writing, to make available reading materials related to the expository writing children are doing, and to read aloud related pieces. A teacher should encourage children to climb into the Author's Chair and read their expository writings to classmates just as they share their stories; a teacher should provide time for students to read the efferent writings of classmates—writings such as the piece in Figure 8.6, which a third-grader wrote in her learning log after reading articles about Rosa Parks and the book *Journey to Jo'burg* during a social studies unit on freedom.

Study Strategies and Content-Area Reading and Writing

Sometimes we forget how important reading is in the various content areas of the curriculum. Bonnie Armbruster (1992/1993) points out the importance of reading in science; she writes, "Reading and doing science are similar processes drawing

DISCUSSION PROMPT

- How can teachers use writing to facilitate children's learning in the social studies? At what points in a social studies lesson is writing a useful response?

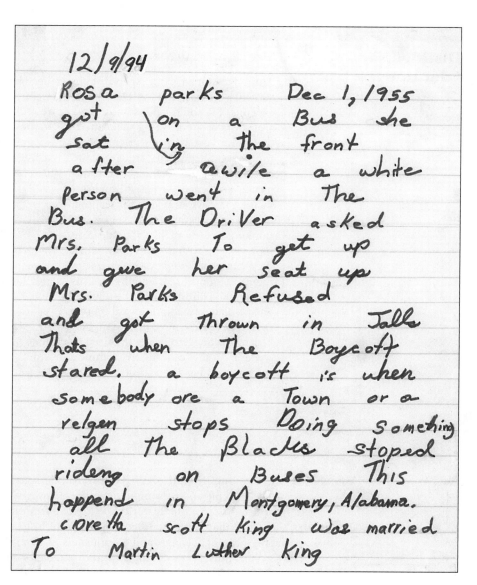

12/9/94

Rosa parks Dec 1, 1955 got on a Bus she sat in the front after awile a white person went in The Bus. The Driver asked Mrs. Parks To get up and give her seat up Mrs. Parks Refused and got Thrown in Jalle Thats when The Boycott stared. a boycott is when somebody ore a Town or a relgen stops Doing something all the Blacks stoped rideng on Buses This happend in Montgomery, Alabama. coretha scott King was married To Martin Luther King

Meet Anthony Manzo

Anthony Manzo is a specialist in content-area reading. As Dr. Manzo explains, "Reading and subject area specialists are redirecting their attention toward creating educational environments in which students are challenged to analyze, reflect, communicate, and create. In such environments, effective strategies for reading, writing, speaking, listening, and thinking are more likely to develop more naturally and easily than when these are addressed as isolated elements. . . . This reorientation shifts the emphasis from reading as a somewhat isolated function toward its role in overall communication and higher-order thinking. Ironically the need to write and to read highly technical information has been greatly intensi-fied by telecomputing and related technologies that once were expected to reduce the demand for every citizen to be highly literate" (*Content Area Literacy: Interactive Teaching for Interactive Learning*. 2nd ed [Upper Saddle River, N.J.: Merrill, 1997], 11).

DISCUSSION PROMPT

Who is responsible for teaching content-area reading—the reading teacher or the subject-content teacher? Why? What kinds of materials should be used to teach content-area reading? Trade books? Subject textbooks? Printouts from the Web? Why? How would you organize content-area reading instruction?

on the same cognitive base. Both are interactive-constructive processes that require thinking and reasoning." Dorothy Hennings (1993) reminds us that "strategies important in reading historical text derive from the nature of historiography—the key ideas that give structure to the study of history: time, place, causation and ultimate meaning, change, and tenuousness of data." Such theorists are implying that teachers must help children acquire strategies to use in making meaning with content-area selections; teachers must help children develop study strategies useful across the curriculum. As Bonnie Bernstein (1995) reports, research studies show a decline in children's reading comprehension as youngsters reach fourth grade—"the very stage at which reading becomes crucial to mastery of other subjects across the curriculum."

Students must have strategies that they can apply knowingly as they study content-area books, especially the textbooks they have to read during their junior high school, senior high school, and college years. One study scheme that some students find useful is SQ3R: survey, question, read, recite, review. Another approach relies on written note making. Other strategies are more visual; they rely on webs, charts, or outlines. In this section we look at some of these ways to study texts.

The Teacher's Message Board

Posted here are comprehension strategies for use in expository contexts.

- **Recapping Strategy (literal comprehension):** Students can identify topic, main idea, and supporting details as they talk about content-area texts. Teacher prompts in this context are "What is this about? What is the big point the author is making about the topic? How do we know that is what the author is getting at? What clue does the author provide: topic sentence, repeating terms, explicitly stated supporting examples? Let's record this idea on our data chart or web or outline. What are the steps in the recapping strategy we have been applying?"

- **Fixing-up Strategy (literal comprehension):** When students have read a segment of text and have trouble recapping, the teacher can suggest, "Let's apply our fix-up strategy. Let's reread, asking ourselves our main idea question: 'What is the author saying to us?'"

- **Vocabulary-Building Strategy (literal or interpretive comprehension):** Students can be encouraged to use context and structure clues to figure out the meaning of an unfamiliar term in science and social studies. Teacher prompts include these: How is this word used in the sentence? What clues does the author supply to help us crack the meaning? What meaningful parts do we see in the word? Do we need dictionary help? Which dictionary meaning applies here? How do we know that? Let's enter our new word in our learning log. What things have we been doing to master the terminology of content-area texts?"

- **Opinion/Proof/Opinion Strategy (critical comprehension):** Students can be prompted to identify an editorial writer's opinion as they read columns from the op-ed pages of a newspaper. Appropriate prompts are as follows: "What is this writer's opinion? What words are clues that this is an opinion piece? What proof does the writer offer in support of his/her opinion? Is that support strong? Weak? What is our opinion? What rationale do we have to support it? What are our personal biases that make us think as we do? Let's review our O/P/O strategy: ferret out the opinion; look for the proof; respond with our own opinion."

(*Note:* In each instance, students are learning a comprehension strategy as they are reading a particular expository text.)

SQ3R

There is a structure to nonfiction that students must be able to handle if they are to make meaning with text. They must learn to use titles and subheadings to predict what a selection is about. They must learn to use subheadings to figure out the organization, or design, of a selection. Most authors of informational prose build clues into their texts to facilitate comprehension: lines such as "There are three major points. . . . This section explains those points"; introductions that give an overview; conclusions that sum up; terms highlighted through italic or boldface type;

GO TO

Pages 339–342 for more on rhetorical structures.

questions at the end; illustrations to accompany each subsection. Most authors also use linguistic clues such as *first, second,* and *finally* to guide readers through the text.

A study scheme called *SQ3R* is helpful in clarifying the structure of an expository piece if "each step is practiced under teacher guidance" (Manzo and Manzo, 1997). SQ3R is a five-step strategy for studying a passage in which readers use the subheadings to develop questions that provide a framework for reading; the steps are **S**urvey, **Q**uestion, **R**ead, **R**ecite, and **R**eview (Robinson, 1961).

■ *Step One: Surveying.* Talking through a passage before reading is an effective strategy for simultaneously teaching SQ3R and the structure of informational texts. First, the teacher and the students *survey* the text together: They read the title and predict what the selection is about, study the headings to figure out the organization, read the introductory and concluding sections, look at the pictures, and note any distinctive aspects. Having surveyed the text, students think and talk about what they already know about the subject. Then they talk about what they have just done; they identify the steps in their getting-ready-to-read strategy. Talking their way through a passage in this way clarifies the structure of the informational selection for students and models how they can use a surveying strategy when they study on their own. It also develops metacognitive awareness—explicit understanding of how to proceed in studying a text. See Figure 8.7 for a checklist upper-graders can use to guide their study survey.

■ *Step Two: Questioning.* In SQ3R, the second step in preparing to read informational texts is *questioning.* Students devise questions to answer when they read, by rephrasing the subheadings as questions. These questions give purpose to reading; students read to find answers.

BEFORE-READING CHECKLIST OF KEY ELEMENTS OF TEXT

Put a check on the line when you have previewed that item. Put a 0 on the line when you preview and do not find the item.

1. Title   _____

2. Key vocabulary listed at the beginning   _____

3. Introductory paragraphs that tell what the selection is about   _____

4. Headings and subheadings   _____

5. Illustrations   _____

6. Italicized or boldfaced terms   _____

7. Summary paragraph at the end   _____

8. Questions at the beginning or end   _____

Figure 8.7
A Checklist for Identifying Key Elements of Expository Text Structure

- **Step Three: Reading.** The next step in SQ3R is *reading*. Students read to find answers to questions they posed before reading.
- **Step Four: Reciting.** Having read a major section of text, students pause to *monitor their comprehension by reciting*. In reciting, students mind talk: They tell themselves answers to the questions devised during the preview survey or retell points from the selection. If students cannot do this, they reread the segment and try again to recite (in their minds) key points about what they have read—main ideas, definitions, and so forth.
- **Step Five: Reviewing.** Finishing the selection, readers *review* again what they have read by mind talking through the main points of the entire selection, again guided by the questions they devised before reading. Reviewing is not a one-shot endeavor; students must review on several occasions to remember what they have read.

The SQ3R study sequence is powerful because surveying and questioning help readers perceive the structure of a selection, which facilitates comprehension by providing a framework for reading. SQ3R is powerful, too, because it provides a means through which readers monitor their comprehension as they study.

Note Making: Connecting Reading and Writing

SQ3R has proven to be a useful study system over the years. One weakness, however, is the limited use of writing; students may write their questions before reading, but that is the extent of the writing activity. Some reading specialists (Burns, Roe, and Ross, 1996) suggest the use of note cards in study reading, especially when students are going to use the information they read as the basis for an oral or written report.

A note card is a simple approach to study reading that teaches children to set a purpose for their reading before they start. If students do not have a purpose clearly in mind, they may write down all manner of detail that may not be useful in the long run. To prevent this from happening, the teacher helps children focus their reading by encouraging them to survey the text to be read (as in SQ3R) and then by asking: "Based on our survey, what is the main question we want to answer? What are one or two related questions?" Children record their main-idea question on one side of a note card and two related questions on the other side. Now when children read the selection, they read to answer their questions. Finishing the selection, they answer the questions on their note cards. During a follow-up discussion or oral reporting time, readers use their note cards as data banks.

Older students may prefer to make notes in a learning log because then they have a continuous record of main ideas and related points to study at the end of a unit. In this context, they can use the same strategy just described, surveying the text, writing down several questions that focus on main and related ideas with space between for answering, and writing explanations after reading. In instances where students have access to laptop computers, children can use the computer screen as their learning log, entering questions directly into the computer before reading and keying in explanations afterward.

Outlines

Although many young people and adults have trouble taking notes in formal outline style, some attention should be given to outlining because (to be completely honest) outlining is often required in high school and some high school teachers just assume that students know how to do it. Also, outlining does help students to perceive connections within a body of data.

A teacher can use some of the same techniques for introducing outlining that he or she used to introduce SQ3R and note cards. Students and teacher begin by together surveying the text, giving particular attention to the system of subheadings. Based on the first-level headings, students brainstorm main topics or questions to be answered through reading. These become the first-level headings in their outlines. Next students look at the second-level headings in the text and use these to flesh out the second-level topics or questions in their outlines. For example, if you were to make an outline of this chapter of *Communication in Action*, you would survey the chapter and write down four topics (or questions) based on the four first-level headings: I. Emergent Literacy; II. Comprehension; III. Study Strategies; and IV. Sustained Silent Reading and Library Visits. The subheadings under these four first-level headings would become items outlined as A., B., C., and so forth under the first-level headings. You can outline subpoints 1., 2., 3., and so forth under the second-level headings. Under each item you entered in your before-reading outline, you leave some space for noting important points while reading. You may want to try making an outline of this section of the text (III. Study Strategies).

Data Webs, or Maps

Another approach to written note making is the data web, or map—a network of interrelated words and phrases connected to a central topic hub and to one another that highlights relationships within a body of information. See Figure 8.8 for an

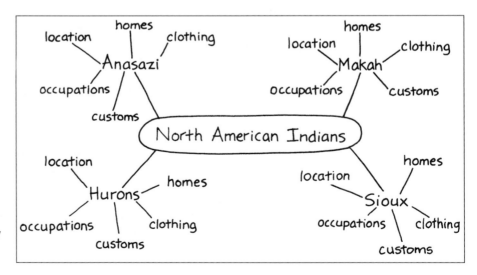

Figure 8.8
A Data Web for Note Taking

ACTIVITY PROMPT

Web the section of *Communication in Action* on study strategies in collaboration with a friend.

READ

Deanne Camp, "It Takes Two: Teaching with Twin Texts of Fact and Fiction," *The Reading Teacher*, 53 (February 2000), 400–408, for visual ways to respond to informational texts.

example. Children who have used a data web to record their knowledge of a topic before and during listening, as described in Chapter 5, can design similar webs to record ideas in reading and in preparation for reporting. Students generally need step-by-step instruction in setting up a reading web. The teacher should model his or her thought processes for designing one web and develop one branch of the web based on a read-aloud. A teacher might say something like this:

> If I were going to read this selection called "Native Americans in North America," that would be my topic, and I would put a shortened version of it in the center of my data web. After that, I would look through the selection, focusing particularly on the subheadings. Let's look at them, one by one. I see that here the subheadings are the names of tribes; those names become the branches on my web. Let's add those to the web. Now let's survey the selection to see the kind of information that the article is supplying. What do I find here? I find information on things like homes, clothing, and so forth. The illustrations help me to see that; so do the words in italics. Here is how I will put those items into my web—branching out from the names of the tribes. Now as I read, I will jot notes extending outward from those words. For example, I'll jot notes about the homes of the Anasazi at that location on my web. Let's do the first tribe as a read-aloud. You tell me how to plot the information from the selection as we go along.

One advantage of a data web is that it is relatively easy to see relationships within the data once the web is completed. This is especially useful if students are reading to gather information for an oral or written report. Sometimes the data web becomes an oral reporting guide, with youngsters using their webs as reminders of what they want to say during their oral presentations; sometimes the web becomes a writing guide, with youngsters numbering in sequential order the items they intend to include in their written reports.

Data Charts

A more difficult task for upper-graders is to take notes on a topic while using several references, searching a number of computer databases, and/or surfing the Internet. One approach to this task is a data synthesis chart, as in Figure 8.9. However, before beginning to read reference materials, search, or surf, youngsters have to know something about their topic. In short, they probably have to carry out some preliminary explorations comparable to the surveying they do as part of SQ3R. Based on knowledge developed in this way, children brainstorm questions that essentially are subtopics of their main problem, much in the way they devise questions and write them on a note card or use their questions to design a data web.

For example, in preparing to read several references on endangered species, some sixth-grade science students posed four questions based on a filmstrip they had viewed: What is an endangered species? What species are endangered today? Where are these species found? Why are they endangered? These questions became labels that students placed as headings on the columns of their charts. In the left-hand column, students listed the references and Internet sites they would check. They completed the chart by consulting each reference and site on each question and placing

DATA CHART ON ENDANGERED SPECIES				
What we want to know ⟶	What Is the Definition of Endangered Species? ↓	What Are Some Endangered Species Today? ↓	Where Are These Species Found? ↓	Why Are Some Species Endangered? ↓
References Used What our science text says ⟶				
What our encyclopedia says ⟶				
What a trade book or Internet site (name: _____) says ⟶				
WRITING FOLLOW-UP: Write four paragraphs. In each paragraph include points from more than one reference. Paragraph 1: Explain the meaning of *endangered species.* Paragraph 2: Describe some endangered species of today. Paragraph 3: Explain some locations in which endangered species are found today. Paragraph 4: Explain why some species are endangered.				

Figure 8.9
A Data Synthesis Chart

ACTIVITY PROMPT
Create a similar chart on global warming. Start by brainstorming questions to guide data collection.

their data in the appropriate box, or cell. They learned that once they had found an answer in one reference and written it in a cell, they did not need to write it down again when they found it in another reference.

As with note cards, outlines, and webs, students can use their charts during oral reporting, speaking informally from their charts or displaying them as they speak. Later they can convert their data charts into writing guides. The directions at the bottom of Figures 8.9 and 8.10 show how to expand a note-taking guide into an oral reporting guide or a writing guide. Figure 8.10 models a different way to organize a

CHART FOR STUDYING ABOUT AND REPORTING ON CULTURE GROUPS					
Organizing: Complete our chart by reading in at least two reference books from the Reading Nook.					
What we want to know →	Kind of Home in Which They Live ↓	Kind of Clothing They Wear ↓	Kinds of Food They Eat ↓	Where They Live ↓	Climate of the Area ↓
The Laplanders →					
The Masai →					
The Thais →					
Making connections: How does the climate of the region where the group lives affect the kinds of homes, clothing, and food they use?					
Writing • Paragraph 1: Describe the Laplanders and how they live. • Paragraph 2: Describe the Masai and how they live. • Paragraph 3: Describe the Thais and how they live. • Paragraph 4: Explain the relationship between climate and food, homes, and clothing of a people. Use examples from your data chart.					

Figure 8.10
Data Synthesis Chart for Studying and Reporting

ACTIVITY PROMPT

Teachers should not provide the data synthesis chart; rather, teacher and children cooperatively create the chart through brainstorming and talking aloud together. Create a similar chart on a topic of your choice.

data chart. It does not itemize the references, which makes it a bit more difficult for children to use.

SQ3R, Note Cards and Learning Logs, Outlines, Webs, and Data Charts

Young people need to develop strategies for studying textbook-type materials; they need to have explicit knowledge, or awareness, of what works best for them as they study. No two readers are the same. Some students—especially those with a learning disability—may function best with an SQ3R approach that provides a step-by-step procedure. Others may prefer a freer, less structured approach that relies more on writing in response, as is the case with note cards and learning logs. Other students may do better with approaches that highlight relationships visually, as is true with outlines and webs. Still others may prefer data charts, especially if they must organize information from a variety of sources, including text references and Internet sites. And still others may vary their approach to study depending on their purpose. Because people differ in what works best for them, teachers must offer a variety of approaches and not insist that all students use the same study strategy in all situations. They must help students to know explicitly what works best for them. In short, they must help students develop metacognitive awareness.

Sustained Silent Reading and Library Visits

READ

Jo Worthy et al., "The Precarious Place of Self-Selected Reading," *Language Arts,* 75 (April 1998), 296–304, for a study of teachers' use of SSR and DEAR.

Children must have a wide variety of experiences with all kinds of texts to become skillful readers. Children learn to construct meanings and interpret text structure related to stories by reading stories; they learn to read poems by reading poems; they learn to read nonfiction by reading informational articles.

To achieve this breadth of skill, many teachers use Sustained Silent Reading (SSR) or Drop Everything and Read (DEAR). Children spend a portion of each day reading independently in material they select, the only prohibition on choice being that they must eventually make selections from key categories: story, biography, science, history, poetry, humor, and so forth. During reading workshops, as a follow-up to SSR, children confer with their teacher, who asks them to retell, rephrase, and summarize; interpret relationships; evaluate content and style; express feelings; and relate what they are reading to their own lives. A truly effective school reading program must include both guided and independent reading.

Visiting the Library Media Center

Children should always have in their desks a book or two that they have chosen for Sustained Silent Reading. To this end, the class should visit the library so that each child can make a selection. Kindergarten is not too early to start these visits. Youngsters squat at their leisure on the floor before the shelves where the picture books are kept and pick books to carry back to the classroom and/or home for reading. The teacher must guide young children as they select books, helping them find books that fit their reading and interest levels; otherwise, a child may return from the library without a book to enjoy. The teacher should send a note home suggesting that the caregiver read the take-home books aloud to the child. To encourage family reading, kindergarten teacher Denise Addona gives an "assignment" to caregivers in her urban school district. They must complete a weekly book report, indicating the name of the book read that week to the child, the number of times they went through the book with the child, and the topics they talked about before and after reading. Ms. Addona has had an amazingly good response to this family-based activity.

READ

Ruth Hayden, "Training Parents as Reading Facilitators," *The Reading Teacher,* 49 (December 1995/ January 1996), 334–336.

Teaching Library Skills in the Primary Grades

As primary children visit the library, they should begin to build alphabetizing skills and learn to alphabetize storybooks. Having read a book, a youngster constructs a large spine from construction paper, printing on it the author's last name and the book title. On the bulletin board, students mount their spines alphabetically according to the authors' last names. The result is a mockup of a library shelf that houses fiction.

In the upper grades, children differentiate between fiction and nonfiction. At this point, they take time to browse in specific areas of the library: science, history, sports, biography, poetry.

Teaching Investigative Skills in the Upper Elementary Grades

More complex library skills should be introduced as early as second grade. These skills include the ability to differentiate among basic library references (encyclopedias, atlases, almanacs, informational books, magazines, newspapers) and the ability to use indexes, tables of contents, topical headings, guide words, the card catalogue, computerized book-search lists, and the Web.

CONSIDER

Topics of mini-lessons include using a computer to find a book, locating books on the library shelf, locating videocassettes, and finding oversized picture-filled books. Basic references include the *Guinness Book of World Records,* atlases, special dictionaries, and encyclopedias.

Basic References   What type of information does an encyclopedia provide? How does this information differ from that in an informational book? Teachers can structure activities to answer these kinds of questions and to familiarize young researchers with basic references as they begin to use them. Here are a few ideas:

- *The encyclopedia.* Introduce the organization of encyclopedias by distributing the various volumes to youngsters who will function collaboratively. By working from front to back of the volumes, the teams discover the organization. They look up particular items in the index of a volume and locate relevant pages. On the spot, students use the volumes to locate information on a content-area unit they are studying, brainstorming subtopics related to the unit, locating them, scanning the sections, and sharing ideas. Where encyclopedias are stored on compact disks, teachers can demonstrate how to access information off a disk.

■ *Magazines.* Schedule comparison times when youngsters compare the content and organization of such magazines as *Ranger Rick, Cricket, Newsweek, Consumer Reports,* and *National Geographic World.* This makes a good group activity, with each group studying a sample of each magazine and writing a summary that begins, "*Consumer Reports* contains articles on. . . ."

■ *Almanacs, atlases, and encyclopedias.* Divide the class into small groups, each to receive copies of an almanac, an atlas, and an encyclopedia volume. Students analyze the volumes and write summary cards for each reference: "An almanac contains . . ."; "An atlas contains . . ."; "An encyclopedia contains. . . ."

■ *Newspapers.* Collect newspapers over several weeks so that each student has one in hand. Ask children to go through their papers page by page, listing the features found in sequence. Later, in groups, students compare their lists and generalize about how newspapers are organized and the kind of information they contain. At some point, demonstrate a newspaper site on the Web.

■ *Informational books.* Distribute a number of informational books on a topic (for example, the American Revolution) and encyclopedia volumes on the same topic. Students scan both to find out how the two types of materials differ. Ask, "Under what conditions would you use an encyclopedia article? Informational books? Both?"

■ *Web.* As part of an ongoing unit, demonstrate how you search the Internet for related information using a browser such as Microsoft Internet Explorer or Netscape Communicator. Model how to log on, enter Web site addresses, search for related sites, click to navigate within a site, access links, download material, print it out, and develop a web or data chart based on it. Today, information on almost any subject is available on the Web. Encourage students to tap into the Web for information about authors of books they are reading to include in their book reports.

Locational and Library Skills   Youngsters need guidance in using indexes and library-search tools. Here are ideas for organizing the activity:

■ *Indexes.* Using the index in their social studies or science book, students locate information on a topic. Provide topics during unit study that can be located in several ways—for example, the automobile, which can be traced by looking under *automobile, car, horseless carriage,* or *gasoline.*

■ *The numbers have it!* Introduce upper-graders to the Dewey decimal system if the school library is organized that way. Start by making a chart showing the numbers used to catalogue nonfiction. Then gather a pile of books. Children decide how to order the books on the library shelves. To aid in teaching the Dewey decimal system, borrow an idea from Eleanor Schwartz, a librarian who has made numerous book spines imprinted with book title, author, and Dewey decimal number copied from library books. Each youngster in the group holds a spine; cooperatively, children decide how to order the books on a shelf. When youngsters visit the library, they use the major Dewey divisions to locate books they need.

CONSIDER

Have children compare a local newspaper to a regional and a national newspaper. Ask, "What kinds of news does each report? What kinds of features does each contain? How do they differ?"

CONSIDER

The major units of the Dewey system are:
000   generalities
100   philosophy
200   religion
300   social sciences
400   language
500   pure sciences
600   technology (applied sciences)
700   the arts
800   literature
900   geography and history

■ *In the computer.* Where possible, demonstrate how to locate a book in a library having a computerized catalogue since many libraries no longer rely on a card catalogue.

A Summary Thought or Two

Reading with Meaning

This chapter develops these major ideas:

■ Specific decoding strategies and oral reading fluency should be developed as part of ongoing purposeful reading and writing activities, not in isolation.

■ Reading is an interactive-constructive process of making meaning with a written text. Activities that increase awareness of meanings and encourage children to explore and clarify meanings support reading comprehension.

■ What readers bring to reading—their world knowledge, linguistic knowledge, text structure knowledge, and metacognitive knowledge—is important in comprehension. Accordingly, teachers should structure before-reading activities that help young readers prepare for full comprehension. Many of these activities are oral.

■ Full comprehension involves the generation of literal, interpretive, critical, and aesthetic meanings. Accordingly, teachers should ask questions and develop activities before reading, during reading, and after reading that help children construct these meanings.

■ Just as oral activity is an integral part of classroom reading, so is writing. Writing provides students with the opportunity to retell, summarize, analyze, apply, invent, and criticize. It is an ideal way to react to reading, for it forces students to organize thought. The result—given oral activity as well—is an integrated, approach to reading instruction.

■ Children need opportunities to develop study skills as they listen, read, and write across the curriculum.

■ Children should have considerable opportunity to read for pleasure and information. To find books for Sustained Silent Reading, children should go to the library and be assisted in using it.

Your Language Arts Portfolio

■ Write a series of lesson plans: a literature-based lesson in which you help children to relate a particular phoneme to its written representation (grapheme); a lesson that incorporates DR-TA; a lesson in which you model some aspect of comprehension; a lesson in which you introduce children to SQ3R through the reading of a particular expository selection that you select. Write your objectives in terms of what children will be able to do or do better by the end of the lesson. If you have the opportunity to teach based on your plan, add samples of children's resulting work and photographs of children's activity.

Related Readings

Blachowicz, Camille, and **Donna Ogle.** *Reading Comprehension: Strategies for Independent Learners.* New York: Guilford Publications, 2001.

Braunger, Jane, and **Jan Lewis.** *Building a Knowledge Base in Reading.* Newark, Del.: International Reading Association, 1997.

Calkins, Lucy. *The Art of Teaching Reading.* Needham Heights, Mass.: Allyn and Bacon, 2001.

Five, Cora Lee, and **Kathryn Egawa,** co-eds. "Reading and Writing Workshop: What Is It and What Does It Look Like?" *School Talk,* 3 (April 1998).

Fountas, Irene, and **Gay Su Pinnell.** *Guiding Readers and Writers (Grades 3–6): Teaching Comprehension, Genre, and Content Literacy.* Westport, Conn.: Heinemann, 2000.

Guthrie, John, and **Allan Wigfield,** eds. *Reading Engagements: Motivating Readers Through Integrated Instruction.* Newark, Del.: International Reading Association, 1997.

Holdaway, Don. *Independence in Reading.* 3rd ed. Portsmouth, N.H.: Heinemann, 1991.

Language Arts, 70 (October 1993). The theme of the issue is "Reading Instruction Today."

Manzo, Anthony, and **Ula Manzo.** *Content Area Literacy: Interactive Teaching for Active Learning.* 2nd ed. Upper Saddle River, N.J.: Merrill/Prentice-Hall, 1997.

May, Frank. *Reading as Communication.* 4th ed. New York: Macmillan, 1994.

McGee, Lea, and **Donald Richgels.** *Literacy's Beginnings: Supporting Young Readers and Writers.* 2nd ed. Boston: Allyn and Bacon, 1996.

Michel, Pamela. *The Child's View of Reading.* Boston: Allyn and Bacon, 1994.

Miller, Heidi, Timothy O'Keefe, and **Diane Stephens.** *Looking Closely: Exploring the Role of Phonics in One Whole Language Classroom.* Urbana, Ill.: National Council of Teachers of English, 1991.

Ministry of Education, Wellington, New Zealand. *Reading for Life: The Learner as a Reader.* Katonah, N.Y.: Richard C. Owen, 1997.

Moustafa, Margaret. *Beyond Traditional Phonics.* Westport, Conn.: Heinemann, 1997.

Richgels, David et al. "Kindergartners Talk About Print: Phonemic Awareness in Meaningful Contexts." *The Reading Teacher,* 49 (May 1996), 632–642.

Routman, Regie, and **Andrea Butler.** "Why Talk About Phonics?" *School Talk,* 1 (November 1995), 1–6.

School Talk, 1 (February 1996). The theme of the issue is "How Do I Actually Teach Reading Now That I Am Using Literation?" *School Talk* is a publication of the National Council of Teachers of English.

Smith, John A. "Singing and Songwriting Support Early Literacy Instruction." *The Reading Teacher,* 53 (May 2000), 646–649.

Smith, John, and **Warwick Elley.** *How Children Learn to Read.* Katonah, N.Y.: Richard C. Owen, 1997.

Wagstaff, Janiel M. "Building Practical Knowledge of Letter-Sound Correspondence: A Beginner's Word Wall and Beyond." *The Reading Teacher,* 51 (December 1997/ January 1998), 298–305.

Writing as Idea Making

Creating Within a Variety of Genres

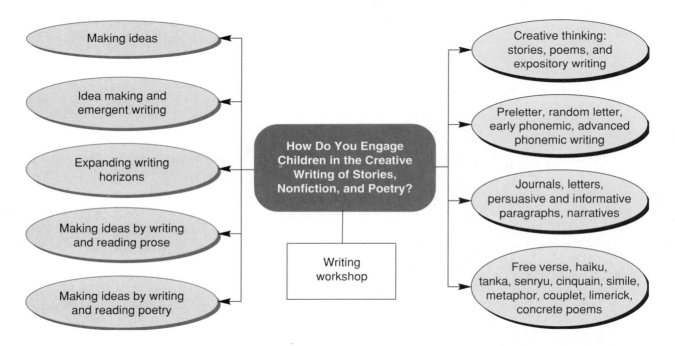

Making ideas

Idea making and emergent writing

Expanding writing horizons

Making ideas by writing and reading prose

Making ideas by writing and reading poetry

How Do You Engage Children in the Creative Writing of Stories, Nonfiction, and Poetry?

Writing workshop

Creative thinking: stories, poems, and expository writing

Preletter, random letter, early phonemic, advanced phonemic writing

Journals, letters, persuasive and informative paragraphs, narratives

Free verse, haiku, tanka, senryu, cinquain, simile, metaphor, couplet, limerick, concrete poems

Workshop in Action | *Journals, Idea Clusters, and Other Ways to Make Ideas During Workshop*

It was a cold December morning, and snow was in the air. Jennifer Chou's fourth-graders came into their room, went to their desks, took out their writing journals, read the replies Ms. Chou had written to them based on their prior entries, and without prompting began to write. After greeting her youngsters, Ms. Chou did the same: She went to her desk, took out her journal, and jotted down ideas.

Making Ideas Through Sharing

When the fourth-graders began looking up to indicate they had written some first thoughts, Ms. Chou told them to gather in the Communication Circle. She asked if any of them wanted to share anything they had written in the past few days—a piece they had worked on during writing workshop or even what they had just written in their journals. The children in this class were accustomed to sharing their drafts, and many were eager to read their work aloud. Using her checklist indicating which students had not shared in the past week, Ms. Chou selected three sharers.

Each child in turn sat in the Author's Chair, which was placed in the Communication Circle, and read what he or she had written. Sean shared sentences he had written about a big fire in his neighborhood. When he had finished, his classmates received his work by first summing up what he had said and then by asking him things about the fire that he had not told them in his writing: How did the fire start? What time had the fire happened? How had he felt? Had anyone been hurt? Sean answered the questions, putting check marks on his paper to remind him of spots where he might add ideas. Then Trudie "celebrated" his writing by telling him, "I liked your story. I liked what you said about the firefighters."

Sean answered, "I'll let you read it when I get it fixed."

Two other youngsters shared what they had written. Their classmates responded as they had with Sean: *receiving* the main points, *asking* for more information, and *celebrating* what they particularly liked.

Making Ideas Through Clustering: A Mini-Lesson

After the three youngsters had shared, Ms. Chou distributed construction paper and crayons. She explained to the fourth-graders, "On my way to school today, I thought about what I would write during journal time. I let my ideas roll around in my head. I made 'mind talk.' By the time I got to school, I was sure I wanted to write about how I felt about winter coming, but I didn't have any specific ideas ready to write, and so this morning I just played with words on paper."

Ms. Chou then went to the board. "Because I did not know where to begin, I drew a circle in the middle of my paper like this, and I wrote *winter* in the circle. Then I began to sort of 'idea doodle.' I drew a line outward from the circle and wrote the word *cold* at the end. I added *snow* to that, and then *ice*. I kept adding words to words as they came to mind." With that, Ms. Chou added the words to her Winter Idea Cluster and asked the students to draw a similar cluster on the construction paper, using their crayons. She asked them to think of words that came to their minds. When many hands went up, she told the students to add their words to their own papers. She continued to "doodle," adding more words to the cluster on the board. After a few moments, she stopped to ask the students to give her words from their clusters, which she added to hers. She told the students that if they ran out of words or phrases to add to their clusters, they could help themselves to ideas from her cluster or from a neighbor's.

When the board was filled with a cluster of thoughts (see Figure 9.1), Ms. Chou asked the children to help her write a first sentence that would get her started writing about winter. She suggested that they write the starting sentence by focusing on one group of thoughts within their webs, then write another by focusing on a different group within the webs. Again, when hands went up, she told the students to write their

READ

Gabriele Rico, *Writing the Natural Way* (Los Angeles: J. P. Tarcher, 1983), for a thorough discussion of idea clustering and writing.

Expand ideas through writing

Expand ideas through sharing

Develop an idea through clustering

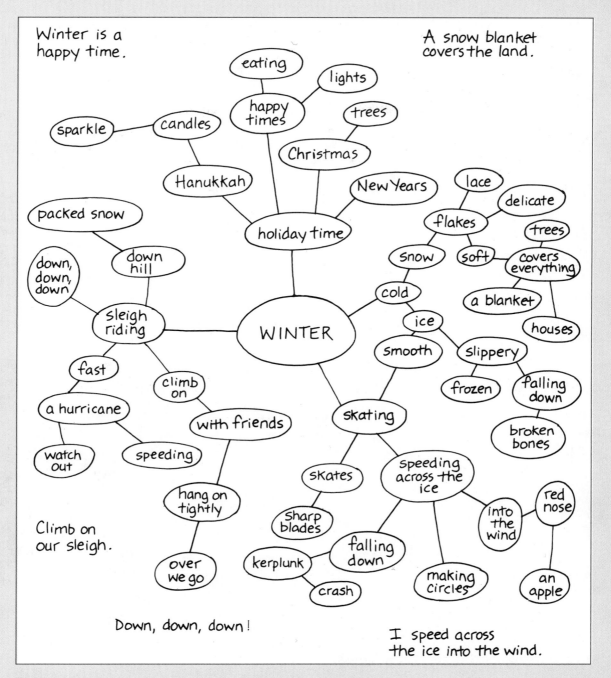

Figure 9.1
An Idea Cluster on Winter

ideas on the edges of their own idea clusters. As the children drafted starting thoughts, she wrote her own ideas on her cluster and then added several offered by the children.

With that, Ms. Chou asked a student to copy the cluster on the board so that she could use it as an idea bank when she wrote in her journal tomorrow. Ms. Chou told the children to fold their idea clusters in half and place them in their active-writing portfolios. She told them that "Winter Thoughts" was an option they could select to write about during writing workshop time or in their journals sometime during the day if that topic appealed to them. She suggested that if they ever had trouble getting started in writing, they could do what she had done that morning: draw an idea cluster and write several possible starting sentences around its edges.

Making Ideas Through Listening, Reading, and Talking

Having modeled the process of idea development through clustering, Ms. Chou dismissed most of the students for the independent phase of workshop. These students needed no additional direction at this point; they knew from prior experiences that they were to take out their active-writing portfolios and work on something "in process." Students like Sean could work on revising a piece they had shared with the class. Some could work on a piece they wanted to share. Others could work with their Writing Editor, sharing and getting feedback on a piece already begun. Some could select a topic from the many options they had recorded on the inside of their

The writing child is a thinking child. (*© Michael Zide*)

writing portfolios and start a new piece. Others could read published pieces by other students, pieces that hung from the classroom clothesline. Still others could read from a book they had in progress. The one thing they all had to do was keep a log of how they spent the time—a log that Ms. Chou looked over each day.

While most students worked independently on writing or reading or collaborated on editing, Ms. Chou worked in the Conferencing Center with seven youngsters who in the past had had trouble getting started in writing. She introduced the poem "Helping" by Shel Silverstein by asking them what thoughts the word *helping* brought to their minds. As the students responded, they recorded the words idea cluster style on paper. Then Ms. Chou read the poem aloud, and the students followed along on their copies. Next, the students orally chorused the poem and talked about what Silverstein was saying (his main idea), how Silverstein had structured the piece, and what they liked about it. They mentioned the repetitive style and the rhyming names. They talked about times when people had given them good help and times when people had given them help they could have done without. They also brainstormed writing possibilities that appealed to them based on "Helping" and recorded those options on the inside of their portfolios for future reference: "What I Like or Don't Like About the Silverstein Poem," "When Someone Gave Me Help I Could Do Without," and a poem structured like "Helping."

Making Ideas Through Conferencing

The seven students who had participated in the mini-lesson returned to their desks. Ms. Chou then called three other youngsters to the Conferencing Center. The night before, these children had placed papers that they believed were ready for a prepublication conference in Ms. Chou's Ready-for-a-Conference basket. Ms. Chou had read the papers in preparation for the conference and jotted her thoughts on sticky notes. During the conference, each child read his or her composition aloud, told what he or she thought were its good points, and indicated where help was needed. Both Ms. Chou and the other two children in the group gave help as requested. Ms. Chou also focused each child's attention on two or three sentences that needed revision. In general, these sentences had the same problem element, which Ms. Chou noted on a conferencing guide that the student took back to his or her desk to refer to during rewriting. Together teacher and students talked about how to make these sentences "better." Finally, with the children helping and watching, Ms. Chou highlighted misspelled words with a yellow highlighting marker to give the young authors guidance in reworking their compositions for publication in the classroom newsletter.

Following the conference, the students went back to work on their own. Ms. Chou began to circulate from desk to desk for "quickie conferences." Students who had run into difficulty while Ms. Chou was working at the Conferencing Center had written their names on a section of the chalkboard labeled "Must Have a Teacher Conference Today." At this point, Ms. Chou helped these students talk through their ideas and problems.

Make ideas through reading

GO TO
Figure 10.6 for a conference guide that identifies problem elements with which a teacher can help a student during a conference. See page 383.

DISCUSSION PROMPT
■ What is Ms. Chou teaching her fourth-graders about the nature of writing? What are key aspects of her approach?

Idea Making in Action

In Ms. Chou's classroom, idea making—or creative thinking—is what writing is all about. Children in her class make ideas as they write spontaneously in their journals, share what they have drafted, "mind talk" before and during writing, and confer with their teacher. Although one of Ms. Chou's objectives is helping children manage the conventions of writing, her initial emphasis is on helping them generate the ideas they express through writing—that is, on the higher-order thinking that is the core of the writing act.

Because idea making is the heart of writing, let us consider the nature of creative thought and what it means in terms of writing in the elementary grades.

What Idea Making Is About

In *On Knowing,* a brief volume that is a classic in education, Jerome Bruner (1962) speaks of the creative process: "The act of a person creating is the act of a whole person. . . . it is this rather than the product that makes it good and worthy." To Bruner, a creative act is one that "produces *effective surprise* . . . that strikes [the creator] with wonder or astonishment." Everyone has experienced the surprise that is part of coming upon a good idea. Often it is this surprise that makes creating a joyous adventure and propels one to complete the physical and mental tasks that are part of bringing a creative idea to fruition.

The word *creative* here does not imply that creativity in writing is restricted to the making of poems and stories. Ronald Cramer (1979) reminds us, "The term *creative* is intended to express the idea that . . . words and sentences are the personal product of the [person's] experience and imagination. The product itself may be a letter, a story, a poem, a report, an observation, or an account." The idea may be an opinion, a conclusion, a hypothesis, a unique relationship.

According to Bruner (1962), creating is a paradoxical process, requiring detachment and commitment, passion and decorum, freedom and domination, deferral and immediacy. To put together fresh combinations, thinkers must detach themselves from existing forms; they must escape the constraints of the expected. But at the same time, creators must care deeply about understanding and discovering. They must be both detached from the available and committed to the novel.

In like manner, people must be both passionate and decorous to create. They must let ideas wing away in the arms of passion, soaring until the mind has explored every ramification. They must thrill to the expansion of ideas, perceiving the beauty of intertwining relationships. But as Bruner explains, "There is a decorum in creative activity: a love of form, an etiquette toward the object of our efforts, a respect for materials." It is decorum that allows the mind to control and shape the random flow of ideas.

In explaining the third paradox, freedom and domination, Bruner describes the point at which a poem in the process of being created takes form. The poem-in-

Creating:
the paradoxes

detachment/
commitment

passion/
decorum

freedom/
domination

deferral/
immediacy

process becomes an entity in its own right, an externalized object, something "out there" that dominates the writer, compelling him or her to complete it. The creating poet begins to serve the poem rather than the poem serving the poet. When that happens, the writer is freed of defenses that prevent him or her from expressing innermost thoughts. Because the piece is "out there," the writer can experiment with style and content without feeling vulnerable.

Deferral and immediacy are paradoxical aspects of creating, too. Creators have a wild flow of ideas that at times cry out to be expressed. They know what they want to say; they rush to record. But as Bruner maintains, only occasionally does the piece "come off lickety-split," finished in first draft in a form the writer likes. Bruner speaks of "precocious completion," suggesting that deferral in producing a finished draft is generally necessary. Writers must stand back; they must "distance" themselves from what they have created and examine it with a fresh eye.

Creating and School Writing

This brief discussion of the paradoxical aspects of creating provides a framework for thinking about writing as it occurs in schools. At some point, children should experience the detachment from what is known and the commitment to know more, the passion to fly with ideas and the decorum ultimately to control them, the freedom to express ideas and the domination by those ideas, the need for immediate expression and the need to defer for review. To this end, school writing *should not*

- Require students to write without opportunity for prior thought. Ideas are not "made" on a topic on command.
- Cast the teacher in the role of external evaluator.
- Emphasize form over ideas. Form follows ideas, and form flows from ideas when the writer recognizes the value of what he or she has created.
- Take away the joy of creating.

To this end, school writing *should*

- Provide youngsters with time to create ideas, strategies for expanding ideas, and opportunities to talk out and share ideas.
- Emphasize idea making in all kinds of contexts—the writing of prose as well as poetry, the writing of critical reports as well as stories. Teachers and students must realize that writing critically is a creative endeavor, for it requires the making of ideas.
- Encourage youngsters to review their writing, to stand back and look with a fresh eye.
- Encourage children to use their peers as sounding boards for idea making and collaborate in authoring groups.
- Enable children to experience the "effective surprise" that is what idea making is all about.

Meet Meredith Ann Pierce

Meredith Ann Pierce, whose novels include *The Darkangel* and *A Gathering of Gargoyles* (Atlantic Monthly/ Little, Brown), describes what happens to her as she writes: "When I sit down to write, I enter a state that is very like dreaming. I become still, relaxed. I lose all track of my surroundings and of the passage of time. I'm not easy to rouse from this state by telephones ringing or my housemates shouting up the stairs, but I surface on my own from time to time, and more often than not, it's to find myself speaking: dialogue mostly, or the closing lines of a scene—replaying them endlessly until I get them right. I'm told that I also talk in my sleep" ("The Queen of the Night," *The New Advocate,* 1 [Fall 1988], 221).

Pierce also talks about the way she feels about writing: "'Tyger! Tyger! burning bright.' I was in love with that poem when I was little. The ferocity and sensuality of its fevered imagery quickened my imagination deliciously and made me think of dark forests, and wandering, and coming unexpectedly upon that which, all unknowingly, I had been seeking—a great cat, incandescently kindled, its fearful symmetry immortally framed. I am in love with it still.

"To write a novel is to be in love. It is to wander dark forests, encountering tigers. I've been referred to as a writer of fantasy stories that have strong female protagonists. Upon reflection, I suppose this is true. I've written four novels, all of them high fantasy, and in three of the four, the main character is female. Yet when people ask me about my heroines, where they come from, on whom they are modeled, and I respond, '"The Tiger" by William Blake,' I'm looked at as though I haven't answered the question" ("A Lion in the Room," *The Horn Book,* 64 [January/February 1988], 35).

DISCUSSION PROMPT

How does Meredith Ann Pierce make her ideas? What relationship do you perceive between what Pierce and Bruner are saying? What can teachers do to engage children in the higher-order thinking operations that are at the heart of the writing process? What approaches did Ms. Chou use in the opening vignette to engage children in creative thinking Why do you think she used those approaches?

Idea Making and Emergent Writing

Making ideas through writing should occur the moment a child sets foot in a classroom. It is not something that must wait until children have learned the alphabet or know how to read. Research indicates that most children are writers before they come to school and are eager to write in preschool and kindergarten.

Young Children as Creative Writers: What the Research Says

The young child is surrounded by print. Print is on cereal boxes on the kitchen table, everywhere in supermarkets, on signs and billboards, on television, on calendars. Print is in books, magazines, and newspapers that family members read and share. Surrounded by print, young children come naturally to understand that print is used to talk about things around them; in time, they come naturally to use print creatively to express their thoughts.

How Young Children Invent Language to Write   In *GNYS AT WRK,* Glenda Bissex (1980) chronicles her son Paul's writing development starting when he was about five. Paul's first writing was the production of a welcome-home banner for his mother. The banner was replete with his unique combination of original letters, a combination that language educators have termed *invented spelling.* A viewer of educational television programs depicting letters and sounds, and a member of a family in which reading and writing played a significant role, within months Paul was spontaneously writing messages like *"RUDF"* (Are you deaf?), a message he used to get his busy mother's attention.

Researchers have documented that at home, young children willingly plunge into creating ideas on paper with an originality all their own. They enthusiastically read back what they have inscribed, in the process adding orally to their written ideas. At this stage and in this context, children's writing departs from conventional letter formation and spelling. Yet, as Diane DeFord and Jerome Harste (1982) maintain, this writing is more than scribble. The writing of typical three- and four-year-olds already demonstrates an impressive understanding by the children of the nature of written messages and the written form of their language. Children begin to exhibit knowledge of linearity, left-to-right and top-to-bottom directionality, and uniformity of size and shape. In addition, Harste (1982) has found evidence in children's early writing of intention (purpose in writing), invention (creativity of ideas), and organization (logical development of ideas). According to Nigel Hall (1987), by the time children enter school, most know that

- The purpose of writing is to communicate messages.
- Written language is composed of various elements.
- Writing takes on certain forms and structures.

Vera Milz (1985) confirms young children's rudimentary understanding of written language. Milz has found that many first-graders are already experimenting with written language to record and request information, to pretend, and to build relationships. In short, first-graders are using higher-order thinking as they function as emerging writers.

Stages in Writing Development   Obviously not all children of the same age or grade level write in the same way. This can be seen in the children's writing in Figures 9.2 through 9.5. All the children whose writing appears in these figures were in kindergarten at the time. The stories are courtesy of DeeJay Schwartz, a kindergarten teacher. The names of stages are after Charles Temple et al. (1993).

Omari's story (Figure 9.2) represents an early developmental stage in making ideas with print: *preletter making,* or line making. His writing, however, is not scribble.

WORD BANK
Preletter making
Random-letter making
Early phonemic stage
Advanced phonemic stage

Figure 9.2
Omari's Story: **Preletter Stage of Writing Development**
Courtesy of Omari Jefferson

DISCUSSION PROMPT

See Omari's name in the box on the left. What does Omari, who is in kindergarten, know about recording ideas on paper?

Figure 9.3
Kerry's Story: **Random Letter-Making Stage of Writing Development**
Courtesy of Kerry Bogert

DISCUSSION PROMPT

What is this kindergartener's conception of writing?

Figure 9.4
Raphael's Story: **Early Phonemic Stage of Writing Development**

Courtesy of Raphael Horowitz

DISCUSSION PROMPT

Raphael's story says, "He has plates like spines. You are too big." What does this kindergartner know about print that Omari and Kerry do not know? Hypothesize why Raphael spells "you" in standard fashion.

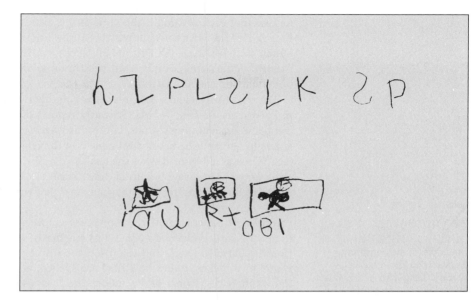

Figure 9.5
Katie's Story: **Advanced Phonemic Stage of Writing Development**

Courtesy of Katie Burk

DISCUSSION PROMPT

Katie is also in kindergarten. What does she know about writing?

Omari has a clear understanding of left-to-right and top-to-bottom progression. He knows that writing tells a story, for he reads his story. His teacher, DeeJay Schwartz, reports that each reading is the same and is almost a perfect rendition of what the tour guide said when the children visited the dinosaur museum, a visit that provided Omari with his ideas for writing. His teacher further reports that although Omari "knows" letters and sounds from preschool, at this stage he does not want to be bothered with them in writing.

Kerry's story (Figure 9.3) represents another developmental stage in writing: *random-letter making*. As Ms. Schwartz reports, Kerry knows that letters exist and can distinguish among sounds, but at this stage words look like bunches of random letters to her, and she has not yet perceived the relationship between sounds and letters. When asked to read what she has written, she says, "Well, I just wrote this, but I don't know what it says because I didn't learn to read yet." But Kerry, too, has a considerable understanding of print; she knows that writing progresses from left to right and from top to bottom.

Raphael's paper (Figure 9.4) represents a more advanced stage in writing development: the *early phonemic stage*. This kindergartner hears and understands the relationship between letters and sounds, especially consonants. He sounds out words he wants to write, estimates how they are spelled, and writes the words that way. He knows there are words and sentences, for he inserts breaks between some words and between sentences. At the early phonemic stage of writing, he is beginning to abide by many conventions of English writing, especially as they apply to the use of consonants.

Katie's paper (Figure 9.5) represents yet another stage: letter name, or *advanced phonemic writing*. Katie has control over both consonants and vowels. She divides her story into discrete word units. And she tells a great story! As Ms. Schwartz reports, Katie loves writing and reading, and she will try any word. Once she starts either activity, she keeps going until her eyes and/or fingers tire. Katie's enthusiasm and confidence are contagious. She reads her story in this way:

> Stegosaurus was a very dumb animal. Stegosaurus was in the field. He was looking for some food. He saw some danger. He suddenly whacked the danger with his tail and he saw that the danger was his friend and he apologized and he lived happily ever after.

Talking, Drawing, and Writing   Especially with preschool, kindergarten, and first-grade children, talking, drawing, and writing blend. Youngsters often use pictures and oral language to flesh out their written stories. Anne Dyson (1981) describes the relationship between the language and visual arts in one young child's writing. To Ms. Dyson, Sara orally told her "Yes Go" story shown in Figure 9.6 in this way:

> Her name's here [pointing to *Sara*]. Somebody yelled "Go." She said "No." Then another girl said, "Yes."

As Dyson explains, "Sara's [written] text is dynamic; it provides the dialogue—the action—of a plot. Her oral language provided the narrative context within which her characters spoke." Sara's writing began with the "selection of an idea, a thought, a thing to put in print—and the discovery of some strategy for making that thought visible." It did not begin with the child's understanding of the alphabetic principles of recording on paper.

READ

Elizabeth Sulzby, "Research Directions: Transitions from Emergent to Conventional Writing," *Language Arts*, 69 (April 1992), 290–297, for a review of fifteen years of research on children's emergent writing.

Figure 9.6
Sara's Story
Courtesy of Anne Dyson and the National Council of Teachers of English

Mary Ellen Giacobbe (1981) has also noted the interrelatedness of writing and drawing. A classroom teacher, Giacobbe gave her newly arrived first-graders journals in which to write. In response, the children tended to produce a combination of drawings and creatively spelled print. Interestingly, the tool given children influences the form of storytelling they choose (Woodward, 1984). Given a crayon, young children are more likely to draw; given a pen or a pencil, children produce more letters and more words using invented spellings.

Writing and Reading   For young children there are no unnatural divisions between writing and reading. Through reading—or through listening to stories read aloud to them—youngsters begin to perceive relationships between print and speech. For example, picture books that use *-ly* words show young listeners how information conveyed through tone of voice is put down on paper; the writer writes, " 'Be quiet,' the teacher said *softly*," to tell how the teacher spoke the words. As Kenneth and Yetta Goodman (1983) summarize so simply and clearly, "Children use in writing what they observe in reading" and in listening to stories. To this end, children must begin to read like writers and notice some of the characteristics of print that are all around them. But ultimately they must write, for it is when children "try to create written language that this observation focuses on how form serves function."

In *What Did I Write?*, Marie Clay (1975) explains why children's early writing has an impact on reading. Children who write—even if they use invented spellings—still manipulate the units of written language: letters, words, and sentences. They must attend to the details of print as they construct words letter by letter; in the process, they become more aware of letter features and sequences. The words children write are the ones they get to know and soon can read on their own.

In summary, the current research on children's early writing emphasizes the following points:

- Young children can write creatively before they can spell, before they know the conventions of written language, and before they read.
- Teachers must provide young children with opportunities for writing. Children should be encouraged to write, inventing their own way of writing down that meets the needs of the creating they are doing at the moment.
- Children should be encouraged to use talk to expand the ideas they have expressed through drawing and print.
- Children need to participate in a host of literacy events—oral encounters with print—so that they have an opportunity to observe the characteristics of print and use them in their writing.

GO TO

Chapter 8, pages 266–280, for more on early literacy events.

Ways to Help Young Children Emerge as Writers

Involving very young children in writing requires thought on the part of the teacher. As many preschool, kindergarten, and first-grade teachers know, young children are egocentric beings whose worlds revolve around themselves. They are curious about that world—a world close at hand. The attention span of kindergartners and first-graders lengthens each day, but attention still lags quickly. At this stage language expands almost exponentially, with new words entering children's speaking vocabularies daily. Just gaining skill as recorders, young learners find printing out letters a time-consuming task.

These characteristics of young learners determine a teacher's approach to beginning composition. Youngsters at this stage must be personally and actively involved in choosing writing topics. Generally, before writing they need to experience and observe, handle, dramatize, and talk out. While writing, they need to talk audibly or subaudibly to themselves.

CONSIDER

Lucy Calkins (1994) stresses that students become involved in their writing when they write on topics important to them.

Because kindergartners and first-graders are only beginning to develop skill in recording ideas on paper, written activity must take into account the level of that skill. Some teachers have found the following activities useful as children start to write.

Drawing and Writing with Invented Spelling   Young children benefit from an approach to writing that does not stress precision in spelling. As children write, they should be encouraged to get their thoughts down on paper in any way they want: drawing, invented spelling, or whatever. The thought is more important than the manner in which it is recorded.

One way of handling invented spelling is to suggest that children think in terms of consonant sounds and provide them with a few consonants to use by teaching those particular sound/symbol correspondences. Donald Graves (Walshe, 1982) has found that youngsters can write using invented spelling "so long as we provide them with six consonants, any six." Children are encouraged to use the consonants they know to "hold the place" of a word or idea. Teachers who celebrate creative spelling realize that excitement about writing is more important in the very early years than precision in recording.

Keeping a Journal   One of the first contexts in which young children should be encouraged to write freely using their invented spellings and pictures is the journal. At the preschool and kindergarten levels, a journal can be a homemade booklet of pieces of construction paper cut in half and stapled together. Children put an illustration, a title, and their name on the cover. They write whatever they want in the journal, at times prompted by classroom experiences, at other times unprompted— just because they feel like it.

After making journal entries, children read them to their teacher or volunteer to share their entries with the class. The teacher also responds to the student by writing back in the journal—creating a written dialogue with the child. In the latter case, the teacher reads what he or she has written to the child, pointing to the words and perhaps asking the child to read along on a second reading. The advantage of this procedure is that it provides the child with a model of letters and words to include in future entries.

GO TO

Pages 233–237 for a description of shared and interactive writing.

Shared and Interactive Writing   Even as children write using drawings and invented spellings, they participate in shared and interactive writing, with the teacher recording dictated sentences on chart paper or on a computer for them. Youngsters contribute letters and punctuation marks to the charts as they learn to construct them. As we saw in Chapter 7, at times the teacher talks out how he or she is translating sounds of words into symbols on paper. For example, in recording, the teacher says, "I want to write the word *dog. Dog*—the sound that I hear at the beginning of the word *dog* is put down on paper with the letter *d*. I hear the same sound at the beginning of my name—Dorothy. That is why I begin my name with the letter *D*." At other times, children individually dictate their thoughts to the teacher or to an assistant who records the sentences for them and stops once in a while to explain how he or she is translating speech sounds into writing. Used in this way, shared and interactive writing provides children with a model of how writing relates to the sounds of speech.

READ

Reading Recovery 1984–1988 (Columbus, Ohio: Ohio State University, 1988). Reading Recovery, a first-grade program to help poor readers, was developed in New Zealand by Marie Clay.

Collaborating at Writing   Reading Recovery, an early intervention program geared at helping at-risk six-year-olds emerge as readers, uses a different approach to emergent writing, an approach based on the one-to-one interaction between a teacher and a child (Clay, 1985). In Reading Recovery, the child writes unaided what he or she can while the teacher watches. When the child reaches a word that he or she cannot write, the teacher asks, "What can you hear? What letters would you expect to see?" In a section of paper above the child's composition, the teacher draws the number of boxes that corresponds to the number of phonemes (speech sounds) in the word the child wants to write. The child writes the letters in the boxes that represent each sound to him or her, and the teacher provides help with silent letters and letters that represent difficult sounds or sounds the child has not mastered. Having drafted the desired word in this way, the child writes it into the ongoing part of his or her composition. Later, as the child reads, the teacher informally reinforces the same sound-symbol correspondences the child has used in writing.

Brainstorming Words for Writing   Without question, first-graders are thwarted in composing by their limited spelling skills. To encourage children to write despite this limitation, some teachers from time to time stand at the board before and while students compose. Children brainstorm words they wish to use, and the teacher writes them on the board. This strategy pays secondary dividends: A word one student identifies may spur others to use it as well.

Some first-grade teachers use a variation on this approach. They post twenty-six charts around the room under the chalkboard areas and label each chart with a

■ ● ● ●

CONSIDER

On the Word Wall
Bb:
1. book
2. ball
3. bridge
4. by
5. Bill

different letter of the alphabet. When children brainstorm a word before writing or call for one while writing, the teachers record it on the appropriate chart. If the word is already on a chart from a previous day, they direct attention to it. In this way, words children are using become part of the classroom Word Walls.

To help children gain skill as recorders, from time to time some teachers organize a more structured activity. To begin, they guide youngsters to brainstorm on a particular topic. For example, Emily Davis had her first-graders brainstorm the months of the year and reasons they liked some months better than others. As the children supplied month names, she listed them in a column on the Word Wall. Then she suggested a structured writing option starting in this way:

> The month I like best is _____ . I like it because _____ . I also like it because _____ .

To complete the composition, the children selected month words from the brainstormed chart and used invented spellings to write their reasons. Note that this activity provided children with a simple introduction to the structure of a paragraph.

Of course, teachers should provide words children need in writing only sparingly. Youngsters should generally try out spellings on their own and have plenty of opportunities to invent spellings as they compose and to use such common words as *I, it,* and *like.*

Emergent Writing in the Early Years

Researchers have noted differences in the way young children approach writing at home and at school. According to R. K. Moss and John Stansell (1983), children's school writing often reflects a teacher's concern that children make their letters and copy words correctly. In contrast, home writing is more creative, revealing children's belief that the purpose of writing is expression and enjoyment.

DeFord and Harste (1982) have found similar differences between classes in which teachers stress form over meaning and those in which meaning takes precedence over form. In the first kind of classroom, youngsters soon learn that "if you can't spell, you can't write" and that finding the right letters to represent word symbols on paper is what writing is all about. In the second kind, children invent spellings as they experiment with the wonder of language and delight in the process of creation. Here idea making is what writing is about.

Expanding Writing Horizons

Writing in the 1980s, Donald Graves (1983), Lucy Calkins (1986), Nancie Atwell (1987), and other teacher-writers proposed that the way to get children involved in writing is to encourage them to write personal narratives that arise out of their own lives (and therefore are personally significant and authentic), and to allow students the freedom to choose their own topics. As a result, in some classrooms, personal narratives became the right and sometimes the only option; students hardly ever tried other kinds of writing and teachers rarely if ever made specific writing assignments.

More recently, many of these same teacher-writers—as well as others—are saying, "Yes, but. . . ." Yes, but there is a need for a writing curriculum that provides a framework for writing workshops (Calkins, 1994; Snowball in Calkins, 1994). Yes, but poetry, fiction, and nonfiction are important (Graves, 1989a, 1989b, 1992). Yes, but it is fine to "require students to do certain types of writing that are common and useful" (Sudol and Sudol, 1995). Yes, but it is all right to "nudge" children in certain directions and "nudging often looks like shoving" (Dudley-Marling, 1995).

Supporting Children in Topic Selection

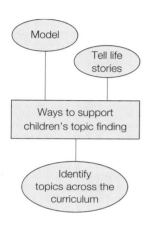

Model

Tell life stories

Ways to support children's topic finding

Identify topics across the curriculum

Most experienced teachers agree with the earlier position of Graves, Calkins, and Atwell that children should have opportunities to choose what they write about; as Nancie Atwell (1991) explains, with choosing comes responsibility. However, experienced teachers also know that children have difficulty identifying topics for writing. These teachers realize that their job is to support children in finding meaningful writing topics.

One way to support children in finding topics that arise out of life's experiences is modeling (Horn, 2001). Earlier in this chapter, we saw Ms. Chou model (in a brief mini-lesson) how she thinks about her topic for writing long before she sits down to write. Her modeling says to the children, "Authors don't just sit down and write; they pause to look around them; they think about ideas when they are doing other things—like coming to school." Her modeling also says, "Sometimes authors have to work on idea making; they need a way to make ideas grow out of their lives. Idea clustering is a way to start ideas flowing."

A second way for teachers to model topic making is to tell stories from their own lives. Terri Miller, a sixth-grade teacher, reserves a number of her own life stories for this purpose. From time to time at the beginning of workshop, she tells one of her stories, something unusual that has happened to her. Students ask her questions to "flesh out her story," which she eventually writes up (not down!) to read during an "Author Share." Having shared her story a second time, Ms. Miller borrows an idea from Lucy Calkins (1994): She explains that to her, writing is not "deskwork"; it is "lifework." She keeps alert for stories as she goes about her life, she tries them in her head, and she tells them aloud—all before she sits down at her desk to put them on paper.

A third way for teachers to help children identify writing topics is to talk about possibilities at the ends of lessons. Ms. Chou did this when she had her instructional group brainstorm writing possibilities based on Silverstein's "Helping" and list these options in their writing portfolios. Advantages of this approach are that writing becomes an integral part of the total curriculum and children start with lots of knowledge about their chosen topics because they have been studying those topics together.

Developing a Writing Curriculum

READ

Gunther Kress, "Genre and the Changing Contexts for English Language Arts," *Language Arts*, 76 (July 1999), 461-469, for a full explanation of Kress's concept of genre.

Today, theorist Gunther Kress (1999) argues for an expanded concept of genre and for a comprehensive writing curriculum with attention to all kinds of genres. According to Kress, genre in the past was conceived in terms of "stereotyped forms" that focused on adhering to the established conventions of these kinds of texts rather than encouraging "variability, unconventionality, or 'creativity.'" This need not be, Kress argues. Genres that have a place in the curriculum include not only what Kress calls "aesthetically valued texts" that society views as the "best" but also culturally salient and mundane texts such as reports, interview scripts, statements of rules and regulations, and even business cards. Out of these genres, writers can create new forms through which they can express their originality. But as Kress contends, originality of expression arises only if writers know about existing genres and know how to handle them.

At some point, teachers must go beyond helping children identify topics based on personal experiences and introduce a full range of genres—their shapes and the contexts in which they typically are used. No child will choose to write a haiku unless he or she knows about haiku, nor will he or she ever invent a piece that is haiku-like but varies in some way. No child will decide to write a tall tale or a modern variation on a tall tale unless he or she knows about exaggeration in story writing. No child will write in the persuasive and the expository modes unless nudged in these directions, nor will a child create original ways to handle opinions or explanations in writing (Kucera, 1995).

At some point, too, teachers must assign writing tasks that clarify the characteristics of different genres; they must involve children in what has been called "demand writing" (Downing, 1995). Teachers have to schedule workshops in which "students are presented with materials and problems that encourage various processes and modes." Having taught a genre, they must require students to try out particular forms and organize samples of those forms of writing in their writing portfolios by the end of a marking period (Kucera, 1995).

Some states and professional organizations are establishing curricular standards that require teachers to provide "many different exposures to writing—as technique, as genre, and as structure—throughout the curriculum" (Phinney, 1998). For example, New Jersey has developed standards that mandate that at grades K–4, all students will begin to

READ

IRA/NCTE Standards for the Language Arts (Newark, Del.: International Reading Association, 1996).

- Write from experiences, thoughts, and feelings.
- Use writing to extend experience.
- Write for a variety of purposes, such as to persuade, enjoy, entertain, learn, inform, record, respond to reading, solve problems.
- Write in a variety of genres such as notes, poems, letters, interviews, journals.
- Write to synthesize information from multiple sources.
- Use figurative language (e.g., simile, metaphor) and analogies to expand meaning.

At grades 5–8, all students will demonstrate a greater ability to do all these tasks, plus:

- Write technical materials that include specific details.
- Cite sources (New Jersey Core Curriculum Standards, 1995).

In addition, New Jersey and some other states have established a testing program to determine whether schools are meeting the standards.

In the next section, we examine prose forms that children should be sampling through their writing and reading. In the final section, we will consider poetry and language forms.

Distinguished Educator

Meet Nancie Atwell

Nancie Atwell is a specialist in middle-school language arts who has taught upper-grade students in public and private schools in Maine for many years and has written widely on the subject in a practical way that teachers appreciate. Her book *In the Middle: New Understandings About Writing, Reading, and Learning* is widely cited.

From the pen of Nancie Atwell, we get these thoughts about the teaching of genre:

"Three years ago I began to teach with a capital T. I planned sequences of mini-lessons. . . . I expected productivity (taking a page from Linda Rief, I asked for three to five pages of rough draft each week and at least two pieces of writing brought to final draft every six weeks). In addition to continued opportunities for students to develop their own projects in the workshop, I expected them to work in particular genres—last year we experimented with short fiction, drama, profiles, book reviews, poetry and songs, and memoir—and I taught about the genres, bombarded kids with great examples, and struggled with them myself in demonstration lessons, writing in front of my students on overhead transparencies. . . . I started workshop every day with a reading and discussion of a poem I loved and thought my kids would, too. I read aloud other writing I loved with themes and characters relevant to my middle-school kids—novels, memoirs, Arthurian legend, short stories, collections of poetry, myths, picture books, the Old and New Testaments. . . ." ("Cultivating Our Garden," *Voices from the Middle*, 3, 4 [November 1996]).

DISCUSSION PROMPT

Atwell talks about providing children with opportunities to write in a variety of genre and about "teaching with a capital T." How do you react to this suggestion? How do you react to the suggestion that teachers should have expectations for their students rather than allowing them always to write just what they want to in whatever manner that they want? How does the suggestion relate to the movement toward accountability and state standards that seems to be sweeping the country—to the anguish of some educators?

Making Ideas by Writing and Reading Prose

■ ● ● ●

READ

Linda Caswell and Nell Duke, "Non-narrative as a Catalyst for Literacy Development," *Language Arts,* 75 (February 1998), 103–117, for a discussion of the reasons for involving children in reading and writing non-narrative texts.

Prose writing can serve a variety of purposes and take a variety of forms. People can write for themselves as in journals or to others as in letter writing. In writing, they can attempt to persuade, inform, or tell a story. Here are some thoughts on ways to encourage a wide range of prose writing and on teaching the characteristics of different kinds of writing.

Journal Writing

In Beverly Cleary's Newbery Award–winning *Dear Mr. Henshaw,* Leigh Botts writes to his favorite author, Mr. Henshaw, asking for answers to questions about writing books. That letter becomes a full-blown correspondence when Henshaw turns the tables and asks Leigh to answer some questions. Mr. Henshaw eventually encourages Leigh to keep a diary. At first Leigh pretends he is writing to Mr. Henshaw, but soon he is consigning to his journal his sad and sometimes humorous thoughts about his divorced parents, the theft of goodies from his lunch bag, and his own writing problems.

■ ● ● ●

READ

■ John Evelyn, *Diary of John Evelyn, 1620–1706* (London: Dent, 1907), and Joseph Plumb Martin, *Narrative of the Adventures, Dangers and Sufferings of a Revolutionary Soldier* (Hallowell, Me.: Glazier, Masters and Co., 1830). Both diaries are available in reprinted editions.

■ Joanne Rocklin, *For Your Eyes Only (FYEO)* (New York: Scholastic, 1997), for another story in journal form.

■ Ann Rinaldi, *Wolf by the Ears* (New York: Scholastic, 1991), fictional biography done in journal form.

In the past, diary keeping preoccupied many people, both the great and the ordinary. For example, John Evelyn kept a diary in which he chronicled events in his life as well as events in the England of his day. An ordinary Revolutionary War foot soldier recorded his day-to-day struggle for survival during that war. These classic diaries, as well as Joan Blos's Newbery Award–winning *A Gathering of Days: A New England Girl's Journal,* are models a teacher can share to introduce children to "journaling."

To encourage children to write in their journals, some teachers, like Ms. Chou, dedicate time each morning to free writing in journals and keep personal journals, which they share from time to time. When children see that their teacher is enjoying writing and they cannot interrupt her, they are less likely to ask for help in spelling and more likely to rely on invented spellings.

Sometimes, too, the teacher can suggest that students pretend, as Leigh Botts does in the Cleary book, that they are writing to a pretend person in conversational style; children write as though they were talking to that person. Of course, the pretend person can be the teacher. For example, Jennifer Chou suggests, "Just start your entry with Dear Ms. Chou."

In this context, as Linda Gambrell (1985), Roger Shuy (1987), and Jana Staton (1988) contend, dialogue journals pay dividends. Using dialogue journals, the teacher reads an entry and writes a reply in the child's journal, not identifying writing errors or criticizing but following up on the ideas. When a child has misspelled a word, the teacher might use and underline that word, correctly spelled, in the reply. On occasion buddies can exchange journals, responding to each other's entries just as their teacher has been doing.

Penny Powell uses communal interest journals with her sixth-graders. An interest journal is one in which students write entries on topics of interest to them and read the entries on those topics written by their peers. To start, Ms. Powell has students brainstorm topics that interest them, such as an upcoming election, a sports figure, a popular story character, a school concern, making friends, keeping friends, or living with a younger sibling. Students record a topic on the outside of a bound notebook. During journal times, they select a topical notebook to write in. In writing, they respond to prior entries or "explore and extend thinking on the topic." Ms. Powell notes that there should be enough journals to go around, that students should sign and date their entries, and that teachers periodically need to look through the journals to see that students' entries are "positive, appropriate, and well thought out" (Bromley and Powell, 1999).

Kindergarten is not too early to begin journals, as teacher Jean Hannon (1999) attests. She introduces the idea of daily journals early in September by modeling how to use a combination of pictures, letter-like shapes, and letters to "hold" ideas on paper. She confers from time to time with the kindergartners, spends some journal time writing in her own journal, and begins to write back to the children in dialogue fashion. In her classroom in North Pole, Alaska, Ms. Hannon writes that journal time is "seldom a quiet time." Children seem "to relish comparing and conferring on their writing and drawing." She also notes that when teacher/student dialogue is part of journal writing, kindergartners develop greater writing fluency and use more "advanced invented spellings."

Letter Writing

For students who have written in journals, letter writing is a feasible next step. Peggy Heller, a creative third-grade teacher, introduced her third-graders to letter writing through a pen pal unit. Youngsters first wrote a cooperatively composed letter to a professor at a nearby college, requesting her to ask her undergraduates if they wanted to be pen pals. The group letter served as the model through which the youngsters learned the structure of a friendly letter. Soon youngsters and college students were exchanging letters. Unfortunately, one youngster did not get a response from her pen pal. Taking matters into her own hands, she decided to make the professor her pen pal and wrote the letter shown in Figure 9.7.

As with journal writing, educators generally propose that children be taught to write letters as though carrying on a face-to-face conversation with the person to whom they are writing. Writers should recognize the reader's interests and anticipate the reader's questions. Modeling helps here because letter writing is a form of demand writing (Downing, 1995). The writer may have little choice about whether to write; circumstances demand it.

In guiding the writing of a class letter to send home to parents to invite them to a class play, the teacher can ask, "If you were talking to your mother or father about our play, what things would you want to tell about? What would your mother or father want to know?" Prompted in this way, children may suggest, "The play is funny. You will laugh a lot," or "I am the clown. I wear a tall hat," or simply "We all get dressed up"—statements that become sentences in the cooperative letter or in children's personalized versions.

The social arena of classroom and community provides innumerable opportunities for conversationally styled letters. Friendly notes can be written to classmates

CONSIDER

■ Paula Danziger and Ann Martin, *P.S. Longer Letter Later: A Novel in Letters* (New York: Scholastic, 1998), with upper-graders who are writing letters.

■ Janet Ahlberg and Allan Ahlberg, *The Jolly Postman or Other People's Letters* (Boston: Little, Brown, 1986) and *The Jolly Christmas Postman* (Boston: Little, Brown, 1991) are useful with primary children.

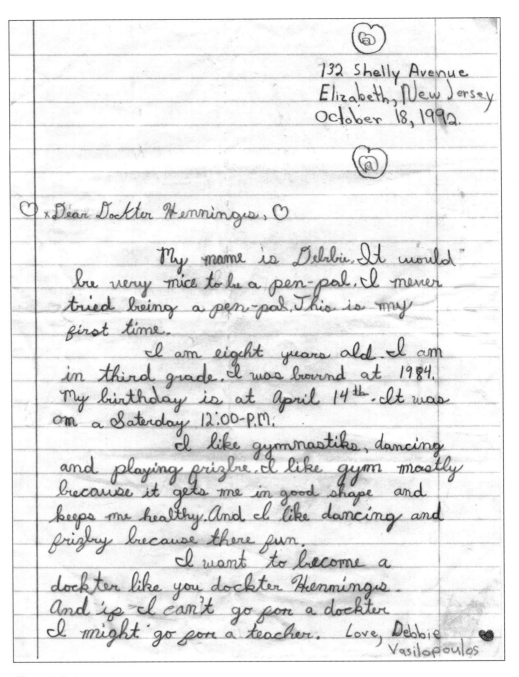

132 Shelly Avenue
Elizabeth, New Jersey
October 18, 1992.

x Dear Dockter Hennings,

My name is Debbie. It would
be very nice to be a pen-pal. I never
tried being a pen-pal. This is my
first time.

I am eight years old. I am
in third grade. I was bournd at 1984.
My birthday is at April 14th. It was
on a Saterday 12:00-P.M.

I like gymnastiks, dancing
and playing frizbre. I like gym mostly
because it gets me in good shape and
keeps me healthy. And I like dancing and
frizby because there fun.

I want to become a
dockter like you dockter Hennings.
And if I can't go for a dockter
I might go for a teacher. Love, Debbie
Vasilopoulos

Figure 9.7
Debbie's Letter to a Pen Pal

DISCUSSION PROMPT

■ For Debbie, writing the letter had a significant purpose: She wanted a pen pal. How can e-mail facilitate letter writing? What problems are there in the use of e-mail in classrooms?

who are at home sick, speakers who have visited the class, or parents who have supplied refreshments. In the upper grades, the class Social Committee, which changes its membership monthly, may take care of the class's social obligations, writing letters during independent study times. In lower grades, letter writing can become a shared writing experience, with all children suggesting possible lines to include in a cooperative letter and selecting those that say what the class wants to express.

In the context of writing letters to real people, schools teach not only conversational style but the conventions of letter writing. Some teachers have found that providing models of social and business letter and envelope forms is helpful. Students analyze elements of a form and then model theirs after it. One teacher printed a letter and envelope on the classroom floor with washable shoe polish. By the time the polish had worn off the floor, students no longer needed the crutch it supplied.

Persuasive Writing: Opinion Paragraphs

As a writing option based on the poem "Helping," Ms. Chou's students proposed a paragraph telling their opinions of what was good and bad about the poem. Writing opinion paragraphs that persuade others is a natural follow-up in many contexts: after reading a selection, after viewing a film, following a general discussion in content-area studies as well as in literature studies.

The teacher should model persuasive writing. Having just discussed the duel between Hamilton and Burr, teacher and students can formulate an opinion about the rightness and wrongness of dueling: "Dueling is a stupid way to settle a dispute." The teacher can write that opinion on the chalkboard as the first, or topic, sentence in an opinion paragraph and suggest, "Let's develop our argument. What reasons do we have to support this opinion?" Children divide into three-person writing teams to complete the paragraph, adding sentences that give supporting reasons—the argument, or proof. Gathering together after team writing, children share their paragraphs and then analyze the structure of what they have written. In this case the structure is deductive, because the paragraph begins with a general point—the opinion—that is followed by supporting detail. Upper-graders can graphically map the structure of their deductively organized paragraph and use their map as a guide for writing opinion paragraphs of their own. The map helps students clarify their thinking and leads to the development of a logical argument. Figure 9.8 shows a graphic organizer for a *deductively* structured paragraph as well as one for an *inductively* structured text in which the support comes first, followed by the topic sentence that states the opinion. In the same way used to model the writing of a deductive paragraph, the teacher should model the writing of an inductive paragraph.

Informative Paragraph and Report Writing

Especially in upper grades, students should write reports as part of content-area studies. Short reports should include information gathered from references, as described in Chapter 8; students experiment with note cards, data webs, data synthesis charts, and informal outlines as ways to organize data. In addition, students should be taught how to go beyond facts to develop relationships to express as conclusions in the reports they write.

READ

Nancy Burkhalter, "A Vygotsky-Based Curriculum for Teaching Persuasive Writing in the Elementary Grades." *Language Arts*, 72 (March 1995), 192–199.

WORD BANK

Deductive design—from general to specific

Inductive design—from specific to general

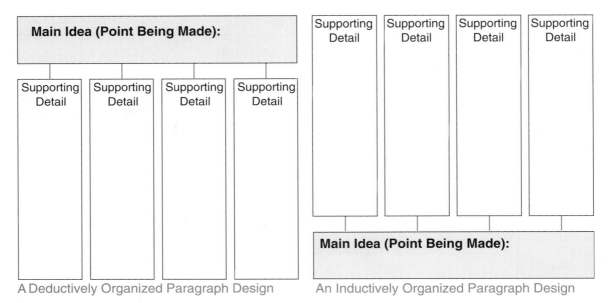

Figure 9.8
Paragraph Organizers. *The teacher models how he or she designs a main idea and supporting detail by plotting them on a main idea/ supporting detail organizer before writing a paragraph.*

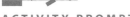

ACTIVITY PROMPT

Write a paragraph using the deductive design in which you express your opinion of states' testing to see if children have met state-mandated standards.

Obviously, content-area teachers should not simply assign children to write reports. Teachers must model the processes of drafting reports just as in mini-lessons they model how to structure opinion-stating paragraphs. The vignette that opens Chapter 10 describes a way to model report writing.

Enumeration   As students begin to write reports, upper-grade language arts teachers should also model some of the rhetorical relationships that characterize informational texts (enumeration, example, comparison/contrast, cause/effect, conditionality) and help upper-graders to feel comfortable with the language writers use to tie content information together (Richards and Gipe, 1995; Moore, 1995). For example, after children have read and discussed several novelettes, students can collaboratively draft a summary that enumerates and elaborates upon elements of a fine story. The teacher can encourage enumeration by suggesting, "Let's think in terms of three or four elements that make us enjoy a story." As students suggest points, a scribe records them on the board to clarify the enumerative relationship, as in Figure 9.9. Together teacher and students interactively craft a topic sentence based on the points enumerated, perhaps something like this: "We look for certain elements in selecting a novel to read: strong characters, exciting events, and an ending that we can believe in."

In coauthoring-pairs, students brainstorm ideas that expand upon the three points they have enumerated and craft a sentence or two about each of them to support the

Figure 9.9
Enumerative Pattern

ACTIVITY PROMPT

With a coauthor, write a paragraph in which you describe three characteristics you look for in a friend.

three elements we look for in a novel:

1. strong characters
2. exciting events
3. a believable ending

topic, or main idea, sentence that the class has drafted together. Students may use words such as *first, next,* and *finally* to organize their ideas. Coauthoring-pairs share their paragraphs, using a diagram, as in Figure 9.9, to clarify the rhetorical relationship.

To strengthen their reading comprehension, students can search content-area texts for similarly crafted paragraphs of enumeration. As they read, upper-graders look for other transitional words that authors use to communicate the enumerative relationship and the way authors use the colon at times as part of a statement of enumeration. In conducting text searches, students may find instances where authors spread enumerated items over a series of paragraphs. Students can explain the rhetorical relationship in these paragraphs and try this more complex application in their own writing.

Examples   In the same way, students can learn to handle and recognize other rhetorical relationships, such as the topic sentence/example(s) relationship. Again as a way to summarize an ongoing discussion, the teacher can interject, "Authors build tension into their stories to keep us reading. Prove that to me in terms of *Nightjohn*. How does Paulsen heighten tension level?" Students identify examples and interactively craft several sentences stating those examples in support of the main idea—that authors build tension into their stories. They share their resulting deductive paragraphs and identify transitional words used to introduce examples: *such as, a case in point, for example, for instance*. Again, upper-graders search for structurally similar paragraphs in their content-area texts. This kind of activity prepares students for demand-writing tasks— essay exams and assignments that they will have to write in high school and written assessments that are part of mandated state testing programs.

Comparison/Contrast   By sixth grade, students may need help with more sophisticated relationships. A case in point is writing that involves a comparison or contrast. During a science unit, a teacher can model the relationship by composing a contrasting paragraph in front of the students. Writing on an overhead transparency, the teacher demonstrates how he or she would start with a main idea sentence such as, "Plant cells differ from animal cells." The teacher demonstrates how he or she would next write several sentences describing plant cells and then a transitional sentence such as, "In contrast, animal cells . . ." that introduces several sentences about animal cells. Here the science teacher is modeling a deductive structure for an informative paragraph that involves a contrast between two things—plant and animal cells. At the same time, children are learning how to express the contrast through a phrase such as *in contrast*. Teachers should list on the Word Wall other words that upper-graders can use in writing reports that contain comparison/contrast: for a comparison—*similarly, as in the case of, like, the same as;* for a contrast, *on the other hand, on the contrary, unlike, whereas, conversely.*

Such instruction is vital, especially at a time when states are testing students' ability to write logically in response to given prompts. The National Assessment of Education Progress reports that a large majority of students in grades 4, 8, and 12 can produce only minimally developed written responses to persuasive and informative writing prompts (as summarized in Moore, 1995). This lack carries over into reading: NAEP assessments consistently report that many students "comprehend expository text only at a basic level" and do not have the strategies necessary to comprehend passages typically found in content-area texts. These findings reinforce the conclusion that writing programs should go beyond the writing of personal accounts and include nonfiction genres as well as the rhetorical structures that are part of these forms.

Narrative Writing

A narrative tells a story of events, either true or fictitious. As Dan Kirby et al. (1988) remind us, "The effective use of narrative is essential to thinking and to intellectual development. Most other forms of writing seem to be permutations or translations. . . . Any writing program that short circuits narrative or uses it only for young or developmentally immature children is simply working against the natural development of language."

In Chapter 4, you saw an outline of the kinds of narratives to which children should be exposed so that they can use these forms to make their own ideas. To introduce children to a narrative form, a teacher can organize a mini-lesson with these components:

- Modeling of the form through oral sharing and/or independent reading of a sample.
- Identifying key elements of the form.
- Engaging children in oral, interactive storymaking with the form.
- Including that kind of narrative as a writing option from which children can choose during workshop.

As children begin to draft narratives either individually or collaboratively, the teacher can also model how he or she uses a tentative plot plan as in Figure 9.10. For example, when introducing talking-beast tales as a genre for writing, the teacher may show how in rehearsing a story he or she thinks about the problem (or conflict) as it relates to a major character. The teacher may say, "My story is going to be about a

TENTATIVE PLOT PLAN
Main characters(s)
Setting (time and place)
The problem (or source of tension) in the story

The steps through which the problem is resolved
  1.
  2.
  3.

The way the problem is finally resolved
The big idea told through the story
The title of the story (Finalize this *after* drafting the story.)

Figure 9.10
A Plot Plan for Storymaking

ACTIVITY PROMPT

With a coauthor, plot out a story using this plan. Be ready to tell your story using your plot plan

lion who can't make friends because he is so proud that he is king of all the lions in the grasslands. When I make a story, I start in my head with a character somewhere who has a problem. I keep working on a problem that would be an appropriate one for that character. Then I ask myself, 'How can I help this character solve his or her problem. What could happen to this lion? What other characters do I need to get to a satisfying ending? What must this lion learn?" As the teacher explains his or her mind talk and involves students in storymaking by raising questions, he or she jots ideas in brief phrases on the plot plan. Students in groups help their teacher expand his or her story idea by talking out possible events.

Making Ideas by Writing and Reading Poetry

Students in Chris Kazal's fifth grade read poems by Cynthia Rylant as part of a unit on life in Appalachia. During their unit, they also wrote poems "in the style of Rylant." Mallika Tarkas wrote:

■ ● ● ●

READ

- Mary Comstock, "Poetry and Process," *Language Arts,* 69 (April 1992), 261–267, for a case study of poetry writing in fifth grade.
- Lisa Lenz, "Crossroads of Literacy and Orality: Reading Poetry Aloud," *Language Arts*, 69 (December 1992), 597–603, for a case study at the primary level.
- Laura Apol and Jodi Harris, "Joyful Noises: Creating Poems for Voices and Ears," *Language Arts,* 76 (March 1999), 314–322, for ideas for using choral reading and poems for two voices.

> ***Going . . . Going . . . Gone***
> *Every evening at dusk,*
> *climb up on our peak,*
> *sit down and pick a*
> *blade of grass.*
> *Chew . . . Chew . . . Chew . . .*
> *Wait . . . Wait . . . Wait . . .*
> *Stop! Wait! Stop!*
> *Sun's losing its rays.*
> *Darkness around the*
> *corner.*
> *In a second now,*
> *Going . . . Going . . . Gone*
> *Darkness has fallen.*

Megan Scully wrote:

> ***Big Ole Black Snake!***
> *Went down to the swimmin' hole*
> *to take a dip.*
> *Saw a snake, big and black*
> *scared more than me,*
> *stepped back not paying attention*
> *and SPLASH!*
> *in the swimmin' hole I went.*
> *Got out of the water as*
> *fast as I could.*
> *Big ole black snake was*
> *still there.*
> *Ran down the road ASAP*
> *'cause that big ole black*
> *snake sure scared me.*

As Mallika's and Megan's poems show us and as Curt Dudley-Marling and Sharon Murphy (1999) remind us, "Poetry is distinguished as a written form by the ways in which it works with line structure." But we all know that poetry is more than the way lines are configured on the page; it is more than architecture. "Good poetry is about the sounds and images made by language" (Hade and Murphy, 2000). It is "imaginative. It deals with emotion and has significance beyond the act of creation. It uses figurative language, yet is compact in thought and expression. Good poetry has an element of beauty and truth, which appears unstable outside the poem" (criteria for judging the Lee Bennett Hopkins Poetry Award, in Hade and Murphy, 2000). In the next sections, we look at ways to bring poetry to life as children create image-filled, ear-striking, and visually sharp poems.

Creating the Images of Poetry

Visualize in your mind's eye the pictures of the crescent and full moon that Emily Dickinson paints in this poem:

> **Moon**
> The moon was but a chin of gold
>   A night or two ago,
> And now she turns her perfect face
>   Upon the world below.

What "makes" the poem is that in only four short lines and with simple, mainly one-syllable words, Dickinson creates two striking ideas: the crescent moon's being "a chin of gold" and the full moon's turning "her perfect face upon the world."

Children should not be asked to analyze to the bone poetic images such as these two that Dickinson gives us; the analytic approach in which children define words and dissect the metaphors and similes may account for some children's aversion to poetry. On the other hand, students should have a multitude of opportunities to listen to poems such as Dickinson's and to visualize pictures in their mind in response. They should have opportunities to chorus poems, as we discussed in Chapter 6, and to use an art medium to transform the verbal image into the visual one they see in their mind's eye. And, of course, students must have time to create their own poetic images using the variety of poetry forms and figurative language devices that have evolved over the years: free verse, haiku, tanka, senryu, cinquain, simile, metaphor.

Free Verse   A *free verse* is an unstructured, unrhymed series of lines that paint a sharply focused word picture and make "the ordinary seem extraordinary" (Hade and Murphy, 2000). A free thought can express a powerful emotion or make the listener laugh at the clever juxtaposition of ideas. Mallika and Megan chose free verse as their form of expression when they wrote about sunsets and snakes.

One approach to free verse is to encourage students to think of an experience, a thing, or a person who means a lot to them—swimming in the rain, racing their scooters, taking a roller coaster ride, walking through fallen leaves, talking to their cat, arguing with their mom, waiting impatiently for a favorite uncle to arrive. Teacher and students orally and interactively free-associate; they call out words and lines that come to their minds as they think about a chosen experience. Then students close their eyes and free-associate on a topic that has personal meaning for them. They speak their words as a peer or the teacher records for them. With some thoughts down on paper, students rearrange their ideas so that "they look like poetry."

WORD BANK

Free verse

First-person free verse

Haiku

Tanka

Senryu

Cinquain

Simile

Metaphor

CONSIDER

A raindrop falls in a puddle and is gone.—A second-grader's thought.

Distinguished Poet

Meet Shel Silverstein (1932–1999)

Shel Silverstein started writing as a young boy and rather quickly developed a style of his own because he had never read the poetry of the master poets of past or present. As Silverstein explained, "I was so lucky that I didn't have anyone to copy, be impressed by. I had developed my own style. I was creating before I knew there was a Thurber, a Benchley, a Price and a Steinberg. I never saw their work until I was about thirty."

Silverstein's books of poetry belong in every elementary teacher's personal library: *A Light in the Attic, Where the Sidewalk Ends,* and *Falling Up.* Children love Silverstein's poems and illustrations for their humor; adults love them for their honest but ironic view of everyday life. Silverstein is also known for his children's stories, especially for *The Giving Tree,* which Silverstein says is a story about two people: one who gives and the other who takes.

You can find out more about Shel Silverstein (who was born "Shelly") by visiting **http://falcon.jmu.edu/~ramseyil/silverstein.htm.** From this site you can access poems Silverstein has written as well as some of his stories with accompanying lesson plans.

READ

The interview between Ai and Elizabeth Farnsworth, November 18, 1999, at **http://www.pbs.org/newshour/bb/poems/july-dec99/nba_11-18.html.** Many of Ai's poems have a violent cast to them, making them inappropriate for use with elementary students.

First-Person Free Verse   A poet who goes simply by the name Ai is a master of a special free verse form. Ai (pronounced with just the long *i* sound) pretends she is someone from the past, climbs into "that person's skin," and speaks in the first person, using the voice and perspective of that someone. In an interview with Elizabeth Farnsworth on *The NewsHour,* Ai described her poetry: "I'm very comfortable in that form. My first poetry teacher said that when you wrote in the first person, that your work was often stronger. And I . . . fell into that. . . . And I love it, because it's so interesting. Every time I write a poem, I'm someone else without actually being that person." Ai, who is half Japanese as well as African American, Irish, and Native American, has assumed in her poems the persona of J. Edgar Hoover, Marilyn Monroe, General George Custer, President Lyndon Johnson, Elvis Presley, and a host of well-known and everyday people. She begins "Jimmy Hoffa's Odyssey," with the words, "I remember summers when the ice man used to come . . ." In 1999, Ai received the National Book Award for her poetry.

Ai's first-person, taking-on-the-point-of-view-of-someone-else type of poem—the dramatic monologue—works well, especially in the upper elementary grades as part of historical studies. Young people who know how Harriet Tubman helped slaves escape to freedom can speak with the voice of Tubman and tell how they felt as they guided escaping slaves northward in the night; they set their words on paper in the line format of poetry. Or youngsters can speak with the voice of Abraham Lincoln, a Revolutionary War soldier, a pioneer who moved west, an immigrant arriving at Ellis Island, or a Native American displaced from his or her land. Working from an emotion-packed perspective, students can create first-person poems that let a reader "feel the feelings."

One group of middle-graders used the form to create a poetic response to *My Brother Sam Is Dead*. They began their poem dramatically: "I was there when they killed / my brother Sam. / They took him out / and shot him dead. / I was there / to stare / and cry / and not believe. / They killed my brother Sam."

The Haiku   For many years, elementary teachers have been inviting students to compose *haiku*, three-line verses that in the hands of Japanese poet masters of the seventeenth century became delicate instruments for expressing feelings about nature, especially seasonal variations. Through their haikus, the early poet masters grasped the "essential quality or essence of reality" and achieved "direct and lucid expression" of this reality. Edward Putzar, a historian of Japanese literature, explains, "The power to reach this goal of understanding lies within a child." The fact that children speak with directness and see the essence of things probably accounts for the success youngsters have in creating haiku moments. Success relates also to the brevity of the form—just seventeen syllables that pattern in three lines: five, seven, five. Here is an example from the pen of a sixth-grader:

> *The pink swamp flower*
> *Has a beauty of its own—*
> *A heavy fragrance.*

READ

William J. Higginson, ed., *Wind in the Long Grass: A Collection of Haiku* (New York: Simon & Schuster, 1992), for a collection of haiku from many parts of the world.

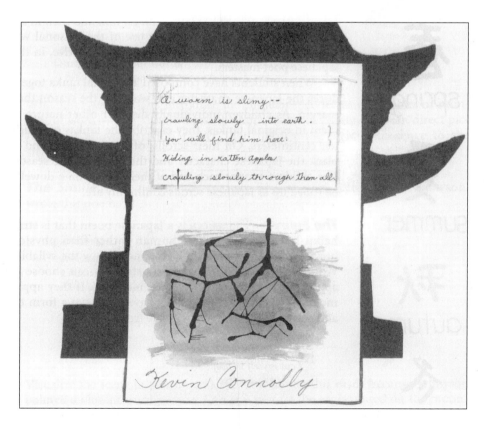

Figure 9.11
A Tanka Drawn in Response to an Original Ink Blowing

DISCUSSION PROMPT

When might this multicultural activity be included in the curriculum?

Because a haiku is comparable to a single image captured on film, colored pictures can evoke the word pictures that are the stuff of haiku, particularly nature shots glorifying the beauty of the earth.

The Tanka   The *tanka* (or *waka,* as it is called in Japanese poetry circles) is more popular in Japan than the haiku and is also much older, dating to the fourth century. Like the haiku, the tanka achieves its poetic flavor through the musical quality of the words and the beauty of the images. The topic is nature and the seasons; the form is short, five lines of thirty-one syllables, distributed according to the pattern five, seven, five, seven, seven, as seen in Figure 9.11. Because the tanka is longer than the haiku, it permits an expanded word picture. Here is a sample that abides by one of the original traditions of Japanese poetry; it names a season:

> *Crystal ice daggers*
> *Glisten in the winter trees—*
> *   Bending branches down.*
> *I listen for gusting wind:*
> *I hear sharp icicles fall.*

spring

summer

autumn

winter

Because traditional tankas express seasonal thoughts, it is possible to combine firsthand seasonal observations with the writing of the Japanese characters and words for the seasons. To introduce the form, one teacher takes youngsters outdoors to see and feel striking moments in nature—a wildflower breaking into bloom, a bird's nest hidden in a remote corner, a clear puddle that reflects the sky, snow sitting on fence posts after a storm. As a class, they capture the moment first on film and then in a tanka. As the children compose, the teacher encourages use of the seasonal word—*autumn, winter, spring, summer*—as a describing word, or adjective, in the manner of the early Japanese poet masters.

When students have composed a seasonal tanka together, the teacher introduces the Japanese character and word for the season through a chart as in the margin. As children individually discover other nature moments and capture them in original tankas, they inscribe the tankas on long scrolls no wider than ten centimeters. On their scrolls, off-center at top and bottom, they paint in black the Japanese character and the word for the season they are describing. The children mount the ends of their scrolls on dowels so that the scrolls can be rolled up as Japanese scrolls commonly are.

The Senryu   The *senryu* is a Japanese poem that is structurally similar to the haiku but concerned with human rather than physical nature. Often humorous, it sometimes does not follow the syllable pattern of the haiku. Working within the senryu form, students can choose topics for writing that appeal to them: surfing, baseball, bicycling. If they apply the syllable requirements of the haiku loosely, they have in senryu a form that requires directness and clarity but allows considerable freedom:

> *Skiing down the mountain:*
> *I cut myself in half*
> *To avoid a tree.*

An English/Japanese dictionary will captivate young poets. A pocket-size version gives Japanese equivalents in both script and characters for terms like *soccer, running, circus*—any one of which could be the subject of a senryu. Students can search an English/Japanese dictionary for words that are the topics of their senryus and paint the Japanese equivalents in both script and characters on their poetry pages.

The Cinquain   Although not of Japanese origin, the *cinquain* is associated with haiku and tanka because of its brevity. As conceived by Adelaide Crapsey, cinquains consist of five lines with a two-four-six-eight-two syllable pattern for a total of twenty-two syllables:

> *The gull*
> *effortlessly*
> *glides on the downward breeze*
> *to land on the soft, sandy beach:*
> *Quiet.*

Some teachers simplify the cinquain so that the number of words rather than syllables per line is the major requirement: first line, one word; second line, two words; third line, three words; fourth line, four words; fifth line, one word. Whichever way teachers introduce the cinquain—in terms of syllables or numbers of words—they should stress the importance of painting a clear, direct picture and allow variation rather than demanding strict adherence to the structural elements.

The Simile   The nineteenth-century English poet Alfred, Lord Tennyson, gave us this poem:

> **The Eagle**
> *He clasps the crag with crooked hands:*
> *Close to the sun in lonely lands,*
> *Ringed with the azure world, he stands.*
>
> *The wrinkled sea beneath him crawls;*
> *He watches from his mountain walls,*
> *And like a thunderbolt he falls.*

Visualize the scene in your mind. You can do this easily because Tennyson painted a vibrant word picture. Can you picture the eagle poised on the mountain crag and then falling "like a thunderbolt" from the blue?

When Tennyson described the eagle as falling like a thunderbolt, he was making an idea through simile. A *simile* is a creative comparison between two things people tend not to associate, in this case between the fall of an eagle and a thunderbolt. A simile relies on the word *like* or *as* to make the connection. Tennyson's simile is effective because he went beyond ordinary associations to create a unique relationship.

A teacher can introduce children to the simile by orally sharing pieces such as that by Tennyson, having children chorus the pieces, and including the writing of a simile series as a writing option. Later, as children read, they keep alert for similes to share from the Author's Chair.

The Metaphor   In composing, one young student called a wasp's nest "an insect condominium." A second equated a bare branch with "a grasping hand." A third called a computer "a boxed mind." A fourth wrote:

CONSIDER

In "The World Outside My Skin," Eve Merriam writes, "Connections, to be sure, are what poetry thrives on, whether through simile or metaphor. This is like That. This is so much like That it can merge and become the other. My love IS a red, red rose." In *Fanfare*, 1 (Norwood, Mass.: Christopher-Gordon, 1993.)

The sun was a pat of butter
melting on a hot potato.
It was juicy and tasty,
and we ate it at night.

READ

Judith Steinbergh, "Mastering Metaphor Through Poetry," *Language Arts,* 76 (March 1999), 324–331.

In making these ideas, these young writers were relying on *metaphors,* creative comparisons that assert an unordinary relationship without the assistance of *like* or *as.* The metaphor and the simile are examples of the figurative, as opposed to the literal, use of language.

Students can write metaphors as last lines in haikus, as parts of free verses, and as lines within stories. To this end, as teacher and children make idea clusters before writing, the teacher should include metaphorical relationships to encourage children to do the same. Review Ms. Chou's idea cluster in Figure 9.1 on page 319 to find a metaphor ready for writing.

As with the simile, students should look for metaphors in their reading and share those they find. They should do this as they read informational prose as well as stories and poems, for metaphors are common in the sciences (the heart as a pump, the computer as a brain).

Technology Notes

You can access poems at **http://www.bartelby.com/verse/.** At the site you can find the following:

- 121 poems from Robert Louis Stevenson's *A Child's Garden of Verses* and *Underwoods.*
- Poems by Robert Frost from *A Boy's Will, North of Boston,* and *Mountain Interval.*
- 597 poems by Emily Dickinson.
- 130 poems by such American masters as Sara Teasdale, Ezra Pound, and Stephen Vincent Benét, as well as 180 poems by such British masters as de la Mare and Kipling, as compiled by the anthologist Louis Untermeyer.

You will also find volumes of poems by A. E. Housman, John Keats, Edgar Lee Masters, Carl Sandburg, Percy Shelley, William Shakespeare, Gertrude Stein, William Wordsworth, and others. Because of the copyright laws, poems found on the World Wide Web predate 1922. However, because the poems are in the public domain, teachers can download, print, and distribute them without copyright infringement.

Another site that encourages the writing and reading of poetry is **http://www.poetry.com.** Here you will find a Haiku of the Day, prizes, and links to other sites. Also visit **http://www.poets.org/npm/npmfrmst.htm,** the Web site for National Poetry Month, which provides practical ideas for teachers on National Poetry Month programs, events, and displays.

WORD BANK

Alliteration

Onomatopoeia

Rhyme

Couplets

Limericks

Playing with the Sounds of Poetry and Language

Sound is an integral element of fine poetry. Listen to the sounds of Edward Lear, whose nonsense verse can be felt "in the mouth" and plays "upon the ear" (Hade and Murphy, 2000):

> A was once an apple-pie,
> > *Pidy,*
> > *Widy,*
> > *Tidy,*
> > *Pidy,*
> *Nice insidy,*
> > *Apple-pie!*

Having listened to such repeating sounds, to onomatopoeia, rhyme, and rhythm, children can create poems with sounds that tease both mouth and ear.

Repeating Sounds   Modern-day poets supply many sound plays to start children on the road to tune-filled composing. Eve Merriam's *It Doesn't Always Have to Rhyme* belongs on every classroom "poet tree." Merriam contributes a delightful piece called "A Jamboree for *J*" that is a fun-laden medium for introducing children to alliterative sounds: "It japes, it jibes, it jingles, / it jitterbugs, it jets." As the Merriam lines demonstrate, *alliteration* is the repetition of the same first sound or letter in a group of words or a line of poetry.

Students can do alliteratively nonsensical things with other letters of the alphabet. For example, after one group heard Merriam's piece, they wrote "A Laugh on *L*," which began similarly: "It's hard to make an *L* sound anything but laughing. / *L* leaps, it leans, it leaks, / it likes, it loves." Titles with which students can play alliteratively in this way include "A Fair for *F*," "A Troubled *T*," "A Play with *P*," "Everywhere with *E*." Children can invent original titles and verses based on the beginning sounds of words, and when they get stuck for a word, they can "pull a Lear": invent one that sounds just right.

Onomatopoeia   *Onomatopoeia* is the use of words that imitate the sound associated with an object, as in *slap, buzz,* and *crash.* The very young love making the sounds of a rooster, cow, lamb, and other barnyard animals, so sound-making time can blend with poetry making as children contribute favorite sounds and add a few descriptive words to make a line of poetry. Oral composition of a series of structured lines— guided by the teacher—provides an easy introduction to onomatopoeia for the kindergartner. Later, the child dictates lines he or she has invented independently— lines that contain different sounds but are structured after lines written together.

Slightly older students enjoy alternating lines of sound with lines of words. Joey did this, writing bee sound effects into his word picture:

> *Bzzzzzzzzzzzzzzzzzzzzzzzz*
> > *The bumblebee buzzes around me!*
> *Bzzzzzzzzzzzzzzzzzzzzzzzz*
> > *He stings me!*
> *OUCH! OUCH! OUCH! OUCH!*

Rhyming Plays, Couplets, and Limericks   The Japanese forms of unrhymed verse developed because the Japanese language is filled with similar vowel sounds and does not lend itself to rhyming. Not so with English. *Rhyme* as well as rhythm accounts for the enduring popularity of such old-time favorites as "One, Two, Buckle Your Shoe."

Some of these favorites can become the means by which youngsters first attempt simple rhymes of their own. For example, teacher and primary pupils can create original versions of "One, Two, Buckle Your Shoe" after they hear the sounds as the teacher shares the poem and after they brainstorm words that end with the same sounds as the words *two, four, six, eight, ten.* The teacher writes rhyming words for each of these number words in five columns on the board and tapes cards already lettered with the alternate lines of the poem—"One, two," "Three, four," "Five, six," "Seven, eight," and "Nine, ten"—on a second board, leaving room beneath each line for suggested rhyming lines. Drawing from their brainstormed pool of rhyming words, children put together original second lines to go with each number line, proposing several possible lines for each. Later children independently select the lines they prefer to go with the number lines and publish them as their original versions of the "Rhyming Number Book." Results may resemble the following, written by a young group at Halloween:

One, two,	*Five, six,*
The witch went boo!	*She was in a fix.*
Three, four,	*Seven, eight,*
She fell through the floor.	*That was her fate.*

GO TO

Pages 205–211 in Chapter 6 for ways to highlight poetry through choral speaking.

One pattern to use for follow-up puts the number sequence in threes rather than twos, as in "One, two, three / I broke my knee! / Four, five, six /. . . ."

Children who have played with pairs of rhyming words in this way are composing *couplets,* two lines that rhyme and are approximately the same length. Again, it is fun to start as a class with a given line and dream up several possible rhyming second lines. Some of the first lines of less familiar nursery rhymes are easy to build into couplets: "Once I saw a little bird," "Barber, barber, shave a pig," "Fishy-fishy in the brook," "Little Robin Redbreast sat upon a tree." Of course, youngsters are not told the "real" second lines, at least until they have created their own pairs.

With older students, there is fun in limericks, especially if the introduction is an oral interpretation session in which each youngster shares a limerick by the nonsense master Edward Lear. Because Lear's nonsense is old (and thus beyond copyright protection), a teacher is free to duplicate his limericks and distribute them to students. A delightful limerick is

> *There was an Old Man with a beard,*
> *Who said, "It is just as I feared!—*
>> *Two Owls and a Hen,*
>> *Four Larks and a Wren,*
> *Have all built their nests in my beard!"*

Children will quickly pick out the five-line pattern of the limerick as well as discover the *aabba* rhyming pattern. They may tap the rhythm of a limerick, perhaps on rhythm instruments, so that they feel the stress on the second, fifth, and eighth syllables of each line.

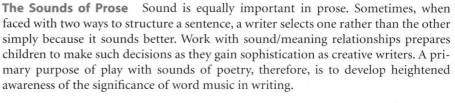

The Sounds of Prose   Sound is equally important in prose. Sometimes, when faced with two ways to structure a sentence, a writer selects one rather than the other simply because it sounds better. Work with sound/meaning relationships prepares children to make such decisions as they gain sophistication as creative writers. A primary purpose of play with sounds of poetry, therefore, is to develop heightened awareness of the significance of word music in writing.

Creating with the Architecture of Poetry

Concrete poetry, or *figured verse,* has a long history. Such poet masters as Robert Herrick, George Herbert, Lewis Carroll, and more recently e.e. cummings have given us figured verse—poems written so that their printed shape communicates a meaning related to the subject. Children delight in seeing and composing poems in which words and visual images interrelate. Young children especially find the concrete more meaningful than the abstract.

Visualizing Words   An easy introduction to writing figured verse is to print a word or phrase so that the design relates to the meaning. Some words lend themselves readily to this picture-word play: *tall, thin, short, narrow, up, down, around, north, above, below, scared, shivery, dark, smile.* Others take more imagination; the margin samples can be used as an invitation to children to play with words in similar fashion.

As Martin Gardner points out in his notes to *The Annotated Alice,* visualizing of words is more significant than it may first appear. Advertisements, book jackets, magazine mastheads, and signboards frequently heighten meanings through the design of words on a page. Students should be able to clip examples from magazines and newspapers to add to a bulletin board that displays samples they have devised and then create original advertisements that include words made visual.

Once children have done some visualizing of words, they incorporate the technique in thoughts they write. They may decide to take just one word and express it visually whenever it occurs in a piece, as a first-grader creatively did in his story entitled "A Vine," or, in visual language: "  James's message says, "A vine grew and grew and grew and grew and grew." He made the vine taller and taller to communicate growth (Figure 9.12).

Squiggling and Shaping   Squiggling is another device for introducing children to the fun of building words into pictures. A squiggle is a series of lines drawn in a design so nonrepresentational that children can read their own impressions into it. One teacher demonstrates the activity by giving children a series of lines on a duplicated sheet. She asks youngsters to hold the sheet in each of the four directions and brainstorm what the lines could represent in each case. Then together they choose one direction and idea and write a thought about that idea, printing the thought along the squiggle lines. Later, on their own, they can choose a different direction and write a thought based on their impression of what the squiggle represents when so viewed. Figure 9.13 is an example that works well because children can see in it not only fireworks but also snakes, water dripping down a windowpane, jet trails in the sky, anchors dropping from boats, Spanish moss hanging from trees—depending, of course, on the direction from which they view it. Students can create original squiggles that will be equally productive. A few examples are shown in the margin.

CONSIDER

A good source of concrete poems is J. Patrick Lewis, *Doodle Dandies: Poems That Take Shape* (New York: Atheneum, 1998).

Figure 9.12
A Composition About a Vine
That Grows

DISCUSSION PROMPT

■ What kind of a thinker is
James?

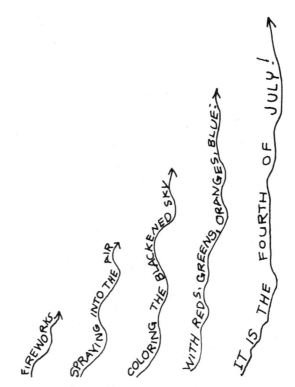

Figure 9.13
Squiggles

The outline of an object like a car, a pair of spectacles, a pair of scissors, a hand, or a shoe also stimulates youngsters to create original word-picture relationships and sometimes motivates the child who is a visual learner. Youngsters compose a poem-like piece and write the lines along the perimeter of the shape drawn on paper or in lines that actually form the shape. One example is the wave in Figure 9.14.

Figure 9.14
A Concrete Poem

ACTIVITY PROMPT
The writing of a concrete poem can be a response to literature or to content-area ideas. Create one.

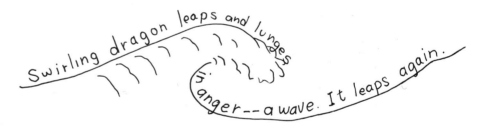

Acrostics

Balloons

Blow up and tie up
A big balloon.
Let it fly free.
Let it dance.
Open up the string!
Out comes the air and
Now the balloon
Spins in crazy, arching zooms.

Wind Thought

W	I	N	D
h	c	o	r
i	y	i	a
s		s	f
t		y	t
l			y
i			
n			
g			
wind:			

"Balloons" and "Wind Thought" are acrostics, or ABC poems. They have a visual dimension in that the letters of the topic word are written in bold print and form the beginning letters of the lines. Even very young children who have just learned to differentiate among beginning sounds of words can write or patch together simple acrostics. The very young write only one word or phrase next to each letter of a word listed downward on their page.

Summary: Visual and Verbal Communication Generally, if a class is engaged in an art activity, enthusiasm reigns as students work on projects. An advantage of involving youngsters in written expression that has a visual component is that enthusiasm for art may be transferred to expressing with words. Also, there is a security factor. Some youngsters are visual learners. When a writing activity has a visual component, these students are more secure than they might have been if the writing were strictly verbal.

A Summary Thought or Two

Writing as Idea Making

This chapter introduces the thesis that writing is idea making—that creating ideas is what fine writing is all about and that an open environment that encourages creativity is essential if ideas are to flow. The chapter describes how idea making through writing begins in preschool, where children write even before they understand alphabetic principles and invent their own ways of recording. It describes ways to integrate writing with reading, drawing, and talking.

A basic principle underlying the chapter is that the teacher must model idea making in writing. The teacher models thinking by writing with the children, demonstrating ways to develop ideas, and structuring experiences so that youngsters learn the varied genres available to them.

When teachers view themselves as authors, initiate writing activities that stimulate children to take off in a multitude of directions, are enthusiastic and filled with ideas of their own, children develop a positive view of writing. Children begin by focusing on ideas as they write. They know they have a story to tell and begin to enjoy writing their stories for others to read.

Your Language Arts Portfolio

- Write a series of plans for mini-lessons: a mini-lesson in which you introduce children to a form of poetry such as the haiku, cinquain, or limerick; a mini-lesson in which you introduce children to the form of a social letter; a mini-lesson in which you help children search their lives for personal writing topics; a mini-lesson in which you teach the design of a persuasive paragraph. Use the plans in the Access Pages as models. Again, keep samples of children's writing if you teach your mini-lesson.
- Become a teacher-writer. Try writing some of the kinds of narratives, expository forms, and poems outlined in Chapter 9. Try to look at your first drafts as tentative.

- Start keeping a personal journal. Write in it at least every other day. Include your impressions of events around you, especially events related to your teaching.

Related Readings

Buss, Kathleen, and **Lee Karnowski.** *Reading and Writing Literary Genres.* Newark, Del.: International Reading Association, 2000.

Calkins, Lucy. *The Art of Teaching Writing.* New ed. Portsmouth, N.H.: Heinemann, 1994.

Clark, Roy Peter. *Free to Write: A Journalist Teaches Young Writers.* Portsmouth, N.H.: Heinemann, 1987.

Cramer, Ronald. *Creative Power: The Nature and Nurture of Children's Writing.* New York: Longman, 2001.

Cullinan, Bernice, Marilyn Scala, and **Virginia Schroder.** *Three Voices: An Invitation to Poetry Across the Curriculum.* York, Me.: Stenhouse Publishers, 1995.

Denman, Gregory. *Sit Tight and I'll Swing You a Tail: Using and Writing Stories with Young People.* Portsmouth, N.H.: Heinemann, 1991.

Downing, Shannon. "Teaching Writing for Today's Demands." *Language Arts,* 72 (March 1995), 200–205.

Dyson, Anne. "Individual Differences in Emerging Writing." In *Children's Early Writing Development.* Ed. M. Farr. Norwood, N.J.: Ablex Publishing, 1985.

Fletcher, Ralph. *What a Writer Needs.* Portsmouth, N.H.: Heinemann, 1992.

Graves, Donald. *Experiment with Fiction.* Portsmouth, N.H.: Heinemann 1989.

———. *Explore Poetry.* Portsmouth, N.H.: Heinemann, 1992.

———. *Investigate Nonfiction.* Portsmouth, N.H.: Heinemann, 1989.

———. *Writing: Teachers and Children at Work.* Portsmouth, N.H.: Heinemann, 1983.

Hall, Nigel, Anne Robinson, and **Leslie Crawford.** *"Some Day You Will No All About Me": Young Children's Explorations in the World of Letters.* Portsmouth, N.H.: Heinemann, 1991.

Hillocks, George. *Teaching Writing as Reflective Practice.* New York: Teachers College Press, 1995.

Indrisano, Roselmina, and **James Squire.** *Perspectives on Writing: Research, Theory, and Practice.* Newark, Del.: International Reading Association, 2000.

Jensen, Julie. "What Do We Know About the Writing of Elementary School Children?" *Language Arts,* 70 (April 1993), 290–294.

Kennedy, Mary Lynch, ed. *Theorizing Composition: A Critical Sourcebook of Theory and Scholarship in Contemporary Composition Studies.* Westport, Conn.: Heinemann, 1998.

Language Arts, 76 (March 1999): The issue focus is the poetic possibilities of language.

McVeigh-Schultz, Jane, and **Mary Lynn Ellis.** *With a Poet's Eye: Children Translate the World.* Westport, Conn.: Heinemann, 1997.

Olson, Janet. *Envisioning Writing: Toward an Integration of Drawing and Writing.* Portsmouth, N.H.: Heinemann, 1992.

Rico, Gabriele. *Writing the Natural Way.* Los Angeles: J. P. Tarcher, 1983.

Smith John, and **Warwick Elley.** *How Children Learn to Write.* Katonah, N.Y.: Richard C. Owen, 1997.

Spandel, Vicki. *Creating Writers Through Six-Trait Writing Assessment and Instruction.* New York: Longman, 2001.

Temple, Charles A., Ruth Nathan, and **Nancy Burris.** *The Beginnings of Writing.* 3d ed. Boston: Allyn and Bacon, 1993.

Writing Processes in a Workshop Environment

The Child Writer as Author

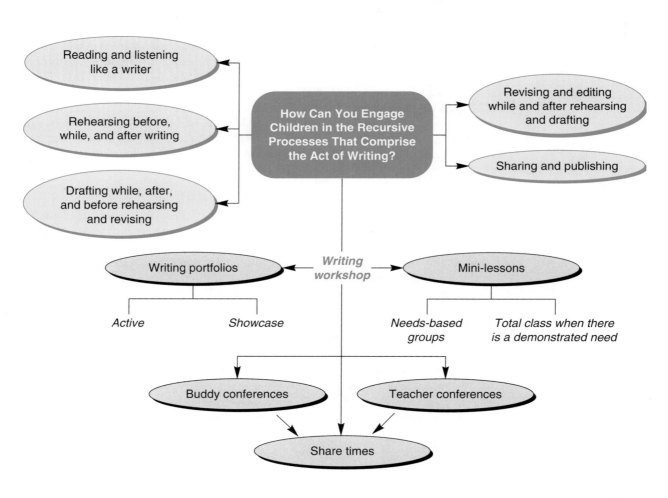

Reading and listening like a writer

Rehearsing before, while, and after writing

Drafting while, after, and before rehearsing and revising

How Can You Engage Children in the Recursive Processes That Comprise the Act of Writing?

Revising and editing while and after rehearsing and drafting

Sharing and publishing

Writing workshop

Writing portfolios

Active   Showcase

Mini-lessons

Needs-based groups   Total class when there is a demonstrated need

Buddy conferences

Teacher conferences

Share times

The Desert

The youngsters in Brad Kamolsky's fourth grade were gathered around three pieces of chart paper posted on the classroom bulletin board. This was the final week of their integrated focus unit on desert regions of the world, and today they were summarizing what they had learned.

Factstorming and Categorizing: Rehearsing for Writing

Searching their learning logs for ideas recorded earlier, the students factstormed: They called out words or facts about deserts as three scribes listed on the charts the points mentioned. When the charts were filled with words and phrases, students and teacher contemplated what they had recorded. Circling in red the word *Sahara*, Mr. Kamolsky asked, "What does the word *Sahara* tell us?" After students had responded, he prompted, "What other words also name desert regions?" At that point, students came forward to circle in red the names of deserts found on their charts. Later, responding to a similar question sequence posed by the teacher, they circled in orange items dealing with topographical features of deserts, in green items pertaining to desert plant life, in blue items related to animal life, and in purple items dealing with human adaptations. They labeled as miscellaneous those items that did not fit any of these categories.

Having helped the students organize their data, Mr. Kamolsky focused on one category: points circled in red. "Let's review," he said, "where all these deserts are located." With that, the children paired off to make a chart in their learning logs with the name of each major desert and next to each its geographic location.

Drafting and Revising Ideas

When everyone had made a chart, the teacher continued, "Before writing a report, I sometimes chart what I know as we have been doing. You may want to try this planning strategy when you compose.

"Now we are going to translate the information from our charts into a paragraph. What is the big, or main, idea that this chart communicates? What do the facts tell us? By the way, these are two questions I often ask myself as I get myself ready to write informational paragraphs." At that point, the teacher recorded his two idea-transforming questions on the board to reinforce their importance in planning-for-writing.

Silence descended, for this was a hard, main-idea question. Then Barbara suggested, "There are really lots of deserts." Ramon volunteered, "They are found all over the world."

"OK," answered Mr. Kamolsky. "Both of your ideas are good. If we were writing a paragraph about where major deserts are located, we could begin with those thoughts. How can we convert Barbara's idea into a sentence to begin a paragraph?"

On the chalkboard, Kamel recorded, "Deserts are all over." Erica wrote, "There are

CONSIDER

In this lesson, children are learning through writing as well as learning to write.

See relationships within data

Get main ideas down

Figure 10.1
First Draft of a Cooperative Composition

> Deserts are all over. There are many deserts in the world. We have the Mohave Desert and the Imperial Valley Desert in the United States. The largest desert is the Sahara. The Sahara Desert is in Africa. There is another desert in South America and there are some deserts in Chile and a desert in Argentina. There is a big desert in Australia.

■ ● ● ●

CONSIDER

Where discipline is a problem, this lesson can be structured as an interactive, small-group session. In small groups, even less interested students are more likely to join in.

many deserts in the world." In this interactive way, the fourth-graders added sentence after sentence until the paragraph in Figure 10.1 emerged.

Next, Mr. Kamolsky guided the fourth-graders in reviewing what they had drafted. "How can we take the thoughts in our first two sentences and expand and combine them into one sentence?" he asked. Orally, students played with the opening sentences, finally settling on, "There are many deserts all over the world." In turn, the students reworked the other sentences they had drafted to eliminate the weak repetitive "There is . . ." construction. Prompted by their teacher's questions, they clarified their thoughts by adding or deleting words, combining sentences, changing word order, and revising punctuation and capitalization. Figure 10.2 shows their revised draft.

Figure 10.2
Revised and Edited Draft of a Cooperative Composition

> **Deserts of the World**
>
> There are many deserts all over the world. The largest deserts are the Sahara, found in Africa, and the desert in central Australia. South America has deserts in Chile and in Argentina. North American deserts are the Mohave Desert and the Imperial Valley Desert.

Collaborative Writing and Publishing

The following morning, the fourth-graders collaborated in writing teams. Each team focused on a set of points circled in a particular color after the factstorming of the previous afternoon. Concentrating on those facts, the teams first made a chart that highlighted relationships within their data. Then they decided what main idea held those facts together and drafted a paragraph that stated it along with supporting points, just as they had done during the teacher-guided group rehearsal for writing on the previous day. As follow-up, they were to revise and edit their paragraphs and produce a clean copy on chart paper.

GO TO

Pages 378–385 for a detailed discussion of revising and editing. See the checklist on pages 391–392 for a guide for profiling children's growth as editors.

DISCUSSION PROMPT

■ What is the content-area teacher's responsibilities in regard to teaching writing processes?

The next day, the writing teams mounted their paragraphs around the room in preparation for a class revising/editing workshop. Now the entire class studied the paragraphs, reworked them, and decided on the best order for grouping the paragraphs into a cohesive composition. When the fourth-graders were satisfied with what they had done, one student volunteered to type the final draft into the computer and print out copies to send to the other fourth grades.

Writing Processes

What were Brad Kamolsky's fourth-graders learning from their unit on deserts? Obviously the students were learning about desert regions, but obviously too they were learning ways to organize paragraphs around a main idea, to combine ideas into complex sentences, and to vary sentences for effect. In addition, they were learning something about writing processes: strategies for planning before and while writing (in this case factstorming, categorizing, and charting ideas), the malleability of first drafts, tools of revision, and the pleasure of sharing ideas through writing. In short, they were learning how to approach writing.

Organizing for Process Writing

S tudies by the National Assessment of Educational Progress (NAEP) confirm the need for ongoing programs through which children learn how to approach writing. Between 1969 and 1974, the NAEP (1975) found "increases in awkwardness, run-on sentences, and incoherent paragraphs." Students expressed themselves in only the simplest sentence patterns and with a limited vocabulary. In 1986, the NAEP further reported that tests of writing showed that young people lacked the ability to use writing to analyze and evaluate what they read (LaPointe, 1986).

Writing Instruction from a Historical Perspective

Granted that the need to teach writing exists, how should teachers go about it? In 1978, Elizabeth Haynes summarized much of the research on the teaching of writing up to that point: "Historically, if there has been any consistency in the teaching of writing in this country, it lies in the fact that most of the approaches used have been negative." One major approach is to teach formal grammar. Studies reviewed by the Curriculum Commission of the National Council of Teachers of English in 1935 and more recently by Ingrid Strom (summarized in Haynes, 1978) show that knowledge of traditional grammar has almost no relationship to the ability to speak or write clearly. To teach grammar is *not* to teach writing.

A second approach is to encourage children to write frequently by assigning topics and then correcting student errors. This technique often begins in the elementary years and continues through secondary schooling. According to Haynes, most studies

indicate that "mere writing does not improve writing. . . . It seems safe to conclude that from the studies to date, intensive correction of errors [by the teacher] is futile."

The Workshop Approach

Today another approach to teaching writing is evolving. This approach emphasizes viewing writing as a composite of interrelated, *recursive processes* and involving children in all aspects of those processes during extended workshops. The outcome is that young authors develop a sense of personal ownership over what they write and a clear understanding of strategies to use in writing.

How Professional Authors Compose   According to Donald Murray (1982), Roy Peter Clark (1987), Pamela Lloyd (1987), and others who have described and analyzed what experienced authors and journalists do when they compose, successful writers generally write for a specific audience on topics about which they feel strongly and have something to say. They plan before and as they write, trying out ideas internally in their heads or externally through sketches, schematics, and/or words listed on paper. In the process, they expand on and transform what they want to say (Bereiter and Scardamalia, 1987).

At some point in their rehearsing, writers begin to organize their ideas in sentence form in a rough draft, realizing full well that what they are crafting is only a beginning that will change many times as they gain control over what they are saying and how they will say it. While and after they draft, most writers revise: They rework ideas, add, delete, modify, cycling back and forth between drafting and revising as they continue to bring forth and transform their ideas. They edit spelling, punctuation, capitalization, and other aspects of language usage.

After some time has passed, they look yet again at what they have written. They ask others within their writing community for advice and make changes in response. They contemplate, they criticize their own writing, and eventually they say, "Enough!" They go to press: They share what they have authored. And as most writers write, they read. In so doing, they learn more about their topic and see how other authors handle words and ideas—even the same ideas—on paper.

In Writers' Workshop   Viewing writing from a "processes" perspective, theorists propose that teachers organize their classrooms as workshops where children function as authors within a community of writers. At the start of workshop, the teacher presents a mini-lesson that lasts about ten minutes and focuses on an idea-generating, idea-transforming, organizational, or language-usage problem that students have encountered in their writing. From time to time, the teacher organizes a more extended instructional segment about twenty minutes in length when the demonstrated problem is a complex one.

Some upper-grade teachers, such as Nancie Atwell (1996), plan "sequences of mini-lessons: a week on how to read a poem, three weeks on character development and other elements of writing fiction, many days throughout the year on the uses of commas, semicolons, colons, and dashes, and the ways that punctuation can bring voice to writing." Others call students together in the middle of workshop to address spontaneously and quickly a composing problem that several authors are experiencing. They set aside the final ten minutes or so of workshop as a time when young authors

What is involved in implementing a process approach to writing instruction?

In *Children's Writing: Perspectives from Research* (an invaluable resource for writing teachers), Karin Dahl and Nancy Farnan describe and caution teachers about the linear, or stage-bound, conception of composing (prewrite-write-revise) that came into vogue in the 1970s; they explain that in some schools this approach became "*the* model of writing process. In-school writing tasks . . . began to take on a predictable format, in which all students would first prewrite, making explicit the ideas they intended to write, through such activities as brainstorming and outlining. Students then wrote the complete text based on their prewriting; only after this stage were they encouraged to revise." Dahl and Farnan note the problems associated with this model: writers' need for flexibility and for cycling back and forth as they plan, draft, and revise.

But Karin Dahl and Nancy Farnan go on to reassure us, "Because writing is process, it is not surprising that instructional strategies that emphasize process elements would contribute to young writers' increasing proficiency. Based on current understandings, the issue is not whether process strategies enhance a writer's ability to write effectively. Rather, the issue centers on which activities and classroom structures will best address individual writers' needs in various task environments and with various writing demands" (Chicago, Ill.: National Reading Conference, and Newark, Del.: International Reading Association, 1998, pp. 8, 15).

DISCUSSION PROMPT

Based on these cautions by Dahl and Farnan, what do you think we should be teaching when we teach writing process? What activities and classroom structures are essential in a program that emphasizes process writing? What problems do you face as a classroom teacher when you organize workshops to involve children in writing processes? What other pitfalls do you see and how can teachers avoid them?

solicit input on problems they are having in their writing-in-progress; emphasis during this segment of workshop is on getting help from fellow writers.

During most of workshop, however, children are writing. Some are rehearsing and reading to find ideas. Some are drafting. Some are doing major editing and revision. Some are preparing publication copies. Most, however, are doing combinations of these things. Throughout, emphasis is on idea making and transformation. It is on cycling back and forth in a to-ing and fro-ing way to draft, revise, and edit. It is on selecting from early drafts some pieces that authors want to publish. In a workshop environment, although students generally are working on individual compositions, a sense of community develops as everyone writes and helps one another. The community of writers includes the teacher, who at times writes individually at his or her desk or models the intertwining processes of drafting and revising by talking out his or her thoughts while developing them on a chalkboard or overhead transparency as children listen, watch, and suggest.

In Chapter 10, we will clarify what happens during workshop by considering the thinking/reading/writing processes in which children are involved as they function as authors:

- **Reading** and **listening** like a writer.
- **Rehearsing** before and while writing.
- **Drafting** with the idea that first words are beginnings.
- **Revising** and **editing** before, while, and after drafting.
- **Publishing** with an audience in mind.

In considering what happens during workshop, we must remember that writing is a nonlinear, recursive act in which there are no divisions among rehearsing, drafting, revising, and sharing—that in authentic writing these processes interrupt one another and ultimately coalesce (see Hayes and Flower, 1980, and Flower and Hayes, 1981, for a model that clarifies the recursive nature of planning, translating, and reviewing in writing).

Reading for background information is an important part of writing, especially expository writing. (© *Richard Orton / Index Stock*)

Reading and Listening Like a Writer

READ

Shirley Koeller and Paula Mitchell, "From Ben's Story to Your Story: Encouraging Young Writers, Authentic Voices, and Learning Engagement," *The Reading Teacher,* 50 (December 1996/ January 1997), 328–336, for ways to relate writing to reading in content learning.

Children become better writers by reading and listening to material written in different styles and modes of discourse. As David Dickinson (1987) states, "Exposure to books influences language and writing. Poor readers often have less control of varied aspects of language structure." They have less control over text structure, especially the structure of expository text. (See Squire, 1983; Stotsky, 1983; Tierney and Pearson, 1983; Moore, 1995.)

Jane Hansen (1987) explains the relationship between writing ability and time spent with books by describing a fourth-grader named Jenny. Having composed a story in which the parts melded beautifully, Jenny remarked during a conference, "I've never written anything before where the parts fit together so well." When the teacher asked her how she had done it, Jenny was unsure at first. She paused to consider. Then she answered, "It must be because I'm reading *Tom's Midnight Garden.* . . . When you read famous authors like Philippa Pearce, you notice how their words fit together." With that, she paged quickly through *Tom's Midnight Garden* to find an example of how Pearce had made her words fit together. As Hansen summarizes, reading fine literature can help children learn to write: "The more children listen, talk, write, and read good books, the more they enjoy the music of language," and the more they begin to see the author as a player in the development of text, manipulating the strings behind the scenes.

Listening for the Writer Behind the Text

The surest way to encourage children to see "the author at work behind a text" is for the teacher to read aloud and zero in on the elements of text as well as on the content (Trelease, 1995; Hansen, 1987; Ray, 1999). As Frank Smith (1992) explains, reading aloud to children not only puts children in the "company of people who read" but also in the "company of authors."

CONSIDER

Russell Freedman's *Lincoln: A Photobiography* (New York: Clarion, 1987) is good for demonstrating paragraphs that focus on one topic. See especially the paragraphs on page 14 of Freedman's Newbery Award–winning book.

Listening "for" the Author   At the beginning of a workshop, teachers can read a selection aloud and use it to focus children's attention on "the writer behind the text." For example, a teacher may read aloud from a story and ask students to listen for *powerlines*—high-tension lines that carry a powerful punch because of the way the author has crafted them. The teacher asks, "What is this author doing here? How is he or she using language to manipulate our emotions?" During another read-aloud/mini-lesson, the teacher may ask students to listen for the way an author uses figurative language or handles dialogue; during another, the teacher may read segments (beginning paragraphs, transitional paragraphs, or concluding paragraphs) from two or three authors, ask students to contrast how various authors ply the writing craft, and suggest that they try these techniques in their own stories.

Chorusing Wondrous Words   Teachers can borrow an instructional strategy from teacher Katie Wood Ray (1999), who helps her students focus on "wondrous words" that authors have crafted. Using a familiar text—one that children have already enjoyed together—she asks them to find a section where "the words are most striking" to them. This is what Ray tells her students:

> *Striking* might mean the words are so beautiful that they just melt in your mouth. *Striking* might mean you like the beat of the words, or the order of the words surprises you in some way. *Striking* could mean the words are so simple and yet so right. *Striking* means you want to read those words again and again. You like the way they sound. (p. 81)

Ray gives her students time to locate "their striking parts" and then insists that they "get that part down to fifteen words or less." She asks them to practice reading and rereading their chosen lines in their best "read-aloud voices"—quietly to themselves, "but loud enough" for themselves to hear. As students try out various renditions, searching for one that best expresses the meaning and the sound, Ray moves about, giving assistance to readers who are struggling with the words. When everyone is ready, students circle round for a "gathering of voices": They read their chosen lines with no breaks between and with the realization that it is perfectly all right to read striking lines that other children have already offered because by doing this, they will see different ways to interpret an author's lines. Ray calls children's oral renderings "poems." Creating such poems orally from the words of prose, Ray suggests that students are celebrating "the beauty of the text." They are filling the classroom with "wondrous words" and are getting "the sound of good writing in their heads."

Time permitting, Ray divides her students into four- to eight-person groups. Groups work together, deciding on the order and the manner in which to render their chosen lines. In talking together, students make decisions about what sounds best and what communicates the meanings they intend. Ray tells her students that these are the same kinds of decisions that authors make as they write and prepare to write; these are the decisions they too must make in writing.

Finding Out About Authors   Students can begin to see the author behind the text by reading or listening to autobiographical and biographical material. Today, students can get background material about authors by going to home pages on the Internet that some authors maintain and from audiotapes and videotapes about children's authors. They also can listen to the speeches of Newbery and Caldecott Award winners published in the *Horn Book Magazine* in the July–August issue each year, to interviews of authors published in *The Reading Teacher,* and to articles by children's authors published in *The New Advocate.* In their speeches, interviews, and articles, authors give clues as to how they write: where they get their ideas, how they change what they write, how dependent they are on the feedback that they get from writers' groups, even how they organize their writing day. With this kind of background, as students read chapter books, they can begin to respond in their literature response journals by writing from the point of view of the author; they become the author and tell "Dear Readers" why they put their words and their stories together as they do.

Informational Read-Alouds   Teachers can and should use comparable approaches as they read aloud from informational texts, for the way writers of factual genres structure text is different from the way writers of fictional genres do it (Pappas and

Pettegrew, 1998). After sharing a segment of a social studies text or trade book, teachers can draw attention to some aspect of text structure: the way a paragraph focuses on a single topic, use of a topic sentence to express the main idea (or what Pappas and Pettegrew [1998] call the "Topic Presentation") of a paragraph, use of chronological sequence to organize a paragraph; use of enumerative words such as *first, second, . . . finally* to clue readers that a transition is in the works; use of a *because* clause to communicate cause/effect, an *if . . . then* pattern to signal a conditional relationship, or the phrase *for example* to signal a supporting example. Any one of these rhetorical patterns from the craft box of informational writers can be the basis of a read-aloud/mini-lesson that teachers organize at the start of workshop when students are wrestling with expository writing (Richard and Gipe, 1995).

Independent Reading from an Author's Perspective

Some schools immerse children in literature and make free reading an important part of the school day. In one school, quiet reigns for twenty minutes a day as students, teachers, principals, secretaries, and custodians settle down with a book they have chosen. In another school, each classroom has a nook reserved for independent reading. The first-grade book nook has a table and a carpet beneath it on which youngsters can stretch out to read. The third-grade nook is an area partitioned off with waist-high pegboard behind which are a few child-size rocking chairs. The fourth-grade nook is an industrial-size carton into which a window has been cut so there is light for the youngster who crawls in to read. The children make weekly excursions to the school library to select books for independent reading in the classroom nook and at home in the evenings and on weekends. Parents are encouraged to talk with children about books the youngsters are reading.

Teachers should motivate children to read from an author's perspective. To do this, Gregory Bartiromo, a second-grade teacher, encourages his students to design bookmarks for stories they are enjoying on their own. On the front of their bookmarks, using both words and visuals, students record names of characters, the progressive settings of a book, the problem the main character faces, and the way the author resolves it. While reading, they use their bookmarks to hold their place; they also record the author's powerlines on the back of their marks. After reading, students design a cut-out to attach to the top—a cut-out of something pivotal in the development of the book they are reading.

Rehearsing for Story and Informational Writing

An early study by Carl Bereiter and M. Scardamalia (1987) seems to indicate that most elementary-school youngsters start to write without pausing beforehand to plan out what they want to say and how they want to say it. Bereiter and Scardamalia discovered that fifth-graders perform almost totally in terms of a knowledge-telling

WORD BANK

Knowledge-transforming
strategies

Pictorializing

Schematic representations

rather than a *knowledge-transforming* construct of writing. Fifth-graders start immediately to write down what they know just as they participate spontaneously in a conversation without an overall plan of development in mind. Composing on paper, they do not mull over what they know in an attempt to make more out of it.

In contrast, expert adult writers take their time in getting started, especially when they know they have plenty of time at their disposal to complete a writing task. They seem to perceive writing from a knowledge-transforming perspective; they see themselves as changing what they want to say through the very act of writing it down, and they use planning strategies that help them develop what they want to say even as they write (Bereiter and Scardamalia, 1987).

Earlier studies suggest that planning, or rehearsal, activities that involve children in transforming, or "growing," ideas have a powerful impact on children's writing. Widvey (Haynes, 1978) found that a process of problem solving that takes place before actual writing-down improves the writing that follows. Similarly, Radcliffe (Haynes, 1978) concluded that writing is facilitated by a talk-write sequence, and Roy Clark (1987) reported on the advantages of note taking, listening and interviewing, observation, and brainstorming in getting ready to write. More recently, utilizing data from the 1992 National Assessment of Educational Progress, Goldstein and Carr (1996) studied children's writing achievement. They found that students whose teachers regularly encouraged them to use planning strategies earned higher scores on the NAEP writing tests than students whose teachers had not stressed rehearsal strategies.

As Karin Dahl and Nancy Farnan (1998) conclude, based on the considerable research carried out in regard to planning-for-writing, "Beginning (and struggling) writers need to have access to strategies for composing, planning, starting, and reformulating (correcting, revising, and rewriting). As writers progress, they can be encouraged to increase their repertoire of strategies and vary how they use them across writing projects. . . . Teachers may especially wish to focus on strategies that support writing as a way of transforming knowledge." In the next subsections, we will look at planning strategies that teachers can model with students, even as Mr. Kamolsky was modeling and clarifying knowledge-transforming strategies in the vignette that opens this chapter.

Rehearsing by Pictorializing

READ

Beth Olshansky, "Picturing Story: An Irresistible Pathway into Literacy," *The Reading Teacher,* 50 (April 1997), 612–613, for an interesting use of picturing story.

Donald Graves and his associates at the University of New Hampshire describe planning strategies that young children find especially useful. One external strategy is *pictorializing*—drawing a picture or series of pictures as part of rehearsing-for-writing. Describing Sarah, a first-grader, one member of Graves's research team notes, "Before Sarah writes, she draws a scene and explains it to the researcher or another young writer, who is usually drawing and talking, too. Then she writes about the scene she drew. Sarah finishes the page and begins the same sequence for her next episode" (Graves and Sowers, 1979).

Because pictorializing appears to be a beneficial way for young authors to plan for their writing, teachers should demonstrate the process of pictorializing in a mini-lesson at some point during workshop. Talking about an event they have recently experienced, youngsters and teacher can cooperatively draw a series of pictures across the chalkboard to tell what happened and then translate their pictures into the words of a shared-writing story. Children should be encouraged to use pictorializing in their own storymaking if they feel comfortable with the strategy. Reports and stories based on a picture series tend to be more organized than those based on memory, for a series of pictures helps young writers keep the sequence of events in mind.

Rehearsing by Talking

As young writers plan for writing by pictorializing, teachers should encourage them to talk about what they want to say and how they want to say it even as young Sarah talked out her story before inscribing it. Talking-through as part of planning-for-writing can take these forms:

- Youngsters talk to themselves (in their heads or aloud) before and as they write. *Mind talk,* a powerful rehearsal tool that professional writers rely on, is internal, hidden from sight inside the head.
- Youngsters talk informally to classmates, describing pictures they are drawing and *schematic representations* they are creating and telling what they want to say and how they want to say it. This kind of soft peer talk during writing workshop should be encouraged; writing is not a silent activity.
- In a peer rehearsal interview, one youngster asks questions of another to get him or her to think through and transform ideas relative to a piece-in-progress. A group of writers may also gather to talk out ideas prior to or during writing. In this context, children ask questions to help one another make more out of what they know. Both the peer rehearsal interview and the talk group reinforce for young authors the fact that they are writing for an audience—in this case, their peers—and the fact that in writing they do not simply tell facts but transform them.
- Youngsters talk informally to the teacher, who moves among them as they plan for writing. The teacher encourages transformation of ideas by asking questions that help young writers gain control over their topic and devise an organizing structure.
- Youngsters talk in teacher-guided groups as part of a mini-lesson. Such talk helps children identify worthwhile topics for writing and think through relationships. It can help them focus on ways to design paragraphs to highlight main ideas. During a mini-lesson, children can also compose interactively, modeling their group compositions after pieces they have heard or read and gaining an understanding of how to organize stories and reports of their own. In the following sections, we will consider ways to use teacher-guided talk and mini-lessons to help children develop planning strategies for story and report writing.

GO TO

Page 343 for a plan for plotting out a story.

Rehearsing for Story Writing

Stories have a structure (Glenn and Stein, 1979). To write a story is not to record a random series of events. It is to design a setting, characters, a problem or conflict, actions through which the conflict is resolved, and an emotionally satisfying ending that reinforces the theme of the story. Reading stories, children begin to grasp story structure, especially if teachers help them plot out these elements as in Figure 10.3.

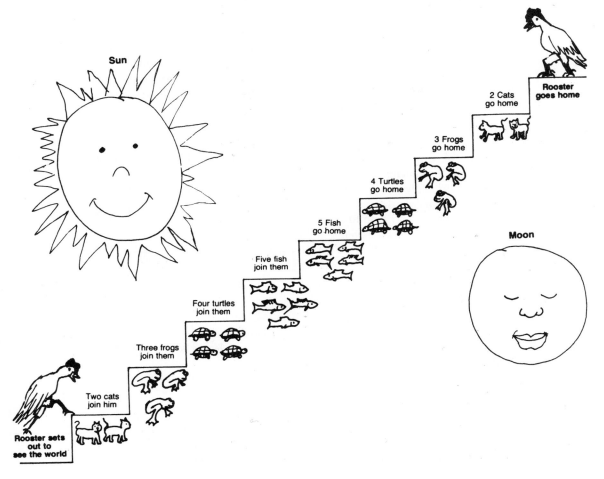

Figure 10.3
A Story Staircase: A Plan for Plotting a Step-by-Step Story
Based on a story by Eric Carle, The Rooster Who Set Out to See the World.

ACTIVITY PROMPT

Try making a story schematic for
a story you have read and for one
you are preparing to write.

A teacher can model how to rehearse a story for writing. Together, students identify the characters and the setting of a class story. They decide on the problem and
possible ways to resolve it. When children write stories on their own, they may follow
the same strategy, making several different plot plans before beginning to draft. Also
before drafting, children can orally share their plans; in so doing, they talk out (or
orally rehearse) their stories.

Story Lines and Story Staircases   The teacher can model how to use story lines and story staircases for storymaking by engaging youngsters in talk about a story they will make together. As the class talks out the events they may want to include in a class story, students and teacher plot them chronologically on a straight or undulating line, incorporating sketches above and below the line. Schematic representations can be relatively complex even in lower grades and include words as children learn to handle them. If students are writing a step-by-step tale in which each event builds on preceding ones, plotting events on a story staircase helps young authors think through the complexities of their tale. On each step, children make a sketch and plot key words that suggest what may happen next in their stories. On the landing, they plot a possible climax. As children rehearse by plotting stories on a staircase, they can think and talk out alternative ways to reach the landing so that story events flow together smoothly and the ending develops out of prior events. Figure 10.3 presents a model of a story staircase based on Eric Carle's *The Rooster Who Set Out to See the World*. A teacher may wish to share that story with a class, model how to make a staircase that maps out major events, and then engage children in interactive storymaking using a staircase as a rehearsal device. Later, as children compose during workshop, they may decide to create their own step-by-step stories using a similar rehearsal device.

Story Flowcharts   A variation of the story staircase is the flowchart, in which arrows connect sketches or verbal descriptions to show direction of story events. Flowcharts (see Figure 10.4) are especially useful as children rehearse circular tales—stories in which a main character leaves home to find adventure but returns at the end. Students plan ahead why the character leaves home, what adventures the charac-

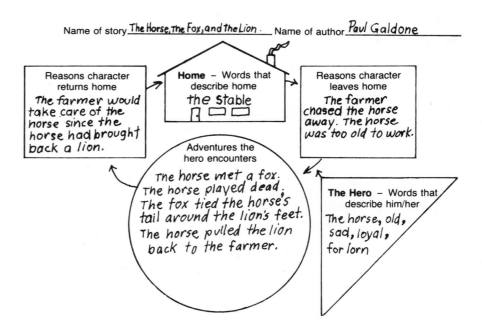

Figure 10.4
A Flowchart for Planning a
Circular Story

ter may experience, and why he or she returns home. In early primary grades, a rehearsal flowchart can be a series of drawings tied together with arrows; in upper grades, students make a story flowchart with words. In either case, the teacher should model how to create a flowchart based on a story read and how to design one in rehearsing for storymaking. Students who have used flowcharts to rehearse stories during interactive writing can use the same type of chart as an independent writing, listening, or reading guide.

Rehearsing for Report Writing

In the collaborative writing-in-action vignette that opens this chapter, students were learning strategies for rehearsing as part of informational report writing. Components of their extended language arts/social studies lesson and the sessions that had preceded it were as follows:

1. *Factfinding.* Through reading, viewing, listening, and talking together, students built background knowledge on the topic about which they were going to write.
2. *Factstorming and categorizing.* Students brainstormed what they knew and grouped these data based on shared relationships.
3. *Charting.* Students studied their data, identified relationships, made a chart highlighting the relationships, and proposed a tentative sequence for reporting the data.
4. *Interactive class writing and rewriting.* Guided by their teacher, students cooperatively drafted a model paragraph based on their chart; together they revised and edited what they had drafted.
5. *Independent writing and rewriting.* In small groups, students made other charts from the data, drafted paragraphs based on their charts, and finalized the sequence of their report.

In this instance, through teacher modeling, the students were learning a rehearsal strategy: factfinding, factstorming and categorizing, and charting.

A teacher can also model how to use a combination of factstorming, categorizing, and webbing as children rehearse for report writing. For example, Florence Amos's fifth-graders went on an elephant-factfinding mission. They searched references and found fascinating elephant facts for factstorming. When they had filled the board with their facts, the children organized items into a web, or map, that highlighted relationships. Guided by the teacher's questions, they categorized the facts—facts that pertain to physical characteristics, habitat, habits, and the importance of elephants. Working from these main categories, they plotted a fact web on the board as in Figure 10.5, projected a tentative sequence for presenting the categories, and cooperatively wrote a first paragraph.

The factfinders then divided into collaborative teams. Each team wrote a short paragraph containing only one category of fact. Later, guided by Ms. Amos, the class sequenced and organized the individual paragraphs into a report on elephants.

The extended lesson in this case included these steps:

1. *Factfinding.* Students located data for report writing.
2. *Factstorming.* Students set out their data where they could analyze them for relationships.

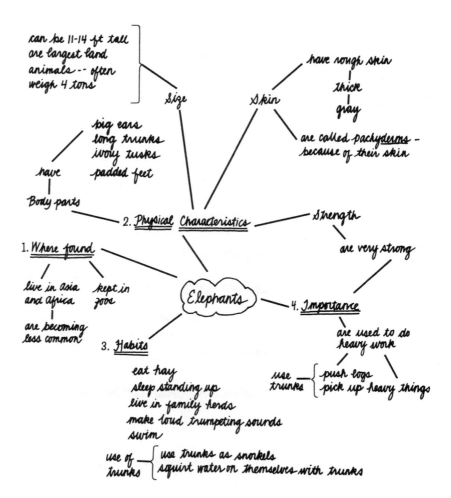

Figure 10.5
A Web of Elephant Relationships

3. *Webbing.* Students searched the data for relationships, organized those data based on relationships perceived, and numbered each web strand to indicate the order in which they would probably present the data (Bromley, 1996).
4. *Interactive class writing and rewriting.* Students cooperatively composed a model paragraph based on one category of data.
5. *Independent writing and rewriting.* Students wrote similar paragraphs, drawing on data from their webs, and sequenced them.

Through these series of activities, Ms. Amos's fifth-graders were learning how to gather data and sequence and organize them for writing. They were learning a rehearsal strategy—webbing and sequencing—that helps writers draft cohesive, logically developed paragraphs. Once children have experienced webbing as part of a teacher-guided group writing experience, they can use webs with numbered strands to plan their own reports.

Rehearsing: What's It All About?

CONSIDER

Internal rehearsal takes place in the mind; external rehearsal relies on activities outside the mind.

As this section has suggested, rehearsing for classroom writing can take a variety of forms; some are primarily internal, others more external. Some young authors talk to themselves in their heads, perhaps for many hours, before they begin to write; they continue to rehearse in their heads as they draft and revise. Some young authors enjoy rehearsing by pictorializing and talking as they choose topics for writing and draft ideas on paper. Rehearsing for and during storymaking, these writers enjoy plotting out stories, basing their rehearsal on their understanding of story structure. They may use story staircases and flowcharts to clarify to themselves what will happen in their stories. Preparing to write reports, some students may factstorm, categorize, chart, and/or web as integral parts of their thinking for writing. Using these strategies during writing workshop, young authors transform their ideas and gain control over them.

Ultimately, the exact form that rehearsal takes for any one writer at any one time is an individual matter. There is no one right way for everyone to rehearse. Labbo, Hoffman, and Roser (1995) suggest that teachers may inadvertently make composing harder rather than easier by insisting on a particular form of rehearsal. They describe seven-year-old Ricardo, who came excitedly to class telling stories of his weekend adventures that entertained and delighted his classmates. Ricardo was a natural storyteller, but his teacher made writing difficult for him by insisting that he list several ideas for writing before he could start to write. Ricardo complied by copying several ideas from other children's lists. In the process, he lost his own story in the "stuff, you know, the other stuff I needed to do before I could do *my* story."

Ricardo teaches us something about when external rehearsal—as distinct from the internalized mind talk that Ricardo had already done—is necessary and when it is not. External rehearsing is most necessary when writers are dealing with demand tasks such as writing longer, expository reports and persuasive pieces. Reports generally do not have a logic of their own; writers must create the logical framework to communicate their ideas. Under these conditions, the need to discover a logical framework makes external rehearsing more necessary; writers may have to scribble points on paper in a way that helps them make sense out of their ideas. In contrast, personal narratives often have a chronological development that makes a story almost tell itself. Here, students may find that externalized rehearsal gets in the way of storymaking.

Drafting

Theorists use the term *drafting* to describe what happens when writers start recording their ideas. Most agree that what is important at this point is how writers view what they are doing. Successful authors know that getting ideas down is crucial in a first draft and that the words they record are only a beginning. They know that they can go back later to fill in holes, transform ideas, check spelling, and smooth out expression. Lucy Calkins (1986) compares the author at this stage to an artist: "Like an artist with a sketch pad, [the writer] begins to find the contours of [the] subject. [The writer] makes light, quick lines; nothing is permanent. Each writer has his or her own style. Some bolt quickly down the page, their momentum building, their pencil leading in unexpected directions. Others work in smaller units, toying with their beginnings, trying a line one way and then another, drawing in to write, then pushing away to see what they have said." Clearly, successful writing requires a mindset about processing words on paper.

First Drafts as Tentative

As children draft, they should start with the assumption that what they are doing is tentative; they will change and shape their writing as they go along. For this reason, youngsters should be taught to cross out, insert new ideas, and draw arrows; invent spellings; use lines, letters, or drawings as placeholders when words and spellings are out of reach; cut apart sections and staple in additions; and use sticky notes for lengthy insertions.

Regie Routman warns teachers not to use the phrase "sloppy copy" in referring to first drafts (1993). That term is "an invitation to turn in messy work with numerous misspellings." Routman says she does not conference with a child until he or she has reread the draft in question and has checked it for basic spelling and punctuation. She teaches her children that even a first draft must be readable, if an author expects someone else to react to it.

Some young writers find Donald Graves's idea of multiple starts helpful. Children who are having trouble getting started with a composition, or part of one, draft a beginning sentence knowing full well that they probably will not use that opening. They then write several more beginnings and choose the one they think will do the trick (Graves, 1979). Use of multiple starts hammers in the fact that what is written on paper is tentative—that changes are the norm, not the exception.

To emphasize the significance of first drafts, the teacher can suggest that children select some of their first drafts for posting on a section of the bulletin board titled "Writing in Process—Our First Drafts." This is important for slower children who may have fewer revised versions for posting; they, too, get a chance to share their written ideas—which is what writing is all about.

Probably the single most significant determinant of how children view the process of drafting ideas is the teacher. The teacher who introduces writing by reminding children to use their best penmanship, keep papers neat, and never erase builds an erroneous picture of first drafts. The teacher must view first drafts as beginnings if young writers are to acquire this more productive view of drafting. Cambourne and Turbill (1987) explain that teachers who are most successful in helping children make meaning with writing "do not expect children's first attempts to be perfect first time around." They understand that "children need to know they can try out their hypotheses and make mistakes, and that their approximations will be accepted, for only then will they be prepared to take risks and experiment in their learning."

The Active-Writing Portfolio

Teachers have found that the use of *active-writing portfolios* affects children's view of writing, especially their view of first drafts. Children place drafts-in-process in their personal writing portfolios, or folders, so that they can keep track of them and have continued access to them. During writing workshops and independent study times, students can

- Rehearse ideas, begin drafting, and add the first drafts to their active-writing portfolios.
- Work on a first-draft-in-process already in the portfolio.
- Edit and revise pieces chosen for publication from those in the portfolio.
- Cull from the portfolio pieces they have begun but lost interest in.

Reworking successive drafts in their portfolios, young authors come to understand that first drafts are exactly that—first, or embryonic, ideas that they will ultimately refine into published writing.

Although students can make their own active-writing portfolios simply by folding a large piece of construction paper, a folder with pockets works especially well. The pockets enable students to organize their work. Children keep first drafts in the left-hand pocket, choosing from them pieces to carry through editing, revision, and publication. They keep pieces they have chosen to publish in the righthand pocket,

Technology Notes

Check out these computer programs and hardware as they relate to children's writing:

- *Word processing programs*—for drafting, revising and editing, and ultimately publishing poems, articles, and stories with columnar format, headings, footers, bulleted lists, tables, and varied fonts. The result is professionally styled newspapers, journals, and short books.

- *Spreadsheet programs*—for preparing labeled graphs and charts to clarify ideas presented in a written report.

- *Drawing programs*—for illustrating publications with original art executed on the computer.

- *Clip art*—for inserting pictures and photographs into publications.

- *Digital cameras*—for taking pictures to include in final drafts.

- *Scanners*—for transferring illustrations into a computer from various sources to be used in publication drafts, especially final drafts of reports and for scanning in student papers.

- *LCD (liquid crystal display) projectors*—for projecting student papers during Help Me! Share-times and presenting student papers as an alternative method of publication.

stapling together the successive drafts of each composition stored there. Younger children may do better using a shoe box or a manila envelope as their portfolio.

Children also write on the surfaces of their active-writing portfolios. On the front cover, they list topics and ideas for future writing; on the back cover, they list topics on which they have written or are currently writing, with a notation about the stage to which a piece-in-process has advanced. On an inside surface, children write points to check during editing. Graves (1983) suggests other uses to which portfolio surfaces can be put: to list skills a student has mastered or wants to master, topics a student knows much about, and books a student already has written.

Revising and Editing

CONSIDER

Knowledge of these copyediting marks is helpful to student authors:

Common editing marks:
/ make lowercase
≡ capitalize
∧ add something
⊙ put a period
⋏ put a comma
⌿ take away
¶ make a paragraph
⌇ reverse order

READ

Barry Lane, *After "THE END": Teaching and Learning Creative Revision* (Portsmouth, N.H.: Heinemann, 1992), for a discussion of revision processes.

Rewriting, which includes revising and editing, is a fundamental part of writing. In *revising*, authors reread what they have written to see where their ideas need restating, expanding, tightening, and/or reorganizing. In *editing*, writers check spelling, capitalization, punctuation, usage, and related elements.

Donald Graves (1983) has studied the revision behavior of beginning writers. He reports that even beginning writers can make changes in their writing; however, "Teachers can play a significant role in releasing a child's potential for revision." What the teacher emphasizes in revising is what child-editors tend to do. The teacher who stresses neatness and handwriting will find that children emphasize "prettiness" in their revisions. In contrast, the teacher who stresses reorganization of text and the addition and deletion of ideas will find that children focus on content and expression.

Mini-Lessons on the Tools of Revision

Some teachers do not give students the opportunity to revise and edit. Instead, they correct children's writing "errors" and ask students to copy the changes. In many instances, students copy unthinkingly and introduce new "errors" in the process. Teachers who use the correction/copy sequence may wonder how to engage children in the active higher-order thinking implicit in the revision process. One way is to provide young writers with revision tools that they can knowingly apply.

Snapshot Tool Basing her ideas on the work of professional author Barry Lane (1992), Laura Harper (1997) explains some specific revising tools that teachers should clarify with their students. One is what Lane has termed the Snapshot Tool—zooming in to enhance the details of a picture and then writing a verbal snapshot with those details. Teachers can read aloud lines from a story where an author has used this tool—for example, a passage from *Little House in the Big Woods* where Wilder describes a zoomed-in view of the way Ma's needle "made little clicking sounds against her thimble and then the thread went softly, swish! through the pretty calico that Pa had traded furs for." Harper shares this passage with her seventh-graders and then has them "take" similar snapshots of their classmates—first by drawing and then by writing. With this as background, the seventh-graders scan their pieces-in-progress for spots they can enrich with a Snapshot.

Thoughtshot Tool A second tool that helps an author develop a story is the Thoughtshot—expounding on the inner thoughts of characters. As Christine Pappas and Barbara Pettegrew (1998) explain, "A major characteristic of description in fictional genres is this presence of characters' mental reactions, their thoughts, feelings, and perceptions." Again, Harper recommends demonstrating how professional writers let readers in on a character's inner thoughts by sharing lines from chapter books. By doing this, young writers see that they can give their characters *flashbacks*—memories of related events; they can give their characters *flashforwards*—anticipations of what will happen; and they can involve their characters in "brain arguments"—debates with the self as to what to do. And again, once young writers perceive how authors use these techniques, they can search their own stories for places where flashbacks, flashforwards, and brain arguments can enhance their writing.

Exploding-a-Moment Tool A third tool that authors use to develop a story is what Lane (1992) calls Exploding a Moment. Rather than rushing through climactic points in their stories, good authors stretch them out; they build in suspense. Harper also shares with her students parts from stories where authors do just that, actually timing with a timer how long an author stretches out the suspenseful parts. Students then explore their own writings to see how they can revise to build in suspense—to explode a moment.

Making-a-Scene Tool A fourth tool is Making a Scene. As Harper explains, most of her students write action into their stories as if they are composing a "laundry list of things a character did." They often do not make a scene that includes dialogue. Revisiting stories they are writing, they apply the Making-a-Scene Tool: They consider the amount of story time they allocate to action, dialogue, Snapshots, and Thoughtshots. They ask themselves, "Will my story be more powerful if I write in more dialogue here, incorporate a flashback or flashforward, write a snapshot that describes details?"

Expansion and Clarification Tools Teachers should organize a series of mini-lessons to teach children some revision tools authors of expository selections use to expand and clarify their ideas: developing the attributes related to a topic, giving supporting examples, providing a contrasting point, using organizing words such as *first, second,* and *finally,* and adding a concluding section that sums up main points. Having spotted these techniques in articles and textbooks they are reading, students ask themselves as they revise, "Will my writing be enriched though inclusion of more attributes? An example? A contrasting point? Do I need transitional words to help my readers follow my thoughts? If so, what words will give my writing a clear structure? Does my concluding section sum up my two or three main points?"

Interactive Writing and Review

Interactive writing is another context in which to teach children how to go about revising and editing. Children who have collaborated to compose a piece, as in the

GO TO

Chapter 7 for a detailed explanation of interactive writing.

vignettes that open Chapters 1 and 10, follow interactive writing with revision and editing. Guided by teacher questions that help them pinpoint ideas, sentences, or words to revise, children reconsider the first draft of an interactive writing piece.

Especially with young authors, a teacher may find that focusing on one writing problem at a time is the most productive. For example, one group of first-graders dictated the following sentences to their teacher in the order in which the thoughts came to mind:

> I like to build a snowman. We like snow. Snowflakes fall on the ground. Frosty the snowman could be alive. Snowflakes are white.

Revisiting their first draft, the first-graders decided that all sentences were not about the same topic; some were about the snow, others about the snowman. With that thought in mind, they reorganized their sentences as two paragraphs, changed some words, and cleaned up their capitalization. Their final draft read as follows:

Snow

We like snow. Snowflakes fall to the ground. They are white.

We like to build a snowman. Frosty the Snowman could be alive.

Questioning-the-Self Tool   In guiding an interactive review, the teacher can model how to ask questions that lead to effective change: Where might we add a word or sentence to expand our picture more fully? Where might we delete words to sharpen our story? Where have we overused a particular word? How can we reorder our sentences (or paragraphs) so that related ideas are together? Can we combine two sentences into one without relying on the *and*-word? What title best sums up our story? The teacher should make children aware of the questions he or she is asking to trigger ideas for revision. Questioning the Self is another tool for revision that Laura Harper is using with good results with her seventh-grade class. This tool applies equally to editing: Student authors at some point must review a composition by asking themselves questions about punctuation, capitalization, and usage.

Read-for-the-Flow Tool   In guiding an interactive review, too, the teacher can demonstrate how he or she keeps going back to read and reread sentences to listen for places where the syntax sounds awkward and where long and short pauses are clues to punctuation. The oral Read-for-the-Flow Tool is a basic editing/revision strategy that the teacher should model even with young children.

Help Me! Share-times

A Help Me! Share-time is a special part of writing workshop, generally scheduled toward the end after students have spent considerable time writing on their own. In

READ

James Swaim, "In Search of an Honest Response," *Language Arts,* 75 (February 1998), 118–125, for ideas to help children react to other children's content and intentions in writing.

GO TO

Chapter 11, pages 401–418, for more on writing conventions.

preparation, each of several students selects a paper he or she has been struggling with. The student shares the selected paper, explaining to classmates what problem or problems remain to be conquered. The sharer may say, "I don't like my beginning (or build-up, or ending, or whatever). Help me with it." Or the sharer may say, "I'm not sure how to punctuate this sentence. Help me with it."

At times, a few students make transparencies of papers they have chosen to revise. During share-time, they take turns displaying their drafts, explaining why they used particular words or developed their ideas as they did, and ask for feedback. "Helpers" start by paraphrasing what they think an author is saying, then identify parts that are most effective, and finally help with the problem the author is mind-wrestling.

As part of share-time, the teacher can also give a writing hint relative to an editing problem that is common to several papers being shared. By doing this, the teacher makes clear that the problem is generic within the community of writers and asks everyone to look through his or her writings-in-progress for possible places for change based on the hint. To clarify the way to apply the hint, the teacher may "lift" exemplars from student papers—for example, run-on sentences or sentences in which subjects and verbs lack agreement. During share-time, students talk about ways to handle the problem and make a note to look at their own writing during the next workshop to edit for similar unconventional usages.

Teacher Conferences

Although mini-lessons, interactive writing and review, and Help Me! Share-times are important in teaching writing, the keystone of a writing program in which children are involved in revision and editing is the *teacher conference.* In *Writing: Teachers and Children at Work* (1983), the definitive and classic reference on writing conferences, Graves notes that the personalized conference between teacher and young writer offers the student an opportunity to develop self-critical powers and learn what to do in reworking a paper. It is the time when the teacher gives one-on-one assistance to help students apply the specific revision/editing tools they have been learning during mini-lessons, interactive writing, and share-times.

The Best-Paper Tool   Pieces that young authors select from among their early drafts and have collected in their active writing portfolios are the content of a conference. Graves proposes that a teacher begin a conference by introducing children to the Best-Paper Tool. The teacher suggests, "I am going to ask you to do something that you can do by yourself as you edit: Look at the papers in your folder and choose the one you think is best, the next best, . . . and then the next best. What makes this the best?" Once a piece has been chosen for review, the teacher's task is to elicit information rather than to tell the child precisely what to do. The teacher proposes, "Read me your most exciting part." If the teacher senses a need for more detail, he or she may suggest, "Let's apply our Exploding-a-Moment Tool. How can we stretch this out to build up the suspense?" Or, "How can we apply our Snapshot Tool? How can we describe the car after the accident to give a picture of what it looked like?" The purpose here is to get young writers talking about ideas that will strengthen their writing and to help them apply the revision tools they have been learning.

A Basic Editing Guide of Common Problems

Check your use of homophones:

It's	means	it is.	Its	means	ownership.
There	means	location.			
They're	means	they are.	Their	means	ownership.
You're	means	you are.	Your	means	ownership.
Who's	means	who is.	Whose	means	ownership.

Check basic capitalization:
 Have you started each sentence with a capital letter?
 Have you started proper nouns with capital letters?

Check your use of sentence-ending punctuation by reading aloud each sentence and listening for the sentence sound:
 Do you have periods at the ends of statements?
 Do you have question marks at the ends of questions?
 Do you have exclamation marks at the ends of exclamations?

Things-to-Edit-For Guide   During a conference, the initial focus is on ideas—on the story being told. Eventually, however, the focus shifts to editing and surface mechanics. The teacher may propose, "You have two thoughts set as one sentence. Read it aloud and listen for the sentence-ending pause (the vocal stop-drop) at the end of the first thought." Or "What kind of punctuation do we need to reflect the excitement here?" At this stage, the teacher may teach one or two points of usage to the child who needs them to clarify his or her writing and have the child list those points on his or her cumulative "Things-to-Edit For" Guide (Atwell, 1998).

Reading-Aloud-to-Self Tool   Because intonation and punctuation are related, students should be encouraged to read parts of their compositions aloud during teacher conferences. By doing this, young writers begin to equate a vocal stop-drop with a period, a shorter stop with a comma, and a stop-rise with a question mark. Likewise, reading aloud helps identify awkwardness, missing word endings, and sometimes misspellings. Later, as students rework compositions on their own, they apply the Reading-Aloud-to-Self Tool as a first step in revision/editing.

Conference Guides   Some teachers—like Ms. Chou, whom we met in Chapter 9—end a conference by listing specific areas for revision and editing on a conference guide, which students affix to their active-writing portfolios to refer to as they rewrite (see Figure 10.6). In developing the guide, teachers select the one or two major concerns on which a student has decided to focus in reworking a paper.

Speculation Tool   Graves (1983) suggests that teachers schedule a final conference before a student makes a publication draft. According to Graves, the student should prepare for the pre-publication conference by making use of the Speculation Tool:

1. Circling possible spelling errors.
2. Putting a box around probable punctuation errors that he or she is unable to resolve.
3. Drawing lines under spots where the language does not sound right.

Graves recommends that the teacher say to children who have trouble locating possible misspellings, "There are five words misspelled here. I want you to sound out each word, listen to the sounds, and circle which of these may be the five." Grave's Speculation Tool provides students with a 1-2-3 step approach for thinking about where to edit.

Buddy Conferences

To encourage oral reading of compositions-in-progress and talking out of ideas, some teachers pair students for peer revision and editing. Buddies work together, reading aloud a piece composed by one, then a piece composed by the other (The Read-Aloud Tool). If children have participated in mini-lessons and teacher conferences where they have been working with other tools of revision, the teacher may suggest that they apply these tools collaboratively and ask the questions of one another that are the essence of these tools. Thus at an initial conference about a particular paper, peers ask their buddies, "What is the most exciting part? What

---

Figure 10.6
A Conference Guide

ACTIVITY PROMPT

This form can be used in both teacher and peer conferences. Use it to confer with a classmate who is editing a paper.

A CONFERENCE GUIDE FOR WRITERS

Author: _____   Title of Piece: _____

Reviewer: _____   Date: _____

• What is the piece saying?

• What is best about it?

• What could make it better? Think about the lead, details, organization, ending, and wording.

• What needs editing? Check spelling, punctuation, capitalization, and usage.

---

more do you want to say about it? Do you need a Snapshot? A Thoughtshot? More dialogue?" During a later conference, students listen together to speculate on spelling and punctuation errors and places where language needs to be smoothed out (The Speculation Tool).

Figure 10.6 can be used during buddy conferences. Some teachers require that a student have his or her buddy go over a paper with him or her before placing it in the Ready-for-a-Teacher-Conference Basket; they also require that a buddy initial a copy of the guide in Figure 10.6 that buddy and writer have completed together and attach the guide to any paper placed in the Conference Basket.

Processing Words—and Ideas—with a Computer

■ • • •

READ

Articles in the January 2001 issue of *Language Arts* that focuses on the theme "Text, Technology, and Thinking."

Personal computers equipped with word processing systems allow a writer to enter a first draft of a composition via a keyboard and display it on a monitor. With knowledge of a few commands, the writer can delete redundancies, transform and add ideas, combine sentences, change the order of presentation, edit punctuation and capitalization, run a spell check, and direct the printer to produce a hard copy. The writer can also use software that checks usage and provides an on-screen thesaurus. He or she can log onto the Internet to locate needed information and organize data as charts and graphs to include in a report.

In the Early Years   Researchers have investigated the effect of word processing on children's early writing. Juanita Avinger (1984) compared stories children dictated to a teacher who inscribed them for the youngsters on paper with stories that the teacher entered for youngsters into a computer. Avinger reported that students whose ideas were recorded via computer contributed more sentences than those whose thoughts were handwritten on paper. Also, children's sentences were more complex and their stories more descriptive. Virginia Bradley (1982) reported similar findings where children dictated in groups. Stories their teacher recorded for them on a computer were longer, perhaps because of the speed with which words can be entered into a computer and the size limitations imposed by a piece of chart paper.

Similarly Bill Barber (1982) reported positive results from use of word processing programs with first-graders. In his study, Barber had youngsters first write individual summaries of an experience using invented spellings. Then youngsters dictated sentences from their papers as contributions to an interactive story—an excellent technique, by the way. Barber noted that "the processes of editing . . . seemed to occur naturally as they (the children) read from the monitor. They quickly noted the difference between my spelling on the monitor and their own invented spellings." The outcome was an in-context spelling lesson on language sounds and the ways those sounds are represented on paper.

In the research just cited, the investigators studied the relationship between computer use and writing when the teacher enters the writing into the computer during interactive composition. Other studies have compared children's pencil-and-paper writing to their computer writing. Using a case-study approach, one group of investigators compared the writing of a five-year-old as she wrote using first one medium and then the other. Use of a computer appeared to help the child focus more on ideas rather than on handwriting and letter formation, and it fostered an environment in which a coach could intervene as the child wrote rather than after (Cochran-Smith, Kahn, and Paris, 1990). In a study of first-graders' computer versus pencil-and-paper writing, another team of researchers made similar findings: Computer use appeared to help youngsters focus on their ideas rather than on mechanics; the children's resulting narratives were more cohesive than when they used pencil-and-paper (Jones and Pellegrini, 1996).

In the Middle Grades   Several studies have looked at the effects of computer use on middle-graders' writing. For example, working with eighth-graders, one team of researchers found that judges rated stories the young people had entered via computer as significantly better than stories the students had written by hand (Owston, Murphy, and Wideman, 1992). Using software that tracked revisions students made, these researchers discovered that their subjects did most of their revising during their initial drafting. Students' revisions tended to be small changes to the text rather than large changes involving reorganization.

Research suggests that the kind of software upper-graders use affects their writing behavior, especially the kinds of revisions they attempt. Software that requires complicated keyboard commands to make changes in text results in lower-quality compositions as compared to software that allows easy manipulation of text via a mouse (Haas, 1989a). However, research also suggests that computer-based writers may not get an overall sense of their text because they can view only small blocks of it on a computer screen (Haas, 1989b). Apparently, for some writers the most effective revision occurs as they consider hard copy of early drafts that they have printed out and can carry along with them to reread, rethink, and transform over time. Furthermore, "numerous studies have shown that students feel more motivated to write and more confident using a computer" for their writing (Rankin, 1997). And finally, evidence exists that computer use encourages more collaborative writing in classrooms, due perhaps to the fact that pieces entered into a computer are more open to the perusal of others than pieces written on paper (Dickinson, 1986). All in all, research seems to confirm the importance of young writers' having access to computers as part of classroom writing programs.

Teachers must realize, however, that use of the computer does not teach children the comprehensive planning and revision tools discussed earlier in Chapter 10. This is especially true when students use computers primarily for emailing messages; emailing may lead to less preplanning and revision since email messages in many ways resemble off-the-top-of-the-head conversations. Therefore, even when composing with a computer, young writers will require mini-lessons that teach the tools of revision; they will need to participate in interactive writing and review, Help Me! Share-times, and teacher and buddy conferences that help them develop planning strategies and revision tools and apply these to their writing-in-process. (See Figure 10.7 for a depiction of these components.)

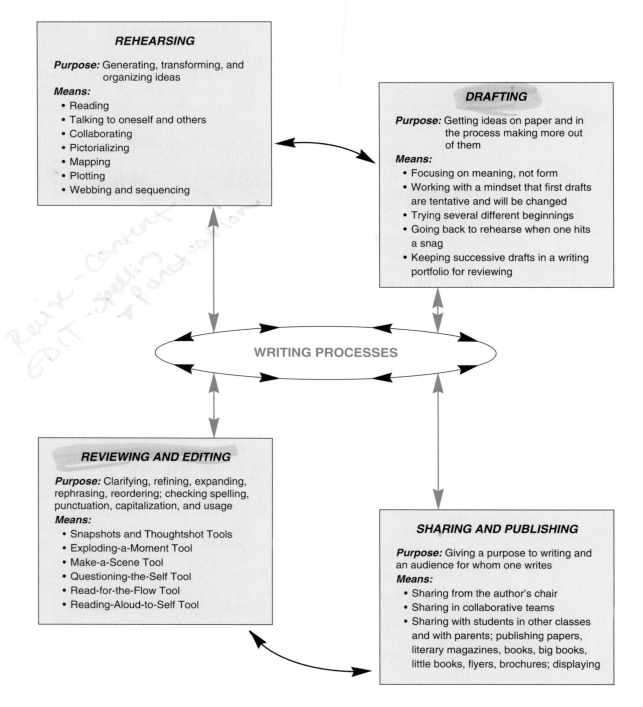

REHEARSING

Purpose: Generating, transforming, and
organizing ideas

Means:
- Reading
- Talking to oneself and others
- Collaborating
- Pictorializing
- Mapping
- Plotting
- Webbing and sequencing

DRAFTING

Purpose: Getting ideas on paper and in
the process making more out
of them

Means:
- Focusing on meaning, not form
- Working with a mindset that first drafts
are tentative and will be changed
- Trying several different beginnings
- Going back to rehearse when one hits
a snag
- Keeping successive drafts in a writing
portfolio for reviewing

WRITING PROCESSES

REVIEWING AND EDITING

Purpose: Clarifying, refining, expanding,
rephrasing, reordering; checking spelling,
punctuation, capitalization, and usage

Means:
- Snapshots and Thoughtshot Tools
- Exploding-a-Moment Tool
- Make-a-Scene Tool
- Questioning-the-Self Tool
- Read-for-the-Flow Tool
- Reading-Aloud-to-Self Tool

SHARING AND PUBLISHING

Purpose: Giving a purpose to writing and
an audience for whom one writes
Means:
- Sharing from the author's chair
- Sharing in collaborative teams
- Sharing with students in other classes
and with parents; publishing papers,
literary magazines, books, big books,
little books, flyers, brochures; displaying

Figure 10.7
Recursive, Nonlinear Writing Processes: Purposes and Means

Sharing and Publishing: The Child Writer as Author

READ

Linda Labbo, James Hoffman, and Nancy Roser, "Ways to Unintentionally Make Writing Difficult," *Language Arts,* 72 (March 1995), 164–170, for a warning: Don't turn the Author's Chair into a "hot seat"—a "place of inquisition"! That destroys the thrill and the joy of writing.

In Ellen Blackburn's first-grade classroom (as in Jennifer Chou's third grade), there is an Author's Chair. Each day, children take turns sitting in the chair to read aloud what they or another child or adult author has written. Listeners respond by first stating what they think a story says and then asking questions of the author. When a child is sitting in for a professional author such as Bill Martin, Ezra Jack Keats, or Dr. Seuss and is sharing a story by that writer, Ms. Blackburn and the children together propose answers the storymaker might give.

Sitting in the Author's Chair, children are participating in another writing process: sharing, or publishing, what they have written. In so doing, children experience the thrill of authoring and the joy of sharing what they have written with an audience.

Oral Sharing of Writing

READ

Marianne Saccardi, "Can We Read You Our Story? The Tale of a School–Public Library Partnership," *The Reading Teacher,* 51 (February 1998), 445–447, for ideas for "story hours" and "poetry hours" through which older students share their creative writings with younger children in a library program.

Opportunities for oral sharing of writing need to be built into writing workshops. First, most youngsters take pleasure in reading aloud what they have written. Second, the fact that they will share with classmates provides young writers with a purpose for writing and an audience for whom they write. Sometimes, too, oral sharing can substitute for more laborious rewriting. The final draft is an oral one, presented to classmates from an intermediate draft on which the author has penciled changes.

Of course, children should be free to decide when not to share. Some ideas are too personal—too close to the heart—to let others hear. Youngsters can keep some of their writing in a Keep Out! folder that only they see. The teacher can establish a special drawer into which writers tuck pieces they want only the teacher to read.

Children can also use other means for sharing their writing. Young poets can lead classmates in choral renditions of their poems. Young playwrights can lead a company in productions of their playlets. Oral sharing blends equally well with art, dance, and music.

Publishing Writing

On the door of one sixth-grade classroom was the sign "Pine Brook Press." Inside upper-graders worked on their own or in authoring/illustrating teams writing original picture storybooks. To interest students in book writing, their teacher had earlier rolled into the room a cart of newly arrived storybooks. Together teacher and students had read and looked at the variety of story and art patterns in the collection and decided that they would become a press, publishing their own books to share with younger children—their audience—and to distribute to local libraries. Now they were engrossed in story writing; they would go on to illustrate the stories, bind stories and pictures together, and design covers. Eventually they would go to the kindergarten and first grades to read their books to the younger children for whom they had geared their writing.

Technology Notes

CONSIDER

Young authors' conferences in some areas of the country provide opportunities for students to share their writings with others.

Young authors take pleasure and pride in publishing books. Cut-out books like Eric Carle's *The Very Hungry Caterpillar* can inspire young writers to conceive of stories that they illustrate graphically as the masters of storybook writing have done. Tiny books like Maurice Sendak's *Nutshell Library* invite children to "think small" and create their own hand-size books about little things like mice, mites, nuts, or even prunes. ABC books, counting books, and day books—in which each page tells a happening for each day of the week—make easy beginnings for young authors/ illustrators. Nonverbal stories in which pictures carry the story line and there are few or no words are helpful in developing understanding of story sequence and structure.

Bookmaking need not be as sophisticated an activity as it was in this sixth-grade class. Very young children can compose simple books made up of a series of illustrated pages, written with invented spellings. Slightly older children can select a piece they have written, revise and edit it, and publish it as a book. Books of these kinds can be placed in the classroom reading nook where children go to browse and read. See Figure 10.8 for a way to make a bound book.

Children can also publish literary magazines and newspapers to which each youngster contributes one or more pieces. A photocopied or computer-printed magazine can simply be a collection of children's writing or can feature Poetry Pages, Laugh Lines (jokes, riddles), Story Spots, Opinion Notes (book, film, and TV reviews), Puzzle Pages, and Advertisements. A newspaper can feature editorials, news stories, letters to the editor, political cartoons, comics, sports, social events, classified advertisements, advice to the lovelorn, and cooking hints. Using desktop-publishing software that enables the writer to print in columns, set visuals in conjunction with print, and use a variety of fonts, students can create rather professional-looking publications, especially if they study real magazines and newspapers for styling ideas.

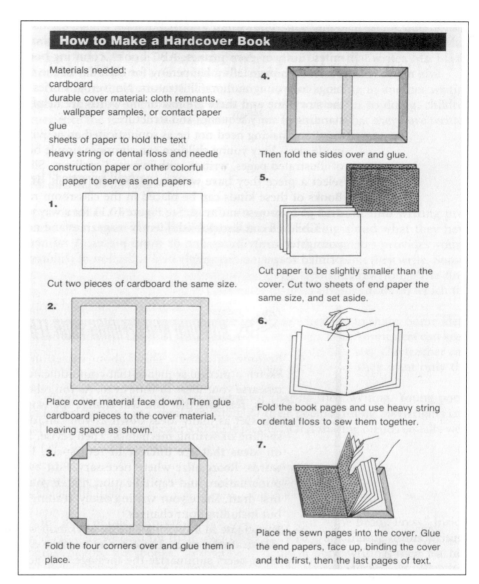

How to Make a Hardcover Book

Materials needed:
cardboard
durable cover material: cloth remnants,
    wallpaper samples, or contact paper
glue
sheets of paper to hold the text
heavy string or dental floss and needle
construction paper or other colorful
    paper to serve as end papers

1.
Cut two pieces of cardboard the same size.

2.
Place cover material face down. Then glue cardboard pieces to the cover material, leaving space as shown.

3.
Fold the four corners over and glue them in place.

4.
Then fold the sides over and glue.

5.
Cut paper to be slightly smaller than the cover. Cut two sheets of end paper the same size, and set aside.

6.
Fold the book pages and use heavy string or dental floss to sew them together.

7.
Place the sewn pages into the cover. Glue the end papers, face up, binding the cover and the first, then the last pages of text.

Figure 10.8
Steps in Making a Bound Book

DISCUSSION PROMPT

- What pitfalls do you see in having children turn their writings into books?

Publishing in classrooms can take other forms. An obvious approach is bulletin board posting in the classroom, the hall, or neighboring classrooms where others outside the class group have the opportunity to read the publication. Important here is the fact that children have a purpose for writing and rewriting; they are getting material ready for publication—for reading by others. When children—all children in a class—know that a piece they have drafted will be published in some form, they are more likely to polish it carefully. Now they have an audience. Now they are authors.

Observing, Profiling, and Assessing Children as Authors

To teach writing is to engage children in an array of recursive writing processes. Given this premise, a teacher cannot simply read students' papers to correct the "errors" and think that he or she has assessed children's progress as writers. Obviously, at some point a teacher reads students' papers, but in a processes workshop approach to writing instruction, the focus in assessment is rather different from that in an assign/correct approach.

Profiles and Portfolios

In a process workshop approach to writing instruction, the teacher studies children's behavior *as they write* to profile their development as authors and to identify the kind of instructional assistance needed (Bunce-Crim, 1992). The teacher studies the successive drafts of children's writing in their active-writing portfolios to note the changes children are making as they review their ideas from one draft to the next. The teacher also notes the topics children choose, specific skills that need attention, and the overall progress of children as writers. Here the focus is on children as rehearsers, drafters, revisers, editors, and sharers. Figure 10.9 is a checklist of concerns the teacher may consider in profiling an upper elementary child's development as an author.

In addition, more and more teachers are asking students to create what Tierney, Carter, and Desai (1991) call *showcase portfolios* to use in assessing progress. To compile a showcase portfolio, students periodically cull from their active-writing portfolios representative samples of their writings-in-process and their published writings that showcase their development as writers. The use of showcase portfolios for assessment arises out of the belief that assessment should focus on "what students are actively doing" and out of a commitment "to student involvement in self-evaluation and helping students to become aware of their own development as . . . writers."

In the 1990s the state of Vermont (Vermont Assessment Program) opted for an assessment of students' writing achievement based on the showcase portfolio model. Fourth- and eighth-graders in the Vermont program compile portfolios that include

1. A table of contents.
2. A dated "best piece," chosen with the teacher's help. A best piece is one "the student feels represents his/her best achievement as a writer."
3. A dated letter from the student to the assessors, explaining the choice of the "best piece" and the process of its composition.
4. A dated poem, short story, play, or personal narration.
5. A dated personal response to a cultural, media, or sports exhibit or event or to a book, current issue, math problem, or scientific phenomenon.
6. At the fourth-grade level, a dated prose piece from any curriculum area that is not "English"; at the eighth-grade level, three dated prose pieces from any curriculum area that is not "English" or "Language Arts."

READ

Marna Bunce-Crim, "Evaluation: Picture of a Portfolio," *Instructor*, 101 (March 1992), 28–29, for a description of one Vermont fourth-grader's portfolio.

Teacher reviewers use the pieces in children's showcase portfolios to analyze whether children maintain a clear purpose in their writing, develop a coherent organization, provide details that support their main points, develop a personal voice or tone, and demonstrate ability to use language (usage, spelling, capitalization, punctuation, and sentence forms) conventionally.

Classroom teachers can use a similar approach, asking students at the end of each quarter to select specific kinds of pieces from their active-writing portfolios to include in their quarter-period showcases (Kucera, 1995). For example, if some writing during the quarter centers on persuasive paragraphs, poetry, and biography, then that quarter-period showcase must contain at least one sample of each carried through to a publication draft, with earlier drafts stapled to the final one. Additionally, students select several other pieces that they think best showcase their progress during the

AN OBSERVATIONAL CHECKLIST OF WRITING BEHAVIORS				
	Always	Generally	Sometimes	Never
A. The child as rehearser				
1. uses pictures to rehearse				
2. uses mind talk before drafting				
3. talks to others before drafting				
4. participates in group rehearsal activities				
5. uses graphic organizers during rehearsal				
6. uses story maps to plot out stories				
B. The child as drafter				
1. views first drafts as beginnings				
2. uses copyediting symbols				
3. crosses out, circles, adds on freely during drafting				
4. goes back for more rehearsing when hitting a snag in drafting				
C. The child as reviser and editor				
1. changes the focus of the composition				
2. revises by adding information				
3. revises to achieve well-organized paragraphs				

Figure 10.9
An Observational Checklist of Writing Behaviors

C. The child as reviser and editor (cont.)	Always	Generally	Sometimes	Never
4. revises to achieve a logical sequence				
5. revises to include transitional words for clarity (*first, however, also*) and to tighten sentences				
6. revises to avoid awkwardness				
7. substitutes more effective words				
8. deletes unnecessary words				
9. edits nonstandard expressions, such as *ain't*				
10. edits for punctuation and capitalization				
11. edits spelling				
12. rewrites for motor aesthetics				
D. The child as sharer				
1. enjoys sharing his/her papers orally				
2. takes pride in compiling a publication copy				

Name of child: _____   Date of observation: _____

Child's comments: _____

_____

Figure 10.9 (continued)

NOTE: In using the checklist, the teacher is profiling the child as writer, not evaluating or grading.

quarter—for whatever reason. Following the guidelines of the Vermont Assessment, students write a brief explanation of why they believe these pieces are their best; they organize with a table of contents.

At the end of the quarter, teacher and student talk about the student's showcase. During a conference, the student explains how he or she has progressed during the quarter. Together, teacher and student identify strengths and weaknesses in idea development, organization, and the mechanics of writing; they identify areas needing attention in the coming quarter. If a school district requires an end-of-quarter grade, teacher and student establish the grade by the end of the conference, based on an analysis of the pieces in the showcase.

Obviously, standardized tests or teacher-made, one-shot tests of writing do not provide the depth of information about children's writing progress that portfolios do (IRA/NCTE Task Force on Assessment, 1994). Sheila Valencia (1990) explains, "No single test, single observation, or single piece of student work could possibly

For grades one and two, the levels represent stages of development based entirely upon the child's ability to communicate meaning in writing. The ability to use the conventions of written expression (correct spelling, punctuation, capitalization, etc.) is not evaluated until grade three.

Beginning Writing

Level 1   The writing does not contain at least three complete thoughts that can be readily understood and are about the same topic.

Level 2   The child can organize some complete thoughts and express them in writing. Some passages may not readily be understood. The ideas tend to be restatements of the same thought or to be a "list of sentences" with only one word different in each sentence.

Level 3   The child can express a number of related ideas about a topic so that each idea after the first says something else about the topic or tells what happens next. Taken as a whole, however, the topic does not have a sense of completeness.

Competent Writing

Level 4   The child can compose a completed series of ideas which are readily understood. The writing, however, consists entirely of basic sentence patterns.

Highly Competent Writing

Level 5   The child can compose a completed series of ideas about a topic, some of which are expressed in non-basic sentence patterns or contain a connecting word to join two main ideas. The ideas, however, tend to be expressed one at a time in simple sentences. The writing does not contain sentences packed with information and ideas.

Superior Writing

Level 6   The child can compose a completed series of ideas about a topic and can compose complicated sentences, each with enough content to have been expressed in three or four simple sentences. The writing, however, does not contain insights or creativity.

Level 7   The child can compose a completed series of ideas about a topic with some complicated sentences and can compose with insight and creativity.

Figure 10.10
Scoring Rubric for Grades 1 and 2, Grosse Pointe, Michigan

DISCUSSION PROMPT
Some schools use "anchor papers" rather than rubrics to establish levels of excellence. Teachers collect a series of papers, each representing a progressively higher level of competence against which they compare a particular sample. Children also compare their final drafts to the anchors. What advantage is there to using anchor papers in contrast to using rubrics?

capture the authentic, continuous, multi-dimensional, interactive requirement" of portfolio assessment. Showcase portfolios pay secondary dividends as a means of communicating this view of assessment to parents. "Portfolios can help parents understand the ongoing development of their children. . . . With this kind of frame, parents are less likely to put undue value on the results of test scores. They come to realize that numerical scores provide only limited information about their children's abilities" (Siu-Runyan, 1991).

Not Competent

Level 1   The writing does not contain an understandable message. It either contains passages that cannot be readily understood or contains an insufficient number of related thoughts to comprise a message.

Level 2   The student can express a message that can be readily understood although the writing contains numerous deficiencies in wording, spelling, punctuation, or capitalization, judged by standards appropriate for the grade.

Marginally Competent

Level 3   The student can express a message that can be readily understood and does not contain numerous gross deficiencies in wording, spelling, punctuation, and capitalization. The writing, however, is not competent in at least one of the following skills:

Completeness of content   Use of several non-basic sentence patterns
Sentence sense   Use of connecting words to join sentences
Spelling   Some use of subordination
Punctuation and capitalization

Competent

Level 4   The student can compose a completed series of ideas about a topic with the basic skills, listed above at a level appropriate for the grade. The writing does not, however, demonstrate the use of good vocabulary, good sentence structure, a controlling idea, and some interpretation.

Highly Competent

Level 5   The student can compose a completed series of ideas about a topic with basic skills at a level appropriate for the grade and with good vocabulary, good sentence structure, a controlling idea, and some interpretation. The writing does not, however, contain passages of superior writing with characteristics such as insight, creativity, or vitality of expression.

Superior

Level 6   The student can compose a completed series of ideas about a topic with excellent skills appropriate for the grade, with good vocabulary and sentence structure, with a controlling idea, and with a passage of superior writing. Superior writing contains characteristics such as insight, creativity, or vitality of expression.

Level 7   The student can compose a completed series of ideas about a topic with excellent basic skills appropriate for the grade, with good vocabulary and sentence structure, with a controlling idea, and with a sustained excellence of expression. The student can compose with insight, creativity, or vitality and richness of expression.

Figure 10.11
Scoring Rubric for Grade 6,
Grosse Pointe, Michigan

Scoring Tables, or Rubrics, for Judging Writing Competency

At some point, a teacher or school may want to make holistic, or general, judgments about the overall competency of child writers. Useful here are competency tables or scales—*rubrics* that describe levels of writing achievement at specific grade levels. Teachers in some school districts are developing such scales to judge the efficacy of the writing program in their district. The Grosse Pointe, Michigan, school district, for example, has devised a sophisticated rubric for assessing performance from grades 1 to 10. The emphasis in the Grosse Pointe scale is on whether the writing communicates a clear message. Level 4 on each grade-level scale represents the achievement expected of students in that grade. Figures 10.10 and 10.11 show the competency levels for grades 1 and 2 and grade 6, respectively.

In contrast to the Grosse Pointe scale, Shannon Downing (1995) uses a relatively simple scoring table with her fourth-graders, especially when her class pursues demand writing—"required writing on an assigned topic completed in a fixed time period." Her students help develop the scoring rubric based on a series of mini-lessons in which Downing introduces them to what is important in demand writing. Three components of one class's rubric are shown here—focus, lead, and ending:

Focus

1	2	3
No! This piece goes all over, or it is too big.	Focus is pretty clear. Only a few things don't fit.	Very clear focus. It stays on track and isn't too big.

Lead

1	2	3
Needs work!	Just okay. Good try.	Great! It catches my readers' attention and gives a clue [as to where the story is going].

Ending

1	2	3
No end in sight. It just stops.	Pretty good. I can tell it is finished without "The End."	Awesome! The end is tied to the beginning and pulls the whole piece together.

Other aspects of writing that these students included in their scale are details, spelling, and punctuation/capitalization (Downing, 1995).

Downing's demand-writing rubric is obviously much simpler than the one developed by the Gross Pointe teachers. Nonetheless, it guides children as they revise and edit, and it guides children and their teacher as they talk at the end of a quarter about students' showcase portfolios. Where schools require a quarter grade (and many schools require this even though the IRA/NCTE Joint Task Force on Assessment states unequivocally that reducing "writing performance to a letter or number grade is unacceptable" [1994]), a rubric of this sort that is devised cooperatively by pupils and teacher is probably the least objectionable way to go.

A Summary Thought or Two

Writing Processes in a Workshop Environment

The major thesis developed in this chapter is that elementary-grade students should participate directly in the processes that comprise the act of writing. They should rehearse before and during writing, draft with the mindset that what they record is simply a beginning, revise and edit their drafts, and from time to time share their writings with others so that they experience the thrill of authorship and of being a member of a community of writers. Simultaneously, youngsters should read all kinds of printed materials; through reading, students begin to comprehend how authors manage ideas in writing.

The chapter also describes strategies for involving children in writing processes during writing workshop: read-alouds and independent reading activity that help children read from a writer's perspective; pictorializing, talking about, and thinking through; factstorming, categorizing, and charting or webbing; story plotting out; developing a mindset about first drafts; active-writing portfolios; mini-lessons on the tools of revision, shared writing and review, Help Me! Share-times, teacher and buddy conferences; the Author's chair, oral sharing, and bookmaking; and the showcase portfolio, rubrics, and anchor papers. Through real authoring, young writers learn what it means to write and how to develop, organize, and sequence their thoughts for sharing with others.

Your Language Arts Portfolio

- Experiment with different ways of rehearsing for writing as described in Chapter 10—webs, pictures, storymaps. Base this on ideas you are trying to get down on paper as you read this book and as you read in other situations.
- Experiment with the revision tools described in Chapter 10. In your portfolio, put a series of drafts that demonstrate your ability to revise your own writing.

Related Readings

Atwell, Nancie. *In the Middle: New Understandings about Writing, Reading, and Learning.* Westport, Conn.: Heinemann, 1998.

Bridges, Lois. *Writing as a Way of Knowing.* York, Me.: Stenhouse Publishers, 1998.

Bright, Robin. *Writing Instruction in the Intermediate Grades: What Is Said, What Is Done, What Is Understood.* Newark, Del.: International Reading Association, 1995.

Calkins, Lucy. *The Art of Teaching Writing.* New ed. Portsmouth, N.H.: Heinemann, 1994.

Clark, Roy Peter. *Free to Write.* Portsmouth, N.H.: Heinemann, 1987.

Cokle, Diane, and Wendy Towle. *Connecting Reading and Writing in the Intermediate Grades: A Workshop Approach.* Newark, Del.: International Reading Association, 2001.

Dahl, Karin, and **Nancy Farnan.** *Children's Writing: Perspectives from Research.* Chicago, Ill., and Newark, Del.: National Reading Conference and International Reading Association, 1998.

Fearn, Leif, and **Nancy Farnan.** *Interactions: Teaching Writing and the Language Arts.* Boston: Houghton Mifflin, 2001.

Graves, Donald. *Writing: Teachers and Children at Work.* Exeter, N.H.: Heinemann, 1983.

————. *A Fresh View of Writing.* Portsmouth, N.H.: Heinemann, 1994.

Hughey, Jane, and **Charlotte Slack.** *Teaching Children to Write: Theory into Practice.* Upper Saddle River, N.J.: Merrill/Prentice Hall, 2001.

Jenkins, Carol. *Inside the Writing Portfolio: What We Need to Know to Assess Children's Writing.* Portsmouth, N.H.: Heinemann, 1996.

Johnson, Paul. *A Book of One's Own: Developing Literacy Through Making Books.* 2nd ed. Westport, Conn.: Heinemann, 1998.

Karelitz, Ellen Blackburn. *The Author's Chair and Beyond: Language and Literacy in a Primary Classroom.* Portsmouth, N.H.: Heinemann, 1993.

Kent, Richard. *Room 109: The Promise of a Portfolio Classroom.* Westport, Conn.: Heinemann, 1997.

Lane, Barry. *After "THE END": Teaching and Learning Creative Revision.* Portsmouth, N.H.: Heinemann, 1992.

Language Arts. March 1995. The theme of the issue is "Revisiting the Teaching of Writing."

Language Arts. May 2001. The theme of the issue is "Rewriting Writing."

Murray, Donald. *Shoptalk: Learning to Write with Writers.* Portsmouth, N.H.: Heinemann, 1990.

National Assessment of Educational Progress. *Write/Rewrite: An Assessment of Revision Skills.* Denver, Colo.: National Assessment of Educational Progress, 1977.

————. *Writing Mechanics, 1969–1974.* Denver, Colo.: National Assessment of Educational Progress, 1975.

————. *Writing Trends Across the Decade, 1974–1985.* Princeton, N.J.: National Assessment of Educational Progress, 1986.

Ray, Katie Wood. *Wondrous Words: Writers and Writing in the Elementary Classroom.* Urbana, Ill.: National Council of Teachers of English, 1999.

Routman, Regie. *Literacy at the Crossroads: Crucial Talk About Reading, Writing, and Other Teaching Dilemmas.* Portsmouth, N.H.: Heinemann, 1996.

————. "The Uses and Abuses of Invented Spelling." *Instructor,* 102 (May/June 1993), 36–39.

Schipper, Beth, and **Joanne Rossi.** *Portfolios in the Classroom: Tools for Learning and Instruction.* York, Me.: Stenhouse Publishers, 1997.

Wilde, Jack. *A Door Opens: Writing in Fifth Grade.* Portsmouth, N.H.: Heinemann, 1993.

Writing, Language Conventions, and Grammar

Managing Word and Sentence Patterns in Writing

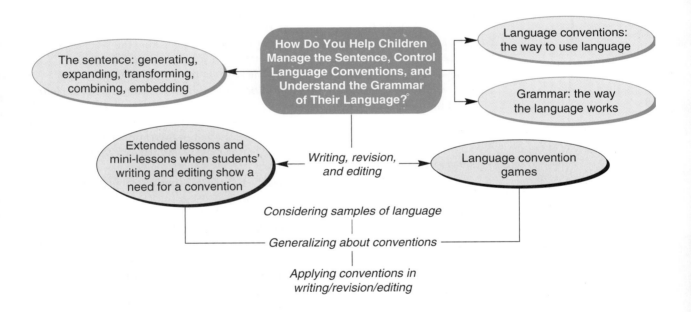

Language conventions: the way to use language

Grammar: the way the language works

How Do You Help Children Manage the Sentence, Control Language Conventions, and Understand the Grammar of Their Language?

The sentence: generating, expanding, transforming, combining, embedding

Extended lessons and mini-lessons when students' writing and editing show a need for a convention

Writing, revision, and editing

Language convention games

Considering samples of language

Generalizing about conventions

Applying conventions in writing/revision/editing

Languaging in Action   *Revising Sentences—A Mini-Lesson*

It was the start of workshop in Rick Riveria's fifth-grade class. "Let's begin with a mini-lesson based on this sentence from someone's writing. Lots of us are writing sentences like this one." With that, Mr. Riveria displayed a sheet of construction paper with this sentence:

> Yesterday we watched TV and we saw "ET" and we saw "Cosby" and we enjoyed the shows.

Students chorused the drag-on sentence, "pausing at the natural breaks between independent clauses" as Rick Riveria suggested. "What do we hear too much of?" their teacher asked. Having orally read the sentence, the students had picked up on the point—the repeated use of the *and*-word. They were able to cut this drag-on sentence into what Mr. Riveria referred to as "four independent clauses, each with a subject and predicate part" by discarding the *and*-words. Eight students volunteered to hold the four resulting clauses and four period cards.

Revise by eliminating the word *and* by combining and embedding ideas

"What is wrong with simply editing by placing a period at the end of each independent clause?" Rick Riveria went on to ask. Rereading the independent clauses aloud as four sentences, the students heard the problem—the short, jerky sentences that had no style. Working first with the second and third independent clauses, the sixth-graders began to remedy the problem by orally composing a sentence with a compound object: *We saw "ET" and "Cosby."* They then worked together to integrate the idea of the first independent clause into their sentence without resorting to the *and*-word: *Yesterday on TV we watched "ET" and "Cosby."* "How can we include the enjoyment notion in our sentence?" Mr. Riveria queried. The students played with possibilities and settled on this revision: *Yesterday on TV we enjoyed watching "ET" and "Cosby."* The sentence manipulation required considerable cutting apart of words; to facilitate the manipulation of sentence parts, other volunteers joined the sentence "train," each to hold a word or punctuation card that was part of the revision.

With that, Mr. Riveria encouraged students holding word cards to move around in the revised version of their sentence to try out different positioning of the words *Yesterday* and *on TV*. They reversed the order and moved them individually and together to the end of the sentence, then moved them back to the front. Mr. Riveria reminded the fifth-graders that *yesterday* was an adverb and *on TV* was a prepositional phrase and hung a sign bearing those labels around the necks of the students who were holding those word cards. He also reminded them that these sentence-building parts were movable; when he revised, he tried his adverbs and prepositional phrases in different positions to discover the spot that best communicated what he wanted to say.

Mr. Riveria suggested that before going on with a writing project-in-progress students spend a few minutes of workshop looking through their recent writings for places where they may have overused the *and*-word. Working with a peer editor, they were to experiment with the Sentence-Embedding Tool they had been applying. At the end of workshop, they would share some of their revised sentences with classmates.

Rick Riveria had two major literacy objectives in mind as he organized this ten-minute mini-lesson at the start of Writing Workshop. One of his objectives was that his students would be better able to tie their thoughts together rather than hinging sentences repetitively with the *and*-word. A second objective was that students would be better able to use punctuation conventions to clarify sentence relationships. At the same time, the mini-lesson allowed this teacher to use terminology such as *independent clause, adverb,* and *prepositional phrase* as students needed that terminology to talk about their sentences.

Writing, Language Conventions, and Grammar

How does a teacher help students to become writers who can manipulate sentences to say what they want to say and at the same time use written language in conventional, or accepted, ways? As Dan Kirby et al. (1988) remind us, teachers do not help youngsters to master language-on-paper by asking them to study traditional, prescriptive grammar, do grammar worksheets, and take punctuation quizzes. The hours students spend memorizing rules, filling in blanks, and underlining words in grammar exercises have no positive impact on children's writing. Numerous research studies and analyses of those studies (Elley et al., 1976; Petrosky, 1977; Haynes, 1978; Newkirk, 1978; Hillocks, 1986, 1987; Weaver, 1996) support that conclusion. What has an effect is a program with the following characteristics:

■ *Children spend considerable time listening to and reading written language.* Helpful are big books that children read along as teachers read aloud. Reading a big book to a class, the teacher runs his or her hand under the lines of print, pointing briefly to highlight sentence beginnings and endings. Children reread the big books together, making their voices show meanings signaled by punctuation. Helpful, too, is story listening, which enables children to hear "book talk" and distinguish it from speech.

■ *Children spend considerable time writing together and alone.* When recording children's writing for them on story charts during interactive writing, the teacher asks youngsters to inscribe the capital letters that begin sentences and the punctuation marks that end them. She or he uses the word *sentence* incidentally to refer to the units of written text children are drafting. Writing independently, children apply the conventions they have picked up during shared and interactive writing to their own drafts.

■ *Children spend considerable time editing what they have written.* In an editing conference, the teacher listens to children read their writings aloud. She or he helps them to translate the sounds of language into the punctuation marks of written language and to think about conventional usage (such as agreement of subject and verb) as writers prepare for publication. Providing instruction when

GO TO

Chapter 10 for ways to use conferences and writing workshops so that children refine their ability to handle the conventions of written language even as they need those conventions to edit.

children are ready to publish pieces, the teacher gathers several youngsters for cooperative editing. Teacher and children consider a piece or two by members of the group; together, with help from the teacher, the students rework sentences, fix punctuation so that it communicates their meaning, or edit for an aspect of conventional usage. Most teachers have found that at any one time, it pays to focus on one major problem rather than on several problems. Youngsters who have worked together in such a group become a self-instructional team; working independently, they edit one another's papers in terms of what they have just learned in the teacher-guided session.

■ *Children are involved in mini-lessons and games in which they play with a convention of written language when their writing demonstrates a need for it.* Donald Graves (1995) explains that a misconception about teaching writing is that "mechanics are not important. . . . In reality, we have very high expectations for children, and teaching conventions is a fundamental part of our approach."

In this chapter, we focus on children's involvement with language conventions, especially as the conventions relate to children's writing and editing. First we consider ways to involve children in sentence building so that they develop a sense of what a sentence is and use that understanding to write complete sentences. Then we consider ways to involve children with written language conventions at the point when they need them to edit their writing. After that, we talk about the place of grammar in the language arts. The reader, however, should keep three assumptions in mind:

■ Conventions and grammar are best taught in the context of students' purposeful reading and writing.
■ Conventions and grammar are only small parts of a comprehensive language arts program.
■ Language arts standards mandated by many states require attention to conventions and grammar. In some states, students are tested on their ability to apply conventions during editing.

Controlling the Sentence

To write with clarity and style, a person must have control over sentences. John Harris (1986) maintains that there is a fundamental difference in the syntactic features of speech and writing. Speech is formed from loosely coordinated chains of words, not all of which are grammatical sentences. Harris uses this oral exchange as an example:

Are you going to the theater tonight?

No. Tomorrow night.

The first string of words is a grammatical *sentence,* a sentence being an independent clause plus the dependent clause(s) or phrase(s) (if any) that are attached to it or embedded within it (Weaver, 1996). A grammatically correct sentence has a subject and a verb. The next two utterances, although ending with periods, are not grammatical sentences in the strict sense of the definition.

Study this unedited composition by a second-grader named John:

> Snow
>
> Snow it is snowing today everywhere there is snow it is fun to play and you can play snow ball fights and we throw snowballs at each other and berry our selfs and make angals in the snow.

Obviously John has exciting ideas and a rather clear concept of a paragraph. He writes of snowball fights and snow angels in a paragraph that focuses neatly on one main idea: having fun in the snow. On the other hand, John does not know where one sentence ends and the next begins; he does not use the signals that indicate sentence beginnings and endings. He does not have a functional concept of a grammatical sentence, including the idea of an independent clause with subject and predicate parts. In short, he has not yet realized that there is a difference between speaking and writing (Harris, 1986).

Sentence Making: What the Research Says

During the late 1960s, the 1970s, and the 1980s, a number of researchers studied children's developing ability to control the sentence. For example, through their studies, Kellogg Hunt and Roy O'Donnell (1970) found that young children generally have trouble building related ideas into one grammatical sentence. Youngsters at this stage string thoughts together using *and*, as in "I saw a dog and he was big and he was with a boy and I called him to come." More mature writers are more likely to combine the thoughts: "I called to the big dog that was with the boy."

Jack Perron (1978) hypothesized that young writers gain control over sentence-combining strategies through "a glacially slow process, currently without much help from teachers." His research indicated that direct experience with sentence combining can help children more rapidly control complex sentence patterns. Perron explained his findings in this way:

> The six-month study demonstrated that a grammar-free program of sentence combining (SC) lessons backed by games, activities, and experiential exercises in SC manipulation, does encourage syntactic growth in the writing of fourth graders. It also demonstrated that games and activities do provide a valuable supplement to the language arts curriculum.

Other studies affirmed Perron's findings. John Mellon (1969) noted a gain in seventh-graders' writing skills through a program in which students systematically

READ

William Strong, *Creative Approaches to Sentence Combining*, and George Hillocks, "Grammar and the Manipulation of Syntax," *Research on Written Composition* (Urbana, Ill.: ERIC Clearinghouse on Reading and Communication Skills, 1986), for reviews of sentence-combining studies.

combined sentences based on symbolic clues for sentence building. Frank O'Hare (1973) found a similar gain among seventh-graders who combined sentences based on word clues. Studies by Hunt and O'Donnell (1970) and Barbara Miller and James Ney (1968) demonstrated similar gains at the fourth-grade level. A study by Elizabeth Stoddard (1982) using SC activities with fifth- and sixth-graders showed gains in syntactic fluency and overall writing quality. In the remaining segments of this section, we look at ways to involve children in the manipulation of sentences at a point when they are beginning to write longer strings of words and need some understanding of how to expand and transform their sentences and to combine and embed their ideas.

Playing with Sentence Parts

Millions of students have memorized the definition, "A sentence is a group of words that expresses a complete thought." However, a sentence is not the only way to express a complete thought. As the example on page 401 shows, in speaking people express complete thoughts through single words and phrases. Today linguists propose that a better approach to building sentence sense is to have children manipulate subjects and predicates and gradually acquire a fundamental understanding of the two-partedness of a sentence and the way writers use capital letters to signal sentence beginnings and punctuation marks to signal sentence ends.

Sentence reconstruction is one way to get a "feel" for the grammatical sentence. At the start of a mini-lesson, the teacher distributes phrase cards to students. Some phrases (such as *a girl in my class*) can function as subjects of sentences, others (such as *made a home run*) as predicates. Students build sentences from the parts by finding a subject or predicate partner and standing next to him or her in sentence order. Once in place with their partners, students read the sentences aloud to hear the sound each sentence makes. They add end punctuation and beginning capitalization. Figure 11.1 shows sentences resulting from this kind of sentence construction.

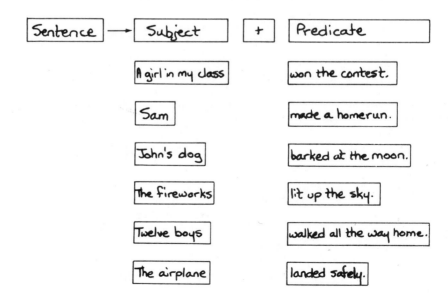

Figure 11.1
Building Sentences (Independent Clauses) from Subject and Predicate Parts

Students who have built sentences from subject and predicate parts can create their own subject and predicate cards. Using their cards, they can locate a friend who has created a subject or predicate part that can form a sentence with one of theirs. Finding an agreeable mate, children read their resulting sentences aloud, testing them to see whether they have the sound of a sentence. Applying their growing sentence sense in editing their own writing, students read their sentences aloud, listening for "the sentence sound."

Expanding Sentences

Children can expand sentences or make them "grow." A fun way is to clip just two words on the sentence clothesline—words such as *alligators* and *swim*—in reverse sentence order: *swim alligators*. Young children can order the pair and then add adjectives, adverbs, and prepositional phrases by writing them on cards and clipping the cards to the line. Then they shift to other patterns, such as "The monkey spied a tiger." "The monkey was afraid." A teacher should keep punctuation cards and capitalization markers ready during the mini-lesson so that pupils include the appropriate signals. Children who have expanded sentences in this way expand their own sentences during revising/editing workshops.

Edward Plank (1992) reports that upper-graders, especially those who learn best when they are physically involved, enjoy "becoming" words in sentences they are expanding. To start what Plank calls a "human-sentence game," three students become the three words in a kernel sentence such as *The dog ran*. Wearing labels with their words, they stand in order before the class. Other students decide what words they will become to join the sentence, encouraged by teacher prompts: "Where do you belong in our sentence? Where else could you fit? What do you do in the sentence? Who names something? Who describes something?" As the sentence grows, other children become punctuation marks. Plank suggests that this mini-lesson reinforces not only children's concept of a sentence but also their understanding of punctuation.

Transforming Sentences

To encourage sentence building with transformations of basic sentence patterns, Mr. Lombard, a third-grade teacher, converts his classroom floor into a composing stage, where children construct sentences. During one mini-lesson, he distributes predicate cards and a number of cards bearing the word *you*. He retains one *you* card, places it on the composing stage, and asks, "Who has a predicate part to complete this sentence?" Mr. Lombard gets half a class of possibilities, which are laid beneath a predicate label card. Other participants contribute their *you* cards under a subject label. Then students say the sentences without the *you*s. By the third grade, students are able to see that the subject parts are unspoken in commanding. The teacher labels *Imperative* the grouping that results by eliminating *you;* having applied that label, he also begins to refer to the basic patterns as *declarative sentences*.

The same technique can be used to highlight interrogative patterns. A teacher can provide phrase cards: *John, has come, Susan and my mother, have gone shopping, my best friend, is the winner, the two cows, are in the barn, the radio, is too loud, the girls, are going to Florida for the winter*. Children build declarative sentences from the parts,

CONSIDER

Students can use a pyramid as a form in which to expand sentences.

Dogs run.
Red dogs run.
Red dogs also run.

CONSIDER

Here are some ideas for phrase cards: *run away, walk slowly, jump the cracks, raise your hand, walk, open the door, get the clock, turn off the radio.*

injecting punctuation and capitalization signals. When asked, "What words must we shift to transform our statements into questions?" they shift linking or helping verbs and change the capitalization and punctuation signals. They go on to write original questions with appropriate punctuation. Eventually, a teacher can introduce other interrogative patterns—patterns beginning with *which, what, where, who, whom, when, why,* and *how* or ending with an upward rise of the voice. Oral work with question patterns is essential to help students to relate the question mark to the upward inflection of voice. The same is true with exclamations, since they, too, have a vocal equivalent: excitement in the voice. This kind of language play relates directly to editing. During editing, children orally read sentences they have written to determine the punctuation needed.

Combining and Embedding Ideas

READ

Don Killgallon and Jenny Killgallon, *Sentence Composing for Elementary School.* Westport, Conn.: Heinemann, 2000, for sentence-building strategies: unscrambling, imitating, combining, and expanding.

As children mature as writers, they begin to write more involved sentences. Not knowing how to handle their longer sentences on paper, upper elementary students are liable to fall into these sentence-writing traps:

- *Drag-on trap:* Writers string several sentences together with *and.* Example: *I saw my friend and I waved and I said, "Hello."*
- *Run-on trap:* Writers craft two or more sentences as one without any punctuation between them. Example: *I saw my friend I waved at him.*
- *Comma-splice trap:* Writers hinge two sentences together with the assistance of only a comma. Example: *Mary was angry, she got red in the face.*
- *Sentence-fragment trap:* Writers craft only partial sentences. Example: *When Mary got red in the face.*

At the point when students' writing exhibits these problems, the teacher should model idea-combining and idea-embedding strategies. Research indicates that sentence-combining activity without a lot of stress on formal grammar is an aid to syntactic fluency, especially when carried out in relationship to actual writing activity (Haynes, 1978).

Combining Ideas   As part of teacher-guided, interactive editing, children can consider how to combine ideas to highlight relationships among them. Suppose, for example, that in composing interactively, third-graders suggest these sentences: *We arrived at the station on time. We missed the train.* The teacher can model how he or she would revise the set to form a compound sentence: *We arrived at the station on time, but we still missed the train.*

Similarly, on another occasion when students have offered as one sentence *Josh went to the movies, Josh's father went to the movies, too,* the teacher can ask the students to chorus the run-on offering and listen for the drop-stop at the ends of the component sentences. Based on the sentence sounds, they edit the comma splice: *Josh went to the movies. Josh's father went to the movies, too.* They chorus the resulting pair of sentences, emphasizing in their oral rendition the drop-stop at the sentence ends. They may further edit to produce a sentence with a compound subject: *Josh and his father went to the movies.* As Katie Wood Ray (1999) suggests, this is the time for the teacher to begin naturally to use such grammatical terms as *conjunction,*

The Teacher's Message Board

Lesson Alert: Here is a plan for a sixth-grade mini-lesson on using the comma in complex sentences that you can use as a model as you plan similar types of mini-lessons.

Context
The mini-lesson is based on a problem that students are encountering in editing.

Objective
As they edit their writings for publication, the children will be able to insert a comma after an initial subordinate clause introduced by the word *When*.

Proposed Sequence of Activities
Anticipatory Set—Explain that many students have been writing declarative sentences that start with the word *When* and that they must use a comma at the short pause after the first clause when they edit those sentences.

Guided Instruction—Display two sentences from children's writing in which the comma is necessary:

> When Sarah came, I was very excited.
> When the storm hit, the family hid in the barn.

Have children orally read the sentences together, listening for the natural short pause, or break, at the comma. Together develop a generalization. Then display two more sentences from the children's writing without the comma punctuation:

> When Sarah went into town I was scared like Caleb.
> When Sarah decided to stay I cried.

Ask students to chorus these sentences to show with their voices where a comma is necessary and add the comma. Invite students to write a sentence that is similar to these and needs a comma. Do a quick oral share of a few sentences. Suggest that students write their sentences with the comma on the inside cover of their writing portfolios to use as models as they edit. Remind students that sometimes the introductory word may be *If, After,* or *Before* rather than *When*. Ask students to look through some paragraphs they have been drafting to find sentences that pattern as their model sentences do. Invite a few students to share their sentences.

Concluding Set—Suggest that students make checking for the comma in this kind of sentence a priority as they edit their writing for publication.

Follow-Up—Children check their use of the comma as they edit during workshop.

Materials
Four sentences from children's papers that focus on the use of a comma after an introductory subordinate clause.

Next Related Mini-Lesson
Handling punctuation when the subordinate clause comes at the end of a sentence.

Assessment
Watch for application in children's writing.

compound sentence, and *compound subject* in talking about the operations the class is performing on their sentences. This is also the time for students to search their textbooks and storybooks for samples of writing in which authors have used compound structures to make their ideas hang logically together.

Eventually, as part of a follow-up mini-lesson, children write equations based on their findings, which in upper elementary grades can include the semicolon as a tool for sentence combining:

$$
\begin{aligned}
&\textit{Compound Sentence} = \text{Subject} + \text{predicate, conjunction}
\begin{cases}
\textit{and} \\
\textit{but} \\
\textit{or} \\
\textit{yet}
\end{cases} \\
&\qquad\qquad\qquad\qquad\quad \text{subject} + \text{predicate.} \\[6pt]
&\textit{Compound Sentence} = \text{Subject} + \text{predicate;} \\
&\qquad\qquad\qquad\qquad\quad \text{subject} + \text{predicate.}
\end{aligned}
$$

Adhering to the patterns set out in their equations, in teams students craft samples, vying with one another to produce the most original examples. Later, they post their sentence-combining patterns on the inside cover of their writing portfolios as guides to use as they edit their own writing and to help them decide whether they have used conjunctions, commas, semicolons, and periods in the conventional manner.

Embedding Ideas   Another way to handle rhetorical relationships among ideas is to draw on the wonderful, meaning-filled power of subordinating conjunctions. For example, as part of interactive writing, students may fall into the comma-splice trap and suggest the following as a sentence: *I ran after Sue, I could not catch her.* This is an ideal situation for the teacher to model how in writing he or she uses a subordinating conjunction to tell readers "what really is happening here." The teacher edits the comma splice to read: *Although I ran after Sue, I could not catch her.* Students and teacher chorus the resulting complex sentence together, "short-pausing" at the comma site to "hear the sound the clauses make."

When students demonstrate in their writing that they need help embedding ideas in this way, the teacher can set up a series of mini-lessons in which children practice building complex sentences by inserting one sentence into another to avoid the drag-on, comma-splice, run-on, and fragment traps. In preparation, several students who need handwriting practice write out the following word, phrase, and punctuation cards:

Connecting words, or subordinators:	*although, since, while, when, after, just as, if, as, wherever, because*
Verb phrases:	*was predicted, rained hard, was late, missed the bus, am her best friend, invited me to her party, was in the gym, put the balls away, arrived here, climbed on, had been in school ten minutes, dismissed us, trusted me, was getting interesting, is right behind me*
Noun phrases:	*she, the school bus, we, the principal, the lesson, my dog, everyone, snow, it, I* (and five additional *I* cards)
Punctuation:	ten comma and ten period cards
Capitals:	Cuisenaire rods to mark capitals
Labels:	SUBJECT, PREDICATE, and SUBORDINATOR

SUBJECT

The principal

Students distribute the cards except the noun phrase card *the principal* and the labels. The teacher places the card with *the principal* on the composing floor or tapes it to the board and asks students to contribute a predicate part to complete the sentence. Children place the period and capitalization marker in the sentence and chorus, listening for the "sentence sound." Those who think they have SUBJECT parts place or tape their cards beneath *the principal,* which they label SUBJECT. Students next try to pair their predicate parts with subjects already in place, labeling that column PREDICATE. By juggling the cards, youngsters can build fifteen sentences. They add punctuation and capitalization markers to form "law-abiding sentences." Incidentally, since punctuation and capitalization are part of the conventions of writing, the phrase *law-abiding* is useful.

With all the parts in place, children check each sentence to identify non–law-abiding sentences. There will be five, since fifteen sentences will have been composed and only ten period cards provided.

Students move to rehabilitate the non–law-abiding sentences. With a little guidance and with the aid of their subordinators, children can embed one sentence within another. A result may be, *Although snow was predicted, it rained.* On the board or floor, students add the comma between the dependent and independent clauses, begin to use those terms as their teacher has been doing, and add labels to clarify the pattern. Students continue to build other complex sentences by placing word and phrase cards below those in the model:

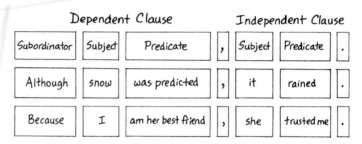

When children have juggled cards to form seven sentences, they shift the subordinator so that it is between the independent and dependent clauses, as in, *It rained although some snow was predicted.* Using the remaining labeling cards, children construct the equation for the pattern as shown here:

A follow-up is for youngsters to write original sentences that adhere to the pattern. Marion Crowhurst's research (1979) has indicated that one way to encourage the construction of complex sentences is to ask youngsters to compose in the argu-

The Teacher's Message Board

Use these kinds of contextually relevant activities to build sentence sense.

- **Shared and interactive writing:** After young children dictate group experience stories, the teacher and students reread their sentences, making the "sentence sound." They then pick out the sentence beginnings and decide how the beginnings are all the same. When the teacher records other stories, the youngsters volunteer to record the beginning capital letters on the story chart.

- **Shared and interactive writing:** When children dictate group stories, they listen for the sentence endings. As they read and reread their sentences, they express the sounds indicated by the sentence-ending punctuation and decide how the endings are different and what makes them different. Now, as the teacher records other stories, the children hold up a period, question mark, or exclamation mark card to indicate the punctuation mark required to end the sentence.

- **Shared reading:** When children reread big books together after an initial reading by the teacher, they express sentence-ending punctuation with their voices. On a third reading, the teacher can mask sentence-ending punctuation marks with sticky notes and the children can "edit" the sentences to make sure that the "sound goes with the sense."

- **Mini-lesson:** When children draft fragments, the teacher can write examples on sentence strips. Children first read a fragment without the rhythm and rise-and-fall of a sentence. Then they transform the fragments into statements, questions, and exclamations and chorus their transformations, making the "sentence sound."

- **Mini-lesson:** When children draft sentences with comma splices, the teacher can write those sentences on strips. Children chorus the poorly crafted sentences, making the sound of two sentences with a stop-drop between. They use scissors to cut the sentence with the splice into its two component independent clauses and then punctuate.

- **Mini-lesson:** When children compose "drag-on sentences"—a series of sentences strung together with *and*s, the teacher writes an example from a student's paper on construction paper without indicating who the student author is. Children cut apart each independent clause and then embed the ideas in one sentence with only limited reliance on the word *and.* For example, one teacher lifted the *drag-on* sentence, "Saturday we went downtown and we saw some friends and we had lunch and we all went to a movie" from a fifth-grader's paper. Youngsters reconstructed it to state, "On Saturday when we went downtown, we had lunch and went to a movie with some friends."

- **Editing:** Students in editing pairs look through stories they have "in process" in their writing portfolios. They check for fragments, run-ons, and drag-ons. After they have located some non–law-abiding sentences, editors rewrite them and share their revisions with the class.

mentative mode. Writing options in this mode include, "Convince your mother to let you look at a particular television program" and "Present an argument about why the afternoon recess break should be extended. Address your argument to the principal." Having written persuasive pieces, youngsters check their sentences against the equation patterns to see whether they have composed any complex sentences and, if so, punctuated them correctly.

A second follow-up is a search of story and textbooks to find comparable sentences and to propose how authors use coordination and subordination in writing. Students will find that textbook writers typically use standard compound and complex sentence forms to highlight relationships among ideas. They discover, however, that sometimes story writers rely on sentence fragments. Now is the time to ask students whether these professional writers "don't know any better." Now is the time to talk about writing style. Now is the time to remind upper-graders that they must know what they are doing with their sentences. If they write a fragment into a story, for example, they must do it knowingly for a stylistic purpose.

One point before moving on to a consideration of other standard conventions. (Did you notice the use right there of a fragment for stylistic purposes?) If teachers are unable to handle coordination and subordination in standard ways in their own writing, they are in no position to help youngsters build sentence sense. Teachers who are still writing fragments, run-ons, comma-splices, and drag-ons without knowing that they are doing it should take three immediate steps:

- Purchase and study an English-language handbook that explains basic conventions of writing. A simple guide intended for upper elementary students is Marvin Terban's *Punctuation Power: Punctuation and How to Use It* (New York: Scholastic, 2000).
- Revise and edit their own writing, listening particularly for the sentence sounds and testing their sentences against the subordinating patterns just laid out; computer grammar checkers can be of some help here because they may tag ungrammatical sentences.
- Run as fast as they can to a writing clinic and sign up for remedial help.

Managing Other Conventions of Written Language

WORD BANK

Conventions

Usage

Hand in hand with the ability to control a variety of sentence patterns in writing goes the ability to manage the *conventions* associated with capitalization, punctuation, and usage. By *usage,* we mean conventional ways of using the language, such as plurals, tenses, and contractions.

Today most school curricular guides include generalizations about language use that have wide application—generalizations about how to manage sentences, paragraphs, capitalization, punctuation, and nouns and verbs in writing. Figure 11.2 addresses some conventions typically included in curricular guides and often tested during state-mandated assessments. It can be used to diagnose children's ability to handle written-language conventions.

A WRITING CONVENTIONS CHECKLIST			
The child is	Never	Some-times	Always
1. Able to compose sentences; specifically he or she			
a. writes a variety of sentence patterns and expansions of them			
b. transforms sentence patterns to gain variety and clarity			
c. combines sentences and inserts one sentence into another in writing			
d. writes complete sentences			
e. uses words other than *and* to connect thoughts in writing			
f. writes effective dialogue			
g. writes sentences in which phrases, clauses, and words are placed so meaning is clear			
2. Able to punctuate			
a. sentence ends			
b. series			
c. dates			
d. addresses			
e. direct address			
f. direct quotations			
g. abbreviations			
h. appositives			
i. parenthetical expressions			
j. yes/no patterns			
k. letter salutations and closings			
l. subordinating and coordinating patterns			
3. Able to capitalize			
a. sentence beginnings			
b. beginnings of direct quotations			
c. proper nouns			
d. proper adjectives			
e. important title words			
f. titles of distinction			

Figure 11.2
A Writing Conventions Checklist

The child is	Never	Some-times	Always
4. Able to write in paragraph units; specifically he/she			
a. starts a new paragraph to show major thought units or units of conversation			
b. sequences ideas logically within and between paragraphs			
c. uses transitional words to indicate rhetorical relationships among ideas			
d. indents the first word of a paragraph			
5. Able to handle nouns and verbs; specifically he/she			
a. makes verbs agree in number with their subject nouns			
b. uses verb tenses and irregular verbs in a standard way			
c. uses helping verbs, or auxiliaries, in a standard way			
d. handles pronouns in constructions like, "She gave it to Mary and them."			
e. spells contractions correctly			
f. handles negative patterns in a standard way			
g. distinguishes between such word pairs as *teach/learn* in writing			
h. restricts *ain't* to informal speech			

Figure 11.2 (continued)

Language Conventions: Playing with Oral Language

Having identified language conventions that children must control to edit their own writing successfully, how does a teacher structure experiences so that children develop the requisite understandings? Because written language to a great extent reflects the spoken language, a teacher can plan mini-lessons in which children orally play with and hear conventional usage patterns so that those patterns begin to sound natural to them. This is fundamental, especially for children whose first language or dialect is not standard English. In these cases, a teacher invites students first to express an idea in their own dialect and then to translate it into standard English. In this way, they work simultaneously with their *everyday talk* and with *school talk*.

Generating and Reconstructing Sentences   It is relatively easy to begin a mini-lesson with language children generate. For example, if a teacher's goal is to help children feel natural with the sounds of nouns and verbs that agree in number, students can make up sentences that adhere to a simple noun-verb-noun pattern and in which present-tense verbs agree with subject nouns. Children make up sentences modeled after two the teacher supplies:

> Elephants pull logs.   An elephant pulls logs.

Models are printed on sentence strips and taped to the chalkboard. As children generate other sentences following the same pattern, they write them on the board

CONSIDER

A *dialect* is a regional or social variation of a language. *Nonstandard* refers to dialects that differ from those used within the general population.

below the appropriate model, depending on the number of "doers." They speak and respeak the sentences they have generated, gradually becoming more comfortable with the sound of the conventional form.

During a follow-up mini-lesson the next day, the teacher displays the strips containing the sentences children generated previously. Now, however, he or she has clipped the sentences between subject and predicate parts. Children play the Agreeable Sentence Game. Each player gets a subject or predicate part and must find an "agreeable buddy" that "sounds right." Children match up subjects and predicates; they read and reread the results so that the language patterns begin to sound natural to them.

Generalizing Based on Samples Generated   Youngsters generalize after they have generated and played orally with sentences that contain the same usage pattern. For example, having generated sentences about actions they performed yesterday (past tense), students study their samples to figure out what clues signal that the action took place in the past. They generalize that the form of the verb and the word *yesterday* are important clues. To test their generalization, students orally transform their sentences to communicate that the action is occurring today or tomorrow. They compare the verb forms to see how those forms change as the time relationship changes.

Having generalized, young linguists record their statements on chart paper and organize their individual chart pages as a big book called "How to Edit It!" that hangs in the classroom. In editing their compositions, writers flip through the pages for a generalization that guides them in handling a particular usage problem. Generally the big book of language conventions is left open to the page of generalizations most recently recorded by the group.

And, of course, writing follows. For example, having identified clues that tell readers that something occurred in the past, youngsters write biographies set in the past. Having clarified clues that tell readers that something is occurring in the present, youngsters write descriptions of themselves as they currently are. Working in pairs, students edit their writing for consistency in tense.

These examples suggest when and how to structure mini-lessons that develop understanding of conventions that are reflected in speech. Lessons should be based on evidence in children's writing that they have a need for a particular convention. Lessons should include:

1. Generation of language samples that are similar (to ensure a comparison pool, the teacher may provide a pattern for sentence generation).
2. Analysis of the samples to discover common features—how we use language.
3. Recording of generalizations to serve as editing guides.
4. Editing based on the samples and generalizations.

Working from Samples of Written Language

In some instances, as with the placement of punctuation marks inside or outside quotation marks, a language convention is a written one that is more arbitrary than logical. As a result, editors have no intonational clues to guide them in deciding whether to capitalize, how to punctuate, or what form to use. In these cases, children

Distinguished
Educator

can get a handle on a conventional usage pattern by starting with samples from stories they are reading. Studying the samples, young language investigators decide what to do in a particular instance—where to place punctuation markers and whether to capitalize.

Modeling Usage After Story Sources   One way to organize activity with conventions of written language is to supply children sentences from good stories they have read and that have been cut between subjects and predicates. Children reconstruct the cut-up version and repunctuate it using the original as a guide.

An alternative approach is to collect a sampling of sentences from stories in which the language is handled in a similar way—for instance, a group of sentences in which commas separate items in a series or proper nouns are capitalized. Youngsters study the models to determine how to manage this problem in editing. Or from time to time, teachers can ask children to play Donald Graves's Language Conventions Game, which is based on the same kind of activity described in the preceding paragraphs. Figure 11.3 explains how to play.

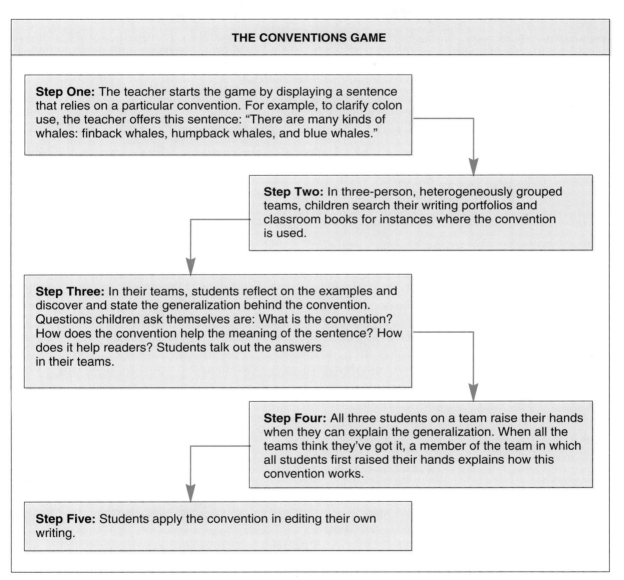

THE CONVENTIONS GAME

Step One: The teacher starts the game by displaying a sentence that relies on a particular convention. For example, to clarify colon use, the teacher offers this sentence: "There are many kinds of whales: finback whales, humpback whales, and blue whales."

Step Two: In three-person, heterogeneously grouped teams, children search their writing portfolios and classroom books for instances where the convention is used.

Step Three: In their teams, students reflect on the examples and discover and state the generalization behind the convention. Questions children ask themselves are: What is the convention? How does the convention help the meaning of the sentence? How does it help readers? Students talk out the answers in their teams.

Step Four: All three students on a team raise their hands when they can explain the generalization. When all the teams think they've got it, a member of the team in which all students first raised their hands explains how this convention works.

Step Five: Students apply the convention in editing their own writing.

Figure 11.3
Donald Graves's Language Conventions Game (Graves, 1994)
Game Time: 10–15 minutes
Frequency of Play: Every 8 to 10 School Days

The Teacher's Message Board

Posted here are ideas for teaching conventions in the context of authentic writing.

- *A class calendar:* Early-primary-graders make a large calendar chart for each month as it arrives and capitalize the name of the month and the days of the week on it. As the days of a month go by, they indicate events in the appropriate blocks, using capitalization where necessary.

- *A class directory:* Middle-graders compile a directory of their names, postal addresses, telephone numbers, and perhaps e-mail addresses. When they do this, students work with capitalization of names, streets, towns, and states, as well as with the punctuation of addresses.

- *A bibliography:* The class compiles a master list of books they have read. Each bibliographic entry should include title, author, and publisher, with capitalization as needed and underscoring of titles. Each time a youngster completes a book not previously read by a classmate, he or she adds an entry to the list, which can be saved in computer memory and periodically printed out.

- *Letters:* Children write letters to students in other schools asking to exchange materials needed for science or social studies, such as leaf, soil, or water samples. They write letters to pen pals, industries, travel bureaus, and agencies. Letter writing requires the punctuation of dates, addresses, salutations, and complimentary closings as well as capitalization of items. If the teacher also composes a letter and does it at the board, his or her letter and envelope serve as models.

- *Summaries:* After children have gone on a field trip, they summarize what they have seen. Serving as scribe, the teacher records sentences on an experience chart. The chart invariably contains items in a series that require commas for separation. On other occasions, the teacher demonstrates how he or she writes a review of the trip by writing his or her thoughts on the board, again with commas to separate items in a series.

- *More summaries:* Children can summarize by enumerating things they have done: games played, books read, activities carried out. Again the result is a series pattern that relies on commas to separate items. Sometimes children dictate a class summary; sometimes the teacher demonstrates how he or she creates a summary by writing in front of the children. Sometimes children write summaries alone or in teams.

- *Still more summaries:* After primary-graders have enjoyed show-and-tell and have listened to a book like Janice Udry's *What Mary Jo Shared*, children can dictate to their teacher a short recap of things shared that day. Participants are more than likely to use possessive forms: Mary Jo's father, Jeff's turtle, Heidi's picture. After other show-and-tell times, children can write individual summaries and edit them for use of the apostrophe to indicate possession, the comma in a series construction, and capitalization for proper names.

- *Editing together:* A teacher can "lift" a paragraph from a student's paper, strip it of punctuation and capitalization, make a transparency of it, and project the paragraph for all to see. Collaboratively, children edit the paragraph based on generalizations they have discovered.

Conventions can be taught on a one-on-one basis to meet individual needs. *(© Susie Fitzhugh)*

Generalizing from Samples in Stories Students generalize based on examples in stories they are reading. For example, they can generalize about *it's* and *its,* from a playful story like this one:

Is It *It's* or Is It *Its?*

"It's a nice day today," said the oak tree to the weeping willow.

The willow shook its branches at the oak and bent its trunk down. "I don't think it's so nice. It looks as if it's about to rain."

The oak waved its highest branches in the air and answered, "It's all in your roots how you view the weather. It's a fine day if you think it is. It's a bit cloudy, but it's spring. Now it's time to wave and toss about." The oak turned its bark upon the weeping willow and waved and tossed its branches higher into the air. "Poor willow!" the oak said to itself. "It's just unfortunate that it cannot forget its troubles and enjoy this fresh spring day."

To guide discovery a teacher asks, "What is the meaning of *it's* in the first sentence? Of *its* in the second sentence?" As is true with homophones, the difference lies in the meaning, which youngsters can figure out for themselves. Having generalized that *it's* is used whenever the meaning is *it is* and *its* is used for ownership, children can check their own first drafts for additional examples.

The structure of this mini-lesson serves as a model for classroom study of a language convention that is not reflected in intonation, although it may have a relationship to meaning. The teacher notices that children need some attention to the convention based on their own usage in writing. As part of workshop, he or she organizes a mini-lesson that includes:

1. A focus on written samples relative to a particular convention.
2. Development of a generalization that explains the samples.
3. Application of the generalization to writing and editing children are doing during workshop.

The immediate application of generalizations about written language conventions to children's writing cannot be overstressed. To encourage this application, the teacher bases mini-lessons and conventions games on children's demonstrated needs. In addition, the teacher may suggest writing options that relate directly to aspects of usage that children have just encountered.

A Warning About Teaching Language Conventions

When involving children with the conventions of language, teachers must remember that the objective is appropriate usage depending on the situation: formal writing, informal writing, formal speech, informal speech. Learning appropriate usage does not come through memorization of rules; rather it comes through considerable oral involvement with forms of language in different communication situations and through editing that requires the conventions.

Accordingly, teachers must take care that stating generalizations does not become the raison d'être—the be all and end all—of language activity. Verbalizing generalizations should simply be a way to sum up what is becoming second nature and to describe the way the language is used. Likewise, teachers should avoid assignments such as, "Memorize the seven uses of the comma," and tests that ask children to list those uses. Bluntly stated, such work is a waste of time.

Grammar: Describing the Language

WORD BANK

Prescriptive grammar
Descriptive grammar
Structural linguistics
Transformational-generative linguistics

Most school language arts programs not only require attention to conventional usage patterns but also introduce youngsters to ways of describing the operations of their language—in other words, *formal grammar*. A grammar describes the syntax of a language—the patterns of sentence and phrase formation in that language.

Robert Hillerich (1985) clarifies the distinction between formal grammar and *usage*. He explains that "grammar has to do with the way words are strung together in order to make intelligible (or 'legal') sentences in the language. 'I brung the pencil' is grammatical; 'I the brung pencil' is not." In contrast, usage is a "matter of language habit" and social acceptability. Hillerich further explains, " 'I don't have a pencil' is socially acceptable usage in school, but 'I ain't got no pencil' is unacceptable."

Traditional, Latin-Based Grammar

For many years, most English grammar was *prescriptive* rather than *descriptive*—hence some educators' confusion of grammar and usage. Early language investigators studied Latin grammar and prescribed how English should be used based on the Latin model. In the 1700s, when a formalized English grammar began to emerge, Latin was believed to be the most eloquent language. Consequently, Latin became the source of precise rules that even today serve in some programs as the content of school grammar.

The problem with this approach is twofold. First, Latin grammar is a poor model for English grammar. Latin is a highly inflectional language. This means that word endings are significant in communicating meaning. In contrast, English depends more on word order than on inflectional endings. Order of words in sentences, not inflectional endings, allows a listener to understand the difference in meaning between "The man killed the tiger" and "The tiger killed the man."

Second, the precise rules devised in the 1700s to describe the language can hardly describe the English of today. Modern linguists accept the fact that language changes. As new words appear, old words acquire new meanings, and others drop from everyday use. It also changes in syntax—the patterns in which speakers put words together. An English grammar must reflect these changes if it is to be accurate. Traditional Latin-based grammar does not.

GO TO

Chapter 3, pages 103 and 106, for a tree and a chart showing that English is a Germanic, not a Romance or Latin-based, language.

Modern-Day Linguistics

The recent past saw the emergence of the scientific study of language: linguistics. Using systematic analysis, *structural linguists* described rather precisely the structures through which speakers communicate meaning in English and the importance of intonation in communication. They also described how we communicate meaning through

- *Sentence patterns:* the order of words in sentences, or the syntax of English.
- *Class words:* nouns, verbs, adjectives, and adverbs.
- *Function words:* words like noun markers, verb markers, phrase markers, clause markers, and question markers that communicate relationships among the four major word classes.
- *Inflectional endings:* endings like the *-s* through which we form a plural noun or the *-ed* we use to show past time.
- *Affixes through which we change words from one class to another:* for example, *govern,* a verb, becomes *government,* a noun, with the addition of the affix *-ment; courage,* a noun, becomes *courageous,* an adjective, with the addition of the affix *-ous.*

To describe English using these features, the structural linguists devised a vocabulary for talking about the language. Instead of talking about only eight parts of speech, linguists recognize four major *word classes*—nouns, verbs, adjectives, and adverbs—and *function words*—prepositions, determiners, pronouns or noun substitutes, auxiliaries, intensifiers, and conjunctions.

Structural linguists also approach the definitions of parts of speech from a different perspective. No longer is a noun defined simply as the name of a person, place, or thing. The structuralists prefer to talk about clues that help distinguish among words as those words work in sentences—clues such as affixes and inflections associated with a particular part of speech, the characteristic positions in a sentence occupied by a part of speech, and the function words that pattern with a particular part of speech. See Figure 11.4 for greater clarification.

More recently, language study has assumed another orientation. Using some of the terminology of the structuralists as well as their analytical approach, *transformational-generative linguists* have described the way speakers use language to generate, or produce, sentences. These linguists have identified basic, or kernel, sentence patterns to describe English syntax and have described the ways speakers expand the basic patterns and the ways speakers transform sentences into questions, commands, and negative statements. They have explained how people insert or embed one sentence in another to produce more complex sentences. The ideas on pages 403–408 of this chapter are derived from transformational-generative linguistics.

Linguistics in the Elementary Grades

Which—if any—aspects of linguistics should be included in the elementary language arts curriculum? To answer this question, teachers must consider why children learn formal grammar in the first place. As we noted earlier, most research indicates that knowing about nouns, verbs, clauses, and phrases makes little difference in children's ability to read and write. No, schools do not teach formal grammar to help young people communicate more effectively. Rather, schools teach grammar to give children the terminology to use in talking about their language as they edit and to help them appreciate and understand the way their language works.

Defending the teaching of grammar from a descriptive perspective, Patrick Groff (1980) argues: "Why cannot modern grammar be defended in the same manner as is other science instruction? We would not dismiss teaching about the circulatory system, for example, because of a complaint that such instruction does not make students' blood flow more properly. Accordingly, one may legitimately argue that a body of scientific knowledge as intrinsically human as is the understanding of how people form intelligible sentences surely is worthy of inclusion in the school curriculum at some level."

Teachers who accept some part of Groff's argument but also believe that the primary goal of the language arts is the ability to communicate effectively are more than likely to be minimalists about the place of formal grammar in the curriculum. Minimalists believe that only aspects of linguistics that contribute to a very general understanding of the structure of English should be taught at the elementary level; some contend that instruction in formal grammar should start not at the elementary but at the secondary level. Teachers who are minimalists limit terminology to words needed to talk about basic aspects of language: names of parts of speech (*noun, verb, singular,* and *plural*) and fundamental terms used to talk about sentences (words such as *subject, predicate,* and *independent clause*). They select content from modern-

	NOUNS	**VERBS**
TRADITIONAL, MEANING-BASED DEFINITION	A noun is the name of a person, place, or thing. In the sentence, ***The horse galloped,*** *horse* is a noun because it names a thing.	A verb indicates action or state of being. In the sentence, ***The horse galloped,*** *galloped* is a verb because it indicates the action in the sentence. In the sentence, ***The horse is brown,*** *is* is a verb because it indicates the state of the horse.
FUNCTION-BASED DEFINITION	A noun functions as the simple subject of a sentence, the object of the verb or preposition, or the verb complement. In the sentence, ***The horse galloped,*** *horse* is a noun because it functions as the simple subject. In the sentence, ***I saw a horse,*** *horse* is a noun because it functions as the object of the verb. In the sentence, ***I gave the horse an apple,*** *horse* is the noun because it functions as the indirect object. In the sentence, ***I rode on the horse,*** *horse* is a noun because it functions as the object of the preposition. In the sentence, ***Jack is a horse,*** *horse* is a noun because it functions as the verb complement.	The verb functions as the simple predicate of a sentence. In the sentence, ***The horse galloped,*** *galloped* is a verb because it is functioning as the simple predicate.
STRUCTURE-BASED DEFINITION	A noun patterns after a determiner or noun marker, which signals that a noun is coming. In the sentence, ***The horse galloped,*** *the* signals that a noun (*horse*) is coming. Other noun marking words include *this, that, these, those, his, her, two, four.* Substitute *the, a, an* to test for nounness.	A verb patterns with helping verbs as in these sentences, **The horse has galloped, The horse will gallop, The horse was galloping.**
INFLECTIONAL-FORM-BASED DEFINITION	A noun can change its form to tell more than one (plural form). In the sentence, ***The horse galloped,*** *horse* is a noun because we can change the sentence to show more than one by changing *horse* to *horses.* A noun can change its form to show possession.	A verb changes form to indicate time or tense. **The horse gallops today; it galloped yesterday.** (Note that some verbs have the same present and past tense forms, as with the verb *hit.* Also the *s* on *gallops* does not indicate more than one.)
WORD-BUILDING-BASED DEFINITION	Some suffixes mark nouns: *-ment* as in *government, -tion* as in *addition, -ness* as in *happiness,* but there are exceptions.	Some suffixes indicate that a word is a verb: *-fy* as in *identify, -ize* as in *generalize, -ate* as in *remediate.*

Figure 11.4
Overview of Two Basic Class Words

DISCUSSION PROMPT

■ Extend this chart to include the same kind of information about adjectives and adverbs where appropriate.

Meet Constance Weaver

Constance Weaver is a professor of English at Western Michigan University. She teaches courses in reading and writing processes and is herself a prolific writer. Her book *Teaching Grammar in Context* (1996) is considered a major contribution to the field of grammar instruction. In this book, Weaver explains her minimalist theory of grammar instruction: "When explaining various aspects of grammar, usage, and punctuation to help students with their writing, minimize the use of grammatical terminology and maximize the use of examples. Teach the minimal terminology primarily by using it in a functional context and through brief lessons as necessary, rather than through memorization of definitions and the analysis of sentences. . . . We should ponder, consider or reconsider the experimental research evidence, and rethink the what, why, and how of our teaching of grammar. . . . Studying grammar as a system, in isolation from its use, is not in fact the best use of instructional time if better writing (or reading) is the intended goal of grammar study. . . . In general, analyzing language—the focus of traditional grammar instruction—is much less helpful to writers than a focus on sentence generating, combining, and manipulating" (*Teaching Grammar in Context* [Portsmouth, N.H.: Heinemann, 1996], 26, 28, 179).

DISCUSSION PROMPT

What does Weaver mean by a minimalist theory of grammar? How does she propose that grammar be taught? Do you agree with her? Why? Why not? Is the teaching of grammar in elementary schools as important as the teaching of communication?

day linguistics that lends itself easily to firsthand manipulation—expanding, cutting-to-the-core, rearranging, substituting. In short, they build a curriculum in which students play "with the 'material' of language to find out what it will and won't do, and what happens when you change some piece" (Hutson, 1980).

Ways to Teach Grammar Opportunistically

Regardless of what you and I might believe about the teaching of formal grammar at the elementary level, most elementary language arts programs have a formal grammar component and many states test students' knowledge of how English works. Given that, we must turn to the next question: How does the teacher involve children in basic grammar—particularly the parts of speech—without diminishing children's delight in language and expression? The answer lies in literature-based activities and mini-lessons in which the teacher uses simple grammatical terms to talk about those samples and children pick up on that terminology as they talk about the way their language works. The answer also lies in referring to the way words function in sentences and using basic grammatical terminology even as children edit and read.

Literature-Based Beginnings   Many schools introduce first-graders to nouns and verbs and second-graders to adjectives and adverbs despite the fact that introduction of grammatical concepts at this level is hard to justify because of young children's difficulty in handling abstractions. If, however, the primary-grade teacher is required to introduce the parts of speech, she or he can do so incidentally as a follow-up to a read-aloud.

Marylou Gillikin uses Eric Carle's *The Very Hungry Caterpillar* as a starting point with her first-graders since introductory work with nouns and verbs is required in her school curriculum. She reads the story aloud and involves children first in a discussion of story meanings. As follow-up, Ms. Gillikin and her students interactively make a phrase chart that lists the things that the caterpillar ate: one apple, two pears, three plums, four strawberries, one piece of pie, one ice cream cone. As students recall items, they list them in two columns, the first labeled *one,* the second labeled *more than one.* The students then draw pictures of other things the caterpillar might have eaten, organizing their pictures on their papers in two labeled clusters: *one* and *more than one.* As students share their words and pictures, this creative first-grade teacher opportunistically begins to use the term *noun* to refer to words that *"change to tell more than one."*

Going on to enjoy other picture storybooks, the first-graders read the titles to find more words that can change to show *one* or *more than one* to add to their noun charts. For example, as their Eric Carle author unit develops, Ms. Gillikin's students read *The Very Quiet Cricket, The Mixed-up Chameleon, The Grouchy Ladybug, The Very Busy Spider,* and *Pancakes, Pancakes!* Meeting these books, they add *cricket/ crickets, chameleon/chameleons, ladybug/ladybugs, spider/spiders,* and *pancake/pancakes* next to one another on their noun chart. Finishing *Pancakes, Pancakes!* they list all the noun words that go into making pancakes on their chart: *the flour, an egg, the milk, the butter, a bowl, a cup, a spoon, a pan.* In the process, they use grammatical terminology—*noun, singular, plural*—correctly to talk about their words. They use these same grammatical terms as they talk about the nouns they meet in Ruth Heller's *Merry-Go-Round: A Book of Nouns* (1990), which this teacher likes to share in its big book form.

On future occasions as students respond to other stories, they expand their noun charts with additional pictures and words, and they categorize story items in the same way: *one* versus *more than one.* Their teacher continues to refer to words that name these items as *nouns* and to use *singular* when she is talking about oneness and *plural* when talking about more than one. In Ms. Gillikin's class, first-graders pick up on and use these terms just as naturally as they acquire less abstract vocabulary words.

Gillikin's findings are in keeping with those of Constance Weaver and Katie Wood Ray. Weaver (1996) suggests that much grammatical terminology "can be learned sufficiently just through incidental exposure—for example, as we discuss selected words and structures in the context of literature and writing" (p. 144). Ray (1999) concurs, proposing that when grammatical terms are embedded in class talk about reading and writing, children pick them up "almost effortlessly, as they do most new words used in sensible ways within real contexts." When, for example, Ray's kindergartners indicate their appreciation of the word *luscious,* she comments, "Oh, yeah, that's an adjective. It tells how something is. Isn't that one wonderful!" (p. 22). In this way, Ray throws "in grammatical names for anything five-year-olds notice" (p. 43). As she explains, "Grammatical names for things are useful. They make it easier to talk about writing. 'Adjective' is easier to say than 'a word that describes a noun'" (p. 44).

Word Study Mini-Lessons   Another way to reinforce children's growing ability to use grammatical terminology to describe the way their language works is through active word study. For instance, in Ms. Gillikin's school district, the distinction between common and proper nouns is part of the required first-grade curriculum. At some point, therefore, after students have begun to use the term *noun* to describe words they are reading in stories, Ms. Gillikin comes in wearing two labels. On her back, she wears the label *the teacher,* on her chest, (with appropriate capital letters) *Ms. Gillikin.* Children create similar labels for themselves (a student/Timothy, a friend/Martha, a reader/Bruce), affix them to their bodies, and wear them all day. The teacher begins to refer to the children's specific names as proper nouns and their general names as common nouns. In a clue-about-language mini-lesson, she draws their attention to the capitalization differences. Now as students listen to stories, they assume the common-noun name and proper-noun name of a character, labeling themselves with those names using the upper-case first letter correctly: the teacher/Miss Nelson; the substitute/Miss Swamp; a student/Melissa.

Similarly, Phyllis Bartkus helps her second-graders to deepen their understanding of nounness by asking each of four children to come forward and wear one of these cards around their necks:

To the other students, she distributes cards labeled with words that can function as nouns in that sentence: *dog, horse, car, friend, boy, fox, teacher, tail, problem, house, toy, bone, box,* and so forth. On the reverse of each noun card is the word in its plural form. One child wears the label *some.* Children physically build sentences using their words, coming forward to join the sentence "train," reversing their noun cards to show more than one, and even creating new cards with adjectives that they add to their growing sentences in the favorite position of describing words—before the noun.

In mini-lessons that follow, students do much the same using other sentence-building patterns: *The _____ jumped. The _____ flew into the _____.* In this context, students may create sentence ladders that highlight the part of speech as shown in Figure 11.5. It is at this point that Ms. Bartkus adds the traditional definition of a noun to children's growing concept of nounness: the name of a person, place, or thing.

Shortly, this teacher develops the same kinds of language plays based on verb functioning. Students play orally with the frame *Charlotte _____.* They brainstorm words that can fit in the empty verb slot and tell what Charlotte did yesterday. They record their words on cards and then turn the cards over and record on the back what spiders do today. Working on several occasions with related test frames such as *The pig _____. The rat _____ the grain,* they

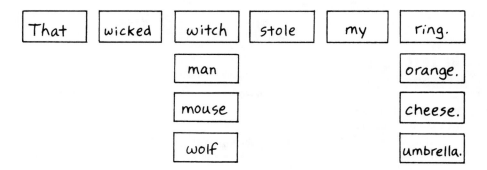

Figure 11.5
A Sentence Ladder

begin to use the term *verb* to talk about words that tell what the noun is doing and that change form to tell the time when an action occurs.

To help her second-graders understand the power of verbs, Ms. Bartkus shares Ruth Heller's *Kites Sail High: A Book About Verbs* (1988) in big book form. Having listened to this book, students talk about some of the energetic verbs that Heller has used. They talk about using energetic verbs in their own stories and compose a class book in the manner of Heller's.

On another occasion, second-graders play with these word and labeling cards: words—*The wind, blew, with terrific force, here, in the early morning;* labels—*What, What happened, How, Where, When.* Together they build a sentence from the word cards, label the meaningful parts, and decide on the subject noun and on the verb that tells what the subject is doing. Students make additional labels (*subject noun* and *verb*) and use those to identify the key parts of this sentence as shown here:

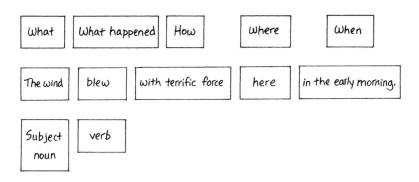

Talking about their sentence-building activity, the teacher begins to use the phrase *subject noun,* and the students pick it up and use it too.

As follow-up, teams of children generate additional sentences, write the words on paper strips, label themselves with the strips, and clarify the function of each of the word units by placing themselves beneath the appropriate *What, What happened, How, Where,* and *When* labels. Middle-grade students who have begun to develop an understanding

The Teacher's Message Board

Posted here are kinds of formula poems (after Koch, 1980) that allow teachers and students to use grammatical terminology to talk about word patterns. Formula poems are pieces written with the architecture of poetry but generally adhere to rather strict construction guidelines.

- *I wish . . . poems.* Each line begins with the pronoun *I* and the verb *wish.*
- *Color poems.* Each line begins with a noun-color word and the verb *is,* as in *Red is . . .*
- *Definition poems.* Each line begins with a noun and the verb *is,* as in *Love is . . .* or *War is . . .*
- *Prepositional phrase poems.* Each line is simply a prepositional phrase. The phrase lines lead up to a final thought as in *In the dark / of the night, / Through my dreams / of days / of joy, / I rest.*
- *If I were . . . poems, When I was . . . poems, After I learned . . . poems, Before I knew . . . poems, Because I am . . . poems, Since I believe . . . poems.* Each line starts with a dependent clause that contains the patterned words. The final line gives the independent clause as in these lines: *Before I knew how to talk, / Before I knew how to feel, / Before I knew how to love, / I could not tell you, "I love you."*

of adverbs and prepositional phrases can shift the *How, Where,* and *When* units around in the sentences they have written. In the process they perceive the impact that such shifts have on sentence meaning and see that one of the characteristics of adverbs and prepositional phrases is that these grammatical structures often are movable.

Patterned Writing   Another activity for reinforcing children's growing understanding of parts of speech is patterned writing. Students who have been playing with adjectives and adverbs and have read Heller's books that use these parts of speech in creative ways (*Many Luscious Lollipops: A Book About Adjectives,* 1989, and *Up, Up and Away: A Book About Adverbs,* 1991) can write their own books in which they use adjectives and adverbs creatively. Students who have begun to develop a concept of prepositional phrases can write original journey stories patterned after *Rosie's Walk* (Hutchins, 1968). In the same way, students who are playing with imperative verbs can write books modeled after *Jump, Frog, Jump!* (Kalan, 1989) and poems modeled after some of Langston Hughes's dream poems ("Dream Dust," "Dreams," "The Dream Keeper"). This kind of writing can be offered as an option after students have listened to and talked about a story or poem.

An excellent poem for patterned writing and for reinforcing understanding of nouns and adjectives is "Beans, Beans, Beans" from *Hooray for Chocolate* by Lucia and James Hymes. Eileen Hoernlein uses it with her second-graders to reinforce their developing understanding of nouns and adjectives. Here is an example of a piece created by a second-grader that follows the Hymes's pattern and that can be used to talk about noun and adjective functioning:

Bugs,
Bugs,
Bugs,
Bad bugs,
Spider bugs,
Daddy long leg bugs,
Dead, smushed up bugs—
Those are just a few.
Cockroach bugs,
Green bugs,
Brown, yellow, black bugs,
Lightning bugs, too.
Don't forget ant bugs.
Last of all, best of all,
I like ladybugs!

  MICHAEL ROBINSON

  The *diamanté* provides a similar pattern for writing, also based on parts of speech. As made clear in the example in Figure 11.6 and in the following sample, the diamanté is a study in contrasts: The last word of the poem, a noun, represents an opposite of the first word, also a noun; adjectives, participles, and nouns in the first half refer to the first noun whereas the words in the second half refer to the last noun.

<table>
<tr><td>*King*</td><td>*noun*</td></tr>
<tr><td>*Rich, Powerful*</td><td>*adjective, adjective*</td></tr>
<tr><td>*Demanding, Commanding, Ruling*</td><td>*-ing, -ing, -ing*</td></tr>
<tr><td>*Leader, Royalty, Low, Peasant*</td><td>*noun, noun, noun, noun*</td></tr>
<tr><td>*Working, Obeying, Despairing*</td><td>*-ing, -ing, -ing*</td></tr>
<tr><td>*Poor, Powerless*</td><td>*adjective, adjective*</td></tr>
<tr><td>*Slave*</td><td>*noun*</td></tr>
<tr><td>*—JOSEPH BORES*</td><td></td></tr>
</table>

  A truncated diamanté centering on one object works equally well. Such a form also introduces youngsters to the simile and the metaphor, for in putting together a last line, they must dream up a creative comparison.

<table>
<tr><td>*Icicle—*</td><td>*noun—*</td></tr>
<tr><td>*Cold, hard, glassy,*</td><td>*adjective, adjective, adjective*</td></tr>
<tr><td>*Shining, dripping, breaking:*</td><td>*participle, participle, participle:*</td></tr>
<tr><td>*Winter's sword.*</td><td>*creative comparison*</td></tr>
</table>

Literature-Based Grammar in Upper Grades Sharon Kane (1997) recommends a creative approach for integrating grammatical considerations into literature studies in upper elementary grades—an approach that simultaneously introduces students to

Figure 11.6
A Group Diamanté
Courtesy of Louise Patterson

style in writing. She shares particularly effective opening and last sentences from stories and chapter books, lines in which favorite authors make characters come alive, and passages in which authors use repetition of words or grammatical structures purposefully. Upper-graders listen to and talk about how the author has used language effectively to create a mood or communicate ideas; in the process, they rely on grammatical terms (*adjectives, verbs, adverbs, prepositional phrases*) to make their points. Later in their independent reading, students identify verbs that make a chapter exciting, expressive adjectives that an author uses to describe the characters and setting, and any series of adverbs or prepositional phrases that set up a rhythm in the text.

For example, in one classroom a literature group compared Patricia MacLachlan's use of color-designating adjectives in the first and third chapters of *Sarah, Plain and Tall* and made a chart of those words. Doing this, they discovered that MacLachlan used color-designating adjectives sparingly in the first chapter, lavishly in the third. "Why did she do that?" the literature group asked. The students hypothesized that Sarah came in the third chapter with her yellow bonnet, bringing color with her into the children's lives.

Another group searched the book for the noun *sea* and discovered that the author used that noun in every chapter. "Why did she keep repeating that noun?" the group also asked. These students hypothesized that the author was making a connection between the "ocean" sea and the sea of grass of the prairie; they decided that the sea was a metaphor for family and "belongingness." Another group searched for flower names (all nouns); another titled each chapter with a determiner and noun that together recapped an important person, place, happening, or thing within the chapter; other groups titled the chapters with verbs or prepositional phrases. These examples demonstrate that as children read, they can expand their understanding of the way their language works and their ability to use grammatical terminology even as they are broadening their understanding of author style.

A slightly different way to integrate grammatical considerations into literature studies is through vocabulary explorations. As part of their reading of a story or chapter book, some teachers ask students to be on the lookout for several words that are new to them. Students jot them down with page numbers. During follow-up discussion, students share their new words. The class uses context clues and word elements to figure out the meaning of each unfamiliar word and decides how it is functioning in the sentence—as a noun, verb, adjective, or adverb. With one student serving as scribe, students formulate a definition, including a part of speech designation. The result is an entry into the cumulative vocabulary chart book, which is exhibited in the classroom as an aid to vocabulary development. Figure 11.7 is an example of a word chart based on Chapter 9 of *Maniac Magee.*

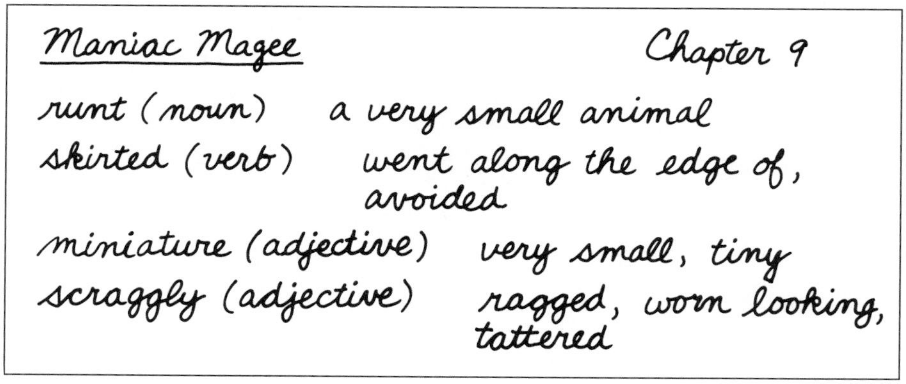

Figure 11.7
A Word Chart Based on a Chapter from *Maniac Magee*

Maniac Magee   Chapter 9

runt (noun)   a very small animal
skirted (verb)   went along the edge of, avoided
miniature (adjective)   very small, tiny
scraggly (adjective)   ragged, worn looking, tattered

The Teacher's Message Board

Teach grammatical terminology opportunistically in these ways.

- **Shared or independent writing:** Students can recap a chapter of a novel they are reading by dictating or writing what each major character does in that chapter. They use the term *proper noun* in referring to a character's name and *verb* in referring to the word that tells what the character does in the chapter.

- **Shared or independent writing:** Students can write brief paragraphs in which they describe a character or place from a story or chapter they have just read. In talking about their paragraphs after having written them jointly or independently, students can explain why they chose particular adjectives to include in their descriptions. Others can comment on why the adjectives chosen are effective.

- **Patterned writing:** Students can write "people couplets" about either story characters or people they know. Each line of a people couplet tells what the person does; the result is a simple noun/verb pattern as shown here in an expanded version that includes an adjective and an adverb:

Our People Poem

Cheerful Anne softly sings.   Loud Joey always talks.
Fast Debbie gracefully springs.   Jolly Mika happily walks.

Speedy Greg quickly races.   Careful Diane leisurely jots.
Talented Alicia accurately traces.   Mysterious Susie cautiously plots.

See Lucy Sprague Mitchell's "Jump or Jiggle" in *Another Here and Now Story Book* (Dutton, 1937) for a model of a simple plural noun/verb poem that works well as a context for opportunistic use of the words *noun* and *verb,* and *subject* and *predicate.* The poem starts: "Frogs jump./ Caterpillars hump." The result is an action poem that clarifies the way in which verbs must agree with their subject nouns.

- **Modeled writing:** When children have listened to or read a piece that incorporates a particular usage convention, they can talk about that convention afterward. For example, having enjoyed Eve Merriam's poem "The Cat Sat on the Mat," in which there are lines such as "They frisk. / They scramble. / They tickle. / They tangle," students can talk about the way the verbs are all the same and agree with the plural subjects. Together they can orally write a singular list poem that might begin with "My cat snarls. / My cat purrs." In this context, discussion and application of singular and plural noun forms are natural. Students also apply the underlying generalization as they individually compose singular or plural list poems.

Grammar and Revision Of course, the best context for enriching children's growing concepts of basic class words and prepositional phrases is during an editing workshop or conference. During editing—class or individual—the teacher can ask, "Can you substitute a more explosive or precise verb?" At the same time, young writers can make charts of explosive verbs to substitute for weaker ones: for the word *went,* children chart words like *ran, hustled, bolted, streaked,* and *sped;* for a verb like *looked,* children chart words like *stared, glared, peeked.* At the same time, they can pantomime action verbs like *hobbled, bowed,* and *swayed.*

In like manner, a teacher can help young writers to revise their early drafts by adding or deleting adjectives, moving adverbs and prepositional phrases, and checking agreement of subject nouns and predicate verbs. In making these suggestions, the teacher should use the terms *agreement, noun, verb, adjective, adverb,* and *prepositional phrase* so that children begin to use those terms to talk about their writing.

A Summary Thought or Two

Language Conventions and Grammar

The primary goal of language arts programs is that children grow in their ability to communicate effectively and in their appreciation and enjoyment of literature—hence the title of this book, *Communication in Action: Teaching Literature-Based Language Arts.* One component of this overarching goal is that children refine their ability to handle the sentence and the conventional usage patterns of English, especially their ability to control punctuation, capitalization, and noun/verb agreement patterns as they write. To this end, teachers need to organize workshops during which children have plenty of time to draft, revise, and edit. To this end, also, teachers need to schedule mini-lessons during workshop periods; within a mini-lesson, students play orally with a particular sentence pattern or language convention, applying their growing understanding as they edit what they are drafting.

Another goal—a lesser one in importance—is that children understand the way their language works, or the grammar of their language. Studying grammar, children see sentences in terms of nouns, verbs, adjectives, adverbs, and other parts of speech. Teachers can schedule mini-lessons in which children orally play with these parts of the language, integrating such study with children's writing and their reading of fine literature. But as John Banitz (1998) warns, "Too much classroom time spent on grammatical analysis is time not spent on writing and reading natural discourse of authentic texts. . . . Too much time spent on grammar exercises is time not spent on learning language functions and strategies." Teachers must remember that the ultimate goal of the language arts is the development of children who not only are able to read, write, speak, listen, and think but who find great joy in all manner of language involvement.

Your Language Arts Portfolio

■ Write a series of plans for mini-lessons in which you introduce children to a particular writing convention, such as commas in a series, the capitalization of place names, the use of the semicolon in compound sentences. Follow the guidelines in the chapter.

After reading a short story or a chapter of a novel, upper-graders refine their under-standing of parts of speech by considering the author's style—his or her use of descriptive adjectives, intensifying adverbs, and expansive prepositional phrases.
(© Elizabeth Crews)

- Reread something of substance that you have written recently. Look for instances of fragments, run-ons, and comma splices. Put some time in editing and revising. Include your successive drafts in your professional portfolio.

Related Readings

Barnitz, John. "Revising Grammar Instruction for Authentic Composing and Comprehending." *The Reading Teacher,* 51 (April 1998), 608–610.

Clark, Roy Peter. "Editing." In *Free to Write.* Portsmouth, N.H.: Heinemann, 1987.

Graves, Donald. "Help Children Learn Conventions." Chapter 12 in *A Fresh View of Writing.* Portsmouth, N.H.: Heinemann, 1994.

———. "Sharing the Tools of the Writing Trade." *Instructor,* 105 (November/December 1995), 38–43. See also the special note on Graves's "If You Write, They Will Too." *Instructor,* 105 (January/February 1996), 40–41.

Hall, Nigel, and Anne Robinson, eds. *Learning About Punctuation.* Avon, England: Multilingual Matters Ltd., 1995.

Hillerich, Robert. "Dealing with Grammar." In *Teaching Children to Write, K–8.* Englewood Cliffs, N.J.: Prentice-Hall, 1985.

Invernizzi, Marcia, et al. "Integrated Word Study: Spelling, Grammar, and Meaning in the Language Arts Classroom." *Language Arts,* 74 (March 1997), 185–192.

Kane, Sharon. "Favorite Sentences: Grammar in Action." *The Reading Teacher,* 51 (September 1997), 70–73.

Killgallon, Don. *Sentence Composing for Middle School: A Worktext on Sentence Variety and Maturity.* Westport, Conn.: Heinemann, 1997.

Kirby, Dan, et al. "Beyond Interior Decorating: Using Writing to Make Meaning in the Elementary School." *Phi Delta Kappan,* 69 (June 1988), 718–724.

Noguchi, Rei. *Grammar and the Teaching of Writing: Limits and Possibilities.* Urbana, Ill.: National Council of Teachers of English, 1991.

Simmons, John, and Lawrence Baines, eds. *Language Study in Middle School, High School, and Beyond.* Newark, Del.: International Reading Association, 1998.

Strong, William. *Creative Approaches to Sentence Combining.* Urbana, Ill.: National Council of Teachers of English, 1986.

Terban, Marvin. *Punctuation Power: Punctuation and How to Use It.* New York: Scholastic, 2000. (This is a punctuation handbook geared for upper elementary students.)

Weaver, Constance. *Teaching Grammar in Context.* Portsmouth, N.H.: Heinemann, 1996.

———. *Lessons to Share on Teaching Grammar in Context.* Westport, Conn.: Heinemann, 1998.

Wilde, Sandra. *You Kan Red This! Spelling and Punctuation for Whole Language Classrooms, K–6.* Portsmouth, N.H.: Heinemann, 1991.

CHAPTER 12

Spelling, Dictionary Use, and Handwriting

Tools of the Editor's Craft

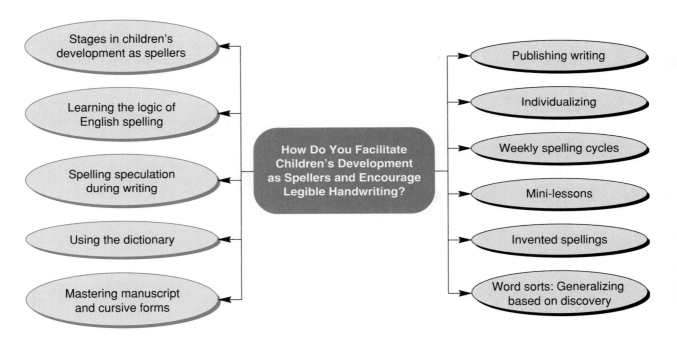

Stages in children's development as spellers

Learning the logic of English spelling

Spelling speculation during writing

Using the dictionary

Mastering manuscript and cursive forms

How Do You Facilitate Children's Development as Spellers and Encourage Legible Handwriting?

Publishing writing

Individualizing

Weekly spelling cycles

Mini-lessons

Invented spellings

Word sorts: Generalizing based on discovery

Spelling in Action   *Spelling Patterns and Writing*

Monday morning! Fred Bronsky's third-graders had entered their room a bit tired and quiet. By ten-thirty they had come to life, so Mr. Bronsky called nine youngsters to the spelling table for a mini-lesson. To start, he asked two students to read aloud pieces they had been writing and explain how they had figured out the spelling of words during proofreading. He asked several others to share words from their writing that they were unsure of; other students in the group suggested spellings for dictionary checking.

Sorting

Look at words with an analytic, appreciative eye; recognize words with structural similarities

Then Mr. Bronsky spread some cards face down and said, "Let's play Word Sorts. Do you recall the rules?" One student explained that players took turns turning over word cards. When they had figured out how the words on the cards were the same, they took a number to show when they had figured it out and turned their backs so they didn't see any more clues.

At that point, the game began. Tom turned over *dark.* Marcia turned over *stars.* Bruce uncovered *porch.* Jack turned over *born.* Pete turned up *door.* Suddenly Marcia's hand shot out to take number one from the pack of cards; then she turned her back. As *Mars, floor, start, lark,* and *story* appeared, other children took numbers and turned away so that they could not see additional clues. They had to figure out the shared feature based on the cards seen at the point when they took a number.

"O.K. Write the word *hypothesis* on a slip of paper, figuring out the spelling using any clues you can think of. Then record your hypothesis, or best guess, about how the words are the same." The children speculated about the spelling of *hypothesis* and wrote their hypotheses regarding the shared feature on strips to which they added their order number. Strips went down on the table and students compared them. They had all figured it out: The words contained a vowel -*r* spelling. "Great!" rewarded Mr. Bronsky, who declared the youngster with the lowest number card the winner.

"Now let's sort the words into related piles." On the desk he placed *stars.* "Pick a word that goes with *stars.*" Five hands shot across the desk to add *dark, start, chart, short,* and *bark.* "All but one!" One hand snaked out to pull *short* from the group. "Explain why." Bruce explained that *short* did not have an *ar.* Ronald added that the word did not have the same sound as the others. With the word *short,* Ronald began a second pile, words that contained *or.* On the spot, the third-graders made labeling cards (*ar* words /är/, *or* words /ôr/) and added them to the applicable piles (see Figure 12.1).

● ● ● ●

CONSIDER

Sorting activities teach that words are objects that can be examined (Henderson, 1990). They can be part of literature and content-area studies. For example, students can sort and search for other /är/ words as they enjoy *Number the Stars,* the title of which contains an /är/ word.

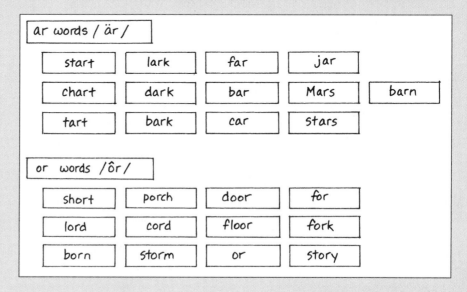

Figure 12.1
Sorted Word Cards

Mr. Bronsky gathered the word cards and handed them to Pete to read without showing the cards to the others. As Pete read, the eight other students pointed to either the *ar* or the *or* label. Pete checked to see whether the letters on the word card corresponded to the letters on the labeling card before placing it in the pile indicated by the pointers. Because a few children pointed incorrectly, the group repeated the activity.

Generalizing About Sound-Symbol Relationships

"Before we pretest on these words," Mr. Bronsky continued, "we'll talk about how in writing we spell words that have the sound as in *bar* and *car* or the sound as in *for* and *door*. When we hear the final sound in *bar*, what letters do we use to represent the sound on paper?"

Pete volunteered, "*Ar.*"

Mr. Bronsky replied, "Give that idea in a sentence, Pete, and put a couple of examples in the sentence." When Pete gave his sentence, Marcia recorded it as Pete's Generalization in the spelling book the group was writing. Because this was a publication copy, she used her best handwriting:

> Pete's Generalization:
>
> We use the letters <u>ar</u> to spell /är/ in words like <u>bar</u> and <u>car</u>.

Robin contributed the next generalization without prompting, modeling hers after Pete's:

> Robin's Generalization:
>
> We use the letters <u>or</u> to spell /ôr/ in words like <u>for</u> and <u>door</u>.

Mr. Bronsky urged, "Look at all our /ôr/ words; in some cases, the symbol is not just *or.*"

Bruce saw the point and amended Robin's generalization by adding "and sometimes *oor.*" He added the generalization to the group's spelling chart book.

Then the youngsters took a pretest as the teacher dictated the list of structurally related words they had been analyzing: *star, start, dark, fork, floor,* and so forth. Students corrected their papers by checking their spellings against those on the game cards and writing the correct spellings next to any incorrect ones.

At that point, Mr. Bronsky had the children compare their spellings of *hypothesis.* Because there were several spellings, the children explained the reasoning behind their inventions. Finally, the Dictionary Sleuth for the day conducted a dictionary search, guided by the other children's suggestions to look first under *highpo-*, then *hipo-*, and finally *hypo-*. Mr. Bronsky summarized, "When I draft ideas during writing, I give longer and harder words my best shot, sounding them out and breaking them into syllables. Often I know that I don't have the spelling right, but that I will go back to check during editing. As I proofread, I circle the words I speculate may be misspelled and check them in the dictionary. Doing this, I identify the various ways a speech sound is recorded on paper. I say to myself, 'That sound could be spelled this way, this way, or even this way. I look up each possible spelling until I find the dictionary spelling.' I think through possible spellings in this way when I proofread. I don't do it while I am drafting because it breaks my train of thought." With that, the third-graders went to their places to write and/or read independently, re-sort the /är/ and /ôr/ words into related groups, and dictate those words to one another.

Components of the Lesson

Fred Bronsky's mini-lesson on a within-word spelling pattern took less than fifteen minutes. During that time, he

1. Helped children edit spellings of words from their writing.
2. Presented children with words that share a relationship.
3. Helped them to sort those words based on similarities and differences.
4. Asked children to state generalizations discovered through analysis of the word sorts.
5. Dictated a list of words related to the generalizations and had children correct their spellings.
6. Modeled a strategy for using one's understanding of sound-symbol relationships to invent spellings while drafting and checking one's inventions against the dictionary while proofreading.

DISCUSSION PROMPT

■ How does this word-study approach to spelling differ from traditional instruction? What are the advantages?

A teacher can use these steps to structure spelling lessons in which children develop an understanding of word patterns and relationships and the ability to invent spellings as a basis for dictionary checking while proofreading. Mr. Bronsky uses these steps because he believes that there is a logic to English spelling, which—if understood—can help children spell well. He also believes that spelling is for writing and it is his job to help children apply their understanding as they write.

What We Know About Spelling Development

The components of a spelling lesson just outlined are founded on current research and theory on how English words are spelled and how children develop as spellers. During the last thirty years, researchers have discovered much about how children develop as spellers. Through their studies of children's invented spellings, researchers such as Edmund Henderson (1990), Charles Read (1971), Darrell Morris (1983), Shane Templeton (1979), Charles Temple et al. (1988), and Marie

Clay (1975) have identified stages through which children progress as they master the spelling of words. Henderson (1990) has categorized these stages as (1) preliterate spelling, (2) letter name spelling, (3) within-word pattern spelling, (4) syllable juncture spelling, and (5) derivational and meaning-based spelling. In this section, we will examine this knowledge base.

Preliterate Spelling

GO TO

Pages 324–332 for more on emergent writing.

As we noted in Chapter 9, if very young children are given a pencil, they "write." At first they make random markings that are more like drawings than writing (Gill, 1992; see Figure 12.2). But at some point children begin to handle the pencil in a way different from that used in drawing (Henderson, 1990). They make markings from left to right, write in left-to-right waves, and incorporate letter- and number-like forms. They ask for letters to write their names; and, in turn, if someone asks them to write a word, they record a letter—the initial consonant of that word or what they hear as the initial consonant. For example, they may write *monster* as *m*, *dressing* as *jr*, *bottom* as *b*. Henderson and his associates describe children who perform in this manner as *preliterate* spellers. Children at this stage "know what writing is and what it does." They know the difference between writing and pictures and imitate writing in creative ways. They do not yet, however, write words with beginnings and endings; in short, they do not have a concept of what a word is (see Figure 12.3 on page 441).

WORD BANK

Preliterate

Letter name

Within-word pattern

Syllable juncture

Derivational

Until children have developed an awareness of word units, are able to map spoken to written words, and are able to "read the spaces" between words, they are "seldom able to represent more than the beginning consonant letter in their invented spelling." Morris (1983) uses finger pointing during oral reading to assess children's concept of word. He reads a poem to children, tracing under the words with his hand as he reads. Children join in to chorus the poem; later they take turns finger pointing as they repeat the poem aloud, trying to synchronize the words they speak with the words they point to.

Morris finds that first-graders fall into three groups based on this diagnostic test. Some youngsters cannot connect spoken with written words as they finger-point; these youngsters generally represent only beginning consonants in their invented spellings and are clearly preliterate spellers. Others can finger-point as they read but only to a degree; when they mismatch written and spoken words, they exhibit only a limited ability to correct their slip-ups. Interestingly, these children demonstrate some ability to include both beginning and ending consonants—syllable barriers— in their invented spellings. On the other hand, youngsters in this group have only limited ability to represent vowels in their spellings. At this stage, children are likely to spell *monster* as *mst*, *dressing* as *jrsn*, *bottom* as *bdm* (Henderson, 1990).

Letter Name Spelling

Still other first-graders have a functional concept of a word. As they read, they can finger-point with a high degree of accuracy. They can identify individual words in a poem they have finger-pointed. They can "sound their way through words," representing consonants and vowels rather accurately. These youngsters are *letter name* spellers; they spell *monster* as *moth*, *mostr*, or *monstr*; *bottom* as *bodm*, *bodu*,

Figure 12.2
A Preschooler's Early Writing with Words He Said as He Read It
Courtesy of Eric Ransom

DISCUSSION PROMPT

- What purpose is served by the teacher's writing down for Eric the words he said as he read his story aloud?

bdim, or *bdm;* and *dressing* as *gasin, jesin,* or *gesg.* Their misspellings reflect the ordered nature of their thinking and the stage of spelling at which they are functioning (see Figure 12.3).

Read (1971) describes how letter name spellers operate. These youngsters start by using the alphabet names of letters to encode. Using this system, children have little difficulty writing down a representation of a sound that equates easily with an alphabetic pronunciation, as is the case with many consonant sounds and the long vowel sounds. Short vowels and blends such as *dr,* however, are a different matter. In working with short vowels, children generally substitute the long vowel that is closest to the sound of the short vowel they want to use; for example, they substitute the letter *a* for the short *e* in *pen,* the letter *i* for the short *o* in *got.* The results are invented spellings like *pan* and *git.* In the case of a blend such as *dr,* they tend to disregard the *d* and write what they hear as *jr.*

That this letter name spelling strategy works to some extent is a result of the rather consistent way speech sounds are represented on paper. Although in the past some educators stressed the inconsistencies in the English spelling system, linguists today highlight the regularities. Take, for example, the way the letter *t* is used to represent the speech sound /t/. According to Paul Hanna, Richard Hodges, and Jean Hanna (1971), *t* is used 96 percent of the time to represent /t/. Linguists call the smallest unit of speech sound a *phoneme* and the written representation of a speech sound a *grapheme.* Thus we can say that the grapheme *t* is predominantly used to represent the phoneme /t/.

Other graphemes serve with equal consistency. Hanna, Hodges, and Hanna (1971) report that *d* represents /d/ in almost 98 percent of the cases in which the speech sound occurs. *B* represents /b/ about 97 percent of the time, and the same is true of the use of *n* and *r* to represent /n/ and /r/. Similarly, the /a/ as in *pan* and *at* is represented by *a* more than 96 percent of the time.

Even some of the spelling demons are more regular than is at first apparent. Hanna, Hodges, and Hanna explain that only parts of a demon depart from expected sound-symbol relationships. For example, *women* is regular except for the /i/ in the first syllable; all the other phonemes are represented by graphemes as expected. According to Hanna et al., the number of spelling demons is small—only 3 percent of the core vocabulary. In sum, we can say that English is an alphabetic language that has important phonetic characteristics. The phonetic characteristics are what young children use as spelling clues as they become letter name spellers. They are also one kind of clue that older children use in checking spellings in a dictionary.

Within-Word Pattern Spelling

But as we all know, English is not strictly phonetic, primarily because it contains words borrowed from other languages and incorporates changes that have occurred over the years. Children must begin to perceive what Henderson (1990) calls the "patterns that exist within words" to master English spelling. One pattern is the presence of two vowels in words in which the long vowel sound occurs (e.g., *cake* and *team*). As children become *within-word pattern* spellers, they tend to spell *cake* as *caek* or perhaps *kake.* They may spell *team* as *teem* or *teme.* These spellings are logical for youngsters at this stage of development. Rather than showing disappointment

STAGE	CHARACTERISTICS	HOW TO HELP CHILDREN AT THIS STAGE
PRE-LITERATE SPELLERS ↓	Children enjoy making marks on paper; they create meaningful scribble by inscribing lines, waves, letterlike shapes, and random letters. Children cannot finger-point precisely; they do not have a concept of a word.	*As Part of Reading and Writing:* Read poetry charts and big books aloud, following the words you read with your hand. Ask children to chorus the charts and books. Ask individuals to finger-point and lead the chorus as the class joins in. Take dictation from children, stretching out the sounds of words as you write them on the chart. Reread the charts, following words and lines with your hand as you read them. Ask children to do the same.
LETTER NAME SPELLERS ↓	Children can finger-point; they have a concept of a word. In their invented spellings they begin to represent a consonant sound with the consonant as they say and hear it in the alphabet; they represent a vowel sound with the vowel from the alphabet with the closest sound to what they hear.	*As Part of Reading and Writing:* As they read and write, give children hints on how to represent language sounds in writing. Celebrate sound/symbol correspondences that children demonstrate in their writing to encourage them to use their emerging understanding. Record for children, modeling your thought processes in deciding word beginnings. *As Part of Developmental Spelling Activity:* Involve children in word sorts (e.g., "let's put all the words in our story that begin with the same sound as *boy* in this pile of words; they all begin with the letter *b*").
WITHIN-WORD PATTERN SPELLERS ↓	Writers begin to vary spellings based on where the sound occurs in a word or how it is used in a word—on the within-word patterns of the English language. They honor short and long vowel markers in their invented spellings.	*As Part of Reading and Writing:* Focus attention on within-word patterns as children edit their invented spellings and read. As part of editing, hint at how certain patterns are spelled, especially vowels. Encourage generalizing based on several words with the same pattern. Model your thought processes in spelling as you write on the board. Encourage proofreading. *As Part of Developmental Spelling Activity:* Across the curriculum, involve children in word sorts to discover some of the within-word patterns of English. Encourage analysis and generalizing about when a sound is spelled in a particular way.
SYLLABLE JUNCTURE SPELLERS ↓	Writers hear the syllables in words and begin to control the spelling at the syllable breaks in multi-syllabic words. Writers control the roots and affixes of the language and use their understanding of word building characteristics of English (such as compound words) in their invented spellings. They begin to manage the schwa in their invented spellings.	*As Part of Reading and Writing:* Focus attention on the word-building characteristics of English as children edit their invented spellings and read. Give hints as part of the editing process about how certain roots and affixes are spelled. Help children to generalize. During shared writing, model your thought processes as you inscribe multisyllabic words. Proofread. *As Part of Developmental Spelling Activity:* Involve children in word sorts to discover some of the word-building characteristics of English. Start with words that include a particular word-building problem, such as words that double a final consonant when a suffix is added. Encourage analysis and generalizing about how to handle similar words in editing.
DERIVA-TIONAL SPELLERS ↓	Writers use their understanding of word origins and related meanings in their invented spellings.	*As Part of Reading and Writing:* Focus attention on words that are related because of a common origin or meaning during reading and editing. Give hints as to why words are inscribed as they are. Help children to generalize about how origin affects orthography. Encourage proofreading. *As Part of Developmental Spelling Activity:* Across the curriculum, involve children in word sorts so that they begin to relate words that share a common origin or meaning. Start with some words that have a common origin, such as words that spell a final long *a* as *et*. Encourage analysis and generalizing.

Figure 12.3
Stages in Spelling Development

with primary youngsters who produce them, teachers should recognize the spellings as evidence that youngsters are beginning to perceive the patterns within words.

Syllable Juncture Spelling

Now too, youngsters show evidence of their growing ability to work with common inflectional endings (*-ed, -ing, -s*), compound words, suffixes and prefixes, and syllable units in their invented spellings. For example, beginning word pattern spellers tend to spell words such as *better* as *betir* or *beter* and *picked* as *pickd* or *pickid*.

Invented spellings such as these represent a natural next stage in children's spelling development. They reflect a growing ability to handle the word-building characteristics of English. Linguists tell us that many English words are built by the addition of inflectional endings: the plural endings on nouns, tense-changing endings on verbs, endings like *-er* and *-est* on adjectives. Through the addition of inflectional endings, *dog* becomes *dogs, walk* becomes *walked,* and *slow* becomes *slower.* Children who have learned to handle these aspects of language have become *syllable juncture* spellers, as set forth in Figure 12.3.

In English, other words are built by adding suffixes and prefixes to roots. Adding affixes, a writer may change how a word functions in a sentence. For example, the word *loose* can function as an adjective; with the addition of *-ly* it becomes *loosely,* which can function as an adverb; with *-ness* it becomes *looseness,* which functions as a noun; with *-en* it becomes *loosen,* which serves as a verb. Still other words are products of compounding, the combining of two short words to form one, as in *anywhere, anthill,* and *sidewalk.* To master English spelling, children must master these challenges that exist within multisyllabic words. Henderson (1990) finds that as children struggle with syllable joinings, invented spellings such as *inocent* for *innocent* and *accomodate* for *accommodate* are common.

Derivational and Meaning-Based Spelling

As they mature as spellers, children perceive the role of meaning in English spelling and begin to function as *derivational* and *meaning-based* spellers. For example, the spelling of *muscle,* with its so-called silent *c* in the middle, makes sense when considered along with the meaning-related *muscular.* The spelling of *bomb,* with its silent *b,* is completely logical when considered in relation to *bombard.* As Templeton (1979) explains, when children begin to handle words in which meaning or derivational relationships are significant, "teachers can point out these regularities, and students can subsequently be on the lookout for similar patterns."

In the same way, spellers think in terms of meaning when considering homophone pairs (e.g., *sewing* and *sowing*). These spellings make sense if one considers the confusion that could result if the orthography system did not clarify different meanings communicated by similar-sounding words. Templeton gives as examples two sets of sentences: "I *herd* the cows" and "I *heard* the cows"; "I run a *sowing* machine" and "I run a *sewing* machine." In each case, spelling differences clarify meaning.

As they mature as spellers, young people also begin to perceive the role of origin, or derivation, in English spelling, for the history of words is one determinant of how

Meet Kimberly Wright, Fourth-Grade Teacher

Kimberly Wright is a fourth-grade teacher at Mapleton Elementary School in Mapleton, Maine. Recently, she dropped "the spelling textbooks and spelling tests in exchange for weekly spelling discussions" that she called Spelling Meetings. Ms. Wright asked her students to bring to a Spelling Meeting three words that "they were wondering about, words they found difficult, or words that made them curious." Her intent was that students would share their words and talk about them during Spelling Meetings. At first, Ms. Wright's innovative approach lacked focus as students just called out their words and the teacher recorded them on the board. Spelling Meetings took off, however, when "the class came to a consensus, agreeing to start keeping charts on different spellings for the same sounds, such as the /shun/ sound and the /er/ sound." In Spelling Meetings that followed, students focused on one sound or one element (such as a suffix) based on a word suggested by a student.

Together, students brainstormed and charted words that were related to the one the student had provided.

As Kimberly Wright explained, "The supportive classroom environment encouraged students to be curious about words. Inquiry based on spelling patterns, the sounds of words, spelling strategies, collaboration, and so on, allowed students to take risks with their spelling . . . and to apply effective spelling practices to everyday writing" ("Weekly Spelling Meetings: Improving Spelling Instruction Through Classroom-Based Inquiry," *Language Arts,* 77 [January 2000], 218–223).

DISCUSSION PROMPT

What merits do you see in Ms. Wright's approach? What kinds of understandings can come about as an outgrowth of Spelling Meetings? What changes to Spelling Meetings could you make to Ms. Wright's approach to make it more productive?

we spell words today. In some instances, linguists can explain current spellings in terms of the way words were pronounced in the past. For example, linguists explain the silent *k* in *knight* in terms of past practice, when speakers pronounced the *k*. They explain the *et* spelling of /a/ in *ballet, buffet,* and *croquet* in terms of a common French origin. Only through mastery of what Henderson (1990) calls "derivational constancy" do children become proficient spellers. The fine spellers—the spelling bee champions—draw on a wide range of semantic (meaning), derivational, and word-building clues, resorting to letter name spelling only when other means fail. These spellers know that there is a multifaceted logic to our spelling system and use all the clues at their command (Hodges, 1982).

Introducing Children to the Logic of English Spelling

Today some spelling authorities advocate that children investigate and discover the multifaceted logic of English so that they build a growing awareness of the principles underlying spelling and do not rely on rote memory for learning word spellings (Schlagal and Schlagal, 1992; Teale, 1992; Invernizzi et al., 1997). Some ways to achieve this goal are to organize children's word study developmentally based on educators' understanding of children's growth as spellers; to rely at some point on grouping, cycles, and individual contracts to meet developmental needs; and to individualize word study based on children's reading and writing (Fresch, 2001; Bear, Invernizzi, Templeton, and Johnston, 2000).

Organizing Developmentally Appropriate Word Study

Spelling instruction often occurs as part of study of the way the English language works. In many classrooms today, learners discover the basic relationships within the English spelling system that govern how words are spelled: Based on their stage of spelling development, children study structurally related words—words that exemplify a particular phoneme-grapheme correspondence, within-word pattern, word-building/syllable-joining principle, meaning relationship, or derivation. Children analyze related words, sort them according to similarities and differences in spelling, search for words that pattern in a similar way, and generalize based on relationships they discover. This is an inductive approach to word study, which can take place as children are reading stories, making exploratory forays into the social and natural science, and editing their writing.

Teaching Related Words Through Discovery   Where word study is based on children's development as spellers, first-graders investigate and discover the graphemes through which onsets and rimes are represented. As you recall, a *grapheme* is a letter or group of letters used to represent a speech sound, or phoneme; an *onset* is a consonant speech sound that occurs at the beginning of a word whereas a *rime* (a phonogram or word family) is a group of speech sounds heard at the end of a word.

In some first-grade classrooms, as children read and write, they sort words based on their onset such as *boy, ball,* and *bat* and *top, tag,* and *tan.* This helps them distinguish between the sound /b/ and the sound /t/ and eventually to connect the sounds with the graphemes used to represent them in spelling. They play, too, with words such as *kit, fit, lit, sit* and *bat, fat, cat, mat,* sorting the words into two groups based on the rime, or final sounds, and searching for other words that belong to the *it* and *at* word families. In each case, youngsters make banners on which they print words organized by onsets and/or rimes and display their word banners in prominent positions in their classroom and at home (Heald-Taylor, 1998).

By fourth grade, many students are able to handle more sophisticated sound-symbol relationships. At some point, perhaps during related content-area studies, they may sort such words as *riddle, muscle, whistle, wrestle, puzzle,* and *nickel, chapel, label, model, can-*

READ

Mary Jo Fresch and Aileen Wheaton, "Sort, Search, and Discover: Spelling in the Child-Centered Classroom," *The Reading Teacher*, 51, 1 (September 1997), 20–31.

GO TO

Page 90 for a list of common rimes.

GO TO

Pages 92–94 for an example of a way to handle affixes and roots.

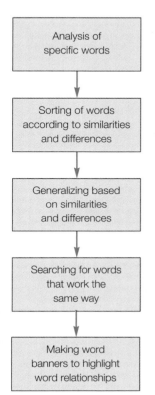

Analysis of specific words

↓

Sorting of words according to similarities and differences

↓

Generalizing based on similarities and differences

↓

Searching for words that work the same way

↓

Making word banners to highlight word relationships

cel, search for words that pattern as these words do, generalize about the spellings, and make banners to post in their living spaces. At another point, perhaps as they read a story that relies on some of these words, they discover relationships among *wagon, gallon, cotton, common,* and *lesson,* as well as *cabin, cousin, satin,* and *ruin.*

Emphasis in upper elementary grades is also on word-building characteristics, word origins, meanings, and use. Notice that the words just listed have two syllables so that the fourth-graders can begin to generalize about syllable joinings. As part of other investigations in which learners are discovering how words are put together rather than memorizing individual words, children add affixes to roots to form multisyllabic words. For example, upper-graders build words by adding *-ed* and *-ing* to roots ending with the letter *y.* During another investigation, they build words using a prefix, a root, and a suffix. During another, they sort and search for words that share a common spelling and origin. At still another time, they relate word spellings to parts of speech, as would be the case in an investigation of the spelling of the final sounds of *marvelous, ridiculous, glorious* (all common adjectives) and *circus, hippopotamus, nucleus* (all nouns).

In each instance, children organize sort-and-search expeditions so that they discover basic relationships for themselves by looking at words that share a feature but also differ in some way. They sort words into groups according to the differences and search for other words that fit into the categories they have devised. Sortings can be based on symbols used to represent a speech sound, on the way a particular affix is added, or on a common origin. Reasoning from the groupings they have formed, students propose generalizations about the spelling of their language, which they apply to other words spelled according to the same principles. Continuing to be alert for related words, students create large banners with their words and post them around the classroom as a visual reminder of the way to spell words such as these.

In inductive, or discovery, learning, students do not memorize generalizations; rather, they put together pieces of a generalization so that it is meaningful to them. Most specialists agree that memorizing generalizations has little effect on ability to spell. Students must work actively with generalizations to make them useful in drafting and editing.

This is especially true of generalizations about word building. Ernest Horn (1960), whose name continues to be associated with spelling instruction after many years, identifies three generalizations that children can discover and use:

- Words ending with a silent *e* usually retain the *e* before suffixes beginning with a consonant (*lone* → *lonely* and *lonesome*). Words ending with a silent *e* usually drop the *e* before suffixes beginning with a vowel (*hike* → *hiking*).
- In words ending with a consonant and a *y,* the *y* is changed to *i* when suffixes—except those beginning with *i*—are added (*lady* → *ladies, cry* → *crying*). In words ending with a vowel and a *y,* the *y* is not changed to *i* when suffixes are added (*lay* → *laying*).
- In words of one syllable and words accented on the last syllable, ending in a single consonant preceded by a single vowel, the final consonant is doubled when a suffix beginning with a vowel is added (*tug* → *tugging, begin* → *beginning*).

To teach these understandings using the discovery approach, the teacher presents a series of words that adhere to a generalization, asks questions that help children sort

Second-graders can learn inductively by sorting words and adding them to word-family banners, which consist of words containing the same sound, even though the sound is represented by different letter patterns. Studying the banners, children generate a theory about the spelling of the sound. In Figure 12.4, they conclude that ay is a common spelling of /ā/ when the sound occurs at the end of the word and ai and a-e are spellings when the /ā/ occurs in the middle of the word. They can add the Kottmeyer symbol for snurk next to words that do not abide by their generalization. Word banners become part of Word Walls.

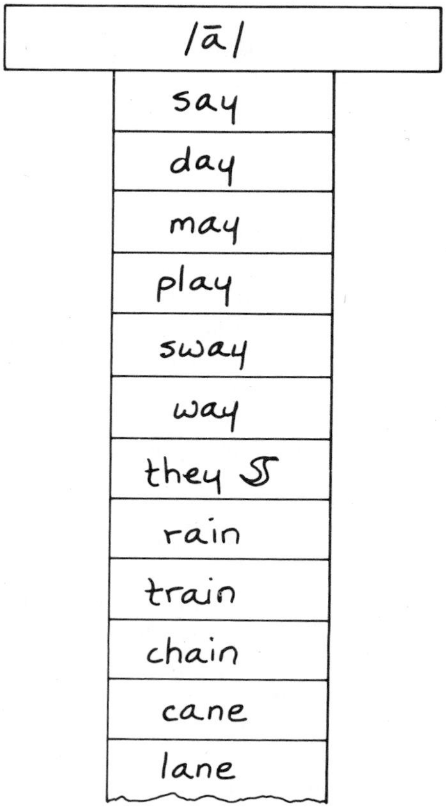

Figure 12.4
A Spelling Banner

the words into groups, and guides children in figuring out the generalization and its limitations. Children search for words that adhere to the generalization and post them on spelling banners.

Teaching Irregular Words Of course, not all words follow predictable sound-symbol relationships, within-word patterns, or word-building principles. William Kottmeyer calls irregularly spelled words *snurks*. He tells his students that to conquer a snurk, they must identify the snurky part to see where it departs from an expected spelling. For example, children identify *key* as a snurk because "we expect to spell /ē/ with *e, ee,* or *ea* at the end of one-syllable words like *me, see,* and *tea.*" In this case, /ē/ is spelled *ey.* Figure 12.4 shows a spelling banner that identifies a snurk.

Hanna, Hodges, and Hanna (1971) propose that irregular words may have to be learned through repeated use, with students relying on visual and kinesthetic clues. This is especially true of frequently used irregular words such as *the.* See Figure 12.5 for the 100 most frequently used words. The word *the* is second on the list.

Some teachers encourage students to print or write irregular words they have mis-spelled in large letters on individual cards. Students tack the cards higgledy-piggledy around the room as visual reminders of the spellings. Other teachers encourage stu-

BASIC SPELLING WORD LIST

1. I	21. at	41. do	61. up	81. think
2. the	22. this	42. been	62. day	82. say
3. and	23. with	43. letter	63. much	83. please
4. to	24. but	44. can	64. out	84. him
5. a	25. on	45. would	65. her	85. his
6. you	26. if	46. she	66. order	86. got
7. of	27. all	47. when	67. yours	87. over
8. in	28. so	48. about	68. now	88. make
9. we	29. me	49. they	69. well	89. may
10. for	30. was	50. any	70. an	90. received
11. it	31. very	51. which	71. here	91. before
12. that	32. my	52. some	72. them	92. two
13. is	33. had	53. has	73. see	93. send
14. your	34. our	54. or	74. go	94. after
15. have	35. from	55. there	75. what	95. work
16. will	36. am	56. us	76. come	96. could
17. be	37. one	57. good	77. were	97. dear
18. are	38. time	58. know	78. no	98. made
19. not	39. he	59. just	79. how	99. glad
20. as	40. get	60. by	80. did	100. like

Figure 12.5
The One Hundred Most Frequently Used Words

DISCUSSION PROMPT

■ How can you help children to master these basic words? Think in terms of Word Walls, word sorts, and Have-a-Go.

dents to make and post banners, collages, or creative finger paintings that include irregular words they are having trouble spelling. Because students have the visual images constantly before them, they use those words in writing and master the spellings. Still other teachers use computer programs that provide practice with irregular words. Ernest Balajthy (1986) suggests that teachers must pick and choose carefully from among computer programs, avoiding those that ask a child to select a correctly spelled word from among incorrect versions that reinforce incorrect visual images.

Relying on Grouping, Contracts, and Cycles to Meet Developmental Needs

Many elementary teachers find it difficult to introduce children to the logic of English spelling through an approach in which all youngsters work with the same generalizations. In any class, there are children who are functioning at different developmental levels. Some are functioning as letter-name spellers, others have control over within-word patterns, whereas still others are able to handle word-building principles and words that share a common origin. Clearly it makes little sense to ask a child who is just beginning to control within-word patterns to study words related by origin simply because he or she is in a class where many of the students are more developmentally advanced spellers.

Organizing Word Study Groups   To meet the diverse spelling levels and needs within a class, some teachers divide students into flexible spelling groups according to the children's development as spellers and use contracts to further individualize work within the groups. Here is how Fred Bronsky—using a weekly spelling cycle—manages the three spelling groups that operate in his third-grade class.

Day 1.   On the first day of a cycle, Mr. Bronsky meets with one group for a discovery mini-lesson. Based on their demonstrated stage of spelling development, children sort words and generalize about them as in the opening vignette. After that, the teacher dictates to students a list of words related to the generalization they have been investigating. Children correct their own spellings by referring to the standard spelling on the word cards they have sorted.

Then Mr. Bronsky explains related word-study options that students will complete later on their own. To meet individual needs, he gives each youngster a spelling contract (see Figure 12.6). The contract specifies a few activities that all children in the group are to complete. To their contracts, youngsters add spelling activities that help them focus on their special needs—options such as re-sorting the words being highlighted during that particular cycle, searching for similarly structured words as well as exceptions to a generalization they are considering, retesting on the words with a spelling buddy, making banners to post at school and at home, concocting original word puzzles to share with buddies, studying personal words misspelled in writing.

Day 2.   Students work independently on activities listed in their contracts. They usually begin with required tasks. Notice that students do not spend spelling study time looking up words in a dictionary, copying definitions, and writing sentences with the words—activities that are not spelling oriented.

Day 3.   Students continue to work independently. They may pair with a spelling buddy for retesting on words, join with others in the group to play a spelling game, practice by using a related computer program, or edit a draft in their active-writing portfolios. They use their word-study plan to master personal words incorporated into their contracts.

Day 4.   Students continue as on Day 3. More students turn to actual writing and begin to draft, revise, and edit stories in their portfolios.

Day 5.   Students work on revising and editing a piece they have drafted. They take a posttest on the words highlighted during the cycle.

Managing the Cycles   Mr. Bronsky usually has three groups functioning in his classroom. The M Group begins a cycle on Monday and completes it on Friday. The W Group begins on Wednesday and ends on Tuesday. The F Group begins on Friday

INDEPENDENT STUDY GUIDE: SPELLING

Spelling agenda for week of _____

Name _____

Mark the time and date when you begin an activity in column 1 and when you complete an activity in column 2. You may add original activities at the bottom of the chart.

1	2	Activity
		• Rewrite each word from your basic spelling list three times so you have three banners with the words, each organized by pattern.
		• Take one banner home to post next to your bed to look at from time to time. Post one on your desk. Cut one banner up and make a collage of the words, highlighting spelling relationships.
		• Search for words that are similar in some way to the words on your study banners. Add these words to the banners. Look for exceptions as well.
		• Run a self-test of your words by having your spelling buddy dictate your words. Have your buddy help you correct your paper.
		• Select, analyze, and study your personal words by writing them on three banners. Again post one at home, post one on your desk, and cut up and sort the words on the third to show relationships.
		• Play one of the spelling sort-and-search games at the spelling table with your buddy.
		• Original activity based on personal words:
		• Original activity of interest to you:

Figure 12.6
A Spelling Contract

DISCUSSION PROMPT

■ Why is a sort-search-banner approach more valid than one that asks students to look up definitions, copy them, and write a sentence for each?

What is the most effective way to teach spelling?

Sharon Murphy and Curt Dudley-Marling propose, "It may be that some writing teachers, in their eagerness to privilege meaning and function over form, have paid too little attention to the conventions of writing to the detriment of their students. . . . The problem has been how best to teach spelling when we know that traditional approaches to the teaching of spelling, especially the reliance on spelling books and rote memorization, are inadequate" ("Editors' Pages," *Language Arts*, 77 [January 2000], 200–201).

Margaret Hughes and Dennis Searle believe that the act of writing supports learning to spell in very specific ways. They explain, "Essentially, writing challenges children to use their knowledge of print to express their thoughts on paper. Writers may spell correctly or incorrectly, but they cannot avoid spelling. Moreover, the process of generating words, making choices about which letters to put down on paper, requires writers to pay attention to the internal details of words in ways that readers do not have to" ("Spelling and the Second 'R,'" *Language Arts*, 77 [January 2000], 203–208).

Irene Gaskins and her colleagues at the Benchmark School in Pennsylvania recognize the importance of writing in the development of spelling facility. On the other hand, they also emphasize that "knowing how our language works is essential to becoming a good reader and speller; thus it does not make sense to leave the development of this knowledge to chance. Instruction needs to be scaffolded so that children develop an awareness of the structure of written language" ("Analyzing Words and Making Discoveries About the Alphabetic System: Activities for Beginning Readers," *Language Arts*, 74 [March 1997], 172–184).

DISCUSSION PROMPT

What is the most effective way to teach spelling—through spelling book lists, memorization, and weekly tests; through a strong writing program in which children are taught to proofread their writing; or through word study in which children sort words into related groupings, search for similar words, and then generalize about the way words work? Given that research shows that traditional approaches to spelling instruction based on memorization do not work, what advantages do you see in an approach in which children learn to spell as a natural part of writing? What advantages do you see in word study as a road to spelling excellence? Is it possible to develop a balanced approach? What would be the characteristics of such an approach? What advantages and disadvantages do you see?

and ends on Thursday. This cycling of three groups frees the teacher on Tuesdays and Thursdays to work with students who need special attention as a result of misunderstanding or absence and with students whose developmental levels are such that they cannot gain from activity with any of the groups. Mr. Bronsky reserves a few minutes during the week to return to a group to dictate words on the final day of a cycle, but this is not always necessary. If words and related sentences have been tape-recorded, children can take a midcycle or end-of-cycle test monitored by a student from another group.

By grouping for instruction, teachers can "place [students] in instructionally appropriate materials," highlighting different words and generalizations with students who are functioning at different developmental levels (Morris, 1987; Bloodgood, 1991; Schlagal and Schlagal, 1992). Emphasis with one group may be on within-word patterns, with another group on word-building principles. By grouping, too, teachers can allot more time to a set of words with youngsters who need more reinforcement of spelling generalizations. In addition, individual students can work on words they have misspelled in writing. Children include these words in their contracts.

Individualizing Word Study Based on Personal Writing Needs

READ

Joan Novelli, "Strategies for Spelling Success," *Instructor*, 102 (May/June 1993), 41–42, 47 for a description of how one first-grade teacher organizes an individualized program.

Another approach to word study is individualized, based on words misspelled in writing. During a writing conference, the teacher helps a student identify five or six personal words that he or she has misspelled. An upper-grader may identify about ten words. Teacher and student talk briefly about the "hard" spots in the misspelled words, relating the errors to generalizations about English spelling. For example, with a child who has spelled *babies* as *babys*, the teacher explains how to form the plural of words that end in *y*. Having focused on such "hard" spots, the child writes the five or six chosen words at the back of his or her learning log.

Working collaboratively with a spelling buddy, the student rewrites the words as the buddy dictates them. Buddies take turns dictating and being tested on their words. They correct their words cooperatively, using the spellings of the words in their learning logs as guides. Spelling buddies collaborate on several occasions until each child thinks he or she has gained ownership over his or her words. At some point, the teacher asks all students to meet with their spelling buddies to dictate and be tested. Words correctly spelled are starred in the student's learning log, at which point teacher and student, during another writing conference, add other words to the student's learning log list, choosing from those the child has misspelled in writing.

An obvious advantage of this approach is that students learn to spell words that they use in speaking and writing; these words therefore are meaningful to them. A second advantage is that students may learn not only their own words but their buddy's words. A disadvantage is that it is relatively difficult to teach children the underlying generalizations that control the spelling of words in English when they are working with individual words rather than with groups of linguistically related words. Children are more or less learning to spell by memorizing individual words rather than by identifying relationships within a group of words.

Personalized Spelling in the Lower Grades   Some teachers modify the personalized spelling approach to overcome this disadvantage. In conferring over a paper to be published, student and teacher select only one or two misspelled words to add to the student's personalized spelling list. For each word chosen, the child brainstorms other words having the same pattern and lists those next to the word he or she originally misspelled. For example, with a very young child who has misspelled *my* as *mi*, the teacher might suggest, "I know that when you write the word *I* you spell the long *i* sound with the letter *i*, just as in the alphabet. But in the word *my*, you write the long *i* sound with the letter *y*. Let's think of other words in which we hear the long *i* sound at the end." As the child suggests such possibilities as *by, fly, why, cry*, the teacher helps the child record these four words next to *my* in his or her log. Once the child has done this, the teacher asks, "When we hear the long sound of *i* at the end of a word, what is a very common way in which we write it down?" Having generalized, student and teacher talk about a second word that the child has misspelled in the prepublication draft. In this way, the child builds a personalized spelling list of related words based on one or two words that he or she has misspelled.

Later, collaborating together, spelling buddies explain their generalizations to each other before they dictate their words. With this approach, children become spelling teachers as well as learners; each explains the generalizations being learned to his or her spelling buddy. Again, buddies correct their words cooperatively, checking against the models in their logs. Again, too, teachers who use this approach have found that not only do children learn their own words and the generalizations that explain them; each learns his or her buddy's words as well.

Personalized Spelling in the Upper Grades   The same approach is possible with older students. If, for example, a third-grade boy spells the word *blew* as *blue* in the sentence "The wind blew through the trees," during a prepublication writing conference the teacher might brainstorm with him words in which this vowel sound is spelled *ew* and words in which it is spelled *ue*, in the process talking about the problem of English homophones. The student brainstorms words such as *flew, knew, dew, chew*, and *clue, true, due*, listing them as a group in his log for later study and testing with a spelling buddy. In the same way, a sixth-grade girl who has spelled *clarify* as *clarafy* brainstorms other words that end as does *clarify—modify, gratify, signify*. She generalizes that when words end with the same sounds as *clarify*, they are spelled with an *-ify*, not an *-afy*; she may also generalize that all these words function as verbs in sentences.

CONSIDER

Regie Routman (1993) writes: "A classroom that encourages children to be good spellers provides . . . lots of mini-lessons to see word patterns, develop rules, notice unusual features of words (these lessons arise from what the teacher notices the children need)." Routman also recommends core lists for each grade level that children should realistically be expected to spell correctly.

Some teachers further modify the personal spelling approach by scheduling mini-lessons with groups of youngsters who exhibit a similar spelling problem (Bartch, 1992). These teachers examine children's papers for common spelling errors such as the spelling of *are/our, their/they're*, contractions, *-ed* endings, silent letters, *qu* spellings, *wr* spellings, possessive forms, and *ie/ei*. When they find that several youngsters exhibit the same difficulty, they gather them together for a discovery lesson that focuses on the problem. Teachers then encourage children to edit their writing based on what they have learned in the mini-lesson. At the same time, these teachers encourage students to keep individual spelling-word banks to use as personal dictionaries during editing and post often-used words on a Word Wall that students also refer to during editing. Teacher Judie Bartch reports that this approach has had the greatest impact "during writer's workshop. As the children write, they use their strategies for spelling their words." They often stop, too, to talk about words and are more aware of words and the relationships among them. The children "are becoming independent spellers."

Making Spelling Speculation a Meaningful Part of Writing

READ

Margaret Hughes and Dennis Searle, "Spelling and 'the Second R,'" *Language Arts,* 77 (January 2000), 203–208, for the importance of writing in the teaching of spelling.

The goal of spelling instruction is for children to use their growing understanding of the logic of English spelling as they draft their ideas, edit what they have written, and later check their spelling inventions in a dictionary. Spelling, after all, is for writing. Therefore, regardless of the approach teachers use to involve children in the logic of English spelling, they must make the writing connection.

Drafting and Invented, or Speculative, Spelling

Teachers should encourage children from the moment they enter school to speculate about the spellings of words as they make first drafts and to use words they know they cannot spell. Mr. Bronsky did this in the opening vignette when he asked children to predict the spelling of *hypothesis*—a word they probably had never before tried to spell—and explained to them how he uses invented, or speculative, spelling during drafting.

Philip DiStefano and Patricia Hagerty (1985) explain, "The first step in teaching spelling is to let the students experiment with language while writing and not worry about their spelling. . . . Students must become risk takers when they use language." By systematically inventing spellings as part of writing, children make the transition from being letter name spellers to using within-word patterns, syllable-joining patterns, and derivational and meaning-based relationships to guide their predictions. Summarizing the research on children's development as spellers (Read, 1971; Bissex, 1980; Ferreiro and Teberosky, 1982; Bouffler, 1984), Brian Cambourne and Jan Turbill (1987) note: "As children continue to write using their temporary or invented spellings, they gradually proceed through a series of approximations to the conventional forms of spelling, experimenting with different unconventional versions of the same word." Cambourne and Turbill give Simon's development as an example: Simon's attempts to write *saw* over a six-month period proceeded from *s* to *sor*, to *swa*, and finally to *saw*.

To help children make the transition from speculative to standard spelling, teachers should model their own thought processes as they serve as scribe during shared writing and brainstorming sessions. Inscribing as children watch, teachers should speak the words clearly in syllable units, stretching out the sounds of the more difficult words, making explicit the thoughts that are going through their minds, and asking children to suggest letters (Scott, 1994). For example, recording during brainstorming, one upper-grade instructor had to write *furry*. She pronounced *fur* as she printed the letters, then stopped to ask herself, "Two *r*s or one?" She then tried out *fury* on the side and said, "That's *fu ry*," going back to record *furry* in the brainstormed list. As she did, she remarked, "Ah, I had to double the *r* because you have to do this when adding a suffix starting with a vowel sound to a single syllable word." When she finished, she asked, "Is that right or should we check the dictionary?" This type of modeling works at all levels, especially with young spellers who are beginning to control graphemes that represent consonant sounds.

GO TO

Page 237 for an instructional strategy to use during shared writing.

Editing and Proofreading

When writers go back to edit their writing, they must give attention to the spelling of words they have used. In this context proofreading becomes a basic skill that people must master if they are to have their writing accorded some respect. According to Jan Turbill (2000), "Proofreading is a special kind of reading that needs to be explicitly taught, so that students, in turn, can understand how it differs from other kinds of reading, such as reading for meaning, skim reading, and critical reading. Proofreading requires readers to *read like spellers.*"

Proofreading Strategies   Turbill provides some good ideas for teaching children to read like spellers. First, she advocates encouraging students to identify and list in their notebooks their personal "trouble-words," simple words that they commonly use but typically misspell. She tells students to keep an eye out for their trouble-words as they read and look carefully at the individual letters in them each time they encounter them in print. In addition, Turbill asks students to become spelling detectives as they go back to proofread their own writing. This means that during the proofreading process, they must "slow down their reading of the text, quite consciously and deliberately, so that each word" is scanned carefully. In doing this, proofreaders can take these steps:

- Fix their focus on each word one by one.
- Read aloud and look at each word as they read.
- Use a pencil to touch each word physically to slow down their reading of the words.
- Place a ruler or piece of paper under the line of text while reading it aloud.
- Read one line of print at a time, beginning from the bottom of the page and working backward.

Once proofreaders locate a possible misspelling, they need strategies for deciding on the conventional spelling. Turbil (2000) recommends that proofreaders use such strategies as these:

- Write the word several times in several ways to see which way "looks" right.
- Sound out and stretch out the word and the syllables in the word.
- Think about spelling generalizations that may apply.
- Find the word in a book where they remember it was used.
- Verify with the dictionary or a computer spell checker.
- Ask others.

Throughout, teachers must model how they go about proofreading their own writing. They must stress the difference between regular reading and reading like a speller.

Roy Peter Clark (1987) suggests that when a proofreader fails to identify a misspelling where one exists, the teacher can put a dot in the margin next to the line in which the word appears and suggest that the child check the hard words on the line in a dictionary. If the student has made many spelling errors and has failed to locate any of them when proofreading, the teacher can pair the poorer speller with a stronger one who can help locate possible errors. Clark reminds us that the teacher

The Teacher's Message Board

Spelling Alert: Posted here are some ideas for developing spelling in functional contexts.

- *Have-a-Go:* Students divide a paper into three columns. In the first column, they inscribe a word from their writing that they may have misspelled. They have a second "go," or try at it—or even a third or fourth try—and enter those attempts in the second column. They speculate in this way with four or five words they are unsure of. Later with a teacher, students write the standard spelling in the third column. Students then record the correct spelling of each word on cards to review from time to time and refer to during drafting and proofreading. This activity can be done by individuals or groups; when done by individuals, the four or five words can become words on the child's personal spelling list (Henry and Routman in Novelli, 1993).

- *Personal Words:* Students create their own personal word lists from words they have misspelled, selecting about five words and listing them correctly in a column. In a second column next to each chosen word, students record structurally or etymologically related words (after Snowball, 1994).

- *Fast Words:* The teacher selects a word misspelled by several students in their writing, asks the class to brainstorm possible correct spellings, and records the possibilities on the board. Students discuss the possibilities, eliminating ones that are unrealistic based on what they already know about sound/symbol relationships, within-word patterns, syllable-juncture rules, and etymology (Henry and Routman in Novelli, 1993).

- *Guess My Word:* The teacher keeps chart paper on view while sharing big books with young children and during content-area reading at the upper levels. After students have enjoyed and talked about the reading, the teacher lists several words from the book that share a spelling feature or asks students to brainstorm words that are similar in onset or rime to one in the text. He or she charts the words; students analyze them and talk about the common feature (Henry and Routman in Novelli, 1993).

- *Fill the Space:* During shared writing, the teacher leaves a space rather than writing one particular word. Children speculate on the spelling of that word, recording their best tries on a nearby chart. Later children and teacher talk about sound-symbol relations, within-word patterns, or syllable-joining rules that govern the spelling, deciding together perhaps through a dictionary check on the correct spelling. They insert that spelling into their language experience chart (after Snowball, 1994).

- *Rhyming Couplets:* Children create original versions of couplets, such as "One, Two, Buckle My Shoe," in the process working with the spelling of rimes, or word families (Henry and Routman in Novelli, 1993).

- *Alphabetic Word Wall:* The teacher lists high-frequency and important words on the Word Wall under the letter of the alphabet found at the beginning of each word. "Once a word is on the wall, the students understand that it is to be spelled correctly in writing" (Hayward, 1998).

- *Spelling Monitor Tables:* The teacher uses a spreadsheet program to list children's names across the top and the high-frequency words they are expected to spell correctly in writing beneath each name. As children master the words, the teacher highlights them in the appropriate row-column of the grid (Hayward, 1998).

should make a final check of a child's spelling before publishing occurs. He states, "Publish a work with the mistakes corrected." Publication tells students, "Here is why these things are important to learn. Now everyone can read what you have to say."

Computer Spell Checkers   In classrooms that have a computer equipped with a word processing program and a spell checker, children can use the checker during the final phase of editing. A spell checker highlights words that do not conform to any words in its dictionary. Students using a checker have to decide whether their spelling of highlighted words is really wrong or whether the highlighted words are simply not in the spelling checker dictionary. As Ruth Betza (1987) explains, the negative aspect of this procedure is that "a spelling checker has limitations in knowing whether all words are correctly spelled or not." A positive aspect is that upper elementary children hypothesize about language and take control of decision making as they edit. They have to decide whether to accept what the checker says or to check on the checker by using a dictionary.

Spelling Across the Curriculum

The kinds of activities just described should occur across the curriculum. In every area of study, elementary teachers should encourage youngsters to identify relationships among words as they read and apply their growing understanding of English spellings as they edit their writing.

For example, children who meet the phrase "Declaration of Independence" can relate the word *declaration* to the word *declare*. By making this relationship, children are less likely to write about the "Decoration of Independence," as one adult of this author's acquaintance still does. In like manner, students of geology identify the word-building elements in the word *geology, geo-* and *-ology;* they talk about the meanings of these elements as they use the word in writing and go back to edit. Similarly, they look at how the vowel sounds are encoded in the word *sedimentary* and talk about the origins of the word *igneous,* which comes from the Latin word meaning "of fire."

Likewise, investigations into the spellings of words can and should be a part of literature studies. For instance, at some point in a *Sarah, Plain and Tall* unit, students divide into word-investigation teams. One team plays with the homophones *plain* and *plane,* brainstorming other words that belong to the *ain* and *ane* phonogram sets and words that rhyme but spell the final sounds differently (*ein, eign, ayne*). Another team compares such story words as *feisty* and *pesky,* generalizes about the spelling of the final vowel sound, brainstorms other words that end with the long *e* sound and are spelled with a final *y,* and thinks about the fact that such words very often function as adjectives in sentences. A third team searches the chapters of the book they are reading for compound words such as *windmill* and *charcoal* (from Chapter 5 of *Sarah, Plain and Tall*) and considers the meanings based on the component words. When children play with the words of a story in investigative ways, they begin to use those words in their written responses and model their spelling after the spelling of words in the story.

Susan Glazer (1996) provides ideas for the kinds of spelling investigations that integrate into literature studies and are fun. In each case children brainstorm related

CONSIDER

To strengthen children's spelling ability, teachers should write important words and phrases on the chalkboard during content-area study and help children see relationships.

words and generalize about the spellings, and the way those words function in sentences:

- common phonograms such as *at, an, et, ight, or, up, it.*
- compound words, such as *bookshelves* and *fogbound.*
- word families such as the *ology* family, the *phobia* family.
- roots such as *phono* and *graph.*
- prefixes such as the *bi* in *bicycle.*
- inflectional endings such as the *-s* on *houses* and the *-es* on *boxes* used to form plurals.
- contractions such as *I'm,* used in informal writing.

Glazer suggests that teachers keep a checklist of the word knowledge children should have based on the items just enumerated, find ways for children to play with words in conjunction with literature and the content areas, and assess children's spelling abilities in terms of the checklist.

Only by thinking about spelling relationships as they meet words in diverse contexts do children develop functional spelling ability. The ultimate success of spelling study is children's ability to edit their own writing as they write across the curriculum, not their ability to spell correctly on a weekly spelling test. In that respect, the very act of writing and reading on a variety of topics provides opportunity for growth in spelling.

Using the Dictionary

Elementary students must master three kinds of dictionary-related learnings if they are to use the dictionary as a spelling and word search tool. First is appreciation of the value of the dictionary as a reference and writing tool. All the skill in the world matters little unless the writer uses a dictionary during proofreading. Second are abilities related to locating and interpreting entries: the abilities to alphabetize, use guide words, find a word of uncertain spelling, interpret definitions to determine how a word should be used, pronounce words based on their phonetic spellings, and interpret etymological notations. The third kind of learning, important in the upper grades, is the ability to handle dictionary-like tools: the thesaurus, a dictionary of synonyms, a rhyming dictionary, and indexes.

Valuing the Dictionary

Perhaps the most effective way to get children to value the dictionary is to make it the most important book in the classroom. Each day a student serves as Dictionary Sleuth; the sleuth's job is to check the spelling of difficult words being recorded on chalkboard or charts. As students brainstorm words and record them on the board, the sleuth keeps the dictionary on standby alert. When writing on the board and

Using a dictionary, children can make great discoveries about words. (© *Bill Aron/PhotoEdit/PictureQuest*)

encountering a tricky word, the teacher nods toward the sleuth to run and check it. When conferring with children who are editing written work, the teacher keeps a dictionary close at hand. Instead of marking a misspelled word, the teacher comments, "Steve, I'm not sure about this word. Let's check it," and hands the dictionary to Steve, who looks it up on the spot.

Alphabetizing and Using Guide Words

ABC books and picture dictionaries are contexts for younger children to learn to alphabetize. On a page a youngster writes a word, perhaps with the teacher's help, and draws a picture about it. If each child works with a word beginning with a different letter, youngsters bind the pages in alphabetical order to form an original ABC book. Slightly older children produce a picture dictionary, each child preparing one page that includes a word, the word used in a sentence, and a descriptive picture.

Children can make shoebox dictionaries by filing individual word cards alphabetically. On the cards are words the child commonly misspells. Looking for a word in his or her file, the child must rely on a growing ability to work with alphabetical order. As files expand, primary children create markers to divide cards into alphabetical groupings.

Ability to handle guide words is essential if students are to turn to a dictionary for assistance. To introduce students to guide words, some teachers have found the following sequence useful:

1. Make word cards, each containing a guide word from a dictionary page. Use guide words from three successive pages of a dictionary, such as *leaf* and *leasing, least* and *leg, legacy* and *leisure.*
2. Make word cards of entries found on those three dictionary pages.
3. Lay out the guide words on the floor.
4. Deal the word cards to students, who place their words in alphabetical order between the appropriate guide words.
5. Clarify use of guide words as students look up words as they edit.

Locating Words of Uncertain Spelling

A major strength of a spelling program that encourages speculative spelling and develops understanding of sound-symbol relationships is that the child has somewhere to begin when looking up a word in a dictionary. How often does a teacher hear, "How can I look it up if I don't know how to spell it in the first place?" The child who has some understanding of the graphemes through which a particular phoneme can be represented has a starting point. The searcher begins with the most common graphemes used to represent the phoneme and systematically checks out possibilities.

Of course, young children are disheartened if they look too long and are unsuccessful. When checking a paper for possible spelling errors, the child who has looked up three or four invented spellings to no avail may turn to a spelling buddy for a consultation. The two search together and, if still unsuccessful, may ask for searching assistance from the general editor—the teacher.

To prevent failure, at times the teacher supplies words in the form of an editing guide. Hanna Walsh, a first-grade teacher, encourages her children to use invented spellings as they draft their ideas in pencil. Later she places a different number above each word that needs to be rewritten. She keys the numbers to a slip of paper that she staples to the corner of the page. By each number on the "dictionary" slip, she writes the word correctly spelled. Children erase their own spellings and replace them with the correct ones. One advantage of this technique is that edited papers are available for bulletin board mounting. A more important advantage is that in drafting, youngsters draw on their understanding of sound-symbol relationships—the same thing they do when looking up a word of uncertain spelling in the dictionary.

Interpreting Dictionary Entries

Much dictionary work should occur as part of content-area study. As children encounter terms of uncertain meaning or pronunciation, they run a dictionary check. At that point, teacher and students puzzle out the notations in an entry. By placing dictionary work in a meaningful context, the teacher helps children see what a helpful tool a dictionary is. For example, as part of children's investigations of life in the colonial period, the teacher can print a related dictionary entry, such as this one from *Webster's II Riverside Beginning Dictionary,* on a transparency:

> **can o py** *noun* (kan′ ə pē), a covering that is usually made of fabric and hangs over a bed, entrance, or throne.

Students draw their conceptions of *canopy* based on the information given. Since the dictionary supplies a picture, children can compare drawings. If one youngster holds the dictionary from which the entry came, that person checks the pronunciation by referring to the model words at the bottom of the page or at the beginning of the dictionary. Once meaning and pronunciation have been clarified, students consider the way the word functions in sentences. In this case the word is a noun, one of the easiest to start with because the word has a concrete referent.

In the upper grades, dictionary entries are more complex and often include information about word relationships. Again children can compare drawings based on verbal definitions to pictures in the dictionary. They check the beginning section of the dictionary to discover how to interpret the etymological information. In some entries, children will encounter information on synonyms, special usages, and frequently confused words. Again, an overhead transparency that all can see turns dictionary study into a discussion time in which youngsters cooperatively solve dictionary puzzles.

Today students can conduct their dictionary searches on the Web because major dictionaries such as *The American Heritage Dictionary of the English Language* and *The Merriam-Webster Dictionary* are available online and provide information about the pronunciation, function, and etymology of words, as well as definitions. For example, accessing the word *orthography* at *The Merriam-Webster Dictionary* site, upper-graders can learn that the word came into English during the fifteenth century from Middle French. The French got the word from the Latin word *orthographia,* which came from the Greek *orth-* meaning "correct," and *graphein,* meaning "to write." They can learn that the English word *orthography* today means "the art of writing words with the proper letters according to standard usage"—a meaning that comes across rather sharply in the derivation. The great thing about an online entry is that the etymology is very clear, which makes working with derivations very interesting. A second advantage is that an entry can be printed out on one piece of paper and then compiled as a notebook or a class book of words.

Meeting Other Dictionary-like References

READ

Kathryn Laframboise, "Said Webs: Remedy for Tired Words," *The Reading Teacher,* 53 (April 2000), 540–542, for an idea for making thesaurus-like webs.

Some people overuse such words as *said, funny, cute, like, put,* and *make.* To avoid overuse, children can construct cards inscribed with alternates or synonyms that have nearly the same meaning as the original but communicate the idea more fully. They print a word such as *funny* on a small strip of paper attached to a rope hanging on the Word Wall. As students discover plausible alternatives—*amusing, entertaining, humorous, laughable*—they print those words on other strips that they clip to the same rope. Eventually, students turn the Word Wall into an original thesaurus by hanging several lengths of rope on it, each containing alternates for an overworked word.

Technology Notes

Check these Web sites for online dictionaries:

http://www.bartleby.com For *The American Heritage Dictionary of the English Language,* 4th ed. Entries include syllabication, pronunciation, function, definitions, related forms, and etymology. At the site is not only *The American Heritage Dictionary* but also *Roget's II: The New Thesaurus.*

http://www.m-w.com:80/cgi-bin/dictionary For *The Merriam-Webster Dictionary.* Entries include pronunciation, function, etymology, date of entry into English, and definitions. You can access a thesaurus at the site.

http://www.wordcentral.com For a student dictionary (*Merriam-Webster*), daily buzz words, and a build-your-own dictionary option. "Merriam-Webster's Word Central" (the name of the site) provides links to other language activities.

The thesaurus is a gold mine for word searchers. The synonyms for *funny* just given are from *In Other Words: A Beginning Thesaurus* by Greet, Jenkins, and Schiller—a splendid volume that should be found in every lower-elementary classroom. *In Other Words* provides synonyms for tired and overused words, defines substitutes, supplies sentences to explain word functioning, and offers antonyms. Upper-graders enjoy *In Other Words: A Junior Thesaurus,* also by Greet et al., as well as online thesauruses.

Teaching Manuscript Letter Forms to Active Young Writers

WORD BANK
Manuscript letter forms
Cursive letter forms

Generally, children are introduced to *manuscript* writing, or structured printing, when they come to school. Some specialists advocate a manuscript for young children composed of letters formed from discrete and unslanted lines, circles, and humps. The rationale is that it is easier for youngsters to distinguish letter parts and form the letters in manuscript than in cursive, where the letters slant and flow into one another. Then, too, most books are written in print; by learning to print, children transfer learnings from one language art (reading) into another (writing). Of course, manuscript writing is not something learned and eventually forgotten; manuscript writing is a lifelong skill. Adults must print signs, charts, and posters and complete forms that require printing rather than writing.

D'Nealian manuscript, developed by Donald Thurber, offers a continuous approach to beginning handwriting: D'Nealian manuscript letters slant in the same manner as in cursive, and letter forms in manuscript and cursive writing are more similar than in other handwriting programs. As a result, the rationale states, "the basic patterns are there when the time comes to learn cursive." See Figure 12.7 for the letters and numbers from the D'Nealian system.

In this section, we will look at ways to introduce children to manuscript and to provide meaningful practice. We will begin by visiting Ms. Robinson's kindergarten, remembering as we do that young children should be encouraged to compose in any form they choose and to invent letter forms as well as spellings to express their ideas. We recall, too, that students should have many opportunities simply to write—for writing is when handwriting is in action.

Handwriting in Action | *Introducing Manuscript Letter Forms to Young Children*

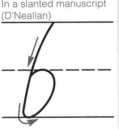

In a line, circle, and hump system

In a slanted manuscript (D'Nealian)

One morning, after her kindergartners had viewed a filmstrip on the characteristics of black bears and had talked about it, Ms. Robinson printed a large *b* on the chalkboard. The children watched as she carefully drew a line down and then a circle around. They used the same strokes to make a *b* in the air and compared Ms. Robinson's *b* to the *b* on the alphabet cards pinned below the board. Then three youngsters came forward to print a *b* on the board. When most children had had a turn, Ms. Robinson erased the board, printed another lowercase *b* on it, and mounted a picture of a black bear there. The children said the word *bear,* and Ms. Robinson told them that *bear* starts with a *b.* She explained that in writing, when she hears a sound like the beginning sound in *bear,* she writes down a *b* to represent it. All day long the *b* and the bear picture remained on the board. After completing other work, the children went to the board to form neat *b*s, erasing what they had written before returning to their seats.

The next day, as part of their science unit on bears, Ms. Robinson shared a filmstrip about brown bears. Afterward, she wrote a *b* and then a *B* on the chalkboard. This time she demonstrated the strokes used to make the lower- and uppercase forms of the letter and asked the students to make the letter strokes with their fingers in the air. In each instance, she presented the component strokes in a rhythmic way and repeated, "Draw a line down, and circle around to make a little *b.*" For the uppercase form she repeated, "Draw a line down. Draw a loop around and another loop around to make the capital *B.*" Left-handed youngsters practiced the rhythm of the strokes by making them with chalk at the board. Others practiced by drawing with crayon on plain paper folded to provide a top and a bottom guideline. As the children practiced, Ms. Robinson reminded them again that when she is writing and hears the sound like the one at the beginning of *bear,* she writes down a *b.* That afternoon, the children wrote informational paragraphs about bears, using the letter *b* to represent the word *bear.*

Figure 12.7
D'Nealian Letter and Number Forms

Source: D'Nealian is a registered trademark of Donald Neal Thurber. Copyright © 1987 by Scott, Foresman and Company.

DISCUSSION PROMPT

■ When printing charts, why is it important to use the letter and number forms of the system in use in the school district?

Early Handwriting: Preschool/Kindergarten

Build manual dexterity

In active kindergarten classrooms, children use their invented spellings to write from the moment they arrive. Their teachers also provide a variety of meaningful activities that increase children's ability to control the fine muscles of the hand and to differentiate among shapes. These activities include

- Drawing with brush and paint at easels in the art area.
- Drawing on large sheets of paper with husky crayons.
- Working with modeling clay, sometimes molding the material into letterlike shapes.
- Manipulating interlocking puzzle blocks.

As youngsters paint, draw, and handle materials, experienced teachers watch to determine which children tend to use the left hand. Of course, there is nothing wrong with being left-handed, and children should be encouraged to use the hand with which they feel more comfortable. The purpose of early identification is to meet the special needs of left-handed youngsters.

Distinguish shapes

Structured Activities   Most kindergarten teachers engage children in some structured handwriting-related activities. One day, for example, Ms. Robinson shared Tana Hoban's *Circles, Triangles, and Squares,* a book of photographs incorporating geometric shapes. In preparation, she had cut a circle, a square, and a triangle from colored construction paper and mounted them on her chalkboard. As the children studied the photographs in the book, they located these shapes and talked about them. As follow-up, the kindergartners made the shapes with crayon, cut them out, and created collages with them.

Form the letters of one's name

Visual Experiences with Words   Additionally, every day, Ms. Robinson provided many visual experiences with words. Before children arrived on the first day of school, she had affixed a nameplate to each desk. Each plate was colored oak tag inscribed with a child's name, starting with an uppercase first letter and followed by lowercase letters. When a youngster completed a drawing or a story with invented spellings, Ms. Robinson wrote the child's name in pencil in the upper right-hand corner, modeling the way to make the component strokes of each letter. With dark crayon, the child then made the letters of her or his own name, following the teacher's model. Because the children produced several papers each day, they had many opportunities to try to write their names. Very soon, the children were writing their names on their papers, using correct upper- and lowercase letter forms.

Each day, too, Ms. Robinson engaged the kindergartners in shared or interactive writing. As she printed words the children dictated, she was careful to make her letters similar to the models posted on the children's desks as well as below the chalkboard. She formed the letters as outlined in the system used in the school district. Not all handwriting systems rely on the same letter shapes or sizes. In some, the manuscript letters are slanted (see Figure 12.7); in others, the letters are straight up and down (Figure 12.8).

At the same time, the children were developing a heightened familiarity with letter shapes. They built skyscrapers from alphabet blocks. They played with alphabet noo-

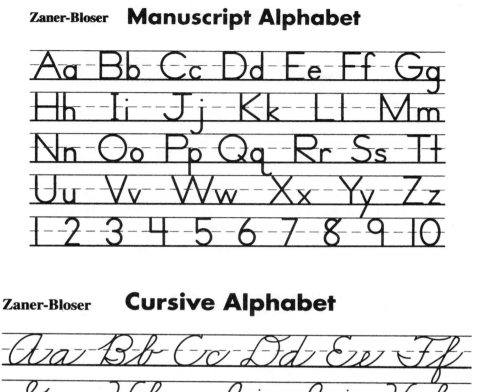

Figure 12.8

Zaner-Bloser Letter and Number Forms

Source: Zaner-Bloser, Inc., P.O. Box 16764, Columbus, Ohio. Used by permission of the publisher.

DISCUSSION PROMPT

■ How do these letter and number forms differ from those on page 463?

CONSIDER

These activities achieve many objectives. They help children perceive differences in shapes, recognize letter shapes, and relate speech sounds to letters.

dles, forming them into collagelike designs by gluing them to small oak tag squares. They matched blocks and noodles to the letters on the guides mounted in the classroom and placed their alphabet pieces in the same order.

More Early Letter-Formation Activities   Working with preschool or kindergarten youngsters, teachers can experiment with some of Ms. Robinson's letter-reinforcing activities. Here are two other ideas:

- *Giant Letters.* Cut child-size upper- and lowercase letters from corrugated cardboard. Children paint the letters bright colors. Throw the large letters on the floor, then the small ones. Children order the letters by picking them up and matching shapes with those on the classroom wall. They also match lower- with uppercase equivalents. For even more fun, young children pick up lowercase letters and dance to music with their uppercase partners. When the music stops, children exchange letters and start again when it resumes.
- *Letter Verses.* One kindergarten teacher composed a little verse to go with each letter and set the verse to music. Her verse for capital *B* is

  I can make the letter B,
  And this is the way I do it.
  A line down and around and around,
  And that is the capital B.

  Her verse for lowercase *b* is almost the same:

  I can make the letter b,
  And this is the way I do it.
  A line down and just once around,
  And that is the little b.

  On the playground, this teacher chalks giant upper- and lowercase *b*s. The children play follow-the-leader as they skip around the outline of a letter and sing the appropriate verse. Teachers can compose original third lines for each of the other letters.

Designing Structured Mini-Lessons to Meet Individual Needs

CONSIDER

Pamela Farris (1991) writes, "Teachers in early childhood education should teach handwriting through direct instruction, for it is a basic and important skill for writing." Do you agree?

Not all children need equal attention to handwriting-related skills. Some can control a pencil at an early age; others have more difficulty controlling the fine muscles of the fingers and perceiving the distinctions in the way letters are made. For example, as some children enter first grade, they may need help in refining the way they form their letters, especially when they begin to use lined paper. At this point, the teacher takes advantage of paper with a lighter guideline between two darker ones and an open area at the top for drawing. He or she structures a mini-lesson for a special needs group and demonstrates letter forms in this way:

Objective: The children will be able to form clear renditions of the letters *l* and *i*. They will be able to form a word with *l* and *i*, spacing the letters within the word and allowing sufficient space between words.

According to a line, circle, and hump system. See Figure 12.8.

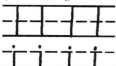

According to D'Nealian

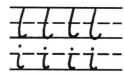

Sequence for the teacher:

1. Within the first double space on your model sheet, write a lowercase *l*. Demonstrate where the top of the letter begins and where it ends. Invite children to do the same on their lined paper.
2. Within the second double space on your sheet, print a lowercase *i*. Again, demonstrate where the top of the letter begins and where the bottom sits. Demonstrate where the dot is placed. Invite children to do the same a few times.
3. Within the third space on your paper, print first an *l* and then an *i*, drawing attention to the space you leave between the letters. Children alternate *l* and *i* across their pages. Encourage them to repeat a rhythmic verse as they print.
4. Talk about how it feels to be sick. Explain to the children that sometimes they say they are "ill" when they are sick. Encourage them to describe times when they were ill. Then print the word *ill* on your paper. Allow time for children to print the word on their papers. Then demonstrate how they can use the width of their pointing finger to figure out how much space to leave between words: "Just one finger's width from the end of the word *ill*; let's begin the word again." Children experiment with the spacing strategy.
5. After children have practiced the letter forms and spacing, suggest that they fold their papers in thirds. Children draw three pictures in the open area at the top to tell a story about when they were sick—a story with a beginning, a middle, and an end. Suggest they write a story about when they were ill, using that sight word somewhere in their story.

On successive days, working with the same special-needs group, a teacher starts handwriting lessons with a brief review and then introduces the form of the lowercase *t*, the uppercase *L*, and the uppercase *T*. Children practice forming and spacing words with those letters and take special care in forming those letters as they make final drafts.

Basic Guidelines for Teaching Letter Forms

The structure of the mini-lesson just described suggests four guidelines for helping first-graders to produce legible forms of manuscript letters:

- *Introduce letters with a similar form together,* such as *i*, *l*, and *t*, since they are formed from a basic downward stroke. However, do not introduce letters that are easily confused (*b*, *d*) together.
- *Provide practice in combining letters into words.* This adds the element of spacing, which makes children gauge distance within and between words. Children can use an index finger or ice cream stick to estimate distance—one finger's width between words, two between sentences, two for indenting. It also makes instruction more meaningful.
- *Provide letter models.* There are two types of models. First are letters the teacher makes when demonstrating how to form a letter. When demonstrating, the teacher draws attention to where to begin a stroke, where to end it, what direction to move in to make circles, and how many strokes to use to form a letter. Second

are the models displayed around the room. Most commonly used are the letter strips placed below or above the chalkboard. To be most effective, models should be placed at eye level, where they can be touched and traced. Another aid is a small card of upper- and lowercase letters. Many teachers tape a card to an upper corner of each student's desk.

■ *Include instruction on how to get ready to write.* The teacher must show youngsters how to sit and how to position the paper. For manuscript writing with no letter slant, the paper is generally held perpendicular to the body and parallel to the edge of the desk for both right- and left-handed writers. If left-handed children find this position awkward, they can experiment with a second position, advocated in the Zaner-Bloser handwriting system (see Figure 12.9).

Some children also need instruction in how to hold their pencils. Observe any group of people—whether first-graders or college students—as they write, and you will see any number holding their pencils in all sorts of weird ways. These ineffective ways may impede writing and should be diagnosed and remediated by an alert teacher.

Functional Opportunities for Refinement

Once children have mastered basic letter forms, they can refine their technique by printing the cards and charts needed for instruction. Children can take turns producing

■ *Cards* to display spelling words; to study subjects and predicates, parts of speech, synonyms, homonyms, antonyms, contractions, alphabetical order, and so forth.

■ *Charts* of words to substitute for worn-out words, spelling generalizations, poetry selections, and procedures used in the classroom during science investigations.

■ *Labels* to affix to objects in the classroom, to desks naming who sits there, and to cabinets identifying what is kept there.

■ *Duplicating masters* of selections for body chants and choral speaking, of material for a class newspaper or magazine, of discussion topics, and of summaries resulting from social science investigations.

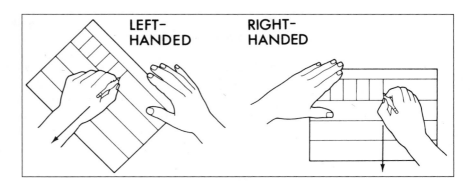

Figure 12.9
Zaner-Bloser Method Writing Positions

GO TO

Chapter 10 for ideas for publications that provide handwriting practice as part of actual writing.

Children can also select some of their own writings to revise and contribute to a class book of stories; each renders in his or her very best handwriting the piece chosen for revision and publication. Bound together, contributions are placed in the reading center or the library for others to enjoy. Students can make a similar collection of hand-printed poems.

Work that children enjoy rendering in their publication manuscript includes

- *Original greeting cards* to give to family members or friends.
- *Invitations* to parents to a class performance, to other classes to share a party or performance, and to speakers requesting that they visit the class.
- *Letters* to pen pals and to editors of local papers.
- *Thank-you notes* to those who have helped the class.

Upper-graders can use the same activities to refine their cursive letter forms.

Since handwriting is a tool for recording thoughts on paper, repeated use as part of actual writing provides the best practice. Children refine their handwriting as they prepare final drafts of stories, poems, and reports. They practice as they write memoranda to teacher and classmates. If children are continuously involved in composing and publishing, they will by necessity be involved in handwriting. After mini-lessons in which letter shapes are introduced and the steps important in forming the shapes are stressed, there is a decreasing need for systematic instruction as children use handwriting on a daily basis and the teacher works with individual children to overcome any special problems.

Diagnosing Children's Handwriting Problems

Six elements result in legible manuscript: shape, size and proportion, slant, spacing, steadiness of line, and styling—the six *S*s of manuscript. As youngsters build skills, problems are diagnosed in terms of the six *S*s so that additional instruction to meet individual needs can be provided. In addition, kidwatching may bring to light problems associated with positioning of paper and pencil. How do children grasp the pencil? Some children may grip it tightly, others may hold it at the point, and still others may hold it between the middle and pointing fingers.

Discovering problems common to several children, a teacher can schedule time for a special-needs mini-lesson. For example, youngsters having difficulty with alignment, or getting letters to rest on the base line, gather together and focus directly on their problem. At other times, a teacher helps an individual child with a special problem.

Children should participate in the assessment process. At first, the teacher supplies youngsters with a simple self-assessment checklist. Later children devise checklists geared to recognized weaknesses. Periodically they select a publication draft to analyze. If the assessment is recorded on the same checklist on several occasions, youngsters can identify areas requiring more practice. Figure 12.10 provides an example of a self-assessment checklist.

LOOKING AT MY OWN HANDWRITING	NAME: _____											
Letters I have trouble making:	Jan 1		Jan 15		Feb 1		Feb 15		Mar 1		Mar 15	
	Yes	No	Yes	No	Yes	No	Yes	No	Yes	No	Yes	No
Do I keep my letters parallel?												
Do my letters stand on the base line?												
Are my uppercase and large lower-case letters filling the space?												
Are my little lowercase letters half-sized?												
Do I space my letters clearly?												
Do I space my words evenly across the page?												
Are my letter lines even and steady?												
Is my paper neat?												

Figure 12.10
A Self-Assessment Handwriting Checklist

Moving from Manuscript Letter Forms into Cursive Forms

Transition cursive:

Adult cursive:

Generally, children are introduced to cursive forms, or script, at the end of second or the beginning of third grade. The cursive children use initially differs to some extent from adult cursive. Because it differs, it is sometimes called *transition cursive*. In some penmanship systems, transition cursive is larger than adult cursive and retains the two-to-one proportion characteristic of manuscript: The small lowercase letters are half the size of uppercase and tall lowercase letters. In adult cursive, the small letters are approximately one-third the height of full-size letters. Transition cursive is commonly used through fourth grade; by fifth grade, youngsters write in adult cursive on paper without central guidelines.

In this section, we will look at ways to help children move from manuscript to cursive letter forms. We will begin by revisiting Fred Bronsky's third grade.

Handwriting in Action   *Introducing Cursive Letter Forms*

When Fred Bronsky's third-graders entered their classroom one late September morning, they noticed a change. Above the manuscript letter strips mounted around the room was a second set of letters—cursive. On each desk, below the letter guide in the right-hand corner, was a second letter guide—cursive. On the board was a series of guidelines.

Mr. Bronsky, a teacher who took little time with preliminaries, jumped into his mini-lesson as soon as the children had settled down. "Watch me," he directed. "I'm going to write something twice. You will have to tell me how each writing differs." He picked up chalk, broke it in two to prevent squeaking, and wrote within the first guidelines:

CONSIDER

In D'Nealian, letters would be slanted.

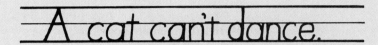

Then he wrote within a second set of guidelines below the first:

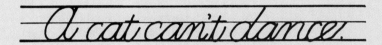

Perceive differences between manuscript and cursive letter forms

"Differences now?" he queried, and the children volunteered explanations: The first was manuscript, the second adult writing; the first was straight up and down, the second slanted; the first had separated letters, the second joined letters; when writing the first, Mr. Bronsky had stopped between letters, while in the second he had kept on going.

"Exactly right," Mr. Bronsky commended. Then he went to a second series of lines on the board. Between the first two, he wrote the word *cat* in manuscript. Between the next two, he wrote *cat* again in manuscript. Between the last two, he wrote *cat* in cursive. Then he demonstrated, using dotted lines added to the middle version (see diagram), how the letters in manuscript relate to the letters in cursive.

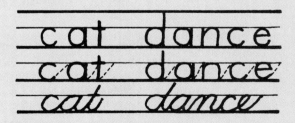

He made a similar connection between the manuscript and cursive letters in the remaining words of his model sentence.

Mr. Bronsky distributed lined paper. The paper was ruled with a heavy base line at half-inch intervals and a lighter midguideline. As he distributed the paper, he visited among the children, showing how to position it on the desk, how to grasp the pencil,

Practice letters that begin with undercurve

and how to position the body for writing. Mr. Bronsky then went to the board to introduce the letters with an undercurve beginning:

He demonstrated the *i*—starting on the base line, moving upward with an undercurve, moving downward toward the base line, moving upward with a second undercurve, and dotting in the space above. The children took pencils in hand and, as Mr. Bronsky rhythmically repeated, "Curve up, move down, curve up with a tail, dot the *i*" and wrote a row of *i*s on the ruled board, they did the same on their papers. A few left-handed children wrote on guidelines on the board next to the teacher's.

Feel the rhythm of cursive writing

Mr. Bronsky demonstrated other letters with an undercurve beginning—*u* and *s*—and rhythmically described the component strokes as he formed them: "Curve up, bring it down, curve up again, bring it down, and up with the tail—the little *u*." "Curve up, bring it down, tie it around, curve up with the tail—the little *s*." He encouraged the children to repeat the jingles to themselves while forming the letters. In short order, the third-graders were joining undercurve letters into words—*it, sit, us*—which they practiced on their sheets.

On successive days, the teacher introduced other letters with undercurve beginnings—*w, e, r*—and letters with undercurve beginnings and large loops—*l, f, b, h, k, p*—essentially following the letter groupings in the handwriting system in use in his school. Soon he was introducing other lowercase groups:

1. Those beginning with an overcurve ( ), the hump letters like *m v x y z.*

2. Those beginning with a downward curve ( ), the small oval letters like *a d g q o c.*

3. Those containing a lower loop like *j g p y z q f.*

Later the third-graders studied the uppercase letter groups, again working concurrently on letters sharing a structural feature.

If Mr. Bronsky had been using a different handwriting system, such as D'Nealian, Palmer, or Noble and Noble, he would have followed a similar sequence. He would have modeled how to hold pencil and paper; taught structurally related letters together; provided classroom models of each letter; introduced letter strokes to a rhythm; and moved quickly from individual letters to words and sentences to develop spacing strategies. There would have been a difference, however, in the final letter shapes, depending on the system in use. Before beginning a mini-lesson series, a teacher should check letter shapes and letter heights to be consistent with what children have learned in previous grades.

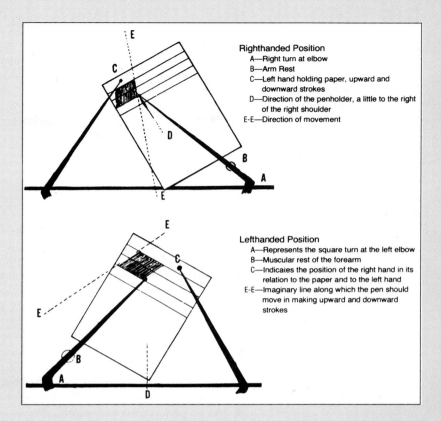

Figure 12.11
Paper and Hand Positions for Cursive Writing

Helping Left-Handed Children

Identify left-handed writers

■ ● ● ●

READ

Thomas Wasylyk, "Teaching Left Handers the Write Stuff," *The Reading Teacher,* 42 (February 1989), 446–447.

During the mini-lesson, Mr. Bronsky checked to make sure children were at ease with the hand they had chosen for manuscript writing. He wanted to be certain which children were right-handed and which were left-handed so that he could help them with the writing position of hands and paper and provide extra time for left-handed students to work at the board.

The recommended position for right-handed writers is to hold the paper so that the bottom forms a thirty-degree angle with the table edge and the left hand is placed in the upper left-hand corner of the paper to steady it. Most handwriting specialists recommend that left-handed writers place the paper in a position that is the mirror image of the one recommended for righties: the right bottom corner pointing toward the writer, the right hand in the right top corner to steady the paper, and the left hand guiding the pencil from left to right, as in Figure 12.11.

Although one left-hander, John Ramsey (1988), has described his own successful use of the rightward-slanting paper position, some left-handed writers find that if they use the position shown in Figure 12.11, they cover with their writing hand the letters and words they have just written. Because of this, lefties cannot look back on their writing. One left-handed person resolved this dilemma by inventing his own system. He pulls his paper down by the left-hand bottom corner so

DISCUSSION PROMPT

■ How does the personality of a teacher such as Mr. Bronsky affect his or her teaching? How does your personality affect your teaching?

that the bottom edge forms at least a fifty-degree angle with the table edge. Without hooking his wrist, he writes uphill, making it possible for him to write most legibly and at the same time see the letters coming from beneath his pen without arching his hand in the upside-down position many left-handed writers adopt. Given the uncertain state of knowledge about left-handed writing, perhaps the logical course to follow is to show left-handed youngsters the traditional position. If that proves unwieldy, children should experiment to find a position that serves them best.

Opportunities for Refinement

Having systematically demonstrated the lower- and uppercase letter forms, a teacher will want to provide continued and meaningful practice with cursive writing first in the transitional and then in the adult style. Many of the activities for refinement described in the manuscript section apply equally to cursive: Upper-graders prepare observational charts, word cards, labels, and so forth. They write letters, invitations, and greeting cards. In addition, they experiment with some of the following publication activities:

■ Youngsters write and send notes to one another. From half-gallon cardboard milk containers, the teacher fashions a series of pigeonholes, one for each student. Students label their pigeonholes, into which others, including the teacher, tuck notes, papers being returned, or special assignments.

■ Upper-graders compose nature haiku and cinquains, which they then render in their best cursive onto pieces of brown paper bag, ripped to form jagged edges. The poems are taken outside, attached with twine to trees and shrubs, and left to weather. They truly become "nature poems."

■ Obtain old wallpaper sample books from a wallpaper store. A student who has written a poem selects a page from the sample book that evokes the same mood as the poem, cuts a rectangle from the page, and writes the poem on it.

■ Scrolls are fun to write, correlate nicely with social science content, and provide meaningful handwriting practice. Children studying colonial America write pseudoproclamations, such as those that might have been written the day after the Boston Tea Party or those that announced the Stamp Tax Act. Children studying ancient Greece and Rome write proclamations that might have been read before the governing councils. Proclamations are written in cursive on the unwaxed side of shelf paper, the ends of the paper are attached to dowels, and the proclamations are delivered as part of a class "We Are There" happening. In this activity, as in the others described here, children use handwriting as a tool for clear communication.

Most of these activities provide practice either as part of ongoing classroom activity or as follow-up to written expression and science or social studies. As in the lower grades, the best practice is repeated use in publishing writing.

In addition, there may be call for more direct instruction, especially as fifth-graders change to adult cursive. To facilitate the transition to adult cursive, youngsters use paper without a central guideline and with lines about 3/8″ apart, the same as the legal-size yellow tablets in common use. Students systematically work on lowercase letters from each letter group, focusing on the letters with undercurve beginnings, downward curve beginnings, upper loops, and lower loops; they work on the upper-case letters as well.

In similar fashion, youngsters work on special weaknesses identified by studying samples of their own cursive. Students can check the legibility of individual letters by punching a hole about one centimeter in diameter in a card. They place the hole on top of a sample of each letter as it appears in their writing. By masking all the other letters, the evaluator can get a better idea of the clarity of individual letters. Failing to close up letters like *a, o,* and *d* is a common problem that can cause confusion and that students can identify by close checking through a masking hole.

The ultimate criterion in judging handwriting is whether the writing is legible. At all levels, but particularly in the middle and junior high schools, students express their individuality through their handwriting. To insist that youngsters' letters be perfect duplicates of the models in a handwriting system is often to ask the impossible and generally to ask the unnecessary. Students above grade five will need to refine skills periodically to ensure continued legibility, but after a point individual styling should be a factor in handwriting.

■ ● ● ●

CONSIDER

Criteria for diagnosing cursive include

1. Consistent slant,
2. Appropriate size and proportion,
3. Consistent spacing,
4. Careful closing of such letters as *a, o,* and *d,*
5. Alignment—letters sitting on the lines,
6. Accurate letter formation,
7. Overall neatness.

Convert items into a diagnostic checklist and evaluate your own penmanship using it.

Keyboarding

Although keyboarding is a skill separate from handwriting, its growing importance must be acknowledged. The ability to produce typed copy has been required primarily by those entering the secretarial professions and those doing a great deal of writing in advanced high school and college programs or in their work. Today, however, the need for keyboarding skill is increasing with the widespread use of relatively inexpensive tabletop and laptop microcomputers. As a result, schools need to reconsider their decision about the point at which they make keyboarding instruction available to students. The elementary grades is not too early to begin.

A Summary Thought or Two

Spelling, Dictionary Use, and Handwriting

To write effectively, people must create the ideas that are the substance of expression. Without ideas to be expressed, writing serves little purpose. For this reason, most writing programs have rightly stressed idea making.

But to make ideas is not enough. To write effectively, people must be able to manipulate language on paper, especially if thoughts are to receive more than cursory attention. Others judge ideas by the words selected to express them, by the way those words are spelled, and even by the appearance of the paper.

Accordingly, spelling, dictionary skills, and handwriting are basic tools that children should acquire in language arts programs. As this chapter explains, schools should be concerned about developing children's ability to

- Handle regular sound-symbol relationships and spell words that do not adhere to expectations.
- Spell multisyllabic words made up of affixes and roots, spell compound words, and handle homonyms.
- Arrange words in alphabetical order and locate words ordered alphabetically.
- Use the dictionary to check spelling, find a substitute for an overworked word, check word meaning, and determine pronunciation.
- Produce readable manuscript in which letters generally conform to conventions regarding size, slant, shape, spacing, line strength, and styling.
- Produce a legible form of cursive, starting in third grade.

As this chapter has also emphasized, children acquire and refine these skills through mini-lessons that focus on particular learnings and through drafting, editing, and publishing as part of actual writing.

A final caveat is in order. Because ideas are basic in writing, the process of recording ideas should not impede expression. Stopping in midthought to check spelling or word meaning in the dictionary and writing painstakingly so that *o*s, *a*s, and *d*s are tightly closed to prevent misinterpretation may cause writers to lose the thoughts they are trying to express. The time for concern about dictionary checking, spelling, and handwriting is not in midthought; it is afterthought, as writers dress up what they have written.

As children compose stories, poems, and reports, teachers should not remind them to check the dictionary and write in their very best penmanship. Editing is the point for checking spelling. Publishing is the point for well-styled handwriting as children select pieces to share. To turn a creative writing experience into a handwriting or spelling test is to take the creativity out of the experience.

Your Language Arts Portfolio

- Write a plan for a discovery-type spelling lesson based on the steps on page 437.
- Write a paragraph or two in which you contrast the forms of the letters in the two handwriting systems pictured in this book (see pages 463 and 465). Write an additional paragraph in which you state your opinion of the two approaches. Write one paragraph in manuscript, one in cursive.
- As Lonnie McDonald writes, "Good handwriting is important for all educators who model before children daily." Teachers-to-be must realize that "it is worth their time and effort to change their life-long poor handwriting habits for the sake of their students." Similarly, teachers-to-be must be able to look at words and see shared features. To this end, sort the following words into categories, decide in what ways they are the same and in what ways they differ, generalize about how to spell the prefix in question, and then (as a demonstration of your ability to produce clear cursive) create a word banner with the words grouped to show relationships. Put your banner in your portfolio. The words: *illegal, ignoble, insecure, immature, irreverent, inappropriate, immaterial, impossible, illicit, irregular, impassable, ignorant.* You may want to check a dictionary for other words to include on your banner.

Related Readings

Barwick, John, and Jenny Barwick. *The Spelling Skills Handbook*. York, Me.: Stenhouse Publishers, 2000.

Bean, Wendy, and Chrys Bouffler. *Read, Write, Spell*. York, Me.: Stenhouse Publishers, 1997.

Bear, Donald, et al. *Words Their Way: Word Study for Phonics, Vocabulary, and Spelling Instruction*. 2nd ed. Upper Saddle River, N.J.: Merrill, 2000.

Bolton, Faye, and Diane Snowball. *Ideas for Spelling*. Portsmouth, N.H.: Heinemann, 1993.

Fresch, Mary Jo. "Journal Entries as a Window on Spelling Knowledge." *The Reading Teacher*, 54 (February 2001), 500–513.

Fresch, Mary Jo, and Aileen Wheaton. "Sort, Search, and Discover: Spelling in the Child-centered Classroom." *The Reading Teacher*, 51,1 (September 1997), 20–31.

Gaskins, Irene, et al. "Analyzing Words and Making Discoveries about the Alphabetic System: Activities for Beginning Readers." *Language Arts*, 74 (March 1997), 172–184.

Gentry, J. Richard. "A Retrospective on Invented Spelling and a Look Forward." *The Reading Teacher*, 54 (November 2000), 318–332.

Gill, Charlene, and Patricia Scharer. " 'Why Do They Get It on Friday and Misspell It on Monday?' Teachers Inquiring About Their Students as Spellers." *Language Arts*, 73 (February 1996), 89–96.

Hayward, Christopher. "Monitoring Spelling Development." *The Reading Teacher*, 31 (February 1998), 444–445.

Heald-Taylor, B. Gail. "Three Paradigms of Spelling Instruction in Grades 3 to 6." *The Reading Teacher*, 51 (February 1998), 404–413.

Henderson, Edmund. *Teaching Spelling*. 2nd ed. Boston: Houghton Mifflin, 1990.

Hillerich, Robert. "Reading Central: Dictionary Skills." *Early Years*, 16 (1986), 14–15.

Hughes, Margaret, and Dennis Searle. *The Violent 6 and Other Tricky Sounds: Learning to Spell from Kindergarten Through Grade 6*. York, Me.: Stenhouse Publishers, 1997.

Invernizzi, Marcia, Mary Abouzerd, and Janet Bloodgood. "Integrated Word Study: Spelling, Grammar, and Meaning in the Language Arts Classroom." *Language Arts*, 74 (March 1997), 185–192.

Koenke, Karl. "Handwriting Instruction: What Do We Know?" *The Reading Teacher*, 40 (November 1986), 214–216.

Language Arts, 69 (October 1992). The theme of the issue is "But What About Spelling?" Check articles by O'Flahavan, Schlagal and Schlagal, and Templeton.

Language Arts, 70 (January 2000). The theme of the issue is "Spelling Out Our Concerns About Spelling." Check articles by Turbil, Hughes and Searle, and Rymer and Williams as well as the editorial comment that opens the issue.

Phenix, Jo. *The Spelling Teacher's Book of Lists*. Ontario, Canada: Pembroke Publishers, 1996.

Pinnell, Gay Su, and Irene Fountas. *Word Matters: Teaching Phonics and Spelling in the Reading/Writing Classroom.* Portsmouth, N.H.: Heinemann, 1998.

Ramsey, John. "Why Is Left Handed Writing Still a Problem in the Last 7th of the 20th Century?" *The Reading Teacher,* 41 (February 1988), 504–506.

Routman, Regie. "The Uses and Abuses of Invented Spelling." *Instructor,* 102 (May/June 1993), 36–39.

————. "Reclaiming the Basics." *Instructor,* 105 (May/June 1996), 49–54, 84.

School Talk (April 1996). The theme of this issue is "Spelling: What It Is and What It Isn't."

Scott, Jill. "Spelling for Readers and Writers." *The Reading Teacher,* 48 (October 1994), 188–189.

Snowball, Diane. "Ten Ways to Encourage Better Spelling." *Teaching K–8* (May 2000), 54–65.

————. "Thinking about Language." *Teaching K–8,* 24, 8 (May 1994), 64–65.

Snowball, Diane, and Faye Bolton. *Spelling K–8: Planning and Teaching.* York, Me.: Stenhouse Publishers, 1999.

Venezky, Richard. *The American Way of Spelling: The Structure and Origins of American English Orthography.* New York: Guilford, 1999.

Communication in Action is based on beliefs about how children become language users.

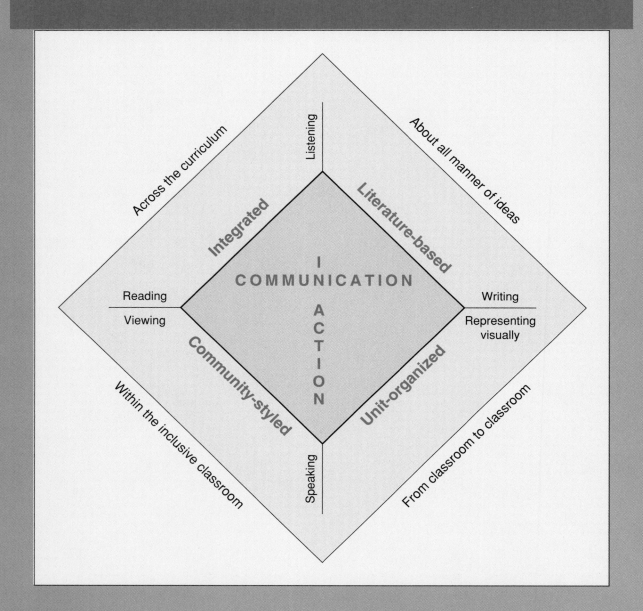

"Will you walk a little faster," said a whiting to a snail.

"There's a porpoise close behind us, and he's treading on my tail.

See how eagerly the lobsters and turtles all advance!

They are waiting on the shingle—will you come and join the dance?

Will you, won't you, will you, won't you, will you join the dance?

Will you, won't you, will you, won't you, won't you join the dance?"

—Lewis Carroll, *Alice's Adventures in Wonderland*

Accepting the Invitation

Deejay Schwartz, a kindergarten teacher, perceives herself as a teacher-researcher. Several years ago, she began to experiment with invented spelling, and now she asks her kindergartners to write daily from the time they arrive at school in the fall. Here she explains how she began to investigate her students' early writing development.

Teacher Inquiry

READ

- *Language Arts*, 73 (February 1996). The theme of the issue is the role of teacher inquiry in language arts.
- Eleanor Kutz, "Teacher Research: Myths and Realities," *Language Arts*, 69 (March 1992), 193–197.

I teach kindergarten in a suburban elementary school. In a typical class, although a few youngsters come to school able to break their thoughts into word units, most have not yet developed a concept of a word; they tend to write in strings of letters without word breaks. Most also come to school knowing that there is a right spelling regardless of how open and encouraging of their invented spellings I am. I asked myself: How can I help the children learn more about words even as they use their invented spellings to write?

Figure Coda.1
Andrew's Early Writing: "If I was president I would fight for my men"; "I wish I could jump higher than a kangaroo."
Courtesy of Andrew Levinson

"To begin, I hypothesized ways in which spelling 'lessons' and eventually handwriting 'lessons' were an integral part of the writing process. I kept trying out these ways, modifying what I was doing as I went along, and discovered two approaches with which I am now experimenting.

"Sometimes—though not always, for I have my children writing daily in many different formats, including journals—I ask children to divide construction paper into three parts. I suggest that they rehearse by drawing whatever story they are planning to write in the first section of the paper as they 'mind talk' their stories. The children use the second section to record using their invented spellings.

"After children have drafted, I confer with each one, asking each child to read his or her story. As the child reads, very lightly in pencil I inscribe the piece in 'dictionary spelling' beneath the child's first draft. The child now reads the revised draft and finger-points the words as he or she reads. Then together, we find correspondences between the child's invented spelling and the dictionary spelling. In every case there are correspondences, because I include some oral work with sound-symbol relationships (especially with beginning consonants) as part of experience story chart writing and the repeated reading of big books. As the child finds the correspondences, I 'celebrate,' making him or her feel good about the writing. In Andrew's case [see Figure Coda.1], I said, 'Look, Andrew! You can write the beginning of *my* and *men*. You know how to use the letter *m* to represent the sound you hear there. Can you find another place where you have a letter that is part of dictionary spelling?'

"Having celebrated their writing in this way, children return to their places elated with themselves and with writing; at their table and independently, they trace over the letters I have inscribed for them in dictionary spelling. For me, this last step comprises a handwriting practice at a point in the writing process where it counts—in the production of a publication draft for bulletin board posting.

"To emphasize words as units of communication and help children develop a concept of word, I vary my approach periodically. As before, children draw as they rehearse their stories through mind talk. But instead of having children record their stories immediately in invented spelling, I have them further rehearse by telling me what they intend to write. As children tell me, I draw word-length lines in paragraph style on the children's papers. Then children draft their stories, putting each word on a separate line, an activity that stresses word units within thought units [see Figure Coda.1]. The after-drafting activities are the same as in my prior treatment: The child orally reads what he or she has written, while I record beneath in dictionary spelling; we identify and 'celebrate' correspondences between the two drafts; the child practices handwriting by tracing over to make a publication copy."

READ

■ Marilyn D'Alessandro et al., "Writing for Publication: Voices from the Classroom," *The Reading Teacher,* 45 (February 1992), 402–414 for a description of how teacher-researchers publish their findings.

■ Karin Dahl, ed., *Teacher as Writer: Entering the Professional Conversation* (Urbana, Ill.: National Council of Teachers of English, 1992).

Reflecting Back

"I have found that when children truly 'celebrate' correspondences between their invented spelling and dictionary spelling, they are not at all miffed. They actually are encouraged in future writing to express themselves in invented spelling, because they

■ What were Ms. Schwartz's objectives in structuring children's writing activity as she did? What advantages do you see in her approach? What disadvantages? How was Ms. Schwartz helping children mature as spellers? How was she helping them appreciate the importance of clear handwriting? Why should teachers function as researchers in their classrooms?

know we will celebrate the correspondences as signs of their growth as writers. As I continue to experiment with these approaches, I find that children keep writing more and are daily adding more dictionary spellings to their repertoire of invented ones. But best of all, they seem to enjoy functioning as authors.

"Are my approaches valid teaching practices? Only more experimentation will tell."

Closing Measures

Today many teachers function as researchers and experiment systematically with ways to help children become more effective users of oral, written, and visual language and more appreciative readers and writers. To these ends, these teachers

■ Engage children in thinking and communicating about all manner of ideas from the world of books and the world all around.
■ Make literature central in the language arts.
■ Integrate listening, speaking, viewing, writing, and reading across the curriculum.
■ Teach language skills and strategies in functional contexts at the point of use rather than through discrete exercises removed from actual reading and writing.
■ Organize their classrooms as social communities.
■ Use a variety of instructional strategies that combine whole class with independent and collaborative learning.
■ Draw upon the latest technology and especially encourage communication beyond the classroom via the Internet.
■ Plan literature-based units to meet the varied needs of children in inclusive classrooms.

Just as Deejay Schwartz is doing, these teachers search for better ways to do things and learn from their successes and their mistakes.

Can you see yourself as a teacher—searching, experimenting, putting ideas together in original ways? To do so, you, too, must "walk a little faster." You must "advance eagerly." You must "come and join the dance."

"Will you, won't you, will you, won't you,
won't you join the dance?"

That is the invitation teachers must accept if students are to acquire the ability to communicate with ease and style, if they are to develop a love of books, and if they are to acquire an understanding of the beauty and power of language.

Your Language Arts Portfolio

- Design a unit plan for early-primary children based on a series of related picture storybooks and poems, as in the thematic plan on fear found in Chapter 1 on pages 34–35. Include opportunities for speaking, listening, viewing, writing, singing, and drawing, as well as reading. State your objectives in terms of student behaviors.
- Design a unit plan for intermediate-grade children based on a core chapter book. Model your plan after the one for *Sarah, Plain and Tall* in the Access Pages, 504–506. Include opportunities for speaking, listening, viewing, reading, and writing. Include some music, art, and social studies opportunities.
- Review your personal statement of beliefs regarding the teaching of the language arts that you wrote earlier. Revise that statement to include any changes in your philosophy of instruction. Create a schematic in the manner of the figure on page 480 to clarify key elements in your philosophy. Take your schematic on position interviews and use it to talk about your instructional beliefs.

Access Pages

The Teacher's Planning Resource Handbook

Caldecott and Newbery Award–Winning Books

Caldecott Award–Winning Books, 1961–2001

Since 1938, the American Library Association has awarded the Caldecott Medal to the most distinguished picture book for children. The illustrators receiving the award since 1961 are shown in bold type. Use the names of these illustrators to guide your search for striking picture books, for these illustrators are among the finest in the United States.

2001   *So You Want to Be President.* **Judith St. George.** Ill. by **David Small.** New York: Philomel Books, 2000.

2000   *Joseph Had a Little Overcoat.* **Simms Taback.** New York: Viking, 1999.

1999   *Snowflake Bentley.* **Jacqueline Martin.** Boston: Houghton Mifflin, 1998.

1998   *Rapunzel.* **Paul Zelinksy.** New York: Dutton, 1997.

1997   *Golem.* **David Wisniewski.** New York: Clarion, 1996.

1996   *Officer Buckle and Gloria.* **Peggy Rathmann.** New York: Putnam's, 1995.

1995   *Smoky Night.* Eve Bunting. Ill. by **David Diaz.** Fort Worth: Harcourt, Brace, 1994.

1994   *Grandfather's Journey.* **Allen Say.** Boston: Houghton Mifflin, 1993.

1993   *Mirette on the High Wire.* **Emily Arnold McCully.** New York: Putnam's, 1992.

1992   *Tuesday.* **David Wiesner.** New York: Clarion, 1991.

1991   *Black and White.* **David Macaulay.** Boston: Houghton Mifflin, 1990.

1990   *Lon Po Po.* **Ed Young.** New York: Philomel, 1989.

1989   *Song and Dance Man.* Jane Ackerman. Ill. by **Stephen Gammell.** New York: Knopf, 1988.

1988   *Owl Moon.* Jane Yolen. Ill. by **John Schoenherr.** New York: Philomel, 1987.

1987   *Hey, Al.* Arthur Yorinks. Ill. by **Richard Egielski.** New York: Farrar, Straus and Giroux, 1986.

1986   *The Polar Express.* **Chris Van Allsburg.** Boston: Houghton Mifflin, 1985.

1985   *Saint George and the Dragon.* Retold by Margaret Hodges. Ill. by **Tina Schart Hyman.** Boston: Little, Brown, 1984.

1984   *The Glorious Flight: Across the Channel with Louis Bleriot.* **Alice and Martin Provensen.** New York: Viking, 1983.

1983   *Shadow.* Blaise Cendrars. Ill. by **Marcia Brown.** New York: Scribner, 1982.

1982   *Jumanji.* **Chris Van Allsburg.** Boston: Houghton Mifflin, 1981.

1981   *Fables.* **Arnold Lobel.** New York: Harper & Row, 1980.

1980   *Ox-Cart Man.* Donald Hall. Ill. by **Barbara Cooney.** New York: Viking, 1979.

1979   *The Girl Who Loved Wild Horses.* **Paul Goble.** New York: Bradbury, 1978.

1978   *Noah's Ark.* **Peter Spier.** New York: Doubleday, 1977.

1977   *Ashanti to Zulu.* Margaret Musgrove. Ill. by **Leo and Diane Dillon.** New York: Dial, 1976.

1976   *Why Mosquitoes Buzz in People's Ears.* Verna Aardema. Ill. by **Leo and Diane Dillon.** New York: Dial, 1975.

1975   *Arrow to the Sun.* **Gerald McDermott.** New York: Viking, 1974.

1974	*Duffy and the Devil.* Retold by Harve Zemach. Ill. by **Margot Zemach.** New York: Farrar, Straus and Giroux, 1973.
1973	*The Funny Little Woman.* Retold by Arlene Mosel. Ill. by **Blair Lent.** New York: Dutton, 1972.
1972	*One Fine Day.* **Nonny Hogrogian.** New York: Macmillan, 1971.
1971	*A Story A Story.* **Gail Haley.** New York: Atheneum, 1970.
1970	*Sylvester and the Magic Pebble.* **William Steig.** New York: Windmill Books, 1969.
1969	*The Fool of the World and the Flying Machine.* Retold by Arthur Ransome. Ill. by **Uri Shulevitz.** New York: Farrar, Straus and Giroux, 1968.
1968	*Drummer Hoff.* Adapted by Barbara Emberley. Ill. by **Ed Emberley.** Englewood Cliffs, N.J.: Prentice-Hall, 1967.
1967	*Sam, Bangs, and Moonshine.* **Evaline Ness.** New York: Holt, Rinehart and Winston, 1966.
1966	*Always Room for One More.* Sorche Nic Leodhas. Ill. by **Nonny Hogrogian.** New York: Holt, Rinehart and Winston, 1965.
1965	*May I Bring a Friend?* Beatrice Schenk de Regniers. Ill. by **Beni Montresor.** New York: Atheneum, 1964.
1964	*Where the Wild Things Are.* **Maurice Sendak.** New York: Harper & Row, 1963.
1963	*The Snowy Day.* **Ezra Jack Keats.** New York: Viking, 1962.
1962	*Once a Mouse.* **Marcia Brown.** New York: Scribner, 1961.
1961	*Baboushka and the Three Kings.* Ruth Robbins. Ill. by **Nicolas Sidjakov.** Orleans, Mass.: Parnassus, 1960.

Newbery Award–Winning Books, 1961–2001

Since 1922, the American Library Association has awarded the Newbery Medal to the most distinguished contribution to children's literature. The writers receiving the award since 1961 are shown in bold type. Use the names of these writers to guide your search for books to recommend to intermediate-level children, for these writers are among the finest in the United States.

2001	*A Year Down Yonder.* **Richard Peck.** New York: Dial Books, 2000.
2000	*Bud, Not Buddy.* **C. P. Curtis.** New York: Delacorte Press, 1999.
1999	*Holes.* **Louis Sachar.** New York: Farrar, Straus, and Giroux, 1998.
1998	*Out of the Dust.* **Karen Hesse.** New York: Scholastic, 1997.
1997	*The View from Saturday.* **E. L. Konigsburg.** New York: Atheneum, 1996.
1996	*The Midwife's Apprentice.* **Karen Cushman.** New York: Clarion, 1995.
1995	*Walk Two Moons.* **Sharon Creech.** New York: HarperCollins, 1994.
1994	*The Giver.* **Lois Lowry.** Boston: Houghton Mifflin, 1993.
1993	*Missing May.* **Cynthia Rylant.** New York: Orchard, 1992.
1992	*Shiloh.* **Phyllis Reynolds Naylor.** New York: Atheneum, 1991.
1991	*Maniac Magee.* **Jerry Spinelli.** Boston: Little, Brown, 1990.
1990	*Number the Stars.* **Lois Lowry.** Boston: Houghton Mifflin, 1989.
1989	*Joyful Noise: Poems for Two Voices.* **Paul Fleischman.** New York: Harper & Row, 1988.

1988   *Abraham Lincoln: A Photobiography.* **Russell Freedman.** Boston: Houghton Mifflin, 1987.

1987   *The Whipping Boy.* **Sid Fleischman.** New York: Greenwillow, 1986.

1986   *Sarah, Plain and Tall.* **Patricia MacLachlan.** New York: Harper & Row, 1985.

1985   *The Hero and the Crown.* **Robin McKinley.** New York: Greenwillow, 1984.

1984   *Dear Mr. Henshaw.* **Beverly Cleary.** New York: William Morrow, 1983.

1983   *Dicey's Song.* **Cynthia Voight.** New York: Atheneum, 1982.

1982   *A Visit to William Blake's Inn: Poems for Innocent and Experienced Travelers.* **Nancy Willard.** San Diego: Harcourt Brace Jovanovich, 1981.

1981   *Jacob Have I Loved.* **Katherine Paterson.** New York: Crowell, 1980.

1980   *A Gathering of Days.* **Joan Blos.** New York: Scribner, 1979.

1979   *The Westing Game.* **Ellen Raskin.** New York: Dutton, 1978.

1978   *Bridge to Terabithia.* **Katherine Paterson.** New York: Crowell, 1977.

1977   *Roll of Thunder, Hear My Cry.* **Mildred Taylor.** New York: Dial, 1976.

1976   *The Grey King.* **Susan Cooper.** New York: Atheneum, 1975.

1975   *M. C. Higgins, the Great.* **Virginia Hamilton.** New York: Macmillan, 1974.

1974   *The Slave Dancer.* **Paula Fox.** New York: Bradbury, 1973.

1973   *Julie of the Wolves.* **Jean Craighead George.** New York: Harper & Row, 1972.

1972   *Mrs. Frisby and the Rats of NIMH.* **Robert O'Brien.** New York: Atheneum, 1971.

1971   *Summer of the Swans.* **Betsy Byars.** New York: Viking, 1970.

1970   *Sounder.* **William H. Armstrong.** New York: Harper & Row, 1969.

1969   *The High King.* **Lloyd Alexander.** New York: Holt, Rinehart and Winston, 1968.

1968   *From the Mixed-up Files of Mrs. Basil E. Frankweiler.* **E. L. Konigsburg.** New York: Atheneum, 1967.

1967   *Up a Road Slowly.* **Irene Hunt.** Chicago: Follett, 1966.

1966   *I, Juan de Pareja.* **Elizabeth Borton de Trevino.** New York: Farrar, Straus and Giroux, 1965.

1965   *Shadow of a Bull.* **Maia Wojciechowska.** New York: Atheneum, 1964.

1964   *It's Like This, Cat.* **Emily Neville.** New York: Harper & Row, 1963.

1963   *A Wrinkle in Time.* **Madeleine L'Engle.** New York: Farrar, Straus and Giroux, 1962.

1962   *The Bronze Bow.* **Elizabeth George Speare.** Boston: Houghton Mifflin, 1961.

1961   *Island of the Blue Dolphins.* **Scott O'Dell.** Boston: Houghton Mifflin, 1960.

Dorothy Hennings's Favorite Books for Organizing Literature-Based Units

Grade levels are approximations. The grade at which a book is read depends on the way the book is used (as a read-aloud, read-along, or read-alone) and children's interests. A book such as *Sarah, Plain and Tall* can be used at almost any level starting at grade three. Theme is what the book means to Dorothy Hennings. Each reader makes multiple meanings with a book. *Starred books have potential for use in multicultural units.* Most are available in paperback.

K-I-2

Burton, Virginia. *The Little House.* Houghton Mifflin. Theme: Things do not stay the same; they change.

Carle, Eric. *The Very Hungry Caterpillar.* World. Theme: Living things change.

Galdone, Paul, reteller. An assortment of traditional folktales. Seabury. *Henny Penny.* Theme: Think before you leap. Don't jump to conclusions. *The Little Red Hen.* Theme: Don't expect to get something for nothing. *The Three Bears.* Theme: You should ask before you help yourself. *The Three Billy Goats Gruff.* Theme: Greed has no reward. *The Three Little Pigs.* Theme: Hard work brings its reward.

Ginsberg, Mirra. *Mushroom in the Rain.* Macmillan. Theme: We need to help one another.*

Hutchins, Pat. *Rosie's Walk.* Macmillan. Theme: Look around you or you will not see all there is to see.

Keats, Ezra Jack. *The Snowy Day.* Viking. Theme: The simple things of life can bring us joy.*

Lobel, Arnold. *Owl at Home.* HarperCollins. Theme: How good it is to be at home despite everything that happens there.

McCloskey, Robert. *Make Way for Ducklings.* Viking. Theme: Families work together.

Rey, Margaret. *Curious George Flies a Kite.* Houghton Mifflin. Theme: The world is filled with many things that make you curious.

Sendak, Maurice. *Where the Wild Things Are.* HarperCollins. Theme: There's no place like home.

Seuss, Dr. *Horton Hatches the Egg.* Random House. Theme: You must be faithful to what you say and keep your promises.

Stevens, Janet. *Tops and Bottoms.* Harcourt Brace. Themes: You can win over hardship by using your wits. If you are not on the ball, you may be taken advantage of.

Taback, Simms. *Joseph Had a Little Overcoat.* Viking. Theme: You can make something out of very little.

Waber, Bernard. *"You Look Ridiculous," Said the Rhinoceros to the Hippopotamus.* Houghton Mifflin. Theme: Believe in yourself.*

Williams, Vera. *A Chair for My Mother.* Greenwillow. Theme: Giving is wonderful.*

I-2-3

Allard, Harry, and James Marshall. *Miss Nelson Is Missing.* Houghton Mifflin. Theme: Appreciate what you have.

Erickson, Russell. *A Toad for Tuesday.* Lothrop, Lee & Shepard. Theme: Everyone needs friends even though he or she sometimes does not realize it.

Lasky, Kathryn. *Marven of the Great North Woods.* Harcourt Brace. Themes: Find courage within yourself. Friends can be far different from you.*

Lionni, Leo. *Leo Lionni Favorites: Six Classic Stories (Swimmy, Tico and the Golden Wings, Fish Is Fish, Alexander and the Wind-up Mouse, The Biggest House in the World,* and *Frederick).* Knopf. Themes: Accept yourself. Differences are good. Recognize your own strengths and build on them. (Note: This book can be the central element in an author-based unit; students read the three simplest stories and listen to the others).*

Lobel, Arnold *Frog and Toad Are Friends.* HarperCollins. Theme: Friends must work together to remain friends.*

Ness, Evelyn. *Sam, Bangs, and Moonshine.* Holt. Theme: Lies are dangerous.

Parish, Peggy. *Amelia Bedelia.* HarperCollins. Theme: Things are not always what you think they are.

Peet, Bill. *Wump World.* Houghton Mifflin. Theme: Take care of the world; don't ruin it by polluting.

Scieszka, Jon. *The True Story of the Three Little Pigs.* Viking. Theme: There may be more than one way to interpret a situation. Good through grade six.*

Sharmat, Marjorie. Books in the *Nate the Great* series, especially *Nate the Great and the Phony Clue.* Coward, McCann, & Geoghegan. Theme: We all have something great about ourselves; use what is great about yourself.

Yolen, Jane. *Owl Moon.* Philomel. Themes: The world of nature is magnificent to behold. Doing something exciting with someone you love is wonderful.

Young, Ed. *Mouse Watch.* Harcourt Brace. Theme: Look into yourself for greatness. This book can be shared with children of almost any age.

2-3-4

Cole, Joanna. Books in *The Magic School Bus* series, especially *The Magic School Bus on the Ocean Floor.* Scholastic. Theme: There is much to discover about the world of nature.

Cleary, Beverly. *Ramona Quimby, Age 8.* Morrow. Theme: Family life has its ups and downs; everyone in a family has responsibilities to the family group and must sacrifice for it.

Dalgliesh, Alice. *The Courage of Sarah Noble.* Scribner. Theme: To be brave, you must reach deep inside yourself.*

Gardiner, John Reynolds. *Stone Fox.* Thomas Crowell. Theme: You must hold fast to your dreams and work hard if you are to achieve them; you cannot give up.*

Lindgren, Astrid. *Pippi Longstocking.* Puffin/Viking. Theme: Life is filled with adventure; you must reach out for it.

Rock, Gail. *Thanksgiving Treasure.* Knopf. Themes: Thanksgiving means a lot more than sitting down to a big dinner. We find friends in the least expected places.

Rockwell, Thomas. *How to Eat Fried Worms.* Watts. Theme: Be careful what you say: You may get stuck eating your words.

Sís, Peter *Starry Messenger.* Farrar, Straus, Giroux. Themes: Sometimes new ideas are frightening. Sometimes a person's ideas can have a big effect.

Sobol, Donald. Books in the *Encyclopedia Brown* series. Thomas Nelson. Theme: Be observant and follow the clues around you.

Viorst, Judith. *Alexander and the Terrible, Horrible, No Good, Very Bad Day.* Macmillan. Theme: We all have days when nothing good seems to happen.

3-4-5

Blume, Judy. *Tales of a Fourth Grade Nothing.* Bradbury. Theme: Everyone is somebody.

Brown, Mary. *Wings Along the Waterway.* Orchard. Theme: The natural world is exciting to behold, and birds are a particularly beautiful part of that world.

Cleary, Beverly. *Dear Mr. Henshaw.* Morrow. Theme: Writing is a way to understand ourselves better.

Coerr, Eleanor. *Sadako and the Thousand Paper Cranes.* Putnam's. Themes: You must have a goal and work toward it no matter what. War is not the way to resolve conflict.*

Fleischman, Sid. *The Whipping Boy.* Greenwillow. Theme: You must take responsibility for what you do; no one can or should take your punishment for you.

Giff, Patricia Reilly. *Lily's Crossing.* Delacorte. Theme: Love and friendship make a difference.*

Lobel, Arnold. *Fables.* HarperCollins. Also Aesop's fables as retold by Brian Wildsmith and Paul Galdone. Theme: Fables teach lessons about people and the world.*

Lowry, Lois. *Number the Stars.* Houghton Mifflin. Theme: You must look out for and help others.*

Naidoo, Beverley. *Journey to Jo'burg.* HarperCollins. Themes: People can be cruel to one another. Discrimination is evil.*

Paterson, Katherine. *The Great Gilly Hopkins.* Crowell. Theme: There is a place for each of us in this world. We must look within ourselves if we are to find it.*

Pringle, Laurence. *An Extraordinary Life: The Story of a Monarch Butterfly.* Orchard. Themes: Nature is fantastic. Observe and learn.

Smith, Doris Buchanan. *A Taste of Blackberries.* HarperCollins. Themes: Friends miss their friends when they are gone. Death hurts those who are left behind.

Spinelli, Jerry. *Wringer.* Harper Collins. Themes: Don't follow the crowd. Stand up for what you believe.

Thayer, Ernest. *Casey at the Bat: A Ballad of the Republic Sung in the Year 1888.* Ill. by Christopher Bing. Handprint Books. Themes: Pride and overconfidence lead to a fall. The design of a book contributes to its message and appeal.

White, E. B. *Charlotte's Web.* HarperCollins. Themes: Each being in this world has value. Life continues.

Wilder, Laura Ingalls. *Little House on the Prairie.* HarperCollins. Theme: Families work together and stick together.

4-5-6

GO TO

Pages 131–132 for a list of great nonfiction books around which to center unit study.

Avi. *The True Confessions of Charlotte Doyle.* Watts. Theme: The roles we are asked to play in this world are not always what we expect.

Hamilton, Virginia. *Zeely.* Macmillan. Theme: Imagination has its purposes, but real beauty is in being true to yourself.*

Konigsburg, E. L. *From the Mixed-up Files of Mrs. Basil E. Frankweiler.* Atheneum. Theme: Life can be a puzzle; you must use all your ingenuity to solve it.

Macaulay, David. *Cathedral.* Houghton Mifflin. Theme: A cathedral is a magnificent architectural and engineering achievement, a monument to humankind's dedication and creativity.

MacLachlan, Patricia. *Sarah, Plain and Tall.* HarperCollins. Theme: We are all searching for a place where we belong and are loved.

Naylor, Phyllis Reynolds. *Shiloh.* Atheneum. Theme: Everyone must function in terms of what he or she believes is right or wrong and is responsible for his or her decisions.

O'Dell, Scott. *Island of the Blue Dolphins.* Houghton Mifflin. Theme: Our survival depends on ourselves and our reactions to problems.*

Paterson, Katherine. *Bridge to Terabithia.* HarperCollins. Themes: Friends miss their friends when they are gone. Death hurts those who are left behind.

Sachar, Louis. *Holes.* Farrar, Straus, and Giroux. Theme: Life can be rough, especially if we do not obey the rules.

Seuss, Dr. *The Lorax.* Random House. Theme: Because our actions affect the environment, we are all responsible for it.

Taylor, Mildred. *Roll of Thunder, Hear My Cry.* Dial. Theme: People have treated others inhumanely; let that not happen anymore.*

5-6-7

Armstrong, William *Sounder.* HarperCollins. Theme: People have treated others inhumanely; let not that happen anymore.*

Avi. *Nothing But the Truth.* Watts. Theme: Truth is not always what it appears to be.

Babbitt, Natalie. *Tuck Everlasting.* Farrar. Theme: The way of life is change and death, yet some things are everlasting.

Bach, Richard. *Jonathan Livingston Seagull.* Macmillan. Theme: To achieve your potential, you must soar to new heights and not be held back by other people's limits.*

Collier, James, and Christopher Collier. *My Brother Sam Is Dead.* Four Winds. Theme: War brings death; people must find peaceful ways to resolve differences.

Freedman, Russell. *Give Me Liberty: The Story of the Declaration of Independence.* Holiday House. Theme: The Declaration of Independence is a timeless document that affirms the rights of people to govern themselves.

———. *Lincoln: A Photobiography.* Clarion. Theme: One person can make a difference. This is a superb example of a biography. See other biographies by Freedman, such as *The Life and Death of Crazy Horse.*

George, Jean Craighead. *Julie of the Wolves.* HarperCollins. Theme: Your survival depends on yourself and your ability to meet the troubles that beset you.*

Paulsen, Gary. *Hatchet.* Puffin. Theme: Your survival depends on yourself and your ability to overcome the unexpected.

Rawls, Wilson. *Where the Red Fern Grows.* Doubleday and Bantam. Theme: You must hold fast to your dreams and work toward them if you are to achieve them.

Spinelli, Jerry. *Maniac Magee.* Little, Brown. Themes: Everyone needs a place where he or she belongs. Belonging is not a matter of race or religion.*

Bibliography of Multicultural Books

Simple Picture Storybooks and Poetry Collections

Altman, Linda, and Enrique Sanchez. *Amelia's Road.* New York: Lee and Low, 1993. The story of how a young migrant girl creates a special place for herself. Grades 1–3. Mexican American.

Best, Cari. *Taxi, Taxi.* New York: Little, Brown, 1994. The story of a Latina girl's day with her father, a taxi driver. Grades K–2. Hispanic American.

Clifton, Lucille. *My Friend Jacob.* Ill. by Thomas DiGrazia. New York: Dutton, 1980. The friendship between an African-American child and an older, European-American boy who has a learning disability. Grades K–3. Multiethnic.

Diakité, Baba Wagué. *The Hatseller and the Monkeys.* New York: Scholastic, 1999. The traditional tale illustrated beautifully. Primary. West African.

Greenfield, Eloise. *Night on Neighborhood Street.* Ill by Jay Gilchrest. New York: Penguin, 1991. Poems highlighting the sights and sounds of an urban evening. Grades K–3. African American.

Griego, Margot. *Tortillitas Para Mama.* Ill. by Barbara Cooney. New York: Henry Holt, 1981. A collection of Spanish nursery rhymes in Spanish and English. Grades K–2. Hispanic American.

James, Betsy. *The Mud Family.* Ill by Paul Morin. New York: Putnam's, 1994. The story of how the rain's coming washes away Sosi's mud family but saves her real family. Grades K–2. Native American.

Keller, Holly. *Grandfather's Dream.* New York: Greenwillow, 1994. The story of the return of the cranes to a village in Vietnam on the Mekong delta and of the balance between traditions and the needs of the future. Grades 1–3. Vietnamese.

Levinson, Riki. *Watch the Stars Come Out.* Ill. by Diane Goode. New York: Dutton, 1985. The story of two children's coming to America. Grades 1–3. European American.

Patrick, Denise. *The Car Washing Street.* Ill. by John Ward. New York: Tambourine Books, 1993. Neighborhood pleasures in an urban environment. Preschool–grade 2. African American.

Paulsen, Gary. *The Tortilla Factory.* Ill. by Ruth Paulsen. San Diego: Harcourt, 1995. A simple, circular account of corn—from earth to seed to corn and back to earth. Preschool–grade 1. Hispanic.

Pinkney, Brian. *Max Found Two Sticks.* New York: Simon and Schuster, 1994. A celebration of the sounds of the city from the point of view of a young boy, who finds two sticks to use in drumming. Preschool–grade 1. African American.

Ringgold, Faith. *Bonjour, Lonnie.* New York: Hyperion, 1996. A search for roots in several cultures. Grades 1–3. Crosscultural.

Spier, Peter. *People.* New York: Doubleday, 1980. The diversity of people. Pre-K–grade 3. Multiethnic.

Williams, Vera. *A Chair for My Mother.* A child's search for something to buy for Mother. Pre-K–grade 2. African American.

———. *"More More More," Said the Baby.* New York: Greenwillow, 1990. The simple pleasures of three babies. Preschool–K. Multiethnic.

More Difficult Picture Storybooks and Other Books

Baylor, Byrd. *The Way to Start a Day.* Ill. by Peter Parnall. A call to the sun. Grades 2–4. Multiethnic.

Bunting, Eve. *How Many Days to America? A Thanksgiving Story.* Boston: Clarion, 1988. A child's view of her family's voyage from Cuba to America. Grades 1–4. Cuban American.

———. *Moonstick: The Seasons of the Sioux.* New York: HarperCollins, 1997. A calendar poem based on the Sioux tradition. Grades 1–4. Native American.

Cohen, Barbara. *Molly's Pilgrim.* Ill. by Michael Deraney. New York: Morrow, 1983. The story of a present-day pilgrim and of how people sometimes treat others who are different from them. Grades 1–4. Russian American.

Garland, Sherry. *The Lotus Seed.* Ill. by Tatsuro Kuichi. San Diego: Harcourt, 1993. The tale of a Vietnamese family forced to flee their homeland. Grades 1–4. Vietnamese American.

Goble, Paul. *The Girl Who Loved Wild Horses.* Scarsdale, N.Y.: Bradbury, 1978. A Native-American legend. (See also Goble's *Buffalo Woman* and *Beyond the Ridge.*) Grades 1–4. Native American.

Heide, Florence, and **Judith Heide Gilliland.** *The House of Wisdom.* D. K. Publishing, 1999. The travels of a young man in search of manuscripts to bring to a tenth-century library. The man discovers the reason to read. Grades 2–5. Arab American.

Jeffers, Susan, ill. *Brother Eagle, Sister Sky: A Message from Chief Seattle.* New York: Penguin, 1991. A plea for the earth. Grades 3–6. Native American.

Johnson, Dolores. *Seminole Diary: Remembrances of a Slave.* New York: Macmillan, 1994. The diary of an African-American girl whose family became slaves to the Seminoles to avoid slavery with the whites. Grades 2–5. African American; Native American.

Knight, Margy Burns. *Talking Walls.* Ill. by Anne O'Brien. Gardiner, Me.: Tilbury House, 1992. A wondrous depiction of walls from around the world that tells about people's past and present. Grades 3–5. Multicultural. (*Note:* In response, students can create their own personal walls that give background on their family histories.) See also *Talking Walls: The Stories Continue*. Both books are available as software packages.

Martel, Cruz. *Yagua Days.* Ill. by Jerry Pinkney. New York: Dial, 1976. The joys of a family reunion in Puerto Rico from the point of view of a young Hispanic-American boy. Grades 1–3. Puerto Rican American.

McKissack, Patricia. *Mirandy and Brother Wind.* Ill. by Jerry Pinkney. New York: Knopf, 1988. A story of a young girl's decision to select her friend—an awkward boy—as her partner in the cakewalk. Grades 1–5. African American.

McKissack, Patricia, and **Federick McKissack.** *Christmas in the Big House, Christmas in the Quarters.* New York. Scholastic, 1994. Grades 2–5. A comparison of Christmas in the South as celebrated by the owners and slaves. African American; Plantation America.

Mochizuki, Ken. *Baseball Saved Us.* Ill. by Dom Lee. New York: Lee & Low Books, 1993. The story of a boy's internment in a Japanese-American camp during World War II and his involvement in baseball. Grades 2–4. Japanese American.

Myers, Walter Dean. *Harlem.* New York: Scholastic, 1997. A poem. Grades 3–5. African American.

Pryor, Bonnie. *The Dream Jar.* Ill. by Mark Graham. New York: Morrow, 1996. A family's dream as they come to America. Grades 1–3. Russian American.

Rappaport, Doreen. *Freedom River.* Ill. by Bryan Collier. New York: Hyperion Books, 2000. One man's efforts to help an African-American family escape from slavery along the Underground Railway. Grades 2–8. African American.

Riggio, Anita. *Secret Signs Along the Underground Railway.* Honesdale, Pa.: Boyds Mills Press, 1997. A story of courage and quick thinking. Grades 1–4. Intercultural.

Say, Allen. *Grandfather's Journey.* Boston: Houghton Mifflin, 1993. Reminiscences of Grandfather's life in America and in Japan. Grades 2–4. Japanese American.

Schmidt, Jeremy, and **Ted Wood.** *Two Lands, One Heart: An American Boy's Journey to His Mother's Vietnam.* The return of a boy—whose father is a white American and whose mother is a Vietnamese who left her country during the war—to his mother's homeland. Grades 2–5. Vietnamese American.

Stanley, Fay. *The Last Princess: The Story of Princess Ka'iulani of Hawai'i.* Ill. by Diane Stanley. New York: Four Winds, 1991. Grades 2–4. An account of the princess who fought annexation. Hawaiian American.

Steptoe, John. *Mufaro's Beautiful Daughters.* New York: Lothrop, Lee and Shepard, 1987. The Cinderella story in an African setting, showing the universality of folklore. Grades 2–4. African folklore.

Uchida, Yoshiko, and **Joanne Yardley.** *The Bracelet.* New York: Philomel, 1993. A Japanese-American girl's memories of internment during World War II. Grades 2–4. Japanese American.

Wells, Rosemary. *Streets of Gold.* Ill. by Dan Andreasen. New York: Dial, 1999. A biographical account of Mary Antin, a Russian Jewish girl, and her family's flight from tyranny in the late 1890s. Grades 4–5. Russian American.

Books for Upper Elementary Grades

Note: Also see starred items on the previous bibliography, grades 3 and up.

Banks, Lynne. *One More River.* New York: Morrow, 1992. The story of a young Canadian girl whose father decides that the family will leave Canada and move to Israel to live on a kibbutz. Grades 4–6. Jewish; Canadian.

Conlon-McKenna, Marita. *Wildflower Girl.* New York: Holiday, 1993. The story of a young Irish girl's immigration to America. Grades 5–8. See also *Under the Hawthorn Tree,* the first in the two-book series. Irish American.

Farmer, Nancy. *A Girl Named Disaster.* New York: Orchard, 1996. A coming-of-age story set in a village in Mozambique. Grades 5–8. African.

Hamilton, Virginia. *The People Could Fly.* Ill. by Leo and Diane Dillon. New York: Knopf, 1985. African-American folktales. Grades 3–8. African American.

Krumgold, Joseph. *…And Now Miguel.* New York: Crowell, 1953. The story of a boy living in Texas who must decide what he wants in his future. Grades 4–6. Mexican American.

Lord, Bette Bao. *In the Year of the Boar and Jackie Robinson.* Ill. by Marc Simont. New York: Harper & Row, 1984. The Americanization of Shirley Temple Wong. Grades 4–6. Chinese American.

Lowry, Lois. *Number the Stars.* Boston: Houghton Mifflin, 1989. Fact-based historical fiction about the Danish people's rescue of the Jews of Denmark during World War II. Grades 4–6. Jewish; Danish.

McKissack, Patricia. *Run Away Home.* New York: Scholastic, 1997. The coming together of two cultures. Grades 4–6. Native American/African American.

O'Dell, Scott. *Sing Down the Moon.* Boston: Houghton Mifflin, 1970. A piece of historical fiction that tells of the white man's destruction of Native Americans. Grades 3–5. Native American.

Paulsen, Gary. *Night John.* New York: Delacorte, 1993. The brutalities of slavery as it existed in America. Grade 7 and up. African American.

Rinaldi, Ann. *Hang a Thousand Trees with Ribbons: The Story of Phillis Wheatley.* San Diego, Calif.: Harcourt Brace, 1996. A fictionalized biography of America's first published black poet. Grades 5 and up. African American.

Say, Allen. *Tea with Milk.* Boston: Houghton Mifflin, 1999. The true story of the struggle of one girl to find a place where she belongs. Grades 5–8. Japanese.

Silton, Faye. *Of Heroes, Hooks, and Heirlooms.* Philadelphia: Jewish Publication Society, 1997. A search for heirlooms when most have been lost in the Holocaust. Grades 4–6. Jewish American.

Taylor, Mildred. *Roll of Thunder, Hear My Cry.* New York: Dial, 1976. A story of racial discrimination somewhere in the South, told from an African-American girl's point of view. Grades 4–8. African American.

Uchida, Yoshiko. *Journey to Topaz.* Ill. by Donald Carrick. New York: Scribner, 1971. The story of the internment of Japanese Americans during World War II. Grades 4–6. Japanese American.

Yep, Lawrence. *Child of the Owl.* New York: Harper & Row, 1988. A Chinese-American girl's acceptance of her ethnicity. Grades 4–6. Chinese American.

Yolen, Jane, collector and reteller. *Not One Damsel in Distress: World Folktales for Strong Girls.* San Diego: Harcourt, 2000. A collection of folktales. Grades 4–8. Strong women.

Zeman, Ludmila, reteller. *Sinbad: Tales from the Thousand and One Nights.* Canada: Tundra Books, 1999. A revisit to the classic tale. Grades 4–6. Arab American.

A Planning Guide for Literature-Based Activities

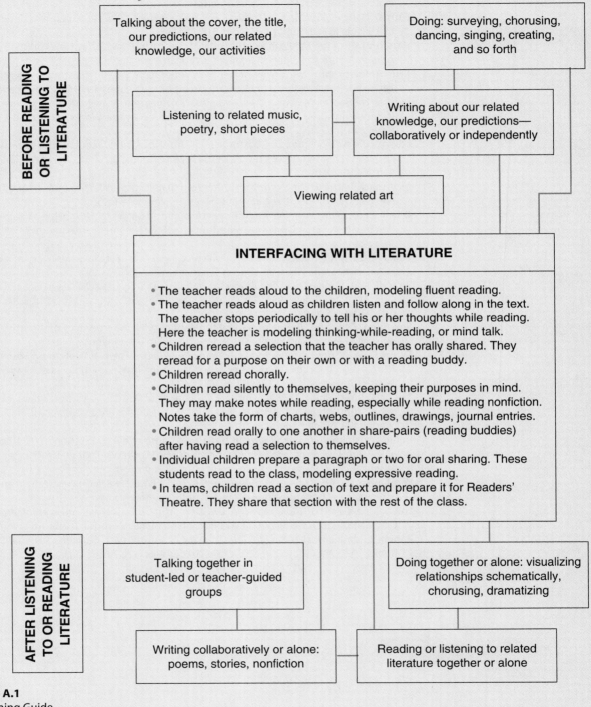

Plans for Literature-Based Units

In this section are plans for literature-based units. The first plan is for an author unit for second grade focusing on the work of Arnold Lobel. This unit is structured with a large independent reading component. It was contributed by Sandra Farina, a teacher in Watchung, New Jersey. The second unit is organized around a chapter book, *Sarah, Plain and Tall*. It demonstrates an approach to literature-based instruction in the upper grades in which all the students are involved in one novel and at the same time read related books on their own. The third plan is for a cross-curricular genre unit on biography and space exploration, intended for fifth grade. The core book of this unit is the biography, *The Story of Guion Bluford*. Bluford was the first African-American astronaut, and his life story provides a way to look at the nature of biography as well as to develop understandings about space and space travel. The unit was contributed by Emilia Marinaro, who planned it for use in conjunction with a basal unit.

Each unit projects more activities than the planner used in teaching. Each one also presents a different way to view literature-based instruction and to organize a unit on paper. A fourth plan is found within the text pages (34–35); it demonstrates a language arts/reading unit in the primary grades in which children read and listen to a number of books on the same theme (a text set). See Figure A.1 for a generic guide for planning literature-based units.

Here are some things to consider as you look over the units:

- The way in which objectives are stated in terms of what students will be able to do as a result of the unit and the way in which the objectives relate to the projected activities.
- The cross-section of objectives including understanding of literature, listening, speaking, writing, visualizing, and language use.
- The relation between independent and integrative dimensions.
- The use of mini-lessons to review or teach skills and strategies.
- The way the plan meets diverse learning styles and talents.
- The integration of technology, art, music, poetry.
- The variety of activities integrated into a unit.
- The cross-section of literature, including story, nonfiction, and poetry, that is part of each unit.
- The levels and kinds of thinking triggered.
- The use of autobiographical material by children's authors (*Note:* The summer issue of *Horn Book* usually has material by Newbery and Caldecott award–winning authors; *The Reading Teacher* features interviews with award-winning authors).

An Author Focus Unit

The Stories and Art of Arnold Lobel: Second Grade

THE WEB

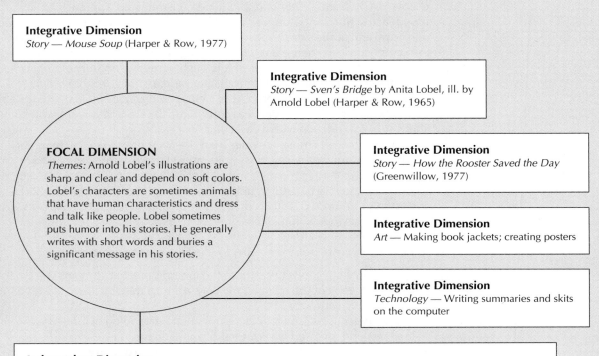

Integrative Dimension
Story — Mouse Soup (Harper & Row, 1977)

Integrative Dimension
Story — Sven's Bridge by Anita Lobel, ill. by
Arnold Lobel (Harper & Row, 1965)

FOCAL DIMENSION
Themes: Arnold Lobel's illustrations are
sharp and clear and depend on soft colors.
Lobel's characters are sometimes animals
that have human characteristics and dress
and talk like people. Lobel sometimes
puts humor into his stories. He generally
writes with short words and buries a
significant message in his stories.

Integrative Dimension
Story — How the Rooster Saved the Day
(Greenwillow, 1977)

Integrative Dimension
Art — Making book jackets; creating posters

Integrative Dimension
*Technology — Writing summaries and skits
on the computer*

Independent Dimension
Other books by Arnold Lobel:
- *The Book of Pigericks* (Harper & Row, 1983)
- *Days with Frog and Toad* (Harper & Row, 1979)
- *Fables* (Harper & Row, 1980)
- *Frog and Toad All Year* (Harper & Row, 1978)
- *Frog and Toad Are Friends* (Harper & Row, 1970)
- *Frog and Toad Together* (Harper & Row, 1971)
- *Giant John* (Harper & Row, 1964)
- *Grasshopper on the Road* (Harper & Row, 1978)
- *A Holiday for Mister Muster* (Harper & Row, 1963)
- *Lucille* (Harper & Row, 1964)
- *Martha the Movie Mouse* (Harper & Row, 1966)
- *Ming Lo Moves the Mountain* (Greenwillow, 1982)
- *Mouse Tales* (Harper & Row, 1972)
- *On Market Street* (Mulburry, 1981)
- *Owl at Home* (Harper & Row, 1975)
- *The Rose in My Garden* (Greenwillow, 1984)
- *Small Pig* (Harper & Row, 1969)
- *A Treeful of Pigs* (Greenwillow, 1979)
- *Uncle Elephant* (Harper & Row, 1981)
- *Whiskers & Rhymes* (Mulburry Books, 1985)
- Another Book by Anita Lobel and illustrated by
  Arnold Lobel: *The Straw Maid* (Greenwillow, 1983)

Unit: Courtesy of Sandra Farina

DEVELOPMENT OF THE UNIT: ARNOLD LOBEL—THE ILLUSTRATOR AND AUTHOR

THE OBJECTIVES

Language Arts Objectives: Through the unit activities, children will be better able to
• listen to make a decision • choose books selectively, based on their knowledge of an author and his or her style • recognize elements of an author's style • recognize examples of humor in writing • recognize personification in stories • listen for the main idea or ideas of a story • write a short summary of a story • create an artistic visualization that highlights a key aspect of a story • use the computer for drafting and revising • underline or italicize the title of a book • form the plural of nouns • share their ideas with their classmates • work cooperatively with classmates • create and present skits based on a story.

PROJECTED ACTIVITIES

Note: This unit is developed around the independent dimension. For this reason, that dimension is given in the left-hand column.

Independent Dimension

Opening Celebration—Book Sale 1: Students participate in a book sale. Copies of books by Lobel are displayed around the room. The teacher tells a little about each—a "teaser." Each child selects a different book, based on the teaser and the book jacket. Students find a cozy spot and settle down to read the books they have chosen.

Independent Activity 1—Summary Writing: The teacher conducts a review mini-lesson on the organization of a story summary. Students go to the computer lab and write summaries for the book each "bought" at the first book sale and finished reading independently. Students print out first drafts for editing and revising; they specifically edit to underline the title of their books. They return to the computer lab to enter their revisions and print out a final draft.

Share-Time: Students share their story summaries with the other second grade.

Book Sale 2: Students participate in a second book sale. At this sale, students who already have read a book present the teaser. Students settle down to read the books they have chosen.

Independent Activity 2—Creating a Poster: Students create posters that will entice someone else to read the book they have bought at the sale. Students display their posters above the books that are displayed along the chalkboard ledge. Students browse the ledge looking at each other's posters.

Book Sale 3: Students use their posters to "sell" the book they have just finished reading to someone else. Students settle down on their own to read the books they have chosen. They write a brief response —whatever they want—in their LRJs.

Integrative Dimension

Whole-Class Activity 1: Students listen to *Mouse Soup* as the teacher reads this book one chapter each day. Students participate in grand conversations about their reactions to the book. Students talk about the fact that stones can't really talk (personification).

They talk about the illustrations in the books they are reading, showing the illustrations to support the points they contribute to the class discussion.

Whole-Class Activity 2: Students listen as the teacher reads aloud the book *Sven's Bridge*. Students talk about the way this story is similar to a story about a town that built a wall down its middle that they have heard in an assembly program. They talk about how walls can create problems and bridges can solve them.

UNIT PLANS

PROJECTED ACTIVITIES

Independent Dimension

Independent Activity 3—Designing a Book Jacket with a Story Summary on the Flap: Students design book jackets with a cover different from Lobel's for the third book they have chosen and read independently. They create a summary for the left inside flap, write a little about the author on the right inside flap, and write their opinion of the story on the back. Each student also goes to at least one other student who has already read the book, interviews that reader about his or her opinion of it, and writes that opinion on the back as well. Students pair off to edit the text of their book jackets before going to final draft.

Book Sale 4: Students participate in a fourth book sale, based on a browse of the book jackets their classmates have made. This time two children bid on a book together and then work as a share-pair to read the book together while sitting next to and facing each other.

Independent Activity 4—Creating Skits: Share-pairs create the text for short skits about their chosen books. They enter the scripts into the computer and practice using the scripts to perform their skits in an expressive way.

Culminating Celebration: Students present their skits to the other second grade.

Integrative Dimension

Whole-Class Activity 3: Students orally share sentences from the books they are reading, select a singular noun from each sentence, and transform the noun into its plural form (a skill-building activity). They search for proper nouns in the Lobel books and classify them in columns as names of places, people, and things (skill building).

Whole-Class Activity 4: Students listen as the teacher reads aloud Lobel's *How the Rooster Saved the Day.* Students join in on the repeating lines. They respond in whatever manner they wish in their LRJs. They share their responses as part of a grand conversation.

Whole-Class Conversation: Students talk as a class about things they like and dislike in the Lobel books they have read.

Whole-Class Conversation: Students talk about their skits and the way they went. They talk about the characteristics of all the Lobel books they have read.

ASSESSMENT ACTIVITIES

• Students compile a portfolio that includes their summaries, posters, book jackets, and skit scripts. • The teacher monitors children's independent reading. • The teacher confers with each child at least twice during the unit, asking the child to summarize a story orally, to give his or her opinion of it, and to read aloud a favorite part and tell why he or she chose that part. • The teacher observes each child's contribution to the share-pair and to class conversations. • At the end of the unit, each child confers with the teacher, talking about items in the portfolio and identifying areas for future growth.

SCRATCH BOARD

Use this page to make your own notes about unit planning; especially note down activities to use in the development of author-focus units.

A Core Book Unit Sarah, Plain and Tall: Fourth or Fifth Grade

THE WEB

Integrative Dimension
Autobiography — Material from Patricia MacLachlan's Newbery Medal acceptance speech, *Horn Book* (July/August, 1986), which describes elements of her life

Integrative Dimension
Poetry — "Dream Dust" and "Dreams" by Langston Hughes; "This is My Rock" by David McCord; "Dakota Dugout" by Ann Turner; "Summer Is Icumen In"

Integrative Dimension
Music — "The Impossible Dream" from *Man of La Mancha; The Four Seasons* by Antonio Vivaldi; "Mail Order Annie"

FOCAL DIMENSION
Core Book: Sarah, Plain and Tall
Themes: We all have a need to belong. Our dreams for a life in which we love and are loved motivate what we do and encourage us to take risks.

Integrative Dimension
Social Studies — Segments from the encyclopedia about sod houses, the plains, and the development of the railroad in the United States; segments from the social studies book about life on the Great Plains; large wall map of the United States; video: *The Land, the Sea, and the Children;* "Song for a Pioneer" by Roger Welsch; "A Sea of Grass" by Duncan Searl

Integrative Dimension
Art — Van Gogh: *Sunflowers;* painting flowers in his style

Independent Dimension
These selections relate to the theme, setting, or the author of the core book. Students select from them to read on their own.
  Other books about prairie life:
■ Harvey's *My Prairie Years: Based on the Diary of Elenore Plaisted* (Holiday House, 1986)
■ Wilder's *Little House on the Prairie* (Harper, 1935) and *Little Town on the Prairie* (Harper, 1941)
■ Anderson's *Christmas on the Prairie* (Clarion, 1988)
■ Conrad's *Prairie Songs* (Harper, 1985), *My Daniel* (Harper, 1989), and *Prairie Vision: The Life and Times of Solomon Butcher* (Harper, 1991)
■ Freedman's *Buffalo Hunt* (Holiday House, 1988)
■ Hesse's *Out of the Dust* (Scholastic, 1997)
  Other poems by Langston Hughes:
■ "Harlem," "Dream Keeper," "In Time of Silver Rain"
  Other books about the need to belong:
■ Spinelli's *Maniac Magee* (Little Brown, 1990)
  Other books by Patricia MacLachlan, especially:
■ *Three Names* (HarperCollins, 1991) and *Skylark* (HarperCollins, 1994)

DEVELOPMENT OF THE UNIT

THE OBJECTIVES: Through interaction with *Sarah, Plain and Tall* (MacLachlan, Harper, 1985) and related literature, children will be better able to
• predict (who, when, where, and what will happen) based on their analysis of the title and cover of a novel and predict continuously as they read • visualize story scenes • infer character traits from character actions • compare events, characters, and places found in a novel • infer time and place • hypothesize reasons and relationships • relate their own feelings to those of a story character and create personal meanings with a book • use context to figure out the meanings of unfamiliar story words and the way those words function in a sentence (e.g., as noun, verb, and so forth) • use story words new to them in talking and writing about the story • create writing topics based on the reading of a book, rehearse and draft in response to reading, and edit and revise what they have written in preparation for sharing • keep a literature response journal and highlight their writing in a portfolio • write a friendly letter in standard form • work in collaborative groups and contribute to a whole-class discussion • orally read favorite lines from a story, using the voice to heighten meaning • find pleasure in reading a chapter book and responding to it by talking and writing.

PROJECTED ACTIVITIES

Focal Dimension

Opening Celebration: Tap prior ideas about the words *plain* and *tall;* predict characters, time, place, and plot based on cover clues.

Chapter One (aloud—class): Listen to infer character traits from what people say and do and to hypothesize time and place; make character webs; chart unfamiliar and interesting words; write to Sarah from the point of view of characters met in the first chapter.

Chapter Two (alone): Share letters to Sarah before reading; read to check predictions in letters to Sarah; expand ideas about character and setting; add to character webs; as Jacob, write to Sarah to tell her to come or write to express feelings.

Chapter Three (share-pair): Retell events from Chapter Two before reading and tell how the characters felt during the events; read to make an events/feeling chart; after reading, list all the color words in Chapters One and Three and decide why there is a difference; chart unfamiliar words, based on context clues; write about your response to Sarah or write to tell how you relate to the story.

Chapter Four (aloud—class): Review the kind of character Sarah is before reading by expanding on a Sarah character web; read to find evidence that Sarah will stay, that Sarah will go; write what you think will happen next or how the chapter makes you feel.

Chapter Five (alone): Review the kind of character Caleb is by expanding his character web; read to propose a title for the chapter; chart unfamiliar words based on context clues; write about your response to Caleb, or write to express your feelings.

Integrative Dimension

Listen to and chorus "This Is My Rock" by David McCord; talk about our own "rocks"; respond in journals.

Chorus again "This Is My Rock" by David McCord; reflect: Who is Caleb's rock? Anna's? Papa's? Listen to "Winter" from *The Four Seasons*. Participate in a mini-lesson on format of a friendly letter.

In collaborative teams, read about life on the Great Plains from the social studies text. Compile a lifestyle map.

Listen to, chorus, and reflect on "Dream Dust" by Langston Hughes. Think about what Sarah's dream was, Anna's, Caleb's. Listen to "Spring" from *The Four Seasons*.

In collaborative groups, prepare "Dreams" by Langston Hughes for oral sharing. Chorus together "Sumer Is Icumen In."

Listen to a recording of "The Impossible Dream" from *Man of La Mancha*. Reflect: Was Anna's dream impossible? Sarah's? Caleb's?

DEVELOPMENT OF THE UNIT   *Continued*

PROJECTED ACTIVITIES

Focal Dimension

Chapter Six (share-pair): Review the kind of character Anna is; read to compare this chapter to the first chapter: How are they different? How are they the same? Why? Write your response to Anna or your response to the way this author writes. Identify similes.

Chapter Seven (alone or share-pair): Review the story by proposing titles for prior chapters; read (1) to decide what the author is trying to tell us about life and what is important to happiness and (2) to create a title for this chapter; write what the story means to you; chart unfamiliar words.

Chapter Eight (alone or share-pair): Review the kind of man Papa is; read to pick the high point of the chapter; be ready to say why you picked it; write your response to Papa or to any of the chapter events.

Chapter Nine (aloud—class): Review story by means of the teacher's dressing up and role-playing Sarah or Jacob; decide what Sarah brought with her (things like courage, hope, fear as well as Seal, the sea stones, and the shells); listen to enjoy, paint pictures in the mind, and grow feelings in the heart; write your response—was Sarah really plain? Write sequels.

Climactic Celebration: In teams, talk about favorite parts; dramatize them; share dramatizations and sequels during a session where everyone dresses up as a character from the novel.

Integrative Dimension

In research teams, read segments from the encyclopedia about sod houses, the development of the railroad in the United States; read "Sea of Grass" and "Song of a Pioneer"; share findings.

In poetry interpretation teams, prepare "Dakota Dugout" by Ann Turner for oral expression. Sing along with "Mail Order Annie." Participate in an art workshop: Study Van Gogh's *Sunflowers;* paint flowers in the style of Van Gogh.

Listen to material from Patricia MacLachlan's Newbery Medal acceptance speech, *Horn Book* (July/August 1986); relate it to the novel.

Use a large wall map of the United States to plot Sarah's travel route from Maine to the Great Plains. Listen to *Going West;* compare it to time, place, and feelings of Sarah. View video on Nebraska and Maine—*The Land, the Sea, and the Children.*

Make a mobile containing things from the story that are key in its development; tell why you included what you did.

ONGOING ASSESSMENT ACTIVITIES

Students will keep a literature response journal in which they record their ongoing responses to what they are reading. They will compile a portfolio of writings and drawings they have made to showcase their response to the novel. While students are reading alone or with a buddy, the teacher conducts individual conferences in which each student talks about personal responses to the novel and to his or her independent reading and discusses his or her literature journal entries. The following assessment activities will be a continuing aspect of the unit:
• informal observations of children's contribution to discussions held before and after reading or listening to a chapter of the book • informal observations of children's interaction with other students in literature groups and as they read to themselves • analysis of students' written responses in their literature logs and written responses that they have revised, edited, published, and showcased in their writing portfolios • checklists based on stated objectives and completed after individual conferences with students • anecdotal records that describe student behavior.

(*Note:* Writing topics are suggestions, not assignments. Children may respond by writing in their journals on topics they choose.)

UNIT PLANS

SCRATCH BOARD

Use this page to make your own notes about unit planning; especially note down activities to use in the development of a core book unit.

A Genre Unit Biography/Space Exploration: Fifth Grade

THE WEB

Integrative Dimension
Books — *Moonwalk: The First Trip to the Moon* by
J. Donnelly (Random House, 1989); *New Technology,
Space, and Aircraft* by N. Hawkes (Twenty-first
Century Books, 1994); segments from *To Space and
Back* by Sally Ride (Beech Tree, 1986); segments from
Our Solar System and the Universe (Silver Burdett and
Ginn, 1990)

Integrative Dimension
Magazine Articles — "Cosmic Close-ups" by
M. Lemonic (*Time*, November 20, 1995); "Orion" by
J. Reston (*National Geographic*, 188:6, 1995)

FOCAL DIMENSION
Core Book: The Story of Guion Bluford
by Jim Haskins and Kathleen Benson
(Carolrhoda Books, 1984)
Themes: We must often struggle to achieve
our dreams. Biography chronicles a person's
struggles to find his or her dreams, is
generally written in the past tense and the
third person singular, and presents fact
and opinion.

Integrative Dimension
Poetry — "Moon" by Myra Cohn Livingston; "The Star
in the Pail" by David McCord

Integrative Dimension
Music — "Twilight," "The Sphynx," and "The Magus"
from *Optimystique* by Yanni, "The Planets" by Holst

Integrative Dimension
Art — *Starry Night* by Vincent Van Gogh

Integrative Dimension
Video — *Being an Astronaut* (Children's Television
Workshop)

Independent Dimension
Nonfiction about space exploration:
- *If You Lived on Mars* by M. Berger (Dutton, 1988)
- *The Dream Is Alive: A Flight of Discovery Aboard the Space Shuttle* by B. Embury (HarperCollins, 1990)
- *The Story of the* Challenger *Disaster* by Z. Kent (Houghton,1994)
- *Apollo 13: Life in Space* by S. Kramer (Grosset & Dunlap,1995)
- *Stars and Planets* by C. Lampton (Doubleday, 1988)
Biographies of other pilots:
- *Amelia Earhart: Aviation Pioneer* by R. Chadwick (Lerner, 1987)
- *Anne Morrow Lindbergh: Pilot and Poet* by R. Chadwick (Lerner, 1987)
- *The Wright Brothers: How They Invented the Airplane* by Russell Freedman (Holiday, 1991)
- Other biographies that children select
Video:
- *Exploring Our Solar System* (National Geographic); *Apollo 13*

*Unit: courtesy of Emilia Marinaro, who developed the unit to use in conjunction with the unit "Fast as the Wind," in Level 5, Volume 2
of Houghton Mifflin's series.*

UNIT PLANS

THE DEVELOPMENT OF THE UNIT: BIOGRAPHY/SPACE EXPLORATION

THE OBJECTIVES:

Language Arts Objectives: Through the unit activities, children will be better able to
• predict the content of a book based on an analysis of its title, cover, illustrations, table of contents, and glossary and predict continuously as they read • infer personal traits of a biographee from his or her actions • use context clues to figure out the meanings of unfamiliar text words and the way those words function in a sentence • write a poem modeled after the style of a particular poet • understand information in nonfiction texts through use of the K-W-L plus strategy (charting) and the survey-and-question strategy (SQ3R) • use time lines to organize dates and events in a biography • infer main ideas and supporting details • summarize a nonfiction selection • identify and analyze the characteristics of biographies and contrast them with the characteristics of other narrative forms • distinguish between facts and opinions • use scientific information to write a short biographical account • maintain a literature response journal • participate in a discussion • share findings.

Content Objectives: Through the unit activities, students will be able to
• explain key ideas about space and space travel • use technical terminology in talking about space • identify problems associated with space travel • identify careers in the space field.

PROJECTED ACTIVITIES

Focal Dimension

Opening Celebration: Students tap prior knowledge about space, predicting what it feels like to be in space and imagining riding a rocket at blastoff; they tap their knowledge of "weighty words" such as *weightless, gravity, anchored;* they discuss the *Challenger* space shuttle explosion. They predict the content of the biography by surveying the cover, illustrations, captions, table of contents, and glossary. They write three questions they hope to answer by reading this biography.

Chapter One (read-aloud—class): Students listen to infer traits of the biographee and create a traits web. After listening, they chart unfamiliar, interesting words. In teams, they pretend to be TV reporters assigned to cover a shuttle flight and write the details of the mission; teams prepare and present news reports, which are evaluated as possessing either an objective reporting style or a subjective style; students distinguish between fact and opinion.

Chapter Two (read-alone): Students share reports, expand ideas about the biographee, analyze the organization of this biography (first chapter = introduction; last chapter = conclusion), and generalize about the structure of a biography. After reading, they discuss Bluford's early interest in aerospace engineering and write a letter requesting information about careers in the space field.

Chapter Three (share-pairs): Students retell events from Chapter Two and explain how Bluford developed an interest in flying. They talk about the K-W-L Plus strategy and use the K and W before reading. They read to identify two main ideas and find supporting details. After reading, they talk about how Bluford overcame early obstacles; they pretend to be Bluford and describe how they would have handled his educational dilemma. In their journals, students relate his struggles with their own personal struggles.

Integrative Dimension

Students listen to and chorus McCord's "The Star in the Pail" and view Van Gogh's *Starry Night;* they talk about human beings' fascination with the celestial realm.

Students listen to Holst's "The Planets" and chorus again McCord's "The Star in the Pail."

Students view *Being an Astronaut;* they identify and discuss personal traits, qualifications, and challenges required of astronauts.

In collaborative teams, students read segments from their science text about the moon, planets, and origin of the universe; they record findings, using graphs and data charts; they share their findings.

PROJECTED ACTIVITIES

Focal Dimension

Chapter Four (read-alone): Students review events from Chapter Three before reading and predict events in Chapter Four. After reading, they select three interesting words and use context clues to make a Word Wall chart. They identify word elements such as prefixes and roots in the words they have selected, especially the element *astro-*.

Chapter Five (share-pairs): Before reading, students use the survey-and-question strategy to get ready, projecting main-idea questions. They read to identify main ideas and supporting details. As a class, they write a summary paragraph about the chapter and analyze the author's style in writing the biography. They start a time line of important dates in Bluford's career and in the history of the United States space program.

Chapter Six (read-alone): Students share their summaries and read the chapter. They work in teams to retitle the first six chapters; they support their titles by citing details.

Chapter Seven (share-pairs): Students talk about Bluford's experiences as known so far. After reading, students compare Bluford's experiences with Ride's. In teams, students locate three opinions and three facts from both sources and evaluate the author's use of facts and opinions. Students update their time lines by adding information they have learned. In teams, students select a portion of a chapter to perform as a Readers' Theatre during the culminating celebration.

Chapter Eight (read-aloud—class): Students talk about the kind of man Bluford is. They listen to infer the author's message—what the author is saying about life and living. Students write in their journals about the meaning of the biography. They identify the three questions they projected during the opening celebration and propose answers.

Final Celebration: Students present their Readers' Theatre readings. They talk about themselves and their hopes for their own lives.

Integrative Dimension

Students in teams read parts of *New Technology, Space, and Aircraft* to find out how space vehicles are designed; they use K-W-L Plus to guide their reading. Students listen to, chorus, and talk about "Moon"; they consider the shape of the poem, the poet's choice of words, the mood the poem creates. They write personal responses in their journals. They create a class poem modeled after "Moon." They begin to create their own poems based on the model.

Students listen to and talk about *Moonwalk: The First Trip to the Moon.* They distinguish between fact and opinion in it. They rechorus "Moon" and the class poem. In their journals, students pretend they are astronauts walking on the moon and describe their feelings.

Students listen to segments from *To Space and Back* and compare its structure or organization to that of the core book. Students begin the writing of biographical paragraphs. Students listen to *Optimystiqe* as they write and work.

Students survey "Cosmic Close-ups" and "Orion: Where Stars are Born" and select one article to read using K-W-L Plus. Students analyze the structure of the article they choose to read in their share-pair.

Students chorus "Moon" and "The Star in the Pail." They share their biographical paragraphs or the K-W-L Plus charts developed around the magazine article they read.

Students share their original poems and reflect upon the music of *Optimystique.*

ASSESSMENT ACTIVITIES

Students compile a portfolio that includes poems, summaries, and paragraphs they write during the unit, time lines and charts they make, and their LRJs. • The teacher monitors children's independent reading, checks samples of daily work, and observes children's contribution to class discussion and team activity. • At the end of the unit, each child confers with the teacher, with his or her portfolio as the focus of the conference.

SCRATCH BOARD

Use this page to make your own notes about unit planning; especially note down activities to use in the development of author-focus units.

Plans for Extended Lessons

This section presents a series of plans that model some of the lessons teachers may develop within a literature-based language arts program. The lessons demonstrate the planning that new teachers generally must do as they prepare for their first years of teaching. More experienced teachers do not often write down each segment in detail; rather, they think through the details and record only major things they plan to accomplish and do.

Important in planning a lesson is conceiving of the lesson as part of a larger unit and relating it to what has gone before and what is to come. In the model plans, the segments labeled "Context" and "Next Related Lessons" focus especially on these aspects.

A Preschool Lesson on Sharing for Four- and Five-Year-Olds to Be Implemented over a Two-Day Period (courtesy of Diane Lauterback)

Literature Base

A Chair for My Mother by Vera B. Williams (Greenwillow).

Context

The lesson is part of a unit focusing on the theme that in this world, we must give to others if we are to be happy.

Objectives

The children will be more likely to share their things with others. They will be able to

- Participate in a conversation about literature in a congenial, sharing way.
- Use the word *border* as they talk and make a border around their own stories.
- Follow text from left to right and top to bottom in reading and writing.
- Recognize the letter *b* when they see it and differentiate it from other letters in a text.

Proposed Sequence of Activities

Anticipatory Set

1. Display a jar of coins and talk about saving up to buy a special gift for someone. Encourage children to talk about what they might want to give a special relative.
2. Show the cover of the book *A Chair for My Mother*. Read aloud the title and author to the children. Have them join in a second reading of title and author.

Draw students' attention to the cover art. Encourage talk and prediction based on the cover and title: Whom is this story about? Where does it take place? What is it about? What will the money be saved for? Show some pages with a border around the pictures. Use the word *border* to talk about this. Encourage student talk, using the word *border*.

3. Suggest that children listen to discover if their predictions about what the story is about are on target and look to see the border on each page.

Guided Instruction

1. Do *A Chair for My Mother* as a read-aloud.
2. Follow with a talk-about: Why did the girl in the story want the chair? Would you have bought the chair for your mom or grandma? Why? Were our predictions right? Next, look at the borders on some of the pages. Encourage talk about how the borders relate to the story. Invite students to talk about what they would save their money to buy and why.
3. Do a shared writing, with several children contributing sentences to be inscribed for them on a literature experience chart: If you saved your money in a jar, what would you buy?
4. Read aloud the story chart, moving a pointing hand from left to right and top to bottom.
5. Encourage children to suggest a title for their story chart. Record the title for them at the top. Reread the title and the chart in choral style with the group, moving a pointing hand from left to right. Invite some children to lead the class in rereading the chart and to point to the sentences as the class reads.
6. Distribute sticky notes with the letter *b* on them. Invite children to match the letter stickies with the letter *b* on the story chart. Make a letter *b* on the chalkboard and ask for volunteers to make the letter on the board while the other children "air write" the letter. Explain to children that they may want to use the letter *b* when they write about what they will buy and need to write down the word *buy*.

Concluding Set

Talk about the kind of border children could put around the edges of their story chart to send a message about what the story is saying. Invite volunteers to add parts of the border. Choral read the story chart, standing up to use the body to express meaning. While children are standing, encourage them to make big letter *b*s in the air with their hands.

Follow-Up Activity

Invite children to write individual stories using invented spellings. They may write about any topic they choose, but they may want to write about the story they have just heard or about what they want to give to or share with someone else. After the writing-about time, gather children in the Communication Circle to share their stories with the others. Stress the importance of sharing ideas as well as things.

Materials

A Chair for My Mother, jar of coins, chart paper, markers, sticky notes.

Next Related Lessons

- *Art activity:* Children will mount their stories on larger paper and draw borders around them. They will explain why they picked the borders they did.
- *Oral/written language activity:* In pairs, children will reread their own stories to a reading buddy. Children will use the pictures to reread *A Chair for My Mother* to their buddies.
- *Math activity:* Open the jar of coins and do counting activities with the pennies, nickels, and dimes in it. Count by tens.
- *Theme lessons to come:* Read-aloud of *Ask Mr. Bear* by Marjorie Flack, which also gets at the importance of giving to others; dramatization of *Ask Mr. Bear;* read-aloud of *Popcorn* by Frank Asch.

Assessment by Kidwatching

Observe children's behavior as they listen, talk, and write. Especially watch for sharing behaviors.

A Second-Grade Lesson on Magic Stories for Children with Neurological Impairments (courtesy of Loretta Zahn)

Literature Base

Anansi and the Moss-Covered Rock by Eric A. Kimmel (Holiday).

Context

The lesson is the first in an extended unit focusing on the nature of magic stories, storytelling, and storytellers.

Objectives

The children will be able to

- Make predictions based on a study of the title and cover of a book.
- Retell a story, mentioning key elements of a magic story—a larger-than-life character, a magic object, a magic word or phrase, the spell.
- Use the words *spell, yam,* and *moss* as they talk.
- Insert appropriate end-of-sentence punctuation and use capital letters at the beginning of sentences.

Proposed Sequence of Activities

Anticipatory Set

1. Hold the Anansi book tightly against the chest to show a love of stories. Encourage children to talk about what magic means to them and how magic has been used in stories they have already read in the unit.

2. Show the cover of *Anansi and the Moss-Covered Rock* and share the title. Encourage talk and prediction based on the cover and title: Whom is this story going to be about? Where does it take place? What is a moss-covered rock? Display a moss-covered rock. Invite children to rub their fingers across the moss and talk about where moss grows. Pass around a yam and tell children this is something from the story. What is it? What do you do with a yam? What could an author do with a yam in a magic spell story?

3. Suggest that children listen to see if their predictions about what the story is about are right.

Guided Instruction

1. Do *Anansi* as a read-aloud. Encourage children to join in to say the magic words, "Isn't this a strange moss-covered rock?" using their most magical story-telling voices.

2. Follow with a talk-about: Were our predictions right? How do we feel about this story? What did the spell do? Use the words *yam, moss,* and *spell* in the talk-about.

3. Ask children to turn to their talk-buddy and tell their favorite part of the story to each other, using their best magic-storytelling voices.

4. Ask children to retell the story as a class. Record dictated points in order on a literature experience chart. Ask children to help insert the sentence-ending punctuation and write in the capital letters at the sentence beginnings. Invite suggestions for a title that sums up the main idea of the story.

Concluding Set

Read the story-retelling chart as a class, "using our voices to signal sentence-ending punctuation." Then talk about the key elements in this story—a larger-than-life character, the magic object, the magic word or phrase, and the spell.

Follow-Up Activities

1. Children write their own stories. They may use Anansi as a character. They may decide to create a magic story with a spell.

2. Children share their stories. They identify the elements of their magic stories.

3. Students reread a version of the literature experience chart that has no punctuation or capital letters. (Make this stripped-down version as children write their stories.) Students collaboratively edit for capital letters and sentence-ending punctuation by listening for the stop-drop of their voices at the end of a sentence. They then work in pairs to edit their own stories in the same way.

Next Related Lessons

■ *Theme lesson:* a viewing of the video of *Sylvester and the Magic Pebble* by William Steig—another magic spell story with a magic phrase.

■ *Independent theme-related activity:* reading (based on the pictures) of other Anansi stories, such as Kimmel's *Anansi Goes Fishing,* and other magic spell stories, such as *Snow White and the Seven Dwarfs*—stories to be found in the classroom library corner.

Materials

Anansi and the Moss-Covered Rock, chart papers, markers.

Assessment

Study children's magic stories written in response to this and previous stories to see if their stories are beginning to embody the key elements and demonstrate appropriate sentence-ending punctuation and capitalization at sentence beginnings. Listen to see if students are using new vocabulary in talking.

A Third- or Fourth-Grade Reading Workshop on Chris Van Allsburg (courtesy of Barbara Malanda)

Literature Base

The Wretched Stone, The Witch's Broom, and *Jumanji* by Chris Van Allsburg.

Context

The lesson is part of an extended unit focusing on the works of Chris Van Allsburg and his literary and artistic style; previous lesson was a total-class encounter with *The Garden of Abdul Gasazi.*

Objectives

The children will be able to

- Work cooperatively in literature interaction groups and share group findings with the class.
- Identify key elements in the literary and artistic styles of Chris Van Allsburg.
- Develop written and schematic responses to a story.

Proposed Sequence of Activities

Anticipatory Set

Discuss together things students remember from *The Garden of Abdul Gasazi,* which was done as a read-aloud in the introductory lesson to the unit on Van Allsburg on the previous day: What comes to mind when we think of *The Garden?* The story? The pictures? How does the cover represent the book? How did this book make us feel at the beginning? How did it make us feel at the end? What ideas did we have at the end? Students refer to the entries in their literature response journals, reading from them and talking to support their points. Encourage students to refer to the class story-structure chart that they made together during the previous lesson, as they talk about the story.

Guided Instruction

1. Do a fast forecast of the books *The Witch's Broom, The Wretched Stone,* and *Jumanji:* Students look quickly at the cover art and predict what each is about. Children select which of these books they will read and talk about in their literature circles.

2. As a result of their choice, students form into triads. Children in each triad read their chosen book to themselves (or aloud together if they prefer) and then talk about it—how the author begins it, how he ends it, how the story makes them feel, how the pictures make them feel. In their triads they may work cooperatively to draw a schematic of some kind to show the structure of the story, following the idea of the structure drawing that the class made for *The Garden of Abdul Gasazi.* If they want, they may also draw a schematic to express the meaning they make with the story, as they have done previously with other stories. Students look at the pictures and compare them to the pictures in *The Garden.* They think about how the two stories are similar and different.

Concluding Set

1. Children gather for a Community Share. Literature-circle triads explain their books to the class, holding up pictures, reading lines from the books, and displaying any schematics they may have made.

2. As a class, students begin to generalize about Chris Van Allsburg as both author and artist: the way his stories leave them feeling at the end, the kinds of subjects he handles, the kinds of characters he draws, the way he uses his pictures, the way he structures his stories, the truths he is trying to communicate, and so forth.

Follow-Up Activity

1. Children write down a sentence or two that tell something about how Chris Van Allsburg writes his stories and makes his illustrations, or about how they feel about his books.

2. Children share their sentences with their classmates.

Next Related Lessons

- *Theme lesson:* Read aloud *Two Bad Ants* (to see if it meets children's expectations about the writing and art of Chris Van Allsburg). Follow the read-aloud with discussion and writing.
- *Theme lesson:* Children view the filmstrip-cassette presentation of *The Polar Express.* Establish the scene for this story by setting up the class as a train and having children sit in its "seats."
- *Theme lesson:* Read aloud *Talking with Artists,* by Pat Cummings, to find out more about Chris Van Allsburg and how he creates a book.
- *Independent reading and writing:* Children independently read and respond in their literature response journals to other Van Allsburg stories, such as *Just a Dream, The Stranger, The Z Was Zapped, The Wreck of the Zephyr.* Afterward children gather to share their responses.

Materials

Multiple copies of *The Witch's Broom, The Wretched Stone,* and *Jumanji;* chart paper for making schematics; markers; single copies of other Van Allsburg books.

Assessment

The teacher assesses children's language growth based on their

1. Contributions to group discussions.
2. Entries in their literature response journals.
3. Schematics of a story and presentation of the schematics to the class.

A Fifth-Grade Lesson on Chapter 1 of *Sarah, Plain and Tall*

Literature Base

Chapter 1 of *Sarah, Plain and Tall* by Patricia MacLachlan.

Context

The lesson is part of an ongoing unit focusing on the theme that we all have a need to belong. See unit plan on pages 504–506.

Objectives

The children will refine their ability to

■ Feel deeply with a character.
■ Predict what characters will do in a story.
■ Infer the kind of person a story character is by what he or she says and does.

Proposed Sequence of Activities

Anticipatory Set

Introduce *Sarah, Plain and Tall* by showing the cover and asking students to brainstorm thoughts brought to mind by the art and by the words *plain* and *tall*. On this prelistening web, record thoughts attached to the appropriate words:

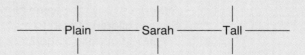

Invite children to predict what the story is about and who the characters are, based on the title and cover art.

Guided Instruction

1. Set a purpose for listening: "Listen to pretend you are Anna. How do you feel? What kind of person are you? What does the author do to make you feel this way and tell you the kind of person Anna is?"

2. Don a coverall of the type Anna might have been wearing. Then do the first chapter of *Sarah, Plain and Tall* as a read-aloud, using the voice to express feelings. Stop just before reaching Anna's final words in the chapter; invite children to suggest what Anna tells Papa to ask Sarah. Why does she ask this?

3. Ask: "How does Anna feel in this chapter? How do you feel in this chapter?" Encourage expression of feelings and rereading of lines that elicit those feelings. Then suggest that students write in their literature response journals, identifying the most powerful sentence in the chapter and telling how that sentence made them feel. Encourage sharing of entries.

4. Ask: "What kind of girl is Anna? How does the author let us know she is that kind of girl?" Begin an Anna character web by plotting her name in the center, placing descriptive adjective words (inferences) around it, and connecting story evidence to the adjectives. Do one adjective as a class to model the process of making inferences. Then organize the class as a workshop in which students collaborate in making an Anna character web.

5. Suggest that each team add one adjective and supporting story evidence to a class chalkboard web. Encourage students to support their additions by reading story lines aloud, indicating location so the class can read along.

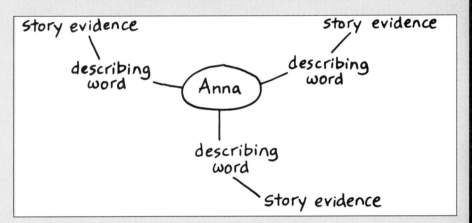

Concluding Set

1. Invite children to identify the other major characters they have met so far in the chapter and to talk about their feelings toward these characters. Ask students to predict the kind of person each character will become, as a way of anticipating where the story is going.

2. Ask students to guess the time and place of the story.

Follow-Up Activity

Tell the children that each of the characters from Chapter 1—Anna, Caleb, and Papa—writes to Sarah. Ask, "If you were one of these people, what would you write in your letter? What questions would you ask? What things would you tell Sarah?" Students write their letters in their literature response journals. The class will share those letters as they get ready to read Chapter 2. (*Note:* Do a mini-lesson later in the afternoon on the form of a social letter.)

Next Related Lessons

- *Vocabulary Development Component:* As a class, children select two power words from Chapter 1. Students use context in which each word is used to project meaning and add the words to the power-word chart that is displayed on the Word Wall of the classroom.
- *Next Theme Lesson:* Children recite orally the poem that they had read as part of the introductory celebration to this focus unit: "This Is My Rock" by David McCord. They talk about these questions: Who or what is Anna's rock? Who or what is Caleb's rock? Does Papa have a rock? How do we know? Does Sarah have a rock? How do we know? Students may choose to write a response in their journals.
- *Ongoing Theme Lesson:* Children share their journal responses: the rock questions, the letters-to-Sarah questions. They talk about the entries. This forms the anticipatory set of the next lesson, in which children read Chapter 2 to themselves.

Materials

Multiple copies of *Sarah, Plain and Tall;* role-playing coverall, literature response journals, a rock, poetry chart of "This Is My Rock."

Assessment

The teacher assesses children's language growth based on their

1. Contributions to group discussions, specifically on the depth of feelings children express and on their ability to make inferences and predictions.
2. Entries in their literature response journals.

A Third- or Fourth-Grade Action Workshop on the First Five Chapters of *Stone Fox*

Literature Base

Stone Fox by John Gardiner.

Context

This lesson is part of an ongoing unit focusing on the theme that we must work hard and sometimes take risks if we are to make our dreams happen. Children will have read the first five chapters of *Stone Fox*.

Objectives

The children will be better able to

- Work cooperatively in collaborative literature activity teams.
- Develop a schematic, or visualization, that highlights some aspect of a story.
- Present their ideas in a clear, organized way to their classmates.
- Make relevant points during a class conversation.

Proposed Sequence of Activities

Anticipatory Set

Describe the way visualizing can help people to see relationships. Talk about ways to visualize story elements, such as through a flowchart, geographic map, or graph. Distribute a list of projects from which children may choose. They organize themselves into teams based on their choice. Students may opt to create a visual of any other kind rather than those listed.

Guided Instruction

1. Children form into three- or four-person circles based on the kind of visual they want to create.
2. Children create their visuals by revisiting segments of the text they have already read and by talking out relationships within their literature circle. Once they have made a schematic on paper, students cooperate in drawing their visuals on the chalkboard.

Concluding Set

The class convenes as a Committee of the Whole. Members of the literature circles take turns coming forward to explain their schematics, answering any questions other classmates may pose.

Follow-Up Activity

In their LRJs, students respond to the ultimate truth of the story—the meaning they make with the story so far.

Next Related Lessons

- *Theme lesson:* Read-aloud of Chapter 6 of *Stone Fox*. The students' LRJ entries written at the end of the previous lesson will serve as the lead-in to this lesson.
- Science activity: Children will continue to monitor the potatoes that they have been growing from cuttings.

Materials

Multiple copies of *Stone Fox,* duplicated copies of the CLAPS (see page 522).

Assessment

The teacher assesses children's language growth based on their

1. Contributions to group activity.
2. Entries in their literature response journals.
3. Participation in class discussions.

Collaborative Literature Action Projects (CLAPS)

1. For any one chapter (Chapters 1–5), make a feelings/mood swing graph. On the *y* axis, plot "very happy" at the top and "very sad" at the bottom. On the *x* axis, plot "beginning of the chapter" on the left and "end of the chapter" on the right. Select one of the first five chapters and graph the mood changes you feel in it.

2. Draw a series of faces (with expressions) to show the changing way little Willy feels in any one of the first five chapters. Connect the faces with arrows to show the direction of story development. Below your first series of faces, draw your own face to show your feelings at each story event.

3. Make a geographic map of the Jackson, Wyoming, area based on the details given in the first five chapters of *Stone Fox.*

4. Make a conflict/tension resolutions graphic in which you diagram the source of the conflict/tension in the story and the varied ways that you could resolve the conflict/tension if you were the author writing the final chapters.

5. Draw two overlapping circles (a Venn diagram). Using your Venn diagram, chart Grandfather's characteristics before he gave up on his dreams and after he gave up. Note: Those characteristics that Grandfather posesses both before and after he gave up go in the part of the diagram where the two circles overlap.

6. Create a roles chart with three columns. In the first column, list all the characters you have met in the first five chapters. In the second, list the role each plays in the community of Jackson. In the third, list the role each plays in the novel. Put a star by the characters you like, an X by the characters you dislike, and an O by the characters about whom you have no opinion.

7. Create an original visual that shows in some way what the story means to you—the truth about life that you have learned from *Stone Fox.* Create a second visual that highlights a second meaning that you learned from the novel.

Plans for Mini-Lessons

A Fifth-Grade Mini-Lesson on the Use of Subheadings in Organizing a Written Report

Context

This mini-lesson takes place during a reading/writing workshop based on an organizational problem that several students are having as they develop written reports.

Objective

The children will be able to use subheadings to ease thought transitions in reports they are organizing.

Proposed Sequence of Activities

Anticipatory Set
Tell students you have noticed that some of them are having trouble moving from one major topic to another in the reports they are writing. You have found a model that will show them how to handle this problem.

Guided Instruction
Display the big book *Rivers of Fire*. Without reading the text, simply turn the pages slowly, showing the subheads. Ask: How is this author using subheads? Why is he doing this? Have children figure out how this big book is organized.

Concluding Set
Suggest that students experiment with subheadings in the reports they are writing.

Follow-Up
Work with individual students as they think through the thought transitions in their own reports.

Materials

The big book *Rivers of Fire*.

Next Related Mini-Lesson

Table of contents in longer reports.

Assessment

Watch for application in children's reports.

A Fourth-Grade Mini-Lesson on List Poems as a Way of Responding to Literature

Context

This mini-lesson takes place during a reading/writing workshop that occurs as children are reading the book *Charlotte's Web* as a class.

Objective

The children will be able to respond to literature through the medium of a list poem.

Proposed Sequence of Activities

Anticipatory Set

Show students Larry Fagin's book *The List Poem* (New York: Teachers and Writers Collaborative, 1991). Explain that you have just come across the book and it provides a poetic form for responding to literature, one that students can use as they respond in their literature journals.

Guided Instruction

Orally share a couple of poems such as "Things That Go Away and Come Back Again" and the "beautiful poems" from the Fagin book. Invite children to write a similar poem together as a class on a topic they pick that connects in some way to *Charlotte's Web*. Develop this on the chalkboard.

Concluding Set

Tell students that the Fagin book is in the reading center. Although it is an adult-level book, they might want to look at some of the poems. They might also use this form as they respond in their journals to *Charlotte's Web*.

Follow-Up

Ask children from time to time if they have tried a list poem. Invite experimenters with the form to sit in the Author's Chair at the end of a workshop to share their poems.

Materials

The List Poem by Larry Fagin.

Next Related Mini-Lesson

Found poems for responding to literature.

Assessment

Study the list poems children write as they respond to literature: Do the poems set a mood? Do they say something worthwhile?

Evaluating Computer-Based Literature and Instructional Software

Checklist to Evaluate Computer-Based Literature

1. Does the story as rendered on the computer maintain the integrity of the original story? Is it an excerpt? Is it an adaptation?
2. Do the illustrations in the computer version maintain the integrity of the illustrations in the original book?
3. Does the way the program breaks up the story into page units detract from the literary appeal?
4. Are the music and sound effects (if any) in keeping with the mood of the story?
5. For what age level is the computer program intended?
6. What are the advantages of the computer-based version over the book version? What are the disadvantages?
7. Will the computer program run on my hardware?

Checklist to Evaluate Instructional Software

1. What does the program teach?
   - Is its primary objective to teach facts? Vocabulary? Basic skills and concepts?
   - Does it involve students in problem solving? Decision making? Evaluative judgments?
   - For what level of student is it intended?
2. Do I want to teach what the program teaches?
3. Do I want to use the computer to teach what the program teaches?
4. Is the content of the program up-to-date and accurate?
5. Is the content presented appropriate for use in an instructional setting?
6. Are the length and pace of the program appropriate for students of the intended age and/or ability level?
7. Are the directions simple and clear? Do they require interpretation by an adult?
8. Is the textual material readable?
9. What role do graphics play in the program?
10. How effective is the system of rewards and corrections?
11. Does the program allow students who have made an error to try a question or program again? Is there opportunity for students to request more practice with the skill or content being studied?
12. Does the program keep track of student progress?
13. Is the program user-friendly, addressing the student by name or allowing slight variations in answering; for example, "y" for yes?

14. Is the program free of glitches, or computer hangups?
15. How is the program protected from accidental wipeouts?
16. What memory is required to run the program?
17. What additional hardware is required?
18. How much does the program disk cost?

Children's References

Asimov, Isaac. *Words from History.* Boston: Houghton Mifflin, 1968.

———. *Words of Science.* Boston: Houghton Mifflin, 1962.

———. *Words on the Map.* Boston: Houghton Mifflin, 1962.

Avi. *Nothing But the Truth.* New York: Orchard, 1991.

Bach, Richard. *Jonathan Livingston Seagull.* New York: Macmillan, 1970.

Bang, Molly. *The Grey Lady and the Strawberry Snatcher.* New York: Four Winds, 1980.

Baylor, Byrd. *Hawk, I'm Your Brother.* New York: Scribner, 1976.

Beim, Lorraine, and Jerold Beim. *Two Is a Team.* New York: Harcourt, Brace, 1945.

Best, Cari. *Taxi, Taxi.* New York: Little, Brown, 1994.

Blos, Joan. *A Gathering of Days: A New England Girl's Journal.* New York: Macmillan, 1979.

Blume, Judy. *Blubber.* Scarsdale, N.Y.: Bradbury, 1974.

———. *Forever.* Scarsdale, N.Y.: Bradbury, 1975.

———. *Tales of a Fourth Grade Nothing.* New York: Dell, 1972.

Bunting, Eve. *How Many Days to America? A Thanksgiving Story.* Boston: Houghton Mifflin, 1988.

Burch, Robert. *Ida Early Comes Over the Mountain.* New York: Viking, 1980.

Byar, Betsy. *The Summer of the Swans.* New York: Viking, 1970.

Carle, Eric. *The Grouchy Ladybug.* New York: Crowell, 1977.

———. *The Mixed-up Chameleon,* 2nd ed. New York: Harper, 1984.

———. *Pancakes, Pancakes.* New York: Scholastic, 1992.

———. *The Rooster Who Set Out to See the World.* New York: Franklin Watts, 1972.

———. *The Very Busy Spider.* New York: Philomel, 1984.

———. *The Very Hungry Caterpillar.* New York: World, 1969.

———. *The Very Quiet Cricket.* New York: Philomel, 1990.

Carrick, Carol. *The Accident.* New York: Seabury, 1976.

Caudill, Rebecca. *My Appalachia: A Reminiscence.* New York: Holt, 1966.

Cleary, Beverly. *Dear Mr. Henshaw.* New York: William Morrow, 1983.

———. *Ramona Quimby, Age 8.* New York: William Morrow, 1981.

Clifford, Eth. *A Bear Before Breakfast.* New York: G. P. Putnam, 1962.

Coerr, Eleanor. *Sadako and the Thousand Paper Cranes.* New York: Putnam, 1977.

Cohen, Barbara. *Molly's Pilgrim.* New York: William Morrow, 1983.

Cole, Joanna. Books in the *Magic School Bus* series. New York: Scholastic, various dates.

Collier, James, and Christopher Collier. *My Brother Sam Is Dead.* New York: Four Winds Press, 1974.

Coombs, Patricia. *The Magic Pot.* New York: Lothrop, Lee, & Shepard, 1977.

Curtis, Christopher Paul. *Bud, Not Buddy.* New York: Delacorte, 1999.

Dahl, Roald. *James and the Giant Peach.* New York: Knopf, 1961.

Danziger, Paula, and Ann Martin. *P.S. Longer Letter Later: A Novel in Letters.* New York: Scholastic, 1998.

Davis, Daniel. *Behind Barbed Wire.* New York: Dutton, 1983.

De Regniers, Beatrice Schenk. *May I Bring a Friend?* New York: Atheneum, 1964.

Emberley, Barbara. *Drummer Hoff.* Ill. by Ed Emberley. Englewood Cliffs, N.J.: Prentice-Hall, 1967.

Ets, Marie Hall. *Play with Me.* New York: Viking, 1955.

Flack, Marjorie. *Ask Mister Bear.* New York: Macmillan, 1986.

Fleischman, Paul. *I Am Phoenix: Poems for Two Voices.* New York: Harper & Row, 1985.

———. *Joyful Noise: Poems for Two Voices.* New York: Harper & Row, 1988.

Fleischman, Sid. *Jim Ugly*. New York: Greenwillow, 1992.

Fox, Paula. *One-Eyed Cat*. New York: Bradbury, 1984; New York: Dell, 1985.

———. *The Slave Dancer*. Scarsdale, N.Y.: Bradbury, 1973.

Freedman, Russell. *Indian Chiefs*. New York: Holiday House, 1987.

———. *Lincoln: A Photobiography*. Boston: Houghton Mifflin, 1987.

———. *The Wright Brothers: How They Invented the Airplane*. New York: Holiday House, 1991.

Freeman, Don. *Tillie Witch*. New York: Viking, 1969.

Galdone, Paul. *The Horse, the Fox, and the Lion*. Boston: Houghton Mifflin, 1968.

———. *The Teeny-Tiny Woman*. Boston: Clarion, 1986.

Gardiner, John. *Stone Fox*. New York: Crowell, 1980.

Giff, Patricia. Books in the *Polk Street School* series. New York: Dell, various dates.

Ginsburg, Mirra. *Mushroom in the Rain*. New York: Macmillan, 1974.

Goble, Paul. *The Girl Who Loved Wild Horses*. Scarsdale, N.Y.: Bradbury, 1978.

———. *Iktomi and the Boulder*. New York: Orchard, 1988.

Grahame, Kenneth. *Wind in the Willows*. New York: Scribner, 1908, 1940.

Greet, W. Cabell, William Jenkins, and Andrew Schiller. *In Other Words: A Beginning Thesaurus (K–2)*. Glenview, Ill.: Scott, Foresman, 1969.

———. *In Other Words: A Junior Thesaurus*. Glenview, Ill.: Scott, Foresman, 1969.

Grifalconi, Ann. *The Village of Round and Square Houses*. Boston: Little, Brown, 1986.

Hader, Berta, and Elmer Hader. *The Big Snow*. New York: Macmillan, 1972.

Haley, Gail. *Jack and the Bean Tree*. New York: Crown, 1986.

Hall, Donald. *Ox-Cart Man*. New York: Viking, 1979.

Heller, Ruth. *Kites Sail High: A Book about Verbs*. Big book ed. New York: Scholastic, 1998.

———. *Many Luscious Lollipops: A Book about Adjectives*. Big book ed. New York: Scholastic, 1989.

———. *Merry-go-round: A Book about Nouns*. Big book ed. New York: Scholastic, 1990.

———. *Up, Up, & Away: A Book about Adverbs*. Big book ed. New York: Scholastic, 1991.

Hendershot, Judith. *In Coal Country*. New York: Knopf, 1987.

Henry, Marguerite. *Cinnabar the One O'Clock Fox*. New York: Rand McNally, 1956.

Hoban, Tana. *Circles, Triangles, and Squares*. New York: Macmillan, 1974.

Hutchins, Pat. *Rosie's Walk*. New York: Macmillan, 1968.

Hymes, Lucia, and James Hymes. *Hooray for Chocolate*. Reading, Mass.: Addison-Wesley, 1960.

James, Joyce. *River of Fire: The 1992 Eruption of Mt. Etna*. Gosford, Australia: Bookshelf, 1992.

Kalan, Robert. *Jump, Frog, Jump!* Big book ed. New York: Scholastic, 1989.

Keats, Ezra Jack. *Apt. 3*. New York: Macmillan, 1983.

———. *The Snowy Day*. New York: Viking, 1962.

Kimmel, Eric. *Four Dollars and Fifty Cents*. New York: Holiday House, 1990.

Klein, Norma. *Mom, the Wolf Man, and Me*. New York: Pantheon, 1972.

Konigsburg, E. L. *Jennifer, Hecate, Macbeth, William McKinley, and Me, Elizabeth*. New York: Atheneum, 1967.

———. *A Proud Taste for Scarlet and Miniver*. New York: Atheneum/Macmillan, 1973; New York: Dell, 1985.

Lear, Edward. *Complete Nonsense Book*. New York: Dodd, Mead, 1912.

Levinson, Riki. *Watch the Stars Come Out*. New York: Dutton, 1985.

Levitin, Sonia. *Journey to America*. New York: Aladdin Books, Macmillan, 1970.

Lindgren, Astrid. *Pippi Longstocking*. New York: Viking, 1969.

Lionni, Leo. *The Biggest House in the World*. New York: Pantheon, 1968.

———. *Pezzetino*. New York: Pantheon, 1975.

———. *Swimmy*. New York: Pantheon, 1968.

———. *Tico and the Golden Wings*. New York: Pantheon, 1964.

Low, Joseph. *Mice Twice*. New York: Atheneum, 1981.

Lowry, Lois. *The Giver*. Boston: Houghton Mifflin, 1993.

———. *Number the Stars*. Boston: Houghton Mifflin, 1989.

———. *Rabble Starkey*. Boston: Houghton Mifflin, 1987.

MacLachlan, Patricia. *Sarah, Plain and Tall*. New York: Harper & Row, 1985.

Martin, Bill. *Brown Bear, Brown Bear, What Do You See?* New York: Holt, 1983.

McCloskey, Robert. *Homer Price.* New York: Viking, 1943; Penguin, 1976.

———. *One Morning in Maine.* New York: Viking, 1952.

———. *Time of Wonder.* New York: Viking, 1957.

McDermott, George. *The Stonecutter.* New York: Viking, 1973.

McKissack, Patricia. *Mirandy and Brother Wind.* New York: Knopf, 1988.

McKissack, Patricia, and Fredrick McKissack. *Christmas in the Big House, Christmas in the Quarters.* Ill. by John Thompson. New York: Scholastic, 1994.

Meltzer, Milton. *Never to Forget: The Jews of the Holocaust.* New York: Harper & Row, 1976.

Merriam, Eve. *It Doesn't Always Have to Rhyme.* New York: Atheneum, 1964.

———. *There Is No Rhyme for Silver.* New York: Atheneum, 1962.

Milne, A. A. *When We Were Very Young.* New York: Dutton, 1961.

Mosel, Arlene. *The Funny Little Woman.* New York: Dutton, 1972.

Naidoo, Beverley. *Journey to Jo'burg.* New York: HarperCollins, 1986.

Naylor, Phyllis Reynolds. *Shiloh.* New York: Atheneum, 1991.

Ness, Evaline. *Sam, Bangs, and Moonshine.* New York: Holt, Rinehart and Winston, 1966.

Paterson, Katherine. *Bridge to Terabithia.* New York: Harper & Row, 1977.

———. *Come Sing, Jimmy Jo.* New York: Dutton, 1985.

———. *The Great Gilly Hopkins.* New York: Crowell, 1978.

———. *Jacob Have I Loved.* New York: Crowell, 1980.

Paulsen, Gary. *Hatchet.* New York: Bradbury, 1987; Puffin, 1988.

———. *Night John.* New York: Delacorte, 1993.

Pearce, Philippa. *Tom's Midnight Garden.* New York: Lippincott, 1984.

Pierce, Meredith Ann. *The Darkangel.* New York: Warner, 1984.

———. *A Gathering of Gargoyles.* New York: Warner, 1985.

Raskin, Ellen. *The Westing Game.* New York: Dutton, 1978.

Rawls, Wilson. *Where the Red Fern Grows: The Story of Two Dogs and a Boy.* Garden City, N.Y.: Doubleday, 1961.

Richter, Hans Peter. *Friedrich.* New York: Puffin Books, 1987.

Rinaldi, Ann. *Wolf by the Ears.* New York: Scholastic, 1991.

Ringgold, Faith. *Tar Beach.* New York: Crown, 1991.

Rock, Gail. *Thanksgiving Treasure.* New York: Knopf, 1974; New York: Dell, 1986.

Rocklin, Joanne. *For Your Eyes Only (FYEO).* New York: Scholastic, 1997.

Roy, Ron. *Three Ducks Went Wandering.* Ill. by Paul Galdone. New York: Clarion, 1979.

Rylant, Cynthia. *Best Wishes.* Katonah, New York: Richard Owen, 1992.

———. *A Blue-Eyed Daisy.* New York: Bradbury, 1985.

———. *Missing May.* New York: Orchard, 1992.

———. *Waiting to Waltz.* New York: Bradbury, undated.

———. *When I Was Young in the Mountains.* New York: Dutton, 1982.

Say, Allen. *Grandfather's Journey.* Boston: Houghton Mifflin, 1993.

Selden, George. *Chester Cricket's Pigeon Ride.* New York: Farrar, Straus, 1981.

———. *The Cricket in Times Square.* New York: Farrar, Straus, 1960.

———. *Harry Cat's Pet Puppy.* New York: Farrar, Straus, 1974

———. *Tucker's Countryside.* New York: Farrar, Straus, 1969.

Sendak, Maurice. *Nutshell Library.* New York: Harper Junior Books, 1962.

———. *Where the Wild Things Are.* New York: Harper & Row, 1963, 1988.

Seuss, Dr. *And to Think That I Saw It on Mulberry Street.* New York: Vanguard, 1937.

———. *The Butter Battle Book.* New York: Random House, 1984.

———. *Green Eggs and Ham.* New York: Random House, 1960.

———. *Horton Hatches the Egg.* New York: Random House, 1940.

———. *The King's Stilts.* New York: Random House, 1939.

———. *The Lorax.* New York: Random House, 1971.

Sharmat, Marjorie. *Frizzy the Fearful.* New York: Holiday, 1983.

———. *Nate the Great.* New York: Dell, 1977.

Silverstein, Shel. *A Light in the Attic.* New York: HarperCollins, 1981.

———. *Where the Sidewalk Ends.* New York: HarperCollins, 1974.

Sis, Peter. *The Starry Messenger.* San Diego: Harcourt Brace, 1995.

Smith, Doris Buchanan. *A Taste of Blackberries.* New York: Crowell, 1973.

Smith, Judith, and Brenda Parkes. *The Three Billy Goats Gruff.* Crystal Lake, Ill.: Rigby, 1986.

Sparks, Beatrice. *Go Ask Alice.* Englewood Cliffs, N.J.: Prentice-Hall, 1971.

Spier, Peter. *People.* New York: Doubleday, 1980.

Spinelli, Jerry. *Maniac Magee.* Boston: Little, Brown, 1990.

Stevens, Janet. *Tops and Bottoms.* San Diego: Harcourt Brace, 1995.

Stockton, Frank Richard. *The Lady, or the Tiger? and Other Stories.* New York: Scribner, 1914.

Stolz, Mary. *Storm in the Night.* New York: Harper & Row, 1988.

Taylor, Mildred. *The Friendship.* New York: Dial, 1987.

———. *Let the Circle Be Unbroken.* New York: Dial, 1981.

———. *Roll of Thunder, Hear My Cry.* New York: Dial, 1976.

Thayer, Ernest. *Casey at the Bat: A Ballad of the Republic Sung in the Year 1888.* Ill. by Christopher Bing. Brooklyn, N.Y.: Handprint Books, 2000.

Travers, Pamela. *Mary Poppins.* New York: Harcourt, Brace, 1934.

Tworkov, Jack. *The Camel Who Took a Walk.* New York: Dutton, 1951.

Udry, Janet. *What Mary Jo Shared.* Niles, Ill.: Whitman, 1966.

Van Allsburg, Chris. *The Garden of Abdul Gasazi.* Boston: Houghton Mifflin, 1979.

———. *Jumanji.* Boston: Houghton Mifflin, 1983.

———. *The Polar Express.* Boston: Houghton Mifflin, 1985.

———. *The Wretched Stone.* Boston: Houghton Mifflin, 1991.

———. *The Z Was Zapped.* Boston: Houghton Mifflin, 1987.

Viorst, Judith. *Alexander and the Terrible, Horrible, No Good, Very Bad Day.* New York: Atheneum, 1972.

———. *I'll Fix Anthony.* New York: Macmillan, 1983, paperback ed.

Voight, Cynthia. *Dicey's Song.* New York: Atheneum/Macmillan, 1982; New York: Fawcett, 1987.

Waber, Bernard. *"You Look Ridiculous," Said the Rhinoceros to the Hippopotamus.* Boston: Houghton Mifflin, 1966.

Webster's II Riverside Beginning Dictionary. Chicago: Riverside Publishing, 1984.

White, E. B. *Charlotte's Web.* New York: Harper & Row, 1952.

Wilder, Laura I. *Little House in the Big Woods.* New York: HarperCollins Children's Books, 1971 (original edition 1956).

Williams, Vera. *A Chair for My Mother.* New York: Greenwillow, 1982.

Yolen, Jane. *Owl Moon.* New York: Philomel, 1987.

Zemach, Harve. *Duffy and the Devil.* New York: Farrar, Straus, Giroux, 1986.

References

Allen, Janet. 1999. *Words, Words, Words: Teaching Vocabulary in Grades 4–12*. York, Me.: Stenhouse Publishers.

Allen, Virginia, et al. 1995. "Amos and Boris: A Window on Teachers' Thinking." *The Reading Teacher*, 48 (February), 384–389.

Alvermann, Donna. 1991. "The Discussion Web: A Graphic Aid for Learning Across the Curriculum." *The Reading Teacher*, 45 (October), 92–99.

Anderson, William, and Patrick Groff. 1972. *A New Look at Children's Literature*. Belmont, Calif.: Wadsworth.

Armbruster, Bonnie, 1992/1993. "Science and Reading." *The Reading Teacher*, 46 (December/January), 346–347.

Armstrong, William. 1997–1998. "Learning to Listen." *American Educator*, 21 (Winter), 24–25, 47.

Atwell, Nancie. 1998. *In the Middle: New Understandings About Writing, Reading, and Learning*. 2nd ed. Portsmouth, N.H.: Heinemann.

———— 1987. *In the Middle: Writing, Reading and Learning with Adolescents*. Portsmouth, N.H.: Heinemann.

————. 1991. *Side by Side: Essays on Teaching to Learn*. Portsmouth, N.H.: Heinemann.

————. 1996. "Cultivating Our Garden." *Voices from the Middle*, 3, 4.

Au, Kathryn. 1997. "Literacy for All Students: Ten Steps Toward Making a Difference." *The Reading Teacher*, 51 (November) 186–195.

Au, Kathryn, and Judith Scheu. 1989. "Guiding Students to Interpret a Novel." *The Reading Teacher*, 43 (November), 104–110.

Aulls, Mark W. 1986. "Actively Teaching Main Idea Skills." In *Teaching Main Idea Comprehension*. Ed. James F. Baumann. Newark, Del.: International Reading Association, 108–115.

Avinger, Juanita. 1984. "Word Processors and Language Experience Stories." *Baylor Educator*, 9 (Spring), 26–28.

Ayers, Donald. 1986. *English Words from Latin and Greek Elements*. 2nd ed., rev. Thomas Worthen. Tucson: University of Arizona Press.

Balajthy, Ernest. 1986. "Using Microcomputers to Teach Spelling." *The Reading Teacher*, 39 (January), 438–443.

Baratz, Joan. 1969. "Language and Cognitive Assessment of Negro Children: Assumptions and Research Needs." *American Speech and Hearing Association Journal*, 11, 88.

Barber, Bill. 1982. "Creating BYTES of Language." *Language Arts*, 59 (May), 472–475.

Barnes, Douglas. 1993. "Supporting Exploratory Talk in Learning." In *Cycles of Meaning*. Eds. Kathryn Pierce and Carol Giles. Portsmouth, N.H.: Heinemann, 17–35.

Barrentine, Shelby. 1996. "Engaging with Reading Through Interactive Read-Alouds." *The Reading Teacher*, 50 (September), 36–43.

Bartch, Judie. 1992. "An Alternative to Spelling: An Integrated Approach." *Language Arts*, 69 (October), 404–408.

Baumann, James, Leah Jones, and Nancy Seifert-Kessell. 1993. "Using Think Alouds to Enhance Children's Comprehension Monitoring Abilities." *The Reading Teacher*, 47 (November), 184–193.

Bear, Donald, Marcia Invernizzi, Shane Templeton, and Francine Johnston. 2000. *Words Their Way: Word Study for Phonics, Vocabulary, and Spelling Instruction*. Upper Saddle River, N.J.: Merrill.

Bereiter, Carl, and M. Scardamalia, eds. 1987. *The Psychology of Written Composition*. Hillsdale, N.J.: Erlbaum.

Berghoff, Beth, and Kathryn Egawa. 1991. "No More 'Rocks': Grouping to Give Students Control of Their Learning." *The Reading Teacher*, 44 (April), 536–541.

Berko, Jean. 1958. "The Child's Learning of English Morphology." *Word*, 14, 150–177.

Bernstein, Bonnie. 1995. "Reading Is Fundamental to Science, Too." *Science Books and Films*, 31 (August/September), 161–163.

Berry, Kathleen. 1985. "Talking to Learn Subject Matter/Learning Subject Matter Talk." *Language Arts*, 62 (January), 34–42.

Betza, Ruth. 1987. "Online: Computerized Spelling Checkers: Friends or Foes?" *Language Arts*, 64 (April), 438–443.

Bianchini, Lori. 2000. "NCTE to You." *Language Arts,* 77 (January), 266.

Bigelow, William. 1992. "Once Upon a Genocide: Christopher Columbus in Children's Literature." *Language Arts,* 69 (February), 112–120.

Bissex, Glenda. 1980. *GNYS AT WRK: A Child Learns to Read and Write.* Cambridge, Mass.: Harvard University Press.

———. 1981. "Growing Writers in Classrooms." *Language Arts,* 58 (October), 787.

Bloodgood, J. 1991. "A New Approach to Spelling in Language Arts Programs." *The Elementary School Journal,* 92, 203–211.

Bosma, Bette. 1987. "The Nature of Critical Thinking: Its Base and Boundary." Paper presented at the National Council of Teachers of English Conference, Los Angeles, November.

Bouffler, C. 1984. "Spelling as a Language Process." In *Reading, Writing, and Spelling: Proceedings of the Fifth Macarthur Reading/Language Symposium.* Ed. L. Unsworth. Sydney, Australia.

Bradley, Virginia. 1982. "Improving Students' Writing with Microcomputers." *Language Arts,* 59 (October), 732–743.

Brent, Rebecca, and Patricia Anderson. 1993. "Developing Children's Classroom Listening Strategies." *The Reading Teacher,* 47 (October), 122–126.

Brock, Cynthia, and James Gavelek. 1998. "Fostering Children's Engagement with Texts: A Sociocultural Perspective." In *Literature-Based Instruction: Reshaping the Curriculum,* ed. by J. Raphael and K. Au. Norwood, Mass.: Christopher-Gordon.

Bromley, Karen D. 1996. *Webbing with Literature: Creating Story Maps with Children's Books.* 2nd ed. Boston: Allyn and Bacon.

Bromley, Karen, and Penny Powell. 1999. "Interest Journals Motivate Student Writers." *The Reading Teacher,* 53 (October), 111–112.

Brown, Ann, et al. 1986. In *Reading Comprehension: From Research to Practice.* Ed. J. Orasanu. Hillsdale, N.J.: Erlbaum, 49.

Brown, Hazel, and Brian Cambourne. 1989. *Read and Retell: A Strategy for the Whole Language/Natural Learning Classroom.* Portsmouth, N.H.: Heinemann.

Brown, Roger. 1958. *Words and Things.* New York: Free Press.

Brown, Roger, and Ursula Bellugi. 1966. "Three Processes in the Child's Acquisition of Syntax." In *Language Learning.* Ed. Janet Emig. New York: Harcourt Brace Jovanovich.

Bruneau, Beverly. 1997. "The Literacy Pyramid Organization of Reading/Writing Activities in Whole Language Classrooms." *The Reading Teacher,* 51 (October), 158–160.

Bruner, Jerome. 1962. *On Knowing.* Cambridge, Mass.: Harvard University Press.

Bunce-Crim, Marna. 1992. "Evaluation: Tracking Daily Progress." *Instructor,* 101 (March), 24–26.

Burke, Constance. 1993. "Talk Within the Kindergarten: Language Supporting a Learning Community." In *Cycles of Meaning.* Ed. Kathryn Pierce and Carol Giles. Portsmouth, N.H.: Heinemann, 79–97.

Burns, Paul, Betty Roe, and Elinor Ross. 1996. *Teaching Reading in Today's Elementary Schools.* 6th ed. Boston: Houghton Mifflin.

———. 1999. *Teaching Reading in Today's Elementary Schools.* 7th ed. Boston: Houghton Mifflin.

Button, Kathryn, Margaret Johnson, and Paige Furgerson. 1996. "Interactive Writing in a Primary Classroom." *The Reading Teacher,* 49 (March), 446–454.

Calkins, Lucy. 1986. *The Art of Teaching Writing.* Portsmouth, N.H.: Heinemann.

———. 1994. *The Art of Teaching Writing.* New ed. Portsmouth, N.H.: Heinemann.

———. 1982. "When Children Want to Punctuate." In *Donald Graves in Australia.* Ed. R. D. Walshe. Portsmouth, N.H.: Heinemann, 89–96.

Cambourne, Brian. 1995. "Toward an Educationally Relevant Theory of Literacy Learning: Twenty Years of Inquiry." *The Reading Teacher,* 49 (November), 186, 188.

Cambourne, Brian, and Jan Turbill. 1987. *Coping with Chaos.* Rozelle, Australia: Primary English Teaching Association.

Cardarelli, Aldo. 1992. "Teachers Under Cover: Promoting the Personal Reading of Teachers." *The Reading Teacher,* 45 (May), 664–668.

Carr, E., and Donna Ogle. 1987. "K-W-L Plus: A Strategy for Comprehension and Summarization." *Journal of Reading,* 30, 626–631.

Carroll, Lewis. *The Annotated Alice.* New York: Clarkson Potter, 1960.

Chomsky, Noam. 1968. *Language and Mind.* New York: Harcourt and World.

———. 1994. In "An Interview with Noam Chomsky." *The Reading Teacher,* 48 (December), 328–333.

Christie, Frances. 1986. "Learning to Mean in Writing." In *Writing and Reading to Learn*. Ed. Nea Stewart-Dore. Rozelle, Australia: Primary English Teaching Association.

Clark, Roy Peter. 1987. *Free to Write: A Journalist Teaches Young Writers*. Portsmouth, N.H.: Heinemann.

Clay, Marie. 1985. *The Early Detection of Reading Difficulties*. Portsmouth, N.H.: Heinemann.

———. 1975. *What Did I Write?* Portsmouth, N.H.: Heinemann.

Cochran-Smith, M., J. L. Kahn, and C. L. Paris. 1990. "Writing with a Felicitous Tool." *Theory into Practice,* 29, 235–247.

Cole, Gerald. 2000. " 'Direct, Explicit, and Systematic'—Bad Reading Science." *Language Arts,* 77 (July), 543–545.

Collins, Allan, John Seely Brown, and Ann Holum. 1991. "Cognitive Apprenticeship: Making Thinking Visible." *American Educator,* 15 (Winter), 6–11, 38–46.

Commeyras, Michelle. 1993. "Promoting Critical Thinking Through Dialogical-Thinking Reading Lessons." *The Reading Teacher,* 46 (March), 486–493.

Congress of the United States. 1975. *Education for All Handicapped Children Act, Public Law 94–142*. Washington, D.C.: U.S. Government Printing Office.

Cooper, Pamela, and Rives Collins. 1991. *Look What Happened to Frog: Storytelling in Education*. Scottsdale, Ariz.: Gorsuch Scarisbrick.

Cooter, Robert. 1989. "Assessment." *The Reading Teacher,* 43 (December), 256–258.

Corson, David. 1985. *The Lexical Bar*. Oxford: Pergamon Press.

Cosgrove, Maryellen. 1987. "Reading Aloud to Children: The Effect of Listening on the Reading Comprehension and Attitudes of Fourth and Sixth Graders in Six Communities in Connecticut." Unpublished doctoral dissertation, University of Connecticut.

Cox, Carole, and Joyce Many. 1992. "Toward an Understanding of the Aesthetic Response to Literature." *Language Arts,* 69 (January), 28–33.

Cramer, Ronald. 1979. *Children's Writing and Language Growth*. Columbus, Ohio: Merrill.

Creighton, Donna. 1997. "Critical Literacy in the Elementary Classroom." *Language Arts,* 74 (October), 438–445.

Crowhurst, Marion. 1979. "Developing Syntactic Skill: Doing What Comes Naturally." *Language Arts,* 56 (May), 522–525.

Cullinan, Bernice, and Lee Galda. 1994. *Literature and the Child*. Fort Worth: Harcourt Brace.

Dahl, Karin, and Nancy Farnan. 1998. *Children's Writing: Perspectives from Research*. Chicago, Ill., and Newark, Del.: National Reading Conference and International Reading Association.

Dahl, Karin, and Patricia Scharer. 2000. "Phonics Teaching and Learning in Whole Language Classrooms: New Evidence from Research." *The Reading Teacher,* 53 (April), 584–594.

Dale, Philip. 1976. *Language Development: Structure and Function*. 2nd ed. New York: Holt, Rinehart and Winston, 18.

D'Alessandro, Marilyn. 1990. "Accommodating Emotionally Handicapped Children Through a Literature-Based Reading Program." *The Reading Teacher,* 44 (December), 288–293.

Davey, Beth. 1983. "Think Aloud—Modeling the Cognitive Processes of Reading Comprehension." *Journal of Reading,* 27 (October), 44–47.

DeFord, Diane, and Jerome Harste. 1982. "Child Language Research and Curriculum." *Language Arts,* 59 (September), 590–600.

DeStephano, Joanna, Harold Pepinsky, and Tobie Sanders. 1982. "Discourse Rules and Literacy Learning in a Classroom." In *Communicating in the Classroom*. Ed. L. Wilkinson. New York: Academic Press.

Dickinson, D. 1986. "Cooperation, Collaboration, and a Computer: Integrating a Computer into a First-Second Grade Writing Program." *Research in the Teaching of English,* 20, 357–378.

———. 1987. "Oral Language, Literacy Skills, and Response to Literature." In *Dynamics of Language Learning*. Ed. James Squire. Urbana, Ill.: National Council of Teachers of English.

Dickinson, Jean. 1993. "Children's Perspectives on Talk: Building a Learning Community." In *Cycles of Meaning*. Ed. Kathryn Pierce and Carol Giles. Portsmouth, N.H.: Heinemann.

Dillon, David, and Dennis Searle. 1981. "The Role of Language in One First Grade Classroom." *Research in the Teaching of English,* 15 (December), 311–328.

DiStefano, Philip, and Patricia Hagerty. 1985. "Teaching Spelling at the Elementary Level." *The Reading Teacher,* 38 (January), 373–377.

Dowhower, S. 1991. "Speaking of Prosody: Fluency's Unnatural Bedfellow." *Theory into Practice,* 30, 502–507.

Downing, Shannon. 1995. "Teaching Writing for Today's Demands." *Language Arts,* 72 (March), 200–205.

Dressman, Mark. 1999. "Mrs. Wilson's University: A Case Study in the Ironies of Good Practice." *Language Arts,* 76 (July), 500–509.

Dudley-Marling, Curt. 1995. "Uncertainty and the Whole Language Teacher." *Language Arts,* 72 (April), 252–257.

Dudley-Marling, Curt, and Sharon Murphy. 1999. "Editors' Pages." *Language Arts,* 76 (March), 288–290.

Dyson, Anne. 1981. "Oral Language: The Rooting System for Learning to Write." *Language Arts,* 58 (October), 776–784.

Dyson, Anne, and Celia Genishi. 1983. "Research Currents: Children's Language for Learning." *Language Arts,* 60 (September), 751–757.

Eeds, Maryann, and Ralph Peterson. 1991. "Teacher as Curator: Learning to Talk About Literature." *The Reading Teacher,* 45 (October), 118–126.

Eeds, Maryann, and Deborah Wells. 1989. "Grand Conversation: An Exploration of Meaning Construction in Literature Study Groups." *Research in the Teaching of English,* 23, 4–29.

Elley, W. B., et al. 1976. "The Role of Grammar in the Secondary School English Curriculum." In *Research in the Teaching of Writing,* 10, 5–21. ED 112 410.

Ennis, Robert. 1987. "A Taxonomy of Critical Thinking Dispositions and Abilities." *Teaching Thinking Skills: Theory and Practice.* Ed. Joan Baron and Robert Sternberg. New York: W. H. Freeman.

Ernst, Franklin. 1968. *Who's Listening?* Addresso Set.

Ernst, Gisela, and Kerri Richard. 1994/1995. "Reading and Writing Pathways to Conversation in the ESL Classroom." *The Reading Teacher,* 48 (December/January), 320–333.

Fagin, Larry. 1991. *The List Poem: A Guide to Teaching and Writing Catalog Verse.* New York: Teachers and Writers Collaborative.

Faix, Thomas. 1975. "Listening as a Human Relations Art." *Elementary English,* 52 (March), 409–413.

Falk-Ross, Francine. 1997. "Developing Metacommunicative Awareness in Children with Language Difficulties: Challenging the Typical Pull-Out System." *Language Arts,* 74 (March), 206–216.

Farr, Roger. 1987. Paper presented at the Great Lakes Regional Conference, International Reading Association, October 1987.

Farr, Roger, and Bruce Tone. 1998. *Portfolio and Performance Assessment: Helping Students Evaluate Their Progress as Readers and Writers.* 2nd ed. Fort Worth, Tex.: Harcourt Brace College Publishers.

Farris, Pamela. 1991. "Views and Other Views: Handwriting Instruction Should Not Become Extinct." *Language Arts,* 68 (April), 312–314.

Ferreiro, E., and A. Teberosky. 1982. *Literacy before Schooling.* Portsmouth, N.H.: Heinemann.

Fitzgerald, Jill. 1999. "What Is This Thing Called Balance?" *The Reading Teacher,* 53 (October), 100–107.

Five, Cora Lee, and Kathryn Egawa. 1998. "Reading and Writing Workshop: What Is It, and What Does It Look Like?" *School Talk,* 3 (April), 1–3.

Flood, James, and Diane Lapp. 1986. "Getting the Main Idea of the Main Idea: A Writing/Reading Process." In *Teaching Main Idea Comprehension.* Ed. James F. Baumann. Newark, Del.: International Reading Association, 227–237.

———. 1987. "Reading and Writing Relations: Assumptions and Directions." In *Dynamics of Language Learning.* Ed. James Squire. Urbana, Ill.: National Council of Teachers of English.

Flower, Linda, and John R. Hayes. 1981. "A Cognitive Process Theory of Writing." *College Composition and Communication,* 32, 365–387.

———. 1994. "The Cognition of Discovery: Defining a Rhetorical Problem." In S. Perl (ed.). *Landmark Essays on Writing Process.* Davis, Calif.: Heragoras Press, 63–74.

Ford, Michael, and Marilyn Ohlhausen. 1988. "Tips from Reading Clinicians for Coping with Disabled Readers in Regular Classrooms." *The Reading Teacher,* 42 (October), 18–22.

Fox, Mem. 1993. "Men Who Weep, Boys Who Dance: The Gender Agenda Between the Lines in Children's Literature." *Language Arts,* 70 (February), 84–88.

Fredericks, Anthony, and Timothy Rasinski. 1990. "Involving Parents in the Assessment Process." *The Reading Teacher,* 44 (December), 346–349.

Fredericksen, Elaine. 2000. "Muted Colors: Gender and Classroom Silence." *Language Arts,* 77 (March), 301–308.

Freire, P., and D. Macedo. 1987. *Literacy: Reading the Word and the World.* South Hadley, Mass.: Bergin & Garvey Publishers.

Fresch, Mary Jo. 2001. "Journal Entries as a Window on Spelling Knowledge." *The Reading Teacher,* 54 (February), 500–513.

Fresch, Mary Jo, and Aileen Wheaton. 1997. "Sort, Search, and Discover: Spelling in the Child-Centered Classroom." *The Reading Teacher,* 51 (September), 20–31.

Fry, Edward. 1998a. "The Most Common Phonograms." *The Reading Teacher,* 51 (April), 620–621.

———. 1998b. *Phonics Patterns: Onset and Rhyme Word Lists.* Laguna Beach, Calif.: Laguna Beach Educational Books.

Funk, Hal, and Gary Funk. 1989. "Guidelines for Developing Listening Skills." *The Reading Teacher,* 42 (May), 660–663.

Gallagher, James. 1975. "The Culturally Different Gifted." In *Teaching the Gifted Child,* 2nd ed. Boston: Allyn and Bacon, 367–387.

Gambrell, Linda. 1985. "Dialogue Journals: Reading-Writing Interaction." *The Reading Teacher,* 38 (February), 512–515.

Gambrell, Linda, Patricia Koskinen, and Barbara Kapinus. 1985. "A Comparison of Retelling and Questioning on Reading Comprehension." Paper presented at the National Reading Conference, San Diego, December 1985.

Gambrell, Linda, Warren Pfeiffer, and Robert Wilson. 1985. "The Effects of Retelling on Reading Comprehension." *Journal of Educational Research,* 78 (July/August), 216–220.

Gardner, Howard. 1993. *Frames of Mind: The Theory of Multiple Intelligences.* 10th anniversary ed. New York: Basic Books.

———. 1995. "Reflections of Multiple Intelligences: Myths and Messages." *Phi Delta Kappan,* 77 (November), 200–209.

Gaskins, Irene. 1997. "Analyzing Words and Making Discoveries About the Alphabetic System: Activities for Beginning Readers." *Language Arts,* 74 (March), 172–184.

Giacobbe, Mary Ellen. 1981. "Kids Can Write the First Week of School." *Learning,* 9 (September), 130–132.

Gill, J. Thomas. 1992. "Focus on Research: Development of Word Knowledge as It Relates to Reading, Spelling, and Instruction." *Language Arts,* 69 (October), 444–453.

Giorgis, Cyndi, and Nancy Johnson. 1999/2000. "Caldecott and Newbery Medal Winners for 1999." *The Reading Teacher,* 53 (December/January), 338–343.

Glasser, William. 1986. *Control Theory in the Classroom.* New York: HarperCollins.

Glazer, Susan. 1996. "Have You Assessed the Balance in Your Reading Program?" *Teaching K–8,* 26 (March), 92–93.

Glenn, C., and N. Stein. 1979. "An Analysis of Story Comprehension in Elementary School Children." In *New Directions in Discourse Processing,* Vol. 2. Ed. R. Freedle. Hillsdale, N.J.: Erlbaum.

Goldenberg, Claude. 1992/1993. "Instructional Conversations: Promoting Comprehension Through Discussion." *The Reading Teacher,* 46, (December/January), 316–326.

Goldstein, A., and P. Carr. 1996. *Can Students Benefit from Process Writing?* (NAEP facts, 1. Report No. NCES-96-845. ED 395 320). Washington, D.C.: U.S. Department of Education, National Center for Educational Statistics.

Goodman, Kenneth, and Yetta Goodman. 1983. "Reading and Writing Relationships: Pragmatic Functions." *Language Arts,* 60 (May), 590–591.

Goodman, Yetta. 1997 reprint. "Reading Diagnosis: Qualitative Versus Quantitiative. *The Reading Teacher,* 50 (April), 534–538.

Goodman, Yetta, and Carolyn Burke. 1972. *Reading Miscue Inventory: Manual Procedures for Diagnosis and Evaluation.* New York: Macmillan.

Graves, Donald. 1989a. *Experiment with Fiction.* Portsmouth, N.H.: Heinemann.

———. 1992. *Explore Poetry.* Portsmouth, N.H.: Heinemann.

———. 1994. *A Fresh Look at Writing.* Portsmouth, N.H.: Heinemann.

———. 1996. "If You Write, They Will Too." *Instructor,* 105 (January/February), 40–41.

———. 1989b. *Investigate Nonfiction.* Portsmouth, N.H.: Heinemann.

———. 1976. "Let's Get Rid of the Welfare Mess in the Teaching of Writing." *Language Arts,* 53 (September), 645–651.

———. 1995. "Sharing the Tools of the Writing Trade." *Instructor,* 105 (November/December), 39–43.

———. 1991. "Trust the Shadows." *The Reading Teacher,* 45 (September), 18–24.

———. 1979. "What Children Show Us about Revision." *Language Arts,* 56 (March), 318–319.

———. 1983. *Writing: Teachers and Children at Work.* Portsmouth, N.H.: Heinemann.

Graves, Donald, and Susan Sowers. 1979. "Research Update— A Six-Year-Old's Writing Process, The First Half of First Grade." *Language Arts,* 56 (October), 831.

Groff, Patrick. 1980. "Is Grammar Teaching Worthwhile?" *Practical Applications of Research,* 2 (March), 4.

Haas, C. 1989a. "Does the Medium Make a Difference: Two Studies of Writing with Computers." *Human Computer Interaction,* 4, 149–169.

———. 1989b. " 'Seeing It on the Screen Isn't Really Seeing It' Computer Writers' Reading Problems." In G. E. Hawisher and C. Selfe, eds. *Critical Perspectives on Computers and Composition Instruction.* New York: Teachers College Press, 16–20.

Hade, Daniel, with Lisa Murphy. 2000. "Voice and Image: A Look at Recent Poetry." *Language Arts,* 77 (March), 344–352.

Hall, Nigel. 1987. *The Emergence of Literacy.* Portsmouth, N.H.: Heinemann.

Hall, Robert. 1960. *Linguistics and Your Language.* New York: Anchor Books.

Halliday, Michael. 1975. *Explorations in the Functions of Language.* New York: Elsevier.

———. 1977. *Learning How to Mean: Explorations in the Development of Language.* New York: Elsevier.

Hancock, Marjorie. 1992. "Literature Response Journals: Insights Beyond the Printed Page." *Language Arts,* 69 (January), 36–42.

Hanna, Paul, Richard Hodges, and Jean Hanna. 1971. *Spelling: Structure and Strategies.* Boston: Houghton Mifflin.

Hannon, Jean. 1999. "Talking Back: Kindergarten Dialogue Journals." *The Reading Teacher,* 53 (November), 200–203.

Hansen, Jane. 1987. *When Writers Read.* Portsmouth, N.H.: Heinemann.

Harman, Susan. 2000. "Resist High-Stakes Testing! High Stakes Are for Tomatoes." *Language Arts,* 77 (March), 332.

Harp, Bill. 1987. "What Are Your Kids Writing During Reading Time?" *The Reading Teacher,* 41 (October), 88–89.

Harper, Laura. 1997. "The Writer's Toolbox: Five Tools for Active Revision Instruction." *Language Arts,* 74 (March), 193–200.

Harris, John. 1986. "Children as Writers." In *Literacy.* Ed. Asher Cashdan. Oxford, England: Basil Blackwell Ltd., 82–111.

Harste, Jerome. 1989. *New Policy Guidelines for Reading: Connecting Research and Practice.* Urbana, Ill.: National Council of Teachers of English.

———. 1982. "What's in a Scribble?" Speech given at the 7th Annual Lester Smith Conference on Educational Research, February 1982, as quoted in DeFord and Harste.

Hayakawa, S. I. 1964. *Language in Thought and Action.* 2nd ed. New York: Harcourt Brace Jovanovich.

Hayes, J. R., and L. Flower. 1980. "Identifying the Organization of Writing Processes." In L. W. Gregg and E. R. Steinberg, eds. *Cognitive Processes in Writing.* Hillsdale, N.J.: Erlbaum, 3–30.

Haynes, Elizabeth. 1978. "Using Research in Preparing to Teach Writing." *English Journal* (January), 82–88.

Hayward, Christopher. 1998. "Monitoring Spelling Development." *The Reading Teacher,* 51 (February), 444–445.

Heald-Taylor, B. Gail. 1987. "Big Books." *Ideas with Insights: Language Arts K–6.* Ed. Dorothy Watson. Urbana, Ill.: National Council of Teachers of English.

———. 1998. "Three Paradigms of Spelling Instruction in Grades 3 to 6." *The Reading Teacher,* 51 (February), 404–413.

Heathcote, Dorothy. 1983. "Learning, Knowing, and Languaging in Drama." *Language Arts,* 60 (September), 695–696.

Henderson, Edmund. 1990. *Teaching Spelling,* 2nd ed. Boston: Houghton Mifflin.

Hennings, Dorothy G. 2000. "Contextually Relevant Word Study." *Journal of Adolescent and Adult Literacy,* 44 (November), 268–279.

———. 1995. "Humanistic, Literature-based Cross-curricular Social Studies." *Reading Instruction Journal,* 39 (Fall), 32–37.

———. 1997/1998. "Modified Found Poems." *The Reading Instruction Journal,* 40 (Fall/Winter), 34–35.

———. 1993. "On Knowing and Reading History." *The Journal of Reading,* 36 (February), 362–370.

———. 1999. *Reading with Meaning: Strategies for College Reading.* Upper Saddle River, N.J.: Prentice-Hall.

———. 1995. "Students' Perceptions of Literature Response Journals Used in Graduate Language Courses." *Reading Research and Instruction,* 35 (Fall), 48–63.

Hennings, Dorothy, and Gail McCreesh. 1994. "Titling and Finding Names that 'Mean.' " *The Reading Teacher,* 48 (October), 186–187.

Hicks, Deborah. 1998. "Narrative Discourses as Inner and Outer Word." *Language Arts,* 75 (January), 28–34. *Note:* In this article, Hicks uses the term "instructional moments," which is a phrase that is synonymous with "teachable moments."

Hildreth, Gertrude. 1966. *Introduction to the Gifted.* New York: McGraw-Hill.

Hillerich, Robert. 1985. "Dealing with Grammar." In *Teaching Children to Write, K–8.* Englewood Cliffs, N.J.: Prentice-Hall.

Hillocks, George. 1986. *Research on Written Composition: New Directions for Teaching.* Urbana, Ill.: ERIC Clearinghouse on Reading and Communication Skills and the National Conference on Research in English.

———. 1987. "Synthesis of Research on Teaching Writing." *Educational Leadership,* 44 (May), 71–82.

Hirsch, E. D. 1987. *Cultural Literacy.* Boston: Houghton Mifflin.

Hodges, Richard. 1982. "On the Development of Spelling Ability." *Language Arts,* 59 (March), 284–290.

Hoffman, James. 1992. "Critical Reading/Thinking Across the Curriculum: Using I-Charts to Support Learning." *Language Arts,* 69 (February), 121–127.

Holdaway, Don. 1982. "The Big Book—A Discussion with Don Holdaway." *Language Arts,* 59 (November/December), 815–821.

———. 1986. "Guiding a Natural Process." *Roles in Literacy Learning.* Newark, Del.: International Reading Association.

Horn, Ernest. 1960. "Spelling." In *Encyclopedia of Educational Research.* 3rd ed. American Educational Association.

Horn, Leigh Van. 2001. "Reading and Writing Essays About Objects of Personal Significance." *Language Arts,* 78 (January), 273–278.

Horn, Thomas. 1947. "The Effect of the Corrected Test on Learning to Spell." *Elementary School Journal,* 47 (January), 277–285.

Howard, Robert. 1987. *Concepts and Schemata: An Introduction.* London: Cassell.

Hoyt, Linda. 1992. "Many Ways of Knowing: Using Drama, Oral Interactions, and the Visual Arts to Enhance Reading Comprehension." *The Reading Teacher,* 45 (April), 580–584.

Huck, Charlotte, et al. 1993. *Children's Literature in the Elementary School.* 5th ed. New York: Holt, Rinehart and Winston; see also 4th ed., 1987.

Hughes, Margaret, and Dennis Searle. 2000. "Spelling and the Second 'R.'" *Language Arts,* 77 (January), 203–208.

Hunt, Kellogg, and Roy O'Donnell. 1970. "An Elementary School Curriculum to Develop Better Writing Skills." U.S. Office of Education Grant. Florida State University.

Hunter, Madeline. 1982. *Mastery Teaching.* El Segundo, Calif.: TIP Publications.

Hutson, Barbara. 1980. "Moving Language Around: Helping Students Become Aware of Language Structure." *Language Arts,* 57 (September), 614–642.

IRA/NCTE Joint Task Force on Assessment. 1994. *Standards for the Assessment of Reading and Writing.* Newark, Del., and Urbana, Ill.: International Reading Association and the National Council of Teachers of English.

Invernizzi, Marcia, Mary Abouzeid, and Janet Bloodgood. 1997. "Integrated Word Study: Spelling, Grammar, and Meaning in the Language Arts Classroom." *Language Arts,* 74 (March), 185–192.

Joint Committee of the National Council of Teachers of English and Children's Theatre Association. 1983. "Forum: Informal Classroom Drama." *Language Arts,* 60 (March), 370–372.

Jones, I., and A. Pellegrini. 1996. "The Effects of Social Relationships, Written Media, and Microgenetic Development on First-grade Students' Written Narratives. *American Educational Research Journal,* 33, 691–718.

Kane, Sharon. 1997. "Favorite Sentences: Grammar in Action." *The Reading Teacher,* 51 (September), 70–73.

Karolides, Nicholas, J. 1999. "Theory and Practice: An Interview with Louise M. Rosenblatt." *Language Arts,* 77 (November), 158–170.

Kellogg, W. N., and L. A. Kellogg. 1933. *The Ape and the Child.* New York: McGraw-Hill.

Kelly, Kevin, and Sidney Moon. 1998. "Personal and Social Talents." *Phi Delta Kappan,* 79 (June), 743–746.

Kelly, Patricia. 1990. "Guiding Young Students' Response to Literature." *The Reading Teacher,* 43 (March), 464–470.

Kirby, Dan, et al. 1988. "Beyond Interior Decorating: Using Writing to Make Meaning in the Elementary School." *Phi Delta Kappan,* 69 (June), 718–724.

Koch, Kenneth. 1980. *Wishes, Lies, and Dreams.* New York: Vintage.

Kolata, Gina. 1987. "Associations or Rules in Language Learning?" *Science,* 237 (July), 133–134.

Koskinen, Patricia, Linda Gambrell, Barbara Kapinus, and Betty Heathington. 1988. "Retelling: A Strategy for Enhancing Students' Reading Comprehension." *The Reading Teacher,* 41 (May), 892–896.

Kress, Gunther. 1999. "Genre and the Changing Contexts for English Language Arts." *Language Arts,* 76 (July), 461–469.

Kucer, Stephen, and Lynn Rhodes. 1986. "Counterpart Strategies: Fine Tuning Language with Language." *Reading Teacher,* 40 (November), 186–193.

Kucera, Cheryl. 1995. "Detours and Destinations: One Teacher's Journey into an Environmental Workshop." *Language Arts,* 72 (March), 179–187.

Kuhl, Patricia, et al. 1992. "Linguistic Experience Alters Phonetic Perception in Infants by 6 Months of Age." *Science,* January 31, 606–608.

Labbo, Linda, James Hoffman, and Nancy Roser. 1995. "Ways to Unintentionally Make Writing Difficult." *Language Arts,* 72 (March), 164–170.

Lane, Barry, 1992. *After "THE END": Teaching and Learning Creative Revision.* Portsmouth, N.H.: Heinemann.

Langer, Judith. 1995. *Envisioning Literature: Literary Understanding and Literature Instruction.* N.Y.: Teachers College Press.

LaPointe, Archie. 1986. "The State of Instruction in Reading and Writing in U.S. Elementary Schools." *Phi Delta Kappan,* 68 (October), 838–847.

Lapp, Diane, et al. 1997. "'Do You Really Want Us To Talk About This Book?': A Closer Look at Book Clubs as an Instructional Tool." In *Peer Talk in the Classroom: Learning from Research,* ed. by Jeanne Paratore and Rachel McCormack. Newark, Del.: International Reading Association.

Lefevre, Carl. 1973. *Linguistics, English, and the Language Arts.* New York: Teachers College Press.

Lehman, B., and D. Hayes. 1985. "Advancing Critical Reading Through Historical Fiction and Biography." *Social Studies,* 76, 165–169.

Lim, Hwa-Ja-Lee, and Dorothy Watson. 1993. "Whole Language Content Classes for Second-Language Learners." *The Reading Teacher,* 46 (February), 384–393.

Lloyd, Pamela. 1987. *How Writers Write.* Portsmouth, N.H.: Heinemann.

Loban, Walter. 1976. *Language Development: Kindergarten Through Grade 12.* Urbana, Ill.: National Council of Teachers of English.

————. 1963. *The Language of Elementary School Children.* Urbana, Ill.: National Council of Teachers of English.

Lopez, Annette. 2000. "The Impact of Changing Demographics—English Language Learners and Programs That Serve Them." *School Connections,* 12 (Fall), 4–10.

Lukens, Rebecca J. 1995. *A Critical Handbook of Children's Literature.* 5th ed. New York: HarperCollins.

Lundsteen, Sara. 1979. *Listening: Its Impact at All Levels on Reading and the Other Language Arts.* Urbana, Ill.: National Council of Teachers of English.

Lunsford, Susan. 1997. "'And They Wrote Happily Ever After': Literature-based Mini-lessons in Writing." *Language Arts,* 74 (January), 42–48.

MacNeil, Robert. 1995. "Language, Reading, and Pleasure." *The Reading Teacher,* 49 (September), 8–14.

Madura, Sandra. 1995. "The Line and Texture of Aesthetic Response: Primary Children Study Authors and Illustrators." *The Reading Teacher,* 49 (October), 110–118.

Manzo, Anthony. 1985. "Expansion Modules for the ReQuest, CAT, GRP, and REAP Reading/Study Procedures." *Journal of Reading,* 28, 498–502.

————. 1975. "Guided Reading Procedure." *Journal of Reading,* 18, 287–291.

Manzo, Anthony, and Ula Manzo. 1997. *Interactive Teaching for Active Learning.* 2nd ed. Upper Saddle River, N.J.: Merrill, Prentice-Hall.

Maria, Katherine. 1989. "Developing Disadvantaged Children's Background Knowledge Interactively." *The Reading Teacher,* 42 (January), 296–300.

Martin, Bill. 1974. *Sounds of Language Series.* New York: Holt, Rinehart and Winston.

Martin, Samuel. 1964. "Review of Greenberg's Universals of Language." *Harvard Review,* 34, 353–355.

McCrone, John. 1991. *The Ape That Spoke.* New York: William Morrow.

McGee, Lea. 1992. "Focus on Research: Exploring the Literature-Based Reading Revolution." *Language Arts,* 69 (November), 529–537.

Mellon, John. 1969. *Transformational Sentence-Combining.* Research Report No. 10. Urbana, Ill.: National Council of Teachers of English.

Miccinati, Jeannette. 1985. "Using Prosodic Cues to Teach Oral Reading Fluency." *The Reading Teacher,* 39 (November), 206–211.

Miller, Barbara, and James Ney. 1968. "The Effect of Systematic Oral Exercises on the Writing of Fourth-Grade Students." *Research in the Teaching of English* (Fall).

Miller, George. 1988. "The Challenge of Universal Literacy." *Science,* September 9, 1293–1300.

Miller, Howard. 2000. "Teaching and Learning About Cultural Diversity: All of Us Together Have a Story to Tell." *The Reading Teacher,* 53 (May), 666–667.

———. 1997. "Teaching and Learning About Cultural Diversity: Breaking the Silence." *The Reading Teacher,* 51 (November), 260–262.

Milz, Vera. 1985. "First Graders' Uses for Writing." In *Observing the Language Learner.* Ed. Angela Jagger and Trika Smith-Burke. Newark, Del.: International Reading Association.

Moe, Alden, and Judith Irwin. 1986. "Cohesion, Coherence, and Comprehension." In *Understanding and Teaching Cohesion Comprehension.* Ed. Judith Irwin. Newark, Del.: International Reading Association.

Moore, Bob, and Maxine Moore. 1997. *NTC's Dictionary of Latin and Greek Origins.* Chicago: NTC Publishing Group.

Moore, Susan. 1995. "Questions for Research into Reading-Writing Relationships and Text Structure Knowledge." *Language Arts,* 72 (December), 598–606.

Morris, Darrell. 1983. "Concept of Word and Phoneme Awareness in the Beginning Reader." *Research in the Teaching of English,* 17 (December), 359–373.

———. 1987. "Meeting the Needs of the Poor Speller in the Elementary School." *Illinois Schools Journal* (Spring), 28–41.

Morrow, Lesley. 1986. "Effects of Structural Guidance in Story Retelling on Children's Dictation of Original Stories." *Journal of Reading Behavior,* 18 (Spring), 135–151.

———. 1985a. "Reading and Retelling Stories: Strategies for Emergent Readers." *The Reading Teacher,* 35 (May), 870–875.

———. 1985b. "Retelling Stories: A Strategy for Improving Young Children's Comprehension, Concept of Story Structure, and Oral Language Complexity." *Elementary School Journal,* 85, 647–661.

Moss, R. K., and John Stansell. 1983. "Wolf Stew: A Recipe for Writing Growth and Enjoyment." *Language Arts,* 60 (March), 346–350.

Murphy, Sharon, and Curt Dudley-Marling. 2000. "Editors' Pages." *Language Arts,* 77 (January), 200–201.

Murray, Donald. 1992. "Focus on Research: Exploring the Literature-Based Reading Revolution." *Language Arts,* 69 (November), 529–537.

———. 1986. Keynote Address. New Hampshire Summer Writing Project. Durham, N.H.

———. 1982. *Learning by Teaching: Selected Articles on Writing and Teaching.* Montclair, N.J.: Boynton Cook.

———. 1990. *Shoptalk: Learning to Write with Writers.* Portsmouth, N.H.: Boynton Cook.

Musthafa, Bachrudin. 1994. "Literacy Response: A Way of Integrating Reading-Writing Activity." *Reading Improvement,* 31, 52–58.

Nathan, Ruth, and Keith Stanovich. 1991. "The Causes and Consequences of Differences in Reading Fluency." *Theory into Practice,* 30, 176–184.

National Assessment of Educational Progress. 1975. *Writing Mechanics, 1969–1974: A Capsule Description of Changes in Writing Mechanics.* Washington, D.C.: U.S. Government Printing Office.

National Council of Teachers of English and International Reading Association. 1996. *Standards for the English Language Arts.* Urbana, Ill., and Newark, Del.: National Council of Teachers of English and International Reading Association.

Newkirk, Thomas. 1978. *Grammar Instruction and Writing: What Does Research Really Prove?* ERIC Document, ED 153 218.

Nicholson, Tom, and Sumner Schachter. 1979. "Spelling Skill and Teaching Practice: Putting Them Back Together Again." *Language Arts,* 56 (October), 804–809.

Nickerson, Raymond. 1986. *Reflections on Reasoning.* Hillsdale, N.J.: Erlbaum.

———. 1987. "Why Teach Thinking?" In *Teaching Thinking Skills: Theory and Practice.* Ed. Joan Baron and Robert Sternberg. New York: W. H. Freeman.

Norwicki, Stephen, and Marshall Duke. 1992. *Helping the Child Who Doesn't Fit In.* Atlanta: Peachtree Press.

Novelli, Joan. 1993. "Strategies for Spelling Success." *Instructor,* 102 (May/June), 41–42, 47.

Ogle, Donna. 1986. "K-W-L: A Teaching Model that Develops Active Reading of Expository Text." *The Reading Teacher,* 39 (February), 564–570.

O'Hare, Frank. 1973. *Sentence Combining.* Research Report No. 15. Urbana, Ill.: National Council of Teachers of English.

Olson, David. 1983. "Perspectives: Children's Language and Language Teaching." *Language Arts,* 60 (February), 227–229.

Owston, P. D., S. Murphy, and H. Widemann. 1992. "The Effects of Word Processing on Students' Writing Quality and Revision Strategies." *Research in the Teaching of English,* 26, 249–276.

Palincsar, Annemarie, and Ann Brown. 1985. In *Reading Education: Foundations for a Literate America.* Ed. J. Osborn et al. Lexington, Mass.: Lexington Books.

———. 1986. "Interactive Teaching to Promote Independent Learning from Text." *The Reading Teacher,* 39 (April), 771–777.

Pappas, Christine, and Barbara Pettegrew. 1998. "The Role of Genre in the Psycholinguistic Guessing Game of Reading." *Language Arts,* 75 (January), 36–44.

Pardo, Laura, and Taffy Raphael. 1991. "Classroom Organization for Instruction in Content Areas." *The Reading Teacher,* 44 (April), 556–564.

Parker, Emilie, et al. 1995. "Teachers' Choices in Classroom Assessment." *The Reading Teacher,* 48 (April), 622.

Paul, Lissa. 2000. "The Naked Truth About Being Literate." *Language Arts,* 77 (March), 335–342.

Pearson, David, and Linda Fielding. 1982. "Research Update: Listening Comprehension." *Language Arts,* 59 (September), 617–629.

Peltzman, Barbara. 1994. "The Art of Story Telling." *Reading Instruction Journal,* 37 (Winter), 7–11.

Perron, Jack. 1978. "Beginning Writing: It's All in the Mind." *Language Arts,* 53 (September), 652–657.

Peterson, Ralph. 1987. "Literature Groups: Intensive and Extensive Reading." In *Ideas with Insights: Language Arts K–6.* Ed. Dorothy Watson. Urbana, Ill.: National Council of Teachers of English.

Peterson, Ralph, and Maryann Eeds. 1990. *Grand Conversations: Literature Groups in Action.* New York: Scholastic.

Petrosky, A. 1977. "Grammar Instruction: What We Know." *English Journal,* 66, 86–88.

Phinney, Margaret. 1998. "Children Writing Themselves: A Glimpse at the Underbelly." *Language Arts,* 75 (January), 19–27.

Piaget, Jean. 1965. *The Language and Thought of the Child.* New York: Meridian Books.

———. 1964. *The Psychology of Intelligence.* Boston: Routledge and Kegan Paul.

Pinker, S., and A. Prince. 1987. "On Language and Connectionism: Analysis of Parallel Distributed Processing Model of Language Acquisition." Occasional Paper No. 33. Cambridge, Mass.: MIT Press.

Pinnell, Gay Su, and Irene Fountas. 1998. *Word Matters: Teaching Phonics and Spelling in the Reading/Writing Classroom.* Westport, Conn.: Heinemann.

Piper, Terry. 1998. *Language and Learning: The Home and School Years.* 2nd ed. Upper Saddle River, N.J.: Merrill/Prentice-Hall.

Plank, Edward. 1992. Personal communication with author.

Porter, Jane. 1972. "Research Report by James Martin—The Development of Sentence Writing Skills at Grades Three, Four, and Five." *Elementary English,* 49 (October), 867–870.

Power, Brenda. 1995. "Bearing Walls and Writing Workshops." *Language Arts,* 72 (November), 482–488.

Price, Debra. 1998. "Explicit Instruction at the Point of Use." *Language Arts,* 76 (September), 19–26.

Purcell-Gates, Victoria, et al. 1995. "Literacy at the Harts' and the Larsens': Diversity Among Poor, Innercity Families." *The Reading Teacher,* 48 (April), 572.

Purves, Alan. 1975. "Research in the Teaching of Literature." *Language Arts,* 52 (April), 463–466.

Putnam, Lillian. 1994. "An Interview with Noam Chomsky." *The Reading Teacher,* 48 (December), 328–333.

Putnam, Lillian, ed. 1996. *How to Become a Better Reading Teacher.* Saddle River, N.J.: Merrill/Prentice-Hall.

Quintero, Elizabeth, and Ana Huerta-Macias. 1990. "All in the Family: Bilingualism and Biliteracy." *The Reading Teacher,* 44 (December), 306–312.

Ralston, Marion. 1993. *An Exchange of Gifts: A Storyteller's Handbook.* Markham, Ontario. Pippin Publishing Ltd.

Ramsey, John. 1988. "Why Is Left Handed Writing Still a Problem in the Last 7th of the 20th Century?" *The Reading Teacher,* 41 (February), 504–506.

Rankin, W. 1997. "The Cyberjournal: Developing Writing, Researching, and Editing Skills Through E-Mail and the World Wide Web." *Educational Technology,* (July/August), 29–31.

Raphael, Taffy. 1992. "Research Directions: Literature and Discussion in the Reading Program." *Language Arts,* 69 (January), 54–61.

Raphael, Taffy, and Susan McMahon. 1994. "Book Club: An Alternative Framework for Reading Instruction." *The Reading Teacher,* 48 (October), 102–116.

Raphael, Taffy, and Kathryn H. Au, eds. 1998. *Literature-Based Instruction: Reshaping the Curriculum.* Norwood, Mass.: Christopher-Gordon.

Rasinski, Timothy. 2000. "Speed Does Matter." *The Reading Teacher,* 54 (October), 146–151.

Raths, Louis. 1978. *Values and Teaching.* Columbus, Ohio: Merrill.

Ravitch, Diane, and Chester Finn. 1987. *What Do Our 17-Year-Olds Know?* New York: Harper & Row.

Ray, Katie Wood. 1999. *Wondrous Words: Writers and Writing in the Elementary Classroom.* Urbana, Ill.: National Council of Teachers of English.

Read, Charles. 1971. "Pre-school Children's Knowledge of English Phonology." *Harvard Educational Review,* 41, 1–34.

Reed, Elaine. 1997–1998. "Projects and Activities: A Means, Not an End." *American Educator,* 21 (Winter), 26–27, 48.

Reutzel, D. Ray, et al. 1995. "Dialogical Books: Connecting Content, Conversation, and Composition." *The Reading Teacher,* 49 (October), 98–109.

Richards, Janet, and Joan Gipe. 1995. "What's the Structure? A Game to Help Middle School Students Recognize Common Writing Patterns." *Journal of Reading,* 38 (May), 667–669.

Richards, Meribethe. 2000. "Be a Good Detective: Solve the Case of Oral Reading Fluency." *The Reading Teacher,* 53 (April), 534–539.

Robinson, Francis. 1961. *Effective Study.* Rev. ed. New York: Harper & Row.

Rodriguez, Richard. 1981. *Hunger of Memory: The Education of Richard Rodriguez.* Boston: David Godine, 60.

Roller, Cathy. 1996. *Variability Not Disability: Struggling Readers in a Workshop Classroom.* Newark, Del.: International Reading Association.

Roller, Cathy, and Penny Beed. 1994. "Sometimes the Conversations Were Grand, and Sometimes. . . ." *Language Arts,* 71 (November), 509–523.

Rosenblatt, Louise. 1995. *Literature as Exploration.* 5th ed. (First published in 1938). New York: Modern Language Association.

———. 1978. *The Reader, the Text, the Poem.* Carbondale, Ill.: Southern Illinois University Press.

Roser, Nancy, and James Hoffman. 1992. "Language Charts: A Record of Story Time Talk." *Language Arts,* 69 (January), 44–52.

Roush, Wade. 1995. "Arguing Over Why Johnnie Can't Read." *Science,* 267 (March), 1896–1898.

Routman, Regie. 1994. *Invitations: Changing as Teachers and Learners K–12.* Rev. ed. Portsmouth, N.H.: Heinemann.

———. 1996. "Reclaiming the Basics." *Instructor,* 105 (May/June), 49–54, 84.

———. 1993. "The Uses and Abuses of Invented Spelling." *Instructor,* 102 (May/June), 36–39.

Routman, Regie, and Angie Butler. 1995. "Why Talk About Phonics?" *School Talk,* 1 (November), 4.

Ruddell, Robert. 1992. "A Whole Language and Literature Perspective: Creating a Meaning-Making Instructional Environment." *Language Arts,* 69 (December), 612–620.

Ruiz, Nadeen. 1995. "A Young Deaf Child Learns to Write." *The Reading Teacher,* 49 (November), 206–217.

Rumelhart, D. E., and J. L. McClelland. 1987. "Learning the Past Tenses of English Verbs: Implicit Rules or Parallel Distributed Processing?" In *Mechanism of Language Acquisition.* Ed. B. MacWhinney. Hillsdale, N.J.: Erlbaum.

Samuels, S. Jay. 1997. "The Method of Repeated Readings." *The Reading Teacher,* 50 (February), 376–381.

Scheflen, Albert. 1972. *Body Language and the Social Order.* Englewood Cliffs, N.J.: Prentice-Hall.

Schlagal, Robert, and Jay Schlagal. 1992. "The Integral Character of Spelling: Teaching Strategies for Multiple Purposes." *Language Arts,* 69 (October), 418–424.

Schreiber, P. A. 1980. "On the Acquisition of Reading Fluency." *Journal of Reading Behavior,* 12, 177–186, as reported by David Pearson and Linda Fielding, "Research Update: Listening Comprehension." *Language Arts,* 59 (September), 617–629.

Schwartz, David. 1995. "Ready, Set, Read—20 Minutes Each Day Is All You'll Need." *Smithsonian,* 25 (February), 82–91.

Scott, Jill. 1994. "Spelling for Readers and Writers." *The Reading Teacher,* 48 (October), 188–189.

Sebesta, Sam. 1997. "Having My Say." *The Reading Teacher,* 50 (April), 542–549.

Shafer, Robert. 1974. "What Teachers Should Know about Children's Language." *Language Arts,* 51 (April), 498–501.

Shanahan, Timothy. 1995. "Avoiding Some of the Pitfalls of Thematic Units." *The Reading Teacher,* 48 (May), 718–719.

———. 1997. "In Pursuit of Effective Integrated Literacy Instruction." *The Reading Teacher,* 51 (September), 12–18.

Shelley, Anne, et al. 1997. "Revisiting the K-W-L: What We Knew; What We Wanted to Know; What We Learned." *Reading Horizons,* 37, 233–242.

Short, Kathy. 1995. "Graffiti Boards and Visual Webs." *School Talk,* 1 (August), 4.

Short, Kathy, Gloria Kaufman, Sandy Kaser, Leslie Kahn, and K. Crawford. 1999. " 'Teacher-Watching': Examining

Teacher Talk in Literature Circles." *Language Arts,* 76 (May), 377–400.

Short, Kathy, and Junardi Armstrong. 1993. " 'More than Facts': Exploring the Role of Talk in Classroom Inquiry." In *Cycles of Meaning.* Ed. Kathryn Pierce and Carol Giles. Portsmouth, N.H.: Heinemann, 119–137.

Shuy, Roger. 1987. "Research Currents: Dialogue as the Heart of Learning." *Language Arts,* 64 (December), 890–897.

Simon, Sidney. 1976. *Values, Concepts, and Techniques.* Washington, D.C.: National Education Association.

Simon, Sidney, et al. 1972. *Values Clarification: A Handbook of Practical Strategies for Teachers and Students.* New York: Hart Publishing.

Siu-Runyan, Yvonne. 1991. "Holistic Assessment in Intermediate Classes: Techniques for Informing Our Teachers." In *Assessment and Evaluation in Whole Language Programs.* Ed. Bill Harp. Norwood, Mass.: Christopher-Gordon.

Smith, Carl. 1991. "The Role of Different Literary Genres." *The Reading Teacher,* 44 (February), 440–441.

———. 1990. "Two Approaches to Critical Thinking." *The Reading Teacher,* 44 (December), 350–351.

Smith, Frank. 1992. "Learning to Read: The Never-Ending Debate." *Phi Delta Kappan,* 73 (February), 432–441.

Snow, C. E. 1977. "The Development of Conversation Between Mothers and Babies." *Journal of Child Language,* 4.

Snowball, Diane. 1994. "Thinking about Language." *Teaching K–8,* 24 (May), 64–65.

Sorensen, Marilou, and Barbara Lehman. 1995. *Teaching with Children's Books: Paths to Literature-based Instruction.* Urbana, Ill.: National Council of Teachers of English.

Spiegel, Dixie. 1995. "A Comparison of Traditional Remedial Reading Programs and Reading Recovery." *The Reading Teacher,* 49 (October), 86–96.

Spivey, Nancy. 1991. "Discourse Synthesis." *The Reading Teacher,* 44 (May), 702–703.

Squire, James. 1983. "Composing and Comprehending: Two Sides of the Same Basic Process." *Language Arts,* 60 (May), 581–589.

Staton, Jana. 1988. "ERIC/RCS Report: Dialogue Journals." *Language Arts,* 65 (February), 198–201.

Stauffer, Russell. 1979. "The Language Experience Approach to Reading Instruction for Deaf and Hearing Impaired Children." *The Reading Teacher,* 33 (October), 21–24.

———. 1980. *The Language Experience Approach to the Teaching of Reading.* 2nd ed. New York: Harper & Row.

Stauffer, Russell, and John Pikulski. 1974. "A Comparison and Measure of Oral Language Growth." *Elementary English,* 51 (November/December), 1151–1155.

Sternberg, Robert. 1984. "Testing Intelligence without I.Q. Tests." *Phi Delta Kappan* (June), 694–698.

Stoddard, Elizabeth. 1982. "The Combined Effect of Creative Thinking and Sentence-Combining Activities on the Writing Abilities of Above Average Fifth and Sixth Grade Students." Ph.D. diss., University of Connecticut.

Stotsky, S. 1983. "Types of Lexical Cohesion in Expository Writing." *College Composition and Communication,* 34, 568–580.

Stout, Hilary. 1992. "Many U.S. Children Don't Read Enough, Can't Analyze the Material, Study Finds." *The Wall Street Journal* (May 29).

Strickland, Dorothy. 1973. "A Program for Linguistically Different Black Children." *Research in the Teaching of English,* 7 (Spring), 79–86.

———. 1994/1995. "Reinventing Our Literacy Programs: Books, Basics, Balance." *The Reading Teacher,* 48 (December/January), 294–301.

Sudol, David, and Peg Sudol. 1995. "Yet Another Story: Writers' Workshop Revisited." *Language Arts,* 72 (March), 171–178.

Swandesh, Morris. 1971. *The Origin and Diversification of Language.* Hawthorne, N.Y.: Aldine.

Taba, Hilda, et al. 1967. "Teaching Strategies for Cognitive Growth." In *Conceptual Models in Teacher Education.* Ed. John Verduin. Washington, D.C.: American Association of Colleges for Teacher Education.

———. 1964. *Thinking in Elementary School Children.* San Francisco: San Francisco State College.

Taylor, Barbara, and Linda Nosbush. 1983. "Oral Reading for Meaning: A Technique for Improving Word Identification Skills." *The Reading Teacher,* 37 (December), 234–237.

Taylor, Denny, and Catherine Dorsey-Gaines. 1988. *Growing Up Literate: Learning from Inner-City Families.* Portsmouth, N.H.: Heinemann.

Teale, William. 1992. "Dear Readers." *Language Arts,* 69 (October), 401–404.

———. 1982. "Toward a Theory of How Children Learn to Read and Write Naturally." *Language Arts,* 59 (September), 555–570.

Temple, Charles. 1993. " 'What If Beauty Had Been Ugly?' Reading Against the Grain of Gender Bias in Children's Books." *Language Arts,* 70 (February), 89–93.

Temple, Charles, et al. 1988. *The Beginnings of Writing.* 2nd ed. Boston: Allyn & Bacon.

Templeton, Shane. 1979. "The Circle Game of English Spelling." *Language Arts,* 56 (October), 789–797.

Terman, Lewis, and Maud Merrill. 1960. *Stanford-Binet Intelligence Scale: Manual for the Third Revision Form L-M.* Boston: Houghton Mifflin.

Thaiss, Christoper. 1990. "Language Across the Curriculum." In *Rhetoric and Composition: A Sourcebook for Teachers and Writers.* Ed. Richard Graves. Portsmouth, N.H.: Boynton/Cook, 33–37.

Tierney, Robert J. 1990. "Learning to Connect Reading and Writing: Critical Thinking Through Transactions with One's Own Subjectivity." In *Reading and Writing Together: New Perspectives for the Classroom.* Ed. Timothy Shanahan. Norwood, Mass.: Christopher-Gordon, 131–143.

Tierney, Robert, Mark Carter, and Laura Desai. 1991. *Portfolio Assessment in the Reading-Writing Classroom.* Norwood, Mass.: Christopher-Gordon.

Tierney, Robert, and F. David Pearson. 1983. "Toward a Composing Model of Reading." *Language Arts,* 60 (May), 568–580.

Trelease, Jim. 1996. "Have You Read to Your Kids Today?" *Instructor,* 105 (May/June), 56–60.

———. 1995. *The New Read-Aloud Handbook.* Rev. ed. New York: Penguin.

Turbill, Jan. 2000. "Developing a Spelling Conscience." *Language Arts,* 77 (January), 209–216.

"Using Nonfiction Literature." 2000. *School Talk,* 5 (January). The entire issue focuses on nonfiction.

Valencia, Sheila. 1990. "A Portfolio Approach to Classroom Reading Assessment: The Whys, Whats and Hows." *The Reading Teacher,* 43 (January), 338–340.

Vermont Assessment Program. 1991. Montpelier, Vt.: Vermont Department of Education, mimeographed document.

Vygotsky, Lev. 1962. *Thought and Action.* Cambridge, Mass.: MIT Press.

———. 1962, 1986. *Thought and Language.* Cambridge, Mass.: MIT Press.

Wagstaff, Janiel. 1997–1998. "Building Practical Knowledge of Letter-sound Correspondence: A Beginner's Word Wall and Beyond." *The Reading Teacher,* 51 (December-January), 298–304.

Walshe, R. D., ed. 1982. *Donald Graves in Australia.* Portsmouth, N.H.: Heinemann.

Watson, Dorothy, ed. 1987. *Ideas with Insights: Language Arts K–6.* Urbana, Ill.: National Council of Teachers of English.

Watson, Dorothy. 1993. "Community Meaning: Personal Knowing Within a Social Place." In *Cycles of Meaning.* Ed. Kathryn Pierce and Carol Giles. Portsmouth, N.H.: Heinemann, 3–15.

———. 1988. "What Do We Find in a Whole-Language Program?" In *Reading Process and Practice.* Ed. Constance Weaver. Portsmouth, N.H.: Heinemann.

Watson, Jerry. 1991. "An Integral Setting Tells More Than When and Where." *The Reading Teacher,* 44 (May), 638–646.

Weaver, Constance. 1991. *Alternatives in Understanding and Educating Attention-Deficit Students.* Urbana, Ill.: National Council of Teachers of English.

———. 1996. *Teaching Grammar in Context.* Portsmouth, N.H.: Boynton/Cook Publishers, Heinemann.

Weiger, Myra. 1971. "Found Poetry." *Elementary English,* 48 (December), 1002–1004.

———. 1976. "Moral Judgment in Children." Ph.D. diss., Rutgers University.

Wells, Gordon. 1979. "Describing Children's Linguistic Development." *British Educational Research Journal,* 5, 75–98.

———. 1986. *The Meaning Makers.* Portsmouth, N.H.: Heinemann.

West, Karen. 1998. "Noticing and Responding to Learners: Literacy Evaluation and Instruction in the Primary Grades." *The Reading Teacher,* 51 (April), 550–559.

Whitin, David, and Phyllis Whitin. 1996. "Inquiry at the Window: The Year of the Birds." *Language Arts,* 73 (February), 82–87.

Whittaker, Catherine. 1997. " 'Voices from the Fields': Including Migrant Farm Workers in the Curriculum." *The Reading Teacher,* 50 (March), 482–489.

Wickelgren, Ingrid. 1999. "Nurture Helps Mold Able Minds." *Science,* 283 (March 19), 1832–1834.

Wilkinson, Andrew. 1970. "The Concept of Oracy." *English Journal,* 59 (January), 70–77.

Willis, Arlette, and Karla Lewis. 1998. "A Conversation with Gloria Ladson-Billings." *Language Arts,* 75 (January), 61–70.

Wilson, T., and M. Hyde. 1997. "The Use of Signed English Pictures to Facilitate Reading Comprehension by Deaf Students." *American Annals of the Deaf,* 142, 333–314.

Winn, Deanna. 1988. "Develop Listening Skills as a Part of the Curriculum." *The Reading Teacher,* 42 (November), 144–146.

Winograd, Peter, Scott Paris, and Connie Bridge. 1991. "Improving the Assessment of Literacy." *The Reading Teacher,* 45 (October), 108–116.

Wittrock, M. C. 1983. "Writing and the Teaching of Reading." *Language Arts,* 60 (May), 600–605.

Wolf, Maryanne, and David Dickinson. 1985. In *The Development of Language.* Ed. Jean Berko-Gleason. Columbus, Ohio: Merrill.

Wood, Karen, and Bob Algozzini, eds. 1994. *Teaching Reading to High-Risk Learners.* Boston: Allyn and Bacon, 346.

Wood, Katie. 1994. "Hearing Voices, Tell Tales: Finding the Power of Reading Aloud." *Language Arts,* 71 (September), 346–349.

Woodward, Virginia. 1984. "Redefining Literacy Development: A Social Interactional Perspective." Speech given at the International Reading Association Convention, May 9, 1984, Atlanta.

Wright, Kimberly. 2000. "Weekly Spelling Meetings: Improving Spelling Instruction Through Classroom-Based Inquiry." *Language Arts,* 77 (January) 218–233.

Yenika-Agbaw, Vivian. 1997. "Taking Children's Literature Seriously: Reading for Pleasure and Social Change." *Language Arts,* 74 (October), 446–453.

Yopp, Hallie. 1995. "A Test for Assessing Phonemic Awareness in Young Children." *The Reading Teacher,* 49 (September), 20–29.

Young, Terrell, and Sylvia Vardell. 1993. "Weaving Readers Theatre and Nonfiction into the Curriculum." *The Reading Teacher,* 46 (February), 396–406.

Youtz, Adella. 1996. "Emotional Difficulties of Disabled Readers." In *How to Become a Better Reading Teacher.* Ed. Lillian Putnam. Saddle River, N.J.: Merrill/Prentice-Hall, 25–34.

Zarrillo, James, 1989. "Teachers' Interpretations of Literature-Based Reading." *The Reading Teacher,* 43 (October), 22–28.

Zindel, Paul. 1992. Paper presented at the 37th Annual Convention of the International Reading Association, Orlando, Fl. (May 1992).

Zutell, J., and Timothy Rasinski. 1991. "Training Teachers to Attend to Their Students' Oral Reading Fluency." *Theory into Practice,* 30, 211–217.

Index

Teaching in Action Vignettes

Chapter	Title	Grade Level	Instructional Strategies Modeled
1	Walking with Rosie	First Grade	read-alouds, visualizing story relationships, communication circle, interactive writing, collaborative revision, language development across the curriculum
2	Preserving Habitats: A Thematic Unit	Third Grade	unit teaching in an inclusive class, language learning across the curriculum, cooperative group activity
3	Mushrooms Now	Family Setting, Preschool	shared reading, family literacy events, phonemic awareness building
4	Racing Life with Willy	Future Teachers, Undergraduates	grand conversations with literature, community shares, reflective responding, literature response journals
5	Getting at the Root of Conflict	Sixth Grade	read-alouds with content-area materials, development of strategic listening, webbing prior knowledge, webbing in response to listening
6	Dramatizing "The Three Billy Goats Gruff"	First Grade	creative storytelling, role-playing across the curriculum
7	Billy Goat	First Grade	shared writing, interactive writing, talking together, language experience approach
	The Lorax	Sixth Grade	higher-order thinking, discussion, patterned writing
8	From Communication Circle into Reading-Writing Workshop	Kindergarten	read aloud, talking together, shared writing, listening to language sounds, independent reading and writing
9	Journals, Idea Clusters, and Other Ways to Make Ideas During Workshop	Third Grade	writing workshop, mini-lessons, teacher modeling, reading to write, topic finding
10	The Desert	Fifth Grade	skills in context, shared writing, collaborative editing and revision, structuring a report
11	Revising Sentences—A Mini-Lesson	Fifth Grade	mini-lesson during workshop, skills in context, active involvement with language conventions
12	Spelling Patterns and Writing	Third Grade	mini-lessons, word sorts, generalizing about spelling patterns, invented spelling and dictionary checks, special needs instruction
	Introducing Manuscript Letter Forms to Young Children	Kindergarten	modeling letter forms, teaching skills in unit contexts
	Introducing Cursive Letter Forms	Third Grade	modeling cursive forms, help for left-handed youngsters